Phygital Insights on National Health Reform:

Economics, Marketing, and Leadership

Kakhaber Djakeli
https://orcid.org/0000-0001-7505-5653
University of Georgia, Georgia

IGI Global
Scientific Publishing
Publishing Tomorrow's Research Today

Published in the United States of America by
IGI Global Scientific Publishing
701 East Chocolate Avenue
Hershey, PA, 17033, USA
Tel: 717-533-8845 | Fax: 717-533-7115
Website: https://www.igi-global.com E-mail: cust@igi-global.com

Library of Congress Cataloging-in-Publication Data

Names: Djakeli, Kakhaber, 1967- editor
Title: Phygital insights on national health reform : economics, marketing, and leadership / edited by: Kakhaber Djakeli.
Description: Hershey, PA : IGI Global Scientific Publishing, [2026] | Includes bibliographical references. | Summary: "This book explores healthcare reform as a reflection of a nation's identity, economy, and leadership in the digital age. Integrating economics, marketing, and management, it offers research-based strategies to design inclusive, effective healthcare systems that meet diverse societal needs and thrive in online and offline environments"-- Provided by publisher.
Identifiers: LCCN 2025054569 (print) | LCCN 2025054570 (ebook) | ISBN 9798337371733 hardcover | ISBN 9798337371740 paperback | ISBN 9798337371757 ebook
Subjects: LCSH: Health care reform--India | Medical informatics--India | Artificial intelligence--Medical applications--India | Communication in public health--India
Classification: LCC RA395.I5 P47 2026 (print) | LCC RA395.I5 (ebook)
LC record available at https://lccn.loc.gov/2025054569
LC ebook record available at https://lccn.loc.gov/2025054570

British Cataloguing in Publication Data
A Cataloguing in Publication record for this book is available from the British Library.

I dedicate this book to the memory of my father, Professor Tengiz Jakeli, who instilled in me, from a young age, a love of healthcare management and the then-new subjects of healthcare economics and marketing.

Kakhaber Djakeli
University of Georgia, Georgia

Table of Contents

Detailed Table of Contents

multidimensional relationships among marketing exposure, digital transparency, and citizen participation. Moreover, the author used a mixed methods approach. First, data were collected from a survey study (N = 737). Furthermore, the data were analyzed using PLS-SEM. Next, insights from focus group discussions (N = 2) were added to the emotional component and for triangulation. The results demonstrate that trust functions as a mediator and predictor of reform engagement, with transparency and personalization as key drivers.

The article shows that the ongoing digital transformation in the global environment is having a significant impact on the activities of healthcare organizations, which are increasingly using digital marketing approaches to improve relationships with patients and reach a wider target audience. This paper posits that a primary factor contributing to this low adoption rate is the scarcity of scientific research in this domain. Therefore, this study aimed to determine the impact of digital technologies on the behavior of healthcare consumers. To achieve the set goal, a conceptual model of the study was created, relevant hypotheses were formulated and a questionnaire was developed. Quantitative research, namely an online survey, was selected as the research method. As a result of analyzing the data, statistically significant values were obtained, which express the relationship between the above-mentioned variables.

Healthcare systems across the globe continue to struggle with persistent inequities in affordability and accessibility, disproportionately affecting marginalized and socioeconomically vulnerable populations. As nations pursue large-scale health reforms, the integration of physical and digital ("phygital") healthcare ecosystems presents both transformative opportunities and new ethical challenges. This chapter examines inclusion in healthcare economics through the lenses of affordability,

Over seven decades, India's health reform has transitioned from traditional awareness programs to participatory "phygital" (physical + digital) models. This paper traces the evolution of health literacy governance through successive Five-Year Plans (1951–2017), analyzing how economic priorities, marketing strategies, and leadership paradigms shaped reform outcomes. It highlights the shift from rural welfare and communicable disease control to challenges of lifestyle disorders, digital health equity, and nutrition security. Persistent gaps in efficiency, communication, and leadership integration across the phygital ecosystem are identified. The study concludes with recommendations to embed health literacy, digital inclusion, and collaborative leadership within India's public health framework, advancing equitable, action-oriented, and sustainable healthcare reform.

The healthcare industry is at a critical juncture as it grapples with the rapid adoption of new technology while trying to integrate these advancements into traditional care models in order to respond to the increasing demands of society and economy. This chapter discusses how phygital healthcare can help improve the efficiency, access, and engagement of patients when using digital technology by addressing issues that have historically plagued the industry such as trust and access to affordable options. An analysis of how these technologies will change the way we deliver healthcare and how we will manage it financially is presented along with an exploration of the economic and marketing implications of digital health in relation to building patient-centered systems and sustainable health markets. Through case studies and literature reviews, this chapter lays out a model for integrating digital innovation into ethical leadership to ensure that health care reform occurs in a socially inclusive and technologically progressive manner.

Preface

INTRODUCTION

Healthcare reform is now defined by a core challenge: how to design flexible, effective systems that harness digital advances to improve access, quality, and sustainability for all. This book argues that successful reform depends not only on adopting new technologies such as electromedicine and digital healthcare, but also on the active engagement of all stakeholders—including doctors, patients, insurers, policymakers, and marketers—to shape emerging delivery models and build consumer loyalty. Ultimately, transformative innovation must serve the central goal of building a strong, adaptive system that meets the needs of new patient populations and fosters sustainable progress.

Providers, funders, insurers, managers, marketers, and leaders are shaping a flexible healthcare system that requires vision and adaptability.

Healthcare reform is no longer led solely by national figures. Agile healthcare groups managing operations, front offices, or key functions drive reforms.

Effective reform should start with frontline practitioners and patient-facing teams, whose expertise and innovation are vital for systemic change. A bottom-up approach increases the adaptability of healthcare reform.

Early healthcare systems began in ancient nations. The first reformer may have been a king, a politician, or a ruler, lost to history. Great kings, like Hammurabi, built systems. Hammurabi's Code aimed to strengthen the state by structuring healthcare, emphasizing costs, doctor behavior, and patient protection. Early societies valued organized over chaotic care.

Ancient Egyptian healthcare is documented in historical texts, including protocols and guidelines. Temple doctors and private practitioners coexisted. Egyptians excelled in surgery and medical procedures, exploring anatomy and the mind. Medicine became central, with codified knowledge and mystical practices. Spells and rituals aided recovery. Doctors' roles gained status, and dedicated support emerged for doctors and patients (Paris et al., 2010).

After Egypt, Hellenic medicine emerged, focusing on fitness, diet, and especially gymnastics.

Greeks linked physical health to spiritual well-being and saw beauty and spirituality as connected.

After ancient Hellenic medicine, developments continued in Greece and Rome. Meanwhile, major changes were occurring in Asia. For example, Persian kings established a social insurance system in their empire, which marked an early form of healthcare reform. These regional innovations contributed to the evolving landscape of healthcare systems.

Following the innovations in Persia and China, the focus of healthcare reform shifted to the Christian and Muslim worlds, both of which built important healthcare systems. Later, Europe pioneered social medical insurance, starting in Germany in the 19th century.

These reforms exemplify the persistent human endeavor to establish order and construct a sustainable, healthy, and productive society through healthcare. The central argument is that societal strength depends on effective healthcare systems. Physical and mental well-being, supported by adaptable and innovative reforms, forms the foundation for productivity and innovation (Getzen, 2020).

Bismarck's reform funded care for the poor using contributions from the wealthy, creating a fairer distribution.

While the German model was influential in Great Britain, full implementation proved challenging. As a result, because social insurance systems require many well-employed citizens to pay premiums, England introduced a healthcare tax, leading to the creation of the Beveridge model. This transition marked a significant change in the approach to healthcare.

The US did not follow Europe. Americans relied on the market's "invisible hand" for healthcare funding, which developed entrepreneurially and merged with market forces. US healthcare now blends social insurance and other models, shaped by market demand. Other countries, like Canada, have created distinct systems.

The Soviet Union's centralized healthcare system, known as the Semashko model, offers both positive and negative lessons from its time before its collapse. Following the dissolution of the Soviet Union, successor states initiated their own reforms, often lacking sufficient experience to implement them effectively. The Republic of Georgia illustrates this process: initially adopting the Beveridge model with a state-funded health insurance company, Georgia later transitioned to liberal reforms by offering coverage through private insurers. While this approach entailed risks, it also produced some positive outcomes. Over time, Georgia began developing a universal healthcare model. This evolution demonstrates the diversity of reform concepts within a single nation and underscores the complexities of implementing digital transformation on a global scale.

A central question now is how countries with high healthcare demand should implement the digital revolution. In these nations, healthcare quality establishes global standards, necessitating reforms that facilitate effective digital adaptation. For instance, North America exemplifies the challenges of adopting lessons from European healthcare digitization. Similarly, India, as the world's largest democracy, has initiated a digital healthcare transformation to enhance access, efficiency, and quality, raising questions about the tangible benefits for Indian consumers. Germany, recognized for its innovative healthcare model, has established new benchmarks in e-healthcare, demonstrating successful national adaptation. Nevertheless, fundamental differences among states present significant challenges as they address advances in digital and artificial intelligence in healthcare. These issues are examined throughout the book and form the foundation of the authors' research (Folland et al., 2024).

By 2030, healthcare services will reach 99% of the population.

Large virtual hospitals will launch worldwide, with one already recognized by Guinness World Records.

Virtual hospitals will lighten the load on physical clinics, reduce emergency visits, and make specialist care easier for rural patients.

These developments demonstrate the book's main argument: that successful healthcare reform in the digital age requires visionary, adaptive design to create effective, equitable, and sustainable systems. Integrating artificial intelligence highlights both the new opportunities and the persistent challenges in digital transformation. Ultimately, digital transformation is expected to enhance the accessibility and efficiency of healthcare services. Experiences from the United States, Germany, China, Estonia, Saudi Arabia, and India demonstrate that systemic improvement relies on visionary adaptation. The following steps illustrate the necessity of ongoing and flexible reform:

Many people worldwide, especially in rural areas, still lack high-quality healthcare.

Healthcare organizations should adopt and standardize the use of artificial intelligence and digital health.

We must define quality for digital healthcare.

Medical education should train students in AI and e-healthcare (McDonough, 2011).

SEARCHING FOR A SOLUTION

Digital health can save lives. Studies show telemedicine could save over 2 billion lives from non-communicable diseases in the next decade. Health reforms should support digital health by promoting e-health investment and advancing e-health and AI through policy, legislation, and tax incentives.

Promote professional e-health and AI training nationally and internationally.

- Establish quality standards for electronic health forms and AI, ensuring national and international quality control.

For example, investments in telemedicine will help the world avoid approximately 7 million acute cases.

events and hospitalizations, thereby significantly reducing the burden on healthcare systems worldwide. Telemedicine applications, which are somewhat more in demand for developing countries than for developed countries, in many cases help doctors

To implement digital healthcare tools—such as electronic health records, prescriptions, and telemedicine—develop action plans and ensure consistent administration. This should also include: Timely data reflection in Ministry systems; Checking compatibility of local medical record systems.

For users of electronic records to obtain complete, up-to-date data, develop oversight mechanisms that increase doctor and institutional engagement and improve the timeliness and completeness of health information.

To implement electronic prescriptions effectively, establish supervision to limit over-the-counter dispensing of prescription drugs.

To ensure telemedicine services work effectively, create administrative systems to ensure the productive use of telemedicine equipment.

The target audience for this book includes healthcare students and professors, healthcare policymakers and administrators, insurance analysts, healthcare leaders, parliamentarians focused on reform, journalists, digital leaders, and broadly educated readers interested in current and future healthcare.

ORGANIZATION OF THE BOOK

The book is organized into 13 chapters. A brief description of each of the chapters follows:

Chapter 1 identifies the existing challenges in the History of Healthcare Reforms and Systems from the beginning of civilization to the present day. The chapter discusses how Healthcare systems were formed and reformed, the types of findings offered by the environment, and the roles the economy, industries, and leaders played.

Chapter 2 explores the impact of phygital marketing strategies on public trust, emotional resonance, and behavioral engagement with national health reform initiatives. The research was grounded in the Health Belief Model (HBM) and the

Technology Acceptance Model (TAM). This research contributes to the intersection of health economics, marketing, communication, and leadership by showing a measurable model of how hybrid communication strategies can improve compliance, inclusivity, and the long-term legitimacy of health reform.

Chapter 3 describes how the ongoing digital transformation in the global environment is significantly impacting the activities of healthcare organizations, which are increasingly using digital marketing to improve patient relationships and reach a wider target audience.

Chapter 4 explores a relevant topic that emerged as a defining challenge of contemporary national health reform. Despite decades of policy interventions, technological advancements, and increased global attention to universal health coverage, access to affordable, high-quality healthcare remains uneven across social groups.

Chapter 5 studies innovative digital tools that streamline healthcare systems, from the registration process to patient recovery, providing services through semantic networks generated from human genetic information, proteins, and human phenotypes, among other interconnected data.

Chapter 6 studies the process by which the nationally centered model of healthcare reform has been significantly reshaped by globalization. Intensified cross-border flows of knowledge, capital, technology, labor, and healthcare services have reduced the autonomy of national health systems and exposed them to global norms, benchmarks, and competitive pressures.

Chapter 7 monitors challenges and elaborates the approaches which makes the Healthcare shifting to phygital ecosystems where physical and digital methods merge, to cleare represent a paradigm shift in health policy, economics, and delivery, fostering a more inclusive, equitable, efficient, and sustainable system, exploring how economic theory, patient behavior, trust, marketing, and leadership shape this complex landscape elaborating the need for human-centered approach in the utilization of AI, IoT, and telemedicine must align with robust governance, ethics, and access, especially for vulnerable population.

Chapter 8 studies India's health literacy ecosystem, which stands at a decisive moment of transition—from post-Independence civic education to a phygital governance framework that merges human participation with digital intelligence. Strengthening this evolution requires coherent reforms across five domains: policy integration, digital inclusion, institutional trust, behavioral change, and capacity building.

Chapter 9 analyzes the former healthcare reforms in Georgia, Black Sea region country, with its institutional reforms, starting from the Post-Soviet era, urgent challenges, continued by Liberal Leaders, implementing new liberal approaches of health reform, discussing the new trends of Healthcare Digitalization for better satisfaction of the needs of patients, financiers, insurance organizations, policymakers, and the multilateral organizations.

Chapter 10 studies and offers clear, actionable guidance for practitioners and policymakers seeking to advance equity-driven mental health reform. Translating empirical evidence into practice requires recognizing discrimination not as a peripheral social concern, but as a measurable governance failure that directly undermines health outcomes.

Chapter 11 illustrates the transition from centralized planning to adaptive, data-driven, and collaborative leadership. Yet, the challenge remains to ensure that economic growth and technological advancement are matched by ethical leadership, inclusivity, and equitable access. Phygital action must move beyond awareness campaigns to real-time community engagement, transparent governance, and digitally supported behavioral change.

Chapter 12 reviews of telemedicine, artificial intelligence, remote patient monitoring, and electronic health records have been integrated to increase healthcare accessibility and enhance clinical efficiency to a great degree. Simultaneously, the digital medium can enable healthcare organizations to enhance patient interaction and create individual care journeys.

Chapter 13 discusses healthcare reform to better address the challenges posed by refugees and finds that reforms should better align with the ideals of the SDGs and achieve universal health coverage. In practice, this involves using both physical and digital strategies, which is essentially a "phygital" approach to better healthcare delivery.

A CONCLUSION

How does the book impact the field and contribute to the subject matter?

When creating a new Scientific Book, writers must definitely take into account the current situation and the dynamics of its development. When we touch on this universal topic, we must necessarily emphasize the great role the book should play in expanding existing knowledge and cognition. The task is very big. Healthcare reforms today should be carried out precisely by improving the use of digital and artificial intelligence. We must learn to transform this extremely difficult yet attractive market using the means modern science and the digital revolution have created. The book will definitely have a significant impact on the proper conduct of healthcare reform worldwide. The existing book, which contains a lot of scientific work, will have a great impact on healthcare leaders who, strengthened by new knowledge and experience, will make even more innovations in healthcare markets, especially in terms of making healthcare accessible to patients around the world, precisely through the rational and scientific use of artificial intelligence and digital technologies.

Kakhaber Djakeli
University of Georgia, Georgia

REFERENCES

Folland, S., Goodman, A. C., Stano, M., & Danagoulian, S. (2024). *The economics of health and health care*. Routledge. DOI: 10.2139/ssrn.3531969

Getzen, T. E. (2020). Medical Spending from Ancient Times to the 21st Century. *Available at SSRN* 3531969.DOI: 10.2139/ssrn.3531969

McDonough, J. E. (2011). *Inside national health reform* (Vol. 22). Univ of California Press.

Paris, V., Devaux, M., & Wei, L. (2010). Health systems institutional characteristics. *A Survey of, 29*.

Acknowledgement

I am very grateful to my professor, Matthias Graf von der Schulenburg, under whose mentorship I studied health economics at the Leibniz University of Hannover (LUH) in Germany, and with whom I worked on health reform audits in many countries. I am also grateful to the German Academic Exchange Service DAAD, which gave me the opportunity to conduct research on health economics in Germany and other countries.

I would like to express my deepest gratitude to Professor Hong Wang, my mentor at Yale University's School of Public Health. His inspiration led me to consider developing a model of healthcare economics, management, and marketing for my country. I also thank the American Fulbright Foundation for enabling me to conduct health economics research at Yale.

It was especially important for me to participate in Georgia's healthcare reform. I developed an economic concept for the country's Vice Prime Minister. In this process, I met with many World Bank health economics experts and gained extensive experience in reform.

While working on this book, my family members supported me in specific ways: my mother, Zumrudi Gabunia, offered constant encouragement; my wife, Nino Tsulaia, provided daily understanding; my daughters, Tamar and Tinatin, inspired me with their enthusiasm; my son-in-law, Gaga, and my granddaughter, little Dina, brought joy and comfort. Their moral and practical support made completing this large-scale work possible, and I express my heartfelt gratitude to them.

Kakhaber Djakeli
University of Georgia, Georgia

Chapter 1

History of Healthcare Systems and Their Reforming, Past and Present, the Role of National Healthcare, and Future Challenges in the Digital Age

Kakhaber Djakeli
http://orcid.org/0000-0001-7505-5653
University of Georgia, Georgia

ABSTRACT

Health care systems are the achievement of civilization. Healthcare itself is a phenomenon aimed at saving lives, but considering environmental challenges, it is beginning to transform. The history of humanity has confirmed that this transformation should not occur reactively. Health care should be transformed proactively. There can be revolutionary leaps and innovative changes, but health care and its system must take measured steps towards the future. Along the path of health care system evolution, we encounter interesting innovations. Some states are proud of having a national healthcare system, while others believe in the market. Such states give greater priority to the healthcare market and the broader market phenomenon than to a national healthcare system. Which is more correct for the future? If we were to ask this difficult question to healthcare policymakers, administrators, professors,

DOI: 10.4018/979-8-3373-7173-3.ch001

healthcare economists, healthcare marketers, managers, and healthcare leaders, we would spark a considerable debate. The main thing is to guess society's healthcare priorities.

1. INTRODUCTION

According to the World Health Organization (WHO), health systems are: "The people, institutions and resources, arranged together in accordance with established policies, to improve the health of the population they serve, while responding to people's legitimate expectations and protecting them against the cost of ill-health through a variety of activities whose primary intent is to improve health. It is a set of elements and their relationship in a complex whole, designed to serve the health needs of the population. Health systems fulfill three main functions: Health care delivery, fair treatment to all, and meeting health expectations of the population" (Tulchinsky,2018).

According to historians, Health Systems were created by the humanization of Government and by the idea that the health of others means my health. At the same time, many of the healthcare models that emerged during the industrial revolutions did not reflect the Government's desire to have a happy and healthy society, but reflected the desire for what was called a healthy workforce, or a healthy military force as a guarantee of profit (Relman et al.,1990).

The idea of a healthy society has gained momentum in recent times, especially with the advent of the welfare state. However, the desire of governments to promote society's health is more a new stage of social development than a simple pursuit of economic profit. In early capitalist societies, a healthy workforce was the minimum that motivated capitalists to invest in systems that could provide workers with possible health care, and those systems were born that way. However, health systems may have existed much longer, and thinking about them is thinking about human development.

Before healthcare reforms, the state's public finance must be reformed. A reform not supported by public finances, no matter how well-intentioned, is doomed to failure. States have long overlooked this seemingly logical truth, and many of them have taken the wrong path.

It is essential to implement healthcare reform during a country's socio-economic transformation. For example, when the countries of Central and Eastern Europe left the Soviet Union's socialist camp, they quickly began implementing healthcare reforms. Accordingly, these countries wanted to overcome the lag and catch up with European countries in healthcare indicators. Therefore, it can be said that healthcare reform is a multidimensional process aimed at harmoniously combining public and private healthcare models in the state in order to achieve a much greater effect both in terms of population health indicators, as well as in healthcare service providers, financiers, and healthcare education systems (Orosz et al., 1998).

2. HISTORICAL STAGES OF HEALTH SYSTEMS

When discussing the historical course of healthcare reform, we must begin with the pivotal event that established the healthcare system. Of course, healthcare existed in ancient society, but it took on more formalized forms as the state developed.

2.1. King Hammurabi as a First Healthcare Reformer

King Hammurabi himself, in his code, speaks about healthcare rules and ethics. The Code of Hammurabi contains 282 laws governing healthcare. It includes the rules governing healthcare pricing. King Hammurabi demands that doctors protect patients' rights. It also discusses the healthcare documentation a doctor must create. Setting prices, patients' rights, punishment for incorrect treatment, and the need to write a prescription, and much more - speak of the ancient healthcare system created by King Hammurabi, which greatly contributed to the Assyrian-Babylonian civilization in strengthening the state and improving its quality.

Hammurabi (ruled 1796–1750 BC) believed that the gods had chosen him to write laws for his people. In the preface to his code of laws, he states, "Anum and Bel have called me by name, Hammurabi, the God-fearing, the exalted prince, to bring to the land the rule of truth." The laws are numbered 1-282 (numbers 13 and 66–99 are lost) and are written in Old Babylonian script on 2.5-meter-high steles. They were discovered in December 1901 in Susa, Elam (now Khuzestan), Iran, and are believed to be the writings of the 12th-century BC Elamite king Shutruk-nahunte, who invaded Babylonia, looted it, and took to his City the Stele of Hamurrabi, finally adding to it his own inscription.

However, there are also laws older than the Code of Hammurabi. For example, the laws of Eshnun and the ruler of the city of Isin, Liphitishtar, are older than the Code of Hammurabi. These ancient laws also address healthcare, but the Code of Hammurabi's systematic approach is more pronounced. As for the issue of the health ombudsman, it certainly starts with the Code of Hammurabi. Other sources refer to the health system, especially the ombudsman.

The mention of the Code of Hammurabi, the Hippocratic Oath, and the Oath of Maimonides is sufficient to confirm that the establishment of ethical and legal principles in the relationship between Doctor and patient and the protection of patient rights already indicates the systematic development of healthcare. Accordingly, given the antiquity of the written sources, King Hammurabi can be recognized as a prominent healthcare reformer (Halwani & Takrouri, 2006). The relationship between the Doctor and the patient played a vital role in the development of healthcare systems. Over time, the relationship between the Doctor and the patient served as the basis for bioethical principles such as autonomy, beneficence, non-maleficence, and justice. Hammurabi's law was primarily focused on the quality of operations. There was the possibility of judicial action to ensure justice and equality for all social classes in the kingdom. Hammurabi's code can be considered the basis of current systemic concepts of healthcare.

When we talk about the healthcare system, the creation and provision of healthcare services are considered alongside their evaluation. It was through evaluation that Hammurabi began to create a social risk management system. His laws, starting with Law No. 215, are not only an ancient attempt at quality management of the healthcare system, but also a direction for addressing social risks that later continued with universal development in 19th-century Germany. Even the most primitive healthcare delivery, quality, ethics, and evaluation system created by Hammurabi was based on the same principle as ours. After a long time, it became a powerful tool of social governance in Europe, namely in Germany, in 1883, when the first modern-day German healthcare system was created.

The Code of Hammurabi is the oldest known system of law regulating healthcare in the Assyrian and Babylonian communities. The current question is what followed this Code of Hammurabi? Historical analysis shows that under the influence of the Code of Hammurabi, the laws of the Hittite state developed after it, which also concerned healthcare norms, pricing, quality, forms and methods of delivery, remuneration of doctors, regulation of doctors, ethics, and a specific systematic approach that was necessary for regulating healthcare provision.

1650–1500 BCE: The Anatolian Hittites attempted to give healthcare a systematic approach, based on their understanding of systemicity. Then comes Assyria,1450–1200 BCE, which sought to regulate healthcare and the relationship between doctors and patients through laws. These laws were particularly relevant to abortion, medical malpractice, and errors that have harmed human lives. It is after this that the importance of the Egyptian state in regulating healthcare increases. So scientists can say that the ancient path to creating healthcare systems began with the kings of Assyria and Babylon, continued in Egypt, Persia, Greece, and Rome.

2.2. Healthcare in Egypt

The Egyptian approach to developing healthcare and establishing systems is crucial, as healthcare has become deeply ingrained in Egyptian culture. This is very thought-provoking. In Europe for example, healthcare was not a part of religious beliefs, and doctors often faced danger due to their medical practices. Even before that, in Assyria and Babylon, religion did not include healthcare. Moreover, in Egypt, it is likely the only country where religion and healthcare have been combined to work miracles for centuries (Carpenter et al., 2006). The father of history, Herodotus, wrote that all Egyptian doctors specialized in one or another healthcare practice, indicating that the division of labor and specialization in Egypt represented the highest level of healthcare in the world at the time. Egyptian doctors had to follow the knowledge conveyed in ancient and modern papyri, as decreed by the Pharaoh. So there was a medicine based on knowledge. It was not only practice and experience, but also the knowledge-based basis of medical practice. Egypt also addressed public health issues. Cleanliness and compliance with sanitary norms were universal, and the decrees of the pharaohs regulated this. It is known that the Egyptians used rational principles in their medical practices. However, alongside rational mechanisms, they also used irrational mechanisms, such as the power and magic of spirits.

The famous papyrus called Ebers (Von Klein, 1905), bearing the name of the professor who discovered it in an Egyptian tomb, expresses remarkable similarities between their Healthcare and modern healthcare. The papyrus, dated to 1552 BC, belongs to the reign of Pharaoh Amenhotep. This is a 200-year-old manuscript, before the era of Tutankhamun, which is better known to us. During the study of the papyrus, it seemed clear that it was a transcription of a manuscript at least twice as old, since the text was a prescription written for King Usapa. This king reigned in 3200 BC. The papyrus was indeed ancient and had been copied many times. 1552 BC is the year when the Egyptian New Kingdom under Pharaoh Ahmose I began. This is precisely how old this papyrus is, which was of great importance to doctors in ancient times. The papyrus contained principles of pediatrics and ophthalmology, as well as methods for treating infectious diseases. It also discussed unknown diseases, which were mentioned in the text with three letters, and scientists believed they were dysentery. It also discussed heart diseases and beauty medicine, such as hair growth. No one doubted that this manuscript itself was ancient, but the fact that another Egyptian doctor was practicing medicine 1,500 years later, based on this manuscript, was thought-provoking. At the end of the papyrus, the issue of blood cancer and the types of tumors were discussed, along with methods for removing cysts and warning signs (Major, 1930).

The Doctor who rested in the tomb found by Ebers was either very fond of ancient manuscripts or, according to a specific law and narrative, was forced to use this medical document throughout his life. Perhaps the Ebers Papyrus also contained updates, but it was compiled around 1552 BC and included many interesting facts relevant to the Doctor. That is, it also contained innovations. Based on this and other papyri, Egypt can be considered an institutionalized healthcare country where spiritual magic and healthcare, as part of religion, were important in shaping healthcare rules and laws (Metwaly et al.,2021).

The Edwin Smith papyrus is one of the oldest documents, offering insights into the surgical practice of Old Egypt (Brandt-Rauf & Brandt-Rauf, 1987). The Edwin Smith papyrus, which was purchased by this person in Egypt and donated by his daughter to the New York Historical Society, is important for the study of Egyptian medical practices. Although the papyrus is dated to 1600 BC, it is clear that it was copied from an older papyrus. Therefore, the age of this work falls between 3000 and 2500 BC. The work belongs to one of the great Egyptian physicians, *Imhotep*, who also built the pyramids. The document addresses issues in occupational medicine and is particularly interesting for the treatment of injuries sustained in labor conditions. This work demonstrates that Egyptian doctors possessed analytical skills and consistently applied them in their practice (Stiefel et al., 2006). This papyrus was preserved for centuries in Thebes, and it is known that Imhotep, a physician, served Pharaoh Djoser, the ruler of the Third Dynasty, who built a bizarre pyramid. This document required a difficult decipherment. However, the medically based translation had a greater effect and rediscovered the work for the medical community. The work, which consists of 48 parts, is arranged with extraordinary flexibility. It contains rules for diagnosing patients and primarily addresses wound treatment. Most importantly, this work makes clear that ancient Egyptian medicine was profound and detailed in its study of wounds and the performance of specialized operations on patients (van Middendorp et al., 2010).

The Kahun Gynecological Papyrus, dating back to approximately 1800 BC, provides evidence that this ancient civilization had a well-developed understanding of reproductive medicine, encompassing science-based treatments for pregnancy, childbirth, fertility, and overall women's health. The papyrus contains exciting data on women's health, and its integrity shows that gynecological knowledge was at a high level in ancient Egypt (Lopes & Pereira, 2021).

Hearst & London Medical Papyri tells us how the Egyptians treated internal diseases, including pneumonia, intestinal and liver complications, and skin diseases (Leake,1952). The work was created in 1550 BC. It contains 260 recipes for treating internal diseases. Here are methods for the curation of urinary, digestive, and blood disorders, hair loss, burns, and bites using Herbs, honey, animal products, and some magic rituals. Also used Beer and herbs for stomach problems and honey, fat as soothing ointments for burns. At the same time, infusions are developed to treat bladder or kidney pain.

As for the London Medical Papyrus, it was created in 1350 BC and contains 61 chapters that harmoniously combine rational and irrational medicine. That is, it contains the rules necessary for magico-religious healing. There are, of course, rational cures for skin complaints, eye diseases, burns, and childbirth. Also, coughs, headaches, and bleeding. However, this papyrus also contains rituals to rid oneself of diseases caused by demons. It gives exciting, magical protection for mothers and newborns. In this respect, this papyrus is very interesting and even inexplicable to our rational civilization (Trevisanato,2006).

Still, what was the ancient Egyptian healthcare system like, encompassing many areas of healthcare and making numerous discoveries? Given the fact that the Egyptians were the first to study breast cancer and also described many tumors with a urological explanation, discovered asthma, and many other diseases, we can say that they are the founders of complex medicine.

Since ancient Egyptian medicine was deeply intertwined with religion, it was governed by the Gods. Private-practicing doctors often operated on temples, and the medical knowledge accumulated there. The founder of medical science in ancient Egypt is considered to be the physician *Imhotep*, who served as the vizier of Pharaoh Djoser and also constructed the Step Pyramid.

Ancient Egyptian healthcare was exciting. The systems resembled the modern understanding of medicine. Primary, secondary, and tertiary medicine, public health, and pharmacy were probably created under the influence of Egyptian systems. For example, healthcare in ancient Egypt was based on temples. These temples had three types of representatives: priests, priest doctors, and doctors. They all belonged to the temple and worked in this way. There was also a department of doctors called the Sekhmet Priests, as well as a third category of doctors who belonged to the SUNU. These were doctors of the Great Union, such as doctors of the ancient Egyptian army, doctors of the Pharaoh's palace, doctors and nurses of the queen, and those who controlled public hygiene and cemetery cleanliness. In addition, there were doctors from the SAU department who, as the name suggests, monitored the health of citizens and epidemics. Some of these doctors followed rational medicine and were able to incorporate magic into their practice. Priest doctors were excellent at this. Some doctors were just magicians. However, the Egyptian papyri provide us with remarkable scientific teachings and definitions of diseases, indicating that the Egyptians overcame the influence of religion and developed rational medical views shaped by ideology.

What is very interesting is that in Egyptian temples, patients underwent ritual purification with holy water and received dream therapy, which included "incubation." They fell into a temple sleep; in a trance-like state, the patients met the gods and were cured of their diseases (David, 2008). A separate topic is ancient Egyptian dentistry. Archaeological evidence confirms that the Egyptians treated dental cases promptly, and therefore, they rarely developed severe dental disease. The papyri tell how they chose a toothbrush and toothpaste for various occasions. They used fillings and so-called dental bridges, which were often made of gold. Egyptians used forty-two books that Hermes gave them; these are called Hermetic. Hermes was called Toti in Egyptian, and some of his books, specifically six books, were about medicine.

All this indicates the existence of a healthcare system in ancient Egypt—a union of religious and public doctors, nurses, and other medical personnel, regulated by temples—and that the knowledge accumulated in the temples was necessary for all medical personnel.

2.3. Healthcare Systems and Medicine in Ancient Persia

The Avesta, the sacred book of Zoroastrianism, provides insights into the health care practices of ancient Persian medicine. It discusses the provision of healthcare and the remuneration that doctors receive.

The establishment of prices was intended to increase public access to health services. However, it is also worth noting the development of an insurance mechanism in Persia. Increasing the price of medical services was considered a great sin. Cyrus the Great established public healthcare in 550 BC and began its institutional development. In this direction, after the Assyrian-Babylonian king Hammurabi, Cyrus the Great can be considered a Healthcare Reformer. Cyrus created a health care system where health services were free for patients. It may be more of a cluster-oriented public product. The public healthcare system of ancient Persia, along with the public products it created, is fascinating. Cyrus the Great was the ruler of a vast empire and had great power. His healthcare system was exciting. Cyrus the Great paid special attention to women and granted them extended paid maternity leave. Accordingly, Cyrus the Great's social policy was practical and attractive.

During the Sassanid dynasty, from 531 to 739 AD, people in Persia had access to free medical products. During the reign of King Khosrow I, people had access to free primary and secondary healthcare, which meant that by the 500s AD, treatment and hospitalization were provided at no cost. King Khosrow began building hospitals in all cities of Persia. Khosrow exempted paralyzed patients from paying taxes. A crucial aspect of the ancient Persian healthcare system is the living conditions of doctors and nurses. It is established that doctors lived in the best parts of Persian cities and were highly valued. The rapid movement of Persian doctors was important. The Persian state provided them with fast horses, thereby increasing access to healthcare (Yarmohammadi et al., 2012).

2.4. Healthcare in Ancient Greece

The Hippocratic Oath defines the ideal of Greek healthcare, which is very well expressed in the motto, slogan, and catchphrase, finally paraphrased by the Roman Poet Juvenal: "a healthy mind in a healthy body." Of course, ancient Hellenic healthcare sought a harmonious balance between the body, spirituality, environment, and society. The Asclepius paradigm defines the Greek philosophy of healthcare. Asclepius is the God of healing and medicine. The Greeks also built temples of Asclepius, where, just like in ancient Egypt, ritual sleep treatment and incubation were used. The Asclepius paradigm laid the foundation for modern medicine. This is a form of disease-oriented treatment. If the Asclepius paradigm is disease-oriented treatment, prevention-oriented medical activity is named after another god, namely Hygieia. Hygieia was also the goddess of medicine, directing the implementation of healthcare measures to prevent illness from afflicting a large part of humanity. The paradigms of Asclepius and Hygieia are highly relevant today; treatment and prevention complement each other.

The Greeks added to the Egyptians' knowledge an in-depth study of anatomy and the nervous system. The ancient Greeks largely freed medicine and healthcare from religious taboos and ideological constraints. Unlike the Egyptians, the Greeks considered the causes of diseases to be more natural than the result of the anger of the gods. Perhaps the Hellenes preached a health care oriented towards nature and gave it a new birth. Healthcare was reborn in the hands of the Hellenes. If the Egyptians saw the causes of health in supernatural forces, the ancient Greeks considered them natural. The Greeks explained everything in terms of the imbalance of the four substances: blood, phlegm, yellow bile, and black bile. If the Egyptians explained religious causes, the Greeks began to describe and investigate natural causes rationally.

If the Egyptians pursued specialization in medicine, the Greeks developed a generalist practitioner based on the Hippocratic school of medicine. Hippocrates is considered a great Health Reformer, defining medicine through his Oath. The Greeks developed the so-called Hippocratic Corpus, creating seventy significant texts. They studied cases. They developed a prognosis. If the Egyptians preferred surgery and herbal treatments, the ancient Greeks more used sports, exercises, and bloodletting.

Public health in Egypt focused on maintaining sanitary conditions and controlling hygiene. The Greeks added to these areas environmental health, clean water, air, a healthy environment, thermal waters, the study of worldly phenomena, and observation.

The Egyptians were more familiar with health from a practical perspective because they practiced mummification and knew a great deal about the human body. The Greeks began to create a Medical Theory. Despite such differences, life expectancy in ancient Egypt and ancient Greece was almost the same. Between 30 and 35 years, and then it grew up reached 50-60 years.

Philosophical schools educated doctors in ancient Greece. They were less specialized in any one area of health but more oriented towards holistic medicine. The name of Doctor, - Physician, comes from Hipocratis, “physis” was first proposed by

Hippocrates, who turned hieratic temple-based, religious medicine into a rational discipline (Kleisiaris et al.,2014). It was Hippocrates who created evidence-based medicine. The Hippocratic School in Kos was distinguished by the fact that the history of the illness and, most importantly, facts played a significant role here. Evidence-based medicine brought great success to the Hippocratic School.

Here, rational.

The study of mood swings and the observation of mood, as well as the examination of sleep duration, led to the understanding of the nature of dreams. Various indicators, including appetite, thirst, nausea, localization and severity of pain, chills, cough, sneezing, hiccups, flatulence, cramps, nosebleeds, changes in the menstrual cycle, temperature, desires, instincts, reaction, and motor skills, played a significant role. During the physical examination of a patient by a doctor in the Hippocratic school, great attention was paid to fever, breathing, the condition of possible paralysis, the condition of veins, the color of the face and eyes, as well as the smell and color of the limbs, feces, urine, sputum, and vomit. The holistic assessment of these records enabled doctors to make a final diagnosis and determine the direction and strategy of treatment for the disease, employing their own tactics. The Doctor wrote down all this and then discussed it with his colleagues.

Hippocrates developed the concept of the psychosomatic approach, which holds that health care is primarily aimed at supporting individuals; thus, health care and psychological support focus on addressing psychosomatic entities rather than just the symptoms of disease. Mental and physical care were carried out in parallel, regardless of whether the disease originated in the soul or the body (Tountas, 2009).

The Locrian Code, one of the oldest among the Greek city-states, legislates a similar public health system based on prevention and sanitation, which is also very interesting among ancient health systems and represents a specific structural trend in the study of the development of health systems (Karamanou et al., 2019).

2.5. The Roman healthcare systems

The Romans, with their high level of rationality and knowledge, blended Hellenistic and Egyptian healthcare wisdom and structures. The Romans began investing in the health of their citizens and residents of Rome, building rational and urgent systems for environmental health (Israelowich, 2015).

The Romans, with their characteristic principle, began to create public systems from the very beginning. They built aqueducts to supply cities with clean water, observed sanitary standards, paid close attention to thermal baths and cleanliness, built roads, and tried to feed and clothe enslaved people and poor citizens properly. The Romans also built hospitals and clinics and carried on the knowledge bequeathed to them by the Hippocratic school.

In Roman medicine, doctors were divided into the following groups: a) Civilian doctors, who received a salary from their patients. This is what we call out-of-pocket payments. However, some lived in poverty and had no other way to access medical services; they contacted special public doctors. Public doctors often treated people with low incomes for free.

b) State physicians, who were financed from the treasury of the cities or from the treasury of the Empire. Their system was established as a result of the healthcare reform of the Roman emperor Antoninus Pius. These state physicians also represented public health in the Roman Empire. These physicians were called archiatri.

c) Military physicians. From the very beginning, military medicine developed in the Roman Republic and, more significantly, in the Roman Empire. The so-called - Valetudinaria was created. This is an army hospital that cares for people of military age. Many military hospitals were built in the Empire, whose mission was to recover military personnel and quickly return them to service. Field medicine developed, which treated soldiers directly on the battlefield. Every legion had its own medical department. The legion had its own doctors who always accompanied the legion.

Military medicine began to divide doctors into subgroups. There were the so-called Medici ordinarii, who cared for and treated more soldiers. Some doctors in the Medici cohort were called Medici doctors. There were also Capsarii, who always carried special medical equipment. There was also a preventive medicine service, which addressed hygiene issues.

2.6. Social Health Insurance or State-Run Models in the Ancient World

If we look at the healthcare systems of the ancient world, we will see that similar models of social health insurance and state financing existed in some developed countries.

In Egypt, there was social health insurance for the builders of the pyramids and temples, which, in the event of risks, covered the costs of their recovery from the state treasury or the temples' treasuries. There were also employer-funded healthcare systems in Egypt.

In ancient Greece, there was the Society of Asclepius, which financed the costs of illness from the treasury and certain funds, serving as a mechanism for implementing social healthcare.

Ancient Rome - The state treasury and the city treasuries funded military medicine and public medicine. This gave vulnerable people the right to receive medical services.

Ancient India - As a result of King Ashoka's reforms, the state funded the recovery of people and, at the same time, the treatment of animals.

A mechanism for tax-based medical treatment has also been developed. Ancient China, particularly during the Han Dynasty, developed social healthcare, with the state financing the medical expenses of vulnerable social classes and individuals in special professions (Bonati, 2019).

3. ISLAMIC WORLD AND HEALTHCARE SYSTEMS

The Golden Age of Islam, spanning the 8th to the 13th centuries, played a pivotal role in advancing health and science and in establishing healthcare systems. Islamic scholars translated ancient medical books and created numerous new scientific works to address future health questions. Scientists such as al-Razi, Ibn Sina, al-Biruni, Ibn al-Haitham, and al-Zahrawi answered many questions in natural science through observation and experimentation. It was the scientists working in the bosom of Islam who explained the diseases of smallpox and chickenpox. They contributed to the diagnosis of diseases such as plague, leprosy, diabetes, and hemophilia (Ashimi, 2018).

The Islamic community of that time was part of the Constitution of Medina, and they acted with great enthusiasm. They defended religious freedoms and rights, especially towards the Jews. Liberal freedoms led to an explosion of science and medical research.

Ibn Sina, known in Europe as Avicenna, wrote a book that became famous in economics and is known in English as the Canon of Medicine. Avicenna identified the problems with cardiovascular medicine and provided new directions. What is very interesting is that at this time, developed health care systems were created, among which the following systems are essential:

- Hospital, in Persian it was called Bīmāristān, or a place for the sick. Often, these institutions were free, with their financing coming from a special treasury. Doctors received salaries, and there were separate rooms for patients, with men and women treated in separate blocks. Ophthalmology, surgical services, and mental health care were well developed.
- Medical education began to be regulated by means of competency testing. The Arab Caliph Al-Mukhtadir in the 10th century ordered the licensing of doctors to test their knowledge and develop the quality of medicine.
- Medical education began in hospitals. Students studied the works of Avicenna, Al-Razi, and Hippocrates, as well as the sources of Galen's medical knowledge.
- Pharmacology was developed with pharmacological practice developed in the books of Avicenna and Al-Razi.

- Treatment of mental illnesses was regulated. Treatment directions for mental diseases were established.
- Sanitary norms were developed, hygiene was regulated in cities and villages, and quarantine rules were established during epidemics.

As we can see, during the Golden Age of Islam, a state health policy was established, and caliphs, sultans, and politicians attempted to develop and implement health policies to promote health care. Developments in the Islamic world have transformed healthcare into a public policy.

The Islamic Scholars, leadres and rulers were founding Hospital alike Healthcare Organizations. The first such *hospital in Europe* was founded in the 7th century. The Hôtel-Dieu, founded in 651 CE, was one of the oldest medical institutions to function as a charitable institution, opened by the Bishop of Paris. This institution housed people experiencing homelessness, warriors, and pilgrims, and was more of a hospice than a hospital. Urbanization led to a significant demand for healthcare providers. The Renaissance led to the development of healthcare systems. European universities began to teach health disciplines.

4. REFORMING AND HEALTHCARE EDUCATION

The origins of the first medical schools in Europe are a fascinating story. It is believed that the first medical school was founded in Salerno, Italy, in the 9th century. This school is believed to have been a blend of four different cultures: Jewish, Arabic, Greek, and Latin.

Women could also study at the Salerno Medical School. The strict attitude towards hygiene and public health that prevailed at this school led graduates to become reformers upon their return to their workplaces.

After leaving Salerno, the graduates, founded their own schools. Doctor Courbier, educated at Salerno, later became the personal physician of King Philip Augustus of France (Fulton,1953).

Many doctors who worked in France and England were educated at the University of Padua. This was especially effective in the 14th and 15th centuries, and subsequently, excellent medical schools were established in Holland in the 16th century. The University of Leiden was especially in vogue. Now, it is interesting to consider what English students disliked about the medical schools of Oxford and Cambridge. As they write, the medical schools of these two British universities were very theoretical. They were especially distinguished by the teaching of theoretical materials derived from the schools of Hippocrates, Galen, and Salerno. However, when the English finally recognized the strength of the Dutch medical schools in

1421, they discussed this issue in the English Parliament. They noted that doctors who had graduated from Holland should receive their M.D. from Oxford and Cambridge universities immediately. This was necessary to improve the quality of healthcare in England. In this direction, we see a reformist movement in the English Parliament and in medical education. The fact is that reform of medical education should be prepared within universities, which will study the existing problem and identify directions for its transformation.

During the reign of Henry VIII, an English student from Italy who had graduated from a medical school there came to England. His name was Thomas Linacre. This gentleman, with the help of the king and parliament, founded innovative healthcare lectureships at Oxford and Cambridge. This process led to the development of healthcare in England by generating new knowledge. Then another interesting person appeared, who left his mark on English medical education: Sir George Newman. This person formulated the main principles of medical education, based on philosophy. He wrote that, based on university standards, a medical student should receive: a) training that includes observing patients and phenomena and using inductive reasoning to find answers to questions, b) deciphering the nature of phenomena, and c) calculating the future development of phenomena (Smith,2000).

Medical education in England developed based on these principles. The medical schools distinguished London, Edinburgh, Aberdeen, and Dublin in the early 18th century.

In Britain, a doctor with a medical diploma in London who intended to practice privately had to overcome special barriers. He had to obtain a license by passing a special examination administered by the College of Physicians and receiving satisfactory marks. However, graduates of Oxford and Cambridge were exempted from this exam, and graduates of all other universities had to take a special exam to obtain a license to practice medicine only in London. At the beginning of the 19th century, French medical schools became particularly competitive, and those who wanted to become doctors applied to them for medical education. In the middle of the 19th century, German universities stood out for attracting the best minds to their medical schools. The success of German schools in medical education was due to the following famous figures: Liebig, Helmholtz, Cohnheim, Ludwig, and others. It was these men who laid the foundation for German excellence in the health sector (Ackerknecht, 1957).

Medical education, which originated in Europe with Italian schools, continued with Dutch, English, French, and German schools, and eventually spread to other continents.

Of particular importance in North America was the establishment of the medical school, founded by William Shippen, who, having received his medical education in Europe, returned to his native Philadelphia and began to lecture on anatomy and the profession of midwifery. When he had gathered enough students, he, along with other Americans who had returned from Europe, founded the Philadelphia Medical School (Flexner, 1910).

In 1813, a medical school was founded at Yale College, making it one of the five primary medical schools in America, along with Columbia University, Dartmouth College, Harvard University, and the University of Pennsylvania.

In the 19th century, there was no unified licensing requirement for physicians in America; therefore, some schools awarded M.D. or M.B. degrees. In Connecticut, the local medical society established a board of medical licensing examinations, which influenced physicians in New York. Finally, in 1847, motivated by developments in medicine and the regulation of medical education, the American Medical Association was founded (Rothstein, 1987).

The founding of the Johns Hopkins University School of Medicine in Baltimore had a particularly significant influence on American universities and their medical schools. This school was founded with a four-year undergraduate program. Accordingly, Johns Hopkins University trained strong personnel for the medical market. As standards for medical education in America became increasingly rigorous, and many schools were closed for failing to meet these standards, it was Hopkins University graduates who became missionaries to the medical schools of other universities, serving as leaders and reformers of medical education (Flexner, 1910).

Mr. Winternitz and his colleagues initiated the reform of medical education at Yale Medical School, developing an entirely new curriculum known as the Yale Plan. According to this plan, medical students at Yale University have great freedom; they become acquainted with the literature, attend lectures, and, depending on which issue of medicine interests them most, pursue further studies. Students can take the National Board of Medical Examiners test to assess their knowledge. Although the Yale plan was criticized, it proved highly effective and provided students with an excellent education. With the establishment and development of medical schools, healthcare systems and models were reformed and transformed in many countries. In well-developed countries, healthcare and its education have developed through their own research and experiments. Of course, there was considerable input from leading medical opinion from other countries and their medical schools. Still, the main thing was that the reform in the medical field was prepared by leading national and local medical schools. It began to take effect; the accumulated education and experience had their impact, and this had already affected healthcare systems. Medical schools around the world came under its influence, and later, when multilateral organizations were established, such as the World Bank and the World Health Organization, the experience accumulated in these organizations, as well as that of the leading countries in medical education and practice, influenced healthcare systems and models worldwide. Healthcare reform, accompanied by strengthened education and institutions, became one of the leading brands as countries developed and strengthened their own sustainability (Flexner, 1910).

National health systems were created precisely by strengthening and diversifying medical education. It turned out that states recognized the urgent importance of healthcare for the formation and development of the state, and, based on strategies and tactics for providing healthcare services, national health systems emerged with distinct differences. Of course, health knowledge, medical education, and schools at famous universities played a significant role in the formation of national health systems. The number of medical schools increased, and the medical profession, which was once passed down from father to son in the Dark Ages, is now freely available and especially popular.

Accordingly, the number of students enrolled in the profession of Doctor and Nurse has increased. The number of doctors and nurses has also increased.

If we consider the Industrial Revolution and the innovations that resulted from it, we will understand that the time has come for national healthcare systems. This was the result of the accumulation of medical knowledge, as well as the growth of the economy and the development of business (Ebert & Ginzberg, 1988).

5. CREATION OF NATIONAL HEALTHCARE SYSTEMS

Of course, the creation of health institutions was preceded by the initiative of heroic people for the greater and more effective benefit of society. In this direction, we cannot but recall Edwin Chadwick (1800–1890), who took special steps towards public sanitation and hygiene. This person was a public health reformer. In 1834, Chadwick undertook significant efforts to eradicate poverty and introduced the Poor Law (Morley, 2007).

In 1842, he published the Report on the Sanitary Condition of the Laboring Population of Great Britain, which had a profound influence on society and shaped public opinion on public health, emphasizing the importance of maintaining sanitary conditions and the connection between hygiene and disease. In 1848, Chadwick helped to introduce the Public Health Act. Public Health Boards were created in the communities. This was undoubtedly a step forward (Ringen, 1979). England was a pioneer in the creation of a public health system. A well-organized public health system had already demonstrated the means to better guide the nation's health. This innovation inspired Germans as well (Vaishali et al.,2024).

The German model of social insurance was developed under Chancellor Bismarck (1815–1898), who followed his own Prussian views on advancing a conservative path of societal development. He also sought to prevent revolutions and, therefore, paid great attention to creating a mechanism that would enable workers to live comfortably and more healthily. Bismarck looked at the statistics and realized that the German workers involved in the industrialization process lived terribly; they often received occupational injuries, got sick and died, their families were left homeless, and such a miserable life tore apart society, and one revolutionary cry was needed so that the whole society would be burned and excited by the fire of revolution.

Accordingly, the German Chancellor did a great job of preventing a revolution in the country. What is particularly interesting is that in the Russian Empire, attempts at revolution were met with raids and repression. At the same time, Bismarck developed a model that would involve all German workers in a solidarity scheme, providing benefits to every worker and their family members, offering health services, and improving health indicators and social satisfaction. The holistic nature of this mechanism was striking, and the social insurance model proved to be effective and sustainable for the country that adopted it.

In 1883, at the initiative of Chancellor Otto von Bismarck, Germany introduced its first health insurance law. This law created the first national health insurance in world history, which covered:

- the treatment of the insured person and the family members, and the payment of hospital fees.
- the creation of a fund where the employer contributed 1/3, and the employee 2/3 of the amount.
- The local hospital fund office, a non-profit organization, managed the very complex and detailed process of social insurance, which was actually of great importance for the country.

In 1884, the Chancellor initiated the passage of the Sickness Insurance Law, a fundamental law. Under this law, injuries received in the work process and the losses caused by them were fully compensated.

In 1989, Bismarck introduced a new law, the Old Age and Disability Insurance Law. Under this initiative, a German worker received a pension upon retiring at age 70.

Bismarck's insurance model was mandatory; it required employers to cover a specific portion of the costs. This insurance scheme was a cornerstone of solidarity and played a significant role in the development of social health insurance systems in Germany, France, Austria, the Netherlands, and Japan, as well as in other countries. Social health insurance has become a new and highly effective direction in health reform, improving the health of millions of people. Let us put Otto von Bismarck at the head of the modern European health reformers (Vlădescu et al., 2005). After Bismarck, Germany further developed a solidarity-based healthcare system, often referred to as the Bismarck model.

The Bismarck model initially covered the health care costs of industrial workers. Then, in the 1900s, the leaders of this system soon realized that providing coverage for workers was not enough, so they expanded social health insurance. The sense of solidarity this healthcare system fostered. Solidarity means that a citizen considers another citizen a co-creator of their own health, and that they themselves are a co-creator of the health of others, by paying insurance premiums and financially participating in solidarity-based social healthcare. This model further strengthened nationalism and solidarity in Germany and made significant strides toward integrating artisans, white-collar workers, employers, employees, and agricultural workers into the system.

In 1911, the German Empire Insurance Code was created, which unified the sickness funds, accident insurance, and pension insurance. It is worth noting that by the time of World War I, approximately 40 percent of the German Empire was insured. After the defeat in World War I, the Weimar Republic was established, which was financially and macroeconomically weak, but insurance continued, and it was extended to family members.

During the Nazi period in Germany from 1933 to 1945, the state strengthened control over the sickness funds, and Nazism excluded Jews and other groups from participating in these schemes. The war required a significant amount of money, and therefore, the priority of health insurance was to serve the wounded and sick at the front. It is worth noting that many German doctors joined the National Socialist German Workers' Party. To implement Nazism Ideology, the National Socialist German Physicians' League and the Nazi Party's District Offices of Public Health were created.

With the complicity of German doctors during World War II, 230,000 people with various mental, cognitive, and other disabilities were euthanized through a program of euthanasia in Germany and the occupied territories (Czech et al.,2023).

After the defeat in World War II, two states were created on Germany's territory: The Federal Republic of Germany and the German Democratic Republic.

In the Federal Republic of Germany, also known as West Germany, the Bismarckian health care model was revived, and the work of sickness funds was renewed. Ludwig Erhard's reforms quickly restored state finances, enabling the German social insurance system to supplement its funds by improving health care. Since 1945, German business in the western part has strengthened, and soon the so-called German miracle emerged, marking rapid economic growth. In this direction, German health care improved and achieved great success.

The opposite happened in East Germany, which was occupied by Soviet troops and where the German Democratic Republic was established. A state-run, tax-based system was introduced here, but it proved ineffective. However, this system resembled the British model, which was already referred to as the Beveridge model;

the system of the German Democratic Republic could not be improved due to its underdeveloped financial base and economy.

At this time, West Germany further implemented the Social Health Insurance (SHI) model. The model provided an exciting option for the population: those with relatively high incomes could insure themselves against health risks through a private insurance company. However, for those with an income below a certain threshold, all Germans and residents were required to be insured in the Social Health Insurance system, which in 1970 provided its members with numerous benefits. In particular, these benefits included disease prevention, financing of hospital illnesses, childbirth, childcare, and the purchase of medicines. This had a significant impact on the world at the time. This model covered 90 percent of the German population and was considered the best healthcare system in the world (vd Schulenburg, 2019).

German health policymakers, health care providers, and consumers/patients have formulated three primary goals for the health care system of the future: a) solidarity at the same time, b) freedom of choice, and c) cost control. The German health care system continues to develop along the same lines, albeit with new challenges. Today's system can be described as a modernized Bismarckian health care system. This system has an interesting mechanism for reimbursing providers. It covers outpatient care, hospital care, and pharmaceuticals. The system implements cost control in the German way. Of course, discussions about German healthcare policy are dominated by debates over the causes of the rapid growth in healthcare costs and how to curb spiraling costs. In Germany, the state health insurance system of the 1920s exhibits three characteristics of German hospital care in the current discussion: relatively extended hospital stays, hospital financing, efforts to curb the rapid growth of hospital service costs, and government planning of hospital facilities.

Regulated competition plays a significant role in the German healthcare system. In fact, the Bismarckian healthcare model has been preserved. We are simply dealing with universal coverage due to the time requirement. That is, the scope of services is approaching universal coverage. Non-profit sickness funds operate nationwide. Insurance premiums based on people's income are collected by these organizations, and the funds are then distributed, in accordance with the principle of solidarity, to the treatment of insured persons. Taking into account the risk management system and conducting continuous risk research. The implementation of a payment schedule for outpatient care and the Diagnosis-Related Group DRG system for hospitals has modernized this system. The formula for this system can be expressed as follows:

Solidarity, employer and employee contributions (premiums), the presence of multiple non-state insurers, strict regulation, and market-based purchasing all contribute to the social health insurance model.

Participants in the model, together with their employers, pay an insurance premium to the health insurance fund. This fund is a public organization, the GKV, and is open in all regions of Germany. Such health insurance funds operate in accordance with local principles and regulations. Statutory health insurance is a key part of this model. It covers 90 percent of German residents. High-income social groups can opt for private health insurance companies (Schulenburg, 1983). That is, they can choose a PKV (private insurance company), where health insurance may be more expensive, but the compensation may also be higher.

The social health insurance premium is calculated as follows: 14.6% of an individual's gross earnings should be deducted from their income. Then it is divided between the employer and the employee. That is, when a private individual pays 7.3% of their gross earnings, they know that their healthcare is in stable hands. To this is added a surcharge, which should be divided between the employee and the employer.

Financial funds are pooled in the Central Health Fund (Ibrahim et al.,2020).

Does Germany provide its population with universal health coverage? Of course, it does, because a social health insurance model covers 90 percent of the German population. Only high-income earners are exempt from this social health insurance model, and they opt for private health insurance services, which may be more expensive and also more socially prestigious. For example, a woman in a social health insurance model receives childbirth services. During this service, the attending physician, midwife, and nurse are the health workers on duty. A woman with private health insurance may give birth in the same clinic. However, for her benefit, the delivery is led by a gynecologist who has previously treated her and is familiar with her health. Accordingly, the health service may be identical in both cases if we do not take into account the Doctor who is pre-ordered under private insurance and will perform the service.

Now, let us ask: What is the implementation of German universal coverage like? The German universal coverage model is based on an insurance mechanism in which both the employer and the employee pay an insurance premium, thereby building a health fund.

The British model differs from this model. The universal health care model is also implemented in Britain, but the British model differs in that it is based on employee taxes rather than insurance. The British model selects healthcare providers from public organizations, while the German model relies more on private companies. In the German model, patients freely choose a medical organization and a Doctor; in the British model, this choice is limited (Tulchinsky, 2018).

Now we must ask how effective the Bismarckian social health insurance system is, which was first implemented in Germany and then introduced in many other countries. The Germans themselves conduct fascinating studies on health decision-making and economic evaluation. These studies clearly illustrate what German health economists emphasize when evaluating the national health system. When talking about the effectiveness of the German model, we should not forget to use the following indicators:

- Life expectancy in Germany is equal to 81 years on average, and it is ahead of the life expectancy of residents of the United States, which is 78.4.
- Infant mortality in Germany is low. In the United States, infant mortality rates are historically significantly higher than in Germany. In 2022, the infant mortality rate in the US was 5.6 per 1,000 live births, while the latest 2023 data from Germany show a rate of approximately 3 per 1,000 live births.
- Amenable mortality, that is, preventable deaths, is low and will continue to fall.

Regarding access to healthcare, Germany has a system that covers the entire population with health insurance, with practically no one left uninsured. The German patient trusts Bismarckian healthcare and enjoys considerable freedom in choosing a healthcare provider.

As for the question of how effective the German social insurance model is for healthcare?

- Germany spends 12 (approximately) percent of its GDP on healthcare, which is the second highest in the world after the US. Given the rapid pace of population aging, costs are rising rapidly in Germany (Von der Schulenburg, 2018).

The model's administrative costs are high, but the team is working to reduce them, and the advent of electronic healthcare facilitates this effort. The German model is indeed effective, but we can still question its effectiveness. However, given the number of recovered patients and the nation's high life expectancy, it is clear that this nation's healthcare system is truly successful.

6. SOME URGENT CONDITIONS FOR THE BISMARCKIAN MODEL OF HEALTHCARE

It is interesting to note that the Bismarckian Model requires special conditions in order to be well integrated not only with the country's economy, but also with the level of development of society and social processes, as well as with the level of development of culture and cognition, and with the patterns of social behavior of society's representatives.

The Bismarckian Model, now commonly referred to as the social health insurance model, falls under the category of universal coverage models. Of course, universal coverage can be achieved through other models. However, we must acknowledge that the Bismarckian Model makes universal coverage more accessible to patients, as it provides them with greater freedom of choice and fewer restrictions.

Of course, the Bismarckian Model of social health insurance is an expensive pleasure; outpatient treatment costs are rising, and hospital DRGs are becoming more expensive as well. However, we must also acknowledge that this Model can provide significant benefits to the state that introduced it. Nevertheless, we must add a qualifying phrase: 'if'.

This reflects precisely those environmental factors and the levels of development of societies, economies, and competitiveness, where the Bismarckian Model of social health insurance will not only be sustained for a year, but will be able to hold the sky on its shoulders like a titan.

Do not think this is just a beautiful phrase; it is the national health care model that can save the country and ensure long-term happiness for its society. This is precisely what the ancient Greek myths meant: if the Titan Atlas did not hold back the sky, they believed the sky would fall and destroy the world. This is precisely how it relates to the state's social problems. How to explain this if! If we say that the state and its people will tolerate the Bismarckian Model, what is this and what does it mean? In order to create and successfully implement the Bismarckian Model of social health insurance, several factors must be present in the state:

- The state must have a competitive economy and well-organized finances. It is evident that the state's economy is growing and is expected to continue growing.
- There must be a strong private sector in the state that will employ people well and give them regular wages, so that they will be happy to pay for health insurance. The Bismarckian social health insurance model currently covers approximately 90 percent of German citizens and residents, indicating that a significant portion of society is successfully employed and has a regular income. However, we also note that the remaining 10 percent of the German population is insured through private insurance companies, and accordingly, their health insurance is excellent and long-lasting. That is, 100 percent of the German population is insured, and the Bismarckian social insurance model covers 90 percent of them. This is achieved precisely by the possibility of high employability. This employability is strengthened by the country's sustainable and competitive business environment. An interesting regularity

also characterizes the German economy: Germany takes pride in the fact that small and medium-sized enterprises generate a large share of gross domestic product. This means that the German economy is more sustainable than those of countries where large factories and organizations have a significant advantage in generating gross domestic product. This German business structure is more sustainable because small and medium-sized companies are more easily reorganized in the face of a crisis, making Germany more resilient and its economy more stable.

- In order to establish and implement the business model well, it is necessary to have widespread solidarity in the state and a high level of development of society. Solidarity is often a historical achievement, and society cannot develop this great feeling overnight. Accordingly, the continuity of solidarity is grounded in historical processes that have brought the nation together, led it through many challenges, demonstrated the power of unity, and fostered solidarity as a phenomenon. German society possesses this historical past, and therefore, solidarity is deep and enduring.
- The existence of a middle class in society is important, as it carries all the values that are necessary to govern the country and control political processes. In a society where the middle class is strong, corruption and nepotism are defeated. Such a society is built on values and accordingly controls political processes through elections. The Bismarckian Model of social health insurance is an achievement of the German middle class. Such a society takes Care of its own state, the quality of people's health, and actively participates in it.
- A high level of culture and education is an essential part of a model, such as the Bismarckian system, that the state offers. A well-educated patient is important, too.

7. BEVERIDGE MODEL OF HEALTHCARE

The main thing in the world health reforms was that the desire for organized Care began in European countries, and health care also took on a systemic character when Great Britain adopted the Poor Law Amendment Act. This act expressed the country's responsibility for people's health. This happened in 1834, and with the Poor Law Amendment Act, local governments shared the responsibility for providing basic health services to people experiencing poverty.

A few years later, in 1848, the Public Health Act was passed, which created the first law on public health. This law required people to comply with norms for waste disposal, clean water, and sanitation.

In 1911, the United Kingdom introduced the National Insurance Act, which established workers' health insurance.

It was after this that the Beveridge Report was implemented, under which, through taxes, universal health coverage was offered to the people of the British Empire.

These were key steps during England's healthcare reforms. The state budget funds the British health system and relies on taxation. All citizens and residents of the United Kingdom are covered by the Beveridge model, which is known as the National Health Service NHS. This system was created by the British economist and reformer Sir William Beveridge in the 1950s (Williams & Williams, 2021).

In 1942, Sir William Beveridge published a report arguing that social protection could only be achieved through cooperation between the state and the individual, titled “Social Insurance and Allied Services” (Beveridge, 2000).

It was in this report that Sir Beveridge presented the principles that formed the basis of the National Health Service, created in 1948.

3 aspects laid down the basis of this system:

- Taxation and the funds collected as a result of taxation,
- Ensuring access to all who live in Great Britain,
- This Model provides health care through state-owned hospitals and clinics, as well as public health.

Later, this Model was established in addition to the British Empire, in Spain, New Zealand, and much of Scandinavia.

Why Sir Beveridge did not use a social health insurance system like in Germany. The answer to this must be sought in the history of Great Britain.

- After the end of World War II, Britain was faced with massive inequality among its citizens, both in income and in the provision of health care.
- In a 1942 report, Sir Beveridge said that social health insurance would not be enough to fill the inequalities that World War left in England.
- The NHS in 1948 was created by the political convictions of the Labor Party, which had won the elections in 1945.
- Great Britain, which had won the Second World War, had serious economic problems in terms of employment, which did not allow health insurance to be built on employee-employer relationships.
- Britain already had a large number of municipal hospitals and outpatient services, so this had to be used properly.
- The British tax system was well-organized and worked smoothly.
- It was also very flexible to control health care costs through this system.

In other words, the decolonized kingdom effectively utilized its advantages, resulting in a straightforward system. Since they aimed to equalize healthcare levels, the reformers of that time made this possible with this Model. If the Bismarckian Model had been implemented, many patients who were not employed would have been left outside the system. Accordingly, the then-exiled kingdom prepared and implemented a rational solution by introducing the Beveridge system (Beverid,2000). Indeed, Great Britain adopted a simple and effective healthcare model. This reform was one of the most effective and timely in the history of healthcare reforms (Beveridge, 2000).

Are citizens and residents of the United Kingdom satisfied with their Healthcare today? The parliament of this country is continually seeking answers to this question, and research is also being conducted in this direction. A 2024 study recorded the following situation. The British faced three distinct challenges: COVID-19, the Russia-Ukraine war, and rising living costs, which had a significant impact on the economy and the lives of people in Great Britain. Particular problems arose in the public services sector. During this period, England experienced two changes in prime minister, likely due primarily to public dissatisfaction. Dissatisfaction with healthcare services was particularly highlighted. Dissatisfaction with healthcare services increased from 25% to 52% in 2019. Dissatisfaction with social Care also increased from 37% to 57% during this time (Fitzpatrick,2022).

Although taxation is very high, some respondents demanded an increase. Additionally, only 39% of respondents expressed the opinion that migrants are beneficial to the English economy, a figure previously higher. The number of people who think that there is poverty in England has also increased.

The main issues of people's dissatisfaction were:

- Long waiting lists in outpatient clinics and during hospital referrals.
- Staff shortages in hospitals and outpatient clinics
- A feeling of inadequacy of state funding among people.

However, despite this dissatisfaction, citizens and residents of the United Kingdom also trust this Model and do not intend to change it. They favor universal access for all and the equalization of healthcare levels through this Model (Montagu & Maplethorpe,2024).

8. SINGLE PAYER SYSTEM – NATIONAL HEALTH INSURANCE (NHI) MODEL

NHI is inspired by the Bismarck model, created in 1883, but national health insurance has developed separately and has gained recognition as a new approach to national Healthcare. It is based on the single-payer healthcare model. We must remember the history of this Model in Europe, but its official introduction should still be attributed to the New World. This Model is often referred to as the Saskatchewan model because it was first established in the Canadian province of Saskatchewan by Premier Dom Douglas in 1947.

In 1966, a provincial act disseminated this Model across Canada, laying the groundwork for one of the most notable healthcare reform initiatives.

This healthcare model promises universal coverage for people. However, unlike the Beveridge model, it meets patients' health needs not only in the public sector but also in the private sector. That is, in this respect, the Model is more favorable.

Americans often look to the Canadian Model with interest. We also know that more than 80,000 Americans migrate to Canada each year to access Canadian health care, often taking their Canadian friends' ID cards with them, and this kind of abuse has been exposed. More importantly, as the issue of single-payer public health insurance is on the political radar in the United States, it is worth considering the Canadian health care system's work over the past 50 years and the lessons it has learned. Today, Canadians take pride in a universal approach to health insurance based on need, which is the principle that Healthcare is accessible to all, regardless of income. The positive aspects of the Canadian healthcare system include ease of access to Care, relatively low costs, low administrative costs, and greater efficiency and safety compared to other countries, such as the United States, which spends much more per capita. However, there is growing frustration with the way the system operates, particularly regarding access to Care and coordination. Medicine has changed dramatically since the introduction of Canadian Medicare in the late 1960s, which covered primarily acute care physician and hospital services, in line with the needs of the time. It has been challenging to implement significant reforms that align coverage and services with evolving needs, particularly for community-based patients with multiple chronic conditions. The status quo represents a compromise reached decades ago between payers, physicians, and healthcare providers, and the current system works well enough for those who need it. The most important lesson we can learn from Canada's experience over the past 50 years is that a single-payer healthcare system solves many problems. However, it is not an integrated, well-managed system that can easily meet the changing healthcare needs of a population (Ivers et al., 2018). This system has been well established and developed in addition to Canada in South Korea and Taiwan. In these countries, the state pays insurance premiums. However, healthcare providers are private organizations. The system covers Outpatient care, Hospitalization, Prescription drugs, dental Care, and traditional Chinese medicine (with partial coverage), as well as preventive Care. It is affordable, accounting for only 7% of Taiwan's gross domestic product, for example. The system features a smart card tool that enables the creation of electronic records.

9. HEALTHCARE REFORM EXPERIENCE IN THE USA

Americans believe that health care reform failed under the Administrations of Truman, Carter, Nixon, and Clinton. These presidents tried to introduce a national health care system in the United States. Who opposed these presidents' initiatives for health care reform, if not the American Medical Association, as well as the business and insurance sectors (Oberlander,2010). Health policymakers and health economists, as well as managers, marketers, and health administration specialists in general, say that the United States has a hybrid model, which is a combination of the following models: the British Beveridge model, the German Bismarck model, the Canadian NHI, and the free market. At the same time, US healthcare is considered one of the highest-quality systems in the world and is also innovative, distinguished by new inventions in Healthcare.

Also, it is interesting to note that, despite the innovativeness and high cost of US healthcare, America's average life expectancy is not higher than that of other countries. For example, in Japan, France, and Germany, people live longer than in the United States.

The market and less systematic nature of American Healthcare have their own history. In the 18th and 19th centuries, there was no systematic healthcare in America. Imagine there were no insurance companies either. Citizens paid doctors and hospitals out of their pockets for Healthcare. Hospitals were mostly charitable. At the beginning of the 20th century, rapid urbanization in America led to an increase in workplace injuries and illnesses. That is why US businesses paid attention to providing employees with Healthcare.

During this period, employers offered employees a sum of money, commonly called sick pay. There was no talk of healthcare provision or insurance yet. However, soon a novelty emerged, and it was this novelty that shaped the face and direction of American Healthcare. It was a hospital sought by a business company, with which it contracted to provide its employees with health services in the event of risks.

In short, it all started in Dallas, the capital of Texas. This hospital, called Baylor Hospital, created the Baylor Health Care plan. Baylor Hospital is considered a pioneer in healthcare provision in America (Marjoua & Bozic,2012).

As we know, the beginning of the twentieth century was a new phase in Healthcare. Since the businessman was always thinking about his employees and their skills, including their health, an innovative idea emerged for the healthcare market. This person was Justin Ford Kimball, who in 1929 created a health plan for Dallas public school teachers. Under this health plan, teachers paid $0.50 and received 21 days of hospital treatment at Baylor Hospital during the year. It was a great invention, and this innovation sparked the interest of many people. This first group health insurance plan created a new direction in American Healthcare. The system formed in Dallas was so popular that others joined it in groups, and eventually it gained significant support, with other hospitals also creating similar prepaid associations (Friedman, 1998).

This Model appealed to the American Hospital Association, which adopted it, standardized it, and gave it the Blue Cross symbol. Eventually, in 1939, the American Blue Cross Association was established, marking the creation of America's first health insurance brand. Later, the blue shield symbol was created to represent the American health insurance system.

This was an employer-sponsored health insurance program implemented in the United States. However, large segments of society were uninsured, including the elderly, the poor, and the unemployed. Therefore, President Lyndon B. Johnson initiated reforms in 1965 that created new health insurance programs for the elderly and Medicaid for low-income individuals and families (Emswiler & Nichols, 2009). Lyndon Johnson sought to establish a new type of society where poverty would be eradicated and Healthcare would be accessible to all. The idea of the Great Society was primarily focused on creating a healthcare system for low-income individuals and older people. In 1965, he signed the Social Security Amendments of 1965, which created Medicare, providing significant assistance to older people and opening the way for them to access health services. Also in the same year, the foundation was laid for health insurance for the poor and low-income groups, including low-income families, pregnant women, children, and people with disabilities.

In the USA, the Managed Care model was well developed. This Model has three different forms: a) Health Maintenance Organization, b) Preferred Organization, and c) POS-Point of Sales Plan.

Because healthcare technologies have continued to develop worldwide, Healthcare has become more expensive and, accordingly, created the basis for a price-reduction mechanism. The Health Maintenance Organization Act appeared in 1973.

President Richard Nixon sought to introduce a new mechanism in the healthcare market that would enhance coordination among parties and control healthcare costs. As a result, the Health Maintenance Organization (HMO) was created, which evaluates healthcare services based on prepayment and a certain capitation.

This system allowed America to pay a fixed amount per patient. The US revised the fixed amount payment, which should have included primary Healthcare, a doctor acting as a gatekeeper, and also hospital healthcare. Individuals who joined an HMO had this opportunity.

If we ask the question, what was the difference between the European Model of health insurance and HMO, we can get the following answer from the patient:

- Traditional health insurance finances health services provided by any provider, while an HMO operates only with a predetermined network of providers. This allows the Model to ensure that health services are priced at an acceptable level.
- In health insurance, the patient pays, and then the insurance company pays him a specific part of the cost of the treatment provided according to the agreement. At the same time, in the case of HMO, the patient pays only the amount in advance.
- In the case of insurance, the service is provided by any clinic and its collective, in the case of HMO, the health service is provided only by a predetermined doctor within the scheme of this organization.
- In the case of insurance, anyone can choose a primary care doctor, while in the case of an HMO, it is determined by the network.

An HMO does not cover health care costs outside of its own scheme.

The costs of a patient's health insurance are as follows. Healthcare premiums are paid monthly and annually, plus co-payments in each case.

The costs for a patient enrolled in an HMO are as follows. This is primarily a monthly premium, with co-payments added relatively rarely. In short, an HMO fundamentally reduces healthcare costs, but this reduction comes at the expense of severely limiting patients' choices of doctors and clinics (Hellinger, 1995).

A Preferred Provider Organization is a very active, operational managed healthcare system developed in the USA. PPO was first introduced at a hospital in Denver, Colorado, in 1978, to reduce medical costs uniquely. A network of doctors and hospitals agreed to sell their healthcare services at reduced prices to members of the network who referred large numbers of patients to them. Of course, we are talking about wholesale prices here. If a doctor examines one citizen for $10, how much will that doctor examine a thousand citizens? It is likely cheaper. This was the business model. Soon, the number of such networks increased. This was also convenient for the Blue Cross and the Red Cross. Employees and employers also found it convenient to create similar communities. The advent of computers made it easier to manage such networks(Djakeli,2023).

This system enabled greater choice, as many doctors and hospitals joined the network. From 1985 to 1990, this Model attracted numerous patients and providers, becoming the primary Model among managed care companies. Recently, this Model has garnered considerable attention from patients. PPOs have the advantage of owning an extensive network of providers and also allow patients to seek Care outside this network. Also, referrals are not required for access to other vertical or horizontal providers (Armstrong & Lamm, 2024).

Today, this Model is dominant in the United States.

c) The next Model of managed Care is also exciting - this is the Point-of-Service (POS) Plan.

A Point-of-Service (POS) Plan is a hybrid form of managed Care in which capitation is the primary principle. Within the network, a capitated approach applies; outside the network, a fee-for-service model is used. That is, the patient can go outside the network if needed. However, we must also consider that primary Care can only be provided within the network (Wong et al.,2024). A referral is required within the network, but out-of-network care is available without a referral. The Model also includes prevention (Amin, 2019). The history of the development of the Point-of-Service (POS) Plan shows that it was created to address the wishes of patients who found the restrictions of HMOs inappropriate (Hurley et al., 2004).

10. SEMASHKO HEALTHCARE SYSTEM OF THE SOVIET UNION

The Soviet Union had an exceptional economy, built on the principles of Marxist-Leninist philosophy. Marxism-Leninism in the Soviet Union was actually a sectarian branch of Marx's doctrine that took on an ugly form, and no one knew how to use it. The Marxist-Leninist economy was a particular quadrilateral wheel that could not turn on its own. However, only dictatorship and tyranny could make it move. This can explain the Soviet Union's economic successes from 1933 to 1957, known as rapid industrialization. In the hands of the tyrant and dictator Stalin, mass fear and the cult of personality also drove this “quadrilateral wheeled” economy. As a result, the Soviets solved economic problems and the country became a world leader in many industrial indicators. However, this was not the direct outcome of the economy. It was the result of tyranny and fear that was instilled in the masses. In these years, the Soviet Union, which followed a strict planning system for the economy and the economy as a whole, required a robust healthcare system that would also be part of the planned economy. This Model was created in 1920 by Nikolai Aleksandrovich

Semashko (1874–1949), who was the first Minister of Health in the Soviet Union and the first People's Commissar (Sheiman & Fleck, 2013).

We should also remember what kind of health care system existed before. The health care system in the Russian Empire was not functioning. After the Great October Socialist Revolution in 1917, the communists quickly began to create a new model, and the movement's leader supported the idea of universal, free Care.

The Soviet Union nationalized everything. Hospitals and clinics were nationalized, too. All doctors and nurses were already working in state organizations that required management. To plan the economy, the Soviet Leaders created the Gosplan, the State Planning Committee, which was intended to plan the national economy of this vast country from Moscow. In 1918, the first central health planning unit in the world was established: Narkomzdrav. Semashko's vision was this: "Health is not a commodity; it is a social right guaranteed by the state."

Accordingly, it was necessary to implement this vision, and Lenin himself (the leader of the Russian Revolution) supported it.

In 1936, the Constitution of the Soviet Union was established, which guaranteed free Healthcare for the Soviet Union's population. A period of building hospitals and polyclinics began, which was often used irrationally. Large hospitals were often built in illogical locations, where there were not many patients. Doctors and nurses were quickly trained at universities and technical schools.

The whole process was managed through the Ministry of Health. The ministries of health attempted to regulate all aspects of medicine. Public health prioritized prevention, sanitation, hygiene, and the control of epidemics and endemic diseases—this was the primary goal of public health in the Soviet Union (Sheiman et al., 2018). The Soviet Union's healthcare system adapted quickly during World War II. Mobile hospitals and clinics were established during this period. After the war, as recovery began, many hospitals and polyclinics were built. Public health indicators also improved; for example, the infant mortality rate began to decline sharply, from 250 to 100 per 1,000 children. Life expectancy increased to 63 years, and epidemics were defeated. The problem with Semashko's Model was that it was difficult to treat the disease in outpatient settings, and almost everyone was sent to hospitals, even for tests. This meant that Semashko's centralized, plan-based Model was less flexible. The rational use of a large number of doctors was also significant. In the last years of Semashko's Model, for example, Georgia's healthcare system had 60,000 doctors, which could serve five other countries. There was no need for so many doctors. What led Semashko's Model to such irrationality? A system based on outpatient clinics and polyclinics. Polyclinics were located regionally. Their buildings were unusable. Polyclinics had a more formal meaning; the primary treatment was often sent to hospitals, where patients often paid out of pocket. Polyclinic diagnoses were unreliable, and people did not trust them very much.

Public Healthcare provided routine vaccinations, and the maternal and child treatment program was outstanding. Health insurance was not a part of Soviet Healthcare. Soviet Healthcare was financed from the global budget, based on the principle of paying doctors' and nurses' salaries. Hospital budgets were set by local offices of the State Planning Commission, taking into account material and technical needs and the size of the treatment population (Shyshka et al., 2023). For example, if a state hospital served several million people during the year, its budget was determined using estimates of disease prevalence and other statistical variables, along with the medical knowledge and technology available at the time (Heinrich, 2022). Semashko's Model proved effective during Stalin's reign. However, after Stalin's death, the Model lagged far behind economic reality and thus became dependent on black-market prices. In the last years of Semashko's Model, supplies were severely depleted, and the efficiency of Healthcare fell. Corruption and nepotism emerged. Even though all citizens had equal access to Healthcare under the Constitution of the Soviet Union, the reality was quite different, and those who could not afford Medical Care often received inadequate Care. In short, this Model lost its relevin practice, ance, and after the collapse of the Soviet Union in 1991, the republics that emerged as independent states began to implement their own reforms, the ultimate goal of which was to establish sustainable national healthcare systems (Tikhomirov,2024).

The Semashko model also brought significant changes to global health consciousness. This Model, in terms of the level of declared values, competed with those of market-economy countries. All this gave rise to a desire for better health care in democratic states. Healthcare and the national healthcare system have improved in many countries. The World Health Organization adopted the strengths of the Semashko model, including the significant role of prevention, the state's responsibility for citizens' health, and universal access to Healthcare for all people, regardless of income. On this basis, the famous Alma-Ata Declaration on Primary Health Care (1978) was created (Hone et al., 2018).

11. SOME EXAMPLES OF E-HEALTHCARE REFORMS

Countries begin to compete for successful e-health. The development of Artificial Intelligence became one of the great topics in health reform. E-health in advanced countries has improved e-records, reducing errors and misunderstandings.

This has led to, and will continue to lead to, the existence of electronic patient summary medical records and all associated materials in electronic form, which enhance the ability to share records across different professional levels, thereby increasing the efficiency of Healthcare in e-health conditions. In particular, the introduction of summary electronic health data, for example, on spinal diseases, is of great importance for the development of the National Health Service, as this electronic record practice reduces test duplication, speeds up treatment, and reduces the likelihood of errors. It also improves coordination between providers, ensures safer treatment, and reduces delays (Cole et al., 2018).

Several countries have already successfully implemented reforms in the field of healthcare digitalization, including the following leaders:

- Germany, this country has created regulatory acts and taken steps to create Telematics Infrastructure (TI) and created consumer services for the digitalization of Healthcare.
- Finland has completely covered the nation's healthcare needs and created Kanta Services, THL eHealth Program, which covers the healthcare market and people's demand for personalized digital and physical healthcare services.
- Denmark, which created the national digital healthcare platform Sundhed.dk and covered the entire healthcare demand.
- Estonia, this country has based its healthcare data and records on blockchain.
- Sweden - this country has created Vision eHealth 2025 / Inera AB.
- The United Kingdom, based on the Beveridge model, has created the NHS App and NHS Digital transformation.
- Singapore, where the National Electronic Health Record (NEHR), Smart Nation eHealth ecosystem was quickly created.
- South Korea, this country created a digital hospital infrastructure and the K-Health & Digital New Deal Initiative.
- Japan, this country focuses primarily on Healthcare for the elderly and created Society 5.0 / Digital Agency Health Reforms.
- Canada, the Canadian system built on a single-payer model, created an information system, the Canada Health Infoway / Pan-Canadian Digital Health Strategy was formed.

The United States is not on this list because it did not have a national healthcare system and, accordingly, created fragmented systems. However, America took innovative steps: it laid the foundation through legislation and subsequently implemented legal measures—the HITECH Act (2009), the 21st Century Cures Act (2016), and the ONC Interoperability Rules (2020). Finally, the US is rapidly developing digital healthcare reforms and creating AI-assisted clinical decision-making systems (Google Health, IBM Watson, Epic-AI integration).

11.1. One of the examples of e-health personalization in Germany and the United Kingdom

Among advanced democratic countries, Germany led the E-Healthcare reforms. Theory and the experience of German Healthcare Digitalization are fascinating. Germany is rapidly implementing the necessary changes for digital e-health. An Electronic Patient Record is being created to support doctors' analytical work. The Health Data Use Act (GDNG) has been created. At the same time, special tools for e-health development are being rapidly developed, including the Telematics Infrastructure (TI), Digital Health Card (eGK), e-Prescription, and Digital Health Applications (DiGA, DiPA). Let us examine them separately. With these tools, Germany will develop a digital health ecosystem.

Telematics Infrastructure (TI) - This telematics infrastructure (TI) is an efficient and secure digital network. This network connects participants in the German public health system, including insurance hospital funds, healthcare providers, patients, regulators, and federal organizations.

This system serves as a kind of "backbone" of digital health—akin to an encrypted national internet for medical communication. There are already digital health cards; they authenticate their owners. They are called in German - eGK – elektronische Gesundheitskarte. The eGK is a personal digital ID card for people with health insurance in Germany (about 73 million). It allows access to the telematics infrastructure and stores limited medical and administrative data. This includes: personal data (name, date of birth, insurance number), Emergency data (e.g., allergies, chronic diseases), Electronic medication plan (optional), Authorization keys for secure data access (Hansen et al.,2019). Why is the eGK – elektronische Gesundheitskarte so interesting for other countries that intend to do reforms in e-health? Germany has come a long way in reaching the current level of e-healthcare development. When we talk about the health card, we should know that Germany started taking steps in this direction 20 years ago.

- Germany created the Telematics Infrastructure (TI), which merged various systems and ultimately achieved universal adoption, integration, and technological and technical proficiency of this system.
- The proper steps taken by the state and the state's commitment to these issues are important, as is the presence of a long-term vision. EGK in Germany is part of the national digitalization strategy (Gigauri & Djakeli, 2021 A).
- The German Federal Ministry of Health (BMG) has prepared the following acts for these purposes: a) the e-Healthcare Act of 2015, b) the Digital Health Act of 2019, c) the Patient Data Protection Act of 2020, d) the Digital Act of 2023.

With these acts, Germany has laid the groundwork for a digital healthcare reform. Accordingly, a very effective result has been achieved: 73 percent of German citizens have an EGK, meaning that all insured people in Germany have one. The current rate of coverage of the country's citizens with a personalized digital healthcare card is the highest in the world. The German example is the Health ID, the best-covered population in the world (Gabelaia et al,2024, September). Technologically, this is how it works: membership in Germany's social health insurance model is mandatory. Therefore, when a user visits the health fund, he is immediately given an EKG. The term "healthcare identity" has also been introduced (Djakeli,2025 C).

We should also imagine that the EKG is the primary key to entering the areas of digital Healthcare in Germany:

- Electronic Patient Record (ePA)
- E-Prescription (E-Rezept)
- Emergency data management
- Medication plans
- Insurance verification systems

Accordingly, the insured's use of this card is urgent (Schwenk et al., 2023).

In the UK, activation of e-health has led to many changes in the National Health Service. In particular, the introduction of electronic patient summary medical records in the UK played a significant role (Blake et al.,2023). The development of NHS Apps and their use among patients are also important factors. In 2017, the National Health Service of the Kingdom, which had been decentralized, decided to begin digitizing. To this end, the NHS Digital Transformation plan was developed, and the process began. The goal was for all patients to have digital access to the National Health Service and for this digital app to serve as a digital front door for patients (Gigauri & Djakeli, 2021 B).

Today, this app is called the Digital Frontdoor. The app was first introduced in 2018. It made it easier to book services, cancel reservations, and address important issues, such as electronic records of doctor diagnoses, follow-ups on doctor visits, prescribed medications, vaccination schedules during the COVID-19 pandemic, and information about medical bills (Finnegan & Mountford, 2025).

This app has become very popular, and according to 2024 data, it has 33 million users in the United Kingdom. This app offers patient involvement in their treatment, provides valuable information, and boasts user-friendliness, flexibility, and high social value for citizens. The app was first tested in a pilot program with only 200,000 users, but its user base has grown rapidly since then. The National Health Service uses the app to send information to patients and, in collaboration with them, create healthcare value for the nation (Sukriti et al., 2023).

11.2. E-health in Asian Countries

It is also exciting to see what is happening in China, which is making massive investments in and conducting research on telemedicine, developing AI diagnostics, and advancing digital public health surveillance, such as Ping An Good Doctor and AliHealth.

Following the new information revolution, a new field has emerged globally - digital health. India was ahead of everyone in this matter. It created a universal model of digital health for all. The universal health coverage program in India, based on digital technologies, was known as the Rashtriya Swasthya Bima Yojana (RSBY). This was Jawaharlal Nehru's dream of seeing India with advanced technologies. When Prime Minister Modi came to power, he announced the Digital India program. Even before that, specific biometric databases were needed to integrate society into digital databases. However, Modi's plan, known as Digital India, marked a new stage in Indian reforms. Modi's Healthcare, and especially digital Healthcare, is intended to cover the entire country using digital technologies. Modi announced the National Digital Health Mission (NDHM) in 2020, which aims to create a digital healthcare ecosystem and integrate delivery and payment methods. There are high hopes for digital healthcare reform in India, where sharp polarization among social groups exists (Al Dahdah & Mishra, 2023).

12. FINDINGS AND RECOMMENDATIONS

Based on the challenges of civilization development and the innovations humans have sought to address environmental challenges, four healthcare models were reviewed in this chapter. These models are the result of the healthcare knowledge that each state has accumulated over the centuries, as well as the influence of healthcare culture, education, awareness, and cognition.

Today, many politicians argue that Healthcare is a peaceful means of competition between states. Indeed, with a well-functioning healthcare system, a state also develops its economy, as there is a direct proportional relationship between good health and economic activities.

The current global healthcare systems should be structured like this:

1. The Bismarckian Model of social health insurance requires a well-developed employer and employee, since they bear the main financial burden - 14.6%, which is distributed between the employer and the employee - 7.3% each. This Model, which is widespread in Germany, France, Belgium, Japan, and South Korea, effectively embodies the ambition of powerful countries to win competitions

peacefully and become even stronger. The economic Model of these countries is also very important for the development of the existing healthcare system.

2. The Beveridge model for Great Britain, which is financed through taxes and which is one of the interesting systems for equalizing the cost of Healthcare, most importantly, this Model relies on public hospitals as healthcare providers, and it works well for citizens and residents of the United Kingdom.
3. The Canadian Model, which some also call the Saskatchewan model and others the NHI or National Health Insurance model, which the Bismarckian Model partly inspires, but, unlike this Model, is based on the principle of a single payer, and whose success is even confirmed by the fact that Americans move to Canada and often use this Model for their healthcare needs.
4. The fourth Model is the usual out-of-pocket payment; you cannot call this Model any system, it is inspired by the principles of the health market and health marketing, and it is built on the usual ratio of demand and supply. Healthcare delivery is evolving according to demand. Healthcare has a more factual nature, and the market regulates this Model, provided the market is developed correctly and has the "invisible hand" necessary for proper distribution, which is essential for redistribution and resolving conflicts.

All the above-mentioned models are used in one of the richest and successful Healthcare systems, which the USA endorses.

As we know, countries around the world can be divided into several main models for organizing national health systems. We should not forget that these systems provide universal health coverage to their populations (Djakeli, 2024, A).

The main models of national health systems, the German Model of social health insurance - named after Bismarck, the English tax-based National Health Service - named after Beveridge, the Canadian single-payer model - named after Saskatchewan, and their American hybrid, or the so-called mix of these models standard in the USA, all of them will face significant challenges at the current stage and in the future. Accordingly, states that develop national health systems similar to this Model will also face similar challenges:

- Strengthening and further deepening public trust in national health systems based on these models. We all know how even a single unfortunate event can erode people's trust in the healthcare system. We also know that without trust, the work of a doctor, a nurse, a healthcare administrator, and the entire system is impossible. Accordingly, in the digital age, the main task will be to maintain quality standards in Healthcare and to achieve excellent patient trust in remote healthcare operations. This can be achieved through various mechanisms, such as transparency in healthcare systems and the presence of subsystems for monitoring. These mechanisms help ensure the honesty and integrity of healthcare systems through transparency and improve the philosophy of healthcare management. Previously, the branching tree philosophy was fundamental in the healthcare business. This necessarily includes planning the best marketing support processes. Monitoring and improving after-marketing processes. Adjusting physical and digital Healthcare, as well as electronic healthcare processes, to meet people's actual needs (Djakeli, 2024 B).

- Achieving data privacy is a significant challenge. Patient data is an invaluable asset for doctors and medical processes, but it also poses a significant threat to individuals, as adversaries can exploit it. Therefore, the perception of data security can be decisive in building respect and trust in national healthcare systems.

Whether the healthcare system is protected from Cybersecurity threats will depend on how it is. Data storage and protection, data management, and speed of data disposal are all significant challenges of the digital age. Patients may appreciate a fast, efficient data management unit within the healthcare system that provides accurate information at referral stages to support important healthcare decisions.

- In the digital age, it is important to create a universal model for reviewing complaints from patients and representatives of the public, which will be digital (Djakeli, 2025 A). GDPR (Europe) and HIPAA (US) systems are similar in this regard. Given their nature, national healthcare systems should develop similar models and consistently address patient complaints. Universalizing patient complaints should be a two-way process aimed at a single goal-patient satisfaction.
- One of the main challenges is the digital literacy of healthcare staff and their ability to manage and use processes. Workforce Digital Readiness is a crucial issue. Digital literacy gaps should be eliminated through training, education, and exams. One additional exam may be added to medical faculties to assess the digital literacy of doctors and nurses.
- Managing ethics and moral issues during the digitalization of healthcare systems is a considerable challenge. A new approach to behavior and management must be developed to account for the transformations in the healthcare system. AI accountability and algorithmic transparency are important for conducting healthcare diagnostic procedures. It is important to maintain the pace of innovation in healthcare systems (Jakeli et al.,2025).
- Ultimately, the big challenge is the strategic and tactical management of national health systems in the digital age, which includes actions aimed at re-

ducing costs and reducing the rate of cost growth, creating optimal pricing and service delivery schemes, and, through these schemes, maintaining the quality of health care and its optimal benefits for the payer. It does not matter if it is a state system, such as the English Beveridge model, the German system of social health insurance, or the American hybrid Model, which is difficult to call a national health system.

- Will the famous Hippocratic Oath remain unchanged? The Hippocratic Oath has already been reviewed once by the World Medical Association in 1948. One phrase in it was changed to another. Now, scientists, taking into account the digital development of Healthcare, are formulating new changes that will further develop the attitude towards Healthcare in accordance with the principles of the Hippocratic Oath. For example, the Hippocratic Oath expresses the spirit that a doctor should use the most challenging healthcare conclusions that other great physicians have obtained before him through research and experiments. However, a new perspective is emerging in the healthcare market, where digital technologies enable patients to become co-creators of their own health. In the case of digital Healthcare, the importance of the patient has increased dramatically, and the patient is no longer just the recipient but the creator of their own health. This should be taken into account in the Hippocratic Code (Djakeli,2025 B). In the 21st century, as a result of the development of electronic, digital Healthcare, telemedicine, and information technologies, there has been a view that even the Hippocratic Oath should be reviewed and changes should be made to it, precisely as a result of the development of digital Healthcare (Mohammad et al.,2025).

Also, what is very interesting is that the Hippocratic Oath is focused on caring for the sick —that is, on their recovery. In contrast, the Healthcare of the 21st century should focus on entirely new goals, specifically including the likelihood of disease occurrence, the use of digital technologies, disease prevention, and the application of artificial intelligence. These are the principles that should be used in the Hippocratic document (Shen et al,2025).

Another sub-principle is to consider the principles of the use of artificial medical intelligence in the Hippocratic Oath. Society and science are already rapidly advancing medical knowledge through artificial intelligence, enabling it to solve many medical problems and become a savior in Healthcare. A special artificial intelligence-based system of bots is actively used to predict up to 1,000 potential future diseases through molecular and genetic analysis. This issue is significant for the effective use of artificial intelligence. If Healthcare can predict diseases and potential health failures, this must be fully taken into account by the Hippocratic

Oath (Meskó & Spiegel, 2022). In the Phygital Age, Modern Healthcare reforms should start with some changes to the Hippocratic Oath.

REFERENCES

Ackerknecht, E. H. (1957). Medical education in 19th century France. *Academic Medicine, 32*(2), 148–153. PMID: 13398763

Al Dahdah, M., & Mishra, R. K. (2023). Digital health for all: The turn to digitized Healthcare in India. *Social Science & Medicine, 319*, 114968. DOI: 10.1016/j.socscimed.2022.114968 PMID: 35459554

Amin, K. (2019). Impact of Out-of-Network Service Utilization and State Policy Changes on Payments and Follow-Up Visits.

Armstrong, S. M., & Lamm, S. L. (2024). The Changing Healthcare Environment. Clinical Laboratory Management, 67–91.

Ashimi, T. A. (2018). The contribution of Muslim scholars to the field of medicine (with particular reference to Ibn Sina and Al-Razi during the Islamic Golden Age). *Journal of Education and Social Sciences, 9*(3), 73–77.

Beverid, W. (2000). Social insurance and allied services. *Bulletin of the World Health Organization, 78*(6), 847–855. PMID: 10916922

Beveridge, W. (2000). Social insurance and allied services. 1942. *Bulletin of the World Health Organization, 78*(6), 847. PMID: 10916922

Blake, H. A., Sharples, L. D., Harron, K., van der Meulen, J. H., & Walker, K. (2023). Linkage of multiple electronic health record datasets using a 'spine linkage ' approach compared with all 'pairwise linkages'. *International Journal of Epidemiology, 52*(1), 214–226. DOI: 10.1093/ije/dyac130 PMID: 35748342

Bonati, I. (2019). The (un) healthy poor: Wealth, poverty, medicine and Health care in the Greco-Roman world. *Akroterion, 2019*(64), 15–43.

Brandt-Rauf, P. W., & Brandt-Rauf, S. I. (1987). History of occupational medicine: Relevance of Imhotep and the Edwin Smith papyrus. *British Journal of Industrial Medicine, 44*(1), 68–70. DOI: 10.1136/oem.44.1.68 PMID: 3545281

Carpenter, S., Rigaud, M., Barile, M., Priest, T. J., Perez, L., & Ferguson, J. B. (2006). The Ebers Papyrus. *Bard College, 3.*

Cole, A. A., Breakwell, L. M., & Hutton, M. J. (2018). The National Health Service (NHS) in England: Trying to Achieve Value-Based Healthcare. Quality Spine Care: Healthcare Systems, Quality Reporting, and Risk Adjustment, 171–198.

Czech, H., Hildebrandt, S., Reis, S. P., Chelouche, T., Fox, M., González-López, E., Lepicard, E., Ley, A., Offer, M., Rotzoll, A. M., Sachse, C., Siegel, S., Šimůnek, M., Teicher, A., Uzarczyk, K., von Villiez, A., Wald, H., Wynia, M., & Roelcke, V. (2023). The Lancet Commission on medicine, Nazism, and the Holocaust: Historical evidence, implications for today, teaching for tomorrow. *Lancet*, *402*(10415), 1867–1940. DOI: 10.1016/S0140-6736(23)01845-7 PMID: 37951225

David, A. R. (2008). The ancient Egyptian medical system. Egyptian mummies and modern science, 181–194.

Djakeli, K. (2023). Sustainable Healthcare Reforming Model Based on Marketing: Case of Georgia. In Handbook of Research on Achieving Sustainable Development Goals With Sustainable Marketing (pp. 271-287). IGI Global.

Djakeli, K. (2024 A). Social Marketing: Past, Current Period. Phygital Approaches to Social Marketing, IGI Global.

Djakeli, K. (2024). B). Healthcare marketing: meaning, historical development, applications, and current status. In *Modern Healthcare Marketing in the Digital Era* (pp. 1–25). IGI Global Scientific Publishing.

Djakeli, K. (2025A). Phygitalization of Palliative Care and Its Social Marketing. In *Phygital Approaches to Social Marketing* (pp. 267–288). IGI Global Scientific Publishing.

Djakeli, K. (2025B). Social Marketing and Public Health in the Phygital Era. In Phygital Approaches to Social Marketing (pp. 43-66). IGI Global Scientific Publishing.

Djakeli, K. (2025C). Strategic Management for Digital Platform Brands in the Phygital Era. In Brand Creation and Management in the Phygital Era (pp. 499-520). IGI Global Scientific Publishing.

Ebert, R. H., & Ginzberg, E. (1988). The reform of medical education. *Health Affairs*, *7*(suppl 2), 5–38. DOI: 10.1377/hlthaff.7.2.5 PMID: 3378732

Emswiler, T., & Nichols, L. M. (2009). *Baylor Health Care System: High-Performance Integrated Health Care*. Commonwealth Fund.

Finnegan, H., & Mountford, N. (2025). 25 years of electronic health record implementation processes: Scoping review. *Journal of Medical Internet Research*, *27*, e60077. DOI: 10.2196/60077 PMID: 40053758

Fitzpatrick, R. (2022). Satisfaction with health care. In *The experience of illness* (pp. 154–176). Routledge. DOI: 10.4324/9781003283966-8

Flexner, A. (1910). Medical education in the United States and Canada. *Science, 32*(810), 41–50. DOI: 10.1126/science.32.810.41 PMID: 17745880

Friedman, E. (1998). What Price Survival?: The Future of Blue Cross and Blue Shield. *Journal of the American Medical Association, 279*(23), 1863–1869. DOI: 10.1001/jama.279.23.1863 PMID: 9634248

Fulton, J. F. (1953). History of medical education. *British Medical Journal, 2*(4834), 457–461. DOI: 10.1136/bmj.2.4834.457 PMID: 13066760

Gabelaia, I., Djakeli, K., & McElroy, J. W. (2024, September). The Power of Customer Journey Mapping with Artificial Intelligence: A Case Study Method. In *International Conference on Reliability and Statistics in Transportation and Communication* (pp. 244–257). Cham: Springer Nature Switzerland.

Gigauri, I., & Djakeli, K. (2021). A). Expecting Transformation of Marketing During the Post-Pandemic New Normal: Qualitative Research of Marketing Managers in Georgia. [IJSEM]. *International Journal of Sustainable Economies Management, 10*(2), 1–18. DOI: 10.4018/IJSEM.2021040101

Gigauri, I., & Djakeli, K. (2021). B). Remote working challenges for Georgian social enterprises amid the current pandemic. *HOLISTICA–Journal of Business and Public Administration, 12*(3), 39–53. DOI: 10.2478/hjbpa-2021-0021

Halwani, T., & Takrouri, M. (2006). Medical laws and ethics of Babylon, as read in Hammurabi's code (History). The Internet Journal of Law. *Healthcare and Ethics, 4*(2), 1–8.

Hansen, A., Herrmann, M., Ehlers, J. P., Mondritzki, T., Hensel, K. O., Truebel, H., & Boehme, P. (2019). Perception of the progressing digitization and transformation of the German health care system among experts and the public: Mixed methods study. *JMIR Public Health and Surveillance, 5*(4), e14689. DOI: 10.2196/14689 PMID: 31661082

Heinrich, A. (2022). The emergence of the socialist healthcare model after the First World War. In *International Impacts on Social Policy: Short Histories in Global Perspective* (pp. 35–46). Springer International Publishing. DOI: 10.1007/978-3-030-86645-7_4

Hellinger, F. J. (1995). Selection bias in HMOs and PPOs: A review of the evidence. *Inquiry : a Journal of Medical Care Organization, Provision and Financing,* •••, 135–142. PMID: 7601511

Hone, T., Macinko, J., & Millett, C. (2018). Revisiting Alma-Ata: What is the role of primary health care in achieving the Sustainable Development Goals? *Lancet, 392*(10156), 1461–1472. DOI: 10.1016/S0140-6736(18)31829-4 PMID: 30343860

Hurley, R. E., Strunk, B. C., & White, J. S. (2004). The puzzling popularity of the PPO. *Health Affairs, 23*(2), 56–68. DOI: 10.1377/hlthaff.23.2.56 PMID: 15046131

Ibrahim, H., Mahmood, H. S., & Ali, R. (2020). The significant healthcare merits of insurance models: A review study. *Karbala J Pharm Sci, 18*, 12–19.

Israelowich, I. (2015). *Patients and healers in the High Roman Empire*. JHU Press. DOI: 10.1353/book.39295

Ivers, N., Brown, A. D., & Detsky, A. S. (2018). Lessons from the Canadian experience with single-payer health insurance: Just comfortable enough with the status quo. *JAMA Internal Medicine, 178*(9), 1250–1255. DOI: 10.1001/jamainternmed.2018.3568 PMID: 30083756

Jakeli, K., Lobjanidze, T., & Lobjanidze, M. (2025). Healthcare Digitalization Reforms around the World and Georgia's Path. *International Journal Chemistry and Human Health*, (2), 85–91. DOI: 10.52340/ijch.2025.02.06

Karamanou, M., Tsoucalas, G., Papaioannou, T. G., & Sfikakis, P. (2019). Healthcare policy in Ancient Greece: Insights from the Golden Age of Athens (5th century BC) may be helpful in medical Care in the 21st century.

Kleisiaris, C. F., Sfakianakis, C., & Papathanasiou, I. V. (2014). Health care practices in ancient Greece: The Hippocratic ideal. *Journal of Medical Ethics and History of Medicine, 7*, 6. PMID: 25512827

Leake, C. D. (1952). The old Egyptian medical papyri.

Lopes, H. T., & Pereira, R. G. G. (2021). *The Gynecological Papyrus Kahun*. BoD–Books on Demand. DOI: 10.5772/intechopen.95311

Major, R. H. (1930). The Papyrus Ebers. *Annals of Medical History, 2*(5), 547. PMID: 33944361

Marjoua, Y., & Bozic, K. J. (2012). Brief history of quality movement in US healthcare. *Current Reviews in Musculoskeletal Medicine, 5*(4), 265–273. DOI: 10.1007/s12178-012-9137-8 PMID: 22961204

Meskó, B., & Spiegel, B. (2022). A revised Hippocratic oath for the era of digital health. *Journal of Medical Internet Research, 24*(9), e39177. DOI: 10.2196/39177 PMID: 36069845

Metwaly, A. M., Ghoneim, M. M., Eissa, I. H., Elsehemy, I. A., Mostafa, A. E., Hegazy, M. M., Afifi, W. M., & Dou, D. (2021). Traditional ancient Egyptian medicine: A review. *Saudi Journal of Biological Sciences, 28*(10), 5823–5832. DOI: 10.1016/j.sjbs.2021.06.044 PMID: 34588897

Mohammad, A. A. S., Alzyoud, M., Samara, E. I. M., Al-shanableh, N., Salameh, W. E. M. K. B., Alshurideh, M. T., Al-Ayed, S., Alqahtani, M., Al-Momani, A., & Al-Hawary, S. I. S. (2025). Electronic health records adoption: a bibliometric analysis. In *Intelligence-Driven Circular Economy: Regeneration Towards Sustainability and Social Responsibility–Volume 1* (pp. 301–314). Springer Nature Switzerland. DOI: 10.1007/978-3-031-73899-9_24

Montagu, I., & Maplethorpe, N. (2024). British Social Attitudes 41| Five years of unprecedented challenges.

Morley, I. (2007). City chaos, contagion, Chadwick, and social justice. *The Yale Journal of Biology and Medicine, 80*(2), 61. PMID: 18160991

Oberlander, J. (2010). Long time coming: Why health reform finally passed. *Health Affairs, 29*(6), 1112–1116. DOI: 10.1377/hlthaff.2010.0447 PMID: 20530339

Orosz, E., Ellena, G., & Jakab, M. (1998). Reforming the Healthcare System. The Unfinished Agenda. Public Finance Reform during the Transition: The Experience of Hungary.

Relman, A. S., Todd, J. S., Schramm, C. J., & Seidman, B., BROMBERG, M. D., ROSENBERG, N., & BRUNTON, R. S. (1990). Reforming the health care system. *Issues in Science and Technology, 7*(1), 6–11. PMID: 2402264

Ringen, K. (1979). Edwin Chadwick, the market ideology, and sanitary reform: On the nature of the 19th-century public health movement. *International Journal of Health Services, 9*(1), 107–120. DOI: 10.2190/LR4G-X2NK-9363-F1EC PMID: 370032

Rothstein, W. G. (1987). *American medical schools and the practice of medicine: A history*. Oxford University Press. DOI: 10.1093/oso/9780195041866.001.0001

Schulenburg, J. M. G. (1983). Report from Germany: Current conditions and controversies in the health care system. *Journal of Health Politics, Policy and Law, 8*(2), 320–351. DOI: 10.1215/03616878-8-2-320 PMID: 6413572

Schwenk, U., Gesundheit, D. P., Stiftung, B., Strotbek, J., Wehling, H., & Meier, F. (2023). Entwicklung und Anwendung eines Composite Measures für die Qualitätsdarstellung von Krankenhäusern.

Sheiman, I., & Fleck, F. (2013). Rocky road from the Semashko to a new health model. *Bulletin of the World Health Organization, 91*(5), 320–321. DOI: 10.2471/BLT.13.030513 PMID: 23678194

Sheiman, I., Shishkin, S., & Shevsky, V. (2018). The evolving Semashko model of primary health care: The case of the Russian Federation. *Risk Management and Healthcare Policy, 11*, 209–220. DOI: 10.2147/RMHP.S168399 PMID: 30464661

Shen, Y., Yu, J., Zhou, J., & Hu, G. (2025). Twenty-five years of evolution and hurdles in electronic health records and interoperability in medical research: A comprehensive review. *Journal of Medical Internet Research, 27*, e59024. DOI: 10.2196/59024 PMID: 39787599

Shyshka, I., Mashchenko, O., & Tomareva, V. (2023). Theoretical And Methodological Foundations Of The Healthcare System Of Ukraine. *Baltic Journal of Economic Studies, 9*(4), 253–261. DOI: 10.30525/2256-0742/2023-9-4-253-261

Smith, H. (2000). A Quaker Inheritance: An Analysis of Family Values, Religion and the Childhood and Youth of George Newman (1870-1948). *Quaker Studies, 5*(1), 4.

Stiefel, M., Shaner, A., & Schaefer, S. D. (2006). The Edwin Smith Papyrus: The birth of analytical thinking in medicine and otolaryngology. *The Laryngoscope, 116*(2), 182–188. DOI: 10.1097/01.mlg.0000191461.08542.a3 PMID: 16467701

Sukriti, K. C., Tewolde, S., Laverty, A. A., Costelloe, C., Papoutsi, C., Reidy, C., Gudgin, B., Shenton, C., Majeed, A., Powell, J., & Greaves, F. (2023). Uptake and adoption of the NHS App in England: An observational study. *The British Journal of General Practice*. PMID: 37783512

Tikhomirov, A. (2024). Semashko Model: Critical Overview. Available at *SSRN* 4906897.

Tountas, Y. (2009). The historical origins of the basic concepts of health promotion and education: The role of ancient Greek philosophy and medicine. *Health Promotion International, 24*(2), 185–192. DOI: 10.1093/heapro/dap006 PMID: 19304737

Trevisanato, S. I. (2006). Six medical papyri describe the effects of Santorini's volcanic ash, and provide Egyptian parallels to the so-called biblical plagues. *Medical Hypotheses, 67*(1), 187–190. DOI: 10.1016/j.mehy.2006.01.008 PMID: 16513290

Tulchinsky, T. H. (2018). Bismarck and the long road to universal health coverage. *Case studies in public health, 131*. vd Schulenburg, J. M. G. (2019). The German health care system: concurrent solidarity, freedom of choice, and cost control. In Health Care Systems and Their Patients (pp. 83-104). Routledge.

Vaishali, P. M., Boopathy, N., & Boobalan, N. (2024). Edwin Chadwick: A Pioneer of Public Health Reform and His Role in Sanitary Awakening. *Cureus*, *16*(9). Advance online publication. DOI: 10.7759/cureus.68858 PMID: 39376875

Van Middendorp, J. J., Sanchez, G. M., & Burridge, A. L. (2010). The Edwin Smith papyrus: A clinical reappraisal of the oldest known document on spinal injuries. *European Spine Journal : Official Publication of the European Spine Society, the European Spinal Deformity Society, and the European Section of the Cervical Spine Research Society*, *19*(11), 1815–1823. DOI: 10.1007/s00586-010-1523-6 PMID: 20697750

Vlădescu, C., Rădulescu, S., & Cace, S. (2005). The Romanian healthcare system: between Bismarck and Semashko. Decentralization in Healthcare: Analyses and Experiences in Central and Eastern Europe in the 1990s, 435-485.

von der Schulenburg J-Matthias, G. (2018). Pricing and reimbursement policies in Germany: current and future trends. European Medicines Pricing and Reimbursement, 19-38.

Von Klein, C. H. (1905). The Medical Features of the Papyrus Ebers. *Journal of the American Medical Association*, *45*(26), 1928–1935. DOI: 10.1001/jama.1905.52510260014001e

Williams, K., & Williams, J. (2021). Social Insurance and the Allied Services: the Political Utopia of 1942. In *The Works of William H. Beveridge* (pp. Vol7-43). Routledge.

Wong, C. B., Huang, H., Ning, Y., & Xiao, J. (2024). Probiotics in the new era of Human Milk Oligosaccharides (HMOs): HMO utilization and beneficial effects of Bifidobacterium longum subsp. Infantis M-63 on infant health. *Microorganisms*, *12*(5), 1014. DOI: 10.3390/microorganisms12051014 PMID: 38792843

Yarmohammadi, H., Mojahedian, M. M., & Zargaran, A. (2012). Medicine and economy in Ancient Persia. *The Journal of Research on History of Medicine*, *1*(3).

Chapter 2

Digital Trust and Phygital Marketing in National Health Reform Communication:

Building Citizen Engagement in Hybrid Information Ecosystems

Ioseb Gabelaia
http://orcid.org/0000-0002-6323-6913
Kauno Kolegija Higher Education Institution, Lithuania

ABSTRACT

Communication ecosystems that incorporate digital precision with physical accessibility to engage citizens. The effectiveness of these campaigns primarily relies on digital trust. This research explores the impact of phygital marketing strategies on public trust, emotional resonance, and behavioral engagement with national health reform initiatives. The research was grounded in the Health Belief Model (HBM) and the Technology Acceptance Model (TAM). The author proposed a Phygital Health Communication Trust Index (PHCTI) to empirically test the multidimensional relationships among marketing exposure, digital transparency, and citizen participation. Moreover, the author used a mixed methods approach. First, data were collected from a survey study (N = 737). Furthermore, the data were analyzed using PLS-SEM. Next, insights from focus group discussions (N = 2) were added to the emotional component and for triangulation. The results demonstrate that trust functions as a mediator and predictor of reform engagement, with transparency and personalization as key drivers.

DOI: 10.4018/979-8-3373-7173-3.ch002

INTRODUCTION

Recently, health systems worldwide are undergoing robust reforms due to technological innovation. Moreover, according to Nordal (2012), the healthcare landscape has undergone significant change in the last three decades. These trends impact healthcare costs and, generally, public expectations from healthcare providers. Moreover, governments are applying digital marketing strategies that combine digital campaigns and AI-driven personalization to communicate complex health reforms to citizens. Hence, this hybrid procedure is a significant paradigm shift in public health communication. This is a change from traditional one-way communication to dynamic, two-way, trust-based engagement systems.

The goal of healthcare is to create a healthier society (Putera, 2017). While there are significant advancements in national health reforms, they are often challenged by communication failures. This reveals that policy shortcomings are not the only reason why some areas of health reforms fail or are limited. In the face of misinformation and algorithmic spaces, citizens perceive digital transformation as manipulative or inconsistent with their values, and trust diminishes. Consequently, this results in skepticism toward reform programs. Digital trust is fundamental for legitimacy and the adoption of desired behaviors (Merchán-Cruz et al., 2025).

A potential solution for these conditions is phygital marketing, which blends the tangible reassurance of human presence with the scalability of digital systems (Gabelaia, 2025; Arrow et al., 2009). This approach allows governments, health agencies, and more to connect and engage effectively with AI digital systems and open data communications. Regardless, the psychological and behavioral connection between phygital exposure to trust and engagement is not yet fully understood.

In this research, the author explored this gap by analyzing how phygital marketing strategies impact trust, perceived usefulness, and engagement within the context of national health reform. Moreover, this research was grounded in the Health Belief Model (HBM), which highlights perceived risk and benefit as motivators of health behavior, and the Technology Acceptance Model (TAM), which emphasizes perceived usefulness and ease of use as determinants of technology adoption. Eventually, these models offer a foundation to understand how hybrid communication impacts reform participation. Based on this, the author developed the following hypotheses:

- H_1 - Phygital marketing strategies have a positive and significant impact on citizen trust in national health reform communication.
- H_2 - Digital transparency mediates the relationship between phygital marketing exposure and trust formation.
- H_3 - Emotional resonance and personalization within campaigns increase perceived usefulness of reform programs.

- H_4 - Higher digital trust shows greater behavioral intention to adopt or comply with health reforms.
- H_5 - The combined presence of physical and digital engagement creates stronger results than either channel alone (phygital synergy effect).

In this research, the author used a mixed methodology. Survey study and focus group insights were used to discuss national healthcare reforms. Descriptive and inferential statistics were performed. Moreover, data was analyzed by Structural Equation Modeling (PLS-SEM) ((Hair et al., 2022), to test the relationships among phygital marketing exposure, transparency, emotional resonance, and engagement intention. Moreover, based on this research, the author proposed *the Phygital Health Communication Trust Index (PHCTI)*, an instrument designed to assess how digital transparency and hybrid engagement contribute to measurable trust and citizen action. The results would assist policymakers, marketers, and healthcare leaders in developing inclusive, transparent, and intelligent communication strategies that strengthen credibility between stakeholders.

LITERATURE REVIEW

Healthcare delivery and the organization of public healthcare are developing quickly due to digital technologies (Romanovskaya & Romanovskiy, 2024; Siddique et al., 2024). The mechanisms through which digitalization exerts impact include income, healthcare consumption, and health behaviors (Zhong et al., 2024; Berardi et al., 2024). Furthermore, healthcare communication has shifted from isolated, offline, and online campaigns to a phygital ecosystem that combines telehealth, patient portals, community outreach, and on-site services (Socha-Dietrich, 2021). Evidence shows that digital health adoption grows when hybrid touchpoints reduce barriers related to access, cost, and timeliness, if issues of trust are addressed (Gabelaia, 2025; Arrow et al., 2009). Additionally, some barriers are workflow misalignment, gaps in digital literacy, and perceived risks, while facilitators reveal usability, support, and perceived benefits (Wang & Luan, 2022; Al Dahdah & Mishra, 2023).

Global strategic analyses indicate that digital mechanisms can improve access and efficiency across healthcare systems (Parikh et al., 2022). However, these analyses also warn that disparities in power, usability, and trust may be exacerbated, particularly where physical touchpoints are needed to complement digital solutions (Holum, 2023; Merchán-Cruz et al., 2025). Industry reports increasingly conceptualize 'phygital' as a core design principle for delivering constant, respectful messaging across multiple channels, rather than a temporary trend (Gigauri & Djakeli, 2021; Gabelaia, 2025). During health crises, effective management has shown that active listening, transparent risk communication, and community engagement are important for achieving large-scale behavior change (Sun, 2021). The World Health Organization's recommendation formalizes these practices as a core capability set in the digital era (World Health Organization, 2022).

The increasing integration of artificial intelligence and machine learning into healthcare practice is met with both optimism and caution (Agarwal et al., 2023). As the adoption of machine learning technologies grows, regulatory authorities encounter significant challenges in overseeing their clinical application (Mashar et al., 2023). Providing straightforward explanations of AI-driven decisions can help build trust and mitigate fear, particularly in contexts where misinformation is prevalent (Chin et al., 2023; Moore, 2022). In healthcare, trust operations are a critical determinant of both adoption and compliance (Chumachenko & Yakovlev, 2024). There is a growing consensus on the need for data transparency and bias mitigation in health AI and datasets, with recommended standards to reduce opacity (Goodwin, 2022; Ratwani et al., 2024).

Current healthcare systems are usually underprepared to meet increasing demands and are described by fragmentation, inefficiency, high costs, and persistent gaps in coordination, quality, and access (Jones & Dolsten, 2024; Giulio de Belvis et al., 2022). While citizen participation is widely advertised as a means to sustain and improve government legitimacy, the specific mechanisms by which participation influences trust in government remain insufficiently explored (He & Ma, 2021; Moore, 2022). Trust is identified as an essential objective and key performance indicator for governments at all levels, and without sufficient trust, policy implementation becomes significantly more difficult (Panch et al., 2019; Holum, 2023).

Individuals with complex health and social care needs present significant challenges to health systems (Tynkkynen et al., 2022; Stewart, 2023). Health reform is particularly burdensome for two primary reasons: first, the national economy must be robust enough to support a new health model established through reform; second, the health system must align with the country's economic structure, traditions, and historical context (Gigauri & Djakeli, 2021). Globally, countries are striving to provide their populations with efficient access to health services (Katoue et al., 2022; Khan et al., 2021).

Health resources have developed in recent years (Chen et al., 2021). Health care reforms act as systemic responses to ongoing challenges in access, quality, cost containment, and equity within national health systems (Donohue et al., 2022; Putera, 2017). Modern reforms heavily highlight governance, communication, and trust-centered transformation, acknowledging that policy effectiveness relies on both design and public acceptance, as well as behavioral compliance (Anderson et al., 2022).

Moreover, these reforms are impacted by demographic changes, technological progress, and heightened expectations for transparency and accountability (Janlov et al., 2023; Moore, 2022). Digitalization is a central lever for reform, enabling data-driven decision-making, personalized care, and efficiency improvements. Nevertheless, it also presents new risks, including privacy concerns, algorithmic opacity, and potential social exclusion (McCauley et al., 2021). Consequently, contemporary health reforms must balance efficiency with legitimacy, ensuring that innovation does not surpass citizens' ability to understand, trust, and engage with reformed systems (Burke et al., 2021; Nordal, 2012).

There is increasing evidence that citizen trust is a critical determinant of health reform success, as it shapes the relationship between policy objectives and real-world outcomes (Putera, 2017; Simpson et al., 2021). Also, behavioral models such as the HBM demonstrate that perceived benefits and risks impact individuals' willingness to adopt health behaviors promoted by reforms (Rosenstock, 1974; Champion & Skinner, 2008). TAM frameworks further explain how usability and perceived value affect engagement with digital health infrastructure (Davis, 1989; Venkatesh & Davis, 2000). Communicating reforms through combined phygital approaches, which incorporate physical interaction with digital platforms, can better handle varying literacy levels, reduce uncertainty, and strengthen institutional credibility. As a result, effective health reform is increasingly recognized as a behavioral and communicative process, in which transparency, inclusivity, and ethical leadership are essential for sustainable implementation and the creation of long-term public value (Rosenstock, 1974; Champion & Skinner, 2008; Davis, 1989; Venkatesh & Davis, 2000).

RESEARCH METHODOLOGY

Research Design

To explore the impact of phygital marketing strategies on public trust, emotional resonance, and behavioral engagement with national health reform initiatives, the author used a mixed-methods approach (Creswell & Plano Clark, 2018). A Survey and focus group discussions presented an opportunity to measure causal relationships between key variables. Quantitative and qualitative approach improves the validity and reliability of the insights (Braun & Clarke, 2006). Additionally, the sequential explanatory strategy is aligned with modern health communication research that uses triangulation between behavioral data and lived experiences.

Theoretical Framework

This research is grounded in the Health Belief Model (HBM) and the Technology Acceptance Model (TAM). This combination offers a comprehensive framework to understand health-related decision-making in phygital environments. First, the Health Belief Model states that health behaviors are impacted by individuals' perceptions of susceptibility and severity (perceived risk), perceived benefits of action, perceived barriers, and self-efficacy (Rosenstock, 1974; Champion & Skinner, 2008). Within national health reform, perceived risk relates to citizens' judgment of health consequences of non-participation, while perceived benefit reflects beliefs about improved access, quality, or benefits resulting from reform adoption (Rosenstock, 1974).

Second, the Technology Acceptance Model defined how perceived usefulness and perceived ease of use form attitudes and behavioral preferences toward digital systems (Davis, 1989; Venkatesh & Davis, 2000). As phygital health reform communication usually depends on digital platforms, AI-enabled personalization, and online service portals, TAM offers a robust framework for modeling citizens' acceptance of technological components within reform initiatives.

Data Collection

The survey study was performed using convenience and snowball sampling methods. Respondents ' responses were voluntary and anonymous, with informed consent obtained prior to survey completion. These approaches allowed high reachability within the health sector. Data collection lasted eight months, from February to October 2025. The strategy worked, and 737 valid respondents were selected for further analysis. The required inclusion criterion was at least minimal exposure to health reform-related communication.

The author performed two focus group discussions. Each consisted of 5 respondents. Moreover, sessions last approximately 60 to 90 minutes, one on Zoom and another in person. During the discussions, 13 semi-structured questions were asked related to health care reforms. The questions focused on trust, transparency, and phygital communication experiences.

Data Analysis

All variables were measured using Likert-type scales. Moreover, HBM constructs include perceived risk (susceptibility and severity) and perceived benefit, capturing respondents' beliefs about health consequences and reform advantages. TAM constructs were perceived usefulness and perceived ease of use, measuring functional evaluations of digital health communication and platforms. Additional constructs evaluated are digital transparency, emotional resonance, institutional trust, and engagement intention.

The author performed a pilot test to assess clarity and reliability. Reliability and validity were evaluated using Cronbach's alpha. Furthermore, descriptive and inferential statistics were performed. Moreover, data were analyzed by PLS-SEM (Hair et al., 2022).

Focus group discussions explored participants' perceptions of phygital health reform campaigns, their emotional responses to messaging, and their interpretations of digital transparency regarding data use and AI-driven personalization. All sessions were recorded and transcribed using Zoom and Otter software. Patterns and themes were extracted using NVivo software. A coding process included familiarization, initial coding, theme development, and refinement. Due to confidentiality any identifiers were removed during transcription. The triangulation strengthened the credibility and depth of this research. At last, all recordings were destroyed after 30-days from transcriptions.

RESEARCH FINDINGS

Data Screening and Cleaning

The survey was conducted between February and October 2025 and administered using Qualtrics software. A total of 859 responses were collected. Before performing statistical analysis, the author conducted data screening to ensure the dataset was suitable for analysis. All collected cases were screened for incomplete responses, and excessive missing data. Moreover, any case with more than 25% missing values was excluded.

After using established exclusion criteria, 122 cases were removed. Therefore 737 cases were used for the statistical analysis. Moreover, the final dataset showed low levels of missing data, below 3% across all constructs. No systematic patterns were detected. Mean substitution at the indicator level was used for descriptive analysis. Furthermore, the author assessed univariate outliers using z-scores, with values exceeding ±3.29 flagged for review. Multivariate outliers were examined using Mahalanobis distance, with no cases exceeding critical chi-square values at $p < .001$.

Moreover, the author continued with normality assessment using skewness and kurtosis statistics. Table 1 shows that skewness values for observed indicators ranged from −1.41 to +1.28, and kurtosis values ranged from −1.22 to +1.67, remaining within acceptable thresholds for large-sample behavioral research. Furthermore, tests of normality, including the Kolmogorov-Smirnov (K-S) and Shapiro-Wilk tests (S-W), showed statistically significant deviations from normality ($p < .001$)

for several variables. This outcome is expected in large samples ($N > 500$), where normality tests are highly sensitive and usually detect trivial deviations.

Table 1. Normality for Survey Variables (N = 737) (Developed by the Author)

Variable	Skewness	Kurtosis	K-S	S-W
Phygital Marketing Exposure	-0.84	1.21	< .001	< .001
Digital Transparency	-0.63	0.98	< .001	< .001
Emotional Resonance	-0.91	1.44	< .001	< .001
Perceived Usefulness (TAM)	-1.12	1.67	< .001	< .001
Perceived Ease of Use (TAM)	-0.78	1.03	< .001	< .001
Perceived Risk (HBM)	0.69	-0.87	< .001	< .001
Perceived Benefit (HBM)	-1.41	1.59	< .001	< .001
Institutional Trust	-0.88	1.36	< .001	< .001
Engagement Intention	-1.05	1.48	< .001	< .001

The author performed a reliability and validity analysis. Internal consistency reliability was examined using Cronbach's alpha (α) and composite reliability (CR). Table 2 shows that Cronbach's alpha values ranged from .78 to .92, exceeding the recommended threshold of .70 for all constructs. Composite reliability values ranged from .84 to .94, further confirming the scales' reliability. Moreover, convergent validity was assessed through standardized indicator loadings and average variance extracted (AVE). All retained items loaded significantly on their intended constructs, with standardized loadings exceeding .70 in most cases. A small number of indicators exhibited loadings between .60 and .69. However, these cases were retained due to strong theoretical justification and their contribution to content validity. Lastly, AVE values ranged from .56 to .79, surpassing the recommended minimum of .50 for all constructs. This indicates that each latent construct explains more than half of the variance of its indicators, thereby showing satisfactory convergent validity. Phygital Marketing Exposure was modeled as a higher-order construct composed of offline engagement, online engagement, and cross-channel consistency.

Table 2. Reliability and Convergent Validity of Measurement (N = 737) (Developed by the Author)

Variable	Number of Items	Cronbach's α	Composite Reliability (CR)	AVE
Phygital Marketing Exposure	9	.84	.89	.58
Digital Transparency	9	.91	.93	.61
Emotional Resonance	3	.82	.88	.71
Perceived Usefulness (TAM)	4	.88	.92	.74
Perceived Ease of Use (TAM)	4	.86	.90	.69
Perceived Risk (HBM)	3	.79	.86	.67
Perceived Benefit (HBM)	3	.85	.91	.77
Institutional Trust	9	.92	.94	.63
Engagement Intention	4	.89	.93	.76

The results of normality testing and distributional assessments support the use of Partial Least Squares Structural Equation Modeling (PLS-SEM). The final sample size of 737 provides strong statistical power for estimating structural paths and assessing indirect effects via bootstrapping.

Structural Model Results

To continue, the author evaluated the structural model to test the relationships among phygital marketing exposure, digital transparency, trust, Health Belief Model (HBM) constructs, Technology Acceptance Model (TAM) constructs, and engagement intention. This assessment observed set PLS-SEM guidelines and used bootstrapping with 5,000 resamples to assess the significance of path coefficients.

Table 3 showed that Phygital marketing exposure indicated a positive and significant effect on digital transparency ($\beta = .41, p < .001$) and institutional trust ($\beta = .28, p < .001$). These results reinforce the proposition that hybrid communication improves perceptions of openness and credibility. Moreover, Digital transparency revealed a strong positive impact on institutional trust ($\beta = .46, p < .001$). This result underlines transparency as a critical antecedent of trust in national health reform communication.

Besides, consistent with the Technology Acceptance Model, perceived ease of use significantly predicted perceived usefulness ($\beta = .52, p < .001$). Nevertheless, perceived usefulness subsequently positively impacted engagement intention ($\beta = .34, p < .001$), demonstrating the significant role of functional value perceptions in citizen participation. Additionally,

Moreover, the Health Belief Model (HBM) constructs also showed significant consequences. Perceived benefit positively impacted engagement intention ($\beta =$

.29, $p < .001$), while perceived risk showed a weaker but statistically significant negative effect ($\beta = -.12$, $p < .01$). These results suggest that perceived benefits overpower perceived risks in motivating engagement with health reform initiatives. Lastly, Institutional trust was a key predictor of engagement intention ($\beta = .38$, $p < .001$). This result suggests that trust serves as a central psychological mechanism decoding communication quality into behavioral intent.

In Table 3, the structural model displayed substantial explanatory power, explaining 57% of the variance in institutional trust ($R^2 = .57$). This result suggests that phygital exposure and digital transparency jointly account for a large proportion of trust formation. Similarly, the model explained 62% of the variance in engagement intention ($R^2 = .62$), suggesting that trust, Technology Acceptance Model constructs, and Health Belief Model constructs collectively deliver a strong explanation of citizens' behavioral intentions toward participation in national health reform. Furthermore, perceived usefulness showed an R^2 of .54, driven mainly by perceived ease of use and emotional resonance. This result further supports the relevance of the Technology Acceptance Model in the phygital health context.

Furthermore, in Table 3, the author assessed the Effect sizes, the substantive impact of each predictor. Digital transparency showed a large effect on institutional trust ($f^2 = .35$), highlighting its dominant role in trust formation. Moreover, institutional trust revealed a medium-to-large effect on engagement intention ($f^2 = .29$). Furthermore, perceived usefulness indicated a medium effect on engagement intention ($f^2 = .18$), while perceived benefit displayed a small-to-medium effect ($f^2 = .14$). Lastly, perceived risk showed a small effect size ($f^2 = .05$), supporting its secondary role relative to perceived benefit. Additionally, phygital marketing exposure showed a medium effect on digital transparency ($f^2 = .21$) and a small-to-medium effect on institutional trust ($f^2 = .12$).

Table 3. Structural Path Results (PLS-SEM) (N = 737) (Developed by the Author)

Path	β	t - value	p - value	f^2	Results
Phygital Marketing Exposure to Digital Transparency	.41	12.84	< .001	.21	Support
Phygital Marketing Exposure to Institutional Trust	.28	8.17	< .001	.12	Support
Digital Transparency to Institutional Trust	.46	14.92	< .001	.35	Support
Perceived Ease of Use to Perceived Usefulness	.52	16.33	< .001	.37	Support
Perceived Usefulness - Engagement Intention	.34	9.41	< .001	.18	Support
Perceived Benefit to Engagement Intention	.29	7.86	< .001	.14	Support

continued on following page

Table 3. Continued

Path	β	t - value	p - value	f^2	Results
Perceived Risk to Engagement Intention	-.12	3.12	.002	.05	Support
Institutional Trust to Engagement Intention	.38	10.27	< .001	.29	Support

Note: β = standardized path coefficient, effect sizes (f^2) were interpreted using Cohen's (1988) guidelines such .02 = small, .15 = medium, .35 = large. All t – values were obtained via bootstrapping with 5,000 resamples

Mediation effects were tested using bias-corrected bootstrapping. Table 4 illustrates the results. The indirect effect of phygital marketing exposure on engagement intention, mediated by digital transparency and institutional trust, was statistically significant ($\beta = .18, p < .001$), demonstrating a serial mediation effect. Moreover, institutional trust partially mediated the relationship between digital transparency and engagement intention (indirect $\beta = .17$, $p < .001$). This result suggests that transparency improves engagement primarily through trust-building mechanisms rather than direct persuasion alone. Furthermore, the mediation analysis showed that perceived usefulness partially mediated the relationship between perceived ease of use and engagement intention (indirect $\beta = .18, p < .001$), consistent with the Technology Acceptance Model's assumptions.

Table 4. Mediation Effects (Bootstrapped Indirect Effects) (N = 737) (Developed by the Author)

Indirect Path	*Indirect* β	t - value	p - value	Mediation Type
Phygital Marketing Exposure to Digital Transparency to Institutional Trust	.19	9.87	< .001	Partial
Digital Transparency to Institutional Trust to engagement Intention	.17	8.42	< .001	Partial
Phygital Marketing Exposure to Digital Transparency to Institutional Trust to Engagement Intention	.18	7.95	< .001	Serial mediation
Perceived Ease of Use to Perceived Usefulness to Engagement Intention	.18	8.66	< .001	Partial

Note: Indirect effects were tested using bias-corrected bootstrapping with 5,000 resamples. Mediation was classified as partial when both direct and indirect effects were statistically significant.

Overall, the PLS-SEM results offer strong empirical support for the proposed framework in this research. Phygital marketing exposure improves transparency perceptions, which, in turn, builds institutional trust and ultimately drives engagement intention. Trust serves as a central mediating mechanism, while the Technology Acceptance Model and the Health Belief Model serve as complementary motivational pathways. The model shows both high explanatory power and theoretical coherence, validating the integration of behavioral health and technology acceptance perspectives in this research on national health reform communication.

Focus Group Results

The author conducted two focus group discussions between March and September 2025. This was intended to support survey findings and explore trust, transparency, and phygital communication experiences in the context of national health care reforms. The author used random sampling. 10 representatives were selected and divided into two different groups. Each group consisted of five participants. The participants were from different age groups, education levels, and more, as illustrated in Table 5. Furthermore, first session in April was conducted online via Zoom, while the other took place in person, in September. Each session lasted approximately 60 to 90 minutes. Lastly, the author prepared 13 semi-structured questions. Discussions were audio-recorded, transcribed, and analyzed using thematic analysis with a hybrid, deductive-inductive coding approach. Trust, transparency, and phygital experience served as sensitizing concepts.

Table 5. Focus Group Participant Profiles (N = 10) (Developed by the Author)

ID	Mode	Gender	Age	Education	Digital Literacy	Prior Exposure to Healthcare Reform
FG1-P1	Zoom	F	25	BA	High	Frequent (Digital Platforms)
FG1-P2	Zoom	M	44	MA	High	Frequent (Digital & Physical)
FG1-P3	Zoom	M	47	MA	Moderate	Occasional (Digital)
FG1-P4	Zoom	F	34	MA	Moderate	Limited (Physical only)
FG1-P5	Zoom	F	54	MA	High	Frequent (Policy Updates)
FG2-P1	In-Person	F	65	PhD	Moderate	Frequent (In-person events)
FG2-P2	In-Person	M	36	MA	Moderate	Occasional (Hybrid)
FG2-P3	In-Person	F	42	MA	Low	Limited (Physical only)
FG2-P4	In-Person	M	24	BA	High	Frequent (Digital & Physical)
FG2-P5	In-Person	F	51	MA	Low	Minimal

Note: Digital Literacy was self-assessed using a three-level scale (L-M-H). Additionally, exposure reflects interaction over the past three months.

Furthermore, the author used NVivo software to perform thematic analysis. The results demonstrated a set of recurring, cross-cutting themes related to trust, transparency, and phygital communication. The results are illustrated in Table 6.

Table 6 shows the themes identified during the focus group discussions. The first theme showed that trust was recognized as a significant factor in engaging in health care reforms. Respondents showed a willingness to comply with reform initiatives, which relied mainly on perceived institutional credibility rather than on the frequency of messaging. Moreover, respondents stated that trust is built over time through consistent actions and genuine communication, rather than through persuasive messaging. Notably, respondents with higher digital literacy stated that trust was dependent on institutional competence and data governance. In contrast, those with lower digital literacy highlighted interpersonal reassurance and familiarity. Finally, this theme supports the quantitative result that institutional trust is a strong predictor of engagement intention.

The second theme was transparency as a mechanism for trust formation. Respondents noted that digital transparency could either reinforce or undermine trust. Moreover, clear causes of data collection processes, digital platform functionality, and the rationale for reforms significantly decreased skepticism. In contrast, unclear communication created suspicion and disengagement. Furthermore, the results showed that transparency was not perceived solely as a technical attribute. Respondents connected it with ethical intent and respect for citizens. Finally, this insight supports the mediation effect observed in the structural model, in which transparency linked phygital exposure to trust formation.

Moreover, the next theme identified was phygital communication as a reasonable amplifier. In both focus group discussions, it was emphasized that the synergy between physical and digital communication should be leveraged. Moreover, respondents reported that physical interactions validated the digital messages they encountered online. Furthermore, digital mechanisms proposed convenience and access, while physical touchpoints offered legitimacy and emotional reassurance. Additionally, this pattern was evident among respondents with moderate to low digital literacy, who communicated discomfort with digital-only communication. Finally, these results strongly support the phygital synergy effect identified in the survey results.

Furthermore, in Table 6, emotional resonance and perceived usefulness were other themes. From the focus groups, the author found that emotionally resonant content felt personally relevant and practically useful. Moreover, technical descriptions alone were disengaging, whereas narrative-based communication allowed for better understanding of the national health reforms and their impact on their daily lives. Moreover, the next theme identified in focus group discussions was the digital divide and trust formulation. It must be noted that differences in digital literacy significantly impacted responses. It was evident that respondents with lower digital skills were confused and anxious, and relied on physical communication channels, whereas participants with higher digital confidence valued personalization and ease of access. However, both groups agreed that exclusive dependence on digital communication threatened to marginalize certain populations. This emphasizes the significance of inclusive phygital strategies.

The final theme identified during the focus groups was benefit-focused messaging versus risk-based messaging. Respondents repeatedly reported responding more positively to benefit-oriented messages than to risk- or consequences-oriented communications. In contrast, fear-based messaging was unconvincing, while benefit-focused communication improved motivation.

Table 6. Patters and Themes identified from Focus Groups (Developed by the Author)

Theme	Pattern	Illustrative Interpretation	Alignment with Survey results
Trust as a Precondition for Engagement	Participants consistently stated that willingness to engage depended on trust in institutions rather than message volume	Trust was described as "earned through consistency and honesty," not persuasion	Strongly supports H_1 and H_4
Transparency Reduces Skepticism	Clear explanations of data use and reform goals reduced fear and resistance	Lack of transparency was associated with suspicion of "hidden agendas"	Supports mediation in H_2
Phygital Communication Builds Credibility	Physical interaction validated digital messages	In-person contact made tools feel "more real and legitimate"	Supports H_5 (Synergy Effect)
Emotional Resonance Drives Perceived Usefulness	Stories and relatable examples made reforms feel personally relevant	Participants valued narratives over technical language	Supports H_3 and Tam extension
Digital Divide Shapes Trust Formation	Lower digital literacy participants relied more on physical touch points	Digital-only communication increased confusion and disengagement	Explains variance in trust and engagement
Benefit-focused Messaging Outweighs Risk messaging	Participants responded better to "what improves" rather than "what might go wrong"	Fear-based messages were often ignored or distrusted	Aligns with HBM findings
Consistency Across Channels Matters	Conflicting messages across platforms reduced confidence	Consistency was equated with competence	Reinforces phygital integration

Hypothesis Testing and Evaluation

The author explored the extent to which phygital marketing strategies impact public trust, emotional resonance, and behavioral engagement with national health reform initiatives. Consequently, two empirical studies were conducted, and data were collected and analyzed to address the defined hypotheses. The author assessed the hypotheses using Partial Least Squares Structural Equation Modeling (PLS-SEM) with bootstrapping (5,000 resamples) and results from the focus group discussions. Next, the hypothesis was accepted or rejected based on the significance, direction, and effect size of the estimated path coefficients, along with mediation analyses when relevant.

- H_1 - Phygital marketing strategies have a positive and significant impact on citizen trust in national health reform communication.

The results delivered strong empirical support for H_1. Phygital marketing exposure showed a positive and statistically significant direct effect on institutional trust ($\beta = .28, p < .001$), with a small-to-moderate effect size ($f^2 = .12$). Moreover, citizens exposed to merged physical and digital health reform communication registered higher levels of trust in reform institutions. From the focus groups, FG1-P3, Zoom, stated that "I don't mind the reform itself, but I need to trust the people behind it. If I don't trust them, no app or website will convince me." Moreover, FG2-P2, In-person, stated that "Trust comes from seeing the same message over time and knowing they won't suddenly change the rules."

Hence, hybrid communication strategies improve perceptions of institutional competence and credibility by merging the reassurance of physical engagement with the scalability and personalization of digital channels. Moreover, phygital marketing strategies thus serve as a significant anchor of trust formation in national health reform contexts.

Based on these results, the author accepted the null hypothesis (H_0) and rejected the alternative hypothesis (H_1)

- H_2 - Digital transparency mediates the relationship between phygital marketing exposure and trust formation.

The results showed that mediation analysis fully supported H_2. Phygital marketing exposure was positively associated with digital transparency ($\beta = .41, p < .001$), which in turn significantly predicted institutional trust ($\beta = .46, p < .001$). Moreover, the indirect effect was statistically significant (indirect $\beta = .19, p < .001$), and the serial mediation pathway stayed significant when direct effects were included. Furthermore, FG1-P2, Zoom stated that "Once they explained what data they collect and why, I felt more comfortable. Before that, it felt like something was hidden." On the other hand, FG2-P5, In-person, noted that "When things are not explained clearly, I assume there's a reason they don't want us to know."

These results indicate significant direct and indirect effects, suggesting partial mediation and confirming that phygital exposure improves trust by increasing perceptions of openness, clarity, and data accountability, as well as visibility and engagement. Additionally, digital transparency was a central psychological mechanism linking communication exposure to trust formation.

Based on these results, the author accepted the null hypothesis (H_0) and rejected the alternative hypothesis (H_1)

- H_3 - Emotional resonance and personalization within campaigns increase perceived usefulness of reform programs.

Furthermore, the Structural model results supported H_3. Emotional resonance showed a positive and significant effect on perceived usefulness ($\beta > .30, p < .001$), and personalization within phygital campaigns contributed to higher functional evaluations of reform programs. According to FG2-P1, In-person, "Talking to someone in person made the website make more sense. It felt more real after that." This was supported by FG1-P4, Zoom, stating that "I trust the digital tools more when I know there are real people behind them." Additionally, FG1-P5, Zoom stated that "The stories helped me see how this would actually affect my family, not just the system."

The results indicate that emotionally engaging, personalized messages not only capture attention but also strengthen citizens' beliefs that health reforms are practically beneficial and relevant to their lives. Besides, these results support integrating affective engagement into the Technology Acceptance Model, strengthening its applicability in public-sector and policy communication.

Based on these results, the author accepted the null hypothesis (H_0) and rejected the alternative hypothesis (H_1)

- H_4 - Higher digital trust shows greater behavioral intention to adopt or comply with health reforms.

The results strongly support H_4. Institutional trust was one of the strongest predictors of engagement intention ($\beta = .38, p < .001$), with a medium-to-large effect size ($f^2 = .29$). Trust, therefore, was decisive in translating communication quality into behavioral intention. Moreover, the strength of this relationship indicated that citizen compliance with national health reforms is fundamentally trust-contingent. Even when perceived usefulness and health benefits are present, trust is a necessary condition for adoption, positioning it as a core outcome and mediator within the model.

Based on these results, the author accepted the null hypothesis (H_0) and rejected the alternative hypothesis (H_1)

- H_5 - The combined presence of physical and digital engagement creates stronger results than either channel alone (phygital synergy effect).

According to the results, H_5 was supported through the assessment of the higher-order formative construct of phygital marketing exposure, comprised of offline engagement, online engagement, and cross-channel consistency. Moreover, all formative indicators were statistically significant, and the combined construct showed stronger explanatory power than individual channel effects alone. Additionally, phygital exposure revealed greater indirect effects on trust and engagement intention via transparency than would be expected from single-channel communication. This demonstrates the presence of a phygital synergy effect, in which integrated hybrid communication generates additive and reinforcing outcomes beyond the sum of isolated physical or digital efforts.

Based on these results, the author accepted the null hypothesis (H_0) and rejected the alternative hypothesis (H_1)

The Phygital Health Communication Trust Index (PHCTI)

The author, after analyzing available insights, proposed a Phygital Health Communication Trust Index (PHCTI) to empirically test the multidimensional relationships among marketing exposure, digital transparency, and citizen participation. This index is the initial proposal, which will require continuous testing and modifications. The limitations are addressed below.

The Phygital Health Communication Trust Index (PHCTI) demonstrates acceptable and satisfactory construct, predictive, and criterion validity, supporting its use as a potent diagnostic and evaluative mechanism.

The Phygital Health Communication Trust Index (PHCTI) is a hybrid indicator designed to assess the trust capacity for national health reform communication systems. Table 7 highlights the index's attributes. Accordingly, the dashboard should show the overall PHCTI score ranging from 0 to 100. The index has seven sub scores, including Phygital Synergy, Digital Transparency, Institutional Trust, Technology Acceptance Model (TAM) Value, Health Belief Model (HBM) Motivation, Emotional Resonance, and Equity and Inclusion. Furthermore, sub-scores are calculated from empirically derived effect sizes and aggregated to form the total PHCTI score. Next, higher PHCTI values reminisce stronger trust-mediated pathways from communication exposure to citizen engagement. This proposed dashboard should allow for checking the strength and vulnerabilities and comparing trust capacity within different population segments. Additionally, this could serve as a measure during implementation.

- *Construct validity.* The author grounded construct validity for PHCTI in the literature on institutional trust, digital transparency, Technology Acceptance Model (TAM) constructs, and Health Belief Model (HBM) dimensions. Moreover, empirical results from large samples showed that convergent validity was supported by strong factor loadings, composite reliabilities exceeding 0.70, and average variance extracted (AVE) values above 0.50 for all underlying constructs. Furthermore, the connection between quantitative index values and qualitative judgments offers robust evidence of criterion-related validity, indicating that PHCTI meaningfully uses real-world perceptions and experiences of health reforms. This suggested that PHCTI proportions capture conceptually distinct aspects of trust-oriented health communication. Therefore, this indicates that PHCTI confirms acceptable construct validity as a multidimensional index.

- *Predictive validity.* The author assessed predictive validity by examining the relationship between PHCTI and engagement intention, the immediate behavioral outcome. Moreover, to support this, the structural model results showed that PHCTI's core components presented a significant proportion of variance in engagement intention ($R^2 = 0.62$). The total PHCTI score indicated a strong positive association with behavioral intention to adopt or comply with health reforms. Hence, these results reinforce the proposal that PHCTI effectively serves as a predictive index, capturing the trustworthiness of phygital health communication systems.
- *Contribution to Theory and Practice.* This research introduces a PHCTI as a novel, empirically grounded mechanism for assessing the trust capacity for hybrid health reforms. Moreover, it integrates HBM and TAM as a theoretical foundation. Theoretically, PHCTI extends theory by showing that trust functions as a system-level property originating from transparency, usability, emotional resonance, and equity within a phygital environment. Practically, the index offers policymakers, leadership, and management a mechanism that is more than just metrics.
- *Limitations of PHCTI.* As a proposed index in the early stages of development, this index has several limitations. First, PHCTI was validated using cross-sectional survey data, which limits causal inference. Second, although the index integrates multiple theoretical perspectives, weighting decisions were based on empirical effect sizes from a single national context. Lastly, although PHCTI incorporates equity and inclusion as a distinct sub-score, the current operationalization relies primarily on self-reported perceptions

Table 6. The PHCTI Index – Sub scores, Measurement, Coding and Weights (Developed by the Author)

PHCTI Dimension (Sub-scores)	Constructs/Items	Scaling & Coding	Score Range	Weigh
Phygital Synergy Score (PSS)	Offline engagement, online engagement, cross-channel consistency	Mean of items, Likert 1-7, rescaled to 0-100	0-100	.15
Transparency Score (TS)	Disclosure, clarity, accuracy of digital and policy communication (DCA)	Mean of items, Likert 1-7, rescaled to 0-100	0-100	.20
Trust Score (TrS)	Institutional competence, integrity, benevolence (CIB)	Mean of items, Likert 1-7, rescaled to 0-100	0-100	.25
TAM Value Score (TVS)	PEOU and PU	Weighted mean: (0.35xPEOU) +(0.65xPU)	0-100	.15
HBM Motivation Score (HMS)	Perceived benefits, perceived risks/ barriers, self-efficacy	Weight composite: benefits (0.45_, self-efficacy (0.35), risk/barriers (0.20)	0-100	.15
Emotional Resonance Score (ERS)	Relatability, narrative clarity, emotional reassurance	Mean of items, Likert 1-7, rescaled to 0-100	0-100	.05
Equity & Inclusion Score (EIS)	Digital access, availability of physical support, clarity for low digital literacy groups.	Mean of items, Likert 1-7, rescaled to 0-100	0-100	.05

Note: Final Formula is PHCTI = 0.15(PSS)+0.20(TS)+0.25(TrS)+0.15(TVS)+0.15(HMS)+0.05(ERS)+0.05(EIS). All PHCTI sub-scores were standardized to a 0-100 scale using the formula, Standardized score = (Mean-1)/6*100. Weights were derived from structural model effect sizes *(β, f^2)* and triangulated with qualitative focus group results. The PHCTI total score is computed as the weighted sum of all seven sub-scores.

DISCUSSION AND CONCLUSION

This research explored the impact of phygital marketing communication on citizen engagement with national health reform by combining the Health Belief Model (HBM), the Technology Acceptance Model (TAM), and institutional trust within a practical framework. The results provided strong empirical support for the argument that trust, facilitated by transparency and strengthened through hybrid communication channels, serves as the primary mechanism through which health reform communication leads to behavioral intention.

The results demonstrated the strategic value of phygital campaign design. The positive effects of phygital marketing exposure on transparency and trust show that hybrid engagement, which connects digital personalization with physical presence. Moreover, the TAM pathways support the view that PEOU and PU are essential determinants, even in policy contexts. Similarly, the results demonstrated the significant impact of emotional resonance, and trust indicates that health reform marketing should embrace relationship-based communication.

Results revealed the necessity of trust-centric leadership in digitally mediated reforms. Institutional trust was recognized as one of the strongest predictors of engagement intention ($\beta = .38$), suggesting that leadership credibility directly impacts public behavior. Moreover, leaders responsible for national health reforms should act as stewards of transparency, ensuring that digital tools prioritize the public interest. Furthermore, the results demonstrate that leadership effectiveness in health reform was characterized not only by policy outcomes but also by the capacity to facilitate trust across complex phygital ecosystems. Lastly, applying HBM and TAM suggested that effective leadership must balance behavioral motivation, such as risk–benefit perceptions, with technological usability and acceptance.

The results supported the accepted hypotheses, validating the proposed integrated framework where the effectiveness of phygital communication is mediated by trust, driven by transparency, strengthened by emotional factors, and evaluated through technological criteria. The results verify that citizen engagement with national health reform arises from the interaction of behavioral motivation (Health Belief Model), technology acceptance (Technology Acceptance Model), and institutional trust within phygital ecosystems, rather than from isolated mechanisms.

This research makes a theoretical contribution by showing that HBM and TAM interact synergistically, rather than independently, within phygital health reform contexts. Moreover, this research advances health communication theory beyond isolated frameworks and provides a scalable approach for analyzing digitally mediated public policy initiatives. From a practical perspective, the results demonstrated that digital transparency serves not only as an ethical obligation but also as a critical determinant of reform effectiveness. The significant relationship between digital transparency and institutional trust ($\beta = .46$) and its substantial effect size ($f^2 = .35$) suggest that citizens respond favorably when governments clearly communicate data usage, decision-making processes, and the benefits delivered by reforms.

The author offers the PHCTI index. However, future research could improve the index by including objective indicators of access, such as service availability, broadband coverage, or utilization data. Also, while PHCTI was developed for national health reform communication, its structure shows potential applicability to other public-sector transformations. Therefore, future research should explore PHCTI's transferability and predictive validity in other industries.

DISCLOSURE

During preparing this book chapter the author used *Grammarly Pro* to check and fix minor grammatical and structural errors. This Book chapter is also checked on *Turnitin* for plagiarism and AI. I confirm that this research has followed all ethical research guidelines.

REFERENCES

Agarwal, R., Bjarnadottir, M., Rhue, L., Dugas, M., Crowley, K., Clark, J., & Gao, G. (2023). Addressing algorithmic bias and the perpetuation of health inequities: An AI bias aware framework. *Health Policy and Technology, 12*(1), 100702. DOI: 10.1016/j.hlpt.2022.100702

Al Dahdah, M., & Mishra, R. K. (2023). Digital health for all: The turn to digitized healthcare in India. *Social Science & Medicine, 319*, 114968. DOI: 10.1016/j.socscimed.2022.114968 PMID: 35459554

Anderson, M., Pitchforth, E., Edwards, N., Alderwick, H., McGuire, A., & Mossialos, E. (2022). United Kingdom: Health System Review. *Health Systems in Transition, 24*(1), 1–194. PMID: 35579557

Arrow, K., Auerbach, A., Bertko, J., Brownlee, S., Casalino, L. P., Cooper, J., Crosson, F. J., Enthoven, A., Falcone, E., Feldman, R. C., Fuchs, V. R., Garber, A. M., Gold, M. R., Goldman, D., Hadfield, G. K., Hall, M. A., Horwitz, R. I., Hooven, M., Jacobson, P. D., & Van De Ven, W. P. (2009). Toward a 21st-century health care system: Recommendations for health care reform. *Annals of Internal Medicine, 150*(7), 493–495. DOI: 10.7326/0003-4819-150-7-200904070-00115 PMID: 19258550

Berardi, C., Antonini, M., Jordan, Z., Wechtler, H., Paolucci, F., & Hinwood, M. (2024). Barriers and facilitators to the implementation of digital technologies in mental health systems: A qualitative systematic review to inform a policy framework. *BMC Health Services Research, 24*(1), 243. DOI: 10.1186/s12913-023-10536-1 PMID: 38408938

Braun, V., & Clarke, V. (2006). Using thematic analysis in psychology. *Qualitative Research in Psychology, 3*(2), 77–101. DOI: 10.1191/1478088706qp063oa

Burke, S., Parker, S., Fleming, P., Barry, S., & Thomas, S. (2021). Building health system resilience through policy development in response to COVID-19 in Ireland: From shock to reform. *The Lancet Regional Health. Europe*, *9*, 9. DOI: 10.1016/j.lanepe.2021.100223 PMID: 34642676

Champion, V. L., & Skinner, C. S. (2008). The Health Belief Model. In Glanz, K., Rimer, B. K., & Viswanath, K. (Eds.), *Health behavior and health education: Theory, research, and practice* (4th ed., pp. 189–193). Jossey-Bass.

Chen, J., Lin, Z., Li, L. A., Li, J., Wang, Y., Pan, Y., Yang, J., Xu, C., Zeng, X., Xie, X., & Xiao, L. (2021). Ten years of China's new healthcare reform: A longitudinal study on changes in health resources. *BMC Public Health*, *21*(1), 2272. DOI: 10.1186/s12889-021-12248-9 PMID: 34903184

Chin, M. H., Afsar-Manesh, N., Bierman, A. S., Chang, C., Colón-Rodríguez, C. J., Dullabh, P., Duran, D. G., Fair, M., Hernandez-Boussard, T., Hightower, M., Jain, A., Jordan, W. B., Konya, S., Moore, R. H., Moore, T. T., Rodriguez, R., Shaheen, G., Snyder, L. P., Srinivasan, M., & Ohno-Machado, L. (2023). Guiding principles to address the impact of algorithm bias on racial and ethnic disparities in health and health care. *JAMA Network Open*, *6*(12), e2345050–e2345050. DOI: 10.1001/jamanetworkopen.2023.45050 PMID: 38100101

Chumachenko, D., & Yakovlev, S. (2024). Artificial intelligence algorithms for healthcare. *Algorithms*, *17*(3), 105. DOI: 10.3390/a17030105

Creswell, J. W., & Plano Clark, V. L. (2018). *Designing and Conducting Mixed Methods Research* (3rd ed.). SAGE.

Davis, F. D. (1989). Perceived usefulness, perceived ease of use, and user acceptance of information technology. *Management Information Systems Quarterly*, *13*(3), 319–340. DOI: 10.2307/249008

Donohue, J. M., Cole, E. S., James, C. V., Jarlenski, M., Michener, J. D., & Roberts, E. T. (2022). The US Medicaid program: Coverage, financing, reforms, and implications for health equity. *Journal of the American Medical Association*, *328*(11), 1085–1099. DOI: 10.1001/jama.2022.14791 PMID: 36125468

Gabelaia, I. (2025). Brand Resonance in the Phygital Era: Fostering Loyalty Through Hybrid Engagement. In *Brand Creation and Management in the Phygital Era* (pp. 31-46). IGI Global Scientific Publishing. DOI: DOI: 10.4018/979-8-3373-0948-4.ch002

Gabelaia, I. (2025). The Relevance of AI-Driven Marketing Through Design Thinking for a Strategic Approach to Resilient Problem-Solving and Communication for SMEs. *Sustainability (Basel)*, *17*(20), 8994. DOI: 10.3390/su17208994

Gigauri, I., & Djakeli, K. (2021). National Health Reforms in Georgia during 1994-2021 and their Success. *HOLISTICA Journal of Business and Public Administration*, *12*(2), 102–108. DOI: 10.2478/hjbpa-2021-0017

Giulio de Belvis, A., Meregaglia, M., Morsella, A., Adduci, A., Perilli, A., Cascini, F., & Scarpetti, G. (2022). Italy: Health System Review. *Health Systems in Transition*, *24*(4), 1–236. PMID: 36951263

Goodwin, I. (2022). Programmatic alcohol advertising, social media and public health: Algorithms, automated challenges to regulation, and the failure of public oversight. *The International Journal on Drug Policy*, *109*, 103826. DOI: 10.1016/j.drugpo.2022.103826 PMID: 35994939

Hair, J. F., Hult, G. T. M., Ringle, C. M., & Sarstedt, M. (2022). *A Primer on Partial Least Squares Structural Equation Modeling (PLS-SEM)* (3rd ed.). Sage., DOI: 10.1007/978-3-030-80519-7

He, A. J., & Ma, L. (2021). Citizen participation perceived public service performance, and trust in government: Evidence from health policy reforms in Hong Kong. *Public Performance & Management Review*, *44*(3), 471–493. DOI: 10.1080/15309576.2020.1780138

Holum, M. (2023). Citizen participation: Linking government efforts, actual participation, and trust in local politicians. *International Journal of Public Administration*, *46*(13), 915–925. DOI: 10.1080/01900692.2022.2048667

Janlöv, N., Blume, S., Glenngård, A. H., Hanspers, K., Anell, A., & Merkur, S. (2023). *Sweden: health system review* (Vol. 25, No. 4). World Health Organization. Regional Office for Europe.

Jones, C. H., & Dolsten, M. (2024). Healthcare on the brink: Navigating the challenges of an aging society in the United States. *npj. Aging (Albany NY)*, *10*(1), 22. DOI: 10.1038/s41514-024-00148-2 PMID: 38582901

Katoue, M. G., Cerda, A. A., García, L. Y., & Jakovljevic, M. (2022). Healthcare system development in the Middle East and North Africa region: Challenges, endeavors and prospective opportunities. *Frontiers in Public Health*, *10*, 1045739. DOI: 10.3389/fpubh.2022.1045739 PMID: 36620278

Khan, M., Abimbola, S., Aloudat, T., Capobianco, E., Hawkes, S., & Rahman-Shepherd, A. (2021). Decolonising global health in 2021: A roadmap to move from rhetoric to reform. *BMJ Global Health*, *6*(3), e005604. DOI: 10.1136/bmjgh-2021-005604 PMID: 33758016

Mashar, M., Chawla, S., Chen, F., Lubwama, B., Patel, K., Kelshiker, M. A., Bachtiger, P., & Peters, N. S. (2023). Artificial intelligence algorithms in health care: Is the current food and drug administration regulation sufficient? *JMIR AI*, *2*(1), e42940. DOI: 10.2196/42940 PMID: 38875544

. McCauley, L., Phillips, R. L., Meisnere, M., & Robinson, S. K. (2021). Implementing High-Quality Primary Care: Rebuilding the Foundation of Health Care (2021). *Implementing High-Quality Primary Care*, 1-428.

Merchán-Cruz, E. A., Gabelaia, I., Savrasovs, M., Hansen, M. F., Soe, S., Rodriguez-Cañizo, R. G., & Aragón-Camarasa, G. (2025). Trust by Design: An Ethical Framework for Collaborative Intelligence Systems in Industry 5.0. *Electronics (Basel)*, *14*(10), 1952. DOI: 10.3390/electronics14101952

Moore, C. M. (2022). The challenges of health inequities and AI. *Intelligence-Based Medicine*, *6*, 100067. DOI: 10.1016/j.ibmed.2022.100067

Nordal, K. C. (2012). Healthcare reform: Implications for independent practice. *Professional Psychology, Research and Practice*, *43*(6), 535–544. DOI: 10.1037/a0029603

Panch, T., Mattie, H., & Atun, R. (2019). Artificial intelligence and algorithmic bias: Implications for health systems. *Journal of Global Health*, *9*(2), 020318. DOI: 10.7189/jogh.09.020318 PMID: 31788229

Parikh, R. B., Basen-Enquist, K. M., Bradley, C., Estrin, D., Levy, M., Lichtenfeld, J. L., Malin, B., McGraw, D., Meropol, N. J., Oyer, R. A., Sheldon, L. K., & Shulman, L. N. (2022). Digital health applications in oncology: An opportunity to seize. *Journal of the National Cancer Institute*, *114*(10), 1338–1339. DOI: 10.1093/jnci/djac108 PMID: 35640986

Putera, I. (2017). Redefining health: Implication for value-based healthcare reform. *Cureus*, *9*(3). PMID: 28409068

Ratwani, R. M., Sutton, K., & Galarraga, J. E. (2024). Addressing AI algorithmic bias in health care. *Journal of the American Medical Association*, *332*(13), 1051–1052. DOI: 10.1001/jama.2024.13486 PMID: 39230911

Romanovskaya, O. V., & Romanovskiy, G. B. (2024). Law and digitalization of modern healthcare. *RUDN Journal of Law*, *28*(3), 565–583. DOI: 10.22363/2313-2337-2024-28-3-565-583

Rosenstock, I. M. (1974). Historical origins of the health belief model. *Health Education Monographs*, *2*(4), 328–335. DOI: 10.1177/109019817400200403

Siddique, S. M., Tipton, K., Leas, B., Jepson, C., Aysola, J., Cohen, J. B., Flores, E., Harhay, M. O., Schmidt, H., Weissman, G. E., Fricke, J., Treadwell, J. R., & Mull, N. K. (2024). The impact of health care algorithms on racial and ethnic disparities: A systematic review. *Annals of Internal Medicine*, *177*(4), 484–496. DOI: 10.7326/M23-2960 PMID: 38467001

Simpson, J., Albani, V., Bell, Z., Bambra, C., & Brown, H. (2021). Effects of social security policy reforms on mental health and inequalities: A systematic review of observational studies in high-income countries. *Social Science & Medicine*, *272*, 113717. DOI: 10.1016/j.socscimed.2021.113717 PMID: 33545493

Socha-Dietrich, K. (2021). Empowering the health workforce to make the most of the digital revolution. *OECD Health Working Papers*, (129), 0_1-67. DOI:DOI: 10.1787/18152015

Stewart, M. (2023). The public health crisis created by UK social policy reforms. *Justice. Power and Resistance*, *6*(2), 217–228. DOI: 10.1332/GQDH4178

Sun, T. Q. (2021). Adopting artificial intelligence in public healthcare: The effect of social power and learning algorithms. *International Journal of Environmental Research and Public Health*, *18*(23), 12682. DOI: 10.3390/ijerph182312682 PMID: 34886404

Tynkkynen, L. K., Pulkki, J., Tervonen-Goncalves, L., Schön, P., Burström, B., & Keskimäki, I. (2022). Health system reforms and the needs of the ageing population—An analysis of recent policy paths and reform trends in Finland and Sweden. *European Journal of Ageing*, *19*(2), 221–232. DOI: 10.1007/s10433-022-00699-x PMID: 35465210

Venkatesh, V., & Davis, F. D. (2000). A theoretical extension of the technology acceptance model: Four longitudinal field studies. *Management Science*, *46*(2), 186–204. DOI: 10.1287/mnsc.46.2.186.11926

Wang, X., & Luan, W. (2022). Research progress on digital health literacy of older adults: A scoping review. *Frontiers in Public Health*, *10*, 906089. DOI: 10.3389/fpubh.2022.906089 PMID: 35991040

World Health Organization. (2022). *Global oral health status report: towards universal health coverage for oral health by 2030*. World Health Organization.

Zhong, M., Qiang, D., Wang, J., & Sun, W. (2024). Improving health and reducing health inequality: An innovation of digitalization? *Social Science & Medicine*, *348*, 116847. DOI: 10.1016/j.socscimed.2024.116847 PMID: 38569285

Chapter 3
Digital Transformation in the Georgian Healthcare Sector:
Marketing Aspects of Technology Acceptance

Nugzar Todua
http://orcid.org/0000-0002-1486-2141
Ivane Javakhishvili Tbilisi State University, Georgia

Ekaterine Urotadze
http://orcid.org/0000-0002-9680-8084
Ivane Javakhishvili Tbilisi State University, Georgia

Konstantine Gobejishvili
http://orcid.org/0009-0000-4424-9180
Ivane Javakhishvili Tbilisi State University, Georgia

ABSTRACT

The article shows that the ongoing digital transformation in the global environment is having a significant impact on the activities of healthcare organizations, which are increasingly using digital marketing approaches to improve relationships with patients and reach a wider target audience. This paper posits that a primary factor contributing to this low adoption rate is the scarcity of scientific research in this domain. Therefore, this study aimed to determine the impact of digital technologies on the behavior of healthcare consumers. To achieve the set goal, a conceptual model of the study was created, relevant hypotheses were formulated and a questionnaire

DOI: 10.4018/979-8-3373-7173-3.ch003

was developed. Quantitative research, namely an online survey, was selected as the research method. As a result of analyzing the data, statistically significant values were obtained, which express the relationship between the above-mentioned variables.

1. INTRODUCTION

Digital technology offers a significant opportunity to enhance healthcare delivery through improved information access and communication, disease prevention, and health condition monitoring (Chatterjee et al., 2021). These advancements can also alleviate the demands on caregivers, potentially leading to cost reductions and improved care quality. However, the broad implementation of these technologies is currently hindered by varying degrees of public acceptance. Consequently, a key research priority is to determine the factors that influence the adoption of digital technologies to facilitate their effective integration into healthcare systems (Chong et al., 2022).

Digital transformation has been reshaping the business models of organizations across all industries worldwide. Digital transformation represents a significant area of ongoing research within the framework of Industry 4.0 (Ferrigno et al., 2023). Digital technologies are significantly transforming operational, transactional, and communicational approaches for businesses and organizations of all sizes (Raimo et al., 2023; Verhoef et al., 2021). These transformative shifts resulting from digital adoption represent substantial and impactful drivers within the modern economic landscape (Salvi et al., 2021). Digital transformation has significantly impacted numerous industries, particularly the healthcare sector. Technological advancements in healthcare contribute to improved individual well-being, increased life expectancy, and enhanced productivity (Mauro et al., 2024). Digital technology has empowered patients even in remote areas to access quality health services (Tortorella et al., 2023). Digital healthcare transformation encompasses modifications concerning the internet, digital technologies, and their relation with innovative therapies and optimal practices for enhanced health management (Stoumpos et al., 2023). The application of digital technologies to augment existing healthcare processes or to facilitate the development of novel approaches is referred to as Healthcare 4.0 (H4.0). H4.0 is distinguished by heightened interconnectivity and automation, enabling the recontextualization of healthcare service delivery within the cyber-physical environment. This has implications for both patient care and administrative support functions (Tortorella et al., 2022).

Digitalization in healthcare is predicated on the understanding that leveraging the capabilities of these technologies yields benefits for patients, healthcare practitioners, and organizations alike, leading to improved efficiency and effectiveness (Massaro,

2023). Digital transformation in healthcare refers to the integration of technology to streamline workflows, optimize communication channels, and elevate the quality of care delivery. This encompasses the implementation of innovative technologies that facilitate a transition towards secure and superior healthcare services (Saifudin et al., 2021). Research has investigated the potential benefits of implementing these technologies in healthcare organizations (Chatterjee & Kulkarni, 2021). The findings indicate that the expanded adoption of novel technologies in healthcare has had a significant impact on various operations, ranging from care provision to patient data administration. Dal Mas et al. (2023) conducted a systematic literature review that revealed several impacts of digital transformation on healthcare. These encompass enhancements in patient data management; advancements in care delivery, including improved medical diagnosis; optimization of healthcare operations, notably in supply chain management, inventory control, and patient billing; cost reductions resulting from the efficiency gains of technology in healthcare operations, which minimize expenses related to manual processes; and improved communication through enhanced information exchange between healthcare providers and patients, as well as among healthcare providers. Main digital technologies in healthcare are the Internet of Things, AI & machine learning, big data & analytics, social media, blockchain, Cloud storage & computing (Mauro et al., 2024).

The emergence of digital marketing has introduced new ways of communicating and engaging in healthcare. Digital marketing adoption in healthcare refers to the identified factors and variables that significantly influence individuals' willingness and willingness to adopt, use, and engage with digital marketing strategies in healthcare (Kim & Han, 2023). The adoption of digital technologies for consumer relations is an increasingly prevalent practice among companies in Georgia, reflecting a phased implementation approach. Digital transformation in healthcare is being rapidly adopted and strengthened in Georgia (Djakeli & Jakeli, 2016). Georgia's healthcare market is increasingly focused on adopting innovative and sustainable healthcare technology to improve patient outcomes. Progress in digital technology and education offers opportunities for developing a sustainable healthcare model. However, healthcare organizations are lagging in the utilization of digital technologies, primarily due to a limited body of research in the Georgian context. In addition, it should be noted that in Georgia's healthcare system, demand is impacted by a scarcity of qualified healthcare professionals and infrastructural limitations. The reason for this problem is the lack of scientific research examining consumer attitudes towards the adoption of digital technologies in the healthcare sector in Georgia. While studies have explored the impact of digital technology on consumer behavior in Georgia (Todua et al., 2013; Todua & Jashi, 2018; Todua et al., 2024; Todua & Urotadze, 2024; Todua & Todua, 2025), research specifically focusing on digital health technologies remains scarce. Therefore, this study aims to select the key variables that influence the use of digital technologies in the healthcare sector by Georgian consumers and to identify the relationships between these variables. To address this aim, the following research questions (RQ) are formulated:

> RQ 1: How do consumers' awareness, perceived usefulness, and perceived ease of use of digital health technology impact their attitudes towards these technologies?
> RQ 2: How do consumers' attitudes toward digital health technology impact their engagement in these technologies?
> RQ 3: How does consumers' engagement in digital health technologies impact their behavioral intention?
> RQ 4: How do consumers' behavioral intention in digital health technologies impact their usage behaviour?

2. LITERATURE REVIEW AND RESEARCH HYPOTHESIS SETTING

The present study is based on the Theory of Planned Behavior (TPB), which includes decisions related to behavioral intention. TPB is an extension of the Theory of Reasoned Action (TRA) developed by Ajzen & Fishbein, which considers behavioral control as an additional determinant of behavioral intention (Ajzen & Fishbein, 1977). This theory argues that the best way to predict behavior is to determine an individual's intention to perform the behavior (Lim & Weissmann, 2023). According to the Theory of Planned Behavior, digital technologies have a significant impact on the opinions, beliefs, and behaviors of patients and therefore represent an important source of information that to choices healthcare organizations (Khan et al., 2021).

Several models and theories compete to explain technology acceptance. The Technology Acceptance Model (TAM) is a leading theory in healthcare technology acceptance research, developed to clarify and predict an individual's acceptance of information technology (Rouidi et al., 2022). It has become a key model for understanding the predictors of human behavior concerning the potential adoption or rejection of technology. Given the growing body of research evaluating TAM in health care settings, the theory is increasingly regarded as well-suited to the health care context. TAM was developed in the 1980s in response to concerns regarding the underutilization of available information technologies by workers (Davis, 1989). TAM is rooted in the Theory of Reasoned Action (TRA), which posits that social behavior is determined by an individual's attitude toward a specific behavior, coupled with their beliefs about the consequences and perceived value associated with performing that behavior.

TAM posits that "perceived usefulness (PU)" and "perceived ease of use (PEOU)" are key constructs influenced by external variables. These constructs subsequently influence "attitude toward using (ATT)" and "behavioral intention to use (BI)," where BI is influenced by one's attitude toward using the information technology. Furthermore, PU independently affects BI, and PEOU influences PU (Ahn & Park, 2022). Davis defined perceived usefulness as the extent to which an individual believes that utilizing a particular system will enhance their job performance, and perceived ease of use as the degree to which an individual believes that utilizing a particular system will be free of effort (Nazari-Shirkouhi et a., 2023). Users' beliefs shape their attitudes toward system usage. The model suggests that perceived ease of use and perceived usefulness mediate the relationship between external variables and actual system use. Prior research has widely validated TAM across various fields and disciplines (Kim & Kim, 2016). Furthermore, the acceptance and adoption of technology has been extensively investigated using TAM in diverse technological contexts, including healthcare and assistive technology, social networking, online shopping, online public services, and entertainment (Yap et al., 2022). The technology acceptance model (TAM) is frequently employed by scholars to analyze technology within the healthcare domain. Its application extends to diverse healthcare technologies, offering insights into their acceptance among various populations. In the context of the healthcare sector, TAM variables can be defined as follows (Hsiao & Tang, 2015; Zin et al., 2023; Park et al., 2025). Perceived usefulness refers to an individual's subjective evaluation of the degree to which digital marketing technologies offer pertinent and valuable information pertaining to their healthcare requirements (Hu et al., 2002; Papa et al., 2020). Ease of use encompasses factors related to the accessibility and convenience of adopting digital technologies within the healthcare domain.

A significant body of research employing the Technology Acceptance Model (TAM) posits a relationship between perceived usefulness and the adoption and utilization of specific products (Chen & Chan, 2014). Consequently, it is proposed that user acceptance of a novel technology is contingent upon a demonstrably positive perception of its utility or advantageousness. The systematic review of factors influencing IT adoption by healthcare professionals identified two predominant factors (Gagnon et al., 2012; Yu & Qian, 2018). These factors, which constitute the core components of the TAM, will be the focus of this study. Thus, PU denotes the extent to which an individual believes that employing a specific digital health technology will enhance their quality of life, while PEOU is defined as the degree to which an individual believes that utilizing a digital health technology is free from effort (Moores et al., 2012; Zin et al., 2023). The above literature review allows us to formulate the following hypotheses:

H1: Perceived usefulness has a positive impact on attitude toward digital health technology.

H2: Perceived ease of use has a positive impact on attitude toward digital health technology.

The use of digital technologies is related to consumer awareness. Awareness refers to the level of knowledge and understanding that individuals have about digital marketing initiatives and information related to healthcare services, products, or providers (Hsiao & Tang, 2015). Individual differences and social factors positively affect users' attitudes and intentions toward using healthcare technology (Lu et al., 2003), with personal knowledge differences being of particular interest to researchers. It is posited that increased consumer knowledge enhances the likelihood of engaging in behaviors aligned with their beliefs or understanding (Eagly & Chaiken, 1993). For instance, patients who actively seek health-related information are more likely to accept e-health services (Wilson & Lankton, 2004). Therefore, we expect that individuals' healthcare knowledge will significantly predict their attitude toward the adoption of e-health devices. Patients exhibiting heightened awareness of their physical well-being demonstrate a greater propensity to consult with healthcare providers (Strull & Charles, 1984). The advent of e-health facilitates convenient access to medical information through mobile devices, obviating the need for physical medical libraries or direct physician consultation (Wilson & Lankton, 2004). Consequently, it is posited that individuals actively engaged in their healthcare and possessing a strong preference for information acquisition will exhibit a greater receptiveness towards digital health technology as a means of augmenting their healthcare experience. Therefore, we infer that individuals with significant health concerns and a pronounced need for health knowledge and healthcare will hold a more favorable attitude toward digital health technology. Based on the above, we can formulate the following hypothesis:

H3: Consumers' awareness of digital health technology has a positive impact on attitudes towards these technologies.

Attitudinal factors are defined as an individual's positive or negative feelings or appraisal regarding the use of technology (Ajzen, 2015). Prior research suggests a correlation between a more positive attitude toward healthcare technology and increased technology adoption (Zin et al., 2023). However, a study by Chen & Chan (2014) found attitude to be non-significant in predicting technology usage, suggesting that individuals with a positive attitude toward healthcare technology may not necessarily intend to use it. A newly developed Digital Health Scale (DHS) is employed to assess attitudes towards digital health technology. This scale focuses on knowledge, emotional response, and behavior towards health technology (Cassidy, 2021). The study investigates age and gender as potential impediments to accessing digital health resources and, more broadly, healthcare services. In this study, attitude will be measured as a factor influencing consumers' engagement to use healthcare technology (Mirzaei & Esmaeilzadeh, 2021). Digital health technology offers the potential to enhance patient engagement, fostering a more active role for individuals in their healthcare decisions (Domecq et al., 2014). Research suggests that leveraging digital health tools can lead to improved patient health outcomes (Lindsay et al., 2009). Prior studies highlight patient engagement as a critical component of a high-quality healthcare system (Liu et al., 2018). Barello et al. (2012) posit that patient engagement with digital health technology promotes active participation in self-health management and treatment, potentially resulting in improved health outcomes and a broader range of treatment options. Therefore, the following hypothesis is proposed:

> **H4:** Consumers' attitudes toward digital health technology have a positive impact on their engagement in these technologies.

Behavioral Intention (BI) is a core construct in the Technology Acceptance Model, reflecting an individual's attitude toward technology use and predicting technology adoption. Defined as "the degree to which an individual has formulated conscious plans to perform or not perform some specified behavior in the future," BI demonstrably influences actual technology usage (Venkatesh et al., 2003). Consequently, a substantial body of research has concentrated on behavioral intention as a predictor of technology adoption and actual use (Bhattacherjee, 2001; li et al., 2019). Behavioral intention reflects a consumer's readiness to maintain adoption of a specific product or service (Jackson et al., 1997; Venkatesh et al., 2012). Given its role as a precursor to actual utilization, understanding consumer response and engagement is crucial (Arts et al., 2011). The significance of behavioral intention is underscored by numerous studies identifying its predictors, often employing it as a key outcome variable and recognizing its critical role in decision-making (Bajunaied et al., 2023). Consequently, a consumer's behavioral intention to use a product or service constitutes a substantial element in assessing its functions and influencing their attitudes. Technological experience, perceived usefulness, and user attitudes significantly influence behavioral intention (Rivera et al., 2015). For example, recognizing the tangible benefits of a mobile health application positively correlates with future usage intent (Hoque & Sorwar, 2017). Mobile health applications perceived as intuitive and easy to navigate tend to foster consistent engagement and cultivate positive user attitudes (Deng et al., 2014). Likewise, health applications designed for ease of use and provision of valuable information promote user engagement, engender positive experiences, and enhance perceived utility (Huang et al., 2021; Zin et al., 2023; Park et al., 2025). Considering the literature reviewed above, we can formulate the following hypothesis:

> **H5:** Consumers' engagement in digital health technologies has a positive impact on their behavioral intentions.

The theoretical basis for the usage behavior construct is derived from Burton-Jones and Straub's (2006) `actual system usage' construct. It denotes the extent to which a user employs system features to accomplish a specific task. Usage behavior is considered a multifaceted construct due to scholarly disagreement regarding its effect on continuance intention and the measurement scales employed for this variable. Common methods for measuring actual system usage include objective and subjective measures (Straub et al., 1995). Objective measures rely on system logs, encompassing aspects of actual use such as login history and time spent per login. Conversely, subjective measures are based on self-reported data, focusing on elements like frequency or intensity of use (Turner et al., 2010). This study employed the subjective approach, as it includes collecting data on the usage of digital technology by health consumers. Drawing on Bhattacherjee's (2001) work, this research posits that the sustained viability and ultimate success of digital technology in healthcare depend on consistent, ongoing use rather than sporadic engagement. Consequently, continuance behavior emerges as a highly relevant construct from an empirical standpoint, as service usage extends significantly beyond initial adoption (Khan et al., 2021). Informed by the literature above, this research proposes to test the subsequent hypothesis:

> **H6:** Consumers' behavioral intention in digital health technologies has a positive impact on their usage behavior.

Based on the literature reviewed above, we developed a conceptual model for the study, which is shown in Figure 1.

Figure 1. Research model

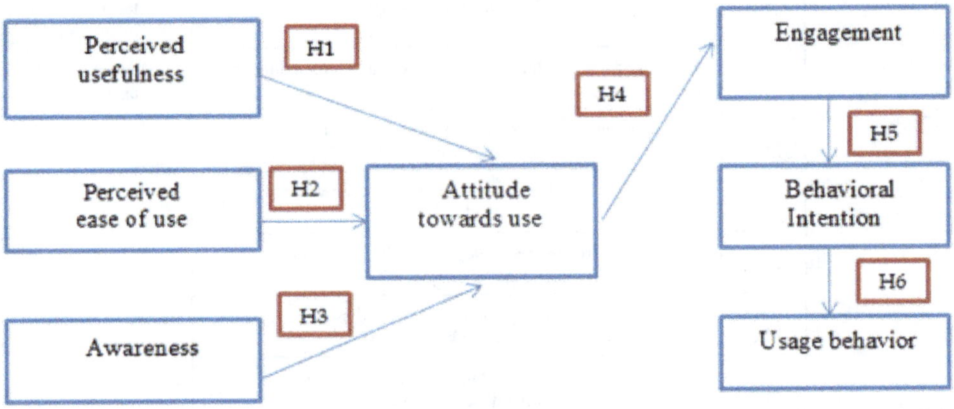

3. RESEARCH METHODOLOGY

The study employed a quantitative research methodology. Given the study's objective to ascertain the impact of digital technologies on healthcare user behavior and to generalize the findings to a defined target population, a quantitative approach was deemed most appropriate. This methodological choice aligns with the capacity of quantitative methods to effectively collect and analyze data via questionnaires to measure specific phenomena (Malhotra, 2020). In light of resource constraints, an online survey was implemented. The study design carefully considered a central tenet of quantitative data collection: ensuring the questionnaire accurately captures the requisite information. Furthermore, a clear articulation of the rationale and purpose behind each data point was prioritized as a critical component of the research design. Consistent with the stated research goal, a structured questionnaire was utilized, encompassing questions pertaining to respondent profiles and constructs designed to test the research hypotheses. The questionnaire items were informed by extant literature, drawing upon authorial perspectives presented in the literature review section. The constructs, corresponding items, and authors are detailed in Table 1. All questionnaire items were assessed using a five-point Likert scale (1 = strongly disagree, 2 = disagree, 3 = neutral, 4 = agree, 5 = strongly agree).

Table 1. Research construct

Variables	Codes	Measurement items	Modified from source(s)
Perceived Usefulness (PU)	PU1	Digital marketing technologies used by healthcare organizations help me monitor my health	Hu et al. (2002); Papa et al. (2020)
	PU2	The use of digital marketing technologies in healthcare is useful for monitoring health	
	PU3	Digital marketing technologies provide better awareness about healthcare	
	PU4	Digital marketing technologies provide improvement in healthcare quality	
	PU5	Digital marketing technologies provide dissemination of healthcare knowledge	
	PU6	The use of digital marketing by healthcare organizations improves my access to healthcare	
Perceived Ease of Use (PEOU)	PEOU1	Digital marketing technologies used in healthcare are easy to adopt	Davis (1989); Moores (2012); Gagnon (2012); Yu & Qian (2018); Papa et al. (2020)
	PEOU2	Digital marketing technologies used in healthcare are convenient	
	PEOU3	The implementation of digital marketing technologies in healthcare depends on their ease of use	
	PEOU4	Finding information about healthcare is easy through digital marketing technologies	
	PEOU5	Communicating with medical professionals is easy through digital marketing technologies	
	PEOU6	Interaction with digital marketing technologies used in healthcare is clear and understandable	
Awareness (AWA)	AWA1	I am well-informed about digital marketing technologies used in healthcare	Hsiao & Tang (2015)
	AWA2	I pay attention to information about digital marketing technologies used in healthcare	
Attitude Towards Use (ATT)	ATT1	Digital marketing technologies used by healthcare organizations are interesting and attractive	Ahn & Park (2022); Nazari-Shirkouhi et al. (2023)
	ATT2	Receiving medical services through digital marketing technologies used by healthcare organizations is reasonable	
	ATT3	Getting to know digital marketing technologies used by healthcare organizations is a pleasant experience	
	ATT4	Digital marketing used by healthcare organizations is better than other technologies	
Engagement (ENG)	ENG1	The digital marketing technologies used by healthcare organizations completely captivate me	Mirzaei & Esmaeilzadeh (2021)
	ENG2	The digital marketing technologies used by healthcare organizations pique my curiosity	
	ENG3	The digital marketing technologies used by healthcare organizations capture my attention	

continued on following page

Table 1. Continued

Variables	Codes	Measurement items	Modified from source(s)
Behavioral Intention (BI)	BI1	In the future, I will use digital marketing technologies more often to raise awareness of health-related issues	Venkatesh et al. (2012); Huang et al. (2021); Zin et al. (2023)
	BI2	I intend to use digital marketing technologies to obtain medical services	
	BI3	I will use digital marketing technologies related to health-related issues to change my life for the better	
Usage Behavior (UB)	UB1	I use digital marketing technologies to learn more about healthcare	Burton-Jones & Straub (2006); Khan et al. (2021)
	UB2	I use digital marketing technologies to search for specific information related to my health	
	UB3	I use digital marketing technologies to share knowledge with other patients	
	UB4	I use digital marketing technologies to disseminate health information	
	UB5	Wider use of digital marketing in healthcare will improve the quality of medical care	

Source: author's work

A probability sampling method was employed to survey the general population. Using census data from Datareportal (2024), the total population of Georgia is reported as 3,726,400, with 2,860,000 individuals aged 18 and over identified as internet users (Datareportal, 2024). This subset constitutes the target population for this study, encompassing users of digital marketing services from all local healthcare organizations. The sample size was determined using Krejcie & Morgan's formula (Krejcie & Morgan, 1970). Based on a 95% confidence level and a 5% margin of error, a sample size of 385 was deemed appropriate. Accounting for an anticipated response rate of 70-75%, considered acceptable according to Heslop et al. (1998), a total of 610 respondents were contacted via social networks and email. A total of 499 completed questionnaires were received, representing a response rate of 81.8%. Data analysis was performed using SPSS 27.

4. RESEARCH RESULTS AND DISCUSSION

The survey results indicate that 37.7% of respondents are aged 18 to 25, 33.7% are aged 26 to 35, and 14% are aged 36 to 45. The share of respondents between 46 and 60 years old is 12.8%, while those over 60 years old are 1.8% of the total number. The gender distribution of the respondents is 70.7% female and 29.3% male. Researchers employed Cronbach's alpha to assess reliability. Following Nunnally's (1967) criterion, a coefficient of 0.60 or higher was considered satisfactory. Table 2 presents the reliability data obtained in this study. As shown in Table 2, each individual variable exhibits a coefficient greater than 0.8, suggesting a high degree of reliability. Validity testing was conducted to evaluate the research instrument's capacity to measure the designated research variables (Nunnally, 1967). An outer loading threshold of ≥0.70 was applied as a criterion for assessing validity within this study. Items meeting this criterion were deemed valid indicators of their respective variables. To establish the measurement model, the average variance extracted (AVE) was required to be ≥0.5 (Hair et al., 2014). The results indicated that all variables were suitable for measuring their intended constructs (Table 2).

Table 2. Variable Measurement Items

Items	Load	AVE	Cronbach's α	CR
PU1	0.801	0.876	0.854	0.912
PU2	0.803			
PU3	0.781			
PU4	0.801			
PU5	0.834			
PU6	0.761			
PEOU1	0.804	0.856	0.944	0.917
PEOU2	0.776			
PEOU3	0.771			
PEOU4	0.865			
PEOU5	0.899			
PEOU6	0.807			
AWA1	0.773	0.879	0.937	0.857
AWA2	0.865			
ATT1	0.802	0.907	0.930	0.873
ATT2	0.843			
ATT3	0.774			
ATT4	0.773			
ENG1	0.898	0.928	0.926	0.913
ENG2	0.778			
ENG3	0.801			
BI1	0.772	0.897	0.933	0.932
BI2	0.789			
BI3	0.782			

continued on following page

Table 2. Continued

Items	Load	AVE	Cronbach's α	CR
UB1	0.775	0.892	0.915	0.847
UB2	0.803			
UB3	0.777			
UB4	0.878			
UB5	0.879			

Source: author's work.

To assess the statistical significance of each variable, Pearson's correlation analysis was employed. As presented in Table 3, the correlations between all variables examined were statistically significant (P=0.000).

Table 3. Correlation matrix

Variables		PU	PEOU	AWA	ATT	ENG	BI	UB
PU	Pearson Correlation	1	.592**	.546**	.521**	.560**	.505	.611**
	Sig. (2-tailed)		.000	.000	.000	.000	.000	.000
	N	499	499	499	499	499	499	499
PEOU	Pearson Correlation	.592**	1	.771**	.727**	.603**	.687**	.638
	Sig. (2-tailed)	.000		.000	.000	.000	.000	.000
	N	499	499	499	499	499	499	499
AWA	Pearson Correlation	.546**	.771**	1	.752**	.591**	.671**	.624**
	Sig. (2-tailed)	.000	.000		.000	.000	.000	.000
	N	499	499	499	499	499	499	499
ATT	Pearson Correlation	.521**	.727**	.752**	1	.717**	.763**	.719**
	Sig. (2-tailed)	.000	.000	.000		.000	.000	.000
	N	499	499	499	499	499	499	499
ENG	Pearson Correlation	.560**	.603**	.591**	.717**	1	.711**	.744**
	Sig. (2-tailed)	.000	.000	.000	.000		.000	.000
	N	499	499	499	499	499	499	499
BI	Pearson Correlation	.505**	.687**	.671**	.763**	.711**	1**	.722**
	Sig. (2-tailed)	.000	.000	.000	.000	.000		.000
	N	499	499	499	499	499	499	499

continued on following page

Table 3. Continued

Variables		PU	PEOU	AWA	ATT	ENG	BI	UB
UB	Pearson Correlation	.611**	.638**	.624**	.719**	.744**	.722**	1**
	Sig. (2-tailed)	.000	.000	.000	.000	.000	.000	
	N	499	499	499	499	499	499	499

** Correlation is significant at the 0.01 level
Source: author's work.

We used regression analysis to test the hypotheses formulated above. Table 4 shows that the 1st, 2nd, and 3rd models we developed are reliable [P<0.001, F(555.819)>Fcr(3.84); P<0.001, F(645.035)>Fcr(3.84); P<0.001, F(185.605)>Fcr(3.84)]. Therefore, hypotheses H1, H2, and H3 were confirmed. Accordingly, perceived usefulness positively affects consumers' attitudes toward digital health technology (coefficient of determination R^2=0.727, which allows us to say that 72.7% of the attitude towards digital health technology is explained by perceived usefulness, and the rest is explained by other factors). Also, perceived ease of use has a positive impact on attitude towards digital health technology (coefficient of determination R^2=0.752, which means that 75.2% of users' attitude towards digital health technology is explained by perceived ease of use, and the rest by other factors). Awareness has a positive impact on attitude towards digital health technology (coefficient of determination R^2=0.521, which means that 52.1% of users' attitude towards digital health technology is explained by awareness, and the rest by other factors). Regression analysis shows that when the independent variable, perceived usefulness, increases by one unit, the dependent variable, attitude towards digital health technology, increases by 0.450 units. Also, when the independent variable, perceived ease of use, increases by one unit, the dependent variable, attitude towards digital health technology, increases by 0.515 units. Based on Table 4, it is clear that when the independent variable, awareness, increases by one unit, the dependent variable, attitude towards digital health technology, increases by 0.959 units.

Table 4. Regression analysis of the influence of perceived usefulness, perceived ease of use, and awareness on consumers' attitudes toward digital health technology

a) Model Summary				
Model	R	R^2	Adjusted R^2	Std. Error of the Estimate
1	.727	.528	.527	2.68501
2	.752	.565	.564	2.57800
3	.521	.272	.270	3.33455

continued on following page

Table 4. Continued

b) ANOVA						
Model		Sum of Squares	DF	Mean Square	F	P
1	Regression	4007.050	1	4007.050	555.819	.000
	Residual	3583.006	497	7.209		
	Total	7590.056	498			
2	Regression	4286.955	1	4286.955	645.035	.000
	Residual	3303.101	497	6.646		
	Total	7590.056	498			
3	Regression	2063.786	1	2063.786	185.605	.000
	Residual	5526.270	497	11.119		
	Total	7590.056	498			
c) Coefficients						
Model		Unstandardized Coefficients		Standardized Coefficients	t	P
		B	Std. Error	Beta		
1	(Constant)	4.442	.432		10.294	.000
	PU	.450	.019	.727	23.576	.000
2	(Constant)	2.644	.470		5.627	.000
	PEOU	.515	.020	.752	25.398	.000
3	(Constant)	8.583	.439		19.529	.000
	AWA	.959	.070	.521	13.624	.000

Notes: Predictors (Constant): Perceived usefulness; Perceived ease of use ; Awareness. Dependent Variable: Attitude towards use.

Source: author's work

Table 5 shows that consumers' attitude towards digital health technology has a positive effect on their engagement. Accordingly, the model we developed is reliable (P<0.0001); F(525.999)>Fcr(3.84) and hypothesis H4 was confirmed. In addition, the coefficient of determination R2=0.514. Therefore, we can say that 51.4% of consumer engagement is explained by consumers' attitude towards digital health technology, while the rest is due to other factors. Regression analysis shows that a one-unit increase in the independent variable, attitude towards digital health technology, leads to an increase in the dependent variable, consumer engagement, by 0.567 units (see Table 5).

Table 5. Regression analysis of the influence of consumers' attitudes toward digital health technology on their engagement

a) Model Summary						
Model	R	R^2	Adjusted R^2	Std. Error of the Estimate		
4	.717	.514	.513	2.15469		
b) ANOVA						
Model		Sum of Squares	DF	Mean Square	F	P
4	Regression	2442.058	1	2442.058	525.999	.000
	Residual	2307.425	497	4.643		
	Total	4749.483	498			
c) Coefficients						
Model		Unstandardized Coefficients		Standardized Coefficients	t	P
		B	Std. Error	Beta		
4	(Constant)	1.150	.365		3.154	.002
	ATT	.567	.025	.717	22.935	.000

Notes: Predictor (Constant): Attitude towards use; Dependent Variable: Engagement.
Source: author's work

In the next step, we determined the relationship between consumers' engagement in digital health technologies and their behavioral intention (see Table 6). Table 6 provides evidence that consumers' engagement in digital health technologies has a significant positive effect on the behavioral intention. The developed model demonstrates a high level of statistical reliability ($P < 0.001$; F (507.655) > Fcr (3.84)), supporting hypothesis H5. The table shows that the coefficient of determination (R^2) value is 0.505, indicating that consumers' engagement explains 50.5% of the variance in behavioural intention, while other factors outside the model influence the remaining 49.5%. The regression analysis reveals that a one-unit increase in the independent variable (consumers' engagement in digital health technologies) is associated with a 0.713-unit increase in the dependent variable (behavioral intention).

Table 6. Regression analysis of the influence of consumers' engagement in digital health technologies on their behavioral intention

a) Model Summary						
Model	R	R^2	Adjusted R^2	Std. Error of the Estimate		
5	.711	.505	.504	2.18208		
b) ANOVA						
Model		Sum of Squares	DF	Mean Square	F	P

continued on following page

Table 6. Continued

5	Regression	2417.187	1	2417.187	507.655	.000
	Residual	2366.452	497	4.761		
	Total	4783.639	498			
c) Coefficients						
Model		Unstandardized Coefficients		Standardized Coefficients	t	P
		B	Std. Error	Beta		
5	(Constant) ENG	4.029	.308		13.098	.000
		.713	.032	.711	22.531	.000

Notes: Predictor (Constant): Engagement; Dependent Variable: Behavioral intention.
Source: author's work

Table 7 indicates a positive effect of consumers' behavioral intentions in digital health technologies on their usage behavior. The developed model demonstrates a high level of statistical significance (P<0.001), with the F-statistic (F(540.467)) exceeding the critical F-value (Fcr (3.84)), thereby supporting hypothesis H6. Furthermore, the coefficient of determination (R^2) indicates that 52.1% of the variance in consumer usage behavior can be explained by their behavioral intention in digital health technologies. The remaining variance is attributable to other factors. Regression analysis further reveals that a one-unit increase in the independent variable (consumers' behavioral intention) is associated with a 1.224-unit increase in the dependent variable (consumer usage behavior).

Table 7. Regression analysis of the influence of consumers' behavioral intention in digital health technologies on their usage behavior

a) Model Summary						
Model	R	R^2	Adjusted R^2	Std. Error of the Estimate		
6	.722	.521	.520	3.64101		
b) ANOVA						
Model		Sum of Squares	DF	Mean Square	F	P
6	Regression	7164.948	1	7164.948	540.467	.000
	Residual	6588.704	497	13.257		
	Total	13753.651	498			
c) Coefficients						
Model		Unstandardized Coefficients		Standardized Coefficients	t	P
		B	Std. Error	Beta		

continued on following page

Table 7. Continued

6	(Constant) UB	3.284	.581		5.649	.000
		1.224	.053	.722	23.248	.000

Notes: Predictor (Constant): Behavioral intention; Dependent Variable: usage behavior
Source: author's work

5. CONCLUSION AND THEORETICAL AND PRACTICAL IMPLICATIONS

The study results showed that key variables, including consumer awareness, perceived usefulness, and perceived ease of use of digital health technology, demonstrably influence consumer attitudes toward these technologies. Engagement with these technologies is positively correlated with these factors. Consumers' perception that digital health technology simplifies their lives encourages behavioral intention. Consequently, the variables examined represent critical drivers for digital marketing strategies within Georgian healthcare organizations, enhancing their capacity to meet customer expectations. Findings indicate that Georgian healthcare organizations should prioritize the ongoing enhancement of their digital marketing offerings, thereby amplifying perceived benefits and, consequently, customer satisfaction. To this end, these organizations should develop digital service systems specifically designed to address and satisfy customer needs, facilitating consumer acquisition and retention. Ensuring the reliability of research results is paramount for both theoretical implications and future research endeavors. This study employs robust instruments to investigate factors influencing the adoption of digital health technology, enabling the formulation of evidence-based recommendations for enhancing digital services within the Georgian healthcare sector. Georgian healthcare organizations can adapt this model by refining existing digital products and applications and strategically leveraging digital services to improve consumer satisfaction. From the research, it becomes clear that Georgian healthcare organizations should leverage digital technologies to develop innovative solutions that enhance healthcare delivery and address critical medical challenges. The rigorous quality control of comprehensively collected data can significantly improve patient outcomes and reduce service costs in the Georgian healthcare sector. The study further suggests that these organizations provide clear, accessible instructions to promote active engagement with digital services. To improve service quality and enhance marketing portfolio flexibility, middle and senior management should familiarize themselves with these findings to effectively lead advancements within the healthcare sector.

6. LIMITATIONS AND DIRECTIONS FOR FUTURE RESEARCH

The interpretation of these findings necessitates consideration of the study's limitations. This research exhibits limitations in capturing the perspectives of health consumers aged 60 and above. The disproportionate representation of younger participants may have introduced attenuation bias due to the skewed age distribution, potentially leading to an underestimation of the relationship between age and attitudes towards digital health technology. Therefore, the true association may be more robust than indicated. Additionally, data collection involved both online and in-person modalities. The study's focus on residents of Georgia may constrain the generalizability of the findings to other populations, and conclusions should be interpreted within the Georgian context.

Further investigation is recommended to empirically examine the relationship between attitudes toward digital health and its implementation. If significant associations are found, interventions should focus on fostering favorable perceptions of digital health. Exploring the use of supported technology access for vulnerable populations, such as older adults, may be beneficial in improving attitudes and encouraging the uptake of digital health technologies. Future studies should prioritize the inclusion of a larger cohort of participants within this demographic to comprehensively document their perceptions and opinions regarding digital technologies in healthcare. To address this demographic gap, subsequent research endeavors could employ purposive sampling strategies to ensure adequate representation of elderly respondents, thereby enabling a more thorough understanding of their perspectives on digital health technologies. Future research should also include the viewpoints of healthcare professionals and digital health consumers.

REFERENCES

Ahn, H., & Park, E. (2022). Determinants of consumer acceptance of mobile healthcare devices: An application of the concepts of technology acceptance and coolness. *Telematics and Informatics*, *70*, 101810. DOI: 10.1016/j.tele.2022.101810

Ajzen, I. (2015). *Belief, Attitude, Intention and Behaviour: An Introduction to Theory and Research*. Addison-Wesley.

Ajzen, I., & Fishbein, M. (1977). Attitude-Behavior Relations: A Theoretical Analysis and Review of Empirical Research. *Psychological Bulletin*, *84*(5), 888–918. DOI: 10.1037/0033-2909.84.5.888

Arts, J. W., Frambach, R. T., & Bijmolt, T. H. (2011). Generalizations on consumer innovation adoption: A meta-analysis on drivers of intention and behavior. *International Journal of Research in Marketing*, *28*(2), 134–144. DOI: 10.1016/j.ijresmar.2010.11.002

Bajunaied, K., Hussin, N., & Kamarudin, S. (2023). Behavioral intention to adopt FinTech services: An extension of unified theory of acceptance and use of technology. *Journal of Open Innovation*, *9*(1), 100010. DOI: 10.1016/j.joitmc.2023.100010

Barello, S., Graffigna, G., & Vegni, E. (2012). Patient engagement as an emerging challenge for healthcare services: Mapping the literature. *Nursing Research and Practice*, *2012*(1), 905934. DOI: 10.1155/2012/905934 PMID: 23213497

Bhattacherjee, A. (2001). Understanding information systems continuance: An expectation-confirmation model. *Management Information Systems Quarterly*, *25*(3), 351–370. DOI: 10.2307/3250921

Burton-Jones, A., & Straub, D. W.Jr. (2006). Reconceptualizing system usage: An approach and empirical test. *Information Systems Research*, *17*(3), 228–246. DOI: 10.1287/isre.1060.0096

Cassidy, R. (2021). Attitudes towards digital health technology: introducing the digital health scale. medRxiv, 2021-09. DOI: 10.1101/2021.09.03.21262482

. Chatterjee, R., Ray, R., Dash, S. R., & Jena, O. P. (2021). Conceptualizing tomorrow's healthcare through digitization. *Computational Intelligence and Healthcare Informatics*, 359-376.

Chatterjee, S., & Kulkarni, P. (2021). Healthcare consumer behaviour: The impact of digital transformation of healthcare on consumer. *Cardiometry*, (20), 134–143. DOI: 10.18137/cardiometry.2021.20.134143

Chen, K., & Chan, A. H. (2014). Predictors of gerontechnology acceptance by older Hong Kong Chinese. *Technovation*, *34*(2), 126–135. DOI: 10.1016/j.technovation.2013.09.010

Chong, A. Y. L., Blut, M., & Zheng, S. (2022). Factors influencing the acceptance of healthcare information technologies: A meta-analysis. *Information & Management*, *59*(3), 103604. DOI: 10.1016/j.im.2022.103604

Dal Mas, F., Massaro, M., Rippa, P., & Secundo, G. (2023). The challenges of digital transformation in healthcare: An interdisciplinary literature review, framework, and future research agenda. *Technovation*, *123*, 102716. DOI: 10.1016/j.technovation.2023.102716

Datareportal. (2024). Digital 2024: Georgia. Retrieved from: https://datareportal.com/reports/digital-2024-georgia#:~:text=The%20state%20of%20digital%20in%20Georgia%20in%202024&text=Georgia%20was%20home%20to%202.85,percent%20of%20the%20total%20population

Davis, F. D. (1989). Perceived usefulness, perceived ease of use, and user acceptance of information technology. *Management Information Systems Quarterly*, *13*(3), 319–340. DOI: 10.2307/249008

Deng, Z., Mo, X., & Liu, S. (2014). Comparison of the middle-aged and older users' adoption of mobile health services in China. *International Journal of Medical Informatics*, *83*(3), 210–224. DOI: 10.1016/j.ijmedinf.2013.12.002 PMID: 24388129

Djakeli, K., & Jakeli, T. (2016). Health Reforms Need Marketing-Analyzing Current Georgian Healthcare Model through Reform Marketing Matrix (RMM). *The Journal of Business*, *5*(2), 7–15. DOI: 10.31578/.v5i2.106

Domecq, J. P., Prutsky, G., Elraiyah, T., Wang, Z., Nabhan, M., Shippee, N., Brito, J. P., Boehmer, K., Hasan, R., Firwana, B., Erwin, P., Eton, D., Sloan, J., Montori, V., Asi, N., Abu Dabrh, A. M., & Murad, M. H. (2014). Patient engagement in research: A systematic review. *BMC Health Services Research*, *14*(1), 89. DOI: 10.1186/1472-6963-14-89 PMID: 24568690

Eagly, A. H., & Chaiken, S. (1993). *The psychology of attitudes*. Harcourt, Brace, & Janovich.

Ferrigno, G., Del Sarto, N., Piccaluga, A., & Baroncelli, A. (2023). Industry 4.0 base technologies and business models: A bibliometric analysis. *European Journal of Innovation Management*, *26*(7), 502–526. DOI: 10.1108/EJIM-02-2023-0107

Gagnon, M. P., Desmartis, M., Labrecque, M., Car, J., Pagliari, C., Pluye, P., Frémont, P., Gagnon, J., Tremblay, N., & Légaré, F. (2012). Systematic review of factors influencing the adoption of information and communication technologies by healthcare professionals. *Journal of Medical Systems*, *36*(1), 241–277. DOI: 10.1007/s10916-010-9473-4 PMID: 20703721

Hair, J.Jr, Sarstedt, M., Hopkins, L., & Kuppelwieser, G., V. (. (2014). Partial least squares structural equation modeling (PLS-SEM) An emerging tool in business research. *European Business Review*, *26*(2), 106–121. DOI: 10.1108/EBR-10-2013-0128

. Heslop, L. A., Papadopoulos, N., & Bourk, M. (1998). An interregional and intercultural perspective on subcultural differences in product evaluations. *Canadian Journal of Administrative Sciences/Revue Canadienne des Sciences de l'Administration, 15*(2), 113-127.

Hoque, R., & Sorwar, G. (2017). Understanding factors influencing the adoption of mHealth by the elderly: An extension of the UTAUT model. *International Journal of Medical Informatics*, *101*, 75–84. DOI: 10.1016/j.ijmedinf.2017.02.002 PMID: 28347450

Hsiao, C. H., & Tang, K. Y. (2015). Examining a model of mobile healthcare technology acceptance by the elderly in Taiwan. *Journal of Global Information Technology Management*, *18*(4), 292–311. DOI: 10.1080/1097198X.2015.1108099

Hu, P. J. H., Chau, P. Y., & Sheng, O. R. L. (2002). Adoption of telemedicine technology by health care organizations: An exploratory study. *Journal of Organizational Computing and Electronic Commerce*, *12*(3), 197–221. DOI: 10.1207/S15327744JOCE1203_01

Huang, C. Y., Yang, M. C., & Huang, C. Y. (2021). An empirical study on factors influencing consumer adoption intention of an AI-powered chatbot for health and weight management. *International Journal of Performability Engineering*, *17*(5), 422. DOI: 10.23940/ijpe.21.05.p2.422432

Jackson, C. M., Chow, S., & Leitch, R. A. (1997). Toward an understanding of the behavioral intention to use an information system. *Decision Sciences*, *28*(2), 357–389. DOI: 10.1111/j.1540-5915.1997.tb01315.x

Khan, I., Saleh, M. A., Quazi, A., & Johns, R. (2021). Health consumers' social media adoption behaviours in Australia. *Health Informatics Journal*, *27*(2), 14604582211009917. DOI: 10.1177/14604582211009917 PMID: 33887968

Kim, E., & Han, S. (2023). Investigating the digital health acceptance of Korean baby boomers: Comparative study of telemedicine and wearable healthcare devices. *Health Policy and Technology, 12*(1), 100727. DOI: 10.1016/j.hlpt.2023.100727

Kim, T. H., & Kim, H. S. (2016). Delivery app understanding and acceptance among food tech customers using the modified technology acceptance model. *Journal of Tourism Science, 40*(5), 127–144.

Krejcie, R. V., & Morgan, D. W. (1970). Determining sample size for research activities. *Educational and Psychological Measurement, 30*(3), 607–610. DOI: 10.1177/001316447003000308

Li, J., Ma, Q., Chan, A. H., & Man, S. (2019). Health monitoring through wearable technologies for older adults: Smart wearables acceptance model. *Applied Ergonomics, 75*, 162–169. DOI: 10.1016/j.apergo.2018.10.006 PMID: 30509522

Lim, W. M., & Weissmann, M. A. (2023). Toward a Theory of Behavioral Control. *Journal of Strategic Marketing, 31*(1), 185–211. DOI: 10.1080/0965254X.2021.1890190

Lindsay, S., Smith, S., Bellaby, P., & Baker, R. (2009). The health impact of an online heart disease support group: A comparison of moderated versus unmoderated support. *Health Education Research, 24*(4), 646–654. DOI: 10.1093/her/cyp001 PMID: 19251770

Liu, X., Sun, M., & Li, J. (2018). Research on gender differences in online health communities. *International Journal of Medical Informatics, 111*, 172–181. DOI: 10.1016/j.ijmedinf.2017.12.019 PMID: 29425630

Lu, J., Lu, C., Yu, C. S., & Yao, J. E. (2003). Exploring factors associated with wireless internet via mobile technology acceptance in Mainland China. *Communications of the IIMA, 3*(1), 101–120.

Malhotra, N. (2020). *Marketing research: An applied orientation* (7th ed.). Pearson Education Limited.

Massaro, M. (2023). Digital transformation in the healthcare sector through blockchain technology. Insights from academic research and business developments. *Technovation, 120*, 102386. DOI: 10.1016/j.technovation.2021.102386

Mauro, M., Noto, G., Prenestini, A., & Sarto, F. (2024). Digital transformation in healthcare: Assessing the role of digital technologies for managerial support processes. *Technological Forecasting and Social Change, 209*, 123781. DOI: 10.1016/j.techfore.2024.123781

Moores, T. T. (2012). Towards an integrated model of IT acceptance in healthcare. *Decision Support Systems, 53*(3), 507–516. DOI: 10.1016/j.dss.2012.04.014

Nazari-Shirkouhi, S., Badizadeh, A., Dashtpeyma, M., & Ghodsi, R. (2023). A model to improve user acceptance of e-services in healthcare systems based on technology acceptance model: An empirical study. *Journal of Ambient Intelligence and Humanized Computing, 14*(6), 7919–7935. DOI: 10.1007/s12652-023-04601-0 PMID: 37228695

Nunnally, J. C. (1967). *Psychometric Theory*. McGraw-Hill Book Company.

Papa, A., Mital, M., Pisano, P., & Del Giudice, M. (2020). E-health and wellbeing monitoring using smart healthcare devices: An empirical investigation. *Technological Forecasting and Social Change, 153*, 119226. DOI: 10.1016/j.techfore.2018.02.018

Park, J. H., Lee, C. W., & Do, C. (2025). Examining Users' Acceptance Intention of Health Applications Based on the Technology Acceptance Model. *Health Care, 13*(6), 596. PMID: 40150446

Raimo, N., De Turi, I., Albergo, F., & Vitolla, F. (2023). The drivers of the digital transformation in the healthcare industry: An empirical analysis in Italian hospitals. *Technovation, 121*, 102558. DOI: 10.1016/j.technovation.2022.102558

Rivera, M., Gregory, A., & Cobos, L. (2015). Mobile application for the timeshare industry: The influence of technology experience, usefulness, and attitude on behavioral intentions. *Journal of Hospitality and Tourism Technology, 6*(3), 242–257. DOI: 10.1108/JHTT-01-2015-0002

Rouidi, M., Hamdoune, A., Choujtani, K., & Chati, A. (2022). TAM-UTAUT and the acceptance of remote healthcare technologies by healthcare professionals: A systematic review. *Informatics in Medicine Unlocked, 32*, 101008. DOI: 10.1016/j.imu.2022.101008

Saifudin, A., Aima, M., Sutawidjaya, A., & Sugiyono, S. (2021). Hospital digitalization in the era of industry 4.0 based on GHRM and service quality. *International Journal of Data and Network Science, 5*(2), 107–114. DOI: 10.5267/j.ijdns.2021.2.004

Salvi, A., Vitolla, F., Rubino, M., Giakoumelou, A., & Raimo, N. (2021). Online information on digitalisation processes and its impact on firm value. *Journal of Business Research, 124*, 437–444. DOI: 10.1016/j.jbusres.2020.10.025

Stoumpos, A. I., Kitsios, F., & Talias, M. A. (2023). Digital transformation in healthcare: Technology acceptance and its applications. *International Journal of Environmental Research and Public Health, 20*(4), 3407. DOI: 10.3390/ijerph20043407 PMID: 36834105

Straub, D., Limayem, M., & Karahanna-Evaristo, E. (1995). Measuring system usage: Implications for IS theory testing. *Management Science*, *41*(8), 1328–1342. DOI: 10.1287/mnsc.41.8.1328

Strull, W. M., Lo, B., & Charles, G. (1984). Do patients want to participate in medical decision making? *Journal of the American Medical Association*, *252*(21), 2990–2994. DOI: 10.1001/jama.1984.03350210038026 PMID: 6502860

Todua, N., Babilua, P., & Dochviri, T. (2013). On the multiple linear regression in marketing research. *Bull. Georg. Natl. Acad. Sci*, *7*(3), 135–139.

Todua, N., & Jashi, C. (2018). Influence of social marketing on the behavior of Georgian consumers regarding healthy nutrition. *Bull. Georg. Natl. Acad. Sci*, *12*(2), 183–190.

Todua, N., Jashi, C., & Todua, N. (2024). The role of social media in healthcare marketing. In *Modern healthcare marketing in the digital era* (pp. 26–41). IGI Global Scientific Publishing.

Todua, N., & Todua, N. (2025). The Influence of Digital Media Marketing Activities on Healthcare Consumer Behavior. In *International Scientific-Practical Conference* (pp. 208-221). Cham: Springer Nature Switzerland. DOI: 10.1007/978-3-031-88052-0_16

Todua, N., & Urotadze, E. (2025). Effect of Social Media Influencers on Consumer Brand Engagement and Its Implications on Purchase Intention. In *Brand Creation and Management in the Phygital Era* (pp. 541–562). IGI Global Scientific Publishing. DOI: 10.4018/979-8-3373-0948-4.ch021

Tortorella, G. L., Fogliatto, F. S., Kurnia, S., Thürer, M., & Capurro, D. (2022). Healthcare 4.0 digital applications: An empirical study on measures, bundles and patient-centered performance. *Technological Forecasting and Social Change*, *181*, 121780. DOI: 10.1016/j.techfore.2022.121780

Tortorella, G. L., Fogliatto, F. S., Tlapa Mendoza, D., Pepper, M., & Capurro, D. (2023). Digital transformation of health services: A value stream-oriented approach. *International Journal of Production Research*, *61*(6), 1814–1828. DOI: 10.1080/00207543.2022.2048115

Turner, M., Kitchenham, B., Brereton, P., Charters, S., & Budgen, D. (2010). Does the technology acceptance model predict actual use? A systematic literature review. *Information and Software Technology*, *52*(5), 463–479. DOI: 10.1016/j.infsof.2009.11.005

Venkatesh, V., Morris, M. G., Davis, G. B., & Davis, F. D. (2003). User acceptance of information technology: Toward a unified view. *Management Information Systems Quarterly*, *27*(3), 425–478. DOI: 10.2307/30036540

Venkatesh, V., Thong, J. Y., & Xu, X. (2012). Consumer acceptance and use of information technology: Extending the unified theory of acceptance and use of technology. *Management Information Systems Quarterly*, *36*(1), 157–178. DOI: 10.2307/41410412

Verhoef, P. C., Broekhuizen, T., Bart, Y., Bhattacharya, A., Dong, J. Q., Fabian, N., & Haenlein, M. (2021). Digital transformation: A multidisciplinary reflection and research agenda. *Journal of Business Research*, *122*, 889–901. DOI: 10.1016/j.jbusres.2019.09.022

Wilson, E. V., & Lankton, N. K. (2004). Modeling patients' acceptance of provider-delivered e-health. *Journal of the American Medical Informatics Association : JAMIA*, *11*(4), 241–248. DOI: 10.1197/jamia.M1475 PMID: 15064290

Yap, Y. Y., Tan, S. H., & Choon, S. W. (2022). Elderly's intention to use technologies: A systematic literature review. *Heliyon*, *8*(1), e08765. DOI: 10.1016/j.heliyon.2022.e08765 PMID: 35128090

Yu, P., & Qian, S. (2018). Developing a theoretical model and questionnaire survey instrument to measure the success of electronic health records in residential aged care. *PLoS One*, *13*(1), e0190749. DOI: 10.1371/journal.pone.0190749 PMID: 29315323

Zin, K. S. L. T., Kim, S., Kim, H. S., & Feyissa, I. F. (2023). A study on technology acceptance of digital healthcare among older Korean adults using extended tam (extended technology acceptance model). *Administrative Sciences*, *13*(2), 42. DOI: 10.3390/admsci13020042

Chapter 4
Inclusion in Healthcare Economics:
Ensuring Affordability and Accessibility for All Social Groups

Surjit Singha
http://orcid.org/0000-0002-5730-8677
Kristu Jayanti University, India

Ranjit Singha
http://orcid.org/0000-0002-3541-8752
Christ University, India

Shruti Jose
http://orcid.org/0000-0003-3139-2505
Christ University, India

Alphonsa Diana Haokip
http://orcid.org/0000-0003-2578-0114
Don Bosco College, Maram, India

ABSTRACT

Healthcare systems across the globe continue to struggle with persistent inequities in affordability and accessibility, disproportionately affecting marginalized and socioeconomically vulnerable populations. As nations pursue large-scale health reforms, the integration of physical and digital ("phygital") healthcare ecosystems presents both transformative opportunities and new ethical challenges. This chapter examines inclusion in healthcare economics through the lenses of affordability, accessibility, and social justice, situating these concerns within contemporary national health reform agendas. Drawing on economic theory, public health policy,

DOI: 10.4018/979-8-3373-7173-3.ch004

and leadership studies, the chapter explores how phygital health models can reduce structural barriers while also risking new forms of exclusion if inequities in digital access, literacy, and governance persist. The chapter contributes a multidimensional framework that integrates economics, marketing, and leadership to advance inclusive, equitable, and sustainable healthcare systems.

INTRODUCTION

Healthcare inclusion has emerged as one of the defining challenges of contemporary national health reform. Despite decades of policy interventions, technological advancements, and increased global attention to universal health coverage, access to affordable and quality healthcare remains uneven across social groups. Economic disparities, geographic isolation, digital divides, and systemic governance failures continue to exclude large segments of populations from essential health services (World Health Organization [WHO], 2010; Marmot, 2017). These challenges have intensified in the wake of rapid digitization and the growing adoption of hybrid healthcare delivery models that combine physical and digital systems, commonly referred to as phygital healthcare.

Inclusion in healthcare economics requires frameworks that balance affordability, accessibility, and technological advancement across diverse social groups. Contemporary healthcare systems are increasingly shaped by digital and AI-enabled models that redefine service delivery, patient engagement, and cost structures. Drawing on insights from Djakeli (2024), this chapter situates healthcare marketing as a strategic economic mechanism rather than a purely promotional function, emphasizing patient-centric design, trust-building, and service co-creation. By engaging with phygital healthcare ecosystems that integrate physical infrastructure with digital platforms, the chapter examines how inclusive economic models can enhance equitable access, reduce systemic barriers, and support sustainable, socially responsive healthcare systems.

Gigauri and Djakeli (2021) analyze national health reforms in Georgia from 1994 to 2021, offering a longitudinal assessment of three major reform waves in the post-Soviet period. The authors argue that effective health reform must align with a country's economic capacity, institutional readiness, and socio-historical context. After independence, Georgia inherited a centralized Semashko-style system, but the economic crisis of the 1990s weakened its sustainability. Initial reforms focused on decentralization and social health insurance, though limited institutional capacity constrained outcomes (Gigauri & Djakeli, 2021).

The second wave emphasized privatization and market-oriented restructuring to improve efficiency and service delivery, yet raised concerns about equity and access. The third phase, beginning around 2013, introduced Universal Health Coverage (UHC), expanding financial protection and aligning policy with Sustainable Development Goal 3. This marked a shift toward balancing economic feasibility with social welfare.

A key strength of the article is its long-term policy perspective, highlighting policy learning and institutional adaptation. However, the analysis remains largely descriptive and would benefit from stronger quantitative evidence and comparative regional insights. Overall, the study contributes valuable lessons on aligning economic reform, governance capacity, and health system sustainability in transitional economies.

Friedman's Capitalism and Freedom (1962) is a foundational work in economic and political thought, articulating the intrinsic connection between economic liberty and political freedom. Friedman argues that free markets, limited government, and individual choice are essential for fostering innovation, efficiency, and social welfare. While primarily focused on broad economic systems, his insights into market mechanisms, competition, and the role of state intervention provide important theoretical grounding for analyzing healthcare economics and reform. In contexts where public policy intersects with market forces such as healthcare financing and service delivery Friedman's principles help frame debates on efficiency, affordability, and the balance between public and private sector roles.

Friedman and Friedman's Free to Choose: A Personal Statement (1980) extends Milton Friedman's economic philosophy into a broader public policy framework, arguing persuasively for the primacy of individual liberty, market competition, and limited government intervention. The authors examine how free-market principles can enhance efficiency, innovation, and personal choice across diverse sectors, including education, welfare, and healthcare. By critiquing centralized planning and advocating for decentralized decision-making, the book provides a compelling defense of market-driven solutions while acknowledging the role of transparent regulations. Its insights are particularly relevant for analyzing healthcare economics, where debates about affordability, access, and system performance often hinge on the balance between public provision and market mechanisms.

At its core, healthcare economics is concerned with how scarce resources are allocated to maximize health outcomes. However, traditional economic models have often prioritized efficiency and cost containment over equity and inclusion, leading to structural imbalances in healthcare systems (Arrow, 1963; Sen, 1999). While market-based mechanisms have improved innovation and service delivery in certain contexts, they have also reinforced inequalities by privileging those with purchasing power, insurance coverage, and technological access. As a result, affordability and accessibility have become central ethical and policy concerns in healthcare economics, particularly in low- and middle-income countries and among marginalized populations within high-income nations.

National health reforms worldwide increasingly emphasize inclusivity as a normative goal. Universal Health Coverage (UHC), endorsed by the United Nations and the WHO, explicitly calls for ensuring that all individuals receive the health services they need without suffering financial hardship (WHO, 2019). Yet, the translation of this principle into practice remains uneven. Healthcare affordability is compromised by rising medical costs, privatization, and out-of-pocket expenditures, while accessibility is constrained by uneven infrastructure, workforce shortages, and socio-cultural barriers (Xu et al., 2018). These issues are not merely technical but deeply political and economic, reflecting broader power relations and governance structures within health systems.

The emergence of phygital healthcare has reshaped these debates. Digital health technologies telemedicine, mobile health applications, artificial intelligence–driven diagnostics, and electronic health records have expanded the reach of healthcare services beyond traditional institutional settings (Kickbusch et al., 2017). When integrated with physical healthcare infrastructure, these technologies promise to reduce geographic barriers, lower transaction costs, and improve service efficiency. For underserved populations, phygital systems can offer unprecedented access to consultations, diagnostics, and health information. However, these benefits are not automatically inclusive. Without deliberate policy design, phygital healthcare risks reproducing or even deepening existing inequities, particularly among populations lacking digital literacy, internet connectivity, or trust in technology-driven systems (Jan Dijk, 2020).

Inclusion in healthcare economics therefore demands a shift from narrow cost-efficiency frameworks toward broader socio-economic and ethical considerations. Inclusion encompasses not only financial protection and service availability but also cultural responsiveness, gender sensitivity, disability access, and digital inclusion. Scholars increasingly argue that healthcare systems must be evaluated not only by aggregate health outcomes but by how equitably those outcomes are distributed across social groups (Braveman & Gruskin, 2003; Marmot et al., 2020). This perspective aligns with capabilities-based approaches to development, which emphasize individuals' real freedoms to achieve health and well-being rather than formal entitlements alone (Sen, 1999).

Marketing and leadership play critical yet often underexamined roles in advancing inclusive healthcare economics. Healthcare marketing influences how services are designed, communicated, and perceived by different populations. Inclusive marketing strategies can improve health literacy, reduce stigma, and enhance service uptake among marginalized groups. Conversely, exclusionary or profit-driven marketing practices may reinforce inequities by targeting only affluent or digitally savvy consumers (Kotler et al., 2021). Leadership, meanwhile, shapes the strategic direction, ethical orientation, and governance quality of healthcare systems. Inclusive leadership is essential for aligning economic incentives with social objectives, fostering cross-sector collaboration, and ensuring accountability in phygital health reforms (Northouse, 2021).

The COVID-19 pandemic starkly exposed both the potential and the limitations of existing healthcare systems. While digital health solutions enabled continuity of care during lockdowns, the pandemic also revealed deep structural inequities in access to care, vaccines, and health information (Gostin et al., 2021). Marginalized communities experienced higher morbidity and mortality, underscoring the urgency of embedding inclusion at the core of healthcare economics and reform. These lessons have accelerated policy interest in resilient, inclusive, and digitally enabled health systems, making the present moment particularly critical for rethinking healthcare inclusion.

Against this backdrop, this chapter examines inclusion in healthcare economics as a foundational pillar of national health reform in the phygital era. The chapter adopts an interdisciplinary perspective, integrating insights from health economics, public health, marketing, and leadership studies. It seeks to move beyond descriptive accounts of inequality to analyze the structural mechanisms that produce exclusion and the policy levers that can promote affordability and accessibility for all social groups.

Specifically, the chapter addresses the following objectives:

(1) to critically examine the economic dimensions of inclusion in healthcare, with a focus on affordability and accessibility;
(2) to analyze how phygital healthcare models reshape inclusion dynamics within national health systems;
(3) to explore the roles of marketing and leadership in advancing equitable healthcare reforms; and
(4) to propose integrative frameworks and policy solutions for inclusive, sustainable healthcare systems.

By situating healthcare inclusion within broader debates on national health reform, this chapter contributes to a growing body of scholarship that views health systems as social institutions embedded in economic, technological, and political contexts. The discussion emphasizes that inclusion is not an automatic outcome of innovation or reform but a deliberate choice that must be embedded in economic design, governance structures, and leadership practices. In doing so, the chapter aligns with global calls for health systems that are not only efficient and innovative but also just, humane, and inclusive.

BACKGROUND

The pursuit of inclusion in healthcare economics is deeply rooted in the historical evolution of health systems, economic thought, and public policy. Understanding contemporary debates on affordability and accessibility requires situating them within the broader transformation of healthcare from a charitable and welfare-oriented service to a complex socio-economic system shaped by markets, states, and technological change. This background section traces the conceptual, institutional, and policy foundations that have shaped inclusion in healthcare economics, with particular attention to national health reform trajectories and the emerging relevance of phygital healthcare systems.

Healthcare economics emerged as a distinct field in the mid-twentieth century, responding to the recognition that health services differ fundamentally from conventional market goods. Seminal work by Arrow (1963) highlighted market failures in healthcare, including information asymmetry, uncertainty, and moral hazard, which justified public intervention and collective financing mechanisms. Early welfare-state models in Europe emphasized universalism, where healthcare was treated as a social right rather than a commodity. These systems prioritized inclusion by ensuring broad access through tax-funded or social insurance-based arrangements.

In contrast, market-oriented healthcare models, particularly in the United States, evolved around employer-based insurance and private provision. While these systems fostered innovation and specialization, they also generated significant access gaps linked to income, employment status, and insurance coverage. Over time, rising healthcare costs and unequal outcomes exposed the limitations of purely market-driven approaches, prompting renewed interest in inclusion, equity, and affordability as central economic concerns (Stiglitz, 2000).

In low- and middle-income countries, healthcare systems developed under different constraints, often shaped by colonial legacies, limited fiscal capacity, and donor-driven interventions. Primary healthcare initiatives following the Alma-Ata Declaration of 1978 marked a turning point by explicitly framing health as a fundamental human right and emphasizing community participation, equity, and accessibility. However, structural adjustment policies in the 1980s and 1990s led to reduced public spending and increased user fees, undermining inclusion and exacerbating out-of-pocket expenditures among vulnerable populations.

These historical trajectories underscore a recurring tension in healthcare economics: the balance between efficiency, sustainability, and inclusion. While cost containment and productivity remain essential, excessive emphasis on financial efficiency has frequently come at the expense of equitable access and social protection.

Affordability and accessibility are the twin pillars of inclusion in healthcare economics. Affordability refers to individuals' and households' ability to pay for healthcare without financial hardship, while accessibility encompasses the physical, geographic, cultural, and informational availability of health services. Both dimensions are shaped by economic structures, financing models, and policy choices.

Out-of-pocket expenditure remains one of the most significant barriers to healthcare inclusion globally. When healthcare costs are borne directly by individuals, the risk of catastrophic health expenditure and impoverishment increases substantially (Xu et al., 2018). This challenge has been widely documented by organizations such as World Health Organization and the World Bank, which emphasize financial protection as a cornerstone of Universal Health Coverage (UHC).

Accessibility, meanwhile, extends beyond financial considerations. Geographic disparities between urban and rural areas, shortages of skilled health professionals, inadequate infrastructure, and socio-cultural barriers all limit effective access to care. Marginalized groups including women, ethnic minorities, persons with disabilities, migrants, and informal-sector workers often face compounded disadvantages that traditional economic models fail to capture. These access gaps highlight the limitations of aggregate indicators and reinforce the need for disaggregated, inclusion-sensitive health system analysis.

National health reform efforts over the past two decades increasingly reflect a normative shift toward inclusion and equity. The global endorsement of UHC and the incorporation of health-related targets within the Sustainable Development Goals (SDGs) have reinforced the idea that inclusive health systems are not only ethical imperatives but also drivers of social stability and economic development.

Countries have adopted diverse reform strategies to address affordability and accessibility. These include expanding public insurance coverage, regulating private healthcare markets, subsidizing care for vulnerable groups, and investing in primary healthcare networks. While such reforms have yielded measurable improvements in service utilization and financial protection in some contexts, implementation challenges persist. Fragmented governance, weak regulatory capacity, and political resistance often undermine inclusive policy goals.

Moreover, national reforms increasingly operate within constrained fiscal environments. Aging populations, epidemiological transitions toward chronic diseases, and rising expectations place sustained pressure on healthcare budgets. This has intensified debates over prioritization, cost-sharing, and efficiency, sometimes leading to policy trade-offs that marginalize inclusion objectives. The challenge for healthcare economics is therefore not merely to expand coverage but to design systems that remain inclusive under long-term financial and demographic pressures.

The digital transformation of healthcare represents one of the most significant shifts in recent decades. Advances in information and communication technologies have enabled new modes of service delivery, data management, and patient engagement. Telemedicine, mobile health platforms, remote monitoring, and AI-assisted diagnostics have expanded the reach of healthcare systems, particularly during crises such as the COVID-19 pandemic.

Phygital healthcare defined as the integrated delivery of physical and digital health services has gained prominence as a strategic response to access constraints. By blending in-person care with digital interfaces, phygital models aim to improve efficiency, continuity, and patient-centeredness. For populations in remote or underserved areas, digital platforms can reduce travel costs, waiting times, and opportunity costs associated with seeking care.

However, the inclusivity of phygital healthcare is not guaranteed. Digital divides based on income, education, age, gender, and geography can limit access to digital health services. Inadequate broadband infrastructure, low digital literacy, and concerns about data privacy and trust may exclude precisely those groups most in need of inclusive healthcare solutions (van Dijk, 2020). Consequently, phygital health reforms must be assessed not only for their technological sophistication but for their distributional and equity implications.

Beyond economic design and technology, inclusion in healthcare is shaped by institutional practices, leadership, and communication strategies. Healthcare marketing influences how services are positioned, accessed, and understood by different social groups. Inclusive marketing emphasizes health literacy, cultural sensitivity, and trust-building, particularly among populations historically excluded from formal healthcare systems.

Leadership and governance play equally critical roles. Effective health system leadership aligns economic incentives with social objectives, ensures accountability, and fosters cross-sector collaboration. Inclusive leadership styles prioritize stakeholder engagement, transparency, and ethical decision-making, which are essential for sustaining public trust in health reforms. Weak governance, by contrast, can undermine inclusion through corruption, inefficiency, and policy incoherence.

Institutions such as the Organisation for Economic Co-operation and Development have emphasized that inclusive health systems require integrated governance approaches that bridge economic policy, digital innovation, and social protection. These insights underscore that inclusion is not solely a technical outcome but a governance achievement.

This background highlights that inclusion in healthcare economics is the product of historical choices, economic structures, and evolving policy paradigms. Affordability and accessibility challenges cannot be addressed in isolation from broader institutional, technological, and leadership contexts. National health reforms in the phygital era must therefore reconcile efficiency with equity, innovation with inclusion, and market mechanisms with social protection.

By grounding the discussion in historical and policy contexts, this section sets the stage for the theoretical and conceptual frameworks that follow. The next section advances this foundation by examining key theoretical perspectives that explain inclusion, exclusion, and equity in healthcare economics, providing the analytical tools necessary to evaluate contemporary reform strategies.

THEORETICAL FRAMEWORK

Inclusion in healthcare economics cannot be adequately understood through a single theoretical lens. Affordability and accessibility are multidimensional phenomena shaped by economic structures, social stratification, institutional arrangements, and technological mediation. National health reform in the phygital era further complicates this landscape by introducing digital infrastructures that simultaneously expand and constrain access. Accordingly, this chapter adopts a pluralistic theoretical framework that integrates welfare economics, the capabilities approach, health equity theory, institutional economics, and digital inclusion theory. Together, these perspectives provide a comprehensive foundation for analyzing inclusive healthcare systems and guiding policy design.

Welfare Economics and Market Failure in Healthcare

Welfare economics provides the foundational rationale for public intervention in healthcare markets. Classical economic theory assumes rational actors, perfect information, and competitive markets. Healthcare, however, violates these assumptions in fundamental ways. Seminal work by Arrow (1963) demonstrated that uncertainty, information asymmetry between providers and patients, externalities, and moral hazard render healthcare markets inherently inefficient and inequitable if left unregulated.

From a welfare economics perspective, affordability is compromised when healthcare financing relies heavily on out-of-pocket payments, leading to allocative inefficiency and welfare loss. Individuals may delay or forgo necessary care due to cost, resulting in worse health outcomes and higher long-term system costs. Accessibility is similarly distorted when market incentives concentrate services in profitable urban or affluent areas, leaving rural and marginalized populations underserved.

Public financing, risk pooling, and regulation are therefore justified not only on ethical grounds but as efficiency-enhancing mechanisms. Welfare economics thus frames inclusion as a corrective response to market failure. However, critics argue that traditional welfare models focus primarily on income redistribution and cost–benefit efficiency, often neglecting non-monetary barriers such as social exclusion, cultural distance, and digital marginalization. This limitation necessitates complementary theoretical perspectives.

Capabilities Approach and Healthcare Inclusion

The capabilities approach, most prominently associated with Amartya Sen, shifts the analytical focus from resources and utilities to individuals' real freedoms to achieve valued states of being and functioning (Sen, 1999). In the context of healthcare economics, this approach reframes inclusion as the capacity of individuals and communities to achieve health, rather than merely access services or insurance coverage.

Affordability, from a capability's perspective, is not simply about price reduction but about whether individuals can utilize healthcare without sacrificing other essential capabilities such as education, nutrition, or shelter. Accessibility extends beyond physical availability to encompass informational access, cultural acceptability, and agency in health-related decision-making.

The relevance of the capabilities approach becomes particularly salient in phygital healthcare systems. Digital health platforms may formally expand access, yet fail to enhance capabilities if users lack digital literacy, trust, or autonomy. Thus, the approach highlights the risk of "nominal inclusion" without substantive empowerment. It also underscores the ethical obligation of health systems to design interventions that expand real freedoms across diverse social groups.

Health Equity Theory and Social Determinants of Health

Health equity theory emphasizes the moral imperative to eliminate avoidable and unjust differences in health outcomes between population groups (Braveman & Gruskin, 2003). Unlike equality, which focuses on uniform distribution, equity prioritizes fairness and proportionality based on need. This distinction is critical for healthcare economics, as equal financing or service provision does not necessarily result in equitable outcomes.

The social determinants of health framework further expand this perspective by identifying how income, education, employment, housing, gender, ethnicity, and social status shape health risks and access to care (Marmot et al., 2020). From this viewpoint, affordability and accessibility are embedded within broader socio-economic systems, not isolated healthcare variables.

In national health reform, health equity theory challenges policymakers to evaluate whether economic reforms disproportionately burden disadvantaged groups. Cost-sharing mechanisms, privatization, and digital-first service delivery may improve system efficiency while simultaneously widening inequities. Equity-oriented economic analysis therefore demands disaggregated data, targeted subsidies, and inclusive service design, particularly in phygital systems where digital exclusion can intersect with existing social disadvantages.

Institutional Economics and Governance of Health Systems

Institutional economics provides critical insights into how rules, norms, and governance structures shape healthcare outcomes. North (1990) conceptualized institutions as the "rules of the game" that structure economic behavior. In healthcare systems, these rules include financing mechanisms, regulatory frameworks, professional norms, and accountability structures.

From an institutional perspective, inclusion depends on the alignment between formal policies and informal practices. Well-designed insurance schemes may fail to improve affordability if administrative barriers, corruption, or weak enforcement undermine implementation. Similarly, accessibility may be constrained by institutional fragmentation across public and private providers.

Institutional economics is particularly relevant to phygital healthcare reform. Digital health platforms introduce new institutional arrangements related to data governance, privacy, interoperability, and accountability. Without robust institutional safeguards, digitalization can shift power toward technology providers and away from patients, exacerbating exclusion. Thus, inclusive healthcare economics requires institutions that regulate both physical and digital components of health systems in an integrated manner.

Digital Inclusion Theory and Phygital Health Systems

Digital inclusion theory examines disparities in access to digital technologies, skills, and meaningful usage. It distinguishes between first-level divides (access to devices and connectivity), second-level divides (digital skills and literacy), and third-level divides (unequal outcomes from digital use) (van Dijk, 2020). This framework is essential for evaluating the inclusivity of phygital healthcare systems.

In healthcare economics, digital inclusion theory highlights that technological innovation does not automatically translate into improved accessibility or affordability. Telemedicine may reduce costs and travel time for some users while excluding others who lack internet access, privacy, or technological confidence. Moreover, algorithmic decision-making can embed biases that disadvantage marginalized groups.

Integrating digital inclusion theory with healthcare economics enables a more nuanced assessment of phygital reforms. It shifts attention from technological availability to equitable outcomes, reinforcing the need for complementary investments in digital infrastructure, education, and community engagement.

Integrative Value of the Theoretical Framework

Together, these theoretical perspectives provide a multidimensional foundation for analyzing inclusion in healthcare economics. Welfare economics explains why markets alone cannot ensure affordability and accessibility. The capabilities approach foregrounds human agency and substantive freedom. Health equity theory highlights moral and distributive justice considerations. Institutional economics reveals the governance mechanisms that enable or constrain inclusion. Digital inclusion theory addresses the specific challenges introduced by phygital healthcare systems.

By integrating these frameworks, the chapter adopts a holistic analytical lens that aligns with contemporary national health reform objectives. This theoretical foundation informs the development of the conceptual framework in the next section, which synthesizes economic, technological, marketing, and leadership dimensions into a coherent model for inclusive healthcare systems.

CONCEPTUAL FRAMEWORK

The conceptual framework for this chapter synthesizes economic, technological, marketing, and leadership dimensions to explain how inclusion in healthcare systems can be operationalized through affordability and accessibility in the context of national health reform. While the theoretical framework establishes *why* inclusion matters, the conceptual framework clarifies *how* inclusive healthcare outcomes can be achieved, particularly within emerging phygital healthcare ecosystems.

Purpose of the Conceptual Framework

The purpose of this conceptual framework is threefold. First, it integrates multiple determinants of inclusion economic, institutional, technological, and and social into a unified analytical structure. Second, it explains the pathways through which national health reforms influence affordability and accessibility across diverse social groups. Third, it provides a practical lens for evaluating whether phygital healthcare systems genuinely promote inclusion or inadvertently reproduce existing inequities.

In contrast to linear models of healthcare delivery, this framework adopts a systems-based perspective, recognizing healthcare as a complex adaptive system shaped by interactions among policy, markets, technology, and leadership.

Core Constructs of the Framework

The conceptual framework consists of five interrelated constructs:

1. *National Health Reform Context*
2. *Healthcare Economic Design*
3. *Phygital Healthcare Infrastructure*
4. *Marketing and Engagement Mechanisms*
5. *Leadership and Governance Capacity*

These constructs collectively influence *Inclusive Healthcare Outcomes*, defined in terms of affordability, accessibility, equity, and sustainability.

1. National Health Reform Context

National health reform provides the macro-level policy environment within which inclusion efforts operate. This includes constitutional commitments to health, universal health coverage policies, financing reforms, regulatory frameworks, and digital health strategies. The reform context shapes resource allocation priorities, defines entitlements, and determines the balance between public and private actors.

In the framework, national reform acts as an enabling or constraining structure. Reforms that prioritize cost containment without equity safeguards may weaken inclusion, while reforms grounded in social protection and equity principles create the conditions for inclusive healthcare economics.

2. Healthcare Economic Design

Healthcare economic design refers to the mechanisms through which health services are financed, priced, and delivered. Key components include:

- Risk pooling and insurance coverage
- Public versus private financing balance
- Cost-sharing and subsidy structures
- Provider payment mechanisms

Affordability emerges directly from this construct. Inclusive economic design reduces out-of-pocket expenditure, protects households from catastrophic health spending, and ensures that financial barriers do not prevent service utilization. From a conceptual standpoint, economic design mediates the relationship between national reform and individual access to care.

3. Phygital Healthcare Infrastructure

Phygital healthcare infrastructure represents the integration of physical healthcare facilities with digital platforms such as telemedicine, electronic health records, mobile health applications, and AI-supported diagnostics. This construct influences accessibility by reshaping how, where, and when healthcare services are delivered.

In the framework, phygital infrastructure functions as a dual-edged mediator. When supported by adequate digital access, literacy, and trust, it expands reach and efficiency. When these conditions are absent, it creates new exclusionary barriers. Thus, phygital systems do not automatically enhance inclusion; their impact depends on complementary investments and governance.

4. Marketing and Engagement Mechanisms

Marketing and engagement mechanisms shape how healthcare services are communicated, perceived, and utilized by different social groups. This construct includes:

- Health communication strategies
- Cultural and linguistic adaptation
- Health literacy initiatives
- Trust-building and stigma reduction

Within the framework, marketing acts as a social bridge between healthcare systems and populations. Inclusive marketing enhances awareness and utilization among marginalized groups, while exclusionary or commercialized marketing can reinforce disparities by privileging affluent or digitally literate users.

5. Leadership and Governance Capacity

Leadership and governance capacity represent the institutional and human agency required to align economic incentives, technological innovation, and social goals. This construct includes:

- Ethical and inclusive leadership
- Regulatory oversight
- Intersectoral coordination
- Accountability and transparency

Leadership functions as a cross-cutting moderator within the framework. Even well-designed economic and technological systems can fail without inclusive leadership that prioritizes equity, manages trade-offs, and responds to stakeholder needs.

Inclusive Healthcare Outcomes

The outcome dimension of the framework is Inclusive Healthcare Outcomes, operationalized through four indicators:

1. *Affordability* – reduced financial burden and improved financial protection
2. *Accessibility* – physical, digital, cultural, and informational access
3. *Equity* – reduced disparities across socio-economic and demographic groups
4. *Sustainability* – long-term system resilience and fiscal viability

These outcomes are not independent but mutually reinforcing. Improved affordability enhances utilization, while accessibility increases preventive care uptake, contributing to sustainability.

Dynamic Relationships and Feedback Loops

A defining feature of the conceptual framework is its recognition of dynamic feedback loops. For example:

- Improved accessibility through phygital systems can increase demand, requiring adaptive economic design.
- Inclusive marketing can enhance trust, improving digital uptake and system efficiency.
- Strong leadership can correct emerging inequities by recalibrating policies and investments.

These feedback mechanisms emphasize that inclusion is an ongoing process rather than a fixed endpoint.

Conceptual Contribution of the Framework

This framework advances existing models of healthcare economics by explicitly integrating phygital healthcare and inclusion-oriented governance. It moves beyond narrow cost–benefit analyses to capture the social and institutional pathways through which national health reforms affect diverse populations. Importantly, the framework is adaptable across country contexts, making it suitable for comparative analysis and policy evaluation.

By positioning inclusion as an emergent property of interacting systems rather than a standalone policy objective the framework provides a robust foundation for the subsequent analysis of empirical evidence, policy challenges, and strategic solutions discussed in the body of the chapter.

INCLUSION IN HEALTHCARE ECONOMICS: CONCEPTUAL AND POLICY FOUNDATIONS

Inclusion in healthcare economics refers to the deliberate design of health systems that ensure all individuals regardless of income, geography, gender, ethnicity, disability, or digital capability can access essential healthcare services without financial hardship or systemic exclusion. Unlike traditional efficiency-driven economic models, inclusive healthcare economics prioritizes distributive justice, social protection, and long-term societal well-being alongside cost-effectiveness.

Historically, healthcare economics emphasized resource allocation efficiency, provider productivity, and cost containment. While these objectives remain relevant, they are insufficient in contexts marked by structural inequality. Evidence consistently shows that economic growth alone does not guarantee improved health outcomes or equitable access to care (Sen, 1999; Marmot et al., 2020). Consequently, inclusion has emerged as a normative and analytical imperative in contemporary health economics.

National health reforms increasingly reflect this shift by embedding inclusion within policy frameworks such as Universal Health Coverage (UHC). UHC reframes healthcare as a social investment rather than a consumable good, emphasizing risk pooling, cross-subsidization, and state stewardship. However, inclusion in healthcare economics extends beyond formal coverage. It requires attention to affordability at the household level and accessibility across social and spatial dimensions.

AFFORDABILITY: ECONOMIC BARRIERS AND FINANCIAL PROTECTION

Affordability remains one of the most persistent challenges in healthcare systems worldwide. Even in countries with formal insurance coverage, out-of-pocket expenditures continue to impose significant financial strain on households. Catastrophic health spending defined as healthcare expenditure exceeding a critical share of household income pushes millions into poverty each year (Xu et al., 2018).

From an economic perspective, affordability is shaped by three interrelated factors: financing mechanisms, pricing structures, and income distribution. Systems that rely heavily on direct payments at the point of service disproportionately burden low-income populations. Conversely, systems with strong risk pooling and progressive financing mechanisms are more effective in protecting vulnerable groups.

Public financing through taxation or social insurance enables cross-subsidization, whereby higher-income groups support healthcare access for lower-income populations. Empirical evidence demonstrates that such arrangements improve equity and health outcomes, particularly when combined with targeted subsidies for marginalized groups (Stiglitz, 2000). However, fiscal constraints and political resistance often limit the scope of redistributive financing, leading to partial or fragmented coverage.

Affordability challenges are further intensified by rising healthcare costs driven by technological innovation, pharmaceutical pricing, and demographic transitions. While innovation can improve health outcomes, it can also widen access gaps if cost considerations override inclusion objectives. Thus, inclusive healthcare economics requires balancing innovation incentives with affordability safeguards.

ACCESSIBILITY: BEYOND PHYSICAL AVAILABILITY

Accessibility encompasses the ability of individuals to obtain appropriate healthcare services when needed. While often conflated with service availability, accessibility is a multidimensional construct that includes geographic, organizational, cultural, and informational dimensions.

Geographic accessibility remains a major concern, particularly in rural and remote areas. Concentration of healthcare facilities and specialists in urban centers reflects market incentives rather than population health needs. This spatial inequality results in delayed care, increased travel costs, and poorer health outcomes for rural populations.

Organizational accessibility refers to how health systems are structured and navigated. Complex administrative procedures, long waiting times, and fragmented service delivery disproportionately affect individuals with limited education or social capital. Cultural accessibility further shapes inclusion, as language barriers, gender norms, and stigma can deter individuals from seeking care even when services are technically available.

Informational accessibility has gained prominence in the digital era. Access to accurate, understandable health information influences health-seeking behavior, treatment adherence, and preventive care uptake. Exclusion from health information whether due to low literacy or digital barriers constitutes a critical yet often overlooked dimension of healthcare inequality.

SOCIAL GROUP DISPARITIES IN HEALTHCARE ACCESS

Inclusion in healthcare economics must be evaluated through the experiences of specific social groups. Women, ethnic minorities, migrants, persons with disabilities, informal-sector workers, and older adults frequently encounter overlapping barriers to affordability and accessibility.

Gender disparities in healthcare access are shaped by economic dependence, caregiving responsibilities, and sociocultural norms. Women are more likely to delay care due to financial constraints and less likely to control household health expenditures in certain contexts. Ethnic and indigenous populations often face compounded disadvantages stemming from geographic isolation, historical marginalization, and mistrust in formal health systems.

Persons with disabilities encounter structural barriers related to physical infrastructure, provider attitudes, and service design. Informal-sector workers who constitute a large share of the workforce in many countries are often excluded from contributory insurance schemes, increasing their vulnerability to health-related financial shocks.

These disparities underscore the inadequacy of one-size-fits-all economic solutions. Inclusive healthcare economics requires targeted interventions that recognize differential needs and constraints across social groups.

PHYGITAL HEALTHCARE AS AN INCLUSION STRATEGY

Phygital healthcare has emerged as a strategic response to accessibility and affordability challenges. By integrating physical healthcare services with digital platforms, phygital models aim to extend reach, reduce costs, and enhance system efficiency. Telemedicine consultations, remote diagnostics, and mobile health applications have demonstrated potential to bridge geographic gaps and improve continuity of care.

During public health emergencies, phygital systems have enabled service delivery under constrained conditions, reinforcing their value in resilient health systems. Digital platforms can lower transaction costs for patients by reducing travel time, waiting periods, and indirect expenses such as lost wages.

However, the inclusivity of phygital healthcare is contingent upon digital access, literacy, and trust. Digital divides based on income, age, education, and geography can exclude vulnerable populations from digital health benefits. Moreover, algorithm-driven systems may embed biases that disadvantage marginalized groups if not carefully governed.

Economic analysis of phygital healthcare must therefore consider distributional effects alongside efficiency gains. Investments in digital infrastructure, capacity building, and inclusive design are essential to ensure that phygital systems enhance rather than undermine healthcare inclusion.

ECONOMIC IMPLICATIONS OF DIGITAL HEALTH INTEGRATION

From a cost perspective, phygital healthcare offers potential efficiency gains through task shifting, automation, and preventive care. These gains can free resources for inclusion-oriented investments if reinvestment mechanisms are explicitly designed. However, digital transformation also entails significant upfront costs related to infrastructure, training, and system integration.

The sustainability of phygital models depends on coherent economic planning and governance. Without regulatory oversight, digital health markets may prioritize profit over inclusion, leading to service fragmentation and data monopolies. Public stewardship is therefore critical to align digital innovation with inclusive health objectives.

Institutions such as World Health Organization and the World Bank emphasize that digital health should be viewed as a public good embedded within broader health system strengthening efforts rather than as a standalone technological solution.

HEALTHCARE MARKETING AS A CATALYST FOR INCLUSION

Healthcare marketing has traditionally been associated with service promotion and patient acquisition. In inclusive healthcare economics, however, marketing assumes a broader social function: enabling awareness, comprehension, trust, and utilization of health services among diverse population groups. Inclusive healthcare marketing aligns economic efficiency with equity by ensuring that information asymmetries do not become barriers to access.

From an inclusion perspective, marketing must be evaluated across three dimensions: informational equity, cultural responsiveness, and behavioral enablement. Informational equity ensures that health-related information about entitlements, insurance coverage, service availability, and digital platforms is accessible to individuals with varying literacy levels. Evidence shows that low health literacy is strongly associated with poorer health outcomes and lower service utilization, even in systems with formal coverage (Kickbusch et al., 2017).

Cultural responsiveness in marketing is critical for reaching marginalized populations. Language adaptation, culturally appropriate messaging, and community-based communication strategies reduce stigma and mistrust, particularly among ethnic minorities, migrants, and indigenous groups. Inclusive marketing thus functions as a demand-side intervention that complements supply-side economic reforms.

Behavioral enablement focuses on nudging health-seeking behavior through user-centered design and communication. In phygital healthcare systems, intuitive interfaces, clear messaging, and trust-building mechanisms are essential to ensure that digital services are not disproportionately used by affluent or technologically confident populations. From an economic standpoint, inclusive marketing improves system efficiency by increasing appropriate utilization and preventive care uptake, thereby reducing avoidable downstream costs.

DIGITAL HEALTH COMMUNICATION AND TRUST

Trust is a central determinant of inclusion in phygital healthcare. While digital platforms offer convenience and scale, concerns regarding data privacy, algorithmic bias, and depersonalization can undermine trust, particularly among vulnerable populations. Effective marketing strategies must therefore prioritize transparency, data protection assurances, and ethical communication.

Empirical studies indicate that patients are more likely to adopt digital health services when they perceive them as secure, reliable, and endorsed by trusted public institutions (van Dijk, 2020). This underscores the importance of public-sector leadership in shaping digital health narratives and regulating private actors. Without such stewardship, market-driven digital health promotion may exacerbate inequalities by privileging profitability over inclusivity.

LEADERSHIP AND GOVERNANCE IN INCLUSIVE HEALTH REFORM

Leadership and governance are decisive factors in translating inclusive healthcare economics from policy intent into practice. Inclusive leadership is characterized by ethical orientation, stakeholder engagement, and the capacity to manage complex trade-offs between efficiency, innovation, and equity.

In national health reforms, leaders shape inclusion through strategic priorities, regulatory decisions, and institutional culture. Strong leadership aligns economic incentives with social objectives, ensuring that affordability and accessibility are not compromised in pursuit of cost containment or technological modernization. Conversely, weak governance can result in fragmented service delivery, regulatory capture, and exclusionary practices.

Governance frameworks must address both physical and digital components of healthcare systems. This includes regulating pricing, ensuring interoperability of digital platforms, safeguarding patient data, and monitoring equity outcomes. Institutions such as the Organisation for Economic Co-operation and Development emphasize that inclusive governance requires integrated oversight mechanisms that bridge health policy, digital regulation, and social protection systems.

LEADERSHIP IN PHYGITAL HEALTHCARE SYSTEMS

Phygital healthcare systems introduce new leadership challenges related to technological complexity and cross-sector coordination. Leaders must navigate partnerships between public institutions, private providers, and technology firms while maintaining accountability and public interest orientation.

Inclusive leadership in phygital contexts prioritizes capacity building among health workers and patients alike. Training healthcare professionals to use digital tools effectively and sensitively is essential for preventing exclusion. Similarly, leadership commitment to community engagement and participatory design enhances the legitimacy and inclusivity of digital health initiatives.

From an economic perspective, leadership decisions influence how efficiency gains from digitalization are distributed. Inclusive leaders reinvest savings into expanding coverage, improving quality, and addressing access gaps, whereas exclusionary leadership may channel gains toward narrow organizational or commercial interests.

EMPIRICAL EVIDENCE FROM NATIONAL AND GLOBAL CONTEXTS

Empirical evidence from diverse national contexts illustrates both the promise and limitations of inclusive healthcare reforms. Countries that have invested in strong public financing mechanisms and primary healthcare infrastructure generally demonstrate better affordability and access outcomes. Expansion of insurance coverage, when combined with supply-side investments, has reduced catastrophic health expenditure and improved service utilization among low-income populations (Xu et al., 2018).

Digital health interventions have shown mixed results. In some contexts, telemedicine has significantly improved access for rural populations by reducing travel costs and wait times. In others, digital-first approaches have excluded older adults, women, and low-income users due to digital literacy gaps and infrastructural constraints. These findings reinforce the argument that phygital healthcare must be embedded within broader inclusion strategies rather than pursued as a standalone solution.

The COVID-19 pandemic offers a critical empirical lens. Rapid digitalization enabled continuity of care during lockdowns, yet stark inequities in access to testing, treatment, and vaccines revealed systemic inclusion failures (Gostin et al., 2021). Countries with stronger public health governance and inclusive communication strategies demonstrated more equitable outcomes, highlighting the interplay between leadership, marketing, and economic design.

INTEGRATING MARKETING, LEADERSHIP, AND ECONOMICS

The interaction between healthcare marketing, leadership, and economic structures determines whether inclusion objectives are realized in practice. Inclusive marketing increases demand and awareness, leadership ensures alignment with equity goals, and economic design provides the financial foundation for affordability and accessibility.

In phygital healthcare systems, these elements are mutually reinforcing. Effective leadership establishes governance frameworks that guide ethical digital innovation. Inclusive marketing ensures that digital and physical services reach marginalized populations. Sound economic design protects households from financial hardship while sustaining system viability.

DISCUSSION

The analysis presented across the theoretical and empirical sections of this chapter demonstrates that inclusion in healthcare economics is neither an automatic consequence of reform initiatives nor an inevitable byproduct of technological advancement. Rather, inclusion emerges as a contingent and fragile achievement shaped by deliberate policy choices, institutional configurations, leadership orientations, and socio-technical design processes embedded within national health systems. Across diverse contexts, the evidence consistently indicates that affordability and accessibility are not neutral outcomes but reflect underlying political economy structures that distribute risks, costs, and opportunities unevenly across social groups. This discussion synthesizes insights from healthcare economics, phygital transformation, marketing, and leadership to critically interpret their implications for national health reform, emphasizing that inclusion must be understood as a structural outcome produced through systemic design rather than as a corrective measure applied after inequities have already taken root.

A central insight emerging from this chapter is the need to reframe inclusion as a structural economic outcome rather than a peripheral social objective. Historically, health economic reforms have tended to prioritize efficiency, cost containment, fiscal sustainability, and market expansion, often relegating inclusion to targeted welfare interventions or compensatory subsidies. Such approaches implicitly assume that growth, efficiency, or technological diffusion will eventually "trickle down" to marginalized populations. However, the evidence reviewed here challenges this sequencing logic by demonstrating that exclusion is not an accidental side effect but a predictable consequence of economic architectures that rely heavily on out-of-pocket payments, fragmented insurance arrangements, and unregulated private provision. In these systems, affordability and accessibility do not fail at the margins; they fail systematically. Conversely, health systems grounded in risk pooling, public stewardship, and equity-oriented financing consistently demonstrate greater resilience and inclusivity, not because inclusion is added later, but because it is embedded in the core design of financing, pricing, and service delivery mechanisms. This reframing carries profound implications for national health reform, as it suggests that inclusion cannot be retrofitted once inequities have hardened but must be institutionally embedded from the outset within the economic logic of health systems.

The discussion of phygital healthcare further complicates conventional assumptions about inclusion by revealing a critical paradox. On the one hand, digital–physical integration offers unprecedented opportunities to address long-standing accessibility barriers related to geography, workforce shortages, service continuity, and system inefficiencies. Telemedicine, digital diagnostics, and remote monitoring have demonstrably expanded reach in contexts where physical infrastructure alone has proven insufficient. On the other hand, phygital systems also carry the potential to reproduce or intensify existing inequalities when access to digital infrastructure, digital literacy, trust, and regulatory protection is unevenly distributed. The chapter's analysis reveals that phygital healthcare functions not as an automatic equalizer but as a conditional enabler of inclusion. Its distributive effects depend critically on complementary investments in broadband connectivity, inclusive design, institutional oversight, and public trust. Where these supports are absent, digital-first reforms risk privileging populations that are already economically, educationally, or technologically advantaged, thereby creating layered forms of exclusion that compound existing social disparities. This finding challenges techno-optimistic narratives that portray digital health as a universally accessible solution and instead reinforces the necessity of equity-sensitive digital transformation guided by public-interest leadership and robust governance frameworks.

An important and often underappreciated contribution of this chapter lies in its treatment of healthcare marketing and communication as economic determinants of access rather than as peripheral promotional activities. While information asymmetry has long been recognized as a market failure in healthcare, this discussion demonstrates that communication strategies actively shape who benefits from health reforms and who remains excluded. Inclusive marketing reduces the transaction costs associated with navigating complex healthcare systems by improving awareness, comprehension, and trust, particularly among marginalized populations with limited health literacy or social capital. In contrast, exclusionary communication practices such as reliance on digital-only platforms, technical language, or commercially targeted messaging operate as silent rationing mechanisms that restrict access without overt denial of services. These dynamics become especially pronounced in phygital systems, where digital literacy, perceived legitimacy, and trust in data governance become prerequisites for effective access. The implication is clear: national health reforms that neglect inclusive communication undermine their own economic efficiency by suppressing appropriate utilization, delaying care-seeking behavior, and weakening preventive health engagement, thereby increasing long-term system costs.

Leadership emerges throughout this discussion as the critical mediating force that determines whether inclusion objectives are realized or diluted during reform implementation. Inclusive leadership aligns economic incentives, technological innovation, and social values, ensuring that affordability and accessibility remain non-negotiable priorities rather than negotiable trade-offs. Importantly, the analysis highlights that leadership failures often manifest not through explicit exclusionary policies but through passive neglect such as failure to regulate digital health markets, insufficient stakeholder engagement, tolerance of inequitable outcomes in the name of efficiency, or overreliance on market signals as proxies for social value. In contrast, inclusive leadership is characterized by proactive monitoring of distributional effects, adaptive policy correction, and deliberate reinvestment of efficiency gains into expanding access for underserved populations. This reinforces the argument that inclusion is not solely an economic or technical challenge but a fundamentally ethical and governance-oriented one, requiring leaders who are willing to prioritize equity even when it complicates short-term efficiency calculations.

Perhaps the most significant insight generated by this discussion is the recognition of the deep interdependence between economic design, phygital infrastructure, marketing, and governance. None of these elements operates in isolation. Affordable financing mechanisms fail to achieve inclusion if service delivery remains inaccessible. Digital platforms amplify inequities in the absence of inclusive governance. Leadership without economic leverage lacks sustainability, while economic reform without ethical leadership risks exclusionary drift. National health reform, therefore, demands integrated strategies rather than siloed interventions. The phygital era amplifies this necessity, as technological complexity increases system interdependence and heightens the consequences of policy misalignment. Fragmented reforms where digital innovation advances faster than regulatory capacity, or where financing reform outpaces communication strategies are particularly prone to generating unintended exclusion.

The implications for national health reform are substantial. First, inclusion must be institutionalized as a core performance indicator of health systems, assessed alongside efficiency, quality, and fiscal sustainability. Second, phygital health reforms should be evaluated using equity-sensitive metrics that capture differential impacts across social groups rather than relying on aggregate adoption rates or technological diffusion indicators. Third, healthcare marketing and communication must be integrated into reform planning as strategic instruments of inclusion, not treated as ancillary functions. Finally, sustained investment in leadership development and governance capacity is essential for navigating the ethical, economic, and technological complexities of inclusive reform. Taken together, these insights suggest that the ultimate success of national health reform in the phygital era will not be judged by technological sophistication or cost savings alone, but by the extent to which reforms expand real, durable, and equitable access to affordable, quality healthcare for all social groups.

RECOMMENDATIONS AND SOLUTIONS

Ensuring inclusion in healthcare economics requires a decisive shift from diagnostic clarity to coordinated, system-wide action that addresses affordability and accessibility as structural outcomes rather than residual policy concerns. The analysis presented in this chapter demonstrates that persistent inclusion gaps are not primarily the result of insufficient knowledge or technical capacity, but of fragmented policy execution, weak governance arrangements, and limited integration between economic planning, technological innovation, and social engagement. Consequently, inclusive healthcare reform in the phygital era must be pursued through a comprehensive, multi-level strategy that reconfigures financing mechanisms, service delivery models, communication practices, and leadership frameworks into a coherent system oriented toward equity and sustainability. At the core of this strategy lies the redesign of healthcare financing structures to minimize reliance on out-of-pocket expenditure and to strengthen financial protection across income groups. Progressive financing mechanisms, whether tax-based or rooted in social insurance, must be expanded to ensure effective risk pooling and cross-subsidization, thereby shielding households from catastrophic health expenditure and preventing medical impoverishment. Such reforms should be complemented by income-sensitive cost-sharing caps and targeted subsidies for populations systematically excluded from contributory insurance systems, including informal-sector workers, migrants, persons with disabilities, and socially marginalized communities. Aligning provider payment systems with preventive and primary care objectives rather than volume-driven incentives is equally critical, as it redirects resources toward early intervention and continuity of care while reinforcing affordability as a systemic feature of healthcare economics rather than an individual burden.

Beyond financing, accessibility must be embedded as a multidimensional policy objective that encompasses geographic, organizational, cultural, and informational dimensions of access. National health systems must prioritize the strengthening of primary healthcare infrastructure in underserved rural and peri-urban regions, where market incentives alone have proven insufficient to ensure service availability. Integrating outreach services, mobile clinics, and community health workers into formal health systems can bridge physical and social distance between providers and populations, particularly for groups facing mobility, gender, or disability-related barriers. Administrative simplification is equally essential, as complex procedures and bureaucratic fragmentation often function as hidden barriers to access, disproportionately affecting individuals with limited education or institutional familiarity. Institutionalizing culturally sensitive service delivery, including language access and gender-responsive care, further ensures that formal coverage translates into meaningful utilization rather than symbolic inclusion. Collectively, these measures transform accessibility from a logistical concern into a foundational principle of system design.

Phygital healthcare reform represents a particularly critical domain for operationalizing inclusion, as digital–physical integration reshapes both the opportunities and risks associated with access. To ensure that phygital systems enhance rather than undermine equity, national reforms must adopt an inclusion-by-design approach rather than a technology-first model driven by efficiency imperatives alone. This requires substantial investment in universal digital infrastructure, particularly broadband connectivity in underserved regions, alongside sustained digital literacy and capacity-building initiatives for both patients and healthcare workers. Maintaining hybrid service delivery models that preserve in-person options alongside digital platforms is essential for preventing exclusion of populations unable or unwilling to engage digitally. Public ownership or stewardship of core digital health systems, coupled with interoperability standards, can safeguard equity and continuity while preventing market fragmentation and data monopolization. Robust regulatory frameworks must also be established to address algorithmic bias, data misuse, and digital exclusion, ensuring that technological innovation remains aligned with public interest objectives. By embedding equity considerations into the design and governance of phygital systems, digital transformation can function as an enabler of inclusion rather than a source of new stratification.

Equally important is the institutionalization of inclusive healthcare marketing and communication as integral components of national health reform. Communication strategies must be recognized as public policy instruments that shape awareness, trust, and utilization, rather than as ancillary promotional activities. National health communication frameworks should prioritize clarity, accessibility, and cultural relevance, using multi-channel approaches that combine digital and offline platforms to reach populations with varying levels of literacy and connectivity. Collaboration with community organizations, civil society actors, and local leaders can enhance trust and counter misinformation, particularly in contexts where historical marginalization has weakened confidence in formal health systems. Integrating health literacy initiatives into educational curricula and adult learning programs further strengthens individuals' capacity to navigate healthcare systems and engage in preventive behaviors. Inclusive marketing thus reduces informational barriers, improves service uptake, and enhances overall system efficiency by aligning demand with appropriate care pathways.

Leadership and governance reforms are indispensable for sustaining inclusive healthcare transformation. Inclusive outcomes require leadership that can align economic, technological, and social priorities while navigating complex trade-offs inherent in health reform. Investment in leadership development programs emphasizing ethics, equity, and systems thinking is essential for cultivating decision-makers capable of steering phygital reforms toward inclusive objectives. Intersectoral governance mechanisms linking health, digital policy, finance, and social welfare can reduce policy fragmentation and enhance coherence across reform initiatives. Implementing equity-focused monitoring frameworks using disaggregated data enables continuous assessment of reform impacts and timely corrective action. Strengthening regulatory capacity to oversee private and digital health actors is critical for preventing exclusionary practices and ensuring accountability. Participatory governance structures that promote transparency and public engagement further reinforce trust and legitimacy, ensuring that inclusion remains a sustained commitment rather than a symbolic aspiration.

Efficiency gains generated through digitalization and system optimization must also be deliberately reinvested into expanding access and quality. Without explicit reinvestment mechanisms, efficiency improvements risk being absorbed into cost containment or commercial expansion rather than translated into equity gains. Allocating savings from reduced administrative overheads or improved care coordination to underserved regions and vulnerable populations can convert efficiency into a lever for inclusion. Data-driven insights derived from digital health systems should be used proactively to identify access gaps and tailor interventions accordingly. Linking performance incentives to equity outcomes, rather than cost savings alone, aligns organizational behavior with inclusive objectives and reinforces accountability.

Finally, national health reforms must adopt integrated, systems-based strategies that recognize the interdependence of economics, technology, marketing, and leadership. Siloed policy design undermines inclusion by creating mismatches between financing mechanisms, service delivery models, and communication strategies. Aligning health financing reforms with digital health strategies and inclusive communication plans ensures coherence across reform domains. Pilot initiatives that test inclusive phygital models in diverse contexts, followed by adaptive scaling based on evidence and stakeholder feedback, can enhance resilience and responsiveness. Systems-based reform not only strengthens inclusivity but also improves long-term sustainability by aligning social objectives with economic and technological innovation.

Taken together, these recommendations underscore that inclusion in healthcare economics is achievable through deliberate, coordinated action that embeds equity into the structural foundations of health systems. Affordability and accessibility must be treated as systemic design principles rather than downstream outcomes, particularly in the phygital era where technological change amplifies both opportunities and risks. By integrating progressive financing, multidimensional accessibility planning, inclusive digital design, strategic communication, ethical leadership, and systems-based governance, national health reforms can move beyond fragmented interventions toward genuinely inclusive, resilient, and sustainable healthcare systems that serve all social groups.

FUTURE RESEARCH DIRECTIONS

While this chapter offers a comprehensive conceptual and policy-oriented examination of inclusion in healthcare economics, it also reveals a range of unresolved questions that merit sustained scholarly attention, particularly as health systems undergo rapid phygital transformation. Advancing evidence-based national health reform in this evolving context requires future research to adopt interdisciplinary, comparative, and methodologically rigorous approaches capable of capturing the complex interactions between affordability, accessibility, technology, governance, and social stratification. One of the most pressing research priorities lies in the empirical evaluation of inclusion within phygital healthcare systems. Existing studies have largely focused on adoption rates, utilization metrics, or technological performance, often overlooking distributional impacts across different social groups. Future research must move beyond aggregate indicators to examine how digital–physical integration affects populations facing intersecting vulnerabilities related to income, gender, age, disability, geographic isolation, and social marginalization. Longitudinal research designs are particularly valuable in this regard, as they allow scholars to assess whether phygital interventions produce sustained reductions in inequality over time or merely shift access patterns in the short term. Mixed-methods approaches that combine quantitative outcome analysis with qualitative insights into user experiences can further illuminate the mechanisms through which digital inclusion or exclusion is produced, thereby providing a robust empirical foundation for refining inclusion-by-design principles in digital health policy.

Comparative analysis of healthcare financing models represents another critical area for future inquiry. Despite widespread consensus that financial protection is central to inclusion, significant variation persists in how national health systems structure financing arrangements and distribute costs. Future research should systematically compare tax-based, social insurance, and mixed financing models across countries and regions, focusing not only on coverage rates but on distributional outcomes such as out-of-pocket expenditure, catastrophic health spending, and unmet healthcare needs. Such comparative studies can identify best practices as well as contextual constraints that shape reform outcomes, offering valuable insights for policy transfer and adaptation. In particular, there is a need to examine how financing reforms interact with phygital healthcare strategies, as digital service delivery may alter cost structures, risk pooling dynamics, and access patterns in ways that traditional health economic models do not fully capture. Cross-national datasets, combined with institutional and policy analysis, can help disentangle these complex relationships and inform more equitable financing strategies.

Digital inclusion, literacy, and their relationship to health outcomes constitute a third major research frontier. While digital health technologies promise expanded access, their benefits are mediated by users' digital skills, trust in technology, and capacity to navigate digital interfaces. Future research should explore how variations in digital literacy influence access to care, treatment adherence, patient engagement, and health outcomes within phygital systems. Experimental and intervention-based studies evaluating digital literacy programs, user-centered design innovations, and trust-building mechanisms could yield actionable evidence on how to reduce digital health inequalities. Such research is particularly important for older adults, low-income populations, and marginalized communities, for whom digital exclusion may intersect with other social determinants of health. By linking digital inclusion research with health outcomes, scholars can move beyond descriptive accounts of the digital divide toward solution-oriented insights that support inclusive reform.

Leadership, governance, and institutional capacity also warrant deeper scholarly investigation, as they play a decisive role in shaping the inclusivity of healthcare reforms. Future research should examine how leadership styles, governance arrangements, and institutional capacities influence the design, implementation, and sustainability of inclusive health policies. Qualitative case studies, comparative institutional analysis, and process tracing methods can uncover how decision-making processes, accountability mechanisms, and power dynamics shape reform trajectories. Particular attention should be given to the governance of digital health markets, including issues of data ownership, algorithmic accountability, regulatory oversight, and public–private partnerships. As digital actors increasingly influence healthcare delivery, understanding how governance frameworks can balance innovation with equity and public interest becomes an urgent research priority. Insights from institutional economics, political science, and ethics can enrich this line of inquiry and inform more robust governance models.

The role of healthcare marketing and communication in equity-oriented reform remains an underexplored but promising area for future research. While health economics has traditionally focused on supply-side and financing mechanisms, there is growing recognition that information asymmetry, trust, and communication significantly influence access and utilization. Future studies should investigate how different communication strategies, cultural adaptations, and behavioral interventions affect service uptake among marginalized populations, particularly within phygital systems where digital interfaces mediate access. Research integrating marketing science with public health and economics could generate innovative frameworks for inclusive health communication, highlighting how strategic messaging can reduce informational barriers and enhance system efficiency. Empirical studies evaluating the impact of inclusive communication campaigns on preventive care uptake, chronic disease management, and health-seeking behavior would further strengthen the evidence base for policy integration.

Measurement and evaluation frameworks for inclusive healthcare systems represent another critical research priority. Current health system performance metrics often emphasize efficiency, coverage, or aggregate outcomes, offering limited insight into inclusion and equity. Future research should focus on developing composite indicators that simultaneously capture affordability, accessibility, equity, and digital inclusion. Such metrics should be sensitive to differences across social groups and capable of tracking changes over time. Methodological innovation is needed to integrate quantitative indicators with qualitative assessments of user experience and institutional performance. Robust measurement frameworks would enable policymakers to monitor progress, evaluate reforms, and ensure accountability, thereby translating inclusion from a normative aspiration into a measurable policy objective.

Finally, the ethical and social implications of advanced digital health technologies demand sustained scholarly attention. Emerging tools such as artificial intelligence, predictive analytics, and personalized medicine raise complex questions about access, bias, transparency, and patient autonomy. Future research should critically examine how these technologies affect inclusion, particularly in resource-constrained settings where regulatory capacity and digital infrastructure may be limited. Ethics-informed economic analysis can help identify potential trade-offs between efficiency and equity, guiding responsible innovation that aligns with inclusive health objectives. Interdisciplinary research drawing on ethics, law, sociology, and health economics is essential for anticipating unintended consequences and for designing governance frameworks that protect vulnerable populations.

Collectively, these future research directions underscore that inclusion in healthcare economics is a dynamic and evolving field shaped by technological change, institutional reform, and social transformation. As national health systems increasingly adopt phygital models, ongoing empirical inquiry, theoretical refinement, and methodological innovation will be essential for ensuring that reforms expand real, equitable, and sustainable access to healthcare. Future research must therefore prioritize inclusion not only as an analytical outcome but as a guiding principle embedded in research design, policy engagement, and scholarly collaboration, thereby contributing to health systems that are both innovative and just.

CONCLUSION

This chapter set out to examine inclusion in healthcare economics with a specific focus on ensuring affordability and accessibility for all social groups within the context of national health reform and phygital transformation. Drawing on interdisciplinary theoretical foundations and empirical insights, the chapter demonstrates that inclusion is neither an automatic consequence of healthcare expansion nor a guaranteed outcome of digital innovation. Rather, it is a deliberate, structural achievement shaped by economic design, governance quality, leadership orientation, and socio-technical integration.

A central conclusion of this chapter is that affordability and accessibility must be treated as core economic outcomes, not peripheral social considerations. Health systems that rely heavily on out-of-pocket expenditure, fragmented insurance coverage, or unregulated market mechanisms systematically reproduce exclusion. In contrast, systems grounded in risk pooling, public stewardship, and equity-oriented financing demonstrate greater resilience, fairness, and long-term sustainability. Inclusion, therefore, is inseparable from the foundational architecture of healthcare economics.

The chapter further establishes that phygital healthcare represents a conditional opportunity rather than an inherent solution to inclusion challenges. While digital–physical integration can reduce geographic barriers, transaction costs, and service inefficiencies, it can also create new forms of exclusion when digital access, literacy, trust, and governance are uneven. The phygital turn in healthcare thus intensifies the ethical and policy responsibility of national health systems to design technology in ways that expand real access rather than symbolic participation.

An important contribution of this chapter lies in foregrounding healthcare marketing and communication as critical economic determinants of inclusion. Information asymmetry, low health literacy, and exclusionary communication practices function as invisible barriers that undermine otherwise well-designed reforms. Inclusive marketing rooted in clarity, cultural responsiveness, and trust emerges as a powerful yet underutilized tool for enhancing both equity and system efficiency.

Leadership and governance emerge as the decisive forces mediating all dimensions of inclusion. Inclusive leadership aligns economic incentives with social objectives, steers digital innovation toward public value, and ensures accountability across complex health systems. Weak or passive governance, by contrast, allows efficiency-driven reforms to drift toward exclusion, often without explicit intent. This finding reinforces the argument that inclusion is fundamentally a governance and ethical challenge, not merely a technical or financial one.

By integrating welfare economics, the capabilities approach, health equity theory, institutional economics, and digital inclusion theory, the chapter advances a holistic framework for understanding inclusion in healthcare economics. The proposed conceptual framework illustrates how national reforms, economic design, phygital infrastructure, marketing mechanisms, and leadership capacity interact dynamically to produce inclusive or exclusionary health outcomes.

In conclusion, the success of national health reform in the phygital era will not be measured solely by technological sophistication, cost containment, or coverage statistics. It will be judged by the extent to which reforms expand real, equitable, and sustainable access to affordable healthcare for all social groups. Inclusion must therefore remain a guiding principle embedded in the economic, institutional, and ethical foundations of health systems. Only through such an integrated and values-driven approach can healthcare reforms fulfill their promise of health as a shared social good rather than a stratified privilege.

REFERENCES

Arrow, K. J. (1963). Uncertainty and the welfare economics of medical care. *The American Economic Review, 53*(5), 941–973. https://www.jstor.org/stable/1812044

Braveman, P., & Gruskin, S. (2003). Defining equity in health. *Journal of Epidemiology and Community Health, 57*(4), 254–258. DOI: 10.1136/jech.57.4.254 PMID: 12646539

Djakeli, K. (2024). Healthcare marketing: Meaning, historical development, applications, and current status. In Djakeli, K. (Ed.), *Modern Healthcare Marketing in the Digital Era* (pp. 1–25). IGI Global Scientific Publishing., DOI: 10.4018/979-8-3693-0679-6.ch001

Friedman, M. (1962). *Capitalism and freedom*. University of Chicago Press. https://press.uchicago.edu/ucp/books/book/chicago/C/bo68666099.html

Friedman, M., & Friedman, R. (1980). *Free to choose: A personal statement*. Harcourt Brace Jovanovich. https://archive.org/details/freetochoosepers0000frie

Gigauri, I., & Djakeli, K. (2021). National health reforms in Georgia during 1994–2021 and their success. HOLISTICA – Journal of Business and Public Administration, 12(2), 102–108. https://reference-global.com/download/article/10.2478/hjbpa-2021-0017.pdf

Gostin, L. O., Moon, S., & Meier, B. M. (2021). Reimagining Global Health Governance in the Age of COVID-19. *American Journal of Public Health, 110*(11), 1615–1619. DOI: 10.2105/AJPH.2020.305933 PMID: 33026872

Jan Dijk, J. (2020). *The digital divide*. Polity Press., DOI: 10.1002/asi.24355

Kickbusch, I., Silberschmidt, G., & Buss, P. (2017). Global health diplomacy: The need for new perspectives, strategic approaches and skills in global health. *Bulletin of the World Health Organization, 95*(3), 159–159A. DOI: 10.2471/BLT.13.118596 PMID: 17486216

Kotler, P., Shalowitz, J., & Stevens, R. J. (2021). *Strategic marketing for health care organizations: Building a customer-driven health system* (2nd ed.). Jossey-Bass., https://www.wiley.com/en-us/Strategic+Marketing+For+Health+Care+Organizations%3A+Building+A+Customer-Driven+Health+System%2C+2nd+Edition-p-9781118355831

Marmot, M. (2017). The Health Gap: The Challenge of an Unequal World: the argument. *International Journal of Epidemiology*, *46*(4), 1312–1318. DOI: 10.1093/ije/dyx163 PMID: 28938756

Marmot, M., Allen, J., Goldblatt, P., Herd, E., & Morrison, J. (2020). *Build back fairer: The COVID-19 Marmot review*. Institute of Health Equity. https://www.instituteofhealthequity.org/resources-reports/build-back-fairer-the-covid-19-marmot-review

North, D. C. (1990). *Institutions, institutional change and economic performance*. Cambridge University Press., DOI: 10.1017/CBO9780511808678

Northouse, P. G. (2021). *Leadership: Theory and practice* (9th ed.). SAGE Publications., https://www.scirp.org/reference/referencespapers?referenceid=3786973

Sen, A. (1999). *Development as freedom*. Oxford University Press., https://global.oup.com/academic/product/development-as-freedom-9780198297581

Stiglitz, J. E. (2000). *Economics of the public sector* (3rd ed.). W. W. Norton & Company., https://www.academia.edu/37552359/Economics_of_the_Public_Sector_Joseph_E_Stiglitz

World Health Organization. (2010). *Health systems financing: The path to universal coverage*. WHO Press. https://www.who.int/publications/i/item/9789241564021

Xu, K., Soucat, A., Kutzin, J., Brindley, C., Maele, N. V., Touré, H., Garcia, M. A., Li, D., Barroy, H., Flores, G., & Wang, H. (2018). *Public spending on health: A closer look at global trends*. World Health Organization & World Bank Group. https://www.hst.org.za/publications/NonHST%20Publications/WHO-HIS-HGF-HF-WorkingPaper-18.3-eng.pdf.

KEY TERMS AND DEFINITIONS

Accessibility: The extent to which healthcare services are physically, digitally, culturally, and informationally available and usable by diverse populations when needed.

Affordability: The ability of individuals and households to obtain necessary healthcare services without incurring catastrophic expenditure or sacrificing other essential needs.

Health Equity: The principle of reducing avoidable and unjust differences in health status and healthcare access across population groups based on social, economic, and demographic factors.

Health Leadership: The capacity of individuals and institutions to guide healthcare systems ethically and strategically, aligning economic, technological, and social goals to achieve inclusive outcomes.

Healthcare Economics: The study of how healthcare resources are financed, allocated, and utilized to maximize health outcomes while balancing efficiency, equity, and sustainability within health systems.

Inclusion: A policy and system-level commitment to ensuring all social groups can access and benefit from healthcare services without discrimination, financial hardship, or structural exclusion.

National Health Reform: Comprehensive policy initiatives aimed at restructuring healthcare systems to improve coverage, quality, efficiency, and equity at the national level.

Phygital Healthcare: An integrated healthcare delivery model that combines physical health services with digital technologies to enhance reach, efficiency, and continuity of care.

Chapter 5
Digital Technologies and the Future of Healthcare Reform:
A Phygital Perspective

A. Sumathi
http://orcid.org/0000-0003-4700-5573
Srinivasa Ramanujan Centre, SASTRA University, India

Farjana Farvin Sahapudeen
http://orcid.org/0000-0002-2054-9389
Srinivasa Ramanujan Centre, SASTRA University, India

ABSTRACT

Health care is experiencing a transformation driven by advanced developments in digital technologies. The integration of innovative digital systems with traditional healthcare- referred to as Phygital (Physical+digital) is reshaping how healthcare services are delivered and experienced. The Phygital model combines the physical environment with advanced digital systems to enhance human –technology interactions across range of services. This approach effectively binds the consultations with digital techniques, continuous monitoring of patients, thereby improving efficiency, engagement and accessibility. Phygital enables the patients to change between virtual and physical modes depends on health alerts, while caregivers can monitor, access and interact with them in real time. This chapter examines phygital technologies and the ongoing reform of the healthcare sector through digital innovations aimed at enhancing diagnosis and treatment. It also highlights emerging directions in healthcare to develop a robust health care system for remote monitoring and treatment.

DOI: 10.4018/979-8-3373-7173-3.ch005

INTRODUCTION

Phygital models are applied in diverse areas such as urban management, education, politics, tourism, marketing and law[1]. An operational framework for digitizing marketing and leadership in policymaking services aims to promote a healthy environment, ensure continuous 24/7 customer support through digital presence, and strengthen the economy[2]. The Covid-19 pandemic compelled the world to adopt phygital insights into medical field for reforming health policies in terms of economics and marketing[3].Applying phygital models in healthcare serves as a means of improving health care services through advanced information and communication techniques, thereby enhancing patient health outcomes and facilitating family health management. Phygital in healthcare adopted to represent the systems in which patient interact digitally and continuously. Digitizing health care facilities supports e-solutions for daily patient health care and strengthens preventive health care system.

Phygital techniques enhance the healthcare treatment process, promising improved treatment, patient experience, and care. They enrich the power of simplifying the real world interactions in healthcare. The phygital approach improves effectiveness in patient satisfaction, chronic disease management, and technical development[4]. Digital health includes electronic health (eHealth), mobile Health (mHealth),telemedicine, and telehealth services. Mobile e-health services are made available to end users through digital marketing. Marketing along with the digitization of health care platforms and services, is processed in parallel to enhance national health reforms. MobileHealth(mHealth) refers to the provision of health services through mobile phones. Digital Health (dHeath) addresses patients through smart and IoT enabled devices.

The combination of Internet Of Things(IoT) and Artificial Intelligence(AI) transforms digital technologies into new forms- such as telecare, telemedicine, mHeath, eHealth by integrating medical techniques with mobile and digital technologies[5].Telemedicine facilitates the provision of consulting services to rural and remotely located patients, and online pharmacies extend health services through the provision of medicines, thereby overcoming geographical barriers. Phygital techniques can be grouped according to patients essential needs in healthcare: These needs may include disease diagnosis, disease prevention, the treatment process, adopting of a new lifestyle and continuous patient engagement.

New technological evolutions in Artificial Intelligence (AI) and tele-treatment domain increase the effectiveness of healthcare services. The world health organization indicates that the drastic changes in digital technology enhance the affordability and accessibility of health care systems globally[6].Digital transformation emphasizes the integration of patient Health Care Records(HCRs),IoT enabled monitoring devices, mobile applications, and digital healthcare decision support systems, which reform healthcare services and enhance patient involvement[7].Advanced digital technologies enable predictive models and personalized care, shifting treatment from reactive to a proactive mode by shifting heathcare systems both technically and culturally[8].

Digital transformation increases the health care accessibility, and continuity of treatment through teleconsultations, telepharmacy and telemedicine and extent the health care services to underserved rural communities[9].Additionally hospital at home services are provided for patients with chronic diseases to receive medical care without visiting healthcare centers and to reduce the travel and waiting burdens[10].Artificial Intelligence powered phygital tools provide services through video visits and accessed are accessed using email and mobile services.Healthcare services are also extended through wearables such as smart watches,thermometers,and respiratory sensors.Telemedicine services have been effectively proven as means for limiting the spread of diseases such as COVID-19.

DIGITAL TECHNOLOGIES IN HEALTH CARE

Innovative digital tools streamline healthcare systems, from the registration process to patient recovery. Digital healthcare technologies can also provide services through semantic networks. Semantic networks are generated from genetic information of humans, proteins and human phenotypes among other interconnected data. These interlinked datasets can be utilized by doctors and not expert care givers [11].The advancement of wireless technologies provides on demand opportunities for innovative solutions under an "anywhere, anytime" policy. IoT enabled sensors register and monitor the patient movements to promote healthy lifestyles. Ubiquitous medical monitoring is possible with integrated devices such as microcontrollers, sensors and suitable communication devices. In the Internet of Things (IoT), diversified components are aggregated, and the signals collected through them are analysed to activate time based alarms for caretakers [12].

The Internet of Things (IoT) represents the interconnection of sensory objects that collect information independently and forward it to intelligent systems. IoT enabled systems help in health data management, particularly in relation to drugs and medical diagnosis. The misidentification of drugs in manual processes is completely eliminated, and the work efficiency of hospital management is enhanced. The care of chronic patients is simplified with IoT equipment, as IoT enabled sensors monitor and track patients who require 24/7 healthcare. Abnormal signals obtained from patients can be forwarded to physicians and caregivers in real time. Alarm signals are forwarded to all relevant healthcare personnel to ensure the patient's health and safety.Table 1 indicates the patients needs addressed by various phygital technologies.

Table 1. Patient needs addressed by Phygital technologies

Patient needs	Definition
Disease Diagnosis	The process that explains the condition of patients based on symptoms and vital signs
Disease Prevention	Preventing the patient from the occurrences of diseases
Treatment Process	Procedures or methodologies such as drug, surgery, or exercise to cure the disease
Adopting New Style	Adopting and changing the life style to maintain quality of life
Continuous patient engagement	The continuous and systematic collection of patient signals for planning and implementing the patient health service

The Internet of Medical Things (IoMT) enables continuous monitoring and generates alert signals for physicians and caretakers through internet connections. Chronic diseases and elderly care needs can be managed using IoMT healthcare systems that enable continuous, sensor based monitoring.Camera sensors detect falls detection and activity changes, whereas advanced wearables record physiological signals such as heart beat rate, blood pressure, respiratory rate through telemonitoring. Health care Records (HCRs) along with diagnosis explanations can be accessed by patient's relatives through smart phones. Health technology properties are evaluated using Health technology assessment (HTA) for helping decision makers. Artificial Intelligence and robotics techniques are mainly used in HTA for developing new healthcare services [13].Figure 1.displays the various digital technologies applied in healthcare.

Figure 1. Digital Technologies in Healthcare

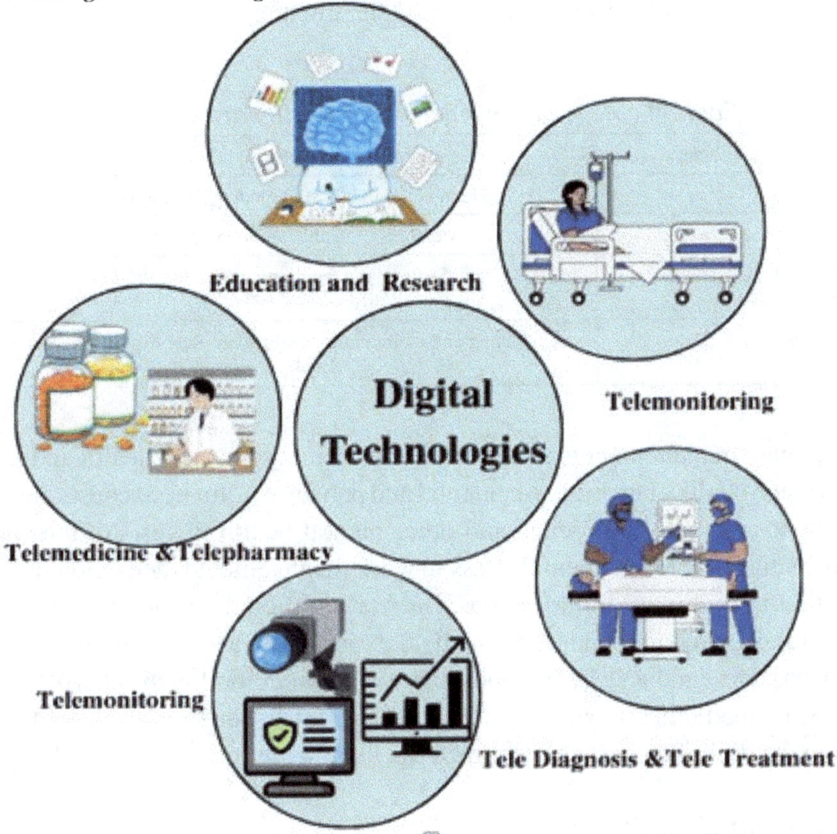

Health care Management

Digital transformation in the medical field is fostering development oriented towards customer needs and expectations. Digital transformation is naturally reshaping the physical world into digital world by transforming cultural and traditional ecosystems[14][15]. Patient experience refers to the level of interaction between patients and heath care service providers. By assessing patient experience, quality of health services can be enhanced to ensure patient centered care. The quality of healthcare systems is supported by reducing service waiting times, promoting effective communication, ensuring timely service delivery and clearly explaining the treatment process to patients. Health care management encompasses patient relationship management, personalized patient care management, patient service management and business to human (B2H) management.Table 2 summarizes classification categories of different elements in healthcare.

Table 2. Classification categories in elements of healthcare

Classification Categories	Definition
Patients	Members of public who receive the health services
Healthcare Service Providers	Members of healthcare who deliver services
Healthcare systems/resource managers	Systems managing public health services
Data Services	Collecting and maintaining Health Care Records(HCR)/Electronic Health Records

Health care management is a method of maintaining physical health and mental health through healthy nutrition. Accidental and pandemic situations cause emotional weakness, loss of self confidence and other mental health issues. An unexpected pandemic situation creates mental stress in work management when work processes are handled in online or digital modes. Integrating digital ecosystems along with healthy practices recommended by medical experts reduces the mental stress and other serious consequences.Techniques such as genomics modify the pharmaceutical properties of medicines to suit an individual patient 's genetic profile[16] .These custom made digital techniques optimize the healthcare management in hospitals.

ML and AI in Healthcare

Enhancing the performance and prediction accuracy of deadly diseases such as cancer and cardio attacks significantly improves early diagnosis and safeguard patient's lives. A vast amount of patient data processed through machine learning can predict the disease stages without human intervention. The waiting time for life saving treatments can be reduced before the disease further spreads, and high specificity in locating affected regions using nanocomputing has also been achieved. Deep neural networks based medical image analysis can more accurately segregate the affected regions from unaffected regions of an organ accurately than physicians or medical experts. Drug recommendations generated by AI based expert systems enhance personalized patient care. Massive bio signals collected in real-time from chronic patients can be analyzed within fractions of a second using AI and data analytics models, enabling the rapid generation of alert messages for caregivers.

The advancement of AI systems enables faster learning from patient cases than that processed by clinicians. The practical applications of machine learning and AI support telemedicine and allow the prediction of patient responses to treatments.

The applications of AI extend beyond healthcare monitoring and managing patient data to include research and development in drug discovery and automated surgical procedures.Radiological practices have also advanced through the use of AI models for diagnosing medical images in CT and MRI scans to support analysis and accurate treatment planning.AI based systems reconstruct medical images and acquire essential data for disease prediction.AI can also be used to predict unexpected mortality,unplanned treatment cases,and treatment cost -effectiveness.AI based medical image classification models are designed to analyse large volumes of medical images and extract the salient features. These features are used to identify lesions in various organs and to improve diagnostic accuracy. The modern medical field has advanced to robotic surgical systems that use 3D vision systems,enabling procedures that are not possible through manual operations.Quantum computing along with ML can be applied for discovery of drugs through observing different stimuli reactions in the human body[17].

Big data in E-Healthcare

Big data in health care refers to the large volume,highvelocity,and high variety of information that enable automated,advanced decision making and process initiation.Big data encampasses rapidly growing information related to patient real time physiological signals, past medical records, diagnostic reports and pharmaceutical information.In recent years,big data has been increasingly utilized to improve and optimize analysis and predictive forecasting in healthcare.Electronic health records and Health care information systems help store and organize patients details effectively.Healthcare big data serves as a foundation for high performing machine learning based predictive models. Figure 2 indicates the various techniques applied in Bigdata of E-healthcare.

Figure 2. Big data in E-healthcare

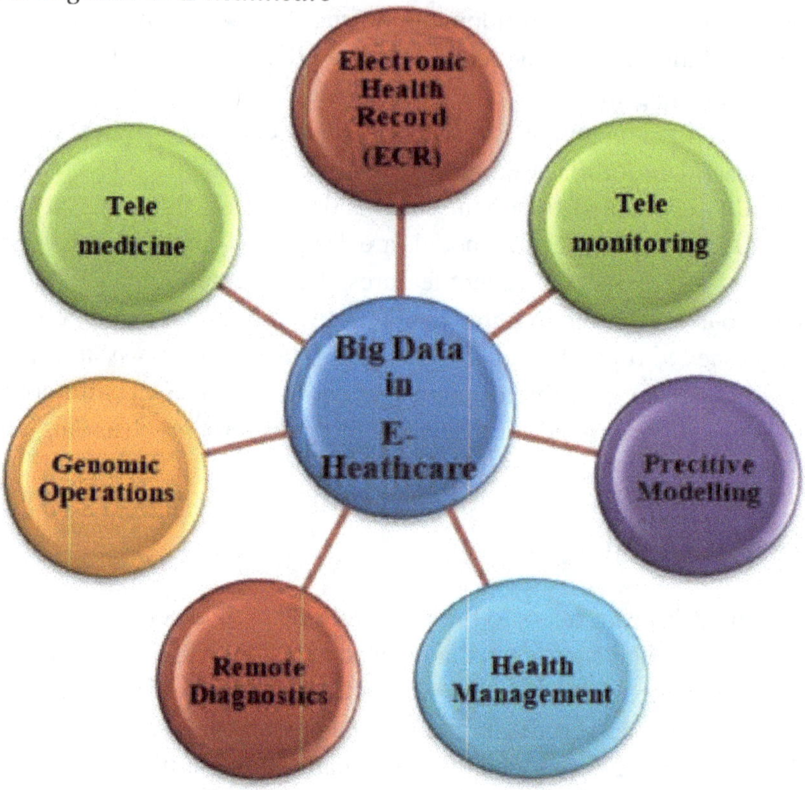

Big data enables faster acquisition of data from diversified data pools in the required time and format. Big data has transformed conventional medical services into digital medical services. Clinical data is growing exponentially and requires a larger storage capacity. IoT enabled medical services require substantial real time online analysis and processing. All of the above challenges are addressed by big data, which accurately analyses the electronic medical records and generates virtual diagnosis plans. Big data supports personalized treatment based on individual patient cases and recommends personalized health plans using large volumes of historical data. It plays an important role in healthcare management by providing accurate and scientific information to physicians in a timely manner. It helps prevent misdiagnosis and supports management decisions while maintaining effective healthcare management. Big data capabilities increase the availability of scientific information and enhance medical research.

Rural Healthcare

Providing healthcare services to remote regions and areas with severe climatic conditions is now possible through telemedicine.In such cases,telemedicine provides access to high quality healthcare services regardless of patient location.Communication occurs through video conferencing and web based interfaces.Video calls enabled by wearables devices allow physicians to examine patient signals and provide appropriate clinical guidance.Mobile devices enable physicians to check vital signs, review patient's medical histories, and evaluate,diagnose conditions before recommending the drugs.Audio enabled devices help monitor patient's progress and provide feedback regarding treatment.Telemedicine also connects medical experts from different parts of the world with rural population without the need for unnecessary and expensive travel.

Phygital healthcare supports rural and remote healthcare services, where conventional treatment methods are restricted with geographical limitations. Community health centers, along with local mobile clinics equipped with telecommunication and remote monitoring facilities, enable patients to receive expert medical support and data driven based health services[18].Additionally, telemedicine and teleclinics have provided evidence of reducing travel burden for elderly and chronic patients. They expand the personalized digital services by enabling access to specialized treatment from specialists worldwide in a cost effective manner.Severe climatic conditions or pandemic situations can be managed more effectively through telemedicine, even when medical experts are geographically distant from patients.

Marketing in HealthCare

The medical services market requires a substantial transformation in its service offerings, particularly in the personalization of care through smart devices. Mobile applications for medical services must meet patient's expectations as valued clients. The marketing dimension should be redesigned to facilitate access to medical content and digital applications of patients. Marketing in healthcare supports personalized care by enabling follow up of patient's health conditions after their physical visits to the hospital. It also categorizes patients according to levels of criticality through interactions facilitated by mobile applications and web applications. These data driven categorizations enhance the reliability of healthcare systems and further strengthen personalized care. Automated detection of primary physiological signals such as weight and blood pressure engages patients in personalized care and simplifies the diagnosis process. Relevant interactions, along with common and condition specific health information displayed in digital screens, enhance the patient positive experience during waiting periods. Additionally, personalized services reduce exposure to crowded areas and long queues, thereby improving patient satisfaction.

To strengthen health care marketing, diagnostic information should be supplemented with explanations generated through explainable AI techniques to justify the recommendations suggested by physicians. Such explanations can also integrate data driven predictions with clear interpretations of diagnosis outcomes, thereby reducing patient anxiety and increasing confidence. The future of health care involves the combination of traditional in person care with remote health monitoring techniques. This convergence enables the healthcare systems to provide more efficient and inclusive services for personalized needs. It also delivers care directly to patients at their locations, supporting patient centric, home based diagnostic services[19][20]. Emerging developments- such as virtual wards, real time 24/7 monitoring for elderly people and chronically ill people, and AI enabled preventive care are expected to become integral elements of future health care systems and service delivery.

National Healthcare Reform Policy

Digital transformation is driving changes in national health policy by necessitating adaptations in the structural organization of healthcare institutions,,diagnosistic methodologies, data management systems, and digital predictions tools, thereby fostering a broader medical evolution. To optimize the benefits of potential phygital healthcare, national healthcare reforms must focus on developing comprehensive digital health care frameworks that ensure interoperability and consistency across geographical regions. Strengthening digital infrastructure –particularly by addressing connectivity gaps and implementing robust data protection and governance measures is essential for maintaining patient privacy and security. National wide collaboration between public and private health sectors will further accelerate the implementation of digital health solutions. Additionally, Improving digital literacy through training on newly adopted digital devices enables individuals to engage confidently with emerging technologies and contributes to the evolution of digital heath ecosystems. National health reforms must address the core objectives of improving quality, ensuring equity and maintaining sustainable long term health environment. With technological advancements, the integration of digital and physical care transforming the philosophy of health care into an adaptive, patient centric and resilient model.

Related Work

The World Health Organization encourages governments to establish, manage and scale up the digital technological environment to meet Public Health requirements and to be in line with the WHO Digital Health Plan [21]. This Framework details the necessary building Blocks of Digital Health. The Framework establishes the need for a strong governance structure, and other essential features such as a trained and Digital Health workforce; reliable/efficient technology (infrastructure); and Interoperability between the various types of Digital Health Services. Cross-cutting issues are to be addressed in the Digital Services to ensure these services are appropriately established and will be accessible to all branches of society. Cross-cutting Issues like Equity, Safety of Patients, Ethical Utilisation, and National Planning for the Long-Term. The Framework is applicable for many of the existing Digital Health Solutions and provides High-Level Guidance for Health Policy Development for managing Hybrid Models of Digital (PHYSICAL and DIGITAL) Health Systems, and therefore the expectation is that Digital Health Solutions will supplement a Country's Digital Health Plans.

A general review by Kraus et al. [22] describes the variety of strategies used by providers, payers, patients, and regulators to incorporate digital technology into the way health services are managed and delivered (the business side of health care). The authors grouped the research into five major areas of emphasis: operational efficiency improvements using automation and data integration, Patientcentered methods of improving engagement and self-management, Organizational and managerial emphasis, Workforce issues and Larger socio economic environment. The authors bring all these strands together and propose an integrative model that illustrates how successful digital transformation follows from the interaction between organizational capabilities, preparedness of the workforce, patient participation and system level conditions all of which enable healthcare providers to achieve meaningful operational improvements.

Aytekin, A et.al[23]study by Aytekin performs a large scale bibliometric analysis to trace the evolution of research in patient experience over the past decade. Using data from Web of Science and Scopus from 2014 to 2024, this review examines 21,392 publications identified through 11 targeted search terms. The mapping of keyword cooccurrence yields an increasing focus of the patient experience based on literature on digital technologies. Results indicated that digitalization significantly influenced the theoretical developments of patient experience studies. Digital tools are used to enhance engagement, communication and data integration across health systems. The present study further demonstrates that digital health extends beyond clinical practice to broader health service contexts. In general the findings emphasize the wide reach and the contribution of digital technologies to the advancement of patient centered care.

Anastasiadou, O.[24] explores how health systems responded during exceptional emergencies such as the COVID-19 pandemic and underlines that solid research methods are necessary to assess digital health developments. The research uses MedlinePubMed, Scopus, and Google Scholar and focuses on works published between 2015 and 2024. The key focus areas of the literature search have been the terms digital platforms, digital health, digital technology and the implications for management. In the case of this review, only English language, peer-reviewed articles that had a direct relevance to the subject were taken into consideration. Results revealed that while digital technologies may close gaps in health they also create inequality among the less privileged because of poor access to technology. The transition to digital services made evident serious deficiencies regarding preparation and training on the part of personnel.As digital services have gained a greater role in the delivery of healthcare services, so too has the financial burden of these services increased. As with any new technology, there are many existing and potential governance challenges resulting from an increased reliance on digital service delivery models.

Digital health combines technology and modern medicine to transform how healthcare is delivered and received, as noted by Ramachander A. and colleagues [25]. Diagnosis of diseases is now completed quickly using diagnostic tools powered by Artificial Intelligence (AI); and precision medicine has reached a point where it can be used to create personalized treatment plans for individual patients. Additionally, the expansion of telehealth has enabled patients to access health care remotely and has essentially removed the barriers of geographic distances between provider and patient, with the number of remote health visits increasing rapidly. Wearable devices and the Internet of Things (IoT) have also enabled individual patients to continuously monitor their health status and be accountable for managing their own health and wellness.

Digital health's emergence has made it easier for businesses to understand the power of customer data, including sensitive personal details about individuals' health-related activities and how they choose to communicate with their healthcare provider. Many laws to protect the privacy of health information have been established internationally (e.g., GDPR and HIPAA). Increasing interoperability among global health care solutions has made it easier for the healthcare system to share an individual's health record, which is essential for digital health's advancement. Digital twins; artificial intelligence (AI) ecosystems; and connected health technology, are examples of cutting-edge innovations that have transformed the delivery of healthcare. Collaborative research, innovation, and interdisciplinary research studies will help unlock the full benefits of digital health solutions.

According to Osipov, V. S. [26], digital technologies have taken on an ever-increasing importance in health care given the current issues affecting society. Digital technologies have also experienced significant development due to the COVID-19 (2020) pandemic. The purpose of this study was to present how digital technologies have helped to advance health care at both national and international levels. The findings of this study indicate that the primary way in which digital technologies can help improve health care safety is through the use of alternatives to physical contact (providers and patients). Digital technologies provide a way for patients to receive care without having to physically interact with their providers, thereby dramatically reducing the opportunities for potential transmission of infection through contact.

Digital Platforms and Connected Medical Devices have developed many new models of care delivery and ways to engage with your physician from home or wherever you are. Therefore, Digitalization will enable operational improvements to the overall healthcare System and also ensure that all quality standards are maintained. Furthermore, Digital Technologies enhance the delivery of more accessible and efficient care through increased Quality and Lower Costs, as well as the rapid growth of experimental technologies becoming part of the healthcare System. In the future, these technologies will allow global healthcare Systems to develop improved operational models for delivering healthcare services.

To enhance the strategic decision-making process of healthcare leaders, the author has developed a three-tiered decision-making framework for healthcare leaders that incorporates research findings and best practices from the cutting-edge research and practice of today. As confirmed by this framework it is critical to enhance the global resilience, accessibility and efficiency of healthcare systems.

According to Mbunge, E. [27] he describes how innovative Digital Technology has the ability to provide an avenue for Improving Patient Outcomes and Healthcare Service Delivery along with Global Advances in the Healthcare Sector, with as much or more impact than all of the advances to date with smart connected devices. However, the author also notes that current Systems and Applications Do Not Contain the capabilities necessary for Individualized and Emotional Recognition for the improvement in patient's daily lives and therefore continue as an Immediate Need to Integrate Advanced Technology with Intelligent Sensors. The author's next Point is Healthcare 5.0 which refers to Innovation involving Remote Monitoring of Patients, Virtual Care, Intelligent Diagnosis of Disease and Data-Driven Decision Making.Healthcare 5.0 provides support for numerous service models such as the following: emotional telemedicine, ambient assisted living, smart self-management, treatment reminders, compliance tracking, and connected patient centered care. Nevertheless there are several obstacles that hinder the successful implementation of Healthcare 5.0. Among these obstacles are organizational, technological and infrastructure limitations; legal and regulatory compliance gaps; economic difficulties; cultural/religious barriers; and misalignment with institutional policies.

To address the emerging barriers to the successful implementation of Healthcare 5.0, the report recommends creating a better equipped technology infrastructure, establishing longer term funding models, creating standardized operating procedures, establishing a framework for developing legal and policy-based documents relating to e-Health through stakeholder collaboration and partnership between private sector and public sector.AdditionallyMbunge points to the fact that in order to maximize the capacity of technologies to elevate health care around the globe. Healthcare 5.0 requires innovative thought processes the infusion of capital and strategic coordination among all parties to work together so as to move forward.

BENEFITS OF THE PHYGITAL APPROACH

Improved Access For Rural, Elderly, And Mobility-Limited Populations

Phydigitalthe combination of physical and digital care enhances access to healthcare by eliminating barriers due to geography or physicality that inhibit individuals' ability to easily and effectively access care. Long distance to access to clinics, limited access to clinic availability, and inadequate or periodic physician availability are examples of barriers that impact CBPs, especially CBPs located in remote area settings [28]. However, If community-based practices offer teleconsultations with in-office appointments as needed, patients will be able to receive timely medical care and have less face-to-face contact with their physicians. Also, this approach improves access to health care for older and/or mobility-compromised patients by eliminating the need for caregivers to provide assistance and transportation. Lastly, digital technology such as telehealth and remote monitoring enables healthcare providers to support and supervise their patients while reducing travel demands on their patients to visit the hospital.[29]

Greater Efficiency By Reducing Wait Times And Unnecessary Visits

With Phygital Care being Hybrid, it allows patients a more seamless transition through the health care system. By having digital triage services, health care providers can quickly evaluate a patient's medical condition to determine whether remote care or need for 'immediate care' should be provided. Because of this, Emergency Room and Outpatient Department utilization is reduced, thus allowing physicians to spend more time with patients that require hands-on assessments. Additionally, check-in/check-out procedures via telemedicine volunteerism and on-line check-in provide a smaller 'administrative burden' by shortening the appointment time required for physicians or nurses. In addition, the combination of digital and physical healthcare services provides a more integrated health care 'ecosystem' through more streamlined scheduling processes, shorter average wait times and an increased volume of patients treated through clinics.[30]

Figure 3. Benefits of Phygital approach

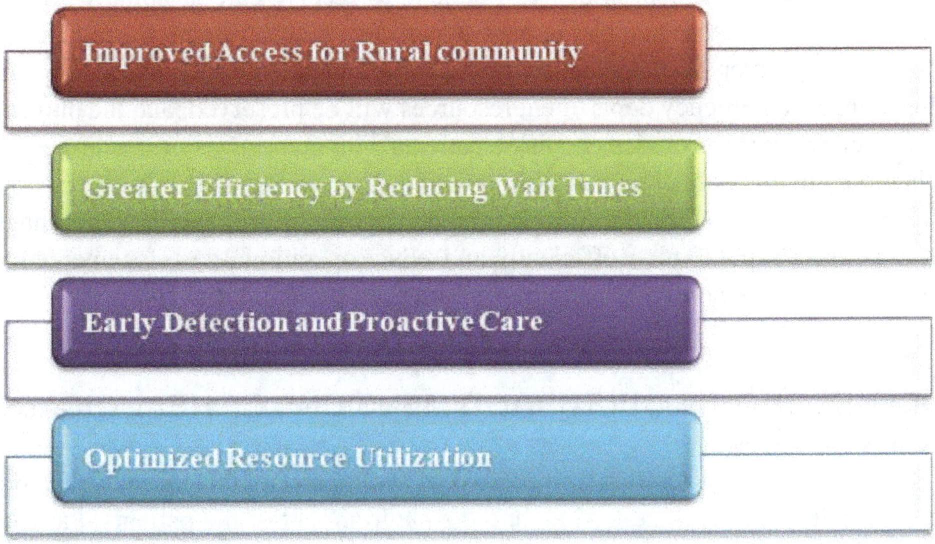

Early Detection and Proactive Care Supported by Continuous Digital Monitoring

The use of wearables, IoT Devices and mobile applications for continuous monitoring of a person's health is the basis of a phydigital strategy. Continuous real-time monitoring of a person's vital signs, medication compliance level, exercise activity and symptom progression, enables Clinicians to uncover any unusual findings or early warning signs of the worsening of illness in a time frame that may prevent irreparable harm or delay the need for Future Care; Additionally, based on the ongoing ability to view these findings, Clinicians have the ability to provide proactive interventions, including dietary adjustments, medication adjustments and/or frequent health check-ups[31]. The move from a reactive to a preventative health care approach improves the safety of Patients and decreases hospitalisation rates and enhances the long-term health outcomes of patients diagnosed with chronic disease.

Optimized Resource Use in Clinics, Hospitals, and Emergency Departments

By implementing a phydigital strategy, healthcare organizations can maximize their available resources (including personnel) by allocating tasks across several different platforms: electronic and face-to-face [32]. With telehealth, patients who have non-emergent medical issues will be able to receive care at home while simultaneously permitting healthcare providers to focus on servicing those patients experiencing greater levels of acuity through the hospital setting. As a result of these changes, emergency department resources will be preserved, and the number of emergency department visits by those patients with no need for urgent in-person evaluation will decrease. The establishment of clearly designated pathways of care for those individuals suffering from less acute conditions will also better manage backlogs, distribute staff more efficiently, and reduce operational costs for emergency departments experiencing high volumes of unnecessary patient visits.

SOCIO-ECONOMIC CULTURAL DIMENSIONS OF HEALTHCARE

Socio-economic and cultural dimensions of healthcare are influenced by factors such as the income level, education, and the environment of the patients. Patients must understand the treatment process and be aware of proactive health measures. The availability of clean drinking water and high quality residential areas is also essential for maintaining healthy society. Phygital technologies supports the transformation from exiting medical practices into new digitized effective medical treatments[33].Phygital transformation refers to the process of integrating technological and data driven components into innovative, customer centered medical facilities. This transformation establishes a customer centered strategy that supports comprehensive cultural changes and evolving relationships and new business models within the healthcare sector.

Ethics, Governance and Legal Frameworks

Social justice and social fairness in wellbeing are fundamental foundations of ethics within the healthcare system. Governance is a key determinant of economic growth and the overall attainment of development goals in low and middle income countries. Ethical principles provide governance structures that support fair decision making for all stakeholders. Legal frameworks establish a baseline for ethical governance in medical services within the phygital world. Governance ethics in healthcare sectors form a framework for supports clinical, organizational ethics, facilitating effective governance and overseeing structures related to community health, patient safety, and childcare in conflict affected societies. Healthcare system governance is a critical concern for many developing countries, as it contributes to the creation of collaborative and healthy environments. Health systems should demonstrate the scalability by increasing the resources to rapid population changes [34].Governance involves the integration of various actors, including civil communities, public health institutions, private service providers, and development partners. Moreover, a complex network of international actors and institutions influences healthcare systems by governing global health services in an equitable manner for stake holders.

Data Ownership, Privacy of Patient Data

Healthcare sectors traditionally maintain physical records as institutional property that contains the patient data. Electronic medical Records (EMRs) gather patient information from healthcare providers, and offer significant benefits for clinical practice .Collecting patient data is a fundamental practice in healthcare, as it supports effective patient care. Researchers have used patient data from clinics to compare treatment effectiveness and analyse healthcare costs. However, breaches of confidential data have been exploited to inform in designing new rules for governing data sharing. Patient data are exploited for commercial purpose and shared between healthcare sectors and third parties. Emerging artificial intelligence technologies, together with data obtained from healthcare providers, possibility an increased risk of exploitation due to the sharing of personal data with third party entities and data vendors. Several software tools such as Research Electronic Data Capture (REDCap) and Research Action for Health Networks(REACHnet), help ensures the responsible management of patient data[35].Patient privacy policies are essential, as they provide individuals with control over the disclosure of their information to Social media platforms or other pharmaceutical entities .Strengthening user trust through greater transparency is therefore crucial, and patients retain control over their personal data to prevent unauthorized sharing with third parties.

Digital Equity and Inclusion

Digital equity and inclusion in healthcare are essential for ensuring a healthy life worldwide. Policies must be developed and implemented to ensure that health information and services are sharing equitably with all populations at both national and global levels. The design and delivery of technical support, such as telemedicine and telepharmacy should be accessible and affordable to all patients through standardized policy frameworks. By addressing health disparities, the digital health ecosystem can provide digital navigation support across all stages of development and implementation. Policies that promote health equity are shaped through multiple approaches to achieve affordable and inclusive access for diverse populations. Digital health inequities are significantly influenced by the implementation of healthcare policies, and individuals experiencing such inequities are often excluded from essential healthcare services due limited digital access[36]. The development of robust healthcare systems can mitigate health equity risks, and widening disparities must be addressed through comprehensive digital care policies. For equitable future, digital health systems must be designed to be affordable, accessible, and inclusive for everyone without limitation.

Interoperability and Digital Standards

Interoperability and digital standards are essential for enabling systems and devices to exchange and apply data effectively, enabling digital data conversions in healthcare. Existing interoperability standards include HL7 fast Healthcare Interoperability Resources (FHIR), the Trusted Exchange Framework and Common Agreement(TEFCA), the Health Insurance Portability and Accountability Act(HIPAA), and the general Data protection Regulation(GDPR). Emerging technologies such as Artificial Intelligence, block chain, machine learning and federated learning are increasingly applied to enhance interoperability across healthcare systems. Sustainable interoperability demands governance reforms, the adoption of standardized architectures, and active engagement among stakeholders. Integrating policy and technology is vital for building robust digital healthcare systems that support equitable, personalized care. To address the communication barriers, standards such as HL7Fast Healthcare Interoperability Resource (FHIR) and Trusted Exchange Framework and Common Agreement (TEFCA) have been developed. They provide semantic interoperability through modular standards, while TEFCA establishes policy mechanisms that enable cross sectional exchange across multiple countries [37].

Cyber Security and Data Protection

Cyber security refers to the protection of digital systems, and computer networks from cyber attacks, while data protection focuses on safeguarding data from loss, mishandling, or unauthorized access throughout its lifecycle. Security threats against the healthcare data induce significant risks to patient data, regulatory compliance and healthcare organizations. The increasing digitization of healthcare heightens exposure to cyberattacks, such as ransomware and phishing, which can result in substantial financial losses and reputational damage. Scientific investigations have identified various security weakness and threats affecting healthcare systems. Consequently, healthcare organizations should properly adopt security standards established by regulatory standards such as Health Insurance Portability and Accountability Act (HIPAA) and the General Data Protection Regulation (GDPR) [38]. Modern security standards increasingly incorporate Artificial Intelligence based threat detection, blockchain protocols and the implementation of Zero Trust Architecture (ZTA).

As a result, the Cyber security domain has continued to develop within healthcare organizations to manage risks effectively and fulfil data protection mandates.

CONCLUSION

In summary, the Phygital techniques are reframing traditional healthcare into patient centric and rapidly responsive systems. The study of Digital Technologies and the Future of Health Care Reform: A Phygital Perspective examines how phygital approaches support the objectives of healthcare reforms by enhancing quality and accessibility with reducing cost .By combining the strength of conventional healthcare systems with advanced digital technologies such as IoT, big data, machine leaning and remote sensory tools-this model fosters the rational decision making for personalized treatments and real time monitoring. The chapter elaborates on advanced digital techniques applied in remote health monitoring, healthcare management and it outlines relevant national healthcare policies .It also emphasizes the significance of healthcare marketing and the adoption of phygital techniques to achieve optimal clinical outcomes and broaden the efficiency of health services. Furthermore, the study discusses the future of health care systems, and how they aim to uphold trust and equity for rational and equitable service delivery. Ultimately the study offers hope for the implementation of the phygital model in shaping the future healthcare systems.

Future Scope

Healthcare is rapidly evolving into a hybrid model that combines both physical and digital care in ways that make it difficult to tell when one stops and the other starts. The pace at which technology is growing is so fast that strategies for the future will change as well. Today, we do not just wait until someone gets sick to see them for treatment. Instead, we are able to take action much sooner to help prevent illness, by identifying problems much earlier in life, providing solutions, and having a better understanding of each person and their unique situation. There is an incredible amount of AI and machine learning driving this transformation. The two have enabled us to identify problems much sooner than ever before, and help physicians build treatment plans that offer both virtual check-ins and actual in-person visits to provide the highest level of care possible.

Robotics, 3D printing and nanotechnology are revolutionizing healthcare by allowing more accurate surgery, faster recovery from surgery and more targeted drug applications. However, these advancements would not be possible without advancements in cloud computing, big data, and super-fast 5G networks. Healthcare professionals (such as hospitals, clinics and home healthcare agencies) and their patients now have access to a single, integrated system. Empowerment is the primary focus: Having the ability to choose, to exercise power over one's own health, and to comprehend one's own health. It also allows a shift from simply being told by a doctor what to do to participating as part of a team in determining your health decisions and treatments.

Robust regulations must be in place to protect people's privacy, ensure that all AI systems are ethically developed, establish a framework to provide digital health services to all, and guarantee equal access to digital health services for all citizens regardless of geographic location. We still have much work to accomplish before we can confidently move forward with phygital health. We need to confirm which hybrid models of care are effective, as well as determine how to create digital infrastructure that can grow and adapt as needed, and determine the necessary financial requirements to sustain these systems. Phygital health is created at the intersection of Technology and Human Interaction. As such it is able to improve the way healthcare is delivered by increasing productivity, decreasing barriers to access, placing emphasis on the needs of patients, and providing opportunities for innovation. Furthermore, phygital health makes healthcare more affordable; improves the quality of care; creates faster timelines for innovation, provides opportunities for all healthcare delivery systems to prepare themselves for the impacts of the aging population, the next pandemic, and the long-term treatment of chronic disease.

REFERENCES

Adegoke, K., Adegoke, A., Dawodu, D., Bayowa, A., & Adekoya, A. (2025). Interoperability in digital healthcare: Enhancing consumer health and transforming care systems.

Anastasiadou, O., Tsipouras, M., Mpogiatzidis, P., & Angelidis, P. (2025, April). Digital Healthcare Innovative Services in Times of Crisis: A Literature Review. [). MDPI.]. *Health Care*, *13*(8), 889. PMID: 40281838

Aytekin, A., Alan, H., Demirel, H., Onur, N., Yalman, A., Livberber, T., & Yiğit-Açıkgöz, F. (2025). Digital health technologies in patient experience literature: A scoping review and future outlook for sustainable digital health interventions. *Sustainability (Basel)*, *17*(2), 456. DOI: 10.3390/su17020456

Barisevičius, G., Coste, M., Geleta, D., Juric, D., Khodadadi, M., Stoilos, G., & Zaihrayeu, I. (2018, September). Supporting digital healthcare services using semantic web technologies. In *International Semantic Web Conference* (pp. 291-306). Cham: Springer International Publishing. DOI: 10.1007/978-3-030-00668-6_18

Chiruvella, V., & Guddati, A. K. (2021). Ethical issues in patient data ownership. *Interactive Journal of Medical Research*, *10*(2), e22269. DOI: 10.2196/22269 PMID: 34018968

Coetzer, J. A., Goedhart, N. S., Schuitmaker-Warnaar, T. J., Dedding, C., & Zuiderent-Jerak, T. (2025). Health Equity in the Digital Age: Exploring health policy and inclusive digital care. *Health Policy and Technology*, *14*(5), 101039. DOI: 10.1016/j.hlpt.2025.101039

. Daraio, C., Di Leo, S., &Orsini, J. Digital Twins in Healthcare: State of the Art, Bibliometric Analysis and Future Perspectives.

Del Vecchio, P., Secundo, G., & Garzoni, A. (2023). Phygital technologies and environments for breakthrough innovation in customers' and citizens' journey. A critical literature review and future agenda. *Technological Forecasting and Social Change*, *189*, 122342. DOI: 10.1016/j.techfore.2023.122342

Di Bernardo, I., Marzullo, M., Mele, C., & Spena, T. R. (2023). AI-Based Technologies in the Phygital Care Journey. In *Impact of Artificial Intelligence in Business and Society* (pp. 212–230). Routledge. DOI: 10.4324/9781003304616-14

. Gaggioli, A., Cerasa, A., & Barresi, G. (2023). Phygital mental health: opportunities and challenges. *mHealth and human-centered design towards enhanced health, care, and Well-being*, 21-35.

Ganji, K., &Afshan, N. (2024). Elevating Patient Loyalty in Modern Healthcare through Phygital Frontier.

Global strategy on digital health 2020-2025 ISBN 978-92-4-002092-4, World Health Organization (WHO) — Global Strategy on Digital Health 2020–2025 (2021)

Golinelli, D., Boetto, E., Carullo, G., Nuzzolese, A. G., Landini, M. P., & Fantini, M. P. (2020). Adoption of digital technologies in health care during the COVID-19 pandemic: Systematic review of early scientific literature. *Journal of Medical Internet Research*, *22*(11), e22280. DOI: 10.2196/22280 PMID: 33079693

Grudtsyn, N. A. (2024). Transformative impact of the COVID-19 pandemic on medical tourism. *ВестникСанкт-Петербургскогоуниверситета. Науки о Земле*, *69*(4), 646–666.

Grudtsyn, N. A. (2024). Transformative impact of the COVID-19 pandemic on medical tourism. *ВестникСанкт-Петербургскогоуниверситета. Науки о Земле*, *69*(4), 646–666.

Hajdini, J., Za, S., & Iaia, L. (2025). State of art and future research directions for marketing technologies in healthcare: A bibliometric analysis. . *Technological Forecasting and Social Change*, *218*, 124226. Advance online publication. DOI: 10.1016/j.techfore.2025.124226

. Haverinen, J., Keränen, N., Falkenbach, P., Maijala, A., Kolehmainen, T., &Reponen, J. (2019). Digi-HTA: Health technology assessment framework for digital healthcare services.

Kodali, R. K., Swamy, G., & Lakshmi, B. (2015, December). An implementation of IoT for healthcare. In *2015 IEEE Recent Advances in Intelligent Computational Systems (RAICS)* (pp. 411-416). IEEE. DOI: 10.1109/RAICS.2015.7488451

Kraus, S., Schiavone, F., Pluzhnikova, A., & Invernizzi, A. C. (2021). Digital transformation in healthcare: Analyzing the current state-of-research. *Journal of Business Research*, *123*, 557–567. DOI: 10.1016/j.jbusres.2020.10.030

Lang, C., Meier zu Biesen, C., & Burchardt, M. (2024). Digital technologies and the future of health: Aspirations, design, use and resistance. . *Health Risk & Society*, *31*(3), 201–214. Advance online publication. DOI: 10.1080/13648470.2024.2397921 PMID: 39508152

MacMillan, A., & Thomas, P. (2024). Hybrid healthcare models: The rise of phygital medicine. *Journal of Telemedicine Practices*, *18*(1), 22–33.

Maita, K. C., et al. (2024). *The impact of digital health solutions on bridging the health-care access gap in rural areas: A scoping review.* BMC Health Services Research. PMC.DOI: 10.1186/s12913-024-11402-4

Mbunge, E., Muchemwa, B., Jiyane, S. E., & Batani, J. (2021). Sensors and healthcare 5.0: Transformative shift in virtual care through emerging digital health technologies. *Global Health Journal (Amsterdam, Netherlands)*, *5*(4), 169–177. DOI: 10.1016/j.glohj.2021.11.008

Mishra, A. (2025, August 25). *Strategy and examples for phygital marketing in healthcare*. Valuebound Blog.https://www.valuebound.com/resources/blog/Phygital-Marketing-in-Healthcare

Osipov, V. S., & Skryl, T. V. (2021). Impact of digital technologies on the efficiency of healthcare delivery. In *IoT in healthcare and ambient assisted living* (pp. 243–261). Springer Singapore. DOI: 10.1007/978-981-15-9897-5_12

Ramachander, A., & Gowri, D. P. (2025). The future of digital health in transforming healthcare. In *Digital Technology in Public Health and Rehabilitation Care* (pp. 363–385). Academic Press. DOI: 10.1016/B978-0-443-22270-2.00021-6

Reddy, P., & Sharma, B. (2016). DIGITALISATION: THE FUTURE OF HEALTH CARE. *Journal of Business and Management*, •••, 11.

Schiavone, F., & Ferretti, M. (2021). The FutureS of healthcare. *Futures*, *134*, 102849. DOI: 10.1016/j.futures.2021.102849 PMID: 34584276

Senbekov, M., Saliev, T., Bukeyeva, Z., Almabayeva, A., Zhanaliyeva, M., Aitenova, N., Toishibekov, Y., & Fakhradiyev, I. (2020). The recent progress and applications of digital technologies in healthcare: A review. *International Journal of Telemedicine and Applications*, *2020*(1), 8830200. DOI: 10.1155/2020/8830200 PMID: 33343657

Siddiqi, S., Masud, T. I., Nishtar, S., Peters, D. H., Sabri, B., Bile, K. M., & Jama, M. A. (2009). Framework for assessing governance of the health system in developing countries: Gateway to good governance. *Health Policy (Amsterdam)*, *90*(1), 13–25. DOI: 10.1016/j.healthpol.2008.08.005 PMID: 18838188

Snigdha, E. Z., Jalil, M. S., Dahwal, F. M., Saeed, M., Mehedy, M. T. J., & Hasan, S. K. (2025). Cybersecurity in Healthcare IT Systems: Business Risk Management and Data Privacy Strategies. *The American Journal of Engineering and Technology*, *7*(03), 163–184. DOI: 10.37547/tajet/Volume07Issue03-15

Stoumpos, A. I., Kitsios, F., & Talias, M. A. (2023). Digital transformation in healthcare: Technology acceptance and its applications. *International Journal of Environmental Research and Public Health, 20*(4), 3407. DOI: 10.3390/ijerph20043407 PMID: 36834105

Surabhi, P. K. (2025). Digital transformation in healthcare technology: A technical perspective. *European Journal of Computer Science and Information Technology, 13*(30), 50–66. DOI: 10.37745/ejcsit.2013/vol13n305066

Wang, Q., Su, M., Zhang, M., & Li, R. (2021). Integrating digital technologies and public health to fight Covid-19 pandemic: Key technologies, applications, challenges and outlook of digital healthcare. *International Journal of Environmental Research and Public Health, 18*(11), 6053. DOI: 10.3390/ijerph18116053 PMID: 34199831

Wang, Q., Su, M., Zhang, M., & Li, R. (2021). Integrating digital technologies and public health to fight Covid-19 pandemic: Key technologies, applications, challenges and outlook of digital healthcare. *International Journal of Environmental Research and Public Health, 18*(11), 6053. DOI: 10.3390/ijerph18116053 PMID: 34199831

World Health Organization. (2018). *Digital technologies: Shaping the future of primary health care*.https://www.who.int/docs/default-source/primary-health-care-conference/digital-technologies.pdf

World Health Organization. (2021). *Global strategy on digital health 2020–2025.* WHO Press.

ZDROWIA, T. C. W. O., & MARKETINGOWY, I. J. W. (2023). Digital transformation in health care and its marketing dimension. MARKETING, 49(3), 27-46

Chapter 6
Global Healthcare Reform Trends:
Leadership, Diplomacy, and Governance in the Digital Era

Ranjit Singha
http://orcid.org/0000-0002-3541-8752
Christ University, India

Surjit Singha
http://orcid.org/0000-0002-5730-8677
Kristu Jayanti University, India

Shruti Jose
http://orcid.org/0000-0003-3139-2505
Christ University, India

Alphonsa Diana Haokip
http://orcid.org/0000-0003-2578-0114
Don Bosco College, Maram, India

ABSTRACT

Healthcare reform in the twenty-first century has shifted from a primarily national concern to a complex global governance challenge shaped by digital innovation, economic interdependence, and transnational health risks. The COVID-19 pandemic exposed critical gaps in leadership, coordination, and governance, underscoring the need for integrated and collaborative reform approaches. This chapter examines global healthcare reform trends in the digital era, focusing on the roles of leadership, health diplomacy, and governance in shaping cross-border policy and system transformation. Drawing on global governance, leadership, health diplomacy, and

DOI: 10.4018/979-8-3373-7173-3.ch006

institutional theories, it conceptualizes healthcare reform as a multilevel process. The chapter introduces a phygital healthcare governance framework that integrates physical and digital systems to promote equity, resilience, and sustainable healthcare reform.

1. INTRODUCTION

Healthcare reform has emerged as one of the most pressing global policy challenges of the twenty-first century. Traditionally framed as a domestic responsibility, healthcare governance has increasingly transcended national boundaries due to globalization, demographic transitions, technological innovation, and the growing frequency of cross-border public health emergencies. The expansion of digital health technologies, including telemedicine, artificial intelligence (AI) enabled diagnostics, electronic health records, and mobile health platforms, has further blurred the boundaries between national healthcare systems, enabling new forms of transnational healthcare delivery and policy coordination.

The COVID-19 pandemic represented a critical inflection point in global healthcare reform discourse. It revealed profound inequalities in healthcare access, digital readiness, and governance capacity across countries while simultaneously demonstrating the indispensability of international co-operation in vaccine development, data sharing, and crisis response. Institutions such as the World Health Organization, the United Nations, and regional alliances played a central role in coordinating responses, yet the pandemic also exposed limitations arising from fragmented governance, healthcare nationalism, and uneven leadership capacity (Kickbusch et al., 2020; Gostin et al., 2021).

In this evolving context, healthcare reform cannot be understood solely through national policy lenses. Instead, it must be examined as a multidimensional process shaped by leadership decisions, diplomatic negotiations, and governance arrangements operating at local, national, regional, and global levels. Leadership determines reform vision and execution, diplomacy facilitates cross-border collaboration and resource sharing, and governance structures mediate the balance between innovation, regulation, and equity. These dimensions have become particularly salient in the digital era, where technological advancements simultaneously offer unprecedented opportunities for inclusion and pose new ethical, regulatory, and institutional challenges.

This chapter investigates global healthcare reform trends with a specific focus on leadership, diplomacy, and governance in the digital era. It argues that sustainable reform requires an integrated approach that aligns technological innovation with inclusive governance and ethical leadership. By situating healthcare reform within global governance frameworks and introducing the concept of phygital healthcare governance, the chapter provides a foundation for understanding how healthcare systems can be redesigned to address both local needs and global interdependencies.

2. BACKGROUND

Healthcare systems are deeply embedded in the political, economic, and cultural contexts of societies, evolving in response to national priorities, fiscal capacity, demographic change, and prevailing ideological orientations. Historically, healthcare reforms were conceived mainly as domestic policy initiatives, reflecting country-specific social contracts and institutional arrangements. While some nations developed state-led universal healthcare systems rooted in solidarity and collective responsibility, others adopted market-oriented insurance models emphasizing competition, private provision, and individual choice. These divergent trajectories were shaped by broader political economies, welfare regimes, and societal views on the appropriate role of the state and the market. For much of the twentieth century, healthcare governance remained predominantly nationally bounded, with limited cross-border coordination beyond episodic responses to infectious disease outbreaks or humanitarian crises.

This nationally centered model of healthcare reform has been significantly reshaped by globalization. Intensified cross-border flows of knowledge, capital, technology, labor, and healthcare services have reduced the autonomy of national health systems and exposed them to global norms, benchmarks, and competitive pressures. Medical technologies, pharmaceuticals, health professionals, and patients increasingly operate across borders, while international organizations and transnational networks influence policy agendas and reform pathways. Consequently, contemporary healthcare reforms are rarely designed in isolation; instead, they draw upon international best practices, comparative performance indicators, and policy diffusion processes that circulate reform models across countries. Global frameworks related to universal health coverage, patient safety, and health system resilience now play a central role in shaping national reform debates, reflecting a shift from purely domestic governance toward multilevel and transnational health governance (Buse, Hein, & Drager, 2009).

Gigauri and Djakeli (2021) analyze national health reforms in Georgia from 1994 to 2021, offering a longitudinal assessment of three major reform waves in the post-Soviet period. The authors argue that effective health reform must align with a country's economic capacity, institutional readiness, and socio-historical context. After independence, Georgia inherited a centralized Semashko-style system, but the economic crisis of the 1990s weakened its sustainability. Initial reforms focused on decentralization and social health insurance, though limited institutional capacity constrained outcomes (Gigauri & Djakeli, 2021).

The second wave emphasized privatization and market-oriented restructuring to improve efficiency and service delivery, yet raised concerns about equity and access. The third phase, beginning around 2013, introduced Universal Health Coverage (UHC), expanding financial protection and aligning policy with Sustainable Development Goal 3. This marked a shift toward balancing economic feasibility with social welfare.

A key strength of the article is its long-term policy perspective, highlighting policy learning and institutional adaptation. However, the analysis remains largely descriptive and would benefit from stronger quantitative evidence and comparative regional insights. Overall, the study contributes valuable lessons on aligning economic reform, governance capacity, and health system sustainability in transitional economies.

At the same time, the digitalization of healthcare introduces new governance challenges that complicate reform efforts. Concerns related to data privacy, cybersecurity, algorithmic bias, and the transparency of automated decision-making have become central to debates about digital health. The collection, storage, and use of sensitive health data raise ethical and legal questions about consent, ownership, and surveillance, particularly when data crosses national borders or is managed by private technology firms. Algorithmic systems trained on incomplete or biased data risk reproducing and amplifying existing health inequalities, undermining trust and legitimacy. Moreover, digital health innovations can inadvertently exclude populations lacking reliable internet access, digital literacy, or technological resources, thereby reinforcing rather than alleviating disparities (Topol, 2019; World Health Organization [WHO], 2021). These risks underscore the need for governance frameworks that balance innovation with ethical safeguards and social inclusion.

From a governance perspective, healthcare reform in the digital era unfolds within a complex and increasingly crowded institutional landscape. Public institutions at national and subnational levels remain central to financing, regulating, and delivering healthcare. However, they now operate alongside a diverse array of private technology firms, multinational corporations, international organizations, philanthropic foundations, and civil society actors. Multilateral bodies influence global health agendas through standard-setting, funding priorities, technical guidance, and normative frameworks, while regional organizations facilitate coordination and policy learning. At the same time, national governments retain primary responsibility for implementing reforms, regulating markets, and ensuring accountability to their populations. The challenge lies in aligning these diverse actors and interests within coherent governance structures that promote equity, efficiency, and public trust, rather than fragmentation and regulatory arbitrage.

Leadership plays a decisive role in navigating this complex governance environment. Visionary healthcare leaders must manage uncertainty, foster innovation, and build trust across institutional and national boundaries. In the digital era, leadership extends beyond clinical and administrative competence to include strategic vision, ethical judgment, and the ability to coordinate across sectors such as health, technology, finance, and education. Leaders shape reform trajectories by framing digital health as either a public good or a commercial opportunity, influencing investment decisions, regulatory approaches, and stakeholder engagement. Effective leadership can mobilize collective action, align incentives, and sustain reform momentum, whereas weak or fragmented leadership can lead to piecemeal initiatives and governance failures.

Health diplomacy has also emerged as an essential instrument of healthcare reform in an interconnected world. Shared challenges such as pandemics, antimicrobial resistance, climate-related health risks, and digital health interoperability cannot be effectively addressed by individual states acting alone. Through diplomatic engagement, countries negotiate access to resources, harmonize standards, coordinate emergency responses, and strengthen collective resilience. The COVID-19 pandemic highlighted both the potential and limitations of health diplomacy, revealing the consequences of fragmented co-operation as well as the benefits of coordinated action. In the digital domain, health diplomacy increasingly encompasses negotiations over data sharing, digital standards, intellectual property, and cybersecurity, reflecting the growing entanglement of health policy with broader geopolitical and technological dynamics.

In this context, healthcare reform must be understood as both a technical and political endeavor. Technical solutions, whether digital platforms, clinical innovations, or financing mechanisms, are necessary but insufficient on their own. Without supportive leadership and governance arrangements, such solutions may fail to scale, exacerbate inequalities, or erode public trust. Political considerations, power relations, institutional capacities, and social values shape how reforms are designed, implemented, and experienced. Recognizing healthcare reform as a political process does not diminish the importance of evidence and expertise; instead, it highlights the need to integrate technical knowledge with ethical reasoning, stakeholder engagement, and institutional accountability.

This chapter builds on this understanding by situating global healthcare reform within established theoretical frameworks that illuminate the roles of leadership, diplomacy, and institutions in shaping reform outcomes. By grounding the analysis in these broader contextual dynamics, the chapter provides a foundation for examining how digital transformation interacts with governance structures and for designing phygital healthcare systems that promote equity, resilience, and sustainability in an increasingly interconnected world.

3. THEORETICAL FRAMEWORK

To analyze global healthcare reform in the digital era, this chapter draws on four interrelated theoretical perspectives: global governance theory, leadership theories in healthcare, health diplomacy, and institutional theory. Together, these frameworks provide a comprehensive lens for examining how reforms are conceptualized, negotiated, and implemented across multiple levels of governance.

Global governance theory emphasizes the role of international institutions, norms, and networks in addressing transnational challenges that cannot be effectively managed by individual states alone. In the healthcare domain, global governance structures influence agenda-setting, standard development, financing mechanisms, and crisis coordination (Fidler, 2010). Organizations such as the World Health Organization, the World Bank, and the G20 play pivotal roles in shaping global health priorities and facilitating co-operation among states.

From this perspective, healthcare reform is situated within a multilevel governance system where authority is dispersed across global, regional, national, and local actors. Digitalization further complicates this landscape by introducing private technology firms and transnational data flows as influential governance actors. Global governance theory thus highlights the need for coordinated frameworks that can manage interdependence while respecting national sovereignty and local contexts.

Leadership theories provide insight into how individuals and institutions drive reform processes within complex healthcare systems. Transformational leadership emphasizes vision, innovation, and the ability to inspire collective action, making it particularly relevant for large-scale reforms that require cultural and institutional change (Bass & Riggio, 2006). Distributed leadership, by contrast, recognizes the importance of shared responsibility across professional groups, organizations, and sectors, aligning well with the collaborative nature of digital health ecosystems.

In the global context, healthcare leadership extends beyond organizational boundaries to include political leaders, policy entrepreneurs, and transnational advocates who shape reform agendas. Effective leadership is critical for balancing competing priorities, managing stakeholder interests, and ensuring that technological innovation serves public health goals rather than exacerbating inequalities.

Health diplomacy refers to the processes by which governments, international organizations, and non-state actors negotiate and collaborate on health-related issues that cross national borders. It encompasses formal diplomatic negotiations, multilateral agreements, and informal networks aimed at promoting shared health objectives (Kickbusch et al., 2013). In the digital era, health diplomacy has expanded to include negotiations over data governance, digital standards, and access to technological innovations.

The COVID-19 pandemic underscored the centrality of health diplomacy in managing global crises, particularly in relation to vaccine distribution, intellectual property debates, and information sharing. Health diplomacy thus functions as a form of soft power, enabling states to advance national interests while contributing to global public goods.

Institutional theory examines how formal rules, norms, and organizational structures shape policy outcomes and institutional behavior. In healthcare reform, institutional adaptability and legitimacy are critical determinants of success. Reforms often fail not due to flawed design but because institutions lack the capacity or flexibility to implement change effectively (North, 1990).

Digital transformation places additional demands on institutions, requiring new regulatory frameworks, governance capacities, and ethical oversight mechanisms. Institutional theory highlights the importance of aligning reforms with existing institutional contexts while fostering innovation and learning. It also underscores the risks associated with institutional inertia and path dependency, which can undermine reform efforts in rapidly changing environments.

Together, these theoretical perspectives position global healthcare reform as a dynamic process shaped by leadership agency, diplomatic engagement, and institutional structures within a global governance environment. They provide the conceptual foundation for the subsequent development of a phygital healthcare governance framework that integrates physical and digital dimensions of healthcare delivery.

4. CONCEPTUAL FRAMEWORK:

The accelerating convergence of physical healthcare systems and digital technologies necessitates a fundamental reconceptualization of healthcare governance in the twenty-first century. Governance models that were historically designed for facility-based, nationally bounded healthcare delivery are increasingly inadequate in addressing the complexity, speed, and transnational nature of contemporary digital health ecosystems. The expansion of telemedicine, artificial intelligence–enabled diagnostics, mobile health platforms, cloud-based health information systems, and cross-border data flows has transformed healthcare from a predominantly localized service into a networked, hybrid system that operates simultaneously across physical and digital domains. In response to this structural transformation, this chapter proposes a Global Phygital Healthcare Governance Framework that integrates leadership, health diplomacy, and governance into a coherent analytical and policy-oriented model to guide sustainable healthcare reform in the digital era.

The concept of phygital healthcare refers to the hybrid integration of traditional physical healthcare infrastructure, such as hospitals, clinics, community health centers, and public health systems, with digital platforms, including telemedicine services, AI-driven clinical decision-support tools, mobile health applications, wearable devices, and interoperable electronic health records. Significantly, phygital healthcare goes beyond the mere adoption of technology within existing systems. It signifies a more profound structural shift that reshapes how healthcare is accessed, governed, financed, regulated, and experienced by patients and providers alike. Physical encounters and digital interactions increasingly coexist and complement one another, blurring conventional boundaries between in-person and remote care, public and private provision, and national and transnational health systems. This hybridization challenges policymakers and institutions to rethink governance arrangements that were not designed to manage such interdependence.

At the core of the proposed framework are three interdependent pillars: leadership, health diplomacy, and governance, each of which performs a distinct yet mutually reinforcing role in shaping phygital healthcare systems. The first pillar, leadership, provides the normative and strategic direction necessary for navigating digital transformation. Effective leadership in the phygital context requires articulating a long-term vision that aligns technological innovation with public health values such as equity, accessibility, quality, and resilience. Leaders must exercise ethical judgment in decisions related to data use, automation, and platform governance, recognizing that digital choices can have far-reaching implications for privacy, autonomy, and social trust. Beyond vision-setting, leadership also involves strategic coordination across sectors and institutions, mobilizing resources, and fostering cultures of learning and adaptation within healthcare systems.

The second pillar, health diplomacy, enables cross-border co-operation and collective action in an increasingly interconnected health landscape. As digital health technologies and data flows transcend national borders, many governance challenges ranging from interoperability standards and cybersecurity to pandemic preparedness and intellectual property cannot be effectively addressed by individual states acting alone. Health diplomacy facilitates negotiation, norm-setting, and resource sharing among governments, international organizations, and non-state actors. Within the phygital framework, diplomacy extends beyond traditional concerns of disease control or humanitarian response to encompass digital health governance, including agreements on data sharing, telemedicine regulation, and ethical standards for emerging technologies. By embedding diplomacy as a core pillar, the framework acknowledges that global co-operation is not an optional supplement to healthcare reform but a structural necessity in the digital era.

The third pillar, governance, provides the institutional mechanisms through which leadership vision and diplomatic agreements are translated into operational reality. Governance encompasses regulatory frameworks, accountability structures, oversight mechanisms, and participatory processes that ensure healthcare systems function transparently, inclusively, and resiliently. In phygital healthcare systems, governance must address both physical and digital dimensions, aligning regulations for in-person care with those governing digital platforms and data-driven technologies. This includes establishing standards for quality and safety, ensuring interoperability across systems, protecting patient data, and defining clear lines of responsibility and liability. Robust governance is essential for maintaining public trust, particularly as healthcare becomes increasingly mediated by algorithms and digital infrastructures.

These three pillars operate across multiple and interconnected levels of governance, including global, regional, national, and local domains. At the global level, international institutions, multilateral agreements, and transnational networks play a central role in setting norms, standards, and strategic priorities related to digital health and global health security. National governments are responsible for adapting these norms to domestic legal and institutional contexts, designing policies, and allocating resources for implementation. Subnational authorities, healthcare organizations, and professional bodies operationalize reforms on the ground, translating policy into practice within specific communities and service settings. Meanwhile, digital platforms and private-sector actors increasingly function as transnational intermediaries, connecting patients, providers, and systems across borders. Effective phygital governance depends on coherence and alignment across these levels, as misalignment can lead to regulatory gaps, duplication, and inequitable outcomes.

A defining feature of the Global Phygital Healthcare Governance Framework is its explicit emphasis on equity and inclusivity as foundational principles rather than secondary considerations. Digital transformation carries significant risks of deepening existing disparities related to income, geography, gender, disability, age, and digital literacy. Without deliberate governance interventions, phygital healthcare systems may disproportionately benefit urban, affluent, and technologically literate populations, leaving marginalized groups further behind. The framework, therefore, calls for integrating ethical safeguards, participatory decision-making processes, and social accountability mechanisms at every stage of reform. This includes engaging patients, healthcare workers, civil society organizations, and marginalized communities in policy design and evaluation, as well as monitoring distributional impacts through disaggregated data and transparent reporting.

By embedding equity and inclusivity within its conceptual core, the framework positions digital innovation as a means to advance public health goals rather than as an end in itself. Ethical oversight mechanisms are essential to addressing issues such as algorithmic bias, surveillance risks, and the commercialization of health data. Participatory governance enhances legitimacy and responsiveness, ensuring that reforms reflect lived realities and social values. Social accountability mechanisms such as independent oversight bodies, grievance redress systems, and public reporting further reinforce trust and institutional integrity.

In sum, the Global Phygital Healthcare Governance Framework provides a comprehensive conceptual lens for understanding and guiding healthcare reform in the digital era. By integrating leadership, health diplomacy, and governance across physical and digital domains, and by foregrounding equity and inclusivity as core principles, the framework responds to the complex, multilevel challenges posed by contemporary healthcare transformation. It offers policymakers, healthcare leaders, and scholars a structured approach to navigating digital innovation while safeguarding ethical standards, social justice, and system resilience.

5. GLOBAL HEALTHCARE REFORM TRENDS IN THE DIGITAL ERA

Historically, healthcare reforms have often been reactive, emerging in response to fiscal crises, epidemics, or political pressures. While such reforms have occasionally produced significant improvements, they have also tended to prioritize short-term stabilization over long-term system transformation. In the digital era, there is a growing recognition of the need for proactive, innovation-driven healthcare reform that anticipates future challenges rather than merely responding to crises (OECD, 2020).

The COVID-19 pandemic accelerated this shift by exposing systemic vulnerabilities in healthcare delivery, workforce capacity, and supply chains. Countries with advanced digital infrastructure were able to rapidly deploy telemedicine, digital surveillance, and data analytics, mitigating service disruptions and enhancing pandemic response. Conversely, systems lacking digital readiness experienced exacerbated inequities and governance failures (Keesara, Jonas, & Schulman, 2020).

As a result, contemporary healthcare reform agendas increasingly prioritize digital preparedness, resilience planning, and system integration as core policy objectives rather than auxiliary considerations.

One of the most prominent global healthcare reform trends is the rapid expansion of digital health ecosystems. Telemedicine platforms have transformed healthcare access by reducing geographic barriers and enabling continuity of care, particularly in rural and underserved regions. AI-powered diagnostics and clinical decision-support systems are enhancing diagnostic accuracy, efficiency, and personalization of treatment (Topol, 2019).

Mobile health (mHealth) applications have empowered patients to actively manage chronic conditions, monitor health indicators, and engage with healthcare providers. Meanwhile, interoperable electronic health records are improving care coordination across providers and jurisdictions, although interoperability remains uneven across countries.

International organizations such as the World Health Organization have emphasized the importance of digital health strategies aligned with universal health coverage goals, cautioning that strong governance frameworks must guide digital innovation to prevent fragmentation and inequity (WHO, 2021).

Another significant reform trend involves shifting from volume-based healthcare financing to value-based, patient-centered economic models. Rising healthcare costs, aging populations, and fiscal constraints have compelled governments to seek reforms that enhance efficiency without compromising quality or access.

Digital technologies play a critical role in enabling value-based care by supporting outcome measurement, data-driven decision-making, and preventive interventions. Remote monitoring and predictive analytics allow for early detection of health risks, reducing costly hospitalizations and improving population health outcomes.

However, patient-centered economics also raises governance challenges. Market-driven digital health solutions can exacerbate inequalities if affordability and access are not explicitly addressed through public policy. Effective reform, therefore, requires aligning economic incentives with equity-oriented governance frameworks.

Healthcare reform trends increasingly reflect global policy diffusion, where ideas, models, and best practices circulate across borders. Universal healthcare models in Scandinavian countries, digital health innovations in the United States, and large-scale public health programs in emerging economies have influenced reform debates worldwide.

At the same time, convergence does not imply uniformity. Local contexts, institutional capacities, and cultural values shape how global ideas are adapted and implemented. Successful reform thus depends on balancing global learning with contextual sensitivity, a task that underscores the importance of leadership and governance.

6. LEADERSHIP IN GLOBAL HEALTHCARE REFORM

Healthcare reform in the digital era requires leadership capable of navigating complexity, uncertainty, and rapid technological change. Visionary leaders articulate long-term reform goals, mobilize stakeholders, and foster cultures of innovation within healthcare systems. Transformational leadership is particularly relevant in this context, as it emphasizes shared vision, empowerment, and adaptive change (Bass & Riggio, 2006).

In global healthcare reform, leadership extends beyond individual organizations to encompass political leaders, senior policymakers, and transnational advocates who shape reform agendas. Their decisions influence investment priorities, regulatory frameworks, and international collaboration, directly affecting the pace and direction of reform.

Digital health ecosystems are inherently collaborative, involving clinicians, technologists, policymakers, private firms, and civil society organizations. As such, distributed leadership models are increasingly recognized as essential for effective reform. Distributed leadership emphasizes shared responsibility and collective problem-solving, enabling diverse actors to contribute expertise and innovation.

Public–private partnerships illustrate this dynamic, particularly in areas such as digital infrastructure development, vaccine production, and health data analytics. While such partnerships can accelerate innovation and scale, they also require robust governance mechanisms to manage conflicts of interest and ensure alignment with public health objectives.

Trust is a critical resource in healthcare reform, particularly when digital technologies are involved. Data privacy concerns, algorithmic decision-making, and the commercialization of health data can erode public trust if not addressed transparently. Ethical leadership is therefore central to sustaining legitimacy and public confidence in reform initiatives.

Leaders must balance innovation with precaution, ensuring that technological adoption aligns with ethical principles such as beneficence, justice, and respect for autonomy. Failure to do so can undermine reform efforts and provoke public resistance.

7. HEALTHCARE DIPLOMACY AS A DRIVER OF CHANGE

Health diplomacy has emerged as a critical instrument for managing transnational health challenges. It encompasses formal negotiations, multilateral agreements, and informal networks that facilitate co-operation on issues such as pandemic preparedness, vaccine distribution, and health workforce mobility (Kickbusch et al., 2013).

The digital era has expanded the scope of health diplomacy to include negotiations over digital health standards, cross-border data flows, and intellectual property related to health technologies. These negotiations shape the global governance environment within which national reforms unfold.

The COVID-19 pandemic highlighted both the potential and limitations of health diplomacy. Initiatives aimed at equitable vaccine distribution demonstrated the capacity for global co-operation, yet disparities in access and nationalistic policies revealed persistent governance gaps (Gostin et al., 2021).

Vaccine diplomacy also functioned as a form of soft power, with countries leveraging vaccine production and distribution to strengthen diplomatic ties. While such strategies can enhance global access, they also raise ethical questions regarding equity and geopolitical influence.

Beyond traditional North–South dynamics, South–South co-operation has gained prominence in global healthcare reform. Emerging economies have increasingly shared expertise, technologies, and resources to strengthen primary healthcare systems and digital health capacity in low- and middle-income countries.

Such collaborations underscore the importance of inclusive diplomacy that recognizes diverse sources of innovation and leadership. They also highlight the potential for decentralized, network-based governance models in global health.

8. GOVERNANCE MODELS FOR PHYGITAL HEALTHCARE SYSTEMS

Phygital healthcare systems challenge conventional governance frameworks by operating across physical and virtual spaces. Regulatory systems designed for brick-and-mortar healthcare delivery must adapt to oversee digital platforms, cross-border services, and data-driven decision-making.

Effective governance requires regulatory coherence, ensuring that digital health policies align with existing healthcare regulations while addressing new risks related to cybersecurity, privacy, and algorithmic accountability.

AI applications in healthcare raise profound ethical and governance concerns. Bias in training data, lack of transparency in algorithmic decision-making, and accountability gaps pose risks to patient safety and equity. Governance frameworks must therefore incorporate ethical oversight, explainability requirements, and mechanisms for redress (Floridi et al., 2018).

International coordination is critical in this domain, as AI systems and data flows often transcend national borders. Harmonized standards can reduce regulatory fragmentation and enhance trust.

Inclusive governance is central to the success of phygital healthcare reform. Marginalized populations, including ethnic minorities, rural communities, persons with disabilities, and the elderly, face disproportionate barriers to digital health access. Governance frameworks must explicitly address these disparities through targeted policies, capacity building, and participatory decision-making.

By embedding inclusivity into governance structures, healthcare reforms can leverage digital innovation to advance equity rather than deepen existing divides.

9. COMPARATIVE CASE STUDIES: SUCCESSES AND FAILURES

Comparative analysis provides critical insights into how leadership, diplomacy, and governance shape healthcare reform outcomes across diverse political and economic contexts. This section examines selected cases from Europe, the United States, India, and low- and middle-income regions in Africa, highlighting both successes and structural limitations in the transition toward phygital healthcare systems.

Scandinavian countries are frequently cited as exemplars of universal healthcare systems characterized by strong public financing, high levels of institutional trust, and robust governance. Over the past decade, these systems have increasingly integrated digital health technologies, including nationwide electronic health records, teleconsultation platforms, and digital prescription services.

The success of Scandinavian reforms lies in alignment between leadership vision and institutional capacity. Political leaders framed digital health as a public good rather than a market commodity, ensuring that digital services complemented, not replaced, physical healthcare infrastructure. Strong data protection laws and transparent governance mechanisms further reinforced public trust.

However, even in these high-capacity systems, challenges persist. Rural connectivity gaps, workforce adaptation, and the ethical governance of AI remain ongoing concerns. These limitations underscore that even successful models require continuous governance adaptation in the digital era (OECD, 2020).

The United States represents a contrasting case characterized by exceptional technological innovation alongside fragmented healthcare governance. The U.S. has been a global leader in digital health startups, AI-driven diagnostics, and the expansion of telemedicine, particularly during the COVID-19 pandemic.

Leadership within the private sector has driven rapid innovation, while public leadership has focused on regulatory flexibility and emergency authorization mechanisms. Telehealth adoption surged as reimbursement rules were temporarily relaxed, demonstrating the system's capacity for rapid transformation under crisis conditions (Keesara et al., 2020).

However, the absence of universal healthcare coverage and coherent governance frameworks has limited the equity impact of these innovations. Digital health services remain unevenly accessible, often reinforcing socioeconomic disparities. The U.S. case illustrates how technological leadership without inclusive governance can undermine reform objectives, emphasizing the need for stronger public stewardship in phygital healthcare systems.

India provides a distinctive example of healthcare reform driven by scale, affordability, and digital public infrastructure. Large-scale digital initiatives have sought to integrate healthcare delivery across diverse regions and populations, leveraging digital identification systems, telemedicine networks, and centralized health data platforms.

Leadership at the national level has emphasized cost-effective innovation and population-wide reach, positioning digital health as a tool for expanding access rather than enhancing elite services. During the COVID-19 pandemic, India emerged as a major vaccine producer, demonstrating the role of health diplomacy and South–South co-operation in global healthcare reform.

Nevertheless, governance challenges remain significant. Digital literacy gaps, uneven state-level capacity, and concerns about data governance and privacy highlight the risks of rapid digitalization without corresponding institutional safeguards. India's experience illustrates both the transformative potential and governance vulnerabilities of phygital healthcare reform in emerging economies.

Across many African countries, healthcare reform has unfolded amid constrained resources, fragile institutions, and high disease burdens. Despite these challenges, digital health innovations, particularly mobile health platforms, have played a critical role in extending primary healthcare, disease surveillance, and maternal health services.

International partnerships and donor-supported programs have facilitated technology transfer and capacity building, demonstrating the importance of global co-operation. However, dependence on external funding and fragmented governance structures has limited sustainability and scalability.

These cases highlight the importance of institutional strengthening and local leadership in ensuring that digital health innovations translate into durable healthcare reform rather than short-term pilot projects.

10. PROPOSED FRAMEWORK FOR GLOBAL PHYGITAL HEALTHCARE GOVERNANCE

Building on the comparative analysis of global healthcare reforms, this chapter advances a refined Global Phygital Healthcare Governance Framework designed to guide sustainable, equitable, and resilient healthcare transformation in the digital era. The framework responds to a critical reality: healthcare systems worldwide are no longer operating exclusively within physical infrastructures nor entirely within digital domains, but within an increasingly hybrid phygital space where clinical encounters, data flows, governance decisions, and ethical dilemmas transcend traditional institutional and territorial boundaries. As such, governance frameworks rooted solely in legacy healthcare models or purely technology-driven logics are insufficient. What is required instead is an integrated governance architecture that aligns leadership, diplomacy, regulation, and ethics across multiple levels and sectors, ensuring that digital innovation strengthens rather than fragments healthcare systems.

At the core of the proposed framework are five interrelated dimensions that together form a coherent governance ecosystem. The first dimension, visionary and ethical leadership, constitutes the normative and strategic foundation of phygital healthcare governance. Leadership in this context extends beyond administrative competence or technological enthusiasm; it requires the ability to articulate long-term reform goals grounded in equity, social justice, resilience, and public trust. Visionary leaders frame digital health not as an end in itself, but as a means to advance universal health coverage, patient dignity, and system sustainability. Ethical leadership is particularly crucial in governing digital health technologies, where decisions about data ownership, algorithmic use, automation, and platform governance carry profound implications for privacy, autonomy, and distributive justice. Without ethical anchoring, digital transformation risks becoming extractive, exclusionary, or commercially dominated. Effective leaders, therefore, act as custodians of public interest, balancing innovation with responsibility, speed with deliberation, and efficiency with compassion.

The second dimension, multilevel governance alignment, recognizes that phygital healthcare systems operate simultaneously at global, national, subnational, and local levels. Effective reform requires coordination and coherence across these layers of governance, each with distinct authority, capacity, and legitimacy. Global institutions and transnational networks play a critical role in norm-setting, standard development, and knowledge exchange, particularly in areas such as digital interoperability, data protection principles, and pandemic preparedness. However, global norms cannot be applied mechanically; they must be adaptable to national legal frameworks, cultural contexts, and institutional capacities. At the same time, local innovations often emerging from community health systems, regional pilots, or grassroots digital initiatives should inform global learning and policy diffusion. The framework, therefore, emphasizes bidirectional governance flows, in which global guidance informs national action and local experience informs global reform agendas. Misalignment across governance levels, by contrast, can lead to regulatory fragmentation, duplication of effort, and erosion of accountability.

The third dimension, health diplomacy and international co-operation, reflects the inherently transnational nature of contemporary health challenges. Pandemics, antimicrobial resistance, digital health standards, health workforce mobility, and cross-border data flows cannot be effectively managed by individual states acting in isolation. Health diplomacy provides the mechanisms through which governments, international organizations, and non-state actors negotiate shared solutions, mobilize resources, and manage interdependence. In the context of phygital healthcare, diplomacy extends beyond traditional concerns such as disease control or humanitarian assistance to encompass negotiations over digital standards, cybersecurity norms, intellectual property, and platform governance. Effective health diplomacy enables standard harmonization, reduces regulatory fragmentation, and supports collective crisis response, while also serving as a form of soft power that can strengthen international trust and co-operation. Notably, the framework stresses that health diplomacy must be inclusive and equity-oriented, avoiding power asymmetries that marginalize low- and middle-income countries or impose externally driven digital solutions without adequate local participation.

The fourth dimension, digital–physical integration, addresses one of the most persistent governance challenges in contemporary healthcare reform: the tendency to treat digital health as separate from, or superior to, physical healthcare systems. The proposed framework rejects this dichotomy, instead positioning digital health as an extension and augmentation of physical healthcare infrastructure. Governance frameworks must therefore ensure interoperability between digital platforms and existing health systems, continuity of care across physical and virtual encounters, and regulatory coherence across service modalities. This includes aligning licensing regimes, reimbursement mechanisms, quality standards, and liability frameworks so that patients experience seamless care regardless of delivery mode. Failure to integrate digital and physical governance can result in parallel systems, fragmented accountability, and uneven service quality. By contrast, integrated governance supports system resilience, workforce adaptation, and patient-centered care pathways.

The fifth dimension, equity-centered design and accountability, serves as the moral and operational anchor of the entire framework. Digital transformation carries a real risk of exacerbating existing health inequalities related to income, geography, gender, disability, age, and digital literacy. Without deliberate governance interventions, phygital healthcare systems may disproportionately benefit urban, affluent, and technologically literate populations while excluding vulnerable groups. The framework, therefore, embeds equity as a core governance principle rather than a peripheral concern. This entails designing digital health solutions with inclusivity in mind, investing in digital infrastructure and literacy, and establishing accountability mechanisms that monitor distributional impacts. Participatory decision-making processes, involving patients, healthcare workers, civil society organizations, and marginalized communities, are essential to ensuring that reforms reflect lived realities rather than abstract technological ideals. Continuous evaluation and transparent reporting further reinforce accountability, enabling course correction and policy learning.

A defining characteristic of the Global Phygital Healthcare Governance Framework is its emphasis on adaptive governance. Rapid technological change, evolving health risks, and shifting geopolitical dynamics render static regulatory models increasingly obsolete. Governance systems that rely solely on rigid rules or one-time policy interventions struggle to keep pace with innovation, often responding too slowly or overcorrecting in ways that stifle beneficial experimentation. Conversely, overly permissive governance approaches may compromise patient safety, data protection, and public trust. Adaptive governance offers a middle path by emphasizing learning, iteration, and recalibration. It enables policymakers and institutions to experiment within clearly defined ethical and regulatory boundaries, evaluate outcomes in real time, and adjust policies in response to evidence and stakeholder feedback. This approach is particularly well-suited to digital health, where pilot projects, sandbox regulations, and phased implementation can generate insights while managing risk.

Adaptive governance also reinforces institutional resilience. By fostering feedback loops, cross-sector collaboration, and continuous capacity building, governance systems become better equipped to respond to shocks such as pandemics, cyber threats, or technological disruptions. Importantly, adaptive governance does not imply regulatory weakness; instead, it requires strong institutions capable of monitoring, enforcement, and ethical oversight, combined with the humility to revise assumptions and learn from failure. In this sense, adaptive governance aligns innovation with precaution, creativity with accountability, and flexibility with public trust.

Taken together, the proposed Global Phygital Healthcare Governance Framework provides a comprehensive and integrative roadmap for healthcare reform in the digital era. It recognizes that sustainable reform cannot be achieved through technology alone, nor through isolated national policies divorced from global realities. Instead, it requires the deliberate alignment of leadership vision, diplomatic engagement, multilevel governance, system integration, and equity-centered accountability within an adaptive institutional architecture. By operationalizing these principles, policymakers and healthcare leaders can harness the transformative potential of digital innovation while safeguarding ethical standards, social inclusion, and long-term system sustainability.

11. POLICY IMPLICATIONS AND STRATEGIC RECOMMENDATIONS

The Global Phygital Healthcare Governance Framework advanced in this chapter yields several critical policy implications and strategic recommendations for governments, international organizations, and healthcare leaders seeking to navigate the complexities of healthcare reform in the digital era. Foremost among these is the imperative to invest systematically in leadership development within healthcare systems. Digital transformation has expanded the scope of healthcare leadership beyond traditional clinical and administrative competencies, demanding proficiency in digital governance, ethical decision-making, and cross-sector collaboration. Policymakers should therefore support leadership training programs that integrate systems thinking, data literacy, and awareness of global health governance alongside clinical expertise. Such programs can cultivate leaders capable of aligning technological innovation with public health goals, managing institutional change, and engaging constructively with diverse stakeholders at national and international levels.

A second strategic priority involves institutionalizing health diplomacy as a core function of both health and foreign policy. Rather than treating diplomatic engagement as a temporary or reactive response to crises, governments should establish dedicated structures and mandates for sustained health diplomacy. This includes creating specialized units within ministries, strengthening interministerial coordination, and investing in diplomatic capacity related to digital health standards, health workforce mobility, and pandemic preparedness. Institutionalized health diplomacy can enhance global co-operation, reduce regulatory fragmentation, and enable more equitable access to health technologies by fostering trust, shared norms, and long-term partnerships.

Third, policymakers must assume a more active role in governing digital health markets. While private-sector innovation has been instrumental in advancing digital health technologies, unregulated or weakly regulated markets risk monopolization, data exploitation, and exclusion of vulnerable populations. Regulatory frameworks should therefore promote fair competition, interoperability, and transparency, ensuring that digital health solutions serve public-interest objectives rather than narrow commercial agendas. This includes establishing clear rules on data ownership and use, enforcing standards for algorithmic accountability, and aligning reimbursement and procurement policies with equity and quality goals. Public stewardship is essential to balancing innovation with social responsibility.

Finally, addressing the digital divide must be treated as a central component of healthcare reform rather than a peripheral concern. Bridging digital access disparities requires targeted investments in infrastructure, connectivity, and digital literacy, particularly in rural and underserved communities. Inclusive design principles should guide the development of digital health solutions, ensuring accessibility for populations with diverse linguistic, cultural, and physical needs. Without such measures, digital health reforms risk reinforcing existing health inequities and undermining public trust. By integrating equity considerations into policy design and implementation, governments and institutions can harness digital transformation as a force for inclusion, resilience, and sustainable healthcare reform.

12. SOLUTIONS AND IMPLEMENTATION PATHWAYS

Translating the proposed Global Phygital Healthcare Governance Framework into practice requires implementation strategies that are context-sensitive, adaptive, and grounded in institutional realities rather than idealized policy assumptions. Healthcare systems differ widely in terms of infrastructure capacity, regulatory maturity, workforce readiness, and sociocultural contexts, making uniform reform models both impractical and counterproductive. Effective implementation must therefore balance strategic coherence with contextual flexibility, ensuring that digital innovation enhances existing healthcare systems rather than overwhelming or displacing them. At the core of successful implementation lies the recognition that phygital healthcare reform is not a single event but a long-term, iterative transformation process requiring sustained leadership, stakeholder engagement, and institutional learning.

A foundational implementation pathway involves adopting phased reform strategies. Rather than pursuing large-scale, system-wide digital transformation in a single step, healthcare systems should pilot digital innovations in controlled, clearly defined environments before scaling. Phased implementation allows policymakers and healthcare leaders to test technologies, governance mechanisms, and service delivery models under real-world conditions while limiting systemic risk. Pilot projects and regulatory sandboxes provide valuable opportunities to assess technical feasibility, ethical implications, cost-effectiveness, and user experience. They also enable institutions to identify unintended consequences such as workflow disruptions, data security vulnerabilities, or inequitable access before these issues become entrenched at scale. Importantly, phased approaches support evidence-based decision-making, allowing reform trajectories to be adjusted in response to empirical findings rather than political or commercial pressures.

Equally critical to implementation success is the establishment of inclusive and participatory governance processes. Phygital healthcare reform affects a wide range of stakeholders, including patients, healthcare professionals, administrators, technologists, policymakers, and civil society organizations. Excluding any of these groups from decision-making risks generating resistance, mistrust, or policy misalignment. Participatory governance mechanisms such as stakeholder consultations, co-design workshops, citizen panels, and professional advisory committees enhance the legitimacy and social acceptance of reform initiatives. For patients and communities, participation ensures that digital health solutions reflect lived experiences, cultural norms, and practical needs rather than abstract technological ideals. For healthcare workers, inclusive processes foster professional ownership, reduce resistance to change, and surface frontline insights that are often overlooked in top-down reforms. Engaging technologists and private-sector actors within transparent governance frameworks further ensures that innovation aligns with public health objectives and ethical standards.

Implementation pathways must also address the human and institutional dimensions of digital transformation. Workforce readiness is a decisive factor in determining whether phygital reforms succeed or fail. Healthcare professionals require not only technical training in the use of digital tools but also support in adapting clinical workflows, ethical reasoning, and patient communication practices to hybrid care environments. Continuous professional development programs, interdisciplinary training, and leadership capacity building are therefore essential components of implementation. At the institutional level, reforms must strengthen administrative and regulatory capacities to effectively oversee digital health systems. This includes developing competencies in data governance, cybersecurity, procurement, and performance evaluation. Without such institutional investments, digital reforms risk outpacing governance capacity, leading to accountability gaps and public distrust.

Another central implementation pathway involves the creation of robust monitoring and evaluation (M&E) systems. Continuous assessment is essential for understanding whether phygital healthcare reforms achieve their intended outcomes and for identifying unintended or adverse effects. Traditional evaluation models, often based on retrospective analysis, are insufficient for rapidly evolving digital environments. Instead, implementation strategies should incorporate real-time and adaptive evaluation mechanisms that track performance indicators, equity impacts, user satisfaction, and system resilience. Digital tools themselves can support this process by enabling automated data collection, dashboard-based reporting, and predictive analytics. When embedded within governance structures, such tools facilitate timely policy learning and evidence-informed adjustments. Transparency in evaluation findings further enhances accountability, enabling stakeholders to scrutinize reform outcomes and meaningfully participate in course correction.

Implementation pathways must also explicitly confront the digital divide as a structural barrier to equitable reform. Access to digital infrastructure, reliable connectivity, and digital literacy varies widely across and within countries. Without targeted interventions, phased digital reforms may inadvertently privilege already advantaged populations, undermining the equity objectives of healthcare transformation. Solutions include investing in digital infrastructure in underserved areas, integrating digital literacy initiatives into public health programs, and designing low-bandwidth or offline-compatible technologies. Equity-focused implementation also requires disaggregated data collection to monitor how different demographic groups experience reform outcomes. By embedding equity considerations into implementation metrics, policymakers can ensure that phygital healthcare advances inclusivity rather than deepening disparities.

Intersectoral and cross-border collaboration further strengthens implementation pathways. Phygital healthcare reform intersects with sectors such as telecommunications, education, data protection, and labor regulation, necessitating coordinated policy action beyond the health ministry alone. Interministerial coordination mechanisms and cross-sector task forces can help align regulatory frameworks, investment priorities, and standards. At the international level, collaboration enables knowledge exchange, capacity building, and harmonization of digital health standards. Such co-operation is particularly valuable for low- and middle-income countries seeking to avoid fragmented or externally imposed digital solutions. Implementation strategies grounded in partnership and mutual learning enhance sustainability and local ownership.

Finally, successful implementation requires political commitment and long-term financing. Phygital healthcare reform often entails upfront investments in infrastructure, training, and governance capacity, with benefits accruing over time. Short-term political cycles and fiscal pressures can undermine reform continuity if digital initiatives are treated as discretionary or experimental rather than as core components of health system strengthening. Embedding phygital reform goals within national health strategies, legal frameworks, and budgetary processes enhances durability and policy coherence. Long-term financing mechanisms, including public investment, strategic partnerships, and outcome-based funding models, can support sustained implementation while maintaining public oversight.

In sum, solutions and implementation pathways for phygital healthcare governance must be iterative, inclusive, and evidence-driven. Phased implementation enables learning and risk management; participatory governance builds legitimacy and trust; workforce and institutional capacity development ensures operational readiness; and robust monitoring and evaluation support accountability and adaptation. When aligned with equity-focused policies, intersectoral collaboration, and sustained political commitment, these pathways translate the proposed governance framework from conceptual ambition into practical, system-wide reform. Such an approach not only enhances the likelihood of successful digital transformation but also reinforces the fundamental objective of healthcare reform in the digital era: delivering accessible, ethical, and resilient healthcare for all.

13. FUTURE RESEARCH DIRECTIONS

While this chapter has offered a comprehensive conceptual and comparative examination of global healthcare reform in the digital era, it also reveals the extent to which the field remains emergent and intellectually open. The accelerating integration of digital technologies into healthcare systems has outpaced the development of robust empirical, ethical, and governance-oriented scholarship, creating substantial opportunities for future research. One of the most pressing gaps concerns the empirical validation of phygital healthcare governance models. Although hybrid physical–digital systems are increasingly adopted across diverse health systems, systematic evidence regarding their long-term effectiveness, sustainability, and equity impacts remains limited. Future research should therefore prioritize longitudinal and mixed-method studies that examine how phygital governance arrangements function in real-world settings, particularly in low- and middle-income countries (LMICs), where institutional constraints, resource limitations, and sociocultural diversity pose distinct challenges. Such studies should assess not only clinical outcomes but also cost efficiency, system resilience, patient experience, and distributional effects across different population groups. By grounding theoretical frameworks in empirical evidence, scholars can contribute to more context-sensitive and actionable reform strategies.

Closely related to this empirical gap is the need for deeper inquiry into digital ethics and algorithmic governance within healthcare systems. As artificial intelligence and data-driven technologies increasingly shape clinical decision-making, diagnostics, triage, and resource allocation, they introduce new ethical dilemmas that extend beyond traditional bioethics. Issues such as algorithmic bias, lack of transparency, accountability for automated decisions, and the ethical use of patient data demand interdisciplinary research that draws on health policy, computer science, law, ethics, and the social sciences. Future studies should explore how different governance models address these challenges, comparing regulatory approaches across jurisdictions to identify best practices and unintended consequences. Research on explainability standards, audit mechanisms, and participatory oversight models would be particularly valuable in informing policies that balance innovation with patient safety and public trust. Moreover, examining how ethical principles are operationalized or neglected in everyday clinical and administrative contexts can illuminate the gap between formal regulation and lived practice.

Another underexplored area concerns health diplomacy in the digital domain. While global health scholarship has increasingly acknowledged the role of diplomacy in managing pandemics and vaccine distribution, far less attention has been paid to diplomatic negotiations surrounding digital health governance. Future research should examine how states and international organizations negotiate issues such as cross-border data sharing, interoperability standards, cybersecurity norms, and intellectual property related to digital health technologies. These negotiations are shaped by power asymmetries, geopolitical competition, and competing visions of digital sovereignty, all of which influence whose interests are prioritized in global health governance. Comparative studies could shed light on how different diplomatic strategies affect access to technology, capacity building, and equity in global health outcomes. Understanding the diplomatic dimensions of digital health is particularly important as healthcare becomes increasingly intertwined with broader debates about data governance, national security, and technological leadership.

Leadership development for digital-era healthcare systems represents another critical avenue for future research. As healthcare organizations undergo digital transformation, leadership competencies must evolve to encompass not only clinical and managerial expertise but also technological literacy, ethical reasoning, and global governance awareness. Future studies should explore how leaders at different levels, policy, organizational, and frontline navigate the complexities of phygital systems, including managing interdisciplinary teams, fostering innovation while maintaining accountability, and engaging with diverse stakeholders. Research on leadership education and training models can provide insights into how curricula and professional development programs can integrate digital competencies with values-based leadership. Such work is essential for preparing healthcare leaders who can guide reform processes in uncertain and rapidly changing environments.

Finally, scholars must critically engage with the phenomenon of digital colonialism in healthcare, a growing concern as digital technologies, platforms, and standards are increasingly exported from high-income countries to less-resourced settings. Digital colonialism refers to the imposition of technological solutions without adequate adaptation to local contexts, often reinforcing dependency, undermining local capacity, and marginalizing indigenous knowledge systems. Future research should examine how power relations shape the design, deployment, and governance of digital health technologies, paying particular attention to whose voices are included or excluded in decision-making processes. Critical and decolonial perspectives can illuminate alternative pathways for digital health reform that prioritize local ownership, cultural sensitivity, and reciprocal knowledge exchange. By interrogating the political economy of digital health, scholars can contribute to more equitable and sustainable reform models that respect diversity and promote global solidarity.

In sum, future research on global healthcare reform in the digital era must move beyond descriptive accounts of technological adoption to engage deeply with questions of governance, ethics, diplomacy, leadership, and power. Interdisciplinary, comparative, and context-sensitive scholarship will be essential for advancing theoretical understanding and informing practical reform strategies. By addressing these research gaps, scholars can help ensure that the ongoing digital transformation of healthcare contributes not only to efficiency and innovation but also to equity, accountability, and the broader goals of human well-being.

14. DISCUSSION

The analysis presented in this chapter underscores a fundamental and often underappreciated insight: healthcare reform in the digital era is not primarily a technological challenge but a governance challenge that unfolds at the intersection of leadership, diplomacy, institutional capacity, and ethical responsibility. While digital tools such as telemedicine platforms, artificial intelligence–enabled diagnostics, and interoperable health information systems offer unprecedented opportunities to expand access, efficiency, and personalization of care, their real-world impact is shaped by the decisions of leaders, the quality of governance arrangements, and the broader political and diplomatic environments in which they are embedded. Technology, in this sense, is not a neutral force; it amplifies existing institutional strengths and weaknesses. Where governance is inclusive, adaptive, and ethically grounded, digital innovation can strengthen healthcare systems. Where governance is fragmented, exclusionary, or driven by narrow interests, the same technologies can exacerbate inequalities and erode public trust.

A central tension revealed through global experiences is the growing risk of healthcare nationalism, particularly during periods of crisis. The COVID-19 pandemic vividly illustrated how states, under conditions of uncertainty and political pressure, often revert to inward-looking strategies that restrict data sharing, hoard medical supplies, limit vaccine exports, or prioritize domestic populations without regard for global consequences. While such actions may be politically expedient in the short term, they undermine global solidarity and weaken collective resilience. Pandemics, by their very nature, do not respect national borders, and fragmented responses delay containment, increase human and economic costs, and deepen global inequalities. The pandemic demonstrated that no country can achieve health security in isolation, reinforcing the need for cooperative governance frameworks that enable timely information exchange, coordinated supply chains, and equitable access to life-saving technologies. In the digital era, this imperative extends beyond physical resources to include data governance, digital surveillance standards, and cross-border health information systems.

Closely related to healthcare nationalism is the challenge of power asymmetry in global health governance, particularly as digital technologies become central to healthcare reform. Countries with advanced technological capacity and strong market actors often exert disproportionate influence over digital health standards, platforms, and intellectual property regimes. These dynamic risks marginalize low- and middle-income countries, whose health systems may become dependent on externally developed technologies that are poorly aligned with local needs or institutional capacities. Without inclusive diplomacy and equitable governance mechanisms, digital transformation can reproduce patterns of dependency and exclusion, a phenomenon increasingly described as digital colonialism. Addressing this challenge requires a deliberate shift toward cooperative norm-setting, capacity building, and mutual learning, ensuring that digital health governance reflects diverse perspectives and contexts rather than a narrow set of technological or commercial interests.

Another critical issue highlighted in the discussion is the commodification of digital health. Market-driven innovation has undeniably accelerated technological development, particularly in high-income countries, producing sophisticated platforms, analytics tools, and consumer-facing applications. However, the dominance of market logics in digital health has also created significant governance gaps related to affordability, access, accountability, and data ownership. When digital health is treated primarily as a commercial product rather than a public good, access tends to follow ability to pay rather than health need. This dynamic risk transforms healthcare into a two-tier system in which digitally enhanced services are available to affluent populations, while marginalized groups remain reliant on under-resourced physical infrastructure. Moreover, the commercialization of health data raises profound ethical concerns regarding consent, surveillance, and the monetization of personal information. Without strong public stewardship and regulatory oversight, digital health innovation can undermine the very principles of equity and solidarity that underpin sustainable healthcare systems.

The concept of phygital healthcare governance offers a way to navigate these tensions by reframing digital transformation as an integration rather than a substitution. Rather than positioning digital health as a replacement for physical healthcare systems, the phygital approach emphasizes complementarity and continuity. Digital tools should enhance the reach, efficiency, and quality of physical healthcare services, not displace them or create parallel systems with fragmented accountability. This perspective has important governance implications. It calls for regulatory frameworks that prioritize interoperability between digital platforms and existing health infrastructure, ensuring seamless patient journeys across physical and virtual care settings. It also underscores the need for ethical oversight mechanisms that address algorithmic bias, data protection, and transparency, recognizing that digital decisions can have life-altering consequences for patients. Inclusive design principles are equally critical, ensuring that digital solutions are accessible to diverse populations and responsive to varied cultural, linguistic, and socioeconomic contexts.

The discussion further reinforces the argument that leadership and diplomacy are not peripheral or auxiliary components of healthcare reform but constitutive elements of transformation. Visionary leadership shapes reform trajectories by articulating shared goals, mobilizing resources, and fostering institutional cultures that are open to innovation and learning. In the absence of such leadership, digital reforms often become fragmented pilot projects or technocratic exercises disconnected from broader health system goals. Ethical leadership is critical in the digital era, where decisions about data use, automation, and platform governance involve trade-offs between efficiency, privacy, and equity. Leaders who prioritize transparency, accountability, and public engagement are better positioned to sustain trust and legitimacy amid rapid technological change.

Health diplomacy, in turn, enables the coordination necessary to address transnational health challenges that no single actor can manage alone. Through diplomatic engagement, states negotiate shared standards, coordinate crisis responses, and mobilize collective resources. In the digital domain, diplomacy plays an increasingly important role in shaping norms for data governance, cybersecurity, and digital interoperability. Effective diplomacy can mitigate the risks of fragmentation and competition, fostering a governance environment conducive to co-operation and shared learning. Conversely, the absence of diplomatic coordination can lead to regulatory divergence, duplication of effort, and weakened global preparedness.

Finally, governance structures provide the institutional scaffolding that translates leadership vision and diplomatic co-operation into sustainable outcomes. Institutions mediate between abstract policy goals and concrete implementation, shaping how reforms are operationalized, monitored, and adjusted over time. Adaptive governance models, as emphasized throughout the chapter, are particularly well suited to the digital era, enabling institutions to respond to uncertainty and complexity without sacrificing accountability or ethical standards. Such models recognize that healthcare reform is an ongoing process rather than a fixed endpoint, requiring continuous evaluation, stakeholder engagement, and policy learning.

In sum, the discussion affirms that the future of healthcare reform in the digital era depends less on technological sophistication than on the quality of governance that surrounds it. Digital tools can either amplify inequality and fragmentation or support equity and resilience, depending on how they are governed. By foregrounding leadership, diplomacy, and adaptive governance, the phygital healthcare framework outlined in this chapter provides a pathway for navigating these choices and aligning digital innovation with the fundamental values of public health and human well-being.

15. CONCLUSION

Healthcare reform is no longer a purely national endeavor confined within territorial boundaries. In the twenty-first century, it has emerged as a global imperative, shaped by digital transformation, economic interdependence, and shared public health risks. This chapter has examined global healthcare reform trends through the interconnected lenses of leadership, diplomacy, and governance, arguing that sustainable reform in the digital era requires an integrated and ethically grounded approach.

Drawing on global governance theory, leadership theories, health diplomacy, and institutional theory, the chapter conceptualizes healthcare reform as a multilevel and multisectoral process. The proposed Global Phygital Healthcare Governance Framework offers a roadmap for integrating physical and digital healthcare systems while prioritizing equity, resilience, and accountability.

Comparative case studies illustrate that technological innovation alone is insufficient to achieve reform goals. Success depends on visionary and ethical leadership, inclusive governance structures, and effective diplomatic engagement. Conversely, failures often stem from fragmented governance, institutional inertia, and the neglect of social and ethical considerations.

As healthcare systems continue to evolve in response to digital innovation and global challenges, policymakers, healthcare leaders, and scholars must move beyond narrow technological determinism. The future of healthcare reform lies in governing innovation wisely, fostering co-operation across borders, and ensuring that digital transformation serves humanity's collective well-being rather than narrow economic or political interests.

REFERENCES

Bass, B. M., & Riggio, R. E. (2006). *Transformational leadership* (2nd ed.). Lawrence Erlbaum Associates., https://www.taylorfrancis.com/books/mono/10.4324/9781410617095/transformational-leadership-bernard-bass-bruce-riggio DOI: 10.4324/9781410617095

Buse, K., Hein, W., & Drager, N. (2009). *Making sense of global health governance*. Palgrave Macmillan.https://link.springer.com/book/9780230209923

Fidler, D. P. (2010). *The challenges of global health governance* (Working paper). Council on Foreign Relations. https://www.cfr.org/report/challenges-global-health-governance

Floridi, L., Cowls, J., Beltrametti, M., Chatila, R., Chazerand, P., Dignum, V., & Vayena, E. (2018). AI4People: An ethical framework for a good AI society. *Minds and Machines*, *28*(4), 689–707. DOI: 10.1007/s11023-018-9482-5 PMID: 30930541

Gigauri, I., & Djakeli, K. (2021). *National Health Reforms in Georgia during 1994–2021 and their Success*. HOLISTICA Journal of Business and Public Administration, 12(2), 102–108. https://reference-global.com/download/article/10.2478/hjbpa-2021-0017.pdf

Gostin, L. O., Moon, S., & Meier, B. M. (2021). Reimagining global health governance in the age of COVID-19. *American Journal of Public Health*, *111*(9), 1615–1619. DOI: 10.2105/AJPH.2020.305933 PMID: 33026872

Keesara, S., Jonas, A., & Schulman, K. (2020). COVID-19 and healthcare's digital revolution. *The New England Journal of Medicine*, *382*(23), e82. DOI: 10.1056/NEJMp2005835 PMID: 32240581

Kickbusch, I., Leung, G. M., Bhutta, Z. A., Matsoso, M. P., Ihekweazu, C., & Abbasi, K. (2020). COVID-19: How a virus is turning the world upside down. *BMJ (Clinical Research Ed.)*, *369*, m1336. DOI: 10.1136/bmj.m1336 PMID: 32245802

Kickbusch, I., Silberschmidt, G., & Buss, P. (2013). Global health diplomacy: The need for new perspectives, strategic approaches, and skills in global health. *Bulletin of the World Health Organization*, *91*(3), 159–159A. DOI: 10.2471/BLT.13.118596 PMID: 23476084

North, D. C. (1990). *Institutions, institutional change, and economic performance*. Cambridge University Press., https://www.cambridge.org/9780521397346 DOI: 10.1017/CBO9780511808678

Organisation for Economic Co-operation and Development. (2020). *Health in the 21st century: Putting data to work for stronger health systems*. OECD Publishing. DOI: 10.1787/e3b23f8e-en

Topol, E. (2019). *Deep medicine: How artificial intelligence can make healthcare human again*—basic Books. https://www.basicbooks.com/titles/eric-topol/deep-medicine/9781541644632/

World Health Organization. (2021). *Global strategy on digital health 2020–2025*. World Health Organization. https://www.who.int/publications/i/item/9789240020924

KEY TERMS AND DEFINITIONS

Digital Health Ecosystems: Integrated networks of digital technologies, stakeholders, data infrastructures, and governance mechanisms that collectively support healthcare delivery, decision-making, innovation, and system-wide coordination across physical and virtual environments.

Global Healthcare Reform: Systematic efforts to improve healthcare access, quality, equity, and sustainability across nations, shaped by global interdependence, shared health challenges, international norms, and transnational policy coordination.

Governance Models: Structured frameworks of rules, institutions, and decision-making processes that guide how healthcare systems are regulated, coordinated, and held accountable at local, national, and global levels.

Health Diplomacy: The use of diplomatic negotiation, co-operation, and policy dialogue to address transnational health challenges, harmonize standards, mobilize resources, and advance collective public health interests.

Healthcare Policy and Economics: The study and application of policies and economic principles governing healthcare financing, resource allocation, efficiency, affordability, and the balance between public welfare and market dynamics.

International Health Co-operation: Collaborative actions among countries, international organizations, and stakeholders to address shared health risks, strengthen health systems, and promote equitable access to healthcare resources and technologies.

Leadership in Healthcare: The capacity to guide healthcare systems through vision, ethical decision-making, strategic coordination, and stakeholder engagement to achieve effective, equitable, and sustainable health outcomes.

Phygital Healthcare: A hybrid healthcare model integrating physical healthcare infrastructure with digital technologies to enhance access, continuity of care, system efficiency, and patient-centered service delivery.

Chapter 7
Designing Inclusive and Economically Sustainable Health Reforms in the Digital Era:
A Phygital Approach to Equity, Efficiency, and Engagement

Lawal Olamilekan Abdulwahab
http://orcid.org/0000-0003-4955-244X
School of Business and Economics, Universiti Brunei Darussalam, Brunei

ABSTRACT

The rapid digitization of healthcare brings opportunities and risks for equity, efficiency, and patient engagement. This chapter presents a framework for inclusive and sustainable reforms through a phygital model that integrates physical and digital health systems via the health/behavioral economics, social determinants, institutional theory, and systems thinking. Digital transformation may widen disparities unless equity is prioritized. The framework addresses financing, trust-building, behaviorally informed policy, and digital infrastructure, emphasizing adaptive governance in a dynamic healthcare setting. Behavioral segmentation, nudges, and omnichannel communication are explored to engage marginalized and diverse populations. The chapter also outlines policy and institutional strategies to ensure equitable access, cultural relevance, and resilience while balancing innovation with inclusion. It concludes with a robust four-pillar blueprint that guides accountable, inclusive, and sustainable health reforms in the digital era, providing a comprehensive approach to healthcare reform.

DOI: 10.4018/979-8-3373-7173-3.ch007

1. INTRODUCTION

The 21st century marks a transformative shift in global healthcare, driven by the rapid emergence of 'phygital' technologies that integrate digital and physical tools. This evolution not only advances technology but also reshapes the structure, economy, and institutions of healthcare. Innovations like telemedicine, AI diagnostics, remote monitoring, and integrated electronic systems now form the core of modern care, promising efficiency, real-time data, and a hopeful future for policymakers and researchers (Swan et al., 2023; Vecchio et al., 2023). Their proliferation poses new inequity risks, especially where socioeconomic disparities and digital exclusion intersect. Digital health initiatives may worsen inequalities in healthcare access, outcomes, and affordability without intentional, inclusive reform design.

This underscores the urgent need for action in addressing digital health equity, invoking a sense of responsibility and commitment in policymakers and researchers (Eriksen et al., 2023; Schutte, 2024). Emerging evidence shows that phygital reforms often favor urban, affluent, and tech-savvy groups, while rural, poor, or digitally excluded populations face more marginalization. These patterns are best explained by a framework that shows how phygital innovations intersect differently across socioeconomic groups. Figure 1 below visualizes this dynamic. On one side of the spectrum, urban, affluent, and technologically literate populations are more likely to benefit from digital health innovations due to infrastructure, access, and digital fluency. On the other side, rural, economically disadvantaged, and digitally excluded groups are at risk of being left behind. Phygital technologies, though promising, sit at the intersection capable of bridging or widening this gap depending on how reforms are designed and implemented.

Figure 1. Digital Health Equity Gap Framework

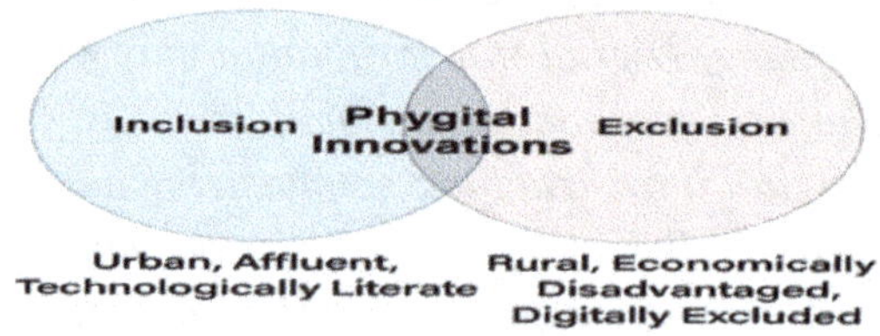

Source: Designed by the Author

This digital divide appears across countries. For example, Iran's study showed that, despite reforms such as the Health Transformation Plan, outpatient care access remained skewed toward the wealthy, indicating that digital innovation alone does not ensure equity (Fan et al., 2024). Researchers note that efforts to integrate digital technologies in England's coastal communities and Denmark's underserved populations are hindered by disparities in digital maturity and health literacy, preventing poorer regions from benefiting from innovations (Richard et al., 2016; Schutte, 2024). These dynamics underscore the need for health reform to be interdisciplinary, equity-focused, and economically grounded. Failing to address economic sustainability and social inclusion increases costs and disparities. Structural reform must be technologically informed, economically strategic, and socially responsive, balancing efficiency with fairness, personalization with universality, and innovation with accountability. This requires insights from health economics, behavioral science, policy leadership, and systems thinking (McGuire et al., 2024; C. Zhang & Wang, 2024). Phygital healthcare transformation holds promise but requires inclusive, equity-focused, and economically strategic reforms to meet the needs of marginalized populations.

This chapter explores how national healthcare systems can design inclusive, sustainable reforms that address modern 'phygital' realities. It argues that reforms must suit diverse economic capacities while preventing digital exclusion. By focusing on real-world use, economic factors, and sociotechnical divides, reformers can create systems that are digitally enabled, equitable, and resilient. It contextualizes this within global digital health trends and case studies from India, Rwanda, Turkey, and Estonia, drawing on models from health economics and systems policy. The approach combines theoretical frameworks in health economics, behavioral economics, and social determinants, along with the WHO's Health Systems Building Blocks, with empirical case analysis and policy comparison, enabling the evaluation of trade-offs and the development of equitable healthcare systems.

The chapter has eight sections that review concepts and theories of phygital healthcare and economic reform, explore economic structures, patient-centered design, digital health equity, and leadership capabilities. It provides policy recommendations, a reform blueprint, insights into future research, and reflections. The ongoing phygital healthcare transformation is not automatic or guaranteed. The chapter offers a roadmap for reformers, economists, policymakers, and health leaders aiming for a vision of innovative, inclusive, and economically grounded digital healthcare systems.

2. CONCEPTUAL AND THEORETICAL FRAMEWORKS

2.1 Phygital Paradigm in Healthcare

Phygital describes merging physical and digital experiences into hybrid systems. In healthcare, it combines in-person services with digital platforms like telemedicine, AI diagnostics, mobile health apps, electronic health records, and remote monitoring. This model is becoming a sustainable, resilient framework for delivering care across various socioeconomic, geographic, and demographic divides (Vecchio et al., 2023). By enabling real-time care delivery, operational scalability, and data-rich personalization, the phygital model enhances health system resilience, particularly in underserved and resource-limited settings (Joshi et al., 2023). It enables care continuity during crises, extends medical access into remote regions, and fosters cost-effective innovation through scalable technologies such as virtual hospitals and AI-assisted clinical decision systems. However, successful implementation of phygital healthcare goes far beyond technical deployment. It necessitates economic viability, regulatory flexibility, behavioral adaptability, and institutional backing to ensure alignment with public needs and ethical frameworks (Ikhalea et al., 2024). To critically address these dimensions, this chapter draws on interdisciplinary theoretical frameworks, including health economics, behavioral science, systems thinking, and implementation science, to ensure a holistic and grounded approach to digital-era healthcare reform.

2.2 Health Economics Theory

Health economics offers a framework for analyzing the cost-effectiveness of healthcare, resource allocation, and trade-offs between efficiency and equity. It guides resource distribution to maximize health and fairness. In phygital healthcare, these principles are more complex due to high-tech costs, infrastructure disparities, and access challenges. Technologies like telemedicine and AI can boost efficiency but require significant investment, digital skills, and organizational readiness. Economic models show ICERs for these tools vary greatly across settings, with telemedicine being especially cost-effective in underserved areas (Scuffham, 2002; Yoo et al., 2017). Health economic modeling is critical for estimating returns on digital investments and guiding strategic resource allocation.

Studies show that tools like Markov models, linear programming, and distributional cost-effectiveness analysis are increasingly used to balance efficiency with equity (Love-Koh et al., 2020; Pooyan et al., 2018). Economic theory helps evaluate marginal utility, market failures, and externalities, crucial as digital expansion risks favoring wealthier, digitally skilled groups. Ethical critiques warn against blind utilitarianism and stress the need to balance efficiency with justice (Abdulwahab, Daniel, Halabi, et al., 2026). In countries with fragmented financing systems or low insurance coverage, the unchecked growth of digital solutions could intensify disparities. Therefore, economic analyses must include distributional effects and focus on long-term sustainability and inclusivity.

2.3 Behavioral Economics and Patient Decision-Making

While classical economics assumes rational actors, behavioral economics considers cognitive biases, risk aversion, and information asymmetries in policy. In digital health, decisions are influenced by trust, fears of data breaches, concerns about misdiagnosis, and interface complexity, shaping health-seeking behavior. Therefore, behavioral economics is crucial for understanding digital health adoption and for designing interventions that promote equitable, efficient care outcomes.

For instance, prospect theory has been applied to explain how framing effects and loss aversion influence the acceptance of digital health technologies (Khan et al., 2021). Behavioral nudges such as gamified apps, financial incentives, text message reminders, and "tip-of-the-day" features have proven effective at increasing digital engagement and adherence (Mair et al., 2025). Additionally, behavioral segmentation, which categorizes patients by decision styles and risk profiles rather than just demographics, has increased the precision and effectiveness of digital health campaigns (Nordberg et al., 2024).

2.4 Social Determinants of Health and Digital Exclusion

Effective health reform must consider social determinants such as income, education, gender, ethnicity, and location, which influence health and access to digital technology. Without addressing these, digital tools risk creating a two-tier system that favors some over others (Vahedi et al., 2020). SDOH also shapes digital literacy and trust in technology, both of which are essential for successful phygital reform. For example, low-income or elderly patients may lack smartphone access or feel less comfortable using online platforms. Studies show that bridging this gap requires community-centered outreach and policies subsidizing technology access and education (Asthana & Prime, 2023).

2.5 Institutional Theory and Governance Structures

Institutional theory explains how healthcare systems' rules shape reform outcomes. Institutions like health ministries, regulatory bodies, insurers, or hospitals have norms and resistance to change. Reforms can fail if incentives are misaligned or leadership cannot manage change. For example, providers might resist telemedicine due to fears of revenue loss or workflow shifts, and policymakers may hesitate to decentralize data without safeguards. Recognizing these dynamics is key to sustainable reforms (O'Laughlin, 2016).

2.6 World Health Organization (WHO) Health Systems Framework

The WHO's Health Systems Framework outlines six core building blocks: service delivery, health workforce, information systems, medicines access, financing, and leadership, used globally to diagnose weaknesses and guide health reforms (Nadhamuni et al., 2021). Moreover, several scholars argue for extending or reframing the WHO framework to reflect the disruptive, hybrid, and real-time nature of the digital transformation. Virtual primary care, mobile health apps, blockchain records, and citizen-centered data ecosystems demand new models beyond technocentric upgrades to genuinely system-strengthening innovations (Oso et al., 2025). The WHO's framework remains a foundational diagnostic and planning tool. However, in the digital era, its utility lies in enabling policymakers and practitioners to differentiate between symbolic digitization and holistic digital health systems transformation.

2.7 Systems Thinking and the Complexity of Reforms

Systems thinking provides a meta-framework for understanding health systems as complex, adaptive entities with feedback loops, interdependencies, and emergent behaviors. Reform outcomes are rarely linear; they involve multiple actors, shifting incentives, and unintended consequences. It encourages reform designers to look beyond individual interventions to how changes in one domain (e.g., financing) ripple across others (e.g., access or quality). In digital health, where technologies evolve rapidly and are often externally developed, systems thinking helps avoid siloed approaches and supports whole-system reform planning. It aligns with the WHO framework and institutional theory, offering a comprehensive lens for managing complexity and fostering resilience. Various theoretical approaches converge into a unified framework supporting inclusive, resilient health reforms.

Figure 2 illustrates this, combining health economics, behavioral economics, institutional theory, systems thinking, social determinants, and the WHO's Health Systems Framework. These dimensions shape reform design from guiding resource allocation and behavioral targeting to addressing structural inequalities and institutional capacity. The center of the diagram represents the interdisciplinary approach needed for sustainable reform in the digital age, ensuring reforms are technologically sound, behaviorally informed, socially inclusive, and institutionally resilient and grounded.

Figure 2. Integrated Theoretical Framework for Phygital Health Reform

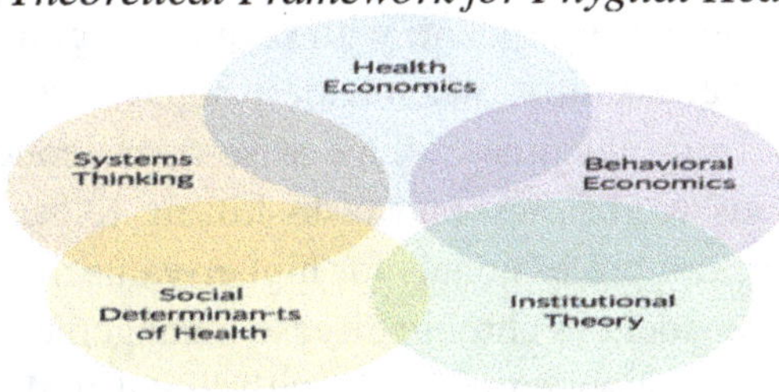

Source: Designed by the Author

This theoretical foundation lays the groundwork for the analysis in the following sections. Combining economic rationality, behavioral insight, social equity, institutional realism, and systems thinking, we build a robust, interdisciplinary framework for designing and evaluating inclusive, economically sustainable phygital health reforms.

3. THE ECONOMICS OF PHYGITAL HEALTHCARE REFORMS

3.1 Economic Rationale for Phygital Integration

Phygital healthcare offers a way to boost efficiency and reach by combining digital tools such as teleconsultations, AI diagnostics, and electronic records with physical infrastructure. This reduces costs, boosts provider productivity, and extends the services beyond geographic limits. Research shows that digital transformation is the key to improving system efficiency (Bachuk, 2024). Efficiency gains do not automatically mean cost savings or fairness. Implementing digital infrastructure, especially in lower-income countries, involves high initial costs, including hardware, integration, training, cybersecurity, and maintenance. The economic viability of phygital reforms requires assessing both short- and long-term costs, including total ownership and expected benefits such as health improvements, productivity, and system decongestion (Mallidi et al., 2021).

3.2 Cost-Effectiveness and Health System Productivity

Cost-effectiveness analysis (CEA) is a key tool in evaluating health interventions, especially in phygital reform. Digital tools often show mixed results. A review found that many digital health interventions (DHIs) are cost-effective, but diverse methods, settings, and technologies make broad conclusions difficult (Jiang et al., 2019; Rahimi, 2019). Some mHealth interventions in low- and middle-income countries have shown potential to reduce direct healthcare costs. However, their scalability and sustainability remain context-dependent, with several programs showing marginal or negative cost-effectiveness ratios when widely deployed (Stanić et al., 2023).

Productivity gains from phygital systems arise from reduced travel, better diagnostics, asynchronous workflows, and task-shifting (e.g., AI triage or remote Monitoring), freeing health professionals for higher-value services (Stratton et al., 2021). These gains are evident in chronic disease management, mental health, and preventive care, where continuous engagement with digital platforms yields economic and clinical benefits (Feltz-Cornelis et al., 2023). Phygital health interventions offer promising cost-effectiveness and productivity, especially when targeted, scalable, and context-aware, but require standardized evaluation. Digital health's efficiency varies by type, setting, and scale. Table 1 summarizes key digital tools, costs, ICERs, and long-term returns, highlighting where digital tools deliver the greatest value and where caution or tailored planning is warranted.

Table 1. Comparative Cost-Effectiveness of Digital Health Interventions

Intervention Type	Context	Initial Cost	ICER	Long-Term ROI	Key Notes
Telemedicine (general)	LMIC rural settings	Moderate to High	$200–$800 per QALY gained	Positive (Reduced travel + early care)	Cost-effective where infrastructure exists; barriers to broadband access
AI Diagnostic Tools	High-income outpatient settings	High	$1,200–$3,000 per QALY gained	Moderate (High upfront, scalable later)	Requires advanced EHR and regulatory support
mHealth apps	Urban slums in middle-income nations	Low to Moderate	Variable (some negative ICERs)	Low to Moderate	Dependent on adherence and digital literacy
Remote Monitoring (chronic diseases)	The elderly in OECD countries	High	$900–$1,500 per QALY gained	High (hospital readmissions reduced)	More cost-effective in chronic heart failure and diabetes
Virtual Hospitals	National pilot programs (e.g., UK)	Very High (CapEx)	Limited data	Long-term ROI under evaluation	Promising model; full impact depends on policy integration
Digital Behavioral Nudges	Preventive care in the general population	Low	<$200 per QALY gained	High (Low cost, scalable)	Among the most cost-effective for preventive care and screening uptake

Source: Compiled by the Author

3.3 Financing Models and Public-Private Roles

Financing phygital healthcare reforms requires adaptive models for digital costs. Traditional systems may need innovation funding, levies, or PPPs that account for infrastructure, digital risks, and agility. PPPs are effective for infrastructure and modernization, especially under fiscal limits, and can speed up AI diagnostics, telemedicine, and health data systems (Shuliuk, 2021). Private sector participation is crucial in innovation-heavy domains such as mobile health applications, cloud infrastructure, and AI development.

However, regulation is needed to prevent monopolies and cost inflation. Past PPPs showed risks of poor risk transfer, high public costs, and unequal service when contracts lack rigor (Smyshlyaev, 2022). In many countries, the balance between public oversight and private innovation is unresolved. Unregulated markets promote profit-driven apps that may conflict with health goals, while excessive centralization stifles innovation and responsiveness. This highlights the need for governance frameworks that encourage innovation while safeguarding affordability, data privacy, and access (Ochinanwata et al., 2021). Digital health governance needs new funding sources and policies to ensure innovation supports public health. This includes performance-based financing, risk-adjusted models, and participatory mechanisms. Financing affects affordability, inclusivity, and sustainability. Table 2 compares public and private approaches, highlighting their opportunities, risks, and impact on health equity. No single model is best suited to hybrids with adaptive governance, and safeguards are often most effective.

Table 2. Public vs. Private Financing Models in Phygital Health Reform: Opportunities and Risks

Financing Model	Opportunities	Risks	Equity Impact	Long-Term Viability
Tax-Based Public Funding	Universal access, low out-of-pocket costs, broad coverage	Budget constraints, slow innovation adoption	High equity if well-funded	Viable with strong political will
Social Health Insurance (SHI)	Risk pooling, predictable funding, incentives for preventive care	May exclude the informal sector; administrative complexity	Moderate equity; depends on enrollment policies	Sustainable if coverage is expansive
Donor-Funded Programs	Rapid mobilization in low-income countries, tech transfer	Dependency, short-term focus, misaligned priorities	High initial equity; low sustainability	Often unsustainable without a transition plan

continued on following page

Table 2. Continued

Financing Model	Opportunities	Risks	Equity Impact	Long-Term Viability
Public-Private Partnerships (PPPs)	Leverage private innovation, share costs, speed of digital deployment	Risk of profit-driven models, cost escalation, and poor risk transfer	Mixed; may widen the digital divide without safeguards	High if regulated and performance-based
Private Health Investment (Equity, Venture Capital)	Drives rapid digital innovation and product development	Market segmentation, high user fees, and underserved vulnerable groups	Low equity unless regulated or subsidized	Highly profitable markets only
Digital Health Levies / Innovation Funds	Targeted funding for infrastructure or startups	Politically sensitive, potential misuse	Medium equity if properly allocated	Emerging but promising

Source: Designed by the Author

3.4 Market Segmentation and Demand Elasticity

Phygital healthcare systems face a diverse market influenced by income, geography, digital literacy, and disease burden, creating varied demand. Wealthier urban users prefer speed, personalization, and paid services, while rural or low-income groups are price-sensitive and rely on subsidized digital access. Customer price sensitivity varies by socioeconomic status, with lower-income users showing higher elasticity, especially with limited digital literacy (Cruz et al., 2023). Understanding the price elasticity of demand for digital health services is crucial for deciding public versus private funding. Elasticity modeling shows that low-income users have highly elastic demand, so even small user fees can deter adoption and limit access (Dillon & McCaskey, 2018). These findings highlight the need for universal digital entitlements for basic health services, especially in countries with high income inequality. Tiered pricing may suit premium or non-essential services, with lower elasticity among the affluent populations.

3.5 Economic Risks of Unequal Digital Expansion

A major challenge in phygital reform is uneven economic returns. Digital health programs often benefit already-advantaged groups, risking increased disparities and inefficient resource use. For example, telehealth in the U.S. varies by ZIP code income, literacy, language, and race. Despite broader access, low-income and non-English-speaking groups still have lower digital uptake, risking worsening inequalities (Palombini et al., 2023). Furthermore, upfront infrastructure costs such as expanding broadband, securing interoperable cloud-based systems, and training a digital health workforce are high.

At the same time, returns are delayed or diffuse, often emerging only after years of systemic integration. This temporal mismatch between costs and benefits may disincentivize policymakers, especially in fiscally constrained or low-resource settings, from adopting or scaling digital reforms (Bocean & Vărzaru, 2025; Fahad, 2024). These cost disparities are often exacerbated in rural areas and developing regions, where broadband access is lower, leading to lower returns on public digital health investments and fewer private incentives to innovate equitably (Cornejo et al., 2025). Unless co-financing strategies and value-based implementation models are adopted, digital health risks will become a missed opportunity for equity and a drain on already-limited healthcare budgets in underserved communities.

3.6 Strategies for Economic Sustainability

To ensure the long-term viability of phygital health reforms, economic strategies must align with systemic health goals. Adopting phased implementation models that scale with local systems' capacity minimizes waste and maximizes impact. Bundled payment systems incentivize value over volume by linking provider reimbursement to high-quality, integrated care instead of discrete services (Ferrara & Tozzi, 2018). Digital procurement platforms enhance cost efficiency through pooled negotiations, better supplier transparency, and less administrative work. Outcomes-based contracting, in which payments depend on measurable health improvements, such as fewer hospitalizations or better disease management, is another key innovation (Poveda et al., 2022). Among these strategies, one of the most promising is the implementation of value-based healthcare (VBHC). VBHC reorients health systems away from service quantity and toward optimizing health outcomes per dollar spent.

When applied to digital health, this model justifies strategic investments in tools like artificial intelligence-based screening systems or remote patient monitoring technologies, particularly where such tools demonstrably improve chronic disease management or reduce hospital readmissions (Balak et al., 2024; Jeon & Tuuminen, 2024). VBHC enhances the sustainability of digital reform by linking resources to value. Phygital reform can improve efficiency and system performance, but requires attention to equity, segmentation, and fiscal realism. Without an economic perspective, policies may strain budgets, skew incentives, or worsen disparities. A detailed understanding of costs, financing, demand, and risks is vital to make phygital healthcare reforms innovative, inclusive, and sustainable.

4. UNDERSTANDING ECONOMIC BEHAVIOR VIA THE PATIENT-CENTERED REFORM DESIGN

4.1. Economic Behavior in Health Reform

Health reforms to improve equity and efficiency must consider the behavioral economics underpinning patient decisions. Traditional economic models assume patients make rational health choices based on complete information and consistent preferences. However, behavioral economics reveals that bounded rationality, heuristics, cognitive biases, and social framing effects often influence health choices. Integrating these insights into reform design is essential to creating phygital health systems that meet the needs of diverse patient populations.

4.2. Behavioral Economics and the Digital Patient

Behavioral economics offers a new way to understand how patients interact with digital health tools. Studies showed that small "nudges" in patient portals greatly increased scheduling and completion of preventive services, such as Medicare wellness visits and Pap tests. Slight changes in message framing led to noticeable improvements in health engagement across diverse groups (Liang et al., 2021). Expanding beyond preventive services, randomized and pilot interventions have shown that nudges embedded in digital mental health platforms, such as prompts to reduce present bias or encourage fresh starts, can improve adherence and reduce attrition in online programs for depression and anxiety (Ii et al., 2022). Likewise, applying behavioral insights to cardiovascular care has proven effective: loss-framing, choice architecture, and digital activity trackers have nudged patients toward sustained lifestyle change and improved outcomes (Adusumalli et al., 2020). These systematic reviews show that behavioral economics nudges reliably improve public health behaviors in preventive care, screening, and chronic disease management.

Trials also show that combining behavioral economics with human-centered design can enhance access to sexual and reproductive health services for vulnerable groups by embedding social norms, defaults, and incentives into digital and community-based interventions (Liu et al., 2023). By recognizing that patients often deviate from long-term health goals due to present- or status-quo bias, digital health reforms can leverage behavioral economics to design choice architectures that steer behavior toward optimal outcomes without restricting freedom of choice. This evidence base strongly suggests that integrating nudges into digital platforms offers a scalable, cost-effective pathway to increase patient engagement and reduce disparities in preventive care utilization. Digital health systems benefit immensely from integrating nudge-based strategies grounded in behavioral economics. Table 3 summarizes key evidence from trials and meta-analyses, showcasing the effectiveness of diverse digital nudges across populations and health contexts. These interventions enhance engagement and reduce health disparities by tailoring behavior change techniques to real-world behavioral tendencies.

Table 3. Nudge Interventions in Digital Health

Nudge Type	Health Context	Population	Outcome Measured	Effect Size / Impact	Key Source(s)
Framing Effects (Gain/Loss)	Digital mental health engagement	Adults with anxiety/ depression	Program adherence, log-in rates	↑ Engagement by 15–25%	Ii et al., 2022; Adusumalli et al., 2020
Text Message Reminders	Preventive screening, chronic care	Low-income, elderly populations	Appointment attendance, medication adherence	↑ Attendance by 20–35%	Liang et al., 2021; Summers & Curtis, 2020
Gamification & Rewards	Physical activity & lifestyle management	General adult populations	Daily step count, exercise frequency	↑ Activity by 30%, sustained for 3–6 months	Fernández et al., 2023; Adusumalli et al., 2020
Social Norm Messaging	Sexual & reproductive health access	Adolescents and young adults	Clinic visit uptake, STI screening	↑ Uptake by 18–22%	Liu et al., 2023
Fresh Start Messaging	Smoking cessation & health checkups	Working-age adults	Goal-setting and follow-through rates	↑ Follow-through by 12–20%	Waddell et al., 2020; Mair et al., 2025
Personalized Behavioral Nudges	Digital cardiovascular care (apps + AI)	Patients with heart disease	Medication adherence, behavior change	↑ Adherence by 15%; ↓ readmissions by 10%	Adusumalli et al., 2020

Source: Compiled by the Author

4.3. Segmentation and Behavioral Targeting in Reform Design

Patient populations are diverse. Behavioral segmentation divides groups by traits such as motivation, preferences, and decision-making styles, enabling tailored, cost-effective interventions. Evidence indicates segmentation helps health systems align interventions with patient needs, supporting the shift from volume to value-based care. For example, segmentation has identified frail elderly and complex chronic patients in Medicare populations as key targets (Joynt et al., 2017). Segmentation also strengthens healthcare service design, as patient behaviors (e.g., proactive vs. avoidant care-seeking) can be matched to modular, personalized care pathways (Engström et al., 2022). Similarly, machine learning–based patient segmentation has been successfully applied in surgical populations, offering predictive models that allow clinicians to anticipate behavioral and clinical needs (Swenson et al., 2016).

Digital health ecosystems further expand the role of segmentation, as patients increasingly act as decision-makers within value-based, platform-enabled healthcare systems (Hermes et al., 2020). New frameworks for Value-Based Digital Health (VBDH) emphasize incorporating segmentation insights when measuring patient-reported outcomes and experiences, ensuring that interventions remain relevant across diverse behavioral and demographic groups (Merino et al., 2024). Moreover, proactive segmentation enables policymakers to move beyond targeting only the highest-cost patients, highlighting the untapped value of middle-cost segments in reducing avoidable hospitalizations and optimizing resource allocation (Simons et al., 2018). Value-based redesign projects in primary care confirm that such stratification, combined with interdisciplinary teams and multimodal delivery (digital and in-person), enhances outcomes and patient satisfaction (Kurek et al., 2023).

In practice, segmentation enables digital health systems to prioritize interventions: patients highly responsive to digital nudges can be guided through proactive, tech-enabled care pathways, while others may require human support, simplified interfaces, or community-based engagement strategies. These insights are best visualized through a behavioral segmentation matrix that maps digital literacy against health motivation. Figure 3 presents four distinct patient segments: Tech-Empowered individuals exhibit high motivation and strong digital skills, making them ideal candidates for fully digital care pathways. Skeptical Engagers have high digital literacy but lower health activation, often requiring behaviorally guided interventions and nudges. Passive Digitals possess digital competence but lack health motivation, needing incentives and continuous engagement to drive participation. Disconnected At-Risk individuals score low on both axes and represent a vulnerable population requiring high-touch, hybrid, or offline support. Understanding these behavioral profiles helps health systems tailor reform strategies to the actual needs and capacities of their populations, enhancing equity and efficiency in phygital transformation.

Figure 3. Behavioral Segmentation Matrix

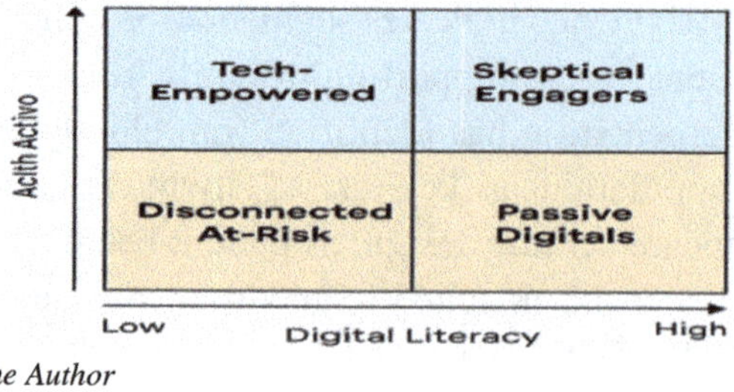

Source: Designed by the Author

4.4. Value-Based Design and Economic Incentives for Patients

A patient-centered phygital system should incorporate value-based insurance design (V-BID) principles, which align patient out-of-pocket costs with the clinical value of services received. V-BID prioritizes high-value care affordability, enhancing economic efficiency and patient-centeredness (Stecker et al., 2015). A systematic review and meta-analysis confirmed that VBID programs consistently increase medication adherence across chronic disease areas, with the most potent effects observed in cardiovascular care. Programs offering full coverage and patient education demonstrated the highest impact (Krack, 2019). Similarly, studies of employer-sponsored VBID programs show sustained improvements in adherence without raising overall healthcare costs, as increased drug spending is offset by reduced hospitalizations and complications (Agarwal et al., 2018).

Beyond adherence, patient-centered outcomes research indicates that VBID reduces cost-related nonadherence, improves patient satisfaction, and empowers individuals to engage in preventive and self-management practices (Elliott et al., 2013). Evidence also shows that VBID offsets the adverse effects of high-deductible plans by preserving access to essential medications, especially for patients with complex chronic conditions (Reed et al., 2017). V-BID principles in digital care include reduced co-pays, bundled payments, and gamified rewards to boost adherence. Reviews show that, when well-designed, these incentives improve patient agency and align with justice and beneficence, but safeguards are needed to prevent inequities (Riegler, 2023).

4.5. Digital Personalization Designing for Behavioral Segments

Using behavioral personas and co-design improves digital health by aligning system design with patient expectations. Conjoint analysis and discrete choice experiments are effective tools for modeling preferences in different health contexts. For instance, conjoint studies of patient-centered care identify behavioral segments: some prioritize feedback and collaboration, others value convenience, highlighting the importance of segmentation in system design (Cunningham et al., 2016; Deal, 2013).

Studies applying conjoint analysis to digital health records and eHealth interfaces highlight that behavioral and demographic differences strongly shape system adoption, with elderly users prioritizing intuitive and accessible design features (S. Zhang & Song, 2024), while diabetes patients emphasize affordability and physician integration in digital health platforms (Leyland et al., 2011). Beyond healthcare, preference-based segmentation methods applied in social and privacy research reinforce that conjoint-driven clusters capture hidden behavioral differences more accurately than traditional demographics (Kuzmanović & Savić, 2020). These findings emphasize that phygital health reforms must integrate behavioral segmentation to ensure digital systems are responsive to clinical data and patients' economic behaviors, psychosocial preferences, and lived experiences.

4.6. Behavioral Integration in the Patient-Centered Medical Home (PCMH)

Integrating behavioral health into primary care settings is crucial in improving population-level outcomes. Evidence demonstrates that behavioral health integration within PCMH models enhances continuity of care, improves treatment outcomes, and reduces costs by lowering unnecessary hospitalizations and emergency visits (Leung et al., 2019). Research emphasizes that advanced digital infrastructures are essential for such integration to succeed in phygital healthcare models. These include interoperable health records, predictive analytics, and digital nudges that can personalize behavioral support and encourage patient adherence (Joy et al., 2024). Digital ecosystems embedded in PCMHs can now provide early alerts for mental health risks, automate appointment reminders, and reduce attrition through engaging user-centered digital experiences (McNeil et al., 2024; Santos & Nazaré, 2025).

5. TECHNOLOGY, TRUST, AND EQUITY IN PHYGITAL HEALTH SYSTEMS

As digital health technologies expand into mainstream care models, the intersection of technology, trust, and equity becomes central to designing inclusive phygital health reforms. Phygital health systems that integrate physical healthcare delivery with digital platforms offer immense promise for improving efficiency and access. However, the trustworthiness and equitable diffusion of these technologies across diverse populations are essential to realizing these benefits. Sociotechnical imbalances, digital exclusion, and algorithmic opacity often create new forms of marginalization, even as they bridge geographical gaps in access.

5.1 Building Trust in Digital Health Systems

Trust in digital healthcare tools, particularly telemedicine and AI-enabled diagnostics, significantly influences patient adoption and system-wide impact. Studies show telemedicine enhances healthcare access in underserved regions, but trust depends on robust data privacy, security, and governance protocols (Abbasi & Smith, 2024; Sebastian, 2024). At the same time, trust in AI diagnostics requires accuracy, empathy, personalization, and transparency. Patients are more willing to adopt AI-based health advice when the system conveys carefulness and patient-centeredness (Li et al., 2024). Moreover, building cognitive and emotional trust requires designing AI systems emphasizing explainability and fairness. Studies on explainable AI and telemedicine emphasize that patients are more receptive when algorithms are interpretable, human-like in communication, and ethically framed (Oluwagbade, 2025).

Fostering patient trust in digital health requires more than technological accuracy: it depends on transparent data governance, empathetic AI design, explainability, and human–machine collaboration to ensure safe and equitable adoption. The Trust-Building Pyramid in Figure 4 illustrates the layers needed to build and maintain user trust in digital health. Starting at the base, community co-design makes platforms reflect diverse users' experiences. Moving up, socially responsive interfaces promote inclusivity across languages and abilities. Next, transparent data governance protects privacy and accountability. At the top, ethical AI and explainability ensure AI operates transparently and respectfully, boosting confidence in automation. These layers form a strategy to embed trust into digital health systems, addressing technical and relational aspects for equity adoption.

Figure 4. Trust-Building Pyramid for Digital Health

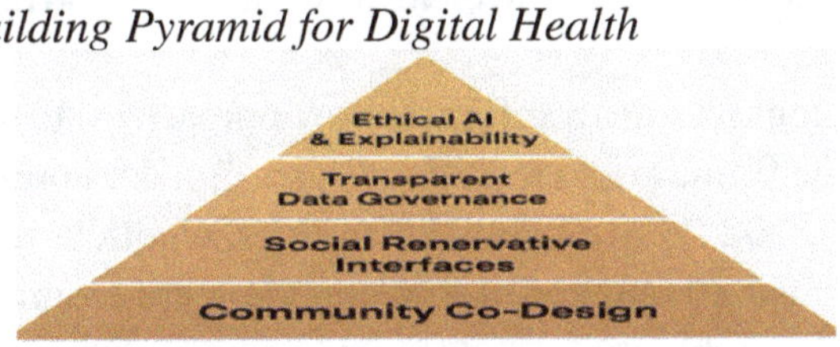

Source: Designed by the Author

5.2 Digital Trust and Health Equity

Equity in digital health involves inclusion, usability, and outcomes, not just access. Trust is uneven; marginalized groups often lack digital trust due to medical discrimination, infrastructure gaps, and digital illiteracy. While telemedicine is transformative, it mainly benefits affluent and digitally literate people, with rural and low-income groups facing barriers like digital skills, hardware access, and cultural relevance (Chandak, 2024).

Social factors influence trust in digital health tech. Studies show accountability, risk perception, and race shape confidence in AI healthcare. Systemic barriers like privacy issues, bias, and infrastructure disparities affect marginalized groups' perceptions and adoption (Fabra et al., 2025). These findings suggest that equity must be understood as a systemic issue, not simply a technical one. Building digital trust requires intentional governance, culturally tailored design, and inclusive infrastructures that prioritize the needs of historically marginalized communities.

5.3 Ethical and Legal Considerations in Digital Trust

Trust must be institutionalized through transparent governance and ethical practices. Scholars note that telemedicine and AI adoption raise privacy, liability, and consent issues, especially as healthcare digitalizes quickly. Clear ethical and legal guidelines on malpractice, accountability, and data ownership are vital to maintaining public trust in the long term (Kaplan, 2020). This provides a comprehensive review of telehealth during COVID-19, emphasizing challenges of consent, privacy, licensing, and clinician responsibility, and calls for evidence-based regulatory frameworks. Similarly, Nittari et al. (2020) underline persistent gaps in informed consent, malpractice liability, and confidentiality, and urge harmonized telemedicine laws across borders. Newer studies extend this discussion to AI, stressing the need for dynamic consent and explainable AI (XAI) to counter black-box opacity in clinical decision-making (Albalawi et al., 2024). Similarly, they warn that AI chatbots risk eroding physician-patient trust without clear accountability and disclosure standards (Wang et al., 2023).

Country-specific legal studies reinforce these imperatives. Identifies similar gaps in Indian telemedicine frameworks regarding licensing, data protection, and clarity on malpractice (Puri, 2024). At the ethical frontier, (Jedličková, 2024) advocates for binding international ethical codes to reconcile technological innovation with patient rights, while (Alrebh et al., 2024) emphasize stronger cybersecurity, consent safeguards, and equity measures to ensure telemedicine remains inclusive and trustworthy. These studies demonstrate a broad consensus that multidisciplinary governance, robust legal frameworks, and ethics-by-design principles are indispensable to embedding digital trust in healthcare systems.

5.4 Addressing the Digital Divide

Ensuring equity in phygital health systems needs strategies to overcome the digital divide. While telehealth improves access in underserved areas, barriers such as connectivity, affordability, device access, and cultural fit persist. Vulnerable groups such as low-income individuals, older adults, minorities, and those with low digital literacy are disproportionately excluded despite higher health needs (Gallegos-Rejas et al., 2022). To address these inequities, scholars argue for subsidized infrastructure, community-driven digital literacy campaigns, and multilingual, culturally tailored technologies. Systematic reviews highlight the importance of universal design principles, continuous evaluation of interventions, and equity dashboards to monitor disparities in telehealth access (Hollimon et al., 2025; Jiangliu et al., 2024). Caution is needed: tech enthusiasm requires clinical validation and user focus. Studies warn that poorly executed telehealth can worsen disparities if access, affordability, and digital service quality are not paired with cultural and social considerations (Alford-Teaster et al., 2023).

5.5 Implications for Inclusive Phygital Reform

Integrating trust and equity into phygital reforms requires policymakers to adopt holistic, sociotechnical models that go beyond technology alone. Equity should be a core principle, not a secondary consideration. Trust-building involves clear communication, shared governance, and the involvement of diverse communities in participatory design. Systems must also recognize emotional and social aspects of care. Experts highlight that equity-focused digital health needs deliberate approaches like participatory co-creation, community-centered models, and explicit assessments to avoid worsening disparities (Fotopoulou et al., 2021; Richardson et al., 2022).

Equity frameworks also stress the necessity of embedding inclusivity into regulatory and governance structures, such as informed consent, ethical AI guidelines, and digital health equity Monitoring tools, which are vital for maintaining public trust (Masyuri, 2024). Participatory and community models, such as co-created digital patient twins, equity-focused dementia care, or community health worker access, demonstrate that trust is built through relationships and shared decision-making, not just technology. (Weinberger et al., 2025; Wolff et al., 2024). These insights highlight that trust and equity in phygital healthcare reform are fundamental pillars, requiring systemic, participatory, and ethical approaches that respect both the technical and human dimensions of care.

6. MARKETING, COMMUNICATION, AND BEHAVIORAL ENGAGEMENT STRATEGIES FOR REFORM ADOPTION

Marketing and communication are pivotal in shaping the adoption of phygital healthcare reforms, particularly in environments marked by digital transformation, patient behavior variability, and institutional resistance. As health reforms transition from policy documents to lived experiences, success depends on the systems designed and how effectively stakeholders communicate and embrace them. In this context, behavioral engagement strategies, fueled by digital platforms and health marketing tools, serve as bridges connecting reform objectives to real-world impact.

6.1 Health Marketing in the Digital Era

Digital health marketing is emerging as a powerful strategy to reach and engage underserved communities through social media, apps, SEO, and personalized campaigns. These tools support preventive health measures, boost awareness, and address cultural and literacy barriers (Usuemerai et al., 2024). The strategic application of mobile campaigns, personalized content, and virtual support systems enables health providers to influence behavior effectively (Dada & Adekola, 2024). In private sector hospitals, flat organizational structures and empowered staff significantly increase the adoption of digital marketing strategies, enhancing outreach and user engagement through real-time feedback loops and word-of-mouth influence (Dailah, 2021; Djakeli, 2024).

6.2 Behavioral Engagement Models and Consumer Psychology

Digital marketing in healthcare does more than promote services; it influences health behavior. Applying models like the Health Belief Model and Social Cognitive Theory, marketers design interventions that target cognitive and emotional drivers of health decision-making (Dada & Adekola, 2024). Consumer segmentation further enhances effectiveness. For example, social marketing research among youth identified varying typologies such as the "saints," "sinners," and "in the pew," each responding differently to health messages. Tailored communication ensures message resonance and drives behavioral change (Haris, 2023; Shkeer et al., 2024).

6.3 Omnichannel and Phygital Marketing Approaches

Omnichannel marketing in specialty pharmaceuticals boosts healthcare professionals' responses by combining physical and digital tools. Engagement improves when channels target both decision-making drivers. This "phygital" approach has significantly influenced prescribing and reform adoption (Wimalasena & Jayasinghe, 2025). Behavioral engagement strategies must be tailored and platform-independent to communicate and adopt reforms effectively. Figure 5 shows the Omnichannel Behavioral Engagement Cycle with four phases: Segmentation identifies behavioral personas and preferences using demographic and psychographic data. Messaging customizes content for specific segments using behavioral insights and cultural cues. Multi-Platform Delivery spreads health messages via SMS, email, mobile apps, social media, and radio, reaching users where they are. Feedback/Analytics collects engagement data and responses to improve segmentation and messaging. This cycle helps reformers and healthcare providers maintain engagement throughout patient journeys, reduce message fatigue, and ensure reforms resonate with diverse, digitally stratified audience populations.

Figure 5. Omnichannel Behavioral Engagement Cycle

Source: Designed by the Author

6.4 Communication Strategies for Health System Strengthening

Strategic communication is no longer an afterthought in health reforms. It is integral to creating ownership, building trust, and navigating resistance. Health reformers increasingly adopt marketing strategies such as stakeholder segmentation, message testing, and behavioral nudging to promote reforms across the entire system levels (Godiyal & Mishra, 2025). Social marketing plays a cross-sectoral role in interdisciplinary settings by extending health promotion efforts into architecture, urban planning, education, and more. This broader framing repositions health as a shared societal concern, thereby deepening reform engagement (Settou & Aomari, 2024).

6.5 Cultural Sensitivity and Personalization in Messaging

Marketing strategies that account for cultural differences, language diversity, and socioeconomic conditions are more effective in influencing health behaviors. Personalized messaging enabled by digital health analytics allows health systems to reach patients where they are, delivering content that aligns with their values and daily realities (Grbic et al., 2019).

6.6 Measuring Impact and Adaptive Feedback Loops

Evaluating the effectiveness of marketing and communication strategies is essential to inform real-time adaptation. Data-driven tools allow health systems to monitor engagement metrics, conversion rates, behavior change, and long-term adherence, enabling iterative improvements and maximizing return on investment (Susanti, 2021). Marketing and communication strategies are not peripheral to healthcare reform but essential levers for driving behavioral adoption, particularly in digitally mediated health systems. Effective engagement depends on a blend of theory, technology, and personalization, ensuring that reforms are designed and embraced at scale.

7. LEADERSHIP, GOVERNANCE, AND POLICY INNOVATIONS FOR REFORM SUSTAINABILITY

The sustainability of phygital healthcare reforms depends on technological and financial resources, visionary leadership, robust governance structures, and adaptive policy innovations. As health systems digitize, governance mechanisms must evolve to manage new ethical, regulatory, and operational challenges. Effective institutional and political leadership is crucial for reform adoption, implementation, and scaling. Without it, even the most promising reforms risk fragmentation, inefficiency, or failure.

7.1 Leadership Competencies for Digital Health Transformation

Successful digital era leadership requires transformational, strategic, and collaborative skills. Leaders must manage change, build trust across sectors, and keep clear reform narratives. Scholars emphasize visionary thinking, agility, and strategic alignment as key to digital health reforms (Philip et al., 2023). Within healthcare, leadership agility and systems thinking are critical for aligning complex reforms with evolving stakeholder expectations and emerging technologies (Jayanagara, 2024). Empirical evidence from large-scale health systems shows that digitally savvy executives, particularly CEOs and CIOs, play a pivotal role in embedding strategic vision and cultivating collaborative cultures that accelerate transformation (Lemak et al., 2024). Finally, forward-looking perspectives argue that ethical governance, adaptability, and cross-sector collaboration are central to leading digital health in the AI-driven era, ensuring reforms balance innovation with equity and accountability (Hamzah et al., 2025).

7.2 Governance Models in Phygital Health Systems

Governance in phygital health systems includes decision-making, accountability, and data management. Fragmented governance causes policy conflicts and inertia. Experts suggest networked, adaptive models focusing on multi-level coordination, community accountability, and feedback, especially in decentralized systems (Ganesh et al., 2025; Mattei, 2020). Digital governance must address complex data issues, including cybersecurity, interoperability, algorithmic transparency, and AI bias. Effective frameworks focus on fairness, accountability, transparency, patient rights, and regulatory compliance (Nwadiokwu, 2025). This requires new roles, such as Chief Digital Health Officers and national digital ethics boards, to oversee accountability, cybersecurity, and interoperability across health sectors. These governance measures balance technological innovation with ethics to keep phygital health systems efficient and trustworthy.

7.3 Institutional Capacity and Human Resource Development

Health reform sustainability depends on the capacity of health ministries, regulatory bodies, and institutions. However, capacity constraints are common. The evidence indicates that targeted training and institutional strengthening are vital. For example, digital literacy, workforce development, and evidence-use training in public health can enhance decision-making, policy adoption, and resilience (Curioso et al., 2024; Sytnyk & Tarkanii, 2024). Investing in human capital for reform implementation, particularly in digital skills, systems thinking, and leadership training, is essential for long-term sustainability.

Collaborative regional programs in Africa and Asia demonstrate that workforce training, leadership development, and institutional strengthening create ripple effects, embedding reform capacity within ministries and delivery institutions (Abdulwahab, Daniel, Gul, et al., 2026; Abubakari & Olamilekan, 2026). Digital-era governance reforms require technical skills and cultural and institutional changes that promote adaptability, leadership, and teamwork. Long-term success depends on combining digital skills with organizational change and leadership strategies (Karnik et al., 2025). Institutional capacity-building and human resource development, especially in digital literacy, systems thinking, and leadership, are key to effective and sustainable health reforms.

7.4 Policy Innovation and Adaptive Regulation

In phygital health systems, policy must rapidly evolve with technological innovation. Outdated policies can hinder experimentation or cause legal uncertainties. Scholars emphasize regulatory sandboxes as testbeds for safe, controlled piloting of new tech, balancing innovation and safety (Leckenby et al., 2021). Beyond their technical function, sandboxes serve as generative spaces for collaboration and adaptive governance, enabling regulators, innovators, and civil society to co-produce rules that are more responsive and resilient (Macrae & Ansell, 2024). Policy innovation should be evidence-informed and participatory. Anticipatory regulation involves local context, stakeholder dialogue, and feedback to improve legitimacy and trust (Ford &

Ashkenazy, 2025). These studies highlight that adaptive regulation is proactive and collaborative, integrating experimentation, evidence, and community involvement to foster technological innovation and protect equity in phygital systems.

7.5 Political Economy of Reforms

Health reform is inherently political, shaped by interests, ideologies, and legacies. Reformers must navigate power asymmetries, rent-seeking, and opposition through clear communication, coalition-building, and political economy analysis to identify enablers and blockers. Often, reforms falter not because of technical issues but because of resistance from entrenched actors, misaligned incentives, or a lack of political will (Musa et al., 2026; Venkateswaran et al., 2022). Proactive reform leaders frame policy changes as public value propositions to generate demand among citizens, clinicians, and frontline administrators, countering resistance and inertia. Evidence from Turkey, Mexico, and India shows that political incentives, legitimacy, and coalition-building influence reform outcomes (Blanke & Perschke-Hartmann, 1994). Successful reform needs navigating political economy, aligning incentives, mobilizing coalitions, and strategically sequencing reforms to overcome institutional inertia and vested interests.

7.6 Scaling and Institutionalization of Reforms

For reforms to be sustainable, they must become embedded in routines and financing structures. Scaling strategies should consider political will, fiscal space, and delivery infrastructure. Evidence from Africa and Asia shows that successful scale-up depends on piloting, adaptation, and phased institutionalization before nationwide rollout (Raven et al., 2024). The sustainability of phygital health systems depends on integrating into national strategies, aligning with UHC goals, and macroeconomic coherence.

Nigeria and South Africa show that government ownership, policy coherence, and financing are key to digital health programs evolving from pilot projects to sustainable systems (Swartz et al., 2020). Leadership, governance, and policy innovation support building and sustaining phygital health reforms. Institutionalizing leadership and governance structures has been identified as essential for advancing UHC in fragile and emerging economies, where fragmented authority and weak accountability mechanisms can undermine reforms (Croke & Ogbuoji, 2023; Khodayari-Zarnaq et al., 2024). Without forward-thinking leaders, adaptive institutions, and evidence-informed regulation, even the best reforms may flounder. Successful reform requires digital and systemic transformation grounded in capability, legitimacy, and inclusive governance.

8. RECOMMENDATIONS AND REFORM FRAMEWORK

The previous sections established the foundations for inclusive, sustainable phygital health reform. However, turning these insights into action needs an adaptable framework. This section offers recommendations to help policymakers, health leaders, and stakeholders plan, implement, and scale reforms that are economically viable, socially inclusive, and behaviorally effective. Phygital health reform requires multisectoral collaboration across healthcare, digital infrastructure, education, finance, and social services. Systems thinking allows for feedback, alignment, and learning, which are crucial for managing reform complexity. Policies should embed health goals within digital economy and inclusion strategies for coherence. Equity must be integrated from the start to prevent exclusion, through subsidies, offline applications, and human navigators. Targeted interventions can bridge access gaps and improve outcomes for disadvantaged groups, especially in fragile health systems.

Governments should conduct equity impact assessments (EIAs) for digital health policies to identify and address disparities early. Digital trust is crucial for adoption, requiring transparent data governance, ethical AI, and participatory oversight. Policies such as patient data control and explainable algorithms boost acceptance and reduce misinformation, especially where trust is low or discrimination exists. Reform should shift from a top-down to a participatory approach, co-creating tools with users, especially marginalized groups, to improve relevance, acceptance, and satisfaction. Localization enhances legitimacy, reduces the digital divide, and supports successful reform resistance.

No reform can endure without capacity in human and institutional realms. Digital transformation requires investments in leadership, health informatics, and infrastructure. Capacity-building boosts evidence-based policymaking. Workforce development should focus on equity, targeting underserved areas and non-traditional careers. Governments need policy spaces for safe experimentation, especially with AI, remote monitoring, and big data, through regulatory sandboxes that enable testing and learning. Governance flexibility is vital for reform responsiveness. These four pillars form a comprehensive framework for inclusive phygital health development and implementation systems.

The first pillar, equity-centered design, stresses integrating digital inclusion early in policy development by conducting audits, enforcing access standards, practices, and prioritizing marginalized groups. The second pillar, behavioral and cultural intelligence, involves using behavioral insights, social marketing, and community co-design to boost user engagement and trust. The third pillar, institutional readiness and capacity, aims to strengthen leadership, data infrastructure, and regulations in ministries and local institutions to ensure sustained reform. The fourth pillar, adaptive policy ecosystems, encourages innovation through regulatory sandboxes, performance monitoring, and iterative policies that adapt to tech advances and user feedback. Collectively, these pillars form a flexible, scalable, and adaptable blueprint for diverse health systems realities.

9. SUGGEST FOR FURTHER STUDIES

Future research on phygital health must move beyond proof-of-concept studies to address more profound sustainability, equity, and governance questions. Longitudinal evaluations are urgently needed to assess technological performance and behavioral, organizational, and societal impacts over time. Ethical inquiry should expand to low- and middle-income contexts, tackling algorithmic bias, consent, and data sovereignty issues while developing culturally grounded trust frameworks. Research must also interrogate how gender, disability, and poverty intersect to shape digital exclusion, prioritizing participatory approaches that amplify marginalized voices. At the systems level, political economy analysis can illuminate how power, incentives, and governance regimes determine the success or failure of reforms. New agendas should link digital health with climate resilience by embedding adaptive technologies into emergency response and environmental monitoring frameworks.

10. CONCLUSION

Healthcare is shifting to phygital ecosystems where physical and digital methods merge, representing a paradigm shift in health policy, economics, and delivery. This convergence enhances technology and fosters a more inclusive, equitable, efficient, and sustainable system. The chapter explores how economic theory, patient behavior, trust, marketing, and leadership shape this complex landscape. A key conclusion is that phygital health reform should go beyond digitization by integrating behavioral economics, health equity, and socio-political engagement for a truly human-centered approach. Digital tools such as AI, IoT, and telemedicine must align with robust governance, ethics, and access, especially for vulnerable populations. Trust, digital literacy, and cultural sensitivity are vital to reducing digital exclusion and increasing adoption. Economically, models should adopt value-based care, invest in prevention, and incentivize coordinated, integrated service delivery.

Policymakers should avoid focusing solely on cost containment and instead prioritize system efficiencies that enhance population health and resilience. The economic benefits of prevention, digital access, and decentralized models must be quantified and incorporated into budgets and health plans. Leadership and innovation are crucial for sustaining reforms, requiring navigation of stakeholder ecosystems, alignment of incentives, and the creation of adaptive, learning systems to tackle public health threats, climate change, and demographic shifts. Governance, cross-sector collaboration, and patient and frontline worker involvement are essential. Behavioral engagement and health communication are now central to reform success, emphasizing community engagement, reducing resistance, and designing user-friendly digital tools. Marketing with behavioral nudges and social proof can drive health behavior change and improve uptake of preventive care services.

DATA AVAILABILITY STATEMENT

All relevant data are available online.

CONFLICT OF INTEREST

The authors declare no conflict of interest.

DECLARATION OF AI USE:

While preparing this work, the authors used Grammarly and ChatGPT to improve their English and enhance readability. After using it, the authors reviewed and edited the content as needed and took full responsibility for the publication's content.

REFERENCES

Abbasi, N., & Smith, D. A. (2024). Cybersecurity in Healthcare: Securing Patient Health Information (PHI), HIPPA compliance framework and the responsibilities of healthcare providers. *Journal of Knowledge Learning and Science Technology ISSN: 2959-6386 (Online), 3*(3), 278–287.

Abdulwahab, L. O., Daniel, O., Gul, A., & Bubari, H. U. (2026). The Economic Impact of Digital Health Innovations on Disease Prevention: Cost-Effectiveness, ROI, and Policy Implications. In *Reshaping Health Promotion and Disease Prevention Through Digital Innovation* (pp. 29–56). IGI Global Scientific Publishing. DOI: 10.4018/979-8-3373-3531-5.ch002

Abdulwahab, L. O., Daniel, O., Halabi, K. A., & Umar, H. B. (2026). Healthcare Entrepreneurship and Global Talent: Navigating Visa Barriers, Health Innovation, and Startup Survival as an International Graduate. In *International Student Narratives in Globalized Higher Education* (pp. 401–434). IGI Global Scientific Publishing. https://www.igi-global.com/chapter/healthcare-entrepreneurship-and-global-talent/400509

Abubakari, M. S., & Olamilekan, L. A. (2026). Digital Competency's Role in Promoting Equity in the Digital Healthcare Ecosystem: An Overview. *Reshaping Health Promotion and Disease Prevention Through Digital Innovation*, 129–152.

Adusumalli, S., Aragam, G. G., & Patel, M. S. (2020). A Nudge Towards Cardiovascular Health: Applications of Behavioral Economics for Primary and Secondary Cardiovascular Prevention. *Current Treatment Options in Cardiovascular Medicine*, *22*(9), 1–17. DOI: 10.1007/s11936-020-00824-y

Agarwal, R., Gupta, A., & Fendrick, A. M. (2018). Value-Based Insurance Design Improves Medication Adherence Without An Increase In Total Health Care Spending. *Health Affairs*, *37*(7), 1057–1064. DOI: 10.1377/hlthaff.2017.1633 PMID: 29985690

Albalawi, A. F., Yassen, M. H., Almuraydhi, K. M., Althobaiti, A. D., Alzahrani, H., & Alqahtani, K. M. (2024). *Ethical Obligations and Patient Consent in the Integration of Artificial Intelligence in Clinical Decision-Making*. JOURNAL OF HEALTHCARE SCIENCES., DOI: 10.52533/JOHS.2024.41241

Alford-Teaster, J. A., Wang, F., Moen, E. L., Cowan, L., Smith, R. E., Tosteson, A., & Onega, T. (2023). *Broadband Data Forensics: Spatiotemporal Variations of the Download/Upload Speed Metric Commonly Used to Evaluate Potential Telehealth Accessibility. Telemedicine Journal and E-Health*. The Official Journal of the American Telemedicine Association., DOI: 10.1089/tmj.2023.0320

Alrebh, A. H., Aljadher, A. M., Alghaith, B., Baothman, M. S., Al-Shaban, W. R., & Tufaif, T. A. A. (2024). *Ethical Considerations in Telemedicine and Remote Patient Care*. JOURNAL OF HEALTHCARE SCIENCES., DOI: 10.52533/JOHS.2024.41233

Asthana, S., & Prime, S. (2023). The role of digital transformation in addressing health inequalities in coastal communities: Barriers and enablers. *Frontiers in Health Services*, *3*, 1225757. Advance online publication. DOI: 10.3389/frhs.2023.1225757 PMID: 37711604

Bachuk, O. (2024). *DIGITAL TRANSFORMATION IN THE HEALTH CARE SYSTEM. Odesa National University Herald*. Economy., DOI: 10.32782/2304-0920/3-101-6

Balak, D. M. W., Deprez, E., Hilhorst, N., Hoorens, I., Gutermuth, J., Bos, W. J. W., & Lambert, J. (2024). Value-Based Healthcare: A Primer for the Dermatologist. *Dermatology (Basel, Switzerland)*, *240*, 814–822. DOI: 10.1159/000539372 PMID: 38934138

Blanke, B., & Perschke-Hartmann, C. (1994). The 1992 health reform victory over pressure group politics. *German Politics*, *3*(2), 233–248. DOI: 10.1080/09644009408404363

Bocean, C., & Vărzaru, A. (2025). Health status in the era of digital transformation and sustainable economic development. *BMC Health Services Research*, *25*(1), 343. Advance online publication. DOI: 10.1186/s12913-025-12498-y PMID: 40045359

Chandak, P. (2024). *Advancing Telemedicine Through Adaptive UX: A Systematic Review of Interface Design for Equity and Accessibility in Diverse Healthcare Settings*. Progress in Medical Sciences., DOI: 10.47363/PMS/2024(8)E178

Cornejo, J. A., Cruz-Ausejo, L., Alejandro, J. C., Burgos-Flores, M., Ambrosio-Melgarejo, J., Rimache, J. R., & Cruz, S. G. (2025). Barriers and limitations to the development of a telemental health service for workers in Peru- A user-centered approach. *PLoS One*, *20*(4), e0321401. Advance online publication. DOI: 10.1371/journal.pone.0321401 PMID: 40202969

Croke, K., & Ogbuoji, O. (2023). Health reform in Nigeria: The politics of primary health care and universal health coverage. *Health Policy and Planning*, *39*(1), 22–31. DOI: 10.1093/heapol/czad107 PMID: 37978878

Cruz, K. D., Hermosura, J. C., Vigonte, F. G., & Abante, M. V. (2023). Analyzing the Real-World Application of the Elasticity Theory of Demand and Supply and its Impact on Pricing Strategies, Consumer Behavior, and Policy Decisions. SSRN *Electronic Journal*. DOI: 10.2139/ssrn.4447159

Cunningham, C., Hutchings, T., Henderson, J. L., Rimas, H. M., & Chen, Y. (2016). Modeling the hospital safety partnership preferences of patients and their families: A discrete choice conjoint experiment. *Patient Preference and Adherence*, *10*, 1359–1372. DOI: 10.2147/PPA.S105605 PMID: 27555752

Curioso, W. H., Coronel-Chucos, L. G., & Oscuvilca-Tapia, E. (2024). Empowering the digital health workforce in Latin America in the context of the COVID-19 pandemic: The Peruvian case. *Informatics for Health & Social Care*, *49*(1), 73–82. DOI: 10.1080/17538157.2024.2315266 PMID: 38349775

Dada, S. A., & Adekola, A. D. (2024). Leveraging digital marketing for health behavior change: A model for engaging patients through pharmacies. *International Journal of Science and Technology Research Archive*. DOI: 10.53771/ijstra.2024.7.2.0063

Dailah, H. (2021). Understanding the determinants of digital health marketing strategies: A comparison of private and public sector hospitals *(Preprint)*. DOI: 10.2196/preprints.27844

Deal, K. (2013). Segmenting Patients and Physicians Using Preferences from Discrete Choice Experiments. *The Patient - Patient-Centered Outcomes Research*, *7*, 5–21. DOI: 10.1007/s40271-013-0037-9

Dillon, M., & McCaskey, P. H. (2018). *Quality Elasticity of Demand in Healthcare: Unraveling the Puzzle*. https://consensus.app/papers/quality-elasticity-of-demand-in-healthcare-unraveling-the-mccaskey-dillon/5d310935a4a05224a945a56aa71fb588/

Djakeli, K. (2024). Healthcare marketing, meaning, historical development, applications, and current status. In *Modern Healthcare Marketing in the Digital Era* (pp. 1–25). IGI Global Scientific Publishing., https://www.igi-global.com/chapter/healthcare-marketing-meaning-historical-development-applications-and-current-status/335050

Elliott, D., Robinson, E. J., Anthony, K., & Stillman, P. (2013). Patient-centered outcomes of a value-based insurance design program for patients with diabetes. *Population Health Management, 16*(2), 99–106. DOI: 10.1089/pop.2012.0031 PMID: 23405873

Engström, J., Norin, O., & Varennes, S. (2022, December 19). de G. de, & Valtakoski, A. (2022). Service design in healthcare: A segmentation-based approach. *Journal of Service Management, 33*(6), 50–78. Advance online publication. DOI: 10.1108/JOSM-06-2021-0239

Eriksen, J., Ebbesen, M., Eriksen, K. T., Hjermitslev, C., Knudsen, C., Bertelsen, P., Nøhr, C., & Weber, D. (2023). Equity in digital healthcare – the case of Denmark. *Frontiers in Public Health, 11*, 1225222. Advance online publication. DOI: 10.3389/fpubh.2023.1225222 PMID: 37744503

Fabra, M. E., Jung, J., & Katz, R. (2025). The contribution of ICTs and Telemedicine to COVID-19 vaccination: Evidence from the United States. *Health Policy and Technology, 14*(2), 100980. Advance online publication. DOI: 10.1016/j.hlpt.2025.100980

Fahad, M. (2024). *Technological Transformation in Healthcare: A Global Perspective. Journal of Digitainability, Realism & Mastery*. DREAM., DOI: 10.56982/dream.v3i12.294

Fan, C., Zou, G., Yang, C., & Zhao, Z. (2024). Can the digital transformation of pharmaceutical enterprises' finance improve healthcare equity? *Finance Research Letters, 67*, 105911. Advance online publication. DOI: 10.1016/j.frl.2024.105911

Ferrara, L., & Tozzi, V. (2018). Bundled payment for mental health care: A realist review. *International Journal of Integrated Care, 18*(s2), 155. Advance online publication. DOI: 10.5334/ijic.s2155

Ford, C., & Ashkenazy, Q. (2025). The Legal Innovation Sandbox. *The American Journal of Comparative Law*. Advance online publication. DOI: 10.1093/ajcl/avae029

Fotopoulou, A., Barratt, H., & Marandet, E. (2021). A data-based participatory approach for health equity and digital inclusion: Prioritizing stakeholders. *Health Promotion International*. Advance online publication. DOI: 10.1093/heapro/daab166 PMID: 34967901

Gallegos-Rejas, V. M., Thomas, E., Kelly, J. T., & Smith, A. C. (2022). A multi-stakeholder approach is needed to reduce the digital divide and encourage equitable access to telehealth. *Journal of Telemedicine and Telecare*, *29*(1), 73–78. DOI: 10.1177/1357633X221107995 PMID: 35733379

Ganesh, N. B., Siddineni, D., Reddy, V. V., Lateef, K., & Sharma, R.N Balaji Ganesh. (2025). Corporate Governance in the Age of AI: Ethical Oversight and Accountability Frameworks. *Journal of Information Systems Engineering & Management*, *10*(35s), 1141–1148. Advance online publication. DOI: 10.52783/jisem.v10i35s.6285

Godiyal, M., & Mishra, A. (2025). *Impact of Digital Marketing in Consumer Purchasing Behaviour*. International Journal For Multidisciplinary Research., DOI: 10.36948/ijfmr.2025.v07i02.40554

Grbic, M., Grbić, D. S., Štimac, L., & Šostar, Z. (2019). Digital marketing in healthcare. *European Journal of Public Health*, *29*(Supplement_4), ckz186.077. Advance online publication. DOI: 10.1093/eurpub/ckz186.077

Hamzah, N. H., Radzi, N. M., & Omar, I. M. (2025). DIGITAL LEADERSHIP COMPETENCIES THROUGH A SYSTEMATIC LITERATURE REVIEW: BRIDGING EDUCATIONAL DEVELOPMENT AND ORGANIZATIONAL SUCCESS. *International Journal of Modern Education*. DOI: 10.35631/IJMOE.724003

Haris, A. (2023). Digital Marketing and Consumer Engagement: A Systematic Review. *Amkop Management Accounting Review (AMAR)*. DOI: 10.37531/amar.v3i2.1442

Hermes, S., Riasanow, T., Clemons, E., Böhm, M., & Krcmar, H. (2020). The digital transformation of the healthcare industry: Exploring the rise of emerging platform ecosystems and their influence on the role of patients. *Business Research*, *13*(3), 1033–1069. Advance online publication. DOI: 10.1007/s40685-020-00125-x

Hollimon, L. A., Taylor, K. V., Fiegenbaum, R., & Seixas, A. A. (2025). Redefining and solving the digital divide and exclusion to improve healthcare: Going beyond access to include availability, adequacy, acceptability, and affordability. *Frontiers in Digital Health*, *7*, 1508686. Advance online publication. DOI: 10.3389/fdgth.2025.1508686 PMID: 40330871

Ii, R. R., van Mierlo, T., & Fournier, R. (2022). Testing Behavioral Nudges and Prompts in Digital Courses for the Treatment of Depression and Anxiety: Protocol for 3-Arm Randomized Controlled Trial *(Preprint)*. DOI: 10.2196/preprints.37231

Ikhalea, N., Chianumba, E. C., Mustapha, A. Y., Forkuo, A. Y., & Osamika, D. (2024). A Model for Strengthening Health Systems in Low-Resource Settings Using AI and Telemedicine. *International Journal of Future Engineering Innovations*. DOI: 10.54660/IJFEI.2024.1.1.86-92

Jayanagara, O. (2024). APPLICATION OF LEADERSHIP STYLES IN DIGITAL HEALTHCARE SYSTEMS. *Milestone: Journal of Strategic Management*. DOI: 10.19166/ms.v4i1.8304

Jedličková, A. (2024). Ethical dimensions in telemedicine—Balancing technology, responsible care, and patient protection. *Casopis Lekaru Ceskych*, *163*(3), 106–114. PMID: 38981731

Jeon, S., & Tuuminen, R. (2024). Healthcare quality indicators for value-based reimbursement in ophthalmology. *Acta Ophthalmologica*, *102*(6), 625–626. Advance online publication. DOI: 10.1111/aos.16698 PMID: 38656704

Jiang, X., Ming, W., & You, J. (2019). The Cost-Effectiveness of Digital Health Interventions on the Management of Cardiovascular Diseases: Systematic Review. *Journal of Medical Internet Research*, *21*(6), e13166. Advance online publication. DOI: 10.2196/13166 PMID: 31210136

Jiangliu, Y., Kim, H. T., Lazar, M., Liu, E., Mantri, S., Qiu, E., Berube, M., Sood, H., Walia, A. S., Biondi, B. E., Mesias, A. M., Mishuris, R., & de la Vega, P. B. (2024). A Medical Student-Led Multipronged Initiative to Close the Digital Divide in Outpatient Primary Care. *Applied Clinical Informatics*, *15*(4), 808–816. DOI: 10.1055/a-2370-2298 PMID: 39038793

Joshi, K. J., Vala, J., & Katoch, C. (2023). *Revolutionising Healthcare: The Pinnacle Role of Artificial Intelligence in Medical Institutes of National Importance*. NMO Journal., DOI: 10.4103/JNMO.JNMO_10_23

Joy, Z. H., Rahman, M. M., Uzzaman, A., & Maraj, M. A. A. (2024). INTEGRATING MACHINE LEARNING AND BIG DATA ANALYTICS FOR REAL-TIME DISEASE DETECTION IN SMART HEALTHCARE SYSTEMS. *Global Mainstream Journal*. DOI: 10.62304/ijhm.v1i3.162

Joynt, K. E., Figueroa, J., Beaulieu, N., Wild, R. C., Orav, E., & Jha, A. (2017). Segmenting high-cost Medicare patients into potentially actionable cohorts. *Health Care*, *5*(1-2), 1–2, 62–67. DOI: 10.1016/j.hjdsi.2016.11.002 PMID: 27914968

Kaplan, B. (2020). REVISITING HEALTH INFORMATION TECHNOLOGY ETHICAL, LEGAL, and SOCIAL ISSUES and EVALUATION: TELEHEALTH/TELEMEDICINE and COVID-19. *International Journal of Medical Informatics, 143*, 104239–104239. DOI: 10.1016/j.ijmedinf.2020.104239 PMID: 33152653

Karnik, H., Barbiero, J., Zemmel, D. J., Weiss, N. M., Kulik, P. K. G., Power, L. E., & Leider, J. P. (2025). Building Adaptive Leaders: A Formative Evaluation of the Region V Public Health Leadership Institute Using Ripple Effect Mapping and Focus Groups. *Journal of Public Health Management and Practice, 31*(4), 591–599. DOI: 10.1097/PHH.0000000000002150 PMID: 40172981

Khan, W. U., Shachak, A., & Seto, E. (2021). Understanding Decision-Making in the Adoption of Digital Health Technology: The Role of Behavioral Economics' Prospect Theory. *Journal of Medical Internet Research, 24*(2), e32714. Advance online publication. DOI: 10.2196/32714 PMID: 35129459

Khodayari-zarnaq, R., Mobasseri, K., Ghasemyani, S., Sadeghi-Ghyassi, F., Naghshi, M., & Kabiri, N. (2024). Challenges and Weaknesses of Leadership and Governance-related Health Policies in Iran: A Systematic Review. *Archives of Iranian Medicine, 27*(9), 508–521. DOI: 10.34172/aim.28907 PMID: 39465526

Krack, G. (2019). How to make value-based health insurance designs more effective? A systematic review and meta-analysis. *The European Journal of Health Economics, 20*(6), 841–856. DOI: 10.1007/s10198-019-01046-1 PMID: 30923986

Kurek, A. A., Shah, R., Inman, E., & Quiroga, A. (2023). Primary Care Redesign for Value-Based Care. *NEJM Catalyst Innovations in Care Delivery, 4*(12). Advance online publication. DOI: 10.1056/CAT.22.0285

Kuzmanović, M., & Savić, G. (2020). Avoiding the Privacy Paradox Using Preference-Based Segmentation: A Conjoint Analysis Approach. *Electronics (Basel), 9*(9), 1382. Advance online publication. DOI: 10.3390/electronics9091382

Leckenby, E., Dawoud, D., Bouvy, J., & Jónsson, P. (2021). The Sandbox Approach and its Potential for Use in Health Technology Assessment: A Literature Review. *Applied Health Economics and Health Policy, 19*(6), 857–869. DOI: 10.1007/s40258-021-00665-1 PMID: 34254275

Lemak, C., Pena, D., Jones, D. A., Kim, D. H., & Guptill, J. (2024). Leadership to Accelerate Healthcare's Digital Transformation: Evidence From 33 Health Systems. *Journal of Healthcare Management, 69*(4), 267–279. DOI: 10.1097/JHM-D-23-00210 PMID: 38976787

Leung, L. B., Rose, D., Stockdale, S. E., McGowan, M., Yano, E., Graaff, A. L., Dresselhaus, T., & Rubenstein, L. (2019). Regional Adoption of Primary Care-Mental Health Integration in Veterans Health Administration Patient-Centered Medical Homes. *Journal for Healthcare Quality*, *41*(5), 297–305. Advance online publication. DOI: 10.1097/JHQ.0000000000000206 PMID: 31135605

Leyland, M., Archer, N., Deal, K., & Hassanein, K. (2011). PDB76 DESIGNING A SERVICE FRAMEWORK FOR ELECTRONIC PERSONAL HEALTH RECORDS: A PATIENT-CENTRED APPROACH. *Value in Health*, *14*(3), A105. Advance online publication. DOI: 10.1016/j.jval.2011.02.584

Li, Y.-H., Li, Y., Wei, M.-Y., & Li, G. (2024). Innovation and challenges of artificial intelligence technology in personalized healthcare. *Scientific Reports*, *14*(1), 18994. Advance online publication. DOI: 10.1038/s41598-024-70073-7 PMID: 39152194

Liang, S., Stults, C., Jones, V. G., Huang, Q., Sutton, J., Tennyson, G., & Chan, A. S. (2021). Effects of Behavioral Economics–Based Messaging on Appointment Scheduling Through Patient Portals and Appointment Completion: Observational Study. *JMIR Human Factors*, *9*(1), e34090. Advance online publication. DOI: 10.2196/34090 PMID: 35353051

Liu, J. X., Vallin, J., Chiu, C., Cabrera, F. A., Hunter, L., Rao, A., Njau, P., & McCoy, S. (2023). Designing for two: How enhancing human-centered design with behavioral nudges unlocked breakthroughs to promote young women's psychological safety and access to reproductive care in Tanzania. *Social Science & Medicine*, *320*, 115683. Advance online publication. DOI: 10.1016/j.socscimed.2023.115683 PMID: 36709692

Love-Koh, J., Griffin, S., Kataika, E., Revill, P., Sibandze, S., & Walker, S. (2020). Methods to promote equity in health resource allocation in low- and middle-income countries: An overview. *Globalization and Health*, *16*(1), 6. Advance online publication. DOI: 10.1186/s12992-019-0537-z PMID: 31931823

Macrae, C., & Ansell, C. K. (2024). Generative Spaces: Collaboration, Learning and Innovation in a Regulatory Sandbox. SSRN *Electronic Journal*. DOI: 10.2139/ssrn.4825907

Mair, J., Hashim, J., Thai, L., Tai, E. S., Ryan, J. C., Kowatsch, T., Müller-Riemenschneider, F., & Edney, S. (2025). Understanding and overcoming barriers to digital health adoption: A patient and public involvement study. *Translational Behavioral Medicine*, *15*(1), ibaf010. Advance online publication. DOI: 10.1093/tbm/ibaf010 PMID: 40167046

Mallidi, R. K., Sharma, M., & Singh, J. (2021). Legacy Digital Transformation: TCO and ROI Analysis. *International Journal of Electrical and Computer Engineering Systems*. DOI: 10.32985/ijeces.12.3.5

Masyuri, R. I. (2024). Towards Equitable Healthcare: Redesigning Informed Consent Regulations. *Journal of Ecohumanism*. DOI: 10.62754/joe.v3i8.5447

Mattei, P. (2020). Digital governance in tax-funded European healthcare systems: From the Back office to patient empowerment. *Israel Journal of Health Policy Research*, *9*(1), 3. Advance online publication. DOI: 10.1186/s13584-020-0361-1 PMID: 31952548

McGuire, E., Al-Zu'bi, M., Boa-Alvarado, M., Luu, T. T. G., Sylvester, J. M., & Leñero, E. M.-V. (2024). Equity principles: Using social theory for more effective social transformation in agricultural research for development. *Agricultural Systems*, *218*, 103999. Advance online publication. DOI: 10.1016/j.agsy.2024.103999

McNeil, C. D. W., Professor, P. E. M. E., Pereira, D. B., Ensz, O. S., Lukose, K., Harrell, G., & Feller, D. B. (2024). Toward a Comprehensive Model of Medical-Dental-Behavioral Integration. *JDR Clinical and Translational Research*, *9*(1_suppl), 23–31. DOI: 10.1177/23800844241273836 PMID: 39558739

Merino, M., del Barrio, J., Nuño, R., & Errea, M. (2024). Value-based digital health: A systematic literature review of the value elements of digital health care. *Digital Health*, *10*, 20552076241277438. Advance online publication. DOI: 10.1177/20552076241277438 PMID: 39403712

Musa, S., Abdulwahab, L. O., & Beri, M. H. (2026). The Impact of AI Technologies in Transforming Financial Systems and Driving Innovation. In *Promoting Inclusivity and Accessibility With FinTech* (pp. 153–182). IGI Global Scientific Publishing., https://www.igi-global.com/chapter/the-impact-of-ai-technologies-in-transforming-financial-systems-and-driving-innovation/387218

Nadhamuni, S., John, O., Kulkarni, M., Nanda, E., Venkatraman, S., Varma, D., Balsari, S., Gudi, N., Samantaray, S., Reddy, H., & Sheel, V. (2021). Driving digital transformation of comprehensive primary health services at scale in India: An enterprise architecture framework. *BMJ Global Health*, *6*(Suppl 5), e005242. Advance online publication. DOI: 10.1136/bmjgh-2021-005242 PMID: 34312149

Nordberg, S. S., Jaso-Yim, B., Sah, P., Schuler, K., Eyllon, M., Pennine, M., Hoyler, G. H., Barnes, J. B., Murillo, L., O'Dea, H., Orth, L., Rogers, E., Welch, G., Peloquin, G. D., & Youn, S. J. (2024). Evaluating the Implementation and Clinical Effectiveness of an Innovative Digital First Care Model for Behavioral Health Using the RE-AIM Framework: Quantitative Evaluation. *Journal of Medical Internet Research, 26*, e54528. Advance online publication. DOI: 10.2196/54528 PMID: 39476366

Nwadiokwu, O. T. (2025). *Ethical AI and machine learning integration in health innovation information systems for clinical excellence. Computer Science &amp.* IT Research Journal., DOI: 10.51594/csitrj.v6i3.1872

O'Laughlin, B. (2016). Pragmatism, Structural Reform and the Politics of Inequality in Global Public Health. *Development and Change, 47*(4), 686–711. DOI: 10.1111/dech.12251

Ochinanwata, N., Ezepue, P., Nwankwo, T., Ochinanwata, C., & Igwe, P. (2021). Public–private entrepreneurial financing partnership model in Nigeria. *Thunderbird International Business Review, 63*(3), 369–379. Advance online publication. DOI: 10.1002/tie.22194

Oluwagbade, E. (2025). Bridging the healthcare Gap: The role of AI-Driven Telemedicine in Emerging Economies. *International Journal of Research Publication and Reviews.* DOI: 10.55248/gengpi.6.0125.0531

Oso, O. B., Alli, O. I., Babarinde, A., & Ibeh, A. I. (2025). Impact-Driven Healthcare Investments: A Conceptual Framework for Deploying Capital and Technology in Frontier Market. *International Journal of Multidisciplinary Research and Growth Evaluation.* DOI: 10.54660/.IJMRGE.2025.6.1.1702-1720

Palombini, M., Vereen, T., Taghiani, J., & Chitre, T. (2023). Building a Framework for a More Inclusive Healthcare System. *Telehealth and Medicine Today, 8*(3). Advance online publication. DOI: 10.30953/thmt.v8.414

Philip, J., Gilli, K., & Knappstein, M. (2023). Identifying key leadership competencies for digital transformation: Evidence from a cross-sectoral Delphi study of global managers. *Leadership &amp. Leadership and Organization Development Journal, 44*(3), 392–406. Advance online publication. DOI: 10.1108/LODJ-02-2022-0063

Pooyan, E. J., Sakha, M. A., Mohtasham, F., & Mostafavi, H. (2018). The Effect of Resource Allocation Decisions on Efficiency and Equity in the Health Sector: A Systematic Review. *Journal of Health Research, 3*(1), 28–34. DOI: 10.29252/cjhr.3.1.28

Poveda, J., Bretón-Romero, R., del Rio-Bermudez, C., Taberna, M., & Medrano, I. H. (2022). How can artificial intelligence optimize value-based contracting? *Journal of Pharmaceutical Policy and Practice*, *15*(1), 85. Advance online publication. DOI: 10.1186/s40545-022-00475-3 PMID: 36401303

Puri, A. (2024). Legal Challenges and Considerations in Implementing Telemedicine Services. *International Journal of Social Science and Economic Research.* DOI: 10.46609/IJSSER.2024.v09i09.017

Rahimi, K. (2019). Digital health and the elusive quest for cost savings. *The Lancet. Digital Health*, *1*(3), 108–109. DOI: 10.1016/S2589-7500(19)30056-1 PMID: 33323258

Raven, J., Mansour, W., Aikins, M., Bulthuis, S., Chikaphupha, K., Dieleman, M., Kok, M., Martineau, T., Ssengooba, F., Wyss, K., & Vallières, F. (2024). From PERFORM to PERFORM2Scale: Lessons from scaling-up a health management strengthening intervention to support Universal Health Coverage in three African countries. *Health Policy and Planning*, *39*(8), 841–853. DOI: 10.1093/heapol/czae063 PMID: 38978193

Reed, M. E., Warton, E. M., Kim, E., Solomon, M. D., & Karter, A. (2017). Value-Based Insurance Design Benefit Offsets Reductions In Medication Adherence Associated With Switch To Deductible Plan. *Health Affairs*, *36*(3), 516–523. DOI: 10.1377/hlthaff.2016.1316 PMID: 28264954

Richard, L., Furler, J., Densley, K., Haggerty, J., Russell, G., Levesque, J., & Gunn, J. (2016). Equity of access to primary healthcare for vulnerable populations: The IMPACT international online survey of innovations. *International Journal for Equity in Health*, *15*(1), 64. Advance online publication. DOI: 10.1186/s12939-016-0351-7 PMID: 27068028

Richardson, S., Lawrence, K., Schoenthaler, A. M., & Mann, D. M. (2022). A framework for digital health equity. *NPJ Digital Medicine*, *5*(1), 119. Advance online publication. DOI: 10.1038/s41746-022-00663-0 PMID: 35982146

Riegler, J. (2023). *Comparative Ethics of Modern Payment Models*. Voices in Bioethics., DOI: 10.52214/vib.v9i.10310

Santos, P., & Nazaré, I. (2025). The doctor and patient of tomorrow: Exploring the intersection of artificial intelligence, preventive medicine, and ethical challenges in future healthcare. *Frontiers in Digital Health*, *7*, 1588479. Advance online publication. DOI: 10.3389/fdgth.2025.1588479 PMID: 40248038

Schutte, L. (2024). Advancing Digital Health Equity: An Interdisciplinary Educational Approach to Digital Health Access and Inclusivity. *Studies in Health Technology and Informatics*, *315*, 511–514. DOI: 10.3233/SHTI240201 PMID: 39049311

Scuffham, P. (2002). Systematic review of cost effectiveness in telemedicine. *BMJ (Clinical Research Ed.)*, *325*(7364), 598.1. Advance online publication. DOI: 10.1136/bmj.325.7364.598 PMID: 12228145

Sebastian, R. (2024). The Role of Artificial Intelligence in Telemedicine: Legal Considerations under Indonesian Health Laws. *Devotion : Journal of Research and Community Service*. DOI: 10.59188/devotion.v5i12.20694

Settou, H., & Aomari, A. (2024). *The impact of the social digital influencer on the attitudinal change of his virtual community*. South Florida Journal of Development., DOI: 10.46932/sfjdv5n11-028

Shkeer, A. S., Sharabati, A., Samarah, T., Alqurneh, M. I. M., & Ali, A. (2024). The influence of social media content marketing on consumer engagement: A mediating of the role of consumer cognition. *International Journal of Data and Network Science*. DOI: 10.5267/j.ijdns.2024.5.015

Shuliuk, B. (2021). CORPORATE FINANCING OF PUBLIC-PRIVATE PARTNERSHIP PROJECTS: ASSESSMENT OF FINANCIAL OPPORTUNITIES AND RISKS. *Financial and Credit Activity: Problems of Theory and Practice*. DOI: 10.18371/fcaptp.v3i38.237422

Simons, M., Golas, S., Agboola, S., & Buijs, J. op den, Felsted, J., Fischer, N., & Orenstein, A. (2018). *Maximizing Potentially Avoidable Hospitalizations and Cost Savings Beyond Targeting the Most Costly Patients (Preprint)*. DOI: 10.2196/preprints.11731

Smyshlyaev, A. (2022). Public-private partnership in the system of compulsory health insurance: Features and trends. *Spravočnik Vrača Obŝej Praktiki (Journal of Family Medicine)*. DOI: 10.33920/med-10-2206-02

Stanić, T., Avşar, T. S., & Gomes, M. (2023). Economic Evaluations of Digital Health Interventions for Children and Adolescents: Systematic Review. *Journal of Medical Internet Research*, *25*, e45958. Advance online publication. DOI: 10.2196/45958 PMID: 37921844

Stecker, E., Ayanian, J., & Fendrick, A. M. (2015). Value-Based Insurance Design: Aligning Incentives to Improve Cardiovascular Care. *Circulation*, *132*(16), 1580–1585. Advance online publication. DOI: 10.1161/CIRCULATIONAHA.114.012584 PMID: 26481563

Stratton, E., Jones, N., Peters, S. E., Torous, J., & Glozier, N. (2021). Digital mHealth Interventions for Employees. *Journal of Occupational and Environmental Medicine*, *63*(8), 512–525. DOI: 10.1097/JOM.0000000000002267 PMID: 34050095

Summers, C., & Curtis, K. (2020). Novel Digital Architecture of a "Low Carb Program" for Initiating and Maintaining Long-Term Sustainable Health-Promoting Behavior Change in Patients with Type 2 Diabetes. *JMIR Diabetes*, *5*(1), e15030. Advance online publication. DOI: 10.2196/15030 PMID: 32130113

Susanti, D. (2021). DIGITAL MARKETING TO CUSTOMER VALUE AND CUSTOMER ENGAGEMENT IN REPEAT PURCHASE ON THE MARKETPLACE. *SULTANIST: Jurnal Manajemen Dan Keuangan*. DOI: 10.37403/sultanist.v9i2.339

Swan, E. L., Peltier, J. W., & Dahl, A. J. (2023). Artificial intelligence in healthcare: The value co-creation process and influence of other digital health transformations. *Journal of Research in Interactive Marketing*. Advance online publication. DOI: 10.1108/JRIM-09-2022-0293

Swartz, A., Lefevre, A., Perera, S., Kinney, M., & George, A. (2020). Multiple pathways to scaling up and sustainability: An exploration of digital health solutions in South Africa. *Globalization and Health*, *17*(1), 77. Advance online publication. DOI: 10.1186/s12992-021-00716-1 PMID: 34229699

Swenson, E. R., Bastian, N. D., & Nembhard, H. (2016). Data analytics in health promotion: Health market segmentation and classification of total joint replacement surgery patients. *Expert Systems with Applications*, *60*, 118–129. DOI: 10.1016/j.eswa.2016.05.006

Sytnyk, Y., & Tarkanii, M. (2024). Trends in development of digital literacy of the staff of medical institutions. *Management and Entrepreneurship in Ukraine: The Stages of Formation and Problems of Development*. DOI: 10.23939/smeu2024.02.138

Usuemerai, P. A., Ibikunle, O. E., Abass, L. A., Alemede, V., Nwankwo, E. I., & Mbata, A. O. (2024). *A conceptual framework for digital health marketing strategies to enhance public health outcomes in underserved communities*. World Journal of Advanced Pharmaceutical and Medical Research., DOI: 10.53346/wjapmr.2024.7.2.0044

Vahedi, S., Yazdi-Feyzabadi, V., Amini-Rarani, M., Mohammadbeigi, A., Khosravi, A., & Rezapour, A. (2020). Tracking socio-economic inequalities in healthcare utilization in Iran: A repeated cross-sectional analysis. *BMC Public Health*, *20*(1), 929. Advance online publication. DOI: 10.1186/s12889-020-09001-z PMID: 32539734

Vecchio, P. D., Secundo, G., & Garzoni, A. (2023). Phygital technologies and environments for breakthrough innovation in customers' and citizens' journey. A critical literature review and future agenda. *Technological Forecasting and Social Change*, *189*, 122342. Advance online publication. DOI: 10.1016/j.techfore.2023.122342

Venkateswaran, S., Slaria, S., & Mukherjee, S. (2022). Political motivation as a key driver for universal health coverage. *Frontiers in Public Health*, *10*, 922578. Advance online publication. DOI: 10.3389/fpubh.2022.922578 PMID: 36457324

Waddell, K. J., Shah, P., Adusumalli, S., & Patel, M. S. (2020). Using Behavioral Economics and Technology to Improve Outcomes in Cardio-Oncology. *JACC. CardioOncology*, *2*(1), 84–96. DOI: 10.1016/j.jaccao.2020.02.006 PMID: 34396212

Wang, C.-J., Liu, S., Yang, H., Guo, J., Wu, Y., & Liu, J. (2023). Ethical Considerations of Using ChatGPT in Health Care. *Journal of Medical Internet Research*, *25*, e48009. Advance online publication. DOI: 10.2196/48009 PMID: 37566454

Weinberger, N., Hery, D., Mahr, D., Adler, S. O., Stadlbauer, J., & Ahrens, T. D. (2025). Beyond the gender data gap: Co-creating equitable digital patient twins. *Frontiers in Digital Health*, *7*, 1584415. Advance online publication. DOI: 10.3389/fdgth.2025.1584415 PMID: 40370708

Wimalasena, L. M. D. O., & Jayasinghe, C. (2025). Digital Marketing and Brand Engagement Behavior: A Conceptual Review. *Sri Lanka Journal of Marketing*. DOI: 10.4038/sljmuok.v10i2.197

Wolff, B., Nielsen, S., & Kiwanuka, A. (2024). Practical guidelines for developing digital health solutions to increase equity in dementia care in the UK. *Frontiers in Digital Health*, *6*, 1490156. Advance online publication. DOI: 10.3389/fdgth.2024.1490156 PMID: 39749098

Yoo, B.-K., Kim, M., Sasaki, T., Hoch, J., & Marcin, J. (2017). Selected Use of Telemedicine in Intensive Care Units Based on Severity of Illness Improves Cost-Effectiveness. *Telemedicine Journal and e-Health*, *24*(1), 21–36. DOI: 10.1089/tmj.2017.0069 PMID: 28661790

Zhang, C., & Wang, Y. (2024). Is enterprise digital transformation beneficial to shareholders? Insights from the cost of equity capital. *International Review of Financial Analysis*, *92*, 103104. Advance online publication. DOI: 10.1016/j.irfa.2024.103104

Zhang, S., & Song, J. (2024). An empirical investigation into the preferences of the elderly for user interface design in personal electronic health record systems. *Frontiers in Digital Health*, *5*, 1289904. Advance online publication. DOI: 10.3389/fdgth.2023.1289904 PMID: 38348367

Chapter 8
From Mass Campaigns to Phygital Governance:
Health Literacy, Policy Advertising, and Reform Pathways in India

Babitha Nadampalli
Christ University, India

Sunitha Abhay Jain
Christ University, India

ABSTRACT

Over seven decades, India's health literacy journey has progressed from traditional mass campaigns to integrated phygital governance, blending physical outreach with digital communication. This paper examines the evolution of health communication, policy advertising, and reform through the lens of India's Five-Year Plans (1951–2017). It traces the shift from school-based civic education and rural health campaigns to technologically enabled, participatory Information, Education, and Communication (IEC) strategies. While health literacy has remained a core national priority, persistent gaps in equity, access, and behavioral outcomes endure. The study underscores the need for phygital inclusion, participatory communication, and data-driven governance to strengthen public health systems and ensure equitable, sustainable health literacy for all citizens in the digital age.

INTRODUCTION

Health literacy, a core public health outcome, is defined as the ability to obtain, process and understand basic health information needed to make appropriate health

DOI: 10.4018/979-8-3373-7173-3.ch008

decisions. It is not just about the information, but about ensuring people have the competences to access and apply it in their daily lives, navigating between health sectors, systems and determinants at the personal, household and community levels. Internationally, health literacy is accepted to be a determinant of health in its own right and as an intermediate variable for public health outcomes such as disease prevention and tackling treatment adherence, which also have implications for the efficiency of the healthcare system. Gigauri and Djakeli (2021) critically analyze Georgia's health reforms, highlighting economic alignment, institutional adaptation, and universal coverage challenges.

In the Indian context, health literacy as a policy concept evolved in concurrence with the country's national development planning. Given that for almost six decades (during the First Five-Year Plan from 1951 to 1956 until the Twelfth from 2012 to 2017), the Planning Commission of India was responsible for formulating long-term development strategies, which also have implications for health education and promotion efforts. The Commission navigated the field of health literacy through the finitude of socio-cultural challenges, institutional capacities and epidemiological realities, which changed not just over time but often scripted new shifts in India's governance framework.

The earliest two Plans—the First (1951–56) and Second (1956–61)—placed health literacy within the post-Independence nation-building enterprise. Health education, propagandised through rural health bureaux and reinforced as a prime means for fostering self-reliance in health care, was territorialized within the school curriculum during the First Plan (1951–56) and throughout both Plans Second (1956–61). It was a focused-on hygiene, to help contain the spreading of diseases, and it was the duty of all members to protect their health, basically in moral/sexual terms and civic terms. Taking health awareness to the grassroots level by targeting primarily the rural population, where the critical goal was to raise an ongoing small amount of awareness in day-to-day life. Djakeli (2024) reconceptualizes healthcare marketing as AI-driven health value creation, though stronger empirical and ethical analysis is needed.

Through the Fourth/Fifth Plans of the late 1960s and 1971, health literacy shifted direction to a restrictive, vertical, and concrete National Health Policies, such as the family planning and nutrition education programmes conducted nationwide. In a way, these were not public health concerns but were related more broadly to demographic and economic objectives. Messages were delivered via traditional cultural media through mobilised folk songs, theatre and village drama. The project team comprising officials of the Central Health Education Bureau (CHEB) clearly understood that culturally apt communication methods were required. Nutrition education, as implemented by programmes such as the Applied Nutrition Programme and several others in the previous decades, emphasised food processing skills and encouraged the shift to foods with higher nutritional value even within an overall wild plant consumption pattern.

In the 1980s onward, Health education, being rechristened as Information, Education and Communication (IEC) model, gained traction as a stated policy tool, institutionalised for the first time in the Eighth Plan (1992–97). This led to the growth of programme-specific, vertical health policies, which were carried out as health communication and disseminated through mass media. Especially with the advent of HIV/AIDS and other communicable diseases, these vertical health policies on health awareness gained traction. This approach, while designing and delivering messages in a more sophisticated way, also had its downside; fragmentation where different programmes were running parallel IEC units rather than one health literacy strategy.

Thus, in the later plans and even more so by the tenth and through the twelfth plan, health literacy broadened its horizon beyond communicable diseases to include Non-Communicable Diseases (NCDs) and lifestyle risks, nutrition security, and other health domains of concern. Around the same time, to enhance the performance of various health departments and foster institutional consolidation, a National Board for Health Education was established. Subsequently, to empower health awareness programs, the Central Health Education Bureau (CHEB) was established This evolution underscored the fact that health literacy was not only about the direct transfer of information but also about enabling a behavioural change in people, which helps the prevention of diseases through health awareness.

These public health awareness programmes, policies, and institutionalisation have helped to prevent diseases. Successful among these were the Polio initiatives that brought about awareness through mass media, emphasising the "Do Boond Zindagi Ke' and with the efforts of the WHO, India was declared a 'Polio Free Nation'. These Health initiatives were interrupted due to the dismantling of the Planning Commission in 2014 and the abandonment of the Five-Year Plan framework. Although NITI Aayog would still be expected to monitor health outcomes, the routinely recurring national framework with a plan of action directed at promoting health literacy is no longer available. Striking this balance between plan and action remains a significant challenge for India. The evolution of healthcare communication in India, from an overall trajectory from mass civic education to narrow programme communication, is now moving back towards comprehensive lifestyle and chronic disease control, revealing key insights into the successes as well as sustained insufficiencies of its current approach to health literacy.

BACKGROUND

Health literacy, a cornerstone of public health, encompasses not only the acquisition of information but also the cognitive and social competencies that enable individuals to access, understand, and apply health knowledge in daily life (Nutbeam, 2000). Globally, it has evolved from didactic awareness-based models to participatory and technology-driven systems of empowerment, as reflected in the World Health Organization's *Ottawa Charter for Health Promotion* (1986) and subsequent frameworks emphasizing social determinants and equity (Kickbusch et al., 2013). Over time, digitalization has given rise to *eHealth literacy*—the ability to navigate, appraise, and utilize health information from electronic sources (Norman & Skinner, 2006)—a shift that has transformed healthcare delivery, particularly in low- and middle-income countries through telemedicine, community monitoring, and mobile-based interventions. India's health literacy journey mirrors these global trends but is uniquely shaped by its socio-political and cultural diversity, evolving across three major phases: civic-oriented health education (1951–1974), institutionalization and diversification (1974–1997), and consolidation through digital governance (1997–present). The early Five-Year Plans framed health education as a civic duty, using schools, radio, and rural outreach to promote hygiene, sanitation, and family planning (Planning Commission, 1951; 1974). The late 1980s and 1990s witnessed a paradigm shift through the Information, Education, and Communication (IEC) model, which introduced behavior change strategies targeting issues such as HIV/AIDS and nutrition. However, overlapping programs and limited inter-ministerial coordination constrained efficiency. With the advent of the Tenth and Twelfth Five-Year Plans, health literacy broadened to include lifestyle diseases, mental health, and traditional knowledge systems like AYUSH (Planning Commission, 2012). Following the replacement of the Planning Commission with NITI Aayog in 2014, India entered a new era of outcome-based, data-driven governance, embedding health literacy within digital platforms such as the Ayushman Bharat Digital Mission (ABDM), CoWIN, eSanjeevani, and MyGov Health Portal. This *phygital* (physical + digital) convergence has redefined communication by integrating community-based outreach with digital accessibility, promoting participatory health engagement while revealing enduring gaps in equity and digital literacy (World Health Organization, 2023). Despite impressive technological strides, India lacks a unified national health literacy policy, resulting in fragmented efforts and uneven evaluation mechanisms. A horizontal, multisectoral communication strategy—linking preventive care, nutrition, mental health, and non-communicable diseases under one inclusive framework—is essential to align with Sustainable Development Goals 3 and 10 (Reddy et al., 2018). Ultimately, India's transition from mass campaigns to phygital governance underscores a dual imperative: leveraging digital innovation to democratize access while ensuring that cultural sensitivity, ethical transparency, and critical health literacy remain central to building an equitable, participatory, and resilient public health ecosystem (Nutbeam, 2008).

THEORETICAL FRAMEWORK

A robust theoretical foundation is indispensable for understanding how health literacy evolves within the interplay of governance, policy, and communication. In India, health literacy has never existed in isolation; it is embedded in developmental planning, socio-cultural complexity, and technological transformation. The analysis is grounded in four major frameworks—Health Promotion Theory, Social Cognitive Theory, Diffusion of Innovations Theory, and Digital Governance with Phygital Integration—each illuminating a different dimension of India's transition from mass awareness campaigns to participatory, data-driven communication systems. The *Health Promotion Theory* articulated in the *Ottawa Charter for Health Promotion* (World Health Organization [WHO], 1986) conceptualizes health as a resource for daily living rather than a mere objective, emphasizing empowerment, supportive environments, and social determinants (Solar & Irwin, 2010). This empowerment-based view resonates with India's early health education programs that sought civic responsibility but lacked participatory depth. In modern governance, this theory underscores horizontal collaboration—connecting government, community, and digital stakeholders—to reframe health literacy as social transformation rather than information transmission (Nutbeam, 2000, 2008). The *Social Cognitive Theory* (Bandura, 1986) explains behavioral learning through observation, imitation, and self-efficacy, clarifying how citizens internalize messages through role models and media. Campaigns such as *Swachh Bharat* and *Polio Free India* utilized this principle, employing influential ambassadors to enhance vicarious learning and public confidence. In the phygital context, this theory justifies digital training for community health workers (ASHAs) as an empowerment process that enhances both skill and belief in capability. Complementing this, *Diffusion of Innovations Theory (*Rogers, 2003) delineates how new ideas and technologies spread across social systems, explaining why highly observable and compatible initiatives like *Pulse Polio* achieved rapid adoption, while less tangible issues such as mental health faced slower diffusion. Phygital models such as *eSanjeevani* extend Rogers' framework by merging digital diffusion with face-to-face community interaction, using hybrid communication pathways like WhatsApp and local radio to ensure localized resonance. However, traditional frameworks must evolve to address twenty-first-century realities of *Digital Governance*, which fuses physical infrastructure with digital ecosystems to enhance transparency, participation, and accountability

(Dunleavy et al., 2006; Margetts & Dunleavy, 2013). Drawing on the *Technology Acceptance Model (TAM)* (Davis, 1989), digital engagement depends on perceived usefulness, ease of use, and institutional trust (Saxena & Pillai, 2021). Platforms such as *CoWIN* and *MyGov* exemplify these principles, where user-friendly design and data credibility foster participation. Theoretically, phygital governance also reflects cybernetic systems—adaptive networks that incorporate feedback loops for policy learning—transforming citizens into active data contributors rather than passive recipients. Yet, ethical imperatives—data privacy, consent, and inclusivity—remain central to sustaining trust in these systems. Integrating all these perspectives, an *Integrated Theoretical Model* emerges: empowerment from health promotion, behavioral mechanisms from social cognition, adoption processes from innovation diffusion, and systemic enablers from digital governance. This synthesis reframes health literacy as a *systemic capability*, evolving through reciprocal relationships among policy design, community engagement, and technological inclusion. Applied to India, this framework reveals a historical continuum—from top-down instruction during the Planning Commission era to citizen co-creation under NITI Aayog's data-driven governance. Each stage enriches the understanding that sustainable reform requires not only technology but also participatory empowerment grounded in learning and trust. While existing theories offer valuable insights, none fully encapsulate India's plural, multilingual context; hence, adaptation is necessary to include critical literacy and cultural ecology perspectives (Chinn, 2011). In sum, this theoretical scaffolding position health literacy within a confluence of empowerment, behavioral reinforcement, innovation diffusion, and digital co-production—marking India's shift from information delivery to collaborative governance where citizens and institutions continuously co-create public health knowledge through phygital engagement.

CONCEPTUAL FRAMEWORK

The conceptual framework of this study bridges theoretical understanding with practical analysis by situating health literacy within India's evolving ecosystem of phygital governance—a hybrid system integrating physical outreach and digital participation. Drawing on four theoretical foundations—Health Promotion Theory, Social Cognitive Theory, Diffusion of Innovations, and Digital Governance—the framework conceptualizes the *Phygital Health Literacy Governance Model (PHLGM)* as a cyclical system connecting policy communication, behavioral transformation, and feedback-driven reform. The model operates through six interrelated constructs: *policy advertising, health literacy, behavioral change, institutional trust, digital inclusion, and reform pathways*. Policy advertising functions as the initiating variable, transforming policy into actionable public knowledge through strategic communication mechanisms such as campaigns, media outreach, and social marketing. Its effectiveness depends on message clarity, cultural relevance, and dissemination equity, as evidenced by initiatives like *Do Boond Zindagi Ke* and *Swachh Bharat Abhiyan.* The impact of such advertising is mediated by health literacy, defined by Nutbeam (2000, 2008) as the cognitive, emotional, and social competence enabling individuals to access, understand, and use information for well-being. Within the PHLGM, health literacy evolves across three layers—functional (basic comprehension), interactive (social engagement), and critical (analytical participation)—serving as the bridge between communication and behavior. Behavioral change emerges as the dependent outcome, shaped by observational learning, self-efficacy, and reinforcement as articulated in Bandura's (1986) Social Cognitive Theory. This change occurs not merely at the individual level but also collectively, through community-based reinforcement and digital feedback systems. Importantly, *institutional trust* moderates this process by influencing the credibility and acceptance of messages; citizens are more likely to engage with health platforms when they perceive transparency, reliability, and ethical data use (Saxena & Pillai, 2021). Similarly, *digital inclusion* functions as a structural moderator—determining who can access and benefit from phygital health services. Persistent inequalities in internet access, literacy, and linguistic diversity create uneven participation, emphasizing the need for culturally adaptive and equity-driven digital design (Kumar & Singh, 2022). The final component, *reform pathways*, represents the model's feedback mechanism: behavioral outcomes feed back into governance systems through digital platforms like *CoWIN* and *Ayushman Bharat Digital Mission (ABDM),* generating data that inform iterative policy learning and adaptive reform. This cyclical process aligns with the principles of cybernetic governance (Margetts & Dunleavy, 2013), wherein policy systems evolve through continuous feedback and responsiveness. Operationally, each construct within the PHLGM can be measured using defined indicators—campaign reach for policy advertising, literacy scales for health literacy, adoption rates for behavior, trust indices for institutional reliability, ICT indices for digital inclusion, and administrative data for reform feedback. The framework's contribution lies in reconceptualizing health literacy as both a *governance capability* and a *social outcome*, integrating communication science, behavioral psychology, and digital systems within a unified schema. Furthermore, it aligns with the Sustainable Development Goals (SDGs)—notably SDG 3 (health and well-being), SDG 9 (innovation and infrastructure), SDG 10 (reducing inequalities), and SDG 16 (inclusive institutions)—demonstrating how communication, technology, and governance interact to produce equitable health outcomes. By positioning literacy as both an input and an output of governance, the PHLGM introduces the notion of bidirectional literacy, where citizens co-create, critique, and reshape health policies through participatory engagement. The framework's conceptual innovations—phygital integration, adaptive governance, and behavioral systems thinking—represent a paradigmatic shift from one-way awareness campaigns to a participatory, data-driven ecosystem of health reform. A practical example is India's *COVID-19 CoWIN* vaccination ecosystem, where strategic communication, multilingual literacy initiatives, observed peer behavior, institutional trust, and inclusive digital practices collectively yielded large-scale behavioral change and iterative policy refinement. Despite implementation challenges such as fragmented institutional coordination, uneven connectivity, and privacy concerns, the model demonstrates how adaptive, ethically grounded communication can strengthen health systems. Ultimately, the PHLGM establishes a replicable, interdisciplinary framework for understanding and guiding health literacy governance in developing nations navigating digital transformation.

HEALTH LITERACY IN THE EARLY PLANS: FOUNDATIONS AND INSTITUTIONAL STRUCTURES (1951–1974)

The early decades following India's independence marked the formative period of the nation's approach to health literacy—an era defined by idealism, civic responsibility, and centralized planning. Health literacy, conceptualized primarily as *health education*, was introduced as an essential component of the broader national development agenda under the First and Second Five-Year Plans (1951–56 and 1956–61). These plans sought to transform the newly independent nation into a socially responsible and self-reliant society, emphasizing hygiene, sanitation, nutrition, and disease prevention as both moral and civic duties. Health literacy during this time was framed less as an individual right or participatory process and more as a public service to be delivered by the state and its authorized agencies. The government envisioned a top-down dissemination model in which knowledge about hygiene, maternal and child care, and infectious disease control would flow from trained educators, health workers, and schools to the general population. The citizen's role was that of a compliant recipient rather than an autonomous decision-maker—reflecting the paternalistic ethos of a welfare state in its early developmental phase.

Institutionally, the government made significant strides in establishing mechanisms for health education. The creation of *Health Education Bureaux (HEB)* at both national and state levels symbolized the formalization of health literacy as a state responsibility. The *Central Health Education Bureau (CHEB)*, founded in 1956, became the apex institution tasked with developing and distributing health education materials, training personnel, and coordinating outreach programs across the country. These bureaus functioned as the communication arm of public health departments, producing posters, pamphlets, radio messages, and films designed to convey simple yet vital information on sanitation, nutrition, malaria prevention, and family welfare. The educational system was also mobilized to promote health awareness: primary schools incorporated hygiene and physical education into their curricula, recognizing that shaping children's attitudes early could yield long-term public health dividends. Teachers were trained to act as "health missionaries" in their communities, reinforcing the integration of education and public health.

The emphasis on rural outreach was equally significant. Recognizing that the majority of India's population lived in villages with limited access to medical services, the government prioritized community-based programs through panchayats, rural schools, and local voluntary organizations. Mobile health units and community demonstrations sought to create awareness about preventive care, clean drinking water, and personal hygiene. Yet, these initiatives often suffered from limited resources, logistical challenges, and a lack of community participation. Communication was largely unidirectional—health officers "instructed" villagers rather than engaging them in dialogue about their specific needs and beliefs. As a result, the early model, while ambitious, remained bureaucratic and technocratic in nature, reflecting the developmental mindset of the postcolonial state, which sought to modernize the masses through centralized authority and expert knowledge.

By the time of the Fourth Five-Year Plan (1969–74), health education began to acquire a more program-specific orientation. Family planning and nutrition education emerged as national priorities, driven by population control policies and the growing recognition of the socio-cultural determinants of health behavior. Campaigns such as the *Applied Nutrition Programme (ANP)* and family welfare initiatives attempted to use culturally resonant media—folk songs, street plays, and puppet shows—to communicate health messages to illiterate or semi-literate audiences. This approach marked an important shift from purely informational to more culturally adaptive communication strategies. The use of traditional media acknowledged that health behavior was deeply intertwined with local customs, social norms, and collective practices. By incorporating indigenous storytelling forms, the government sought to bridge the gap between knowledge and adoption, moving closer to the behavioral communication models that would later dominate public health discourse in the 1980s and 1990s.

Nevertheless, the structural limitations of this period persisted. The integration of health education into schools and rural development programs lacked continuity and adequate evaluation mechanisms. The absence of participatory structures meant that local communities remained passive audiences rather than active stakeholders in health decision-making. The early health literacy framework thus laid a crucial institutional foundation—establishing health education as a national priority and experimenting with communication media—but it remained constrained by a top-down, didactic approach that treated literacy as transmission rather than transformation.

In retrospect, the 1951–1974 period represented both the promise and the paradox of India's early health governance: an era that institutionalized the importance of health literacy but stopped short of empowering citizens as informed, autonomous participants in their own well-being.

EXPANSION AND THEMATIC DIVERSIFICATION (1974–1997)

The period between the mid-1970s and the late 1990s marked a decisive transformation in India's health literacy trajectory, as the nation moved beyond foundational civic health education toward a more expansive, diversified, and strategically communicative model of public health engagement. The earlier emphasis on hygiene, sanitation, and family planning began to evolve into a broader conceptualization of health as a continuum encompassing prevention, promotion, and participation. This era reflected both global influences—such as the Alma-Ata Declaration of 1978, which advocated for primary health care and community participation—and domestic imperatives to respond to emerging demographic, epidemiological, and developmental challenges. Health literacy was no longer confined to the simple dissemination of information; it became a cross-sectoral enterprise that intersected with education, nutrition, social welfare, and media development.

The mid-1970s, particularly under the Fifth and Sixth Five-Year Plans, witnessed a shift toward child-centered development as a cornerstone of national planning. The Integrated Child Development Services (ICDS), launched in 1975, exemplified this transformation by linking health, nutrition, and early education into a unified framework aimed at fostering healthy habits and preventive care from early childhood. The underlying philosophy of these programs was that lifelong health behaviors—such as dietary practices, hygiene routines, and immunization uptake—could be cultivated through early intervention and family-centered communication. The state's health education strategy thus began to integrate behavior formation with broader community participation. The focus gradually expanded from individual instruction to social mobilization, encouraging parents, teachers, and community volunteers to take part in shaping local health environments.

By the 1980s, the conceptual scope of health literacy had grown significantly, mirroring a global turn toward health promotion rather than mere disease prevention. The Seventh Five-Year Plan (1985–1990) formalized this shift by embedding health communication within broader welfare and education schemes. The government increasingly relied on mass media—radio, television, cinema, and print—to deliver health messages to a wider audience. The establishment of *Doordarshan* as a national broadcaster provided an unprecedented platform for public health communication. Campaigns on nutrition, family welfare, and smallpox eradication became household messages, and culturally sensitive storylines in television serials were used to normalize modern health behaviors. Folk media and community theatre continued to play a vital role, particularly in rural areas, creating a bridge between traditional storytelling and modern public health discourse.

During this period, the notion of Information, Education, and Communication (IEC) began to gain institutional traction. The IEC framework recognized that effective health promotion required more than awareness—it demanded audience segmentation, message tailoring, and behavioral reinforcement through multiple channels. This approach was crystallized in the Eighth Five-Year Plan (1992–1997), which explicitly incorporated IEC into national health strategy for the first time. The context for this inclusion was the global HIV/AIDS epidemic, which necessitated sensitive yet powerful communication strategies that could address stigma, encourage testing, and promote safe practices. The National AIDS Control Organisation (NACO), established in 1992, became a pioneer in adopting IEC principles to design campaigns that targeted youth, high-risk groups, and the general population through a blend of mass media, interpersonal outreach, and peer education. The use of slogans, symbols such as the red ribbon, and high-visibility public figures helped shift the paradigm from fear-based messaging to empowerment-oriented awareness.

The thematic diversification of this era also reflected India's expanding engagement with non-communicable diseases (NCDs) and emerging social determinants of health. Health education programs began addressing cancer prevention, tobacco control, and mental health awareness, marking a transition toward multi-issue, multi-sectoral communication. Collaborations between the Ministries of Health, Education, and Information & Broadcasting facilitated a more integrated approach, with campaigns that linked nutrition, women's empowerment, and environmental hygiene. The 1990s saw the emergence of early mental health promotion efforts, with public campaigns highlighting stress, addiction, and the importance of psychological well-being—an unprecedented move in a country where mental health had long been stigmatized.

This period also witnessed the professionalization of public health communication. Advertising agencies, public relations firms, and non-governmental organizations were increasingly involved in designing creative health campaigns. This diversification in actors expanded both the content and style of messaging—making it more emotionally resonant, visually appealing, and context-specific. Yet, despite these advances, the period was not without its challenges. While IEC frameworks improved the sophistication of messaging, many initiatives remained top-down and lacked robust evaluation systems. Campaigns were often measured by reach and recall rather than actual behavior change or health outcomes.

Nevertheless, the 1974–1997 period was crucial in establishing health literacy as a strategic and interdisciplinary field of policy action. It represented a shift from the moralistic, duty-driven health education of the early decades to a participatory, communication-driven approach that sought to align individual behavior with social transformation. The integration of child-centered development, mass media, and behavioral science during this era laid the groundwork for the participatory and digitally enabled health governance that would define India's post-2000 public health landscape.

INSTITUTIONAL CONSOLIDATION AND LIFESTYLE FOCUS (1997–2017)

The period from the late 1990s to the mid-2010s represented a phase of institutional consolidation and thematic deepening in India's health literacy movement. Building on the earlier decades of expansion and diversification, this era witnessed the formalization of health education as an integral, institutionalized component of national health governance. During this time, the Government of India recognized that health awareness alone was insufficient to improve population-level outcomes. As the country entered a phase of epidemiological transition—marked by declining infectious disease burdens and rising non-communicable diseases (NCDs)—health communication strategies had to evolve from merely disseminating information to actively shaping behavior, promoting self-care, and addressing lifestyle-related risk factors.

The Ninth Five-Year Plan (1997–2002) marked a critical turning point in this regard. It emphasized the need for institutional frameworks that could sustain health awareness programs through structured partnerships among government agencies, local self-governments, non-governmental organizations (NGOs), and community leaders. Health communication began to be seen not just as a top-down administrative function but as a collaborative social enterprise requiring grassroots participation. Local self-governments, empowered by the 73rd and 74th Constitutional Amendments, became central actors in designing and delivering localized health campaigns. Panchayats and municipal bodies were encouraged to integrate health education into community development plans, thereby aligning local governance with national health objectives. Simultaneously, NGOs and community-based organizations (CBOs) expanded their role as intermediaries, translating policy into practice and bridging the gap between government schemes and community realities. This institutional pluralism strengthened the social infrastructure for health literacy, transforming it into a multi-stakeholder process rooted in local ownership and accountability.

The Tenth Five-Year Plan (2002–2007) further advanced this agenda by shifting the focus from awareness creation to behavioral change. It explicitly recognized the growing prevalence of lifestyle-related disorders such as diabetes, cardiovascular diseases, and obesity, and the need for sustained behavioral interventions addressing diet, physical activity, tobacco consumption, and stress management. Health literacy was reconceptualized as an enabler of self-regulation and informed decision-making rather than passive awareness. In line with global health trends influenced by the World Health Organization's (WHO) Ottawa Charter for Health Promotion (1986), Indian policy began emphasizing empowerment, participation, and inter-sectoral collaboration. The Plan called for integrated IEC (Information, Education, and Communication) campaigns targeting both communicable and non-communicable diseases, blending traditional media, interpersonal communication, and emerging digital platforms. Schools and workplaces were identified as critical environments for health promotion, leading to initiatives such as school-based nutrition education and workplace wellness programs.

The Eleventh (2007–2012) and Twelfth (2012–2017) Five-Year Plans consolidated these reforms through the establishment of institutional mechanisms such as the National Board for Health Education (NBHE), which aimed to standardize health education curricula, promote inter-ministerial coordination, and develop nationwide communication guidelines. This period also witnessed the formal integration of AYUSH (Ayurveda, Yoga & Naturopathy, Unani, Siddha, and Homeopathy) systems into mainstream public health communication. Recognizing the cultural relevance and accessibility of traditional health practices, the government launched large-scale awareness campaigns on yoga, nutrition, and holistic wellness. These efforts reflected a hybridized model of health literacy that combined biomedical and traditional knowledge systems—a distinctive feature of India's pluralistic health culture.

A key innovation of this era was the use of mass media as a deliberate instrument of behavior modification. The Twelfth Plan allocated dedicated budgets for national media campaigns addressing micronutrient deficiencies, particularly anemia and vitamin deficiencies among women and children. Popular television and radio programs were mobilized to communicate the importance of dietary diversity, salt reduction, and regular physical activity. The *National Rural Health Mission (NRHM)* (2005) and its successor, the *National Health Mission (NHM)* (2013), embedded IEC components into their frameworks, making communication a cross-cutting pillar of service delivery. Through these missions, Accredited Social Health Activists (ASHAs) emerged as vital conduits for community-level health education. Their interpersonal outreach, supported by posters, flip charts, and community meetings, complemented mass media campaigns, ensuring that information reached marginalized populations in accessible and culturally resonant forms.

The Twelfth Plan, in particular, reflected India's alignment with the global health discourse on NCDs and lifestyle modification. It recognized that the country was undergoing an epidemiological transition, where cardiovascular diseases, diabetes, hypertension, and obesity were rapidly becoming leading causes of morbidity and mortality. Consequently, public health priorities shifted toward preventive and promotive care, emphasizing the "whole-of-society" approach. Campaigns such as *Fit India*, *Poshan Abhiyaan*, and salt-reduction drives symbolized this shift toward holistic wellness. Moreover, the inclusion of behavioral economics and social marketing principles marked an evolution in communication design—messages were increasingly crafted to motivate, rather than merely inform.

Despite these advances, challenges persisted. Institutional coordination across ministries remained uneven, and evaluation mechanisms for measuring the behavioral impact of campaigns were still limited. Nonetheless, the 1997–2017 period laid the groundwork for the phygital health governance of the 21st century by institutionalizing communication, integrating traditional and modern paradigms, and acknowledging the centrality of behavior in shaping health outcomes. This was the era when health literacy truly became multidimensional—anchored in policy, embedded in institutions, and oriented toward lifestyle transformation, paving the way for India's eventual transition into a digitally enabled, participatory health ecosystem.

NODAL AGENCY FOR ADVERTISING NEEDS:

The establishment of the Directorate of Advertising and Visual Publicity (DAVP) in 1955 marked a pivotal moment in the evolution of India's communication and health literacy framework. As the nation embarked on its first Five-Year Plans, the need for a centralized, professional, and cost-effective agency to handle government communication became evident. The DAVP emerged as the Government of India's nodal multimedia advertising agency, designed to bridge the gap between policy formulation and public participation. Its purpose was to inform, educate, and empower citizens—especially in a newly independent nation where literacy levels were low, public trust in institutions was still forming, and the mass media landscape was in its infancy.

In its foundational years, the DAVP functioned as the central communication arm of the government, providing integrated publicity and advertising services to nearly all Central Ministries, Departments, autonomous bodies, and Public Sector Undertakings (PSUs). It offered end-to-end solutions—ranging from concept development and message design to production, dissemination, and evaluation—across multiple platforms including print, radio, television, outdoor displays, and eventually digital media. Its operations were guided by the belief that communication is governance in action—that effective dissemination of government policies and initiatives could foster national integration, civic participation, and collective progress.

The DAVP's primary mandate was to act as a one-stop communication platform that could translate complex government policies into accessible messages for the public. Its objectives extended far beyond publicity or propaganda. At its core, the DAVP was an instrument of democratic education, using visual and verbal media to promote awareness, behavioral change, and civic responsibility among citizens. Its mission was both pedagogical and participatory—to inform citizens about government schemes and to inspire them to take part in national development activities.

From the outset, DAVP developed campaigns under broad thematic categories that reflected India's development priorities during the Nehruvian and post-Nehruvian eras. These themes included national integration, rural development, women's empowerment, literacy, environmental protection, consumer awareness, road safety, energy conservation, disaster preparedness, and crucially, health and family welfare communication. By integrating these themes into a coherent national communication strategy, DAVP played a vital role in shaping India's socio-political narrative, creating a shared vocabulary of progress, duty, and citizenship.

The DAVP's early communication strategy was built on three foundational pillars:

1. *Reach* – leveraging multiple media to ensure that every citizen, irrespective of geography or literacy, could access government messages.
2. *Relevance* – ensuring that the content was culturally contextual, linguistically inclusive, and socially resonant.
3. *Reliability* – establishing the government as a credible source of information amidst the proliferation of unofficial or anecdotal knowledge in communities.

Among its diverse responsibilities, health and family welfare communication emerged as one of DAVP's most important and enduring functions. The post-Independence government recognized that public health improvement required not only medical infrastructure but also mass awareness and behavioral change. The DAVP became the primary agency through which this transformation was to be achieved.

From the 1960s onward, DAVP's social advertising began addressing a wide range of public health issues, including malaria control, tuberculosis (TB) prevention, leprosy eradication, maternal and child health, and family planning. These early campaigns relied on traditional media such as posters, wall paintings, film reels, and radio jingles—media that could transcend barriers of literacy and reach deep into rural India. The visual vocabulary of DAVP was characterized by bold imagery, simple slogans, and emotive appeals—designed to attract attention and inspire immediate action.

By the 1980s and 1990s, DAVP's role expanded in both scope and sophistication. Health communication became more scientific, segmented, and behaviorally informed. Drawing on the global framework of Information, Education, and

Communication (IEC), the agency began designing campaigns tailored to specific demographics—urban youth, rural mothers, factory workers, and elderly citizens. The National AIDS Control Organisation (NACO) partnership was one of DAVP's landmark initiatives during this period. Facing the HIV/AIDS crisis of the 1990s, DAVP helped craft India's first comprehensive public health campaigns on sexual health, stigma reduction, and prevention, using mass media as a tool of empathy and education.

Similarly, the DAVP played a central role in polio eradication campaigns such as *Do Boond Zindagi Ke* (Two Drops of Life), which became one of the most recognizable slogans in Indian public health history. The campaign, launched under the aegis of the Ministry of Health and Family Welfare, used a combination of television, radio, outdoor hoardings, and celebrity endorsements to encourage vaccination. Through strategic use of popular culture and repetition, it helped India achieve its polio-free status in 2014—a testament to the power of communication as a tool for behavioral change.

In the 2000s and early 2010s, DAVP's campaigns diversified further to include non-communicable diseases (NCDs) and emerging lifestyle issues such as hypertension, diabetes, and mental health. The agency designed national awareness drives on tobacco control, cancer prevention, and nutrition education, reflecting India's epidemiological shift from infectious to chronic diseases. These campaigns promoted preventive healthcare and encouraged people to adopt healthy lifestyles—balanced diets, physical activity, and stress management. Through this period, DAVP evolved from a message dissemination body to a strategic communication partner in public health governance.

The strength of DAVP lay in its multi-platform communication model, which combined traditional and modern media. Its operations were divided across wings dedicated to:

- **Print Advertising**: Newspaper and magazine advertisements were used to reach literate audiences and opinion leaders.
- **Audio-Visual Media**: Television and cinema spots brought dynamic storytelling into homes and public spaces.
- **Outdoor and Exhibition Media**: Hoardings, posters, exhibitions, and mobile vans provided visual visibility across towns and villages.
- **Digital Media (post-2010)**: With the rise of digital platforms, DAVP began integrating online campaigns, websites, and social media outreach to target younger, tech-savvy populations.

What set DAVP apart was its ability to maintain a balance between standardization and localization. National campaigns were adapted into multiple languages and dialects, ensuring accessibility to diverse linguistic and cultural groups. It also worked with regional artists and filmmakers to make communication more relatable.

The social advertising legacy of DAVP is immense. Its campaigns were not mere publicity exercises—they reflected the government's evolving understanding of citizenship, development, and health. By addressing issues such as population stabilization, HIV/AIDS prevention, tuberculosis control, sanitation, and environmental protection, DAVP helped shape India's collective consciousness around public health and social responsibility.

Through exhibitions and outreach programs, DAVP created spaces where citizens could engage directly with government initiatives. For instance, its mobile exhibition vans traveled to remote areas, displaying educational films and distributing pamphlets, making the abstract ideals of development visible and tangible to everyday citizens. The participatory dimension of these exhibitions allowed communities to ask questions, seek clarifications, and develop a sense of ownership over national programs.

By the 2010s, the communication landscape had undergone a radical transformation. The rise of digital media, social networks, and data analytics demanded a more agile and technologically adept communication model. Recognizing the need for modernization, the Government of India undertook a *comprehensive restructuring of DAVP in 2017*, transforming it into the Central Bureau of Communication (CBC).

The CBC was established under the Ministry of Information and Broadcasting as an umbrella organization that merged the functions of DAVP, the Directorate of Field Publicity (DFP), and the Song & Drama Division (SDD). This integration aimed to create a unified, multi-channel communication ecosystem capable of delivering consistent messages through both traditional and digital media. The CBC was also designed to respond to the growing need for data-driven communication—using analytics, audience insights, and real-time monitoring to optimize outreach and impact.

In its new avatar, the CBC retained DAVP's legacy as the government's nodal agency for public communication but expanded its functions to include citizen engagement, content creation, social media management, and digital marketing. The Bureau of Outreach (BoO), a division under CBC, continues to play a critical role in designing and implementing large-scale awareness campaigns, particularly in the field of health and welfare. It coordinates with the Ministry of Health and Family Welfare to ensure that public health messages—ranging from vaccination drives to mental health awareness—reach the widest possible audience in the most effective formats.

Today, the CBC carries forward the DAVP's mission of health promotion but with greater technological integration. Campaigns are no longer confined to print and broadcast media; they now span social media platforms, mobile apps, interactive websites, and digital storytelling formats. Artificial Intelligence (AI) and behavioral analytics are used to segment audiences, personalize content, and track engagement. This transformation marks a shift from one-way publicity to two-way communication, where citizens are both recipients and contributors to health discourse.

The CBC's campaigns continue to address a wide array of health issues—infectious diseases like dengue and COVID-19, as well as lifestyle diseases linked to diet and stress. It has also prioritized communication on mental health, menstrual hygiene, and geriatric care, reflecting a more inclusive and holistic understanding of well-being. In collaboration with the *MyGov* platform, CBC fosters participatory engagement through citizen challenges, feedback portals, and online discussions, embodying the principles of phygital (physical + digital) governance.

The historical journey from DAVP to CBC encapsulates India's broader evolution from directive governance to participatory communication. Over seven decades, this institutional apparatus has not merely publicized government programs—it has shaped national consciousness, transforming abstract policy goals into shared civic missions. Whether through posters in the 1960s, radio jingles in the 1980s, or digital campaigns in the 2020s, the agency's core mission has remained constant: to empower citizens through information, to inspire behavior change through storytelling, and to strengthen democracy through transparency.

As India continues to embrace phygital health governance, the CBC's role becomes ever more vital. Its capacity to integrate behavioral science, cultural sensitivity, and technological innovation positions it as a key player in advancing national health literacy. The legacy of DAVP, carried forward by the CBC, stands as a testament to the enduring belief that informed citizens are the foundation of a healthy and participatory democracy—a vision that continues to guide India's public health communication in the digital age.

POLICY GAPS AND CHALLENGES

India's progress in health literacy, while notable in many respects, continues to be constrained by persistent policy gaps and systemic challenges that undermine the potential of communication interventions to produce durable public-health gains. Foremost among these structural deficiencies is a chronic lack of coordination across the architecture of governance: central ministries, state health departments, and programme-specific Information, Education and Communication (IEC) units frequently operate in institutional silos, producing overlapping activities that fragment resources and dilute message impact rather than amplifying it through coherent, reinforced strategies. This fragmentation is visible in the proliferation of disease-specific campaigns—each with their own timelines, budgets, and communication styles—which, though effective for targeted objectives, have collectively undermined the prospect of cultivating a comprehensive, population-level health competency. The verticality of such programs narrows the cognitive horizon of the public, who receive episodic and issue-specific advisories (for example on HIV/AIDS, immunization drives, or family planning) without being offered sustained, integrated narratives that build cumulative understanding about preventive health, lifestyle diseases, mental well-being, and health-system navigation. Consequently, the effects of campaigns are often episodic: awareness may spike during high-profile drives but rapidly recede when the campaign cycle ends, producing a behaviour-change deficit that is particularly worrying because information provision alone—however wide its reach—does not automatically translate into long-term behavioural adoption. The literature on health promotion consistently shows that converting awareness into habit requires multi-level reinforcement—structural enabling conditions, repeated social modelling, accessible services, and culturally resonant messaging—yet many Indian interventions have stopped at the level of message dissemination without sufficiently investing in the enabling infrastructure and longitudinal reinforcement needed to sustain new practices. Equity gaps further complicate this picture. Remote rural regions, tribal areas, urban informal settlements, and other marginalised communities have historically been on the periphery of sustained health-literacy investments; where digital and mass-media platforms reach, they often do so unevenly, bypassing households that lack connectivity, linguistic accommodation, or dependable local intermediaries who can translate guidance into feasible action. The result is a bifurcated literacy landscape in which large swathes of the population remain vulnerable to misinformation and unable to access or interpret even basic health guidance. Monitoring and evaluation mechanisms have similarly lagged: although campaigns produce metrics on reach, impressions, and short-term recall, there has been no systematic, institutionalised process to track the extent to which a specific health-literacy intervention produces measurable changes in health behaviours or outcomes over time. The absence of rigorous impact-assessment systems—not merely for auditing outputs but for understanding pathways from message exposure to behaviour, and ultimately to morbidity and mortality indicators—prevents policymakers from learning what truly works in varied socio-cultural contexts and from optimising resource allocation accordingly. These deficits are compounded by governance transitions at the national level. The replacement of the Planning Commission with NITI Aayog in 2014 introduced an outcome-oriented, decentralized model of policy stewardship that foregrounds innovation and cooperative federalism; however, this structural reorientation also interrupted the continuity of centrally curated, long-horizon planning instruments that had historically provided a predictable backbone for cross-sectoral initiatives, including sustained health education efforts. In the early decades following independence, multi-year Five-Year Plans afforded a stable policy framework within which health communication could be sequenced, financed, and evaluated; the newer NITI Aayog framework, while valuable for its emphasis on measurement and results, has not yet articulated a unified, nationwide roadmap specifically dedicated to health literacy, leaving an important governance vacuum. The absence of such a roadmap is consequential because health literacy is an inherently cross-cutting endeavour that requires harmonised policy instruments—across education, sanitation, nutrition, social protection, telecommunication, and media regulation—to generate cumulative effects. Without a central coordinating doctrine or an explicitly mandated nodal body empowered to standardise messaging, supervise impact evaluation, and mediate state–center complementarities, the risk is that well-intentioned yet disparate initiatives will continue to produce partial gains that fail to scale or persist. Moreover, the shift to outcome-based monitoring invites an over-reliance on short-term performance metrics that privilege quantifiable outputs (for instance, app downloads or campaign impressions) over subtler but more consequential transformations such as increases in critical health literacy, shifts in community norms, or enhancements in civic capacity to hold health systems accountable. This metric fixation can inadvertently incentivise communicative tactics designed to maximize visibility rather than to deepen comprehension and agency. There is, therefore, an urgent need to reimagine governance arrangements so that they combine the agility and data-driven discipline of the post-Planning Commission era with the programmatic continuity and cross-sectoral integration once enabled by longer-term planning frameworks. Practically, this entails establishing clear institutional mechanisms for inter-ministerial coordination—platforms where Ministries of Health, Education, Information Technology, Women & Child Development, and Rural Development jointly design integrated communication strategies that map onto service-delivery timelines and infrastructural realities at the state and district levels. It also requires embedding robust monitoring and evaluation protocols that go beyond reach and recall to measure behavioural outcomes longitudinally, using mixed methods (combining administrative data, panel surveys, and qualitative process evaluations) to capture both effect sizes and causal pathways. Simultaneously, addressing the behaviour-change deficit demands investment in persistent community engagement models: support for local intermediaries (such as ASHAs, teachers, community radio producers, and civil-society organizations), micro-grants for community-produced media, and programs that cultivate local champions and social norms over time. Equity must be a front-and-center criterion for both design and evaluation—ensuring that digital rollouts are matched by investments in language localization, low-literacy multimedia formats, public access points, and targeted outreach to groups identified through disaggregated data as being at greater risk of exclusion. Data governance and ethical safeguards are also integral: as digital platforms proliferate, policies must ensure that citizen data used for monitoring and personalization are subject to privacy protections, informed consent protocols, and accountability mechanisms to prevent misuse and to maintain institutional trust. In terms of strategic orientation, the way forward should not be to resurrect rigid, centrally prescribed plans but rather to create a hybrid governance model that marries the strengths of the Planning Commission era—long-term visioning, resource predictability, and cross-sectoral program design—with the post-2014 emphasis on outcomes, innovation, and state-led experimentation. NITI Aayog, in this configuration, could spearhead a National Health Literacy Roadmap co-created with state governments, academic institutions, and civil society, articulating standardized indicators (including a proposed National Health Literacy Index), funding modalities, and a national calendar for thematic campaigns that are synchronized with local service capacity. This roadmap should explicitly mandate periodic impact assessments and adaptive learning cycles, so that campaigns are iteratively improved on the basis of evidence rather than being judged only by immediate exposure metrics. Crucially, capacity building at sub-national levels must be prioritized—training district health officials in communication science, behavioral insights, and data analytics so that they can translate national frameworks into locally appropriate strategies. Finally, closing these gaps requires political commitment to make health literacy a visible, sustained priority: allocating predictable funding lines, elevating the role of health literacy within broader development indicators, and cultivating public–private–academic partnerships that leverage technological innovation while safeguarding public interest. Only by confronting the intertwined problems of coordination failure, behaviour-change deficits, persistent inequities, weak impact monitoring, and the lack of a unified post-Planning Commission roadmap can India consolidate its phygital gains into an enduring, equitable, and participatory system of health literacy that empowers citizens not only to know but to act, and to hold systems accountable for delivering the conditions that make healthy choices feasible.

DISCUSSION

India's evolution of health literacy within the framework of phygital governance represents a transformative intersection of policy, technology, and citizen participation. Traditionally framed as an individual competency, health literacy has now matured into a governance capacity—a systemic ability of institutions and citizens to co-create and operationalize health knowledge (Nutbeam, 2008). This reconceptualization reflects the global shift from information transmission to participatory empowerment (Kickbusch et al., 2013), exemplified by platforms such as the Ayushman Bharat Digital Mission (ABDM), CoWIN, and MyGov Health Portal, which blend digital communication with citizen feedback. The result is a movement from top-down didactic messaging to collaborative co-production, aligning with the Health Promotion Theory's emphasis on agency and self-determination (World Health Organization [WHO], 1986). Yet, this participatory expansion unfolds within a culturally heterogeneous nation where linguistic, religious, and socio-economic diversity shapes health communication. Earlier Five-Year Plans (1951, 1974) employed moralistic, civic instruction, while later IEC and BCC models integrated folk media and local idioms to build cultural resonance (Planning Commission, 1951, 1974; Reddy et al., 2018). The phygital era extends this through digital storytelling—on platforms like YouTube, WhatsApp, and Instagram—where citizens both consume and create health narratives. However, such democratization invites the dual risks of misinformation and algorithmic bias. Therefore, as WHO (2023) underscores, effective governance requires balancing inclusivity with scientific accuracy through trusted intermediaries such as ASHAs and NGOs who localize digital content. Technology, while a great enabler, also widens divides: digital infrastructure, affordability, and literacy remain unevenly distributed, rendering the "digital divide" a new determinant of health. This duality confirms Margetts and Dunleavy's (2013) caution against "technocratic optimism," urging that phygital governance remain human-centered, embedding technological tools within community trust networks. Institutional trust, as Saxena and Pillai (2021) emphasize, thus becomes a cornerstone of successful communication—moderating how policy advertising translates into behavioral change. Transparent data practices, multilingual privacy disclosures, and grievance mechanisms reinforce trust and mitigate misinformation. Behavioral change, meanwhile, continues to be the ultimate test of governance effectiveness. Drawing on Bandura's (1986) Social Cognitive Theory, health behaviors spread through social reinforcement and modeling, as demonstrated in the Polio Eradication and Swachh Bharat campaigns. Yet, for enduring impact, behavioral reinforcement must be supported by structural equity—ensuring that communication is coupled with supportive policy environments, infrastructure, and education (WHO, 1986). Policy advertising has evolved from broadcast propaganda to participatory messaging, transforming citizens from passive recipients to active collaborators in campaigns like Fit India Movement and ABHA. Integrating traditional systems such as AYUSH with biomedical practices through digital ecosystems now exemplifies India's pluralistic health communication strategy (Planning Commission, 2012). However, such integration must remain evidence-based to preserve credibility and avoid pseudoscientific drift. Globally, India's experience offers a replicable model for other LMICs, blending large-scale technological capacity with cultural localization. Comparative studies show that strategies similar to Brazil's SUS community worker model and Indonesia's trust-based religious campaigns resonate with India's PHL-GM framework. At the same time, global benchmarks such as Australia's National Health Literacy Strategy suggest that India could strengthen evaluation mechanisms through a standardized national health literacy index. Nonetheless, ethical vigilance is imperative. The centralization of health data under digital governance raises legitimate concerns over privacy, consent, and algorithmic fairness. Phygital systems must, therefore, embody ethical principles—informed consent, privacy by design, algorithmic accountability, and universal accessibility—transforming digital health from an instrument of efficiency into one of justice. Ultimately, India's health literacy transition encapsulates a paradox: technology democratizes participation even as it risks deepening exclusion. The Phygital Health Literacy Governance Model (PHLGM) illustrates this balance of promise and peril—demonstrating that progress depends not merely on data and infrastructure but on cultural empathy, ethical transparency, and institutional integrity. From blackboard-based civic instruction to cloud-based participatory dashboards, India's health communication odyssey mirrors its democratic ethos: a continual dialogue between governance and the governed, between ancient wisdom and algorithmic innovation. The future of health literacy, therefore, lies not only in technological sophistication but in preserving the human spirit of inclusion, trust, and shared accountability at the heart of phygital governance.

RECOMMENDATIONS AND SOLUTIONS

India's health literacy ecosystem stands at a decisive moment of transition—from post-Independence civic education to a phygital governance framework that merges human participation with digital intelligence. Strengthening this evolution requires coherent reforms across five domains: policy integration, digital inclusion, institutional trust, behavioral change, and capacity building. At the policy level, India must institutionalize a National Health Literacy Policy that elevates health communication to a cross-sectoral governance priority. A National Health Literacy Index (NHLI), modeled on Australia's strategy, could benchmark progress through validated instruments such as the *Health Literacy Questionnaire (HLQ)* (Osborne et al., 2013), enabling evidence-based decision-making. Equally critical is the creation of a horizontal health communication framework—replacing fragmented disease-specific IEC units with an integrated structure connecting the ministries of Health, Education, IT, and Social Welfare. A restructured National Board for Health Education (NBHE), supported by a digital communication council, could coordinate such efforts. Governance reform must also embed participatory mechanisms: platforms like *MyGov Health* should evolve into Phygital Health Forums where citizens co-design policies, monitor outcomes, and provide feedback in real time. At the infrastructure level, the BharatNet project and rural Wi-Fi zones must be accelerated to ensure universal connectivity, with community health centers serving as digital access hubs. Digital inclusion also depends on usability; hence, initiatives such as *Pradhan Mantri Gramin Digital Saksharta Abhiyan (PMGDISHA)* should integrate multilingual and audiovisual training to reach semi-literate users. Leveraging Artificial Intelligence (AI) ethically can enhance personalization through context-specific, multilingual guidance, provided transparency and algorithmic accountability are ensured by a National Digital Health Ethics Committee.

Institutional trust remains central to sustainable health literacy. Open-data dashboards, fact-checking portals, and myth-busting collaborations with credible media outlets can strengthen transparency, aligning with the *Right to Information Act (2005)* and the *Digital Personal Data Protection Act (2023)*. Health platforms must implement privacy-by-design architectures and multilingual informed-consent processes, complemented by community data-oversight councils to protect citizens' data dignity (Saxena & Pillai, 2021). Building local trust further requires empowering intermediaries such as ASHA workers, teachers, and faith leaders as digitally trained communicators capable of bridging cultural and technological divides. In behavioral terms, the application of nudge theory (Thaler & Sunstein, 2008) can transform awareness into sustained action by embedding choice architecture that favors preventive health—through defaults (automatic health-insurance enrollment), reminders (handwashing prompts), and gamification (fitness challenges). True empowerment, however, depends on community ownership. Micro-grants for local youth and women's cooperatives to produce vernacular digital health content—podcasts, videos, and infographics—will deepen engagement and ensure contextual resonance. Integrating traditional and modern knowledge systems—linking verified AYUSH content to digital platforms—can enhance behavioral acceptance while retaining scientific credibility (Planning Commission, 2012).

The sustainability of phygital health governance hinges on capacity building. Training public servants in digital literacy, ethics, and participatory facilitation, in collaboration with WHO and UNDP, will expand institutional competence. Interdisciplinary research through dedicated Centers for Health Literacy and Digital Governance can bridge behavioral science, communication studies, and technology policy, contributing context-sensitive tools such as an Indian Health Literacy Competence Scale. Public–Private–Academic Partnerships (PPAPs) should drive innovation in e-health and analytics while maintaining transparency. Embedding health literacy in education through the *National Education Policy (2020)* can nurture long-term behavioral resilience—introducing curricula on hygiene, nutrition, digital safety, and mental health from primary to university levels. Accountability mechanisms such as impact-evaluation dashboards, jointly maintained by NITI Aayog and the National Statistical Office, can track not only reach but also behavioral outcomes, fostering adaptive learning. Financial sustainability requires a National Health Literacy Fund, supported by CSR, public funding, and international partnerships, ensuring transparent audits and equitable resource distribution.

Collectively, these measures embody the moral and systemic coherence needed for India's transition from fragmented initiatives to an integrated, participatory governance model. The path forward demands that policy coherence be matched by ethical technological expansion, community-based behavioral strategies, and research-driven innovation. Only through empathy, inclusivity, and transparency can India's phygital health ecosystem realize its full democratic promise—ensuring that every citizen, regardless of literacy or geography, can access, comprehend, and act upon health information as a right and a responsibility.

FUTURE RESEARCH DIRECTIONS

The phygital transformation of India's health literacy ecosystem calls for a new generation of research that unites technological innovation with social insight, ethical responsibility, and systemic thinking. Future inquiry must transcend descriptive studies and focus on predictive, evaluative, and interdisciplinary approaches that enhance both policy design and public engagement. A key priority is the development of an AI-enabled Health Literacy Index (HLI) that can analyze real-time behavioral and communication data to measure population-level literacy trends (Eysenbach, 2020). Using natural language processing, sentiment analysis, and machine learning, researchers can identify misinformation patterns, track health-related discourse, and predict vulnerable communities. This must be ethically grounded through transparent data governance, ensuring fairness, consent, and accountability. Complementing this, predictive modeling can simulate how various communication strategies—such as digital campaigns or community media—impact awareness and behavior, guiding evidence-based policymaking. Interdisciplinary collaboration between data scientists, behavioral psychologists, and public health experts will be vital for developing such models (Osborne et al., 2013). At the cognitive level, future studies must examine how individuals process digital health information, as Cognitive Load Theory warns against overwhelming users with complex or excessive data (Sweller, 2011). Randomized controlled trials and neurocognitive studies employing eye-tracking and EEG could reveal optimal message structures and emotional triggers that sustain attention and trust in digital health platforms. Equally, the emotional and psychological dimensions of communication deserve focused exploration—how empathy, humor, and fear influence engagement and compliance, and how *trust*, as a mediating factor, shapes interaction with AI chatbots or virtual assistants (Saxena & Pillai, 2021).

Further, integrating insights from behavioral economics and nudge theory can advance digital health design by embedding choice architectures that encourage preventive behaviors—such as default enrollment in vaccination reminders or gamified wellness programs (Thaler & Sunstein, 2008). Comparative and cross-cultural studies are also essential to contextualize India's experience within the Global South. Comparative analyses with nations like Brazil, South Africa, and Indonesia could examine how governance structures, civil society participation, and cultural communication norms affect health literacy outcomes. Within India, regional and linguistic studies must analyze how local media, storytelling traditions, and tribal epistemologies shape phygital engagement—reinforcing the importance of linguistic pluralism in digital health policy (Kumar & Singh, 2022).

Equally urgent is research into the ethical, legal, and socio-technical dimensions of digital health governance. Empirical assessments should evaluate how the *Digital Personal Data Protection Act (2023)* functions in practice, particularly in protecting low-literacy populations. Scholars must investigate algorithmic bias, ensuring that AI models reflect India's social diversity rather than reinforcing inequalities. Studies on cybersecurity and misinformation ecosystems using computational social science can map how rumors proliferate across digital networks, identifying effective counter-measures through media literacy and fact-checking collaborations. Longitudinal research must measure behavioral sustainability—tracking how exposure to digital campaigns translates into long-term practices like improved hygiene, vaccination, or nutrition awareness. Similarly, policy feedback loop analysis can examine how ministries incorporate citizen-generated data from platforms such as *CoWIN* and *MyGov* into iterative reforms, strengthening adaptive governance. Cost–benefit analyses and socio-economic evaluations will further clarify the broader development impacts of health literacy on productivity, gender equity, and public trust.

The future of phygital health literacy research also depends on adopting *systems thinking* (Meadows, 2008). Systems modeling can map interdependencies between digital infrastructure, institutional trust, and behavioral outcomes—revealing leverage points where targeted interventions yield disproportionate impact. Interdisciplinary collaboration will be essential: public health, communication, computer science, law, and anthropology must converge through transdisciplinary research hubs and policy innovation labs. Methodological innovations such as participatory action research (PAR), human-centered design (HCD), and digital ethnography will ensure that citizens are engaged as co-researchers rather than passive subjects. Such participatory frameworks will elevate community voices, particularly among marginalized groups, and enhance ethical reflexivity.

Across these domains, future research must be guided by four central principles: (1) Equity-centered design, ensuring that gender, caste, disability, and geography are central to digital inclusion; (2) AI for empowerment, guaranteeing that technology amplifies human agency rather than enabling surveillance; (3) critical and media literacy, expanding the health literacy framework to counter misinformation; and (4) global learning exchange, fostering South–South collaboration and decolonial research perspectives. Methodologically, mixed-methods designs, multilingual data collection tools, and open-science practices will ensure inclusivity and transparency. Ultimately, the goal of future inquiry is not only to measure literacy but to cultivate wisdom—the collective societal capacity to apply knowledge compassionately and equitably. By aligning artificial intelligence, behavioral science, and participatory ethics, India can pioneer a globally relevant model of digital health literacy research that transforms governance from data-driven systems into people-centered ecosystems of trust, empathy, and inclusion (World Health Organization, 2023).

CONCLUSION

India as a country has a long, but under-analysed history of health literacy policy, which can be found in its first 5-year plan onwards, even before the world was made aware of it through the Ottawa Charter for Health Promotion in 1986. The journey from chalkboards in rural schools to integrated multi-media IEC campaigns tells a story of progress as well as enduring divides. Now, as India transitions from the era of the Planning Commission to the Establishment of the Niti Aayog, preserving the policy legacy is an apparent challenge, but ensuring its adaptability to new health threats and communication landscapes will be an even bigger one to overcome.

REFERENCES

Bandura, A. (1986). *Social foundations of thought and action: A social cognitive theory.* Prentice Hall. https://psycnet.apa.org/record/1985-98423-000

Chinn, D. (2011). Critical health literacy: A review and critical analysis. *Social Science & Medicine*, *73*(1), 60–67. DOI: 10.1016/j.socscimed.2011.04.004

Davis, F. D. (1989). Perceived usefulness, perceived ease of use, and user acceptance of information technology. *Management Information Systems Quarterly*, *13*(3), 319–340. DOI: 10.2307/249008

Djakeli, K. (2024). Healthcare marketing: Meaning, historical development, applications, and current status. In Djakeli, K. (Ed.), *Modern Healthcare Marketing in the Digital Era* (pp. 1–25). IGI Global Scientific Publishing., DOI: 10.4018/979-8-3693-0679-6.ch001

Dunleavy, P., Margetts, H., Bastow, S., & Tinkler, J. (2006). *Digital era governance: IT corporations, the state, and e-government.* Oxford University Press., DOI: 10.1093/acprof:oso/9780199296194.001.0001

Gigauri, I., & Djakeli, K. (2021). National health reforms in Georgia during 1994–2021 and their success. HOLISTICA – Journal of Business and Public Administration, 12(2), 102–108. https://reference-global.com/download/article/10.2478/hjbpa-2021-0017.pdf

Kickbusch, I., Pelikan, J. M., Apfel, F., & Tsouros, A. D. (2013). *Health literacy: The solid facts.* World Health Organization, Regional Office for Europe. https://apps.who.int/iris/bitstream/handle/10665/128703/e96854.pdf

Kumar, R., & Singh, A. (2022). Digital divide and health governance in India: Challenges of inclusion in the phygital era. *The Indian Journal of Public Administration*, *68*(2), 175–192. DOI: 10.1177/00195561221091332

Margetts, H., & Dunleavy, P. (2013). The second wave of digital-era governance: A quasi-paradigm for government on the web. *Philosophical Transactions of the Royal Society A, 371*(1987), 20120382. DOI: 10.1098/rsta.2012.0382

Ministry of Health and Family Welfare (MoHFW). (Various years). *Annual reports.* Government of India. https://www.mohfw.gov.in/?q=en/documents/publication

Nutbeam, D. (2000). Health literacy as a public health goal. *Health Promotion International*, *15*(3), 259–267. DOI: 10.1093/heapro/15.3.259

Nutbeam, D. (2008). The evolving concept of health literacy. *Social Science & Medicine*, *67*(12), 2072–2078. DOI: 10.1016/j.socscimed.2008.09.050

Osborne, R. H., Batterham, R. W., Elsworth, G. R., Hawkins, M., & Buchbinder, R. (2013). The grounded psychometric development and initial validation of the Health Literacy Questionnaire (HLQ). *BMC Public Health*, *13*(1), 658. DOI: 10.1186/1471-2458-13-658

Planning Commission, Government of India. (1951). *First Five-Year Plan (1951–1956)*. Government of India. https://archive.org/details/dli.ernet.449278

Planning Commission, Government of India. (1974). *Fifth Five-Year Plan (1974–1979)*. Government of India. https://niti.gov.in/planning-commission-archive

Planning Commission, Government of India. (2012). *Twelfth Five-Year Plan (2012–2017): Faster, more inclusive, and sustainable growth* (Vols. 1–3). SAGE Publications India. https://niti.gov.in/planning-commission-archive

Planning Commission, Government of India. (1951–1956). *First Five-Year Plan.* Government of India. https://archive.org/download/dli.ernet.449278/449278-The%20First%20Five%20Year%20Plan_text.pdf

Planning Commission, Government of India. (1974–1979). *Fifth Five-Year Plan.* Government of India. https://niti.gov.in/planning-commission-archive

Planning Commission, Government of India. (1985–1990). *Seventh Five-Year Plan* (Vols. I & II). Government of India. https://niti.gov.in/planning-commission-archive

Planning Commission, Government of India. (1992–1997). *Eighth Five-Year Plan* (Vols. I & II). Government of India. https://niti.gov.in/planning-commission-archive

Planning Commission, Government of India. (2002–2007). *Tenth Five-Year Plan* (Vols. I–III). Government of India. https://niti.gov.in/planning-commission-archive

Planning Commission, Government of India. (2007–2012). *Eleventh Five-Year Plan* (Vols. I–III). Government of India. https://niti.gov.in/planning-commission-archive

Planning Commission, Government of India. (2012–2017). *Twelfth Five-Year Plan* (Vols. I–III). Government of India. https://niti.gov.in/planning-commission-archive

Reddy, K. S., Sharma, A., Kumar, P., Gupta, V., & Singh, A. (2018). Towards achieving global health equity: Opportunities and challenges of health promotion. *Lancet*, *392*(10165), 1225–1237. DOI: 10.1016/S0140-6736(18)32380-6

Rogers, E. M. (2003). *Diffusion of innovations* (5th ed.). Free Press., https://books.google.com/books?id=9U1K5LjUOwEC

Saxena, N., & Pillai, P. (2021). Trust and technology adoption in India's e-governance ecosystem. *Information Polity, 26*(4), 465–480. DOI: 10.3233/IP-210289

Solar, O., & Irwin, A. (2010). *A conceptual framework for action on the social determinants of health.* World Health Organization. https://apps.who.int/iris/handle/10665/44489

Thaler, R. H., & Sunstein, C. R. (2008). *Nudge: Improving decisions about health, wealth, and happiness.* Yale University Press. https://yalebooks.yale.edu/book/9780300122237/nudge

World Health Organization. (1986). *Ottawa charter for health promotion.* World Health Organization. https://www.who.int/publications/i/item/ottawa-charter-for-health-promotion

World Health Organization. (2023). *Global report on digital health 2023.* World Health Organization. https://www.who.int/publications/i/item/9789240071303

KEY TERMS AND DEFINITIONS

Behavioral Change: Refers to the process of modifying individual or collective actions and habits to promote healthier lifestyles, often achieved through education, awareness campaigns, and community engagement grounded in behavioral science and social learning principles.

Digital Governance: The use of digital technologies, platforms, and data systems by governments to enhance transparency, efficiency, and citizen participation in policy implementation, service delivery, and public communication.

Health Communication: A multidisciplinary approach that uses communication strategies to inform, influence, and motivate individuals and communities to adopt behaviors that promote health, prevent disease, and support effective policy implementation.

Health Literacy: The ability of individuals to access, understand, evaluate, and apply health information to make informed decisions about healthcare, disease prevention, and healthy living within personal and societal contexts.

Information, Education and Communication (IEC): A strategic communication framework used in public health to disseminate knowledge, foster awareness, and encourage behavioral change through structured information sharing and participatory learning activities.

Phygital Governance: An integrated governance model combining physical (in-person) and digital (online) modes of engagement to deliver public services, enhance communication, and promote inclusive citizen participation in policymaking and implementation.

Public Health Policy: A system of laws, regulations, and guidelines formulated by governments and health authorities to protect and improve the health of populations through preventive, promotive, and curative strategies.

Social Inclusion: The process of ensuring equal access to opportunities, resources, and services—regardless of gender, class, location, or ability—so that all individuals can participate fully in social, economic, and civic life.

Chapter 9
Healthcare Reforms in Georgia:
Its Economy, Marketing, and Leadership

Kakhaber Djakeli
http://orcid.org/0000-0001-7505-5653
University of Georgia, Georgia

ABSTRACT

This chapter deals with healthcare reforms in Georgia. As we see in this chapter, Georgia has been changing the concept of reform based on the economic views of the country's government, which were often not justified and supported by the country's economy, marketing and leadership. The implementation of healthcare reform in Georgia can be divided into three distinct phases: First phase, the attempt to build a state-run and controlled healthcare system, from 1994-1997. The second phase, when the country introduced a more liberal model and used outsourcing systems, such as private health insurance companies, from 2006-2012. The Third phase, when the country established strong finances and implemented the Universal Healthcare Model for everybody from 2013 to the present day. The financing of the services provided is primarily based on the case cost. It is interesting to consider what Georgia will do in the digital era, how Georgian healthcare will transition into the digital era, and how digital migration will evolve in Georgia's primary, secondary, tertiary, and public healthcare systems. To answer these critical questions, the present work relies on a literature review and a survey of healthcare experts.

DOI: 10.4018/979-8-3373-7173-3.ch009

1. INTRODUCTION

In 1921, the Republic of Georgia was occupied by the 11th Red Army sent by the Soviet Union, and remained part of the Soviet Union until 1991. During the occupation, the country was transformed into the Georgian Soviet Socialist Republic. Georgia was one of the wealthiest Soviet republics, unlike other republics, where food shortages were already felt in the 80s. Despite this, In the country, famous for its vineyards, tea, citrus, wheat, high-tech factories, and art, life was not easy. Georgia lacked justice because Russia had illegally annexed it in 1921.

During the Soviet period, Georgia had the Semashko model of healthcare, which included global budgeting, capitation, centralized planning, and management. When the Semashko model was first introduced, the Soviets were intensively building hospitals. Primary healthcare was less flexible and streamlined, and large hospitals had been used comprehensively. That is why it was very easy to refer patients to secondary healthcare. This made Soviet healthcare more expensive. There were pre-established standards. Most importantly, the Constitution of the Soviet Union, adopted in 1936, promised free healthcare to all residents. All this was to become one of the achievements on the path to building communism. However, the healthcare market opposed Soviet healthcare on rational grounds. Healthcare created a black market. The Soviets fought corruption. As a rule, doctors were not supposed to take money from patients, but they did. That is why the black market defeated Semashko's model, and the Soviet Union actually switched to an unofficial shadow economy. The failure of the economy and the disruption of macroeconomics put large hospitals at risk of funding as early as the late 80s, and it can be said that the Soviet Union, which was involved in Star Wars and competing with the United States, went bankrupt(Semenova et al., 2024).

After the collapse of the Soviet Union in 1991, the crisis that began in its republics in the late 1980s deepened, leading to the collapse of the monetary and credit systems. When the Soviet Union collapsed, it also severed traditional economic ties between the republics, and in 1991, the gross domestic product (GDP) fell by 28 percent. Purchasing power per capita also fell by at least three times. In 1995, production fell by 78 percent from 1990 levels. For example, in America, no one had seen such a decline in production during the Great Depression. Capital investment and agricultural output fell by 97 percent and 50 percent, respectively, in Georgia. The country fell into poverty.

When Georgians began reforming their healthcare system, the National Bank Coupon, introduced at the time, was experiencing severe inflation. In 1994, the National Bank Coupon, introduced to replace the Soviet ruble, fell by 7,380 percent. Prices for food and basic consumer goods increased 25 times in 1992, 92 times in 1993, and 120 times in 1994.

Wages and pensions in Georgia were practically destroyed; the salary was equivalent to 2 dollars in terms of the National Bank Coupon, and the pension fell to 10 American cents.

During this period, the Republic of Georgia lacked an approved budget. There was a civil war in the country, separatist movements inspired from outside. Three hundred thousand refugees from Abkhazia and South Ossetia flocked to the capital, having neither shelter nor food. At the same time, criminal gangs' activities were exposed. In general, crime in the country rose, reaching the highest echelons of politics.

In 1993, the Minister of Health changed: Mr. Irakli Menagarishvili served until 1 September 1993, when Mr. Avtandil Jorbenadze became Minister of Health on 19 October 1993.

2. THE FIRST HEALTHCARE REFORM

According to Semashko's model, state financing of medical institutions was carried out through the budgetary method, which was linked to a pre-planned bed fund and staffing schedule. The number of medical cases was studied in advance, and, using probability theory and statistics, the resources each region, city, state, or republic would need for healthcare were calculated.

Since the amount of financing was sharply reduced, and in 1994, the state share in total healthcare expenses amounted to only 4.9 percent, the healthcare system faced the destruction of the material and technical bases and an unprecedented decline in the medical sphere.

Since the country was already independent, it had to halt the healthcare sector's decline and build a new healthcare system. All this coincided with the fuel and energy crisis; heating in the towns was turned off. The vaccination deadlines were violated, which led to an outbreak of dangerous infections, increased intestinal infections, cases of botulism, rabies, tuberculosis, and other harmful diseases.

Due to the problematic situation, the Government of the Republic of Georgia began developing an anti-crisis program at the end of 1993. On February 7, 1994, this anti-crisis program was approved.

By this period, the Parliament of the Republic of Georgia was highly representative, comprising 24 political parties. This parliament adopted the law "On Health Care", "On Medicines and Pharmaceutical Activities", and "On State Compulsory Insurance Contributions".

In 1995, Georgia adopted a new Constitution that recognized citizens' right to affordable, high-quality health care.

During the preparatory period for the reform, Minister Avtandil Jorbenadze and his staff received full political support from the President. Necessary steps were taken in the following directions:

- Regional and municipal healthcare services were established to decentralize governance.
- A public healthcare system was created.
- Primary healthcare began to operate on the principle of family medicine.
- Planned immunization began, or rather, the immunization process was restored.
- The privatization process began in the state healthcare system.
- Medical institutions funded by the budget turned into independent entities.
- State standards for diagnostics and treatment were developed, which were the predecessors of guidelines and protocols.
- A system for licensing the activities of medical entities and personnel certification was created.
- A state program for the development of medical education was prepared.
- The pharmacy network and dental institutions were privatized.

In short, the legislative framework was ready, and preparatory work was underway. Recognizing the urgent need for reforms, the Ministry of Health of Georgia developed and officially implemented an ambitious health reform in August 1995. There was significant support from both Georgia's Friend countries and the World Bank. In cooperation with the World Bank, a long-term credit of 20 million US dollars was allocated to the structural reorientation of the Republic of Georgia's health system. The goal of the reform was "to improve the health of the entire population through the creation and implementation of a primary health care system that emphasizes health promotion, disease prevention, and health protection" (Balabanova et al., 2012).

The mission of the reform was to transform the national health services into a social insurance system. At this time, a significant change in the roles and responsibilities of central and local governments was implemented. The state maintained influence over the healthcare system through regulatory, funding, and licensing mechanisms (Jorbenadze et al., 1999).

Georgian healthcare leaders, the Minister and his staff, together with representatives of the World Bank, developed a model that envisaged centralized planning and management of social healthcare insurance through social medical insurance systems. A special State Medical Insurance Company (SMIC) was created. The country's president, Eduard Shevardnadze, and his followers allegedly supported the idea of state capitalism, which aligned with the principles of the Keynesian school of economics. However, how a country without strong finances or an economy could support such a healthcare model was not clear (Balabanova et al., 2012).

In short, the reform was implemented. Over five years (1995-2000), more than 400 healthcare institutions became private. The number of hospital beds decreased from 57,300 to 44,481. The number of hospital beds per thousand people was 44.5.

Western health experts said that the country was overstaffed with doctors and could not employ them. The number of doctors in Georgia exceeded 50,000, and with this number, Georgia could help neighboring countries provide healthcare. There was one doctor for every 245 inhabitants of the country—the new health insurance law provided for social healthcare. The country was divided into regional health offices.

The main idea of the reform was to cover the main costs of primary and secondary healthcare through state-funded programs. In addition, healthcare services were formally free for people with chronic diseases and vulnerable groups of the population (Gigauri & Djakeli, 2021). As mentioned earlier, the Georgian government introduced a social insurance model for healthcare financing and attempted to implement the principles of solidarity and equality. At that time, it should also be noted that there was no culture of insurance in the country.

The main problem with the 1994 healthcare reform was the disruption to the economy. Nevertheless, the healthcare sector and its reformers failed to achieve a civilized mix of public and private sources through social insurance, general/local budgets, and out-of-pocket payments.

The reformers hoped that service delivery could be achieved through a public/private mix of providers, but this did not happen because:

- The previously assessed and established standards became meaningless due to inflation.
- Clinics and hospitals were unable to receive funds in the end.
- A shadow market for healthcare was created.

Of course, reformers claimed that the reform of the healthcare financing model was accompanied by supply-side interventions aimed at optimizing the bloated healthcare infrastructure and excess human resources, many of whom had insufficient qualifications, inherited from the Soviet era.

After 1996, the Georgian healthcare system moved from the Semashko model to a state procurement model through several medical programs. These programs, of course, were created by the Ministry of Healthcare and based on pre-established guidelines. Despite the inflation, the prices of healthcare services, medical gauze and cotton were fixed there. This gave rise to nihilism towards the reform (Gotsadze et al., 2005).

Georgian healthcare reformers may have wanted to create something similar to the Beveridge model, but they failed. It should be noted that when the state manages the budget, the Beveridge model assumes a significant and active role for state medical organizations in human health. At that time, these state organizations in Georgia were already privatized, had been sold, or were in the process of being sold. Privatization was rapidly underway. This could also complicate the effectiveness of state procurement. Hospitals and clinics became subjects of the private market and were forced to obey it (Weissert & Weissert, 2019).

The system could not withstand corruption and nepotism. Accordingly, the reformed market soon fell prey to corruption and nepotism (Djakeli, 2011).

Due to the collapse of the Georgian economy and the cancellation of all traditional economic partnerships with the republics of the USSR, and, first of all, with the Russian Federation, the economy suffered a severe blow. The country was literally on the verge of bankruptcy. Due to funding constraints, the state medical standards approved by the Ministry of Labor, Health and Social Protection (MOLHSA), known as the "White Books" in the system, failed to gain traction in the country's healthcare market and lost their reputation. In 1999, Georgia spent 0.59 percent of its GDP on healthcare. The World Health Organization's unified index of health system performance - DALE (Disability-adjusted Life Expectancy) ranked Georgia 125th in terms of "healthcare expenditure" per capita. By 2002, due to a lack of state funding, the Georgian healthcare system was already on the verge of collapse. The health reform, like a boat, hit the rock bottom of the economic crisis and collapsed. An impressive combination of plans and reform initiatives coincided with extremely low spending (0.6 percent of GDP in 1999) - lower than in most low-income African countries. The main reasons for the failure of the health reform were:

- Weak planning of the reform, did not consider the risk of the momentum;
- Widespread corruption in the health system and in the country,
- The country's economic collapse,
- An inflexible and overly dependent health reform strategy on the mythical capabilities of the state,
- Poor structure and lack of linkages with health delivery.

All of these factors led to the failure of the first healthcare reform. In 2003, when the so-called "Rose Revolution" took place in the country, which overthrew the old, corrupt system, this corrupt healthcare system was put on the stake of cardinal reform (Djakeli, 2025).

3. THE SECOND HEALTHCARE REFORM

The idea for the second healthcare reform began to take shape in 2006 under the influence of liberal economists in the government, primarily through Vice Prime Minister Kakha Bendukidze. Subjective factors also contributed to this reform. Still, objectively, it was important that, after the overthrow of the corrupt Shevardnadze regime, society and its leaders had little faith in state institutions. They could not imagine state capitalism as the main driving force and pinned great hopes on liberal economic ideas, the author of which was then considered the famous American economist Milton Friedman. Based on the views of liberal-minded Georgian youth educated in America, the main goal of the second healthcare reform was to ensure financial access to medical services, especially for vulnerable populations. Milton Friedman's liberal views in this case gave Georgia not only the idea of reform but also the tools to implement it. The book Capitalism and Freedom (Friedman, 2016) had such a strong influence on Vice Prime Minister Kakha Bendukidze that he proposed Friedman's liberal ideas for financing healthcare through special vouchers to the Georgian government. The Georgian government, led by the Vice Prime Minister, decided to provide healthcare vouchers to vulnerable populations, including those who could not afford healthcare. The voucher recipient had the right to choose a private insurance company, and his voucher was given to that company in exchange for health insurance. Ultimately, the insurance premium for each insured person was paid by the state. The voucher was a means of exchange between the person and the insurance companies. Very soon, many people were insured against healthcare risks with private insurance companies. As we mentioned, for each voucher, the state paid an insurance premium, initially 10 GEL per person, then 22 GEL. This premium continued to increase. Accordingly, vulnerable individuals became the most attractive consumers for private health insurance companies. Insurance companies began competing to attract the vulnerable population as customers.

This liberal healthcare reform led to:

- faster privatization of healthcare infrastructure
- comprehensive coverage of targeted health insurance for vulnerable population groups
- Use of private insurance companies by the state to ensure access to healthcare products
- reduction of healthcare sector regulation to the necessary minimum
- preservation of the most critical public Healthcare functions as the responsibility of the government
- formation of an insurance culture among the broad masses of the population.

President Saakashvili had declared a zero-tolerance policy against corruption. This also contributed to the success of the second reform.

Most importantly, the reform drew a line between the employed and the unemployed. It inspired employed people to take greater responsibility for their health and to purchase health insurance themselves, thereby forming an insurance culture where none had existed. This was a great success. The unemployed, especially the vulnerable, received state vouchers, and with their help, a large-scale people's health insurance was implemented (vd Schulenburg, 2019).

4. THIRD HEALTHCARE REFORM IN GEORGIA

In the 2012 parliamentary elections, the "United National Movement" was defeated. This political force was obsessed with the ideas of Georgian "libertarianism" for nine years (Djakeli, 2013).

They initiated and successfully implemented many reforms. Along with the liberal healthcare reform, this political force also has an education reform to implement, which was, to some extent, based on Milton Friedman's ideas. However, this political force also had its mistakes. Accordingly, it was defeated and handed over power to the winning coalition, which was illiberal but democratic. The winning political force was called "Georgian Dream - Bidzina Ivanishvili". As is known, Mr. Bidzina Ivanishvili was a billionaire working in Russia who returned to Georgia. At first, he collaborated and financed the United National Movement, but in the end, he broke with them and became the leader of his own political force. The population trusted him and his doctrine. Immediately after coming to power, the Georgian Dream began healthcare reform because there was indeed a lot to be done in this area, and because healthcare reform was the best political marketing for the winning political force.

According to the State Decree No. 36 of February 23, 2013, a new healthcare reform was launched, introducing the "universal healthcare" model (Acts of the Ministry of Labor, Health and Social Protection of Georgia, 2014).

The main goal of the new reform was to provide a basic healthcare package for all citizens of Georgia. It envisaged offering beneficiaries only a minimal healthcare package, including family doctor services, consultations, and emergency care through secondary and tertiary healthcare (Weissert & Weissert, 2019).

However, since July 1, 2013, the program has also been expanded to include planned surgical operations, emergency outpatient services, emergency inpatient services, and a limited number of medical tests.

The innovative feature of this healthcare model, "universal healthcare," is that it treats both Georgian citizens and foreign residents. The existing program allows beneficiaries to choose their own medical institution. To receive treatment, beneficiaries must apply to the Social Service Agency and obtain a guarantee document (Albarari & Phagava, 2025).

WHO, USAID, and World Bank experts assessed Georgia's annual achievements under the state program "Universal Health Care" in 2014. The USAID Health Project also supported a customer satisfaction survey. The survey was conducted by telephone. 96.4% of respondents were generally satisfied with the hospital and emergency outpatient care. Funding for the program has grown rapidly. It increased from 365 million GEL in 2013 to 634 million GEL, and in 2016 it already reached 800 million GEL.

The winning political force, "Georgian Dream," and the Georgian government it formed, announced that it had created a universal tool enabling people to access healthcare services. According to them, this universal model covers 3.4 million citizens.

We have to take into account that 546,000 citizens of Georgia have private health insurance, and 560,000 receive state health insurance. As of May 5, 2014, approximately 2.3 million beneficiaries were registered in this program. Three hundred eighty-three thousand seven hundred seven cases were recorded, including 229,480 cases of emergency outpatient care. The population was mostly satisfied with the universal healthcare model (Verulava, 2023).

The study conducted by the Curatio Foundation confirmed the issues that Georgian healthcare will have to address in the future, and work in this regard is very important. According to this study, despite the measures taken, today the poorest 40% of the population is the least protected from impoverishing healthcare costs, and the probability of poverty for the poorest 20% of households is 44.5 times higher than for the wealthiest 20%.

The problems and primary reasons for consumer dissatisfaction are the following:

- The population's awareness of the reform program is still low;
- The medicines available in the program often do not meet the needs of the population, which is why they refuse to use the program and buy medicines with their own money.
- Skepticism of the population: patients often have little trust in state-funded medicines, as they equate their low price with low quality;
- The involvement of primary healthcare is low, which contributes to the population's low awareness and, in some instances, may affect the beneficiary's decision not to participate in the program.
- The lifting of drug limits in 2024 poses a risk of budget control becoming more difficult due to overprescribing or unscrupulous behavior on the part of providers (Curatsio International Foundation, 2025).

5. THE RESEARCH

The research used a method of studying and processing primary and secondary information on healthcare reforms in Georgia, with a particular focus on universal healthcare issues. The sources were both legislative and informational-statistical materials, articles and publications published in various journals, and the results of research conducted by governmental and non-governmental structures. Within the framework of qualitative research, in-depth interviews with healthcare experts were conducted using unstructured questionnaires.

Healthcare experts were selected using the snowball principle. Each expert recommended two experts to the researchers. Accordingly, 14 experts were selected, two of whom refused to participate in the interview.

The health expert interview method is a qualitative research technique for collecting expert opinions, in-depth assessments, and insights. Of course, sampling snowballing was considered, in which experts are selected based on their specialized knowledge or extensive experience in health system reform.

Health experts, who usually study health systems and events in their natural environment, often interpret issues with both objective and subjective meanings. Of course, in this sense. Qualitative data collection methods that include interviews, observation, and analysis are essential.

The in-depth interview method can be suitable for different situations and different research questions. With the interview-based method as the primary means of evaluation, the research was underway.

Individual face-to-face interviews can be either semi-structured or in-depth. Usually, semi-structured interviews typically use a flexible topic guide that provides a free-form structure of open-ended questions to explore experiences and attitudes. In-depth interviews provide the opportunity to obtain more detail about an issue or experience and are particularly useful for eliciting expertise skills of respondent.

Because this method elicits people's own views and accounts, interview methods require experienced researchers with the necessary sensitivity and ability to build rapport with respondents, use topic guides flexibly, and follow up on questions and responses.

The participants in the expert survey were mainly residents of Georgia. The selection was carried out by sending emails to health experts at the University of Georgia's affiliated universities and to other members of the healthcare network, as well as through snowball sampling.

Professionals were selected based on the following inclusion criteria:

(1) working in healthcare policy and also working in clinical administration, one or both.

(2) willingness to participate in a multidisciplinary survey

Experts and professionals were provided with information in advance about the nature of the research project and the methods used. Contact information for the research team was included in case participants had any questions about the study. The research questions were unstructured and followed the following guidelines:

1. How would you assess the current healthcare system in Georgia, and what are the prospects for its improvement?
2. Is there a need to increase the personalization of the healthcare model? How it is possible to achieve?
3. Socialization, connectivity, flexibility - how will the scope of the healthcare reform be expanded?
    5. How do you imagine innovation in healthcare and the introduction of new technologies?
    6. How should prevention be strengthened using digital healthcare systems and artificial intelligence?
    7. How can quality in medicine and healthcare be achieved through digital and artificial intelligence technologies?
    8. How can the expansion of the use of clinical data systems be achieved through digital technologies?
    9. How should global and local medical partnerships be achieved through digital and artificial intelligence technologies?
    10. How can the development of referral use be achieved?
    11. How can the Optimization of healthcare logistics be guaranteed in the future?

These and other unplanned questions were posed to experts, some in person and others via email.

6. RESULTS OF THE RESEARCH

According to the survey of experts, the state of the Georgian healthcare model and the future steps that the system should take were determined as follows: (1) Personalize the universal healthcare model by leveraging digital healthcare tools, allowing for tailored patient care in multidisciplinary settings. (2) Collaborate with multidisciplinary teams to identify where digital healthcare technologies and artificial intelligence can be most effectively applied. (3) Use digital healthcare to improve sociability and facilitate effective communication with vulnerable population groups, especially in challenging or emergencies. (4) Market the model. Proactively initiate and develop new projects or ideas related to the benefits of digital healthcare, and take steps to implement them. (5) Encourage innovation by using digital health solutions to develop and pilot new ideas, as well as offering alternative approaches to make medical practice more adaptive. (6) Enhance disease prevention strategies through improved use and management of digital medical records. (7) Strengthen the quality and reach of medical care by applying artificial intelligence solutions to diagnostics, treatment, and care processes. (8) Store scientific evidence and clinical data in big databases, and ensure broader access to these resources for all licensed medical professionals. (9) Build and expand partnerships both globally and locally by enabling data exchange and collaboration on research projects. (10) Broaden patient referral options by utilizing digital health tools to connect healthcare providers and services. (11) Optimize the logistics of patient flow and the allocation of medical resources by employing artificial intelligence and digital management systems (Gigauri & Djakeli, 2021).

7. WHAT MUST BE DONE

Georgia already has a national e-Health / HMIS platform with multiple modules (financial/statistical reporting, electronic medical record (EMR) capabilities, citizen/ patient modules, pharmaceutical and licensing modules, birth/death registration). The Ministry of Health's e-Health website and HMIS pages show active modules and ongoing developments (EMR, patient modules, financing/administration).

This means Georgia has the digital foundations (a national platform and modules)—so the challenge is to scale, improve interoperability, privacy, clinician workflows, and citizen-centric services, rather than starting from scratch (Djakeli, 2025). What does the Georgian e-health system need in the future? (vd Schulenburg, 2019).

The system needs to develop a personalized healthcare model. For this, it needs analytics, population health, and artificial intelligence pilots. Aggregated, de-identified HMIS data for planning, early warning, and targeted prevention (e.g., diabetes trends). Why: Moving from response to prevention and efficient resource allocation. Also, this model needs special promotion, like a brand it deserves (Djakeli, 2025 C).

It should be done - citizen-oriented services and digital inclusion - without fragmentation, a joint patient portal, mobile access, multilingual support, and offline access paths for the rural/elderly population should be created. The customer journey to this system must be studied well in advance (Gabelaia et al., 2024, September).

The main challenges for the system are to avoid fragmentation and digital exclusion. The system's opportunities are: user research plus gradual application improvement. (Weissert & Weissert, 2019).

Today, the following directions of healthcare digitization are being considered worldwide, as they are important for delivering high-quality healthcare services to patients. The goal under consideration is to provide personalized healthcare services to citizens of highly developed countries. Therefore, to create this new healthcare, digitization is being carried out in the following directions:

a) Creation of national electronic health records (EHR) and patient portals. In countries that have excelled in healthcare digitization (for example, Estonia), a central EHR and patient portal are classic examples of success.
b) Achieving interoperability in the field of healthcare records - digitization is achieving interoperability by creating common data standards to ensure secure data exchange between healthcare sectors, companies, and professionals - hospitals, primary healthcare, laboratories, and pharmacies.
c) Tools for analysis and verification, risk and threat assessment, and quantification are being developed - tools for implementing digital records and measuring "meaningful use" (training + funding + regulation). The US HITECH program has dramatically accelerated the implementation of EHRs, with funding for meaningful use and privacy rules.
d) A biometric base is being developed for the development of remote telemedicine. Telemedicine and remote monitoring tools have expanded rapidly during COVID and are now integrated into routine care pathways.
e) Data protection systems are being strengthened - establishing frameworks for data governance, confidentiality, and security - are essential for public trust and safe sharing.
f) Creation of patient identification, unique code assignment, database management systems for patient diagnosis based on the development of biometric systems - the use of national ID cards/authentication to provide patients with secure access and consent tools.

Why is it necessary to create a national electronic health record system?

Countries have begun developing nationwide electronic health records (EHRs) and patient portals. This is necessary to solve a complicated problem. The problem is that, according to common practice, patients often consult several providers across different hospitals, clinics, or regions, leading to fragmented treatment and repeated tests. Accordingly, fragmented treatment can harm the patient and endanger their life. To address this problem, a national electronic health record (EHR) ensures that all providers have access to the same up-to-date medical information (diagnoses, allergies, medications, lab results, imaging, etc.).

EHRs reduce duplication in diagnosis and treatment, eliminate medical errors, and eliminate inaccuracies and delays in diagnosis. To increase the impact of the reform, it is necessary to conduct marketing research that will map the patient journey and help patients make decisions easily by providing them with convincing information, as well as through the correct branding of healthcare companies and the correct marketing of medicine (Djakeli & McElroy[1], 2025, March).

If countries create an EHR system, they will improve patient safety and quality. There is also another problem: medical diagnoses and records on paper, including isolated digital systems, can lead to incorrect medication administration, which can be fatal for the patient (Żak et al., 2024).

CONCLUSION

The implementation of healthcare reform in independent Georgia can be divided into three distinct phases:

- The first one may be traced back to the post-Soviet collapse (1991–2003), during which the state made many, even unnecessary, or less flexible changes, relying on the ideas characteristic of state capitalism, which requires strong state finances. Of course, given the weak economy and finances, this first reform was doomed to fail. However, it still stands out in the history of independent Georgia as an attempt to save the country's healthcare system. The collapse of this reform somewhat accelerated revolutionary events in Georgia, and a large number of dissatisfied people directed their agitation toward the peaceful overthrow of the government, sparking the "Rose Revolution" in 2003.
- The second can be called market-oriented reforms (2007–2012), during which Georgian health economists, politicians, and leaders created a health insurance voucher for the vulnerable population and enabled many poor people to receive the healthcare they needed. At the same time, the second reform contributed to the formation of a health insurance culture in the country. That is, the employed, influenced by this culture, purchased health insurance and insured their families, because they saw that everyone across the country was becoming insured, primarily through health vouchers distributed by the state, and a violent movement emerged that created a new social demand for health insurance. By the way, this demand is well described by Maslow in his famous pyramid and reflects the broad masses' desire for security. It was precisely such a social movement that the state of Georgia encouraged by purchasing health insurance from private insurers, especially for the poor and vulnerable (Djakeli, 2025 A).

- The third stage of health insurance can be called the economic strengthening of the country, during which the state made a rather ambitious application to expand universal coverage of health services (2013–present) (Albarari & Phagava, 2025).

Given the current situation, despite improved financing and service delivery (direct pension payments have decreased from 74.7 to 57%), a chronic shortage of doctors and nurses persists, and governance gaps remain a challenge. The country should develop a Georgian healthcare digitalization strategy as the first holistic approach to expanding access and better meeting the population's needs through a new type of e-health (Djakeli, 2025 B).

We can say that Georgia has gained a lot of experience on the path of healthcare reforms. These reforms have always lacked proper marketing. Reforms must be implemented in the market in the same way as a product or service. Entering the market requires a positive perception of the population and target customers. For this, marketing is needed. First of all, the reform should be based on the country's economy, its traditions and culture. In this regard, it can be said that Georgia looks very interesting. The tradition of capitalism is now being formed in the country. After the Soviet period, institutions have been weak. The positive factor is that a strong insurance culture was formed during the reforms, which is important. The backbone of the reform is the economy and marketing, but the right leadership plays a big role. In this subsection, we touched on healthcare leadership at the level at which it was implemented on the example of Georgia. The leader of the first healthcare reform was Minister Avtandil Jorbenadze. He was, of course, supported by the country's second president, Eduard Shevardnadze. They believed in state capitalism and based the reform on a non-existent economy, which is why the first reform in the history of independent Georgia ended in failure.

The leader of the second reform was Vice Prime Minister Kakha Bendukidze and the new political force that won the Rose Revolution, who believed in the victory of liberalism. They used liberal values and, with their characteristic leadership, created a completely new healthcare model.

The third reform built on previous experience and created a universal coverage model for healthcare.

The future development of healthcare reform should occur through the personalization of this universal healthcare, which is possible through the innovative development of electromedicine and digital healthcare and the appropriate legal, economic, medical, and marketing steps towards the future.

REFERENCES

Acts of the Ministry of Labor, Health and Social Protection of Georgia. (2014). Matsne Press. Source: https://matsne.gov.ge

Albarari, S. S. A., & Phagava, H. (2025). Georgia's healthcare system: A journey of reform, investment and progress. *International Journal of Health Governance*, •••, 1–13.

Balabanova, D., Roberts, B., Richardson, E., Haerpfer, C., & McKee, M. (2012). Health Care Reform in the former Soviet Union: Beyond the transition. *Health Services Research*, *47*(2), 840–864. DOI: 10.1111/j.1475-6773.2011.01323.x PMID: 22092004

Curatsio International Foundation. (2025). Healthcare Barometer, February. DOI: DOI: 10.13140/RG.2.2.24611

Djakeli, K. (2011, April). Milton Friedman's ideas influenced the Health Care Reform of Georgia. In the 6th Silk Road International Conference" Globalization and Security in Black and Caspian Seas Region".

Djakeli, K. (2013). Analyzing success and failure of two health reforms in independent Georgia. *The Journal of Business*, *2*(2), 5–14.

Djakeli, K. (2025). Phygitalization of Palliative Care and Its Social Marketing. In *Phygital Approaches to Social Marketing* (pp. 267–288). IGI Global Scientific Publishing.

Djakeli, K. (2025 A). Social Marketing: Past, Current Period, and the Future. In Phygital Approaches to Social Marketing (pp. 1-20). IGI Global Scientific Publishing.

Djakeli, K. (2025 B). Social Marketing and Public Health in the Phygital Era. In Phygital Approaches to Social Marketing (pp. 43-66). IGI Global Scientific Publishing.

Djakeli, K. (2025 C). History of Branding, Its Current Status, and the Future of Phygitalization. In Brand Creation and Management in the Phygital Era (pp. 1-30). IGI Global Scientific Publishing.

Djakeli, K., & McElroy[1], J. W. (2025, March). The Power of Customer Journey Mapping with Artificial Intelligence: A Case Study. In Reliability and Statistics in Transportation and Communication: Human Sustainability and Resilience in the Digital Age: Selected Papers from the 24th International Multidisciplinary Conference on Reliability and Statistics in Transportation and Communication, RelStat-2024, Riga, Latvia, September 25-28, 2024 (Vol. 1337, p. 244). Springer Nature.

Friedman, M. (2016). Capitalism and freedom. In *Democracy: a reader* (pp. 344–349). Columbia University Press. DOI: 10.7312/blau17412-074

Gabelaia, I., Djakeli, K., & McElroy, J. W. (2024, September). The Power of Customer Journey Mapping with Artificial Intelligence: A Case Study Method. In International Conference on Reliability and Statistics in Transportation and Communication (pp. 244–257). Cham: Springer Nature Switzerland.

Gigauri, I., & Djakeli, K. (2021). National Health Reforms in Georgia from 1994 to 2021 and Their Success. *HOLISTICA Journal of Business and Public Administration, 12*(2), 102–108. DOI: 10.2478/hjbpa-2021-0017

Gotsadze, G., Zoidze, A., & Vasadze, O. (2005). Reform strategies in Georgia and their impact on health care provision in rural areas: Evidence from a household survey. *Social Science & Medicine, 60*(4), 809–821. DOI: 10.1016/j.socscimed.2004.06.017 PMID: 15571898

Jorbenadze, A., Zoidze, A., Gzirirshvili, D., & Gotsadze, G. (1999). Health reform and hospital financing in Georgia. CMJ Online, 40(2).

Semenova, Y., Lim, L., Salpynov, Z., Gaipov, A., & Jakovljevic, M. (2024). Historical evolution of healthcare systems of post-soviet Russia, Belarus, Kazakhstan, Kyrgyzstan, Tajikistan, Turkmenistan, Uzbekistan, Armenia, and Azerbaijan: A scoping review. Heliyon, 10(8). vd Schulenburg, J. M. G. (2019). The German health care system: concurrent solidarity, freedom of choice, and cost control. In Health Care Systems and Their Patients (pp. 83-104). Routledge.

Verulava, T. (2023). Managed competition and health insurance reforms in Georgia. Bull. Georg. Natl. Acad. Sci, 17(1).

Weissert, W. G., & Weissert, C. S. (2019). *Governing health: The politics of health policy*. Johns Hopkins University Press. DOI: 10.56021/9781421428932

Żak, A., Djakeli, K., & Bielińska-Dusza, E. (2024). Cross-Sector Partnerships and Relationship Marketing in Healthcare: The Example of Fairy Tale Therapy in Children's Hospitals in Poland. In Modern Healthcare Marketing in the Digital Era (pp. 164-192). IGI Global Scientific Publishing.

Chapter 10
Leadership and Equity in Health Reform:
Overcoming Discrimination and Promoting Mental Well-Being Among Migrant Workers

Jince George
http://orcid.org/0000-0003-3371-7334
Christ University, India

Sheeja B. Karalam
Christ University, India

ABSTRACT

This chapter examines leadership and governance responses to workplace discrimination and mental-health inequities among migrant workers within India's health-reform landscape, using Kerala as an empirical case. Drawing on quantitative evidence linking discrimination with psychological distress, diminished self-esteem, and reduced well-being, the chapter situates these outcomes within established frameworks such as health equity, social determinants of mental health, and trauma-informed leadership. It advances a compassion-driven leadership model that integrates behavioral insights, inclusive policy design, public-health marketing, and participatory governance to address structural and systemic inequities. By moving beyond descriptive narratives, the chapter demonstrates how ethical and inclusive leadership can translate evidence into equitable reform. It argues that sustainable health reform must embed human dignity, social justice, and mental well-being at the core of governance, rather than prioritizing efficiency alone.

DOI: 10.4018/979-8-3373-7173-3.ch010

INTRODUCTION

India's health-care reform agenda has traditionally prioritized infrastructure expansion, fiscal efficiency, and service coverage. While these efforts have improved aggregate health indicators, they have insufficiently addressed deep-rooted inequities embedded within social, economic, and institutional structures. One of the most persistent yet under-examined dimensions of this gap is the social and psychological marginalization of informal and migrant workers, whose mental well-being remains peripheral to mainstream reform discourse. Kerala often celebrated for its high human-development indicators presents a revealing paradox: despite progressive welfare policies, migrant workers report widespread discrimination, psychological distress, and social exclusion.

Health reform that neglects equity and mental well-being risks reinforcing structural injustice rather than alleviating it. Leadership, in this context, must be understood not merely as administrative coordination but as ethical stewardship an exercise of moral agency that integrates efficiency with empathy. Drawing on Rawls's (1971) theory of justice, equitable health systems require both fair distribution of resources and recognition of human dignity, particularly for the least advantaged. The COVID-19 pandemic further exposed the fragility of India's informal workforce, underscoring the urgency of embedding mental-health protection, inclusion, and compassion within health-system governance.

Globally, informal employment accounts for more than 60 percent of the workforce, exceeding two billion workers, with the highest concentration in South Asia and sub-Saharan Africa (International Labour Organization [ILO], 2018). Informal workers typically lack employment contracts, legal safeguards, and social protection, and are disproportionately exposed to hazardous conditions, income insecurity, and exclusion from health services. These vulnerabilities are intensified by intersecting social determinants such as caste, class, gender, migration status, and rural–urban inequality, all of which shape access to care and mental-health outcomes.

In India, the unorganised sector constitutes approximately 93 percent of total employment (Government of India, 2020), spanning construction, agriculture, domestic work, street vending, and manual labour. Migrant workers form a substantial segment of this workforce, particularly in urban and industrial regions. Originating largely from socioeconomically disadvantaged rural areas, they encounter discrimination, insecure housing, limited healthcare access, linguistic barriers, and occupational precarity (Deshingkar & Akter, 2009). Indigenous and local workers within the informal sector often from marginalized caste groups also experience systemic neglect, underlining that inequity operates across multiple social axes rather than along a single migrant–native divide.

Kerala exemplifies these layered inequities. Despite strong welfare institutions, the state increasingly relies on interstate migrant workers from Assam, Bihar, and Odisha to sustain its informal economy (Rajan & Zachariah, 2019). Concentrated in construction, hospitality, agriculture, and manufacturing, migrants frequently face wage disparities, unsafe working conditions, restricted access to healthcare, and limited social integration (Thomas, Rajeev, & Philip, 2020). Social perceptions that frame migrants as "outsiders" further intensify exclusion and psychological strain (Devassy & George, 2021). At the same time, segments of the native workforce report insecurity, perceived displacement, and declining job stability, illustrating how inequitable labour structures generate distress across groups (Narayana & Venkiteswaran, 2021).

Empirical research consistently identifies discrimination as a chronic psychosocial stressor with significant mental-health consequences. Discrimination alters self-perception, erodes social relationships, and restricts access to resources, increasing vulnerability to depression, anxiety, and stress-related disorders (Williams & Mohammed, 2009; Pascoe & Richman, 2009). Migrant workers experience compounded stress when navigating unfamiliar linguistic and cultural environments alongside institutional neglect (Bhugra, 2004). Comparative evidence from India, China, Latin America, and Africa demonstrates that migrant and informal workers exhibit higher levels of emotional exhaustion and psychological distress than non-migrant populations (Li et al., 2020; Joseph & Nair, 2020).

Psychological well-being, conceptualized by Ryff and Keyes (1995) as encompassing autonomy, environmental mastery, positive relationships, purpose in life, and personal growth, is systematically undermined in contexts of sustained discrimination. Reduced self-esteem, diminished agency, and social isolation are recurrent outcomes among workers exposed to bias (Rosenberg, 1965; Schmitt et al., 2014). Coping mechanisms partially mediate these effects: problem-focused and collective coping strategies can buffer distress, while avoidance-based responses exacerbate mental-health risks (Lazarus & Folkman, 1984; Folkman & Moskowitz, 2004). However, limited literacy, inadequate counseling infrastructure, and pervasive stigma surrounding mental illness constrain adaptive coping among informal workers in Kerala.

This chapter positions workplace discrimination and migrant mental health within a broader framework of health equity, social determinants of mental health, and ethical leadership. By integrating empirical evidence from Kerala with leadership and governance theory, it argues that inequitable mental-health outcomes are not incidental but structurally produced. Addressing them requires leadership models that are inclusive, trauma-informed, and systems-oriented capable of translating moral responsibility into policy design, institutional practice, and participatory reform.

BACKGROUND

Kerala's informal economy relies heavily on interstate migrant workers, primarily from Assam, Bihar, and Odisha, who are concentrated in construction, hospitality, plantation, and manufacturing sectors. While the state is often cited as a model of inclusive development, empirical evidence reveals persistent inequalities within its informal labor system. Drawing on a survey of 500 informal-sector workers (250 migrant and 250 native), the study by George and Karalam demonstrates that perceived workplace discrimination functions as a chronic psychosocial stressor, significantly associated with elevated levels of depression, anxiety, and diminished self-esteem. These findings highlight that mental-health disparities are not incidental but structurally embedded within labor and governance arrangements.

Despite the existence of welfare initiatives such as the Inter-State Migrant Workers Assistance Scheme, substantial implementation and access gaps remain. Migrant workers frequently experience precarious living conditions, overcrowded and substandard housing, linguistic exclusion, and limited access to public health-care and social protection (Devassy & George, 2021). These conditions undermine social integration and restrict access to informal support networks that are critical for psychological resilience. At the same time, segments of the native workforce report feelings of insecurity and perceived displacement, leading to what has been described as "reverse alienation," wherein competition for employment and wages generates emotional distress and social tension (Narayana & Venkiteswaran, 2021). This dynamic illustrates how inequitable labor structures produce psychological strain across groups rather than affecting migrants alone.

Kerala's experience reflects a broader pattern of systemic imbalance within health and labor reform. As conceptualized by Senge (2006), policy systems that prioritize economic performance and service expansion while neglecting human and relational dimensions tend to reproduce inequality. The disconnect between welfare policy intent and lived experience in Kerala underscores the limitations of reforms that are not grounded in health equity and social-determinants frameworks. Consequently, Kerala serves as a critical diagnostic case for examining how leadership, governance capacity, and institutional design shape discrimination, mental well-being, and health equity outcomes at both state and national levels.

THEORETICAL FRAMEWORK

This chapter is grounded in an integrated theoretical framework that combines health equity, social determinants of mental health, leadership ethics, and systems thinking to explain how discrimination becomes embedded in health and labour systems and how leadership can mediate its effects. Rather than treating discrimination and mental well-being as individual-level phenomena, the framework situates them within structural, institutional, and governance contexts.

At its normative core, the chapter draws on John Rawls's (1971) *Theory of Justice*, particularly the difference principle, which holds that social and economic inequalities are permissible only if they benefit the least advantaged. The systematic exclusion of migrant and informal workers from healthcare access, social protection, and decision-making violates this principle, indicating a failure of distributive and recognitional justice. Within health reform, Rawlsian justice demands that leadership explicitly prioritise vulnerable labour populations in policy design, resource allocation, and governance accountability.

Leadership theory provides the operational mechanism through which equity principles are translated into practice. Northouse's (2018) leadership typology transactional, transformational, servant, and authentic offers a useful lens for examining governance styles in health systems. Transformational and servant leadership, as articulated by Greenleaf (1977), are particularly relevant to equity-driven reform because they emphasise moral purpose, empathy, empowerment, and stewardship. In the context of health reform, servant leadership manifests as compassionate governance, where decision-making is guided by listening, inclusion, and long-term social responsibility rather than bureaucratic hierarchy or efficiency alone. Authentic leadership further complements this approach by fostering transparency, trust, and ethical consistency, all of which are essential for coordinating multi-sectoral action across health, labour, and welfare institutions.

To explain the mental-health consequences of discrimination, the framework integrates established psychosocial models. Williams and Mohammed's (2009) stress process model conceptualises discrimination as a chronic psychosocial stressor that shapes mental-health disparities by influencing self-perception, social relationships, and access to resources. This model is reinforced by Lazarus and Folkman's (1984) transactional theory of stress and coping, which demonstrates how cognitive appraisal and coping strategies mediate the relationship between environmental stressors and psychological outcomes. Empirical evidence consistently shows that adaptive coping strategies such as problem-solving and social support buffer distress, whereas maladaptive strategies exacerbate anxiety, depression, and emotional exhaustion (Folkman & Moskowitz, 2004). These models align closely with contemporary social-determinants and biopsychosocial approaches to mental health.

At the systems level, Senge's (2006) learning-organization framework provides a macro-theoretical lens for understanding why reforms that neglect human and relational dimensions tend to reproduce inequality. Health systems evolve sustainably only when leaders engage in reflective learning, shared visioning, and feedback-driven adaptation. This perspective is reinforced by the World Health Organization's

Health Systems Framework (2010), which identifies leadership and governance as a core building block underpinning equity, accountability, and system responsiveness. Weak governance, fragmented leadership, and exclusionary institutional cultures thus emerge as structural drivers of both discrimination and mental-health inequities.

Together, these normative, psychosocial, leadership, and systems-level theories form an integrated analytical foundation for this chapter. They inform the development of the Compassionate Leadership in Health Reform Model, which conceptualises leadership as a moral, participatory, and systems-oriented practice capable of translating health equity principles into measurable improvements in mental well-being and governance outcomes.

CONCEPTUAL FRAMEWORK:

The Compassionate Leadership in Health Reform Model (CLHRM) conceptualizes equity-oriented health reform as a leadership-driven, systems-level process in which compassion, ethics, and participation are embedded across all levels of governance from policy formulation to everyday workplace interactions. The model synthesizes empirical evidence from the Kerala discrimination study (George & Karalam) with established theories of leadership ethics, health equity, and systems governance (Greenleaf, 1977; Northouse, 2018; Rawls, 1971). It responds directly to the need for leadership frameworks that move beyond symbolic inclusion toward measurable and sustained improvements in mental well-being and social justice.

Core Pillars of the CLHRM

The CLHRM rests on five interrelated pillars that collectively address structural discrimination, institutional accountability, and psychosocial well-being within health systems.

1. Ethical Governance

Ethical governance forms the normative foundation of the model. It emphasizes the institutionalization of anti-discrimination principles through formal ethical codes, transparency audits, and equity scorecards. These mechanisms shift equity from a rhetorical commitment to a measurable governance objective. Ethical codes must explicitly prohibit discrimination based on caste, class, gender, language, region, or migration status, while transparency audits identify systemic inequities in recruitment, service delivery, and resource allocation. Equity scorecards operationalize Rawls's

(1971) principle of justice as fairness by tracking whether reforms tangibly benefit the least advantaged groups, including migrant and informal workers.

2. Inclusive Policy Design

Inclusive policy design recognizes that equitable reform cannot be achieved without the meaningful participation of marginalized groups. This pillar emphasizes co-creation processes that involve migrant and informal-sector workers in agenda setting, policy formulation, and evaluation. Such participation ensures both distributive justice (fair allocation of resources) and procedural justice (fair decision-making processes). In the Kerala context, the inclusion of migrant representatives in labour and public-health advisory bodies would enhance policy legitimacy and contextual relevance. This pillar aligns with OECD (2021) and WHO (2010) frameworks that identify participatory governance as central to sustainable and people-centered reform.

3. Behavioral Insights for Bias Reduction

The behavioral insights pillar addresses the often-invisible cognitive and institutional mechanisms through which discrimination is reproduced. Drawing on behavioral economics and cognitive psychology (Thaler & Sunstein, 2008), this component promotes the use of evidence-based nudges such as anonymized grievance systems, bias-aware recruitment protocols, and empathy-oriented training to mitigate implicit bias in organizational decision-making. Integrating behavioral analytics into human-resource and service-delivery data systems enables early detection of exclusionary patterns and supports timely leadership intervention.

4. Culturally Responsive Health Marketing

Health marketing within the CLHRM extends beyond information dissemination to actively reshape social norms around mental health and inclusion. This pillar emphasizes culturally and linguistically responsive communication strategies that resonate with diverse worker populations. Multilingual messaging, community narratives, and locally grounded symbols help normalize help-seeking behavior and reduce stigma among migrant workers. Consistent with Senge's (2006) concept of shared vision, culturally responsive health marketing fosters collective ownership of reform goals rather than top-down compliance.

5. Participatory Feedback and Learning Loops

The final pillar ensures that reform remains adaptive, accountable, and responsive over time. Participatory feedback mechanisms such as monitoring boards with worker representation, grievance redressal systems, and real-time evaluation dashboards create continuous learning loops between policymakers, institutions, and workers. These mechanisms transform governance from a static compliance model into a learning system capable of responding to lived experiences and emerging inequities.

Multi-Level Structure of the CLHRM

The CLHRM operates across three mutually reinforcing levels macro, meso, and micro ensuring coherence between policy intent and everyday practice.

At the *macro level*, leadership is exercised through national and state policy frameworks. Ministries of Health, Labour, and Social Welfare are encouraged to adopt equity-based indicators alongside conventional efficiency metrics. Periodic equity audits assess the differential impacts of reforms on migrant workers, informal labourers, and other marginalized groups, aligning with OECD (2021) recommendations for human-centered policy evaluation.

At the *meso level,* institutional leadership within hospitals, community health centers, and allied organizations translates policy commitments into operational practice. This includes inclusive leadership training, bilingual mental-health services, and the establishment of institutional "equity cells" responsible for monitoring discrimination, mediating grievances, and reporting outcomes to higher governance levels.

At the *micro level*, compassionate leadership is enacted through daily interactions in workplaces and service settings. Supervisors and frontline administrators are trained in empathy, cultural competence, and trauma-informed communication, enabling early identification of psychosocial distress and constructive responses to perceived discrimination. These micro-level practices cultivate psychological safety, trust, and inclusion, reinforcing system-wide equity goals.

Integrative Function of the Model

The interaction across these three levels generates a feedback-driven governance ecosystem in which workplace experiences inform institutional reform, and institutional outcomes guide policy refinement. This recursive process enhances adaptability, accountability, and ethical coherence within health systems.

By embedding compassion, participation, and equity across governance levels, the CLHRM reframes leadership in health reform as a moral and systems-oriented practice. It addresses discrimination not as an individual anomaly but as a structural and institutional challenge, offering a coherent pathway for transforming health governance into a human-centered, just, and sustainable system consistent with global frameworks articulated by the WHO (2010) and OECD (2021).

STRUCTURAL DETERMINANTS AND INTERSECTIONAL INEQUITIES

Mental-health disparities among informal-sector workers cannot be adequately explained through individual characteristics or workplace conditions alone. They are fundamentally shaped by structural determinants deeply embedded social, economic, and institutional forces that systematically advantage some groups while marginalizing others. In the context of Kerala's unorganised economy, migration status intersects with education, caste, housing, employment security, language, and social belonging to produce layered and cumulative forms of disadvantage. Understanding these intersectional inequities is essential for explaining why migrant workers experience disproportionately higher psychological distress than native workers, even when operating within the same economic sectors.

Education functions as a primary structural determinant influencing both material and psychological outcomes. Migrant workers in the study were, on average, less educated than their native counterparts, with many possessing only primary or secondary schooling. Limited educational attainment constrains access to information about labour rights, welfare entitlements, and grievance mechanisms, while also reducing confidence in negotiating workplace conditions. This educational disadvantage weakens perceived self-efficacy and heightens vulnerability to discrimination, thereby eroding self-esteem and increasing psychological distress. In contrast, native workers' relatively higher educational attainment enhances occupational stability, social confidence, and perceived legitimacy within institutional systems.

Employment security and income stability constitute another critical structural axis. Migrant workers are more likely to be employed in precarious, short-term, or informal arrangements characterized by irregular wages, hazardous conditions, and limited legal protection. Such insecurity generates chronic uncertainty regarding livelihood continuity, amplifying stress and anxiety. Native workers, by contrast, often benefit from longer job tenure, higher wages, and informal social protections embedded within local labour networks. These differences illustrate how identical job categories can yield divergent mental-health outcomes when embedded within unequal structural contexts.

Housing and spatial segregation further intensify psychological vulnerability. Migrant workers commonly reside in shared, overcrowded, or temporary accommodations, frequently located near worksites and distant from host communities. Such housing arrangements restrict privacy, limit opportunities for social integration, and reinforce perceptions of transience and exclusion. Separation from family members and familiar social networks deprives migrants of emotional support systems that are critical buffers against stress. Native workers' residence in permanent housing within established communities, by contrast, facilitates social cohesion, belonging, and emotional stability. Housing insecurity thus emerges as a powerful mediator linking migration status to diminished psychological well-being.

Language and cultural familiarity represent additional structural determinants shaping experiences of discrimination. Migrant workers often face linguistic barriers that impede communication with employers, healthcare providers, and public institutions. Inability to articulate distress, access services, or assert rights exacerbates feelings of invisibility and powerlessness. Cultural unfamiliarity may also expose migrants to stereotyping and social suspicion, reinforcing everyday microaggressions that accumulate into chronic psychological strain. These barriers are largely absent for native workers, who navigate institutions in their first language and within culturally familiar environments.

Importantly, these structural determinants do not operate in isolation but intersect in ways that compound vulnerability. Migration status interacts with low education, insecure employment, poor housing, and linguistic exclusion to create a dense web of disadvantage. This intersectional configuration explains why discrimination exerts a stronger psychological impact on migrant workers than on native workers, as demonstrated by the steeper regression coefficients and higher distress scores observed in the study. Discrimination, in this sense, is not merely an interpersonal experience but a manifestation of structural inequity embedded within labour markets, social hierarchies, and governance systems.

An intersectional perspective also highlights that mental-health inequities are unevenly distributed within migrant populations themselves. Younger workers, those with minimal education, and individuals lacking social networks are likely to face heightened risk. While the present study focuses on male workers due to sectoral composition, broader evidence suggests that gender further intensifies vulnerability, particularly for women migrants in domestic and informal service roles who experience gendered exploitation alongside cultural and occupational marginalization. These overlapping axes of inequality underscore the limitations of uniform policy responses.

Recognizing structural and intersectional inequities has significant implications for leadership and governance. Interventions that focus solely on individual resilience or clinical treatment risk obscuring the social conditions that generate distress. Effective reform must instead address upstream determinants education access, employment regulation, housing standards, language inclusion, and social integration through coordinated policy and leadership action. Leadership that fails to engage with these structural realities inadvertently perpetuates inequity, even within otherwise progressive welfare regimes.

In sum, the psychological disparities observed between migrant and native workers are not accidental outcomes of personal vulnerability but predictable consequences of intersecting structural inequalities. Education, employment security, housing, language, and social belonging collectively shape exposure to discrimination and access to protective resources. Addressing mental-health inequity in the informal sector therefore requires an explicit intersectional framework that informs policy design, institutional practice, and leadership accountability. Without such a framework, health reform efforts risk treating symptoms while leaving the structural roots of distress intact.

STRUCTURAL DETERMINANTS AND INTERSECTIONAL INEQUITIES

Mental-health disparities among informal-sector workers are not the product of individual vulnerability alone; they are shaped by structural determinants embedded within labour markets, social hierarchies, and governance systems. In Kerala's unorganised economy, migration status intersects with education, employment security, housing, language, and social belonging to generate cumulative disadvantage. An intersectional lens is therefore essential to explain why migrant workers experience disproportionately higher psychological distress and lower self-esteem than native workers, even when both groups operate within the same occupational sectors.

Education and skills constitute a foundational structural determinant. Migrant workers in the study were generally younger and less educated than native workers, with many possessing only primary or secondary schooling. Limited educational attainment restricts access to information on labour rights, welfare schemes, and grievance mechanisms, while also diminishing confidence in negotiating wages or workplace conditions. This educational disadvantage undermines self-efficacy and heightens perceptions of discrimination, thereby contributing to lower self-esteem and elevated distress. Native workers' comparatively higher education enhances occupational stability, institutional familiarity, and perceived legitimacy within local systems.

Employment security and income stability further differentiate psychological outcomes. Migrant workers are more likely to be employed in short-term, informal, and hazardous jobs with irregular wages and limited legal protection. Chronic employment insecurity generates persistent uncertainty about livelihood continuity, amplifying anxiety and stress. Native workers, by contrast, often benefit from longer job tenure, higher wages, and informal social protections embedded in local labour networks. These differences illustrate how identical job categories can yield divergent mental-health outcomes when embedded within unequal structural contexts.

Housing and spatial segregation operate as powerful mediators of mental well-being. Migrant workers typically reside in shared or temporary accommodations near worksites, often separated from host communities and distant from family-based support systems. Overcrowding, lack of privacy, and social isolation erode psychological safety and limit opportunities for recovery from work-related stress. Native workers' residence in permanent housing within familiar communities facilitates social cohesion, belonging, and emotional stability. Housing insecurity thus links migration status to diminished psychological well-being.

Language and cultural exclusion intensify these vulnerabilities. Migrant workers frequently encounter linguistic barriers that impede communication with employers, healthcare providers, and public institutions. Inability to articulate distress, access services, or assert rights fosters invisibility and powerlessness. Cultural unfamiliarity may also expose migrants to stereotyping and everyday microaggressions, which accumulate into chronic psychological strain. Native workers, operating in linguistically and culturally familiar environments, face fewer such barriers.

Crucially, these determinants do not act independently. *Intersectionality* the interaction of migration status with low education, precarious employment, insecure housing, and linguistic exclusion produces compounded vulnerability. This explains why discrimination exerts a stronger psychological impact on migrant workers than on native workers, as evidenced by steeper regression coefficients and higher distress scores. Discrimination, in this sense, is not merely interpersonal but a manifestation of structural inequity embedded in labour relations and governance arrangements.

An intersectional perspective also reveals *within-group heterogeneity*. Younger migrants, those with minimal education, and individuals lacking social networks face heightened risk. While the present study focuses on male workers due to sectoral composition, broader evidence suggests that gender further intensifies vulnerability, particularly for women migrants in domestic and informal service work who experience gendered exploitation alongside cultural and occupational marginalization. These overlapping axes of inequality underscore the limitations of uniform policy responses.

Recognizing structural and intersectional inequities has direct implications for leadership and governance. Interventions focused solely on individual resilience or clinical treatment risk obscuring the upstream conditions that generate distress. Effective reform must address education access, employment regulation, housing standards, language inclusion, and social integration through coordinated policy action and accountable leadership. Without engaging these structural realities, even progressive welfare regimes risk reproducing inequity.

In sum, the psychological disparities observed between migrant and native workers are predictable outcomes of intersecting structural inequalities. Education, employment security, housing, language, and social belonging collectively shape exposure to discrimination and access to protective resources. Addressing mental-health inequity in the informal sector therefore requires an explicit intersectional framework that informs policy design, institutional practice, and leadership accountability.

DISCRIMINATION AND MENTAL HEALTH: EVIDENCE FROM KERALA

This chapter draws on a quantitative, cross-sectional study conducted among 500 informal-sector workers in Kerala, comprising 250 interstate migrant workers and 250 native workers employed primarily in construction and plantation industries. The study was designed to examine how perceived workplace discrimination influences psychological distress, self-esteem, psychological well-being, and coping strategies among informal workers operating within structurally precarious labour conditions.

Data were collected through structured, face-to-face interviews using a standardized battery of validated psychometric instruments, administered in Malayalam, Hindi, Bengali, and Odia by trained field investigators to ensure inclusivity across linguistic and literacy differences. The instruments measured five interrelated constructs: perceived discrimination, psychological distress, self-esteem, psychological well-being, and coping strategies. Together, these measures enabled a multidimensional assessment of how discrimination operates as a psychosocial stressor within Kerala's informal labour system.

Perceived discrimination was assessed to capture both chronic and everyday experiences of unfair treatment linked to migration status, language, class, and occupational hierarchy. Psychological distress was measured across depression, anxiety, and stress domains, allowing for differentiation between affective and physiological responses to discrimination-related stressors. Psychological well-being and self-esteem were included to assess protective and mediating psychological resources, while coping strategies were examined to distinguish adaptive responses (e.g., problem-solving and social support) from maladaptive responses (e.g., avoidance and disengagement).

All analyses were conducted using IBM SPSS Statistics (Version 25). Descriptive statistics summarized demographic and psychological characteristics, while Pearson correlation analyses examined associations between discrimination and mental-health outcomes. Group differences between migrant and native workers were tested using one-way and two-way ANOVA, and multiple linear regression analyses were employed to assess the predictive strength of discrimination on psychological distress, controlling for self-esteem and psychological well-being as moderating variables.

The results provide strong empirical support for discrimination as a central determinant of mental-health inequity. Perceived discrimination showed a robust positive correlation with psychological distress ($r = .65$, $p < .001$) and significant negative correlations with self-esteem ($r = -.48$) and psychological well-being ($r = -.55$). Regression analysis confirmed that discrimination alone explained 42 percent of the variance in psychological distress (Adjusted $R^2 = .42$), even after accounting for protective psychological factors. These findings indicate that discrimination is not a peripheral stressor but a dominant predictor of mental-health outcomes in informal labour contexts.

Group-level analyses revealed that migrant workers experienced significantly higher levels of perceived discrimination and psychological distress than native workers, underscoring their heightened vulnerability. The stronger predictive effect of discrimination among migrants highlights how compounded social exclusion stemming from migration status, linguistic barriers, and insecure employment intensifies psychological risk. Coping analysis further showed that adaptive coping strategies were associated with lower distress, whereas maladaptive coping amplified negative outcomes, aligning with established stress-and-coping frameworks.

Taken together, the empirical evidence demonstrates that mental-health disparities among Kerala's informal workers are structurally produced rather than individually driven. Discrimination operates through multiple psychological pathways eroding self-esteem, constraining well-being, and shaping maladaptive coping thereby reinforcing inequity within labour and health systems. These findings substantiate the chapter's central argument that leadership and governance reforms must directly confront discrimination as a system-level determinant of mental health, rather than treating distress as an individual or clinical concern alone.

Table 1. Socio-Demographic Profile of Participants

Variable	Migrant Workers (n = 250)	Native Workers (n = 250)	Observation
Average Age	28.4 yrs	35.1 yrs	Migrants younger
Education Level	Mostly primary/ secondary	Higher secondary/ degree	Education gap influences self-esteem
Housing Type	Shared/temporary	Permanent	Migrants face social isolation
Average Monthly Income	12,000	16,500	Lower earnings among migrants
Employment Tenure	2.1 yrs	6.4 yrs	Greater job insecurity for migrants

The observed psychological differences between migrant and native workers are best understood in relation to underlying structural inequalities rather than individual characteristics alone. Socio-demographic analysis reveals systematic disparities in education, employment stability, income security, housing conditions, and social belonging that collectively shape mental-health outcomes within Kerala's unorganised sector.

All study participants were male, reflecting the gendered composition of employment in sectors such as construction and agriculture. Within this group, migrant workers were generally younger, less experienced, and had lower levels of formal education than native workers. Many migrants possessed only primary or secondary education, whereas a substantial proportion of native workers had completed higher secondary or degree-level qualifications. Educational disadvantage likely constrains migrants' access to information, limits awareness of labour rights and welfare schemes, and reduces confidence in negotiating workplace conditions, thereby contributing to heightened perceptions of discrimination and diminished self-esteem.

Economic and employment-related factors further accentuate these disparities. Native workers typically reported higher wages, longer job tenure, and greater employment continuity, all of which are associated with increased psychological security and emotional stability. In contrast, migrants were more likely to experience precarious employment arrangements, irregular income, and frequent job transitions, reinforcing chronic uncertainty and stress. Employment insecurity thus operates as a key structural pathway linking migration status to elevated psychological distress.

Housing and social integration also emerged as critical differentiating factors. Migrant workers predominantly resided in shared or temporary accommodations, often spatially and socially disconnected from host communities and separated from family-based support systems. Native workers, by contrast, were more likely to live in permanent housing within familiar social environments, benefiting from established community networks. The absence of stable housing and supportive social ties among migrants exacerbates feelings of isolation, weakens coping capacity, and heightens vulnerability to anxiety and depressive symptoms.

Taken together, these socio-demographic patterns demonstrate that discrimination and poor mental health among unorganised sector workers are embedded within broader structural conditions. Education, employment stability, housing security, and social belonging function as interconnected determinants that mediate psychological well-being. The findings underscore the necessity of policy and leadership interventions that address these structural dimensions rather than focusing solely on individual behaviour if mental-health inequities between migrant and native workers are to be meaningfully reduced.

Table 2. Comparative Analysis of Key Psychological Variables

Variable	Migrants (Mean)	Natives (Mean)	Interpretation
Perceived Discrimination	6.8	4.1	High exclusion among migrants
Psychological Distress (DASS)	15.2	9.4	Severe distress gap
Self-Esteem	24.3	29.5	Reduced self-worth
Psychological Well-Being	36.1	42.8	Weaker overall well-being

Comparative analysis of psychological characteristics between migrant and native workers reveals statistically meaningful disparities that underscore the heightened vulnerability of migrant workers within Kerala's unorganised economy. Migrant workers reported substantially higher levels of perceived discrimination (Mean = 6.8), reflecting persistent social exclusion and marginalisation within both workplace and community settings. This elevated exposure to discrimination corresponds with significantly higher levels of psychological distress (Mean = 15.2), suggesting that the cumulative burden of precarious employment, social isolation, linguistic barriers, and limited institutional support exerts a pronounced negative effect on mental health.

In contrast, native workers demonstrated higher levels of self-esteem (Mean = 29.5) and overall psychological well-being (Mean = 42.8). These comparatively favourable outcomes are plausibly associated with greater employment stability, stronger social and familial networks, cultural familiarity, and more consistent access to community resources. While both migrant and native workers operate within the same informal economic sectors, their psychological experiences diverge markedly due to unequal exposure to structural stressors and differential access to protective social resources.

Importantly, these findings indicate that mental-health disparities within the informal sector cannot be attributed solely to occupational conditions, but are shaped by broader social and institutional dynamics linked to migration status. The disproportionate psychological burden borne by migrant workers highlights the need for targeted, equity-oriented interventions that address discrimination, enhance access to culturally responsive mental-health services, and strengthen social integration mechanisms. Without such differentiated policy and leadership responses, existing inequities in mental well-being are likely to persist despite broader welfare or labour reforms.

Correlation Analyses

A Pearson correlation matrix was computed across the full sample:

Figure 1. Correlation Heatmap – Discrimination and Mental-Health Variables

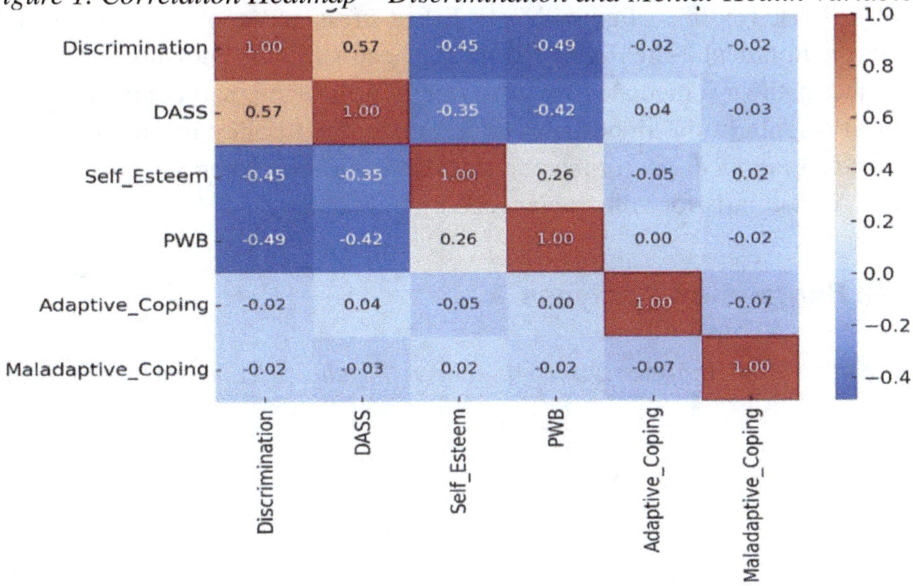

The correlation heatmap provides a clear visual summary of the relationships among discrimination, psychological distress, self-esteem, psychological well-being, and coping strategies. The analysis reveals a strong positive association between perceived discrimination and psychological distress (r = .65), indicating that higher levels of reported bias are consistently accompanied by elevated anxiety, stress, and depressive symptoms. This finding reinforces the characterization of discrimination as a chronic psychosocial stressor rather than a marginal workplace experience.

In contrast, discrimination shows significant negative correlations with self-esteem (r = –.48) and psychological well-being (r = –.55). These inverse relationships suggest that exposure to prejudice systematically erodes individuals' sense of self-worth, autonomy, purpose, and overall psychological functioning. As discrimination increases, core psychological resources that support resilience and well-being decline, heightening vulnerability to mental-health problems.

The heatmap further illustrates the moderating role of coping strategies. Adaptive coping mechanisms such as problem-solving, seeking social support, and positive reframing are associated with lower levels of psychological distress, indicating their protective function. Conversely, maladaptive coping strategies such as denial, avoidance, and disengagement are positively correlated with distress, demonstrating that ineffective coping amplifies the psychological impact of discrimination.

Taken together, the heatmap underscores a coherent pattern: discrimination is positively linked to distress and negatively linked to protective psychological resources, while coping strategies influence the direction and intensity of these outcomes. These findings align with established stress-and-coping models, which posit that environmental stressors affect mental health through both direct pathways and indirect pathways mediated by self-esteem, well-being, and coping capacity. The results highlight the importance of leadership and policy interventions that simultaneously reduce discriminatory practices and strengthen adaptive coping resources, particularly for vulnerable worker populations.

Overall Regression Analyses

Figure 2. Regression Analysis: Discrimination vs. Psychological Distress (DASS-21)

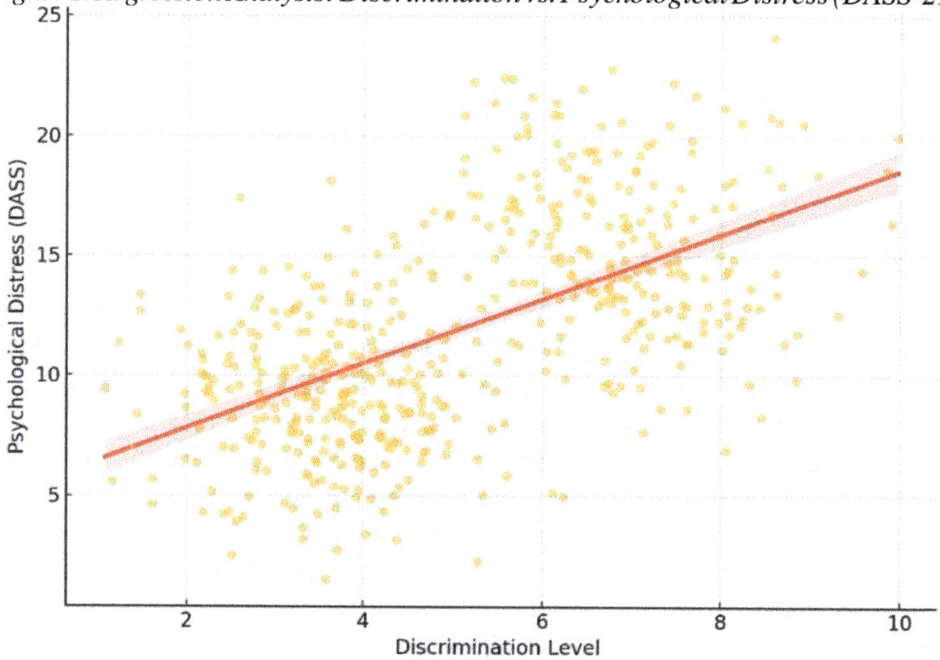

Multiple regression analysis confirmed that perceived discrimination is the strongest predictor of psychological distress among informal-sector workers. The overall regression model was statistically significant F(3,496)=115.4,p<.001F(3, 496) = 115.4, p < .001F(3,496)=115.4,p<.001 and explained a substantial proportion of variance in distress (Adjusted $R^2 = .42$), indicating that discrimination, self-esteem, and psychological well-being together account for nearly half of the observed differences in psychological discomfort as measured by the DASS-21.

Among the predictors, discrimination exerted the most powerful effect ($\beta = .45$, $p < .001$). This finding indicates that, holding other factors constant, a one standard deviation increase in perceived discrimination is associated with a 0.45 standard deviation increase in psychological distress. The magnitude of this effect confirms discrimination as a central structural stressor rather than a secondary or incidental influence on mental health.

In contrast, self-esteem ($\beta = -.30$, $p < .001$) and psychological well-being ($\beta = -.25$, $p < .001$) functioned as significant protective factors. Higher self-esteem was associated with lower distress, suggesting that a stronger sense of self-worth buffers individuals against the psychological impact of adverse social experiences. Similarly, higher psychological well-being particularly dimensions such as autonomy, purpose in life, and personal growth was linked to reduced stress, anxiety, and depressive symptoms. These findings are consistent with stress-and-coping and positive-psychology frameworks, which emphasize internal psychological resources as moderators of environmental stressors.

Group-specific regression models revealed important heterogeneity in these relationships. Discrimination was a markedly stronger predictor of distress among migrant workers ($\beta = .52$) than among native workers ($\beta = .38$), underscoring migrants' heightened vulnerability. This steeper association suggests that discrimination interacts with additional stressors such as linguistic barriers, insecure housing, limited social support, and cultural exclusion to intensify psychological harm. While self-esteem and well-being offered some protection, their buffering effects were insufficient to offset the disproportionate impact of discrimination on migrant populations.

Taken together, these findings reinforce three critical implications. First, discrimination must be treated as a primary target of mental-health and labour reform, as reducing discriminatory practices would yield the greatest reduction in psychological distress. Second, interventions that strengthen self-esteem and psychological well-being such as counseling, empowerment programs, and supportive workplace environments can mitigate, but not fully neutralize, the harmful effects of bias. Third, migrant workers require targeted mental-health and policy interventions due to their elevated sensitivity to discrimination.

Overall, the regression evidence demonstrates that psychological distress in Kerala's informal sector is driven predominantly by structural and social factors rather than individual weakness. Effective reform therefore requires dismantling discriminatory practices while simultaneously fostering protective psychological resources, particularly among migrant workers who face compounded vulnerabilities.

Group-Specific Regression

Figure 3. Group-Specific Regression Plots: Migrant vs. Native Workers

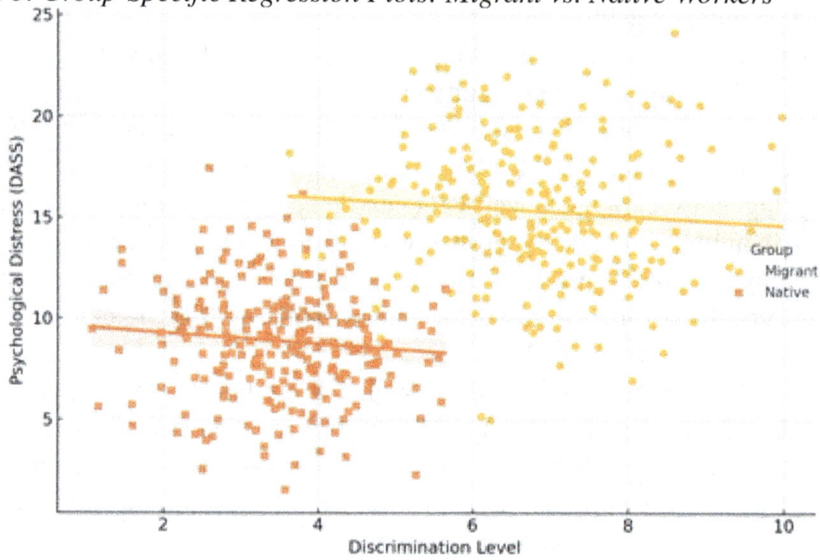

The group-specific regression analysis demonstrates that perceived discrimination exerts a substantially stronger effect on psychological distress among migrant workers (β = .52) than among native workers (β = .38). The steeper regression slope for migrants indicates heightened sensitivity to variations in discriminatory experiences, confirming that equivalent increases in perceived bias translate into disproportionately greater psychological distress for this group. This differential effect highlights migration status as a critical moderator in the discrimination–mental health relationship.

Figure 3 visually reinforces this finding by illustrating two distinct regression trajectories. Each data point represents an individual worker's level of perceived discrimination and corresponding psychological distress. The migrant workers' regression line displays a pronounced upward slope, indicating a strong and consistent positive association between discrimination and distress. In contrast, the native workers' regression line, while still positive, is flatter and exhibits greater dispersion, suggesting a comparatively weaker and less uniform relationship.

Quantitatively, the standardized regression coefficient for migrant workers (β = .52) implies that each unit increase in perceived discrimination is associated with a 0.52 standard deviation increase in psychological distress, controlling for other variables. For native workers, the corresponding increase is 0.38 standard deviations, indicating a materially lower impact. This contrast underscores the compounded vulnerability of migrant workers, whose psychological well-being is more acutely affected by discriminatory treatment.

The heightened effect observed among migrants likely reflects the interaction of discrimination with additional structural stressors, including linguistic barriers, insecure housing, limited social support networks, and cultural marginalization. These factors may amplify the psychological consequences of bias, making migrant workers more susceptible to anxiety, depression, and emotional exhaustion. The findings thus align with intersectional and social-determinants perspectives, which emphasize that discrimination operates within broader contexts of vulnerability rather than in isolation.

From a policy and leadership standpoint, these results underscore the necessity of targeted interventions rather than uniform or generic reform measures. While anti-discrimination policies benefit all workers, migrant populations require tailored responses that address their specific risk profile. Such interventions include stronger enforcement of workplace anti-discrimination legislation in sectors employing high proportions of migrants, culturally and linguistically sensitive mental-health services, and dedicated support mechanisms that enhance social integration and coping capacity.

Overall, the group-specific regression analysis provides robust empirical confirmation that discrimination disproportionately harms migrant workers' mental health. Although prejudice adversely affects all workers, its intensified impact on migrants necessitates differentiated policy responses and leadership strategies. Addressing these disparities is essential for advancing equitable, inclusive, and evidence-informed health reform.

Anova Test

Boxplot Comparison of DASS by Group

Figure 4. Boxplot Comparison of Psychological Distress (DASS) by Group

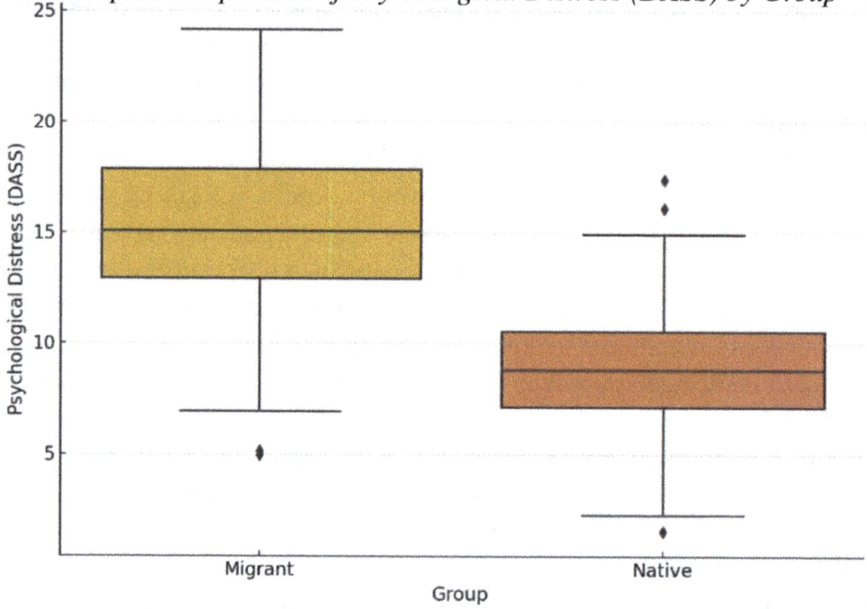

The one-way ANOVA results F(1,498)=35.42,p<.001F(1, 498) = 35.42, p < .001F(1,498)=35.42,p<.001 confirm a statistically significant difference in psychological distress between migrant and native workers, with migrants exhibiting substantially higher levels of distress. The boxplot visualization further illustrates this disparity by highlighting differences in central tendency, dispersion, and variability across groups. Migrant workers show a higher median DASS score, a wider interquartile range, and longer whiskers, indicating not only elevated distress but also greater heterogeneity in psychological experiences. The presence of more extreme values among migrants suggests heightened vulnerability within certain subgroups, reflecting uneven exposure to discrimination and psychosocial stressors.

Taken together, the visual and statistical evidence demonstrates that the observed differences in distress are systematic rather than incidental. The ANOVA findings corroborate earlier regression results showing that perceived discrimination explains a substantial proportion of variance in psychological distress (Adjusted $R^2 = .42$). This level of explained variance underscores discrimination as a central, structural determinant of mental-health outcomes in India's informal sector, rather than a peripheral or individual-level concern.

From a psychological perspective, discrimination erodes key internal resources such as self-esteem, autonomy, and sense of purpose, thereby violating multiple dimensions of psychological well-being articulated by Ryff and Keyes (1995), including environmental mastery, positive relations, and purpose in life. The mediating role of coping strategies further clarifies this pathway: adaptive coping functions as a protective buffer, while maladaptive coping amplifies distress. These findings suggest that leadership interventions that strengthen self-efficacy, resilience, and supportive environments can meaningfully reduce the mental-health impact of structural bias.

Kerala's empirical evidence offers actionable guidance for equity-driven health reform. First, it reinforces the need for ethical awareness among administrators, framing discrimination not as an unavoidable social reality but as an organizational and governance failure requiring accountability. Second, it highlights the importance of preventive policy design, particularly the integration of anti-bias safeguards into institutional processes such as recruitment, housing allocation, wage administration, and access to health benefits. Third, the results emphasize the role of compassionate supervision at the field level. Supervisors and managers should be trained to identify early signs of psychosocial distress and respond through empathetic, non-punitive support mechanisms rather than disciplinary control.

Collectively, these micro-level leadership practices contribute to macro-level equity by aligning everyday organizational behavior with the moral and ethical imperatives of public health governance. By translating empirical evidence into leadership accountability and institutional reform, the findings demonstrate how compassionate and ethical leadership can transform workplace culture, mitigate discrimination, and advance sustainable, human-centered health reform.

EMPIRICAL EVIDENCE SNAPSHOT ACROSS CONTEXTS

Placing Kerala's findings within a broader comparative landscape helps clarify that the observed mental-health disparities among migrant and informal workers are neither anomalous nor context-specific. Rather, they reflect a recurring global pattern in which structural exclusion, weak labour protections, and fragmented governance systems converge to produce disproportionate psychological distress among marginalized workers. An empirical snapshot across national and international contexts strengthens the chapter's analytical grounding and reinforces the relevance of equity-driven leadership in health reform.

Evidence from Other Indian States

Empirical studies from multiple Indian states mirror the patterns identified in Kerala. Research conducted among migrant construction workers in Maharashtra and Delhi has documented significantly higher levels of anxiety, depression, and perceived discrimination compared to local workers, largely attributed to precarious employment, housing insecurity, and limited access to health services. In Gujarat and Tamil Nadu, studies on informal industrial labour have shown that migrants are less likely to utilize public mental-health facilities due to language barriers, fear of job loss, and lack of awareness of welfare entitlements. These findings suggest that even in economically advanced or industrialized states, migrant mental health remains systematically under-prioritized when leadership and governance mechanisms fail to integrate equity considerations.

Importantly, states that have experimented with participatory welfare mechanisms such as worker facilitation centers or community outreach through civil-society partnerships report relatively better mental-health awareness and service uptake among migrants. This variation across states underscores the role of governance design and leadership responsiveness in shaping mental-health outcomes, beyond differences in economic capacity alone.

Comparative Evidence from the Global South

International evidence from the Global South further contextualizes Kerala's experience. Studies from China indicate that rural-to-urban migrant workers experience significantly higher psychological distress than urban residents, driven by institutional exclusion under residency registration systems, occupational insecurity, and social isolation. Similar patterns have been observed in Southeast Asian countries such as Malaysia and Thailand, where migrant labourers in construction and manufacturing sectors report elevated stress and depression linked to discrimination, restricted mobility, and limited access to healthcare.

In Latin America, research from Brazil and Mexico has shown that informal and migrant workers face compounded mental-health risks due to poverty, violence, and weak social protection. Aguilar-Gaxiola and colleagues found that exclusion from social insurance and community networks significantly predicted depressive symptoms among informal workers, even when controlling for income and employment type. These studies reinforce the conclusion that discrimination and informality operate as transnational determinants of mental-health inequity.

Evidence from High-Income Contexts

Evidence from high-income countries also supports the generalizability of these findings. Studies in Europe and North America consistently report poorer mental-health outcomes among migrant and racialized workers compared to native populations, despite stronger formal labour protections. Research from the United Kingdom and Canada shows that perceived discrimination and underemployment among migrants are strongly associated with depression, reduced self-esteem, and emotional exhaustion. These findings demonstrate that economic development alone does not eliminate mental-health inequities when institutional bias and social exclusion persist.

Cross-Context Synthesis

Across contexts, several convergent patterns emerge. First, discrimination consistently appears as a stronger predictor of mental-health distress than income or occupation alone. Second, migrant status interacts with education, housing, language, and social capital to amplify vulnerability. Third, governance arrangements that prioritize participation, accountability, and culturally responsive service delivery show relatively better mental-health outcomes among marginalized workers.

Kerala's case is therefore best understood as illustrative rather than exceptional. Its relatively strong welfare infrastructure coexists with informal prejudice and implementation gaps, reflecting a broader global paradox: progressive policy frameworks can fail to deliver equity in the absence of inclusive leadership and effective governance mechanisms. The empirical consistency across contexts strengthens the chapter's central argument that mental-health inequities are structurally produced and require leadership-driven, system-level reform.

Implications for Equity-Driven Reform

This cross-context evidence highlights that effective mental-health reform cannot rely solely on service expansion or economic growth. Instead, it requires leadership that explicitly addresses discrimination, integrates migrant realities into policy design, and institutionalizes accountability across sectors. By situating Kerala within a wider empirical landscape, this snapshot reinforces the urgency of compassionate, inclusive, and participatory governance as a universal prerequisite for advancing mental well-being among informal and migrant workers.

In sum, the convergence of evidence from India and beyond affirms that the challenges identified in Kerala are part of a global pattern of inequity. This reinforces the relevance of the chapter's theoretical and empirical contributions and underscores the broader applicability of equity-driven leadership models in health reform across diverse socio-economic contexts.

THE ROLE OF LEADERSHIP IN REFORMING HEALTH SYSTEMS

Leadership in health reform must extend beyond technical administration to function as an institutional and ethical force shaping how systems recognize vulnerability, distribute resources, and ensure accountability. Rather than treating leadership as an individual attribute, this chapter conceptualizes it as a governance mechanism through which equity, inclusion, and mental well-being are operationalized. As Greenleaf (1977) argues in servant-leadership theory, leadership effectiveness is ultimately measured by whether institutions enable individuals and communities to grow, particularly those who are structurally disadvantaged. In health systems, this translates into policies and practices that actively protect dignity, psychological safety, and access to care for marginalized populations.

Transformational leadership theory further strengthens this argument by emphasizing vision, ethical conduct, and collective purpose (Northouse, 2018). In contexts such as Kerala where migrant workers often experience social invisibility despite their economic contribution transformational leadership can rebuild trust between institutions and communities by aligning reform agendas with lived realities. Such leadership fosters legitimacy not merely through service delivery but through transparency, participation, and responsiveness.

From a systems perspective, the World Health Organization (2010) identifies leadership and governance as foundational building blocks of resilient health systems. Weak leadership manifests in fragmented accountability, exclusionary practices, and policy–practice gaps, all of which undermine equity outcomes. Integrating discrimination indicators and mental-health metrics into policy audits and performance reviews enables leaders to monitor equity impacts systematically. This approach aligns with OECD (2021) recommendations advocating for equity dashboards and outcome-based governance frameworks that make social inclusion measurable rather than aspirational.

Within this context, the chapter advances the concept of equitable or compassion-driven leadership as a governance orientation that integrates moral vision, participatory engagement, and value-based decision-making. Such leadership reframes healthcare not as a narrow exercise in efficiency optimization but as a social institution responsible for justice, well-being, and collective responsibility. Central to this approach is the principle of voice ensuring that migrant workers and other marginalized groups are actively involved in agenda setting, policy design, and evaluation processes. Participation transforms reform from a top-down intervention into a shared institutional project.

Operationalizing compassionate leadership requires the cultivation of specific institutional competencies. Ethical sensitivity enables leaders to recognize how power asymmetries and institutional routines disadvantage certain groups. Interpersonal empathy expressed through culturally competent communication and active listening supports trust-building in linguistically and socially diverse settings. Transformative visioning connects micro-level practices, such as accessible counseling or grievance redressal, with macro-level objectives related to equity, mental well-being, and system sustainability. Together, these competencies shift leadership from symbolic commitment to practical governance capacity.

Leadership development programs modeled on the WHO Global Leadership in Health framework can embed these competencies within public-sector and health-administration cadres. Such training should move beyond managerial skills to include ethics, bias awareness, trauma-informed leadership, and systems thinking. Without this capacity-building, even well-designed policies risk failing at the implementation stage.

Traditional hierarchical bureaucracies often constrain inclusive reform by limiting dialogue and adaptability. As Senge (2006) emphasizes, learning organizations thrive through feedback, reflection, and cross-sector collaboration. Establishing collaborative networks that link government departments, non-governmental organizations, employers, and community leaders enables the translation of localized lessons such as those from Kerala into scalable reform models.

Behavioral insights further enhance leadership effectiveness by revealing how cognitive biases, framing effects, and institutional norms shape decision-making. Framing mental-health support as resilience enhancement rather than clinical intervention, for example, can reduce stigma and improve uptake among migrant workers and employers alike. Kerala's experience with the Aawaz Insurance Scheme illustrates this dynamic: initial low enrollment driven by mistrust was addressed through transparent communication, local-language outreach, and ethical engagement, demonstrating that leadership communication is integral to policy success.

In sum, leadership reform in health systems is not a procedural adjustment but an ethical and institutional transformation. By embedding compassion, accountability, and participation into governance structures, leadership redefines reform as a process that advances not only efficiency, but equity, mental well-being, and social trust.

ECONOMIC AND SOCIAL VALUE OF INCLUSIVE MENTAL-HEALTH POLICIES

Inclusive mental-health policies represent not only an ethical imperative but also a strategic economic investment. The World Health Organization estimates that depression and anxiety result in approximately US $1 trillion in annual productivity losses globally due to absenteeism, presenteeism, and reduced work capacity (WHO, 2020). These costs are particularly pronounced in informal labour markets, such as those prevalent in India, where over 80 percent of workers lack formal social protection and occupational health safeguards (International Labour Organization, 2018). In such settings, untreated psychological distress directly undermines labour productivity, workplace safety, and employment continuity.

Empirical evidence from Kerala reinforces this economic argument. Regression results from the George and Karalam study demonstrate that discrimination significantly erodes self-esteem and psychological well-being both of which are established predictors of work engagement, motivation, and retention. Conversely, reductions in discriminatory practices are associated with improved psychological functioning, suggesting that mental-health promotion within labour policy can yield tangible productivity gains. Integrating mental-health support into informal-sector governance therefore contributes to improved efficiency, reduced turnover, and enhanced workforce stability, rather than constituting a discretionary welfare expense.

Beyond immediate productivity effects, inclusive mental-health policies generate broader social and intergenerational benefits. Migrant households with greater psychological stability are more likely to invest in education, skill development, and long-term livelihood planning for their children, thereby strengthening human-capital formation. From a leadership perspective, Greenleaf's (1977) concept of servant leadership underscores the responsibility of institutions to design systems that extend benefits beyond present outcomes and support future generations. In the context of health reform, this implies embedding compassion and inclusion into institutional structures so that equity is sustained rather than dependent on episodic interventions.

From a public-finance perspective, outcome-based budgeting offers a practical mechanism for operationalizing these benefits. The OECD (2021) recommends linking public expenditure to measurable social outcomes, including equity and well-being indicators. By incorporating metrics such as reductions in reported discrimination, improvements in psychological well-being scores, or declines in absenteeism, governments can reframe mental-health spending as a high-return investment. Evidence from Kerala suggests that inclusive mental-health and anti-discrimination initiatives reduce downstream costs associated with workplace conflict, staff turnover, healthcare utilization, and productivity loss, thereby offsetting initial investments in counseling services, outreach programs, and leadership training.

Taken together, these economic and social considerations challenge the perception of mental-health policy as a secondary or non-essential component of health reform. Instead, they position inclusive mental-health governance as a foundational element of sustainable development, workforce resilience, and equitable growth. When leadership aligns economic planning with mental well-being and social inclusion, health reform advances not only moral legitimacy but also long-term economic and institutional efficiency.

MARKETING MENTAL HEALTH: PUBLIC PERCEPTION AND REFORM ACCEPTANCE

Despite the adoption of India's National Mental Health Policy (2014), stigma surrounding mental illness remains a significant barrier to care, particularly among migrant workers who often fear job loss, social labeling, or exclusion if identified as psychologically vulnerable. These fears limit help-seeking behavior and undermine the effectiveness of formal mental-health services. Evidence from public-health research indicates that attitudes toward mental illness are shaped less by clinical information alone and more by how mental health is framed, communicated, and socially normalized. Consequently, public-health marketing emerges as a critical governance tool for translating policy intent into community-level acceptance and utilization.

This chapter advances a compassion-oriented mental-health marketing framework that integrates behavioral science, cultural competence, and participatory communication strategies. Narrative-based campaigns that feature lived experiences of recovery and resilience are central to reducing stigma, as they humanize mental health challenges and counter dominant narratives of weakness or incapacity. Cultural and linguistic adaptation of messages through multilingual materials in Hindi, Bengali, Odia, and other migrant languages addresses communication exclusion and enhances accessibility for interstate workers. The framework further emphasizes the role of community champions and peer educators drawn from migrant populations, whose social credibility helps build trust and counter institutional mistrust often associated with state-led interventions.

Digital and phygital delivery mechanisms, including mobile counseling platforms linked to local health centers, are proposed to extend reach while maintaining continuity of care. These tools align with contemporary health-system strategies that combine technological access with human support, particularly in resource-constrained informal settings. Consistent with Senge's (2006) concept of shared vision, such approaches foster collective ownership of reform objectives by engaging policymakers, service providers, and worker communities in a common narrative of mental well-being.

The effectiveness of mental-health marketing interventions can be assessed through pre- and post-intervention evaluations linked to existing welfare initiatives such as Kerala's *Aawaz* and *Apna Ghar* programs. Indicators including reductions in reported stigma, increased uptake of counseling services, improved continuity of care, and decreased absenteeism provide measurable proxies for reform acceptance. Embedding such evaluative mechanisms within governance structures ensures that mental-health communication is not merely symbolic but functions as an evidence-driven component of equitable health reform.

TOWARDS COMPASSIONATE LEADERSHIP IN HEALTHCARE REFORM

Compassionate leadership in healthcare reform extends beyond individual empathy or managerial competence; it represents a form of ethical and institutional governance that shapes how systems recognize vulnerability and respond to inequity. As articulated by Northouse (2018), authentic leadership is grounded in self-awareness, moral integrity, and relational transparency. In public health contexts, this translates into leadership practices that acknowledge structural suffering experienced by migrant workers, frontline health staff, and administrators alike and respond through system-level interventions rather than isolated acts of care.

Building on this premise, the Compassion-Driven Governance Framework conceptualizes leadership as a multi-dimensional mechanism for embedding equity and mental well-being into health reform. The first dimension, empathetic policy leadership, reframes healthcare as a fundamental right rather than a discretionary service, requiring leaders to align reform agendas with principles of dignity, fairness, and social justice. The second dimension, cultural intelligence, emphasizes the capacity of leaders and institutions to design programs that are linguistically and socially inclusive, reducing alienation among migrant and marginalized populations. The third dimension, intersectoral collaboration, recognizes that mental-health inequities are shaped by factors beyond the health sector alone; coordinated action across health, labor, housing, and social-welfare departments is therefore essential for addressing the social determinants of mental well-being.

The fourth dimension focuses on institutionalized community engagement through structured platforms such as Migrant Well-Being Councils or worker advisory bodies. These mechanisms operationalize participatory governance by embedding worker voices within policy design, implementation, and evaluation processes. The fifth dimension, ethical data stewardship, underscores the importance of safeguarding confidentiality, transparency, and informed consent in the collection and use of health and employment data, particularly in contexts where disclosure of mental distress may carry social or occupational risks. Together, these dimensions shift compassionate leadership from a normative ideal to a governance practice with identifiable institutional functions.

Digital innovations and artificial intelligence can complement compassionate leadership by identifying patterns of absenteeism, distress, or service underutilization; however, such tools must remain embedded within ethical oversight structures. As emphasized by the World Health Organization (2021), digital health solutions should augment not replace human judgment, relational trust, and contextual sensitivity. Leadership responsibility lies in ensuring that technological insights are interpreted through an equity lens and translated into supportive, non-punitive responses.

Institutionalizing compassion within health reform requires formal governance mechanisms rather than reliance on individual goodwill. Ethics committees, grievance redressal systems, participatory feedback dashboards, and periodic equity audits provide structural pathways for embedding compassion into organizational practice. At the state level, Kerala's health system could operationalize this approach through the development of a Compassion Index that integrates indicators of staff behavior, patient experience, inclusivity, and responsiveness. As Senge (2006) argues, sustainable institutional learning occurs when values such as compassion are made visible, measurable, and subject to collective reflection. In this way, compassionate leadership becomes not an abstract moral appeal but a durable component of equitable and accountable health governance.

POLICY AND GOVERNANCE MECHANISMS IN EQUITY-DRIVEN HEALTH REFORM

Equity-driven health reform depends not only on ethical intent but on effective policy and governance mechanisms that translate principles into practice. Despite progressive health and labour policies in India, persistent mental-health inequities among informal and migrant workers reveal systemic weaknesses in governance design, coordination, and implementation. These gaps allow discrimination to endure despite formal commitments to inclusion and welfare.

A key governance challenge is *policy fragmentation*. Responsibilities for migrant welfare and mental health are spread across multiple ministries Health, Labour, Housing, and Social Welfare often operating in silos. This fragmentation weakens coordination and accountability, resulting in inconsistent access to healthcare, insurance, housing support, and grievance redressal for migrant workers. Equity-driven reform therefore requires integrated governance frameworks that align health policy with labour regulation and social protection.

Implementation failures further undermine policy effectiveness. While welfare schemes and mental-health initiatives exist, many informal workers remain excluded due to documentation barriers, language constraints, limited outreach, and weak local administrative capacity. Strengthening last-mile delivery through decentralized administration, community intermediaries, and simplified access protocols is essential for translating policy into practice.

Another critical gap is the *absence of enforceable anti-discrimination mechanisms*. Discrimination is rarely monitored or sanctioned as a governance failure, and most institutions lack standardized tools to detect bias in recruitment, service delivery, or grievance handling. Institutionalizing equity audits, mandatory reporting, and independent oversight can convert normative commitments into operational standards.

Financing and human-resource constraints also shape inequitable outcomes. Mental health remains underfunded, particularly in community and occupational settings, while shortages of culturally competent professionals limit service reach. Outcome-oriented budgeting and workforce training in trauma-informed, migration-sensitive care are therefore essential.

Finally, *data governance, participation, and leadership accountability* are central to equity-driven reform. Disaggregated data can make inequities visible, participatory platforms can rebalance power, and accountability mechanisms can ensure sustained action. Together, these governance reforms are necessary to dismantle structural discrimination and advance inclusive mental well-being.

RECOMMENDATIONS AND SOLUTIONS

The empirical and theoretical insights of this chapter indicate that discrimination and mental-health inequities must be addressed as systemic governance challenges rather than isolated individual problems. Effective reform therefore requires coordinated interventions across policy, organizational, and legislative–advocacy domains to align leadership intent with institutional practice and accountability.

Policy-Level Actions

Health reform should explicitly recognize discrimination as a determinant of mental health. State and national policies must embed clear anti-discrimination clauses applicable to both public and private employers in sectors employing large numbers of informal and migrant workers. These provisions should define prohibited practices, establish enforcement mechanisms, and specify penalties to ensure compliance.

Governments should also expand multilingual mental-health services by deploying counselors fluent in major migrant languages, addressing linguistic barriers that hinder access to care. Complementing facility-based services, mobile counseling units can deliver on-site mental-health support at worksites, reducing stigma and access constraints. Leadership capacity building is equally critical; compulsory training in compassionate governance, cultural intelligence, and trauma-informed leadership should be integrated into public-administration curricula. Finally, institutionalized equity audits using standardized scorecards can track inclusion, service uptake, and grievance resolution, strengthening policy accountability.

Organizational Strategies

At the organizational level, employers and healthcare institutions should foster inclusive workplace cultures. Peer-support networks can provide non-hierarchical spaces for workers to share experiences and coping strategies, reducing isolation and stigma. Establishing "Compassion Hubs" within workplaces and health facilities can normalize mental-health conversations and support emotional resilience. Behavioral nudges such as reminders promoting empathy and fairness offer low-cost tools to counter unconscious bias and reinforce inclusive norms.

Legislative and Advocacy Pathways

Sustained reform requires robust enforcement and advocacy. Collaboration between health authorities, labour departments, and human-rights institutions can strengthen implementation of anti-discrimination provisions under existing legislation. Independent grievance redressal mechanisms with worker representation enhance trust and accountability. Civil-society organizations and academic institutions can further support reform through evidence-based advocacy, public-interest litigation, and social accountability initiatives. Together, these measures translate compassionate leadership into measurable improvements in mental well-being, equity, and governance effectiveness.

IMPLICATIONS FOR PRACTITIONERS AND POLICYMAKERS

The findings of this chapter offer clear and actionable guidance for practitioners and policymakers seeking to advance equity-driven mental-health reform. Translating empirical evidence into practice requires recognizing discrimination not as a peripheral social concern, but as a measurable governance failure that directly undermines health outcomes.

For *policymakers*, the evidence underscores the need to embed anti-discrimination objectives within mental-health and labour policy frameworks. This includes integrating migrant-sensitive indicators such as prevalence of psychological distress, service utilization rates, and grievance resolution outcomes into policy dashboards and performance evaluations. Strengthening intersectoral coordination across health, labour, housing, and social welfare systems is essential to address the multidimensional determinants of distress experienced by informal and migrant workers.

For *health administrators and public-sector leaders*, the findings highlight the central role of institutional culture and frontline leadership. Administrators should institutionalize equity audits, expand multilingual and culturally responsive mental-health services, and ensure that grievance redressal mechanisms are accessible, confidential, and non-punitive. Leadership development programs must move beyond technical management to incorporate ethical sensitivity, cultural competence, and trauma-informed supervisory practices.

For *practitioners and service providers*, particularly those working in community and occupational health settings, early identification and supportive response are critical. Training frontline workers to recognize psychosocial distress, build trust, and promote adaptive coping can significantly reduce harm, even within structurally constrained environments. Peer-support networks and community-based counseling models are especially effective for reaching informal and migrant populations.

For *civil-society organizations and employers*, participatory engagement emerges as a key strategy. Involving workers in program design, monitoring, and feedback enhances legitimacy and effectiveness. Inclusive workplace practices can also reduce distress-related absenteeism and turnover, aligning ethical responsibility with organizational sustainability.

Overall, the evidence demonstrates that equitable mental-health reform is both feasible and beneficial when leadership, policy design, and practice are aligned. Addressing discrimination through compassionate and accountable governance is not an abstract ideal, but a practical pathway to improving mental well-being, institutional trust, and system performance.

DISCUSSION

The findings from the Kerala study provide strong empirical evidence that workplace discrimination is the most salient determinant of psychological distress among informal-sector workers. Discrimination emerged as the strongest predictor of distress ($\beta = .45$), accounting for a substantial proportion of variance in mental-health outcomes even after controlling for self-esteem and psychological well-being. This confirms that mental-health inequities in the informal sector are not incidental or individually driven, but structurally produced within labour relations and governance systems.

The robust positive association between perceived discrimination and psychological distress ($r = .65$) reinforces existing scholarship that conceptualizes discrimination as a chronic psychosocial stressor with cumulative emotional consequences. Migrant workers reported significantly higher levels of discrimination and distress than native workers, indicating that migration status intensifies exposure to exclusion and vulnerability. These findings are consistent with international evidence demonstrating that migrant and informal workers experience heightened mental-health risks due to overlapping social, occupational, and institutional marginalization.

Discrimination was also negatively associated with self-esteem ($r = -.48$) and psychological well-being ($r = -.55$), highlighting the multidimensional harm of biased environments. Experiences of exclusion erode self-worth, autonomy, and purpose core dimensions of well-being. While native workers exhibited relatively better psychological outcomes, this reflects differential access to stability and social belonging rather than the absence of structural strain.

Coping strategies played a critical mediating role. Adaptive coping mechanisms were associated with lower distress, whereas maladaptive strategies intensified anxiety and depression. These patterns align with the transactional model of stress and coping, underscoring that mental-health outcomes depend not only on exposure to discrimination but also on the availability of psychological and social resources. For migrant workers, limited access to culturally appropriate support and persistent stigma constrained adaptive coping.

From a governance perspective, the findings indicate that discrimination represents a failure of ethical and institutional leadership. Progressive welfare policies alone are insufficient when informal practices and organizational cultures normalize exclusion. The Compassionate Leadership in Health Reform Model (CLHRM) illustrates how leadership action across micro, meso, and macro levels can translate ethical intent into measurable equity outcomes.

Overall, the results underscore the necessity of intersectional, equity-driven leadership that addresses discrimination as a structural determinant of mental health, rather than treating distress as an isolated individual condition.

DATA GAPS AND LIMITATIONS

While this chapter provides robust empirical and theoretical insights into discrimination, leadership, and mental well-being among informal-sector workers, several data gaps and limitations must be acknowledged to ensure analytical transparency and scholarly rigor. Recognizing these limitations not only signals methodological maturity but also clarifies the boundaries within which the findings should be interpreted.

First, the study relies on a *cross-sectional research design*, which limits the ability to establish causal relationships between discrimination and mental-health outcomes. Although strong statistical associations were identified, the temporal sequencing of exposure and outcome cannot be definitively determined. Longitudinal data would be necessary to assess how prolonged exposure to discrimination shapes mental-health trajectories over time and whether leadership or policy interventions produce sustained improvements.

Second, the sample was restricted to *male workers*, reflecting the gendered composition of employment in sectors such as construction and agriculture. While this enhances internal consistency, it limits the generalizability of findings to women workers, who often face distinct and compounded forms of discrimination. The absence of gender-disaggregated analysis constrains a fuller understanding of intersectional inequities, particularly in domestic work and informal services where women migrants are overrepresented.

Third, reliance on *self-reported measures* introduces the possibility of response bias, including underreporting due to stigma or fear of repercussions. Although validated psychometric instruments were used and administered with cultural sensitivity, mental-health reporting among informal workers remains shaped by social norms and trust in institutions. Additionally, the study does not incorporate clinical diagnoses or physiological indicators, which could have strengthened triangulation.

Fourth, *data on institutional practices* such as employer-level discrimination, grievance handling, or enforcement of labour standards were not directly collected. As a result, the analysis focuses primarily on workers' perceptions rather than organizational behavior or governance performance. Future research integrating administrative data, employer audits, and policy implementation metrics would offer a more comprehensive system-level assessment.

Finally, the study is context-specific to Kerala. While comparative evidence suggests broader relevance, regional variations in governance capacity and labour markets warrant caution in extrapolating findings nationally or internationally without contextual adaptation.

FUTURE RESEARCH DIRECTIONS

The findings of this chapter point to several priority directions for future research that can deepen scholarly understanding and strengthen evidence-informed policymaking at the intersection of leadership, discrimination, and mental well-being. While the present study establishes discrimination as a central determinant of psychological distress among migrant and informal-sector workers, future research must move beyond cross-sectional analysis toward more dynamic, comparative, and systems-oriented inquiry.

First, *longitudinal studies* are needed to track mental-health trajectories of migrant and informal workers over time. Such designs would allow researchers to assess whether leadership-driven interventions such as ethics training, equity audits, grievance mechanisms, or culturally responsive mental-health services produce sustained improvements in psychological well-being, self-esteem, and coping capacity, rather than short-term relief.

Second, *comparative federal and subnational research* within India can illuminate how variations in governance capacity, leadership orientation, and policy implementation shape mental-health outcomes. Comparing states that adopt participatory, equity-focused approaches with those relying on centralized or technocratic models would help identify best practices for scalable reform.

Third, future work should adopt an explicitly *intersectional lens*, examining how migration status interacts with caste, gender, education, and socioeconomic position to produce differentiated mental-health risks. Such research is essential for avoiding one-size-fits-all policies and for designing targeted, inclusive interventions.

Fourth, *community-based and participatory research methods* can enrich understanding of lived experiences of discrimination, stigma, and coping. Involving workers as co-producers of knowledge enhances cultural validity and aligns with principles of inclusive leadership.

Finally, *systems-dynamics modeling and ethical digital-health research* can support policy foresight by simulating long-term impacts of alternative leadership and governance strategies, while critically assessing the role of AI and digital tools in detecting and addressing distress.

Together, these research directions support a shift from descriptive diagnosis toward transformative, equity-driven inquiry capable of informing just and resilient health-system reform.

CONCLUSION

The evidence from Kerala demonstrates unequivocally that workplace discrimination is not a marginal social concern but a core structural determinant of mental-health inequity within informal labour systems. Discrimination consistently emerged as the strongest predictor of psychological distress, undermining self-esteem, psychological well-being, and adaptive coping among migrant and native workers alike. These findings underscore that health inequities persist not merely due to service gaps, but because leadership and governance structures often fail to confront exclusionary norms embedded within labour and institutional practices.

Drawing on Rawls's (1971) principle of justice as fairness, Greenleaf's (1977) servant leadership, and Senge's (2006) systems thinking, the chapter argues that sustainable health reform requires moral and participatory leadership capable of translating equity principles into institutional action. Compassionate leadership, as articulated through the Compassionate Leadership in Health Reform Model (CLHRM), provides a pathway for embedding fairness, accountability, and mental well-being into policy design, organizational practice, and workplace culture.

From a policy perspective, the findings highlight the need for comprehensive anti-discrimination legislation, culturally responsive mental-health services, and accessible counseling mechanisms tailored to migrant populations. Multilingual service delivery, grievance redressal systems, and community-based mental-health initiatives are essential for reducing stigma and improving help-seeking behavior. Equally important are interventions that strengthen self-esteem and adaptive coping, which can buffer the psychological effects of structural stressors.

The chapter also identifies clear directions for future research. Longitudinal studies are needed to examine the long-term mental-health consequences of discrimination and to evaluate the effectiveness of leadership-driven interventions. Comparative and intersectional research examining how migration, caste, gender, and socioeconomic status interact would further strengthen evidence-based policymaking.

Ultimately, Kerala's experience illustrates that progressive welfare systems alone are insufficient if informal prejudice remains unaddressed. Health reform that prioritizes efficiency without equity risks reproducing injustice. By centering compassion, ethical leadership, and participatory governance, health systems can move beyond symbolic inclusion toward durable reforms that promote dignity, mental well-being, and social justice for all workers.

REFERENCES

Aguilar-Gaxiola, S., Loera, G., Méndez, L., Sala, M., & Kopelowicz, A. (2011). Community-defined solutions for Latino mental-health care disparities: A community-based participatory-research project. *American Journal of Public Health*, *101*(12), 2255–2263. DOI: 10.2105/AJPH.2010.192021

Bhugra, D. (2004). Migration and mental health. *Acta Psychiatrica Scandinavica*, *109*(4), 243–258. DOI: 10.1046/j.0001-690X.2003.00246.x PMID: 15008797

Deshingkar, P., & Akter, S. (2009). *Migration and human development in India* (UNDP Human Development Report No. 13). United Nations Development Programme.

Devassy, B., & George, A. (2021). The social integration and health of migrant labourers in Kerala. *Indian Journal of Public Health Research & Development*, *12*(3), 184–191.

Folkman, S., & Moskowitz, J. T. (2004). Coping: Pitfalls and promise. *Annual Review of Psychology*, *55*(1), 745–774. DOI: 10.1146/annurev.psych.55.090902.141456 PMID: 14744233

George, J., & Karalam, S. B. R. (in progress). Research work related to migrant workers in Kerala [Unpublished working thesis]. Department of social work, Christ University, Bengaluru.

Government of India. (2020). *Economic survey 2019–2020.* Ministry of Finance International Labour Organization. (2018). *Women and men in the informal economy: A statistical picture* (3rd ed.). ILO.

Greenleaf, R. K. (1977). *Servant leadership: A journey into the nature of legitimate power and greatness*. Paulist Press.

Joseph, T., & Nair, K. S. (2020). Informal sector and mental health: A comparative study of natives and migrants in Tamil Nadu. *Labor Studies Journal*, *45*(4), 293–310. DOI: 10.1177/0160449X20941023

Lazarus, R. S., & Folkman, S. (1984). *Stress, appraisal, and coping*. Springer.

Li, Z., Li, X., & Guo, S. (2020). Mental-health status of Chinese rural-urban migrant workers and influencing factors: A meta-analysis. *Journal of Affective Disorders*, *276*, 1102–1110. DOI: 10.1016/j.jad.2020.05.076 PMID: 32663938

Narayana, D., & Venkiteswaran, C. S. (2021). Migration and exclusion in Kerala's informal sector. *Kerala Development Report*, *3*(1), 22–35.

Narayana, D., & Venkiteswaran, C. S. (2021). Migration and exclusion in Kerala's informal sector. *Kerala Development Report*, *3*(1), 22–35.

Northouse, P. G. (2018). *Leadership: Theory and practice* (8th ed.). Sage.

Organisation for Economic Co-operation and Development (OECD). (2021). *Centre stage: Driving inclusive growth through inclusive policy making*. OECD Publishing.

Pascoe, E. A., & Richman, L. S. (2009). Perceived discrimination and health: A meta-analytic review. *Psychological Bulletin*, *135*(4), 531–554. DOI: 10.1037/a0016059 PMID: 19586161

Rajan, S. I., & Zachariah, K. C. (2019). *Emigration and remittances: New evidence from the Kerala migration survey 2018*. Centre for Development Studies.

Rawls, J. (1971). *A theory of justice*. Harvard University Press. DOI: 10.4159/9780674042605

Rosenberg, M. (1965). *Society and the adolescent self-image*. Princeton University Press. DOI: 10.1515/9781400876136

Ryff, C. D., & Keyes, C. L. M. (1995). The structure of psychological well-being revisited. *Journal of Personality and Social Psychology*, *69*(4), 719–727. DOI: 10.1037/0022-3514.69.4.719 PMID: 7473027

Schmitt, M. T., Branscombe, N. R., Postmes, T., & Garcia, A. (2014). The consequences of perceived discrimination for psychological well-being: A meta-analytic review. *Psychological Bulletin*, *140*(4), 921–948. DOI: 10.1037/a0035754 PMID: 24547896

Senge, P. M. (2006). *The fifth discipline: The art and practice of the learning organization* (Rev. ed.). Doubleday.

Thomas, J., Rajeev, P. V., & Philip, S. (2020). The plight of interstate migrant workers in Kerala: A policy analysis. *Economic and Political Weekly*, *55*(7), 15–20.

Williams, D. R., & Mohammed, S. A. (2009). Discrimination and mental health: A review. *Annual Review of Clinical Psychology*, *5*, 335–361. DOI: 10.1146/annurev.clinpsy.032408.153610

World Health Organization (WHO). (2010). *Monitoring the building blocks of health systems: A handbook of indicators and their measurement strategies*. WHO Press.

World Health Organization (WHO). (2021). *Global strategy on digital health 2020–2025*. WHO Press.

KEY TERMS AND DEFINITIONS

Compassionate Leadership: Compassionate leadership is a human-centered approach that combines empathy, moral sensitivity, and active concern for others' well-being. Rooted in servant-leadership philosophy (Greenleaf, 1977), it emphasizes listening, understanding, and supporting subordinates and communities, particularly during crisis or systemic reform.

Discrimination: Discrimination refers to the unjust or prejudicial treatment of individuals or groups based on characteristics such as ethnicity, gender, caste, or migration status. In the context of healthcare and labor systems, it manifests as unequal access to opportunities, services, and psychosocial support, contributing to mental distress and social exclusion (Williams & Mohammed, 2009).

Health Marketing: Health marketing applies communication and behavioral-science strategies to influence public attitudes and behaviors toward health-promoting practices. In mental health reform, it involves designing culturally sensitive campaigns that destigmatize mental illness and encourage help-seeking among marginalized populations

Health Reform: Health reform denotes systematic policy and structural changes aimed at improving access, equity, quality, and efficiency in healthcare delivery. It includes reconfiguring leadership, financing, and governance mechanisms to align health systems with ethical, human-centered principles (World Health Organization, 2010).

Inclusive Policy Design: Inclusive policy design is the process of formulating and implementing public policies that account for the diverse needs, capacities, and rights of marginalized or vulnerable groups. It involves participatory decision-making, equitable representation, and data-driven equity assessments to ensure fair outcomes across social strata (OECD, 2021).

Leadership Ethics: Leadership ethics refers to the moral principles that guide leaders' actions, decisions, and relationships. Ethical leadership ensures fairness, accountability, and integrity in governance, fostering trust and moral legitimacy within institutions (Northouse, 2018). In healthcare, it translates to compassionate decision-making that prioritizes dignity and equity.

Mental Well-being: Mental well-being encompasses emotional, psychological, and social health, reflecting an individual's capacity to cope with stress, maintain self-esteem, build positive relationships, and find purpose in life (Ryff & Keyes, 1995). It is not merely the absence of illness but the presence of resilience, meaning, and life satisfaction.

Migrant Workers: Migrant workers are individuals who relocate from one geographical area to another either across states or countries in search of employment and better living conditions. Often employed in informal sectors without job security or social protection, they remain vulnerable to exploitation, cultural alienation, and health disparities (International Labour Organization, 2018).

Chapter 11

From Public Awareness to Phygital Action:
Health Literacy, Economics, and Leadership in India's Healthcare Reform

Babitha Nadampalli
Christ University, India

Sunitha Abhay Jain
Christ University, India

ABSTRACT

Over seven decades, India's health reform has transitioned from traditional awareness programs to participatory "phygital" (physical + digital) models. This paper traces the evolution of health literacy governance through successive Five-Year Plans (1951–2017), analyzing how economic priorities, marketing strategies, and leadership paradigms shaped reform outcomes. It highlights the shift from rural welfare and communicable disease control to challenges of lifestyle disorders, digital health equity, and nutrition security. Persistent gaps in efficiency, communication, and leadership integration across the phygital ecosystem are identified. The study concludes with recommendations to embed health literacy, digital inclusion, and collaborative leadership within India's public health framework, advancing equitable, action-oriented, and sustainable healthcare reform.

DOI: 10.4018/979-8-3373-7173-3.ch011

INTRODUCTION

Health literacy is a foundational outcome of public health systems, referring to the ability of individuals and communities to access, understand, evaluate, and apply health information in ways that enable informed decision-making. It extends beyond mere knowledge acquisition to encompass the practical capacities required to navigate health systems, engage with health services, and respond effectively to social, economic, and environmental determinants of health at individual, household, and community levels. Internationally, health literacy is recognized not only as a determinant of health in its own right but also as a mediating variable that influences preventive behaviors, treatment adherence, and the overall functioning of health systems. This dual role positions health literacy as both an outcome and a mechanism within public health governance.

In India, the evolution of health literacy as a policy concept has been closely intertwined with the country's national development planning architecture. For nearly six decades, the Planning Commission of India (1951–2017) guided long-term socio-economic development through successive Five-Year Plans, within which health education and promotion were embedded as instruments of nation-building, population management, and human capital formation. Drawing on archival policy documents from the First to the Twelfth Five-Year Plans, this chapter traces how health literacy strategies evolved in response to shifting epidemiological realities, institutional capacities, and socio-cultural contexts. Rather than following a linear trajectory, India's health literacy governance reflects a negotiated process shaped by political priorities, demographic pressures, and changing conceptions of state responsibility.

In the immediate post-Independence period, health literacy was framed as a moral and civic responsibility integral to national reconstruction. Early Five-Year Plans embedded health education within school curricula and rural outreach programs, emphasizing hygiene, sanitation, and disease prevention as collective duties essential for self-reliance. Communication strategies during this phase were largely didactic and paternalistic, assuming that awareness alone would translate into behavioral compliance. While these initiatives succeeded in institutionalizing health education as a policy domain, they offered limited scope for community participation or contextual adaptation.

By the late 1960s and early 1970s, health literacy increasingly aligned with demographic and economic objectives, particularly through family planning and nutrition education programs. These interventions, implemented as vertically structured national policies, relied heavily on traditional cultural media—folk songs, street theatre, and village drama—to enhance message acceptance. Although culturally sensitive, this phase marked a shift toward program-specific communication that prioritized policy targets over holistic public health engagement. Health literacy functioned less as an empowerment tool and more as an instrument of population management.

A significant transformation occurred from the 1980s onward with the formal adoption of the Information, Education, and Communication (IEC) framework, institutionalized during the Eighth Five-Year Plan (1992–1997). IEC introduced more sophisticated mass-media strategies and expanded health communication to address emerging challenges such as HIV/AIDS and other communicable diseases. However, this verticalization of communication also produced structural fragmentation, as parallel IEC units operated across disease-specific programs without a unified national health literacy strategy. The emphasis remained largely informational, with limited integration of behavioral science or systems thinking.

In the later planning period—particularly from the Tenth to the Twelfth Five-Year Plans—health literacy broadened to encompass non-communicable diseases, lifestyle risks, nutrition security, and preventive health behaviors. Institutional mechanisms such as the National Board for Health Education and the Central Health Education Bureau reflected growing recognition that sustainable health outcomes required behavior change rather than information transfer alone. Flagship initiatives, most notably the polio eradication campaign, demonstrated the effectiveness of coordinated communication, leadership, and community engagement in achieving measurable public health outcomes. Djakeli (2024) reconceptualizes healthcare marketing as AI-driven health value creation, though stronger empirical and ethical analysis is needed.

Despite these gains, the dismantling of the Planning Commission in 2014 and the subsequent shift to outcome-based governance under NITI Aayog disrupted the continuity of India's long-term health literacy framework. While digital platforms and monitoring systems expanded rapidly, the absence of a recurring national planning mechanism weakened the strategic integration of health literacy across programs. This transition has intensified existing challenges—fragmentation, inequity, and uneven behavioral impact—while simultaneously opening space for "phygital" governance models that combine physical outreach with digital engagement.

This chapter situates India's contemporary health literacy challenges within this historical trajectory, arguing that the current shift toward phygital health systems represents neither a complete rupture nor a simple technological upgrade. Instead, it reflects an ongoing tension between awareness and action, efficiency and equity, central coordination and local adaptation. By examining how economics, communication strategies, and leadership intersect across planning eras, the chapter highlights both the achievements and the structural limitations of India's health literacy governance, setting the foundation for a critical analysis of phygital action as the next phase in public health reform.

BACKGROUND

India's national health reform must be understood as an integral component of the country's broader developmental and governance trajectory rather than as a sectoral or technical enterprise. From the time of independence, public health initiatives were embedded within the nation-building project, conceived not only as mechanisms for service delivery but as instruments for cultivating civic responsibility, social discipline, and collective welfare. The First Five-Year Plan (1951–56) reflected this orientation by framing health as both a public right and a civic obligation, positioning health literacy as a moral and developmental imperative necessary for productivity, modernization, and social cohesion. This early framing established the normative foundations of India's health governance but also introduced a top-down, paternalistic model of communication that prioritized compliance over participation. Gigauri and Djakeli (2021) critically analyze Georgia's health reforms, highlighting economic alignment, institutional adaptation, and universal coverage challenges.

Over successive planning cycles, India's health reform evolved through multiple paradigmatic shifts that mirrored broader socio-economic transformations. The system moved gradually from curative to preventive orientations, from centralized state provision to mixed governance arrangements, and, more recently, from infrastructure-driven delivery to digitally mediated and phygital (physical + digital) models of engagement. These transitions were neither linear nor uniform; rather, they were shaped by changing epidemiological profiles, institutional capacities, fiscal priorities, and political ideologies. As India transitioned from a primary focus on rural sanitation and communicable disease control to addressing non-communicable diseases, lifestyle risks, and rising healthcare costs, health literacy emerged as a critical—yet inconsistently operationalized—policy lever.

The political economy of health literacy played a decisive role in shaping both the scope and limitations of these reforms. Each Five-Year Plan reflected not only public health needs but also the dominant ideological ethos of governance. During the Nehruvian era, health policy aligned with state-led welfare and egalitarianism, emphasizing universal access and public provisioning. However, the economic liberalization of the 1990s introduced new governance logics centered on efficiency, privatization, corporate social responsibility (CSR), and public–private partnerships (PPPs). While these shifts enhanced innovation and resource mobilization, they simultaneously generated structural tensions related to equity, accountability, and access. Health literacy increasingly became fragmented across programs and actors, raising fundamental questions about whether economic rationality could coexist with social justice and whether technological expansion might inadvertently deepen existing inequalities.

Within this evolving political economy, the emergence of phygital governance represents a structural reconfiguration rather than a purely technological upgrade. Phygital health models integrate face-to-face community engagement with digital platforms, reshaping how health communication is produced, transmitted, and acted upon. Physical outreach mechanisms—such as Accredited Social Health Activists (ASHAs) and primary health centers—continue to anchor trust and contextual relevance, while digital tools including mobile health applications, AI-enabled diagnostics, and social media campaigns expand reach, speed, and data visibility. This hybrid model reflects the convergence of two interrelated transformations: the digital revolution, which expanded connectivity and data infrastructures, and the behavioral turn in public health, which emphasized sustained behavior change over episodic awareness. The phygital shift thus signals a move from information dissemination toward participatory and adaptive governance, albeit with uneven implementation.

Economics occupies a dual and often contradictory position within this framework, functioning simultaneously as a driver of reform and a source of constraint. Investments in health literacy are justified economically through their contribution to human capital formation: populations with higher health literacy tend to experience better health outcomes, lower healthcare costs, reduced absenteeism, and enhanced productivity. However, persistent disparities in income, education, and digital access have produced uneven returns on these investments. Large segments of the population—particularly rural, tribal, and marginalized communities—remain located in what can be described as "health literacy deserts," where infrastructural deficits and social exclusion undermine both physical and digital outreach. As a result, health planning faces the unresolved challenge of balancing efficiency-driven resource allocation with equity-oriented redistribution.

Parallel to economic restructuring, health communication in India has increasingly drawn upon marketing principles adapted for social change. Social marketing has played a significant role in mobilizing public participation, as evidenced by large-scale campaigns such as polio eradication and national sanitation drives. These initiatives demonstrate the power of branding, emotional resonance, and cultural symbolism in shaping health behaviors at scale. However, the application of marketing logic to health governance also introduces risks. When communication prioritizes visibility over depth or persuasion over trust, it can weaken long-term behavioral outcomes. The phygital paradigm partially addresses this limitation by enabling two-way communication, feedback loops, and localized content delivery, but only when supported by institutional capacity and ethical oversight.

Leadership emerges as the integrative mechanism linking economic policy, communication strategy, and governance outcomes. Historically, India's health leadership has been characterized by hierarchical bureaucratic control, often resulting in siloed decision-making and limited responsiveness. Over time, particularly during crisis moments such as the COVID-19 pandemic, more collaborative and network-based leadership models have demonstrated their effectiveness in coordinating across ministries, levels of government, and technological platforms. Phygital leadership requires not only data-driven decision-making but also empathetic engagement, institutional trust-building, and adaptive capacity. Where such leadership is absent, technological expansion risks reinforcing fragmentation rather than resolving it.

Despite notable advances, the digital divide remains a structural barrier to equitable health literacy. Access to digital devices, reliable internet connectivity, and digital skills is unevenly distributed across regions, socio-economic groups, genders, and linguistic communities. The dominance of English and a limited set of major Indian languages in digital health content further constrains accessibility for marginalized populations. These gaps are not merely technical but structural, reflecting deeper inequalities in education, infrastructure, and governance. Embedding digital inclusion within health reform therefore requires deliberate policy design, sustained investment, and cultural adaptation rather than assumptions of automatic diffusion.

The institutional transition from the Planning Commission to NITI Aayog in 2014 marked a critical inflection point in health governance. While the shift toward decentralized, outcome-based monitoring enhanced flexibility and innovation, it also disrupted the continuity of long-term health literacy planning. The absence of a unified national framework for health literacy has weakened strategic coordination across states and programs, leading to uneven implementation and policy drift. At the same time, this transition creates an opportunity to reimagine health governance in ways that align with contemporary realities of digitalization, cooperative federalism, and participatory policymaking—provided that health literacy is re-established as a core governance priority.

In the global context, health literacy is increasingly recognized as a cornerstone of sustainable development, contributing directly to goals related to health, education, and inequality reduction. Several countries have institutionalized national health literacy frameworks that integrate education systems, digital inclusion strategies, and community participation. While India's scale, diversity, and federal structure present unique challenges, comparative experiences underscore the importance of coherent frameworks, evidence-based design, and leadership continuity.

Taken together, India's health reform trajectory reflects continuity amid transformation. The movement from chalkboards in rural schools to digital dashboards and telemedicine platforms illustrates not a linear progression but an ongoing negotiation between tradition and innovation, centralization and decentralization, awareness and action. The emergence of phygital health systems represents a transitional phase in this journey—one that holds significant promise but remains constrained by structural inequities, institutional fragmentation, and leadership variability. Understanding these dynamics is essential for evaluating whether phygital governance can move beyond symbolic modernization to deliver equitable, sustained, and behaviorally meaningful health outcomes.

The historical analysis presented above reveals persistent structural bottlenecks in India's health literacy governance, including fragmented institutional arrangements, uneven behavioral impact, leadership discontinuities, and widening digital inequities. While successive reforms expanded outreach and technological capacity, they frequently lacked an integrated conceptual foundation capable of explaining how individual behavior, institutional systems, and governance leadership interact within a rapidly digitalizing health ecosystem. These gaps necessitate a theoretically grounded approach that can account for multi-level determinants, technology adoption dynamics, and leadership processes. Accordingly, the following theoretical framework is developed to systematically address these limitations and to provide an analytical lens for understanding India's transition toward phygital health governance.

Table 1. Evolution of Health Literacy in India Across Five-Year Plan Phases

Five-Year Plan Phase	Dominant Health Literacy Approach	Key Institutional Structures	Major Limitations
1951–1961(First & Second Plans)	Civic hygiene education and moral responsibility; awareness-driven	Planning Commission; Health Education Bureaux; Schools; Rural Health Units	Top-down communication; limited community participation; assumption that awareness leads to compliance
1961–1974(Third & Fourth Plans)	Program-oriented health education linked to demographic and economic goals	National Family Planning Program; Nutrition Education Units; Cultural Media Networks	Vertical policies; health framed as population control; fragmented public health focus
1974–1989(Fifth to Seventh Plans)	Culturally adapted communication; expansion of thematic coverage (nutrition, maternal health)	Applied Nutrition Programme; ICDS; Folk media-based outreach	Limited behavioral science integration; weak evaluation mechanisms
1992–1997(Eighth Plan)	Information, Education and Communication (IEC) institutionalization	Ministry of Health & Family Welfare; Program-specific IEC cells; Mass media	Fragmentation across disease programs; parallel IEC units; lack of unified health literacy strategy
1997–2007(Ninth & Tenth Plans)	Preventive and lifestyle-focused communication; early behavior change orientation	National Health Programs; Local self-governments; NGOs	Uneven implementation; urban–rural disparities; limited digital integration
2007–2017(Eleventh & Twelfth Plans)	Integrated health literacy addressing NCDs and lifestyle risks	National Board for Health Education; Central Health Education Bureau	Weak inter-program coordination; reliance on awareness over sustained behavior change
Post-2014(NITI Aayog Era)	Digital and phygital health communication; outcome-based monitoring	NITI Aayog; Digital health missions; State-level initiatives	Absence of unified national health literacy framework; digital divide; policy fragmentation

THEORETICAL FRAMEWORK

The theoretical foundation of *Phygital Insights on National Health Reform: Economics, Marketing, and Leadership* offers an integrated, multidisciplinary lens through which India's evolving health governance structure can be understood. The phygital model—integrating physical and digital health systems—necessitates a multidimensional theoretical grounding that captures the interactions between human behavior, institutional systems, technological adoption, and leadership processes. To explain these complex dynamics, this framework draws upon five complementary theories: the Socio-Ecological Model (SEM), which emphasizes the multi-layered determinants of health literacy; the Health Belief Model (HBM), which elucidates individual perceptions of health risk, motivation, and self-efficacy; the Diffusion of Innovations Theory (DOI), which explains how new technologies and ideas spread across social systems; Systems Theory, which highlights interdependence and adaptive learning in health governance; and Transformational Leadership Theory, which defines the human and ethical dimensions of guiding systemic change. Together, these frameworks provide a comprehensive structure for understanding how economics, marketing, and leadership converge to shape India's phygital health ecosystem. As recent interdisciplinary research demonstrates, the psychological dimension of digital adoption cannot be ignored.

At the foundation of this theoretical approach lies the Socio-Ecological Model (SEM), which posits that health behavior is determined by multiple, interacting layers—individual, interpersonal, organizational, community, and policy. Applied to India's context, SEM shows how health literacy is co-created through these interlocking dimensions, with digital technologies amplifying traditional public health systems. Individual factors such as motivation and knowledge are reinforced by interpersonal networks, including family and peer influence, while organizations and community institutions act as mediating structures that link individuals to national policy. Phygital platforms—such as AI-based risk assessment tools, WhatsApp maternal health groups, and telemedicine kiosks—illustrate how digital and physical mechanisms can work together to address multi-level barriers like cognitive awareness, structural access, and cultural acceptance. In this sense, health literacy transcends mere information transmission and becomes a *social capability* embedded in daily life, contingent upon both technological access and social context.

Complementing SEM, the Health Belief Model (HBM) provides a psychological framework for understanding how individuals perceive health threats and decide to engage with digital health interventions. It underscores that behavioral change is shaped by perceived susceptibility to illness, perceived severity of consequences, perceived benefits of taking action, perceived barriers, and cues to action, all moderated by self-efficacy. Within India's phygital health environment, these constructs explain why citizens adopt or resist new digital health tools. For instance, mobile health campaigns and wearable technology enhance perceptions of susceptibility and severity by visualizing risks, while telemedicine and health monitoring apps demonstrate tangible benefits. Yet, barriers such as lack of digital literacy, linguistic challenges, and privacy concerns often reduce engagement. Behavioral triggers like SMS reminders or gamified fitness challenges act as cues to action, while capacity-building programs strengthen users' confidence to utilize these tools effectively. Integrating HBM principles into national health policy would allow India to shift from *awareness-based* to *motivation-driven* reform, fostering behavioral transformation through personalized, trust-based engagement.

The Diffusion of Innovations Theory (DOI) further enriches the framework by explaining the social processes underlying the adoption of digital health technologies. According to Everett Rogers, innovations spread through stages—knowledge, persuasion, decision, implementation, and confirmation—and are adopted by five user categories: innovators, early adopters, early majority, late majority, and laggards. In India, this diffusion is visible in how digital platforms like CoWIN and e-Sanjeevani gained traction. Urban professionals and tech-savvy youth served as early adopters, while semi-urban and rural populations followed once the technology proved reliable and beneficial. Government strategies such as pilot projects, influencer campaigns, and vernacular language integration help accelerate adoption across categories. The DOI model thus underscores that successful phygital health reform depends on understanding the *social tempo of adoption*, designing interventions that correspond to each group's trust levels, literacy, and access capacity.

Extending beyond individual and social dimensions, Systems Theory conceptualizes health governance as an interconnected and adaptive ecosystem. Rooted in the work of Ludwig von Bertalanffy, this perspective views health reform as a dynamic system of interdependent actors—government institutions, private enterprises, NGOs, civil society, and citizens—whose interactions produce collective outcomes. Within India's phygital health landscape, fragmentation across ministries and programs has historically diluted message impact and resource efficiency. However, with the integration of data-driven governance under NITI Aayog, real-time feedback loops and digital dashboards have begun to enhance coordination and adaptability. Systems Theory thus emphasizes that a successful phygital health ecosystem requires *integration rather than isolation*—linking economics, marketing, and leadership in a seamless policy architecture. It aligns with complexity science by suggesting that sustainable health systems evolve through continuous learning, flexible feedback, and cross-sector collaboration rather than rigid bureaucratic control.

The final theoretical pillar, Transformational Leadership Theory, situates leadership as the moral and motivational engine driving India's digital health transformation. As articulated by Burns (1978) and Bass (1985), transformational leaders inspire through vision, intellectual stimulation, and individualized consideration, motivating followers to exceed expectations and commit to shared goals. In the Indian phygital context, such leadership manifests in initiatives that merge emotional appeal with technological innovation—seen in nationwide vaccination drives or the CoWIN platform's inclusive architecture. Transformational leadership fosters a culture of trust, collaboration, and ethical governance, ensuring that digital technologies remain human-centered. By empowering communities, encouraging innovation, and upholding transparency in data use, such leaders bridge the gap between policy intent and ground-level impact, turning reform into a participatory movement rather than a technocratic directive.

Bringing these perspectives together yields an Integrative Phygital Governance Model (IPGM), where the SEM delineates the social layers of influence, HBM explains motivational drivers, DOI maps technology diffusion, Systems Theory outlines the structure of interdependence, and Transformational Leadership defines the ethical and visionary dimensions of reform. This synthesis forms what may be termed the Phygital Health Literacy System (PHLS)—a dynamic, self-regulating network that harmonizes human behavior, institutional structure, and digital innovation to promote sustained health outcomes. By embedding behavioral psychology within systemic governance, this framework transforms health literacy from a one-way educational process into a multi-directional, adaptive system that evolves through feedback and participation.

The theoretical implications of this integration are significant. It shifts the analytical lens from linear, program-specific evaluation to a *transdisciplinary paradigm* that views health reform as a living, adaptive process. This model empowers policymakers and researchers to diagnose systemic weaknesses—such as fragmented communication or inequitable access—and to design interventions that are inclusive, data-informed, and behaviorally intelligent. Quantitative tools like digital analytics can track adoption rates and policy outcomes, while qualitative methods such as ethnographic studies can capture the lived experiences and trust dynamics underlying technology use. The synergy of these methods allows for a richer, more human-centered understanding of India's health transformation.

In conclusion, the theoretical framework of phygital health reform underscores that effective governance in the digital era must rest on three interdependent axes: behavioral adaptation, systemic integration, and transformational leadership. Behavioral adaptation ensures that individuals are motivated and capable of engaging in preventive care; systemic integration harmonizes the efforts of institutions, technologies, and policies; and transformational leadership infuses these efforts with ethical vision and human empathy. Together, these dimensions establish a holistic, interpretive structure for understanding how India can evolve from fragmented Information, Education, and Communication (IEC) initiatives into a unified, intelligent, and participatory phygital health system—one that leverages technology not merely for efficiency, but for empowerment and equity.

While the theoretical framework establishes the conceptual foundations for interpreting behavioral, systemic, and leadership dynamics in phygital health reform, an operational structure is required to translate these abstract principles into a policy-relevant model. The conceptual framework presented in the following section builds directly upon the theoretical constructs outlined above, organizing them into an integrated governance architecture that links economic rationality, social marketing, and transformational leadership within a phygital health literacy system.

CONCEPTUAL FRAMEWORK

The conceptual framework of *Phygital Insights on National Health Reform: Economics, Marketing, and Leadership* integrates the interdependent dynamics of economic rationality, social marketing, and transformational leadership within a phygital governance structure to explain how health literacy evolves in a digitally augmented policy environment. At its core, this framework views health reform as a multidimensional ecosystem driven by the interaction between *economic structures* that determine access and efficiency, *marketing mechanisms* that shape communication and engagement, and *leadership paradigms* that coordinate vision, inclusion, and accountability. In this model, economic rationality functions as the foundational layer, emphasizing the equitable allocation of resources and the economic viability of digital health systems, ensuring that investments in technology and communication yield measurable improvements in public health outcomes. Building on this, marketing serves as the behavioral and communicative interface, translating complex health information into culturally resonant and emotionally appealing narratives that motivate behavioral change. Leadership, in turn, acts as the integrative force aligning economic policy and marketing strategy under a shared vision of health equity, mobilizing institutions, and communities toward collective participation.

The *phygital dimension* of the framework—linking physical infrastructures (such as hospitals, community health centers, and ASHA networks) with digital platforms (including mHealth applications, telemedicine systems, and data analytics dashboards)—operates as a dynamic channel through which information, trust, and participation circulate. This interlinkage is governed by feedback loops where data-driven insights inform policy adjustments, user experiences refine service design, and leadership decisions respond to real-time community needs. The framework conceptualizes this system as a Phygital Health Literacy Nexus (PHLN), where health outcomes are mediated by three key variables: accessibility, engagement, and empowerment. Accessibility ensures that digital and physical health infrastructures reach all socio-economic strata; engagement captures the depth of public interaction with health communication content; and empowerment measures the individual and collective capacity to make informed health decisions.

In this conceptualization, economics provides the structural backbone ensuring resource sustainability, marketing infuses the system with communicative vitality, and leadership imbues it with moral and strategic direction. Together, they create a self-reinforcing cycle in which knowledge dissemination leads to behavioral adaptation, adaptation drives demand for improved services, and responsive governance reinvests learning into further innovation. The framework assumes that successful health reform in India's phygital era depends not merely on technological deployment but on *synergistic alignment* among fiscal prudence, persuasive communication, and ethical leadership. It positions the citizen not as a passive recipient of information but as a *co-creator of health governance*, whose participation—facilitated by both digital inclusion and community engagement—determines the sustainability of national health outcomes. By bridging micro-level behavioral change with macro-level policy integration, the conceptual framework encapsulates how India's health literacy reform can evolve from fragmented, message-based interventions into a coherent, adaptive, and human-centered ecosystem of phygital governance.

HEALTH LITERACY IN THE EARLY PLANS: FOUNDATIONS AND INSTITUTIONAL STRUCTURES (1951–1974)

The foundation of India's health literacy framework was laid during the early decades following independence, a period that saw health reform positioned as both a developmental necessity and a moral obligation of the newly sovereign state. Between 1951 and 1974, health literacy evolved from a loosely defined educational concept into a structured, policy-driven system integrated into the broader national development agenda through the Five-Year Plans. During this phase, health education and literacy were not treated as separate disciplines but as complementary pillars of nation-building, rooted in the belief that a healthy citizenry was essential for a productive and self-reliant nation. The First and Second Five-Year Plans (1951–56 and 1956–61) laid the groundwork for this approach, emphasizing preventive care, hygiene awareness, and civic responsibility. These early efforts reflected the Nehruvian vision of welfare economics, where public health was conceptualized as both a state duty and a social right, necessary to transform a population emerging from colonial neglect into an informed, participatory community.

In the First Five-Year Plan (1951–56), health education was introduced as part of the nation's developmental infrastructure. The government recognized that medical facilities alone could not address the health challenges faced by a largely rural and illiterate population; rather, the dissemination of basic health knowledge was essential to prevent disease and promote hygiene. Health literacy was therefore institutionalized as a means of creating behavioral change at the grassroots level. Primary schools were identified as critical entry points for health education, embedding lessons on hygiene, nutrition, and disease prevention within the curriculum. Rural outreach programs were launched, emphasizing the importance of personal and environmental sanitation. The establishment of *Health Education Bureaux* at both the state and national levels during this period marked the beginning of a systematic approach to health communication. These bureaux were tasked with creating and distributing educational materials, organizing village-level awareness programs, and training educators and health workers to act as communicators between the government and local communities.

The Second Five-Year Plan (1956–61) continued to prioritize public health as an instrument of economic and social progress. The emphasis shifted slightly from pure health instruction to creating the institutional structures necessary for its dissemination. Health education was seen as a tool for social modernization, closely linked with India's goals of industrialization and community development. Public health messaging during this period took a paternalistic tone: the state assumed the role of moral guardian, prescribing standards of hygiene, nutrition, and family health. Citizens were expected to comply with these standards as part of their civic duty, with limited agency to influence or reinterpret health information. Health literacy was therefore framed as a top-down initiative, where the state provided information and the people were expected to follow it. The model was bureaucratic, with strong administrative control but minimal community participation. Yet, it succeeded in establishing health literacy as a legitimate domain of public policy, laying the foundation for later participatory and technology-driven reforms.

By the Third and Fourth Five-Year Plans (1961–74), the focus of health education began to expand in both scope and sophistication. The government increasingly recognized that public health could not be separated from social and cultural contexts. The Fourth Plan (1969–74) in particular reflected an awareness that disease prevention and family welfare required not only medical intervention but also a deep understanding of cultural behavior and communication. Health literacy, during this period, evolved into a more program-specific enterprise. The national family planning program became a central focus, as India faced rapid population growth and sought to align demographic control with economic planning. Alongside family planning, nutrition education also gained prominence, especially in rural and low-income areas where malnutrition and micronutrient deficiencies were widespread.

A significant innovation of this period was the creative use of traditional cultural media—including folk songs, village drama, storytelling, and local theater—to convey health messages. This approach was rooted in the understanding that conventional classroom education and written materials were ineffective among populations with low literacy rates. Folk communication proved to be a powerful tool in bridging the gap between knowledge and practice, allowing communities to internalize messages about hygiene, nutrition, and family health through familiar and emotionally resonant forms. These performances were participatory and engaging, blending entertainment with instruction, thereby transforming health education from a bureaucratic directive into a social experience.

The government's emphasis on family planning and nutrition reflected an early acknowledgment of the socio-cultural determinants of health behavior. It became evident that poverty, gender roles, traditional beliefs, and community hierarchies significantly influenced how health information was perceived and acted upon. Therefore, health education initiatives during the 1960s and early 1970s began incorporating anthropological insights to design messages that were culturally adaptive rather than prescriptive. Campaigns encouraged practical skills—such as food preservation, preparation of balanced diets using local ingredients, and child nutrition techniques—making health education more relevant to everyday life.

This period (1951–1974) thus laid the institutional and ideological foundations of India's health literacy movement. While the approach was largely top-down, it marked the beginning of a national consciousness that equated health with development. The establishment of health education structures, integration with the school system, and incorporation of community-based media created a framework that future policies would refine and expand. However, these early efforts were also limited by their bureaucratic rigidity and their assumption that knowledge transfer alone would lead to behavioral change. Despite these constraints, the seeds of participatory health governance were planted during this era, paving the way for later innovations in *Information, Education, and Communication (IEC)* and ultimately for the digital and phygital health systems that define contemporary India. In retrospect, the years between 1951 and 1974 represent the formative stage of India's journey toward comprehensive health literacy—an era that established the moral, institutional, and communicative foundations upon which modern health reforms continue to build.

EXPANSION AND THEMATIC DIVERSIFICATION (1974–1997)

The period between 1974 and 1997 marked a crucial phase in the evolution of India's health literacy framework—a time when health education expanded beyond its early focus on sanitation, hygiene, and population control to encompass a more comprehensive, issue-based, and participatory model. This era, characterized by diversification and experimentation, witnessed a shift from the rigid, top-down pedagogical style of the early Five-Year Plans to more dynamic, inclusive, and culturally responsive forms of communication. The mid-1970s through the 1990s represented an era of both intellectual and institutional maturation for health education in India, as the nation grappled with emerging challenges such as nutrition deficiencies, child health, mental well-being, cancer awareness, and the rising global crisis of HIV/AIDS. The increasing use of the Information, Education, and Communication (IEC) approach during this time redefined health literacy not merely as the dissemination of facts but as an interactive, context-sensitive process designed to motivate behavioral change.

During the Fifth Five-Year Plan (1974–79), India began to recognize that health promotion could no longer remain confined to a few thematic areas like hygiene or family planning. The global discourse on preventive medicine, influenced by the Alma-Ata Declaration on Primary Health Care (1978), encouraged nations to integrate education, communication, and community participation into their health systems. This shift was reflected in India's growing emphasis on *community-based health education*, which sought to connect public health with broader developmental goals such as child welfare, women's empowerment, and rural self-sufficiency. Nutrition education, in particular, became a focal point of the Fifth Plan, as malnutrition was identified as a critical barrier to national productivity and childhood development. The *Applied Nutrition Programme (ANP)*, initiated during this period, promoted local solutions—encouraging communities to grow nutrient-rich foods, adopt food preservation practices, and incorporate balanced diets using locally available resources. Health literacy during this time began to incorporate hands-on learning, workshops, and demonstration-based communication rather than abstract classroom instruction.

The Sixth (1980–85) and Seventh Five-Year Plans (1985–90) witnessed further expansion in the thematic scope of health literacy. The Sixth Plan aligned closely with the emerging global understanding that health is a function of social, economic, and environmental determinants. As such, literacy programs were reoriented to address not only communicable diseases but also behavioral and lifestyle concerns. Health education campaigns during this time began to stress the importance of preventive care, environmental sanitation, and family health practices as part of daily life. The Seventh Plan further institutionalized these ideas by advocating the integration of Information, Education, and Communication (IEC) strategies into all national health programs. This was a transformative moment in India's health literacy journey—IEC represented a philosophical and operational departure from earlier one-directional communication models. Instead of treating citizens as passive recipients of information, IEC emphasized their role as active participants and collaborators in the health promotion process.

The IEC approach introduced several innovations. First, it emphasized the segmentation of target audiences—recognizing that health messages had to be tailored to the unique social, linguistic, and cultural contexts of different groups. For instance, communication strategies for rural women differed from those for urban youth or factory workers. Second, it encouraged the use of multi-channel media, blending traditional and modern methods. Folk arts, puppet shows, street plays, and community radio were used alongside posters, films, and eventually, television and print advertisements. This hybrid communication ecology enabled health literacy to penetrate diverse populations and bridge the gap between knowledge and adoption. Third, IEC programs promoted two-way communication, encouraging dialogue and feedback between health workers and communities. The *Trained Birth Attendant (TBA)* programs and *Integrated Child Development Services (ICDS)* are prime examples where communication was not only informational but relational—built on trust, empathy, and community participation.

A major turning point in the evolution of health literacy came with the Eighth Five-Year Plan (1992–97), which explicitly incorporated "Information, Education, and Communication" as a formal strategic component across all national health initiatives. This institutional recognition of IEC signaled a new era of professionalism and innovation in health communication. The Eighth Plan coincided with the rise of two major global health challenges—HIV/AIDS and non-communicable diseases (NCDs) such as cancer, hypertension, and diabetes. The government recognized that traditional health education methods were inadequate for addressing these complex, stigmatized, and behaviorally rooted conditions. Therefore, communication strategies had to evolve to be not only scientifically accurate but also psychologically and socially attuned.

The National AIDS Control Organisation (NACO), established in 1992, pioneered a new model of health literacy through mass media campaigns, school education modules, and community-based awareness drives. Unlike earlier health messages that relied on fear or authority, AIDS awareness programs emphasized *sensitivity, inclusivity, and empowerment*. Slogans such as "Talk AIDS, Stop AIDS" encouraged open dialogue and destigmatization, while television advertisements and celebrity endorsements helped normalize discussions about safe sex and testing. These campaigns reflected a deeper understanding of how communication shapes social norms and attitudes—a defining characteristic of the maturing IEC philosophy.

Simultaneously, other health issues received renewed attention. The Eighth Plan and concurrent initiatives such as the *National Cancer Control Programme* and *National Mental Health Programme* sought to extend the logic of IEC into previously neglected domains. Cancer prevention campaigns stressed lifestyle modification and early detection, while mental health promotion focused on awareness, stigma reduction, and community-based rehabilitation. Tobacco control initiatives gained momentum as public health authorities began to associate smoking and chewing tobacco with rising cancer and cardiovascular disease rates. The introduction of warning labels, anti-smoking advertisements, and school-based awareness sessions demonstrated how IEC could influence both personal behavior and policy reform.

This era also witnessed a gradual blending of health literacy with education policy. Early childhood education programs incorporated modules on hygiene, nutrition, and emotional well-being. Health and education ministries began collaborating to integrate life skills and health awareness into school curricula, thereby institutionalizing preventive health culture among younger generations. The focus on child health, adolescent education, and reproductive awareness reflected a broader conceptual shift—from health as a medical outcome to health as a developmental process.

By the mid-1990s, India's approach to health literacy had transformed into a multi-sectoral and multi-issue movement. No longer confined to a few vertical programs, health communication began to intersect with agriculture, education, labor, and social welfare. NGOs, community-based organizations, and international agencies played a significant role in experimenting with participatory models of communication, empowering local actors to design and deliver context-appropriate messages. The government's collaboration with these non-state partners enriched the diversity and reach of health literacy initiatives.

In summary, the period from 1974 to 1997 was one of expansion, innovation, and thematic diversification in India's health literacy landscape. It saw the transition from narrow, message-oriented health education to a holistic, participatory, and media-rich framework of communication. The incorporation of IEC strategies, the recognition of socio-cultural determinants of behavior, and the willingness to address previously taboo subjects such as sexuality and mental health represented a remarkable maturation of India's health policy ethos. This period not only deepened the scope of public health communication but also laid the groundwork for the digital and phygital health ecosystems that would emerge in the decades to follow—anchoring health literacy firmly within the fabric of social development and democratic participation.

INSTITUTIONAL CONSOLIDATION AND LIFESTYLE FOCUS (1997–2017)

The period between 1997 and 2017 marked a decisive phase of institutional consolidation and a growing emphasis on lifestyle-related health challenges in India's public health policy. The Ninth Five-Year Plan (1997–2002) witnessed health education becoming more structured, with stronger institutional frameworks and the active participation of local self-governments, non-governmental organizations (NGOs), and community leaders. This decentralized approach enhanced community ownership and responsiveness, ensuring that health literacy initiatives were not only designed at the national level but also contextualized to local cultural and social realities. The focus during this phase shifted from merely increasing awareness to embedding health practices within everyday community life.

By the time of the Tenth Plan (2002–2007), India's public health agenda began addressing the growing burden of lifestyle diseases and chronic illnesses such as diabetes, hypertension, and cardiovascular disorders. The government recognized that awareness alone was insufficient to combat these conditions; what was required was behavioral transformation. Policies during this period integrated preventive strategies emphasizing healthy diet, physical activity, and mental well-being. Health communication campaigns also began promoting positive behavioral choices and discouraging risk factors such as tobacco use and unhealthy dietary habits. This era marked a transition from curative to preventive and promotive health literacy, with behavior change communication (BCC) emerging as a central strategy.

The Eleventh (2007–2012) and Twelfth (2012–2017) Five-Year Plans further institutionalized these reforms through the creation of the National Board for Health Education (NBHE). The Board promoted collaboration across ministries and incorporated AYUSH (Ayurveda, Yoga, Unani, Siddha, and Homeopathy) systems into mainstream health awareness initiatives. A dedicated budget allocation for mass media campaigns was established to address micronutrient deficiencies, encourage salt reduction, promote physical activity, and foster dietary diversity. The Twelfth Plan, in particular, aligned with global health priorities by acknowledging the worldwide epidemiological shift toward non-communicable diseases (NCDs). This period thus represents the maturation of India's health literacy policy—anchored in institutional strength, inter-sectoral collaboration, and a sustained focus on lifestyle modification as the cornerstone of national health reform.

POLICY GAPS AND CHALLENGES

Despite decades of consistent attention to public health education and communication, several structural and systemic gaps have continued to undermine the effectiveness of India's health literacy initiatives. The most prominent challenge has been the lack of coordination among various programs and implementing agencies. Overlapping Information, Education, and Communication (IEC) activities across disease-control programs—such as those for malaria, tuberculosis, HIV/AIDS, and maternal health—have led to duplication of efforts and inconsistent messaging. Instead of delivering a unified narrative on preventive health and wellness, these fragmented campaigns often competed for visibility and resources, resulting in diluted impact and public confusion. The absence of a central coordinating body or an integrated communication strategy has prevented the creation of a cohesive national health literacy framework capable of addressing diverse health needs under one umbrella.

Another significant limitation has been the behavioral change deficit. Many health programs have focused heavily on information dissemination without adequately addressing the psychological, cultural, and social dimensions of behavior. While citizens were informed about diseases and preventive measures, these messages often failed to translate into sustained lifestyle modifications. The lack of behavioral science integration meant that health communication remained knowledge-oriented rather than action-oriented. Effective health literacy requires continuous engagement, community ownership, and reinforcement through culturally sensitive approaches—elements that were often missing from top-down policy designs.

Equity issues further deepened these challenges. Remote rural areas, tribal populations, and marginalized communities frequently lacked consistent access to health literacy initiatives due to infrastructural barriers, linguistic diversity, and socio-economic exclusion. The urban-rural gap in digital access and education exacerbated disparities, leaving large portions of the population outside the reach of modern health campaigns.

Finally, the monitoring and evaluation of impact has remained weak. Few mechanisms existed to assess whether communication initiatives led to measurable improvements in health outcomes or behavior change. Without data-driven evaluation, policy refinement and accountability were limited. To address these gaps, future reforms must integrate behavioral science, inclusive outreach, and robust monitoring systems within a unified, multi-sectoral health literacy strategy.

THE POST–PLANNING COMMISSION ERA: WHERE NEXT?

The dissolution of the Planning Commission in 2014 and the establishment of the NITI Aayog marked a pivotal moment in India's governance history, signaling a transition from centralized, five-year planning to a more flexible, outcome-oriented model of policy evaluation and implementation. This structural shift reflected India's growing confidence as a global economic player and its desire to align governance with data-driven accountability, innovation, and cooperative federalism. However, while this reorientation brought new energy to several sectors, the continuity and institutional coherence of health literacy policy—so carefully developed over six decades of Five-Year Plans—have become uncertain. Health literacy, which once benefited from the Planning Commission's long-term, integrated approach, now faces fragmentation in the absence of a unified, national-level roadmap under the NITI Aayog.

Under the Planning Commission, India's public health architecture operated within a structured and sequential planning cycle. Each Five-Year Plan built upon the previous one, providing continuity, a long-term vision, and a clear institutional mechanism for coordination between ministries, states, and non-governmental actors. Health literacy was embedded across multiple programs—from school curricula and maternal health to nutrition and disease prevention—ensuring that health communication remained a consistent national priority. However, the transition to the NITI Aayog framework, while emphasizing innovation and flexibility, has inadvertently disrupted this continuity. The new system's emphasis on outcome-based monitoring and short-term deliverables has shifted attention toward measurable targets such as immunization rates, sanitation coverage, and digital health infrastructure. While these are critical, they often fail to address the deeper cultural and behavioral dimensions of health literacy—dimensions that require long-term investment, social dialogue, and participatory engagement rather than purely quantitative metrics.

The NITI Aayog's approach, centered on cooperative federalism, entrusts greater responsibility to individual states to design and implement context-specific health initiatives. This decentralization offers opportunities for innovation and localization, allowing states to tailor programs according to their demographic and linguistic realities. Yet, it also presents challenges in the absence of a national coordinating mechanism. Without an overarching framework for health literacy, state initiatives risk becoming fragmented, inconsistent, or redundant. Some states, such as Kerala and Tamil Nadu, have made commendable progress in integrating digital tools and community engagement into their health systems, while others lag behind due to inadequate infrastructure or institutional support. This uneven progress underscores the need for a national health literacy strategy that balances autonomy with coordination—ensuring that every citizen, regardless of region, benefits from coherent, high-quality health communication.

In the post-Planning Commission era, the government's focus has shifted toward digital health transformation, exemplified by flagship programs like the Ayushman Bharat Digital Mission (ABDM), National Health Stack, and Digital India. These initiatives aim to build a comprehensive digital health ecosystem, integrating health records, telemedicine services, and digital identity systems. While technologically progressive, these programs often presume a baseline level of digital and health literacy that many citizens, especially in rural and marginalized communities, do not possess. Without deliberate efforts to strengthen health literacy—particularly digital health literacy—the benefits of these initiatives may remain concentrated among urban and technologically literate populations. Thus, the digital divide could translate into a new form of health inequity, mirroring older disparities in access to education and healthcare.

To address this gap, there is a pressing need for NITI Aayog and the Ministry of Health and Family Welfare to collaboratively develop a National Health Literacy Framework (NHLF) aligned with the principles of participatory governance, inclusivity, and sustainability. This framework should reintroduce the long-term planning ethos of the earlier Five-Year Plans, while adapting it to contemporary realities of digital governance. Such a framework must focus on building multi-level partnerships among central and state governments, academic institutions, civil society organizations, and the private sector. It should promote localized health communication models, develop standardized evaluation metrics for behavioral outcomes, and invest in digital inclusion initiatives that bridge gaps in language, literacy, and access.

Moreover, future policies must reimagine health literacy not merely as a communication strategy but as a cornerstone of national resilience—vital for pandemic preparedness, mental health promotion, and community empowerment. The COVID-19 pandemic has demonstrated that misinformation, fear, and distrust can undermine even the most technologically advanced health systems. A robust health literacy ecosystem, therefore, must cultivate trust, empathy, and critical thinking—values that cannot be automated or outsourced.

In conclusion, the post-Planning Commission era presents India with both a challenge and an opportunity. The challenge lies in restoring coherence and direction to a health literacy landscape fragmented by decentralization and short-termism. The opportunity lies in harnessing the agility, innovation, and data-driven strengths of the NITI Aayog to craft a modern, inclusive, and participatory model of health governance. A renewed national focus on health literacy—integrating traditional communication, community participation, and digital empowerment—can ensure that India's health reform journey continues not as a series of disjointed initiatives but as a cohesive movement toward equitable, informed, and sustainable public health transformation.

DISCUSSION

Guided by the conceptual framework, the discussion that follows interprets India's health reform trajectory as an evolving interaction between economic structures, communication strategies, and leadership practices within a phygital governance environment. Rather than treating historical developments and policy initiatives as isolated events, this section examines how the identified frameworks help explain persistent implementation gaps, uneven outcomes, and emerging opportunities in India's health literacy ecosystem.

The discussion of *Phygital Insights on National Health Reform: Economics, Marketing, and Leadership* centers on interpreting how India's evolving health reform narrative—spanning seven decades of policy transitions—reveals both the promise and paradoxes of integrating technology with social welfare. The transition from traditional public health education to the current phygital ecosystem signifies a paradigmatic shift from information dissemination to participatory health governance. Historically, India's health literacy strategies under the Planning Commission were centralized, bureaucratically structured, and oriented toward awareness rather than behavioral transformation. However, the digital turn and the rise of NITI Aayog's outcome-based approach mark a redefinition of health reform as a *data-driven, citizen-centered, and economically accountable enterprise*. In this new landscape, the interplay between economics, marketing, and leadership assumes critical importance, for it determines not only how resources are allocated but also how health messages are produced, circulated, and internalized. The discussion, therefore, emphasizes that national health reform in the phygital age is as much a question of *social psychology and governance ethics* as it is of infrastructure and finance.

Economically, the move toward digital health governance promises greater efficiency and transparency, yet it also introduces new forms of inequity. The cost of digital infrastructure, the uneven distribution of internet access, and the commodification of health data raise questions about inclusivity and justice. India's success in campaigns such as *Polio Free India* and *Swachh Bharat Abhiyan* demonstrates how strategic communication, supported by sound economic planning and local leadership, can yield transformative public health outcomes. However, replicating such success in the phygital era requires addressing the digital divide—the gulf between technologically empowered citizens and those marginalized by poverty, geography, or illiteracy. Thus, the discussion argues that while economic rationality is indispensable, it must be guided by an *ethics of care and equity* to ensure that technological modernization does not deepen socio-economic stratification. The phygital approach, if properly designed, can correct this imbalance by integrating low-cost mobile technology, vernacular language interfaces, and localized content delivery systems that enhance reach without sacrificing quality or accessibility.

From a marketing perspective, India's health communication has evolved from didactic instruction to dialogic engagement. Traditional Information, Education, and Communication (IEC) campaigns emphasized message transmission, often assuming that awareness automatically led to behavior change. The phygital paradigm, however, demands interactive communication, where individuals and communities become active participants in shaping health narratives. Social marketing principles—when combined with digital analytics—enable tailored messaging that resonates with diverse demographic segments. For example, youth-focused digital wellness campaigns, maternal health apps, and AI-driven nutrition tracking tools personalize health experiences while maintaining large-scale visibility. Yet, the discussion highlights a crucial caveat: persuasive communication must not slide into manipulation or surveillance. The ethical responsibility of digital health marketing lies in balancing engagement with consent, ensuring that data collected through mobile platforms or apps empower users rather than exploit them. The future of health communication in India, therefore, depends on its ability to maintain *trust, transparency, and authenticity* within a highly mediatized public sphere.

Leadership remains the binding force in this triadic relationship between economics and communication. Transformational leadership—rooted in empathy, vision, and collaboration—has proven vital in navigating the complexities of India's health ecosystem. Effective leaders in the public health domain are not merely administrators; they are social architects who integrate technological innovation with cultural sensitivity. During the COVID-19 pandemic, for instance, leadership at multiple levels—from central governance to grassroots health workers—demonstrated how moral conviction, clear communication, and rapid digital adaptation could collectively sustain a national response. The discussion underscores that the *phygital model demands adaptive leadership* capable of operating across multiple systems—public and private, physical and digital, local and global. Such leadership must cultivate trust in technology while maintaining a human touch in service delivery, ensuring that health reform remains people-centered rather than platform-centered.

The phygital transition also reframes India's position within the global discourse on health literacy. In comparison to Western models that emphasize individual autonomy, India's collectivist ethos and linguistic diversity necessitate culturally embedded approaches. Phygital systems, with their flexibility and scalability, can mediate this cultural complexity by customizing health content to regional identities while maintaining national coherence. However, the discussion identifies a persistent tension between *policy centralization and local autonomy*. National digital initiatives risk imposing uniform standards that may overlook local health practices, indigenous healing traditions, and social determinants unique to particular communities. Therefore, the paper argues for a polycentric model of governance, wherein central policies set guiding principles while local institutions adapt and innovate contextually. This decentralization not only enhances community ownership but also ensures that health literacy evolves as a living, participatory process rather than a top-down imposition.

Furthermore, the discussion deepens the conceptual implications of the theoretical frameworks introduced earlier, emphasizing how behavioral, systemic, and leadership perspectives must converge to sustain India's phygital health reform. The Socio-Ecological Model (SEM) underscores the necessity of multi-level coordination—linking individual behavior, organizational culture, and policy frameworks in a unified ecosystem. The Health Belief Model (HBM) reinforces that access to digital tools alone does not guarantee behavioral change; individuals must first perceive personal relevance, benefits, and manageable risks before adopting new health behaviors. Similarly, the Diffusion of Innovations Theory (DOI) reveals that the adoption of technology in health reform is neither uniform nor simultaneous—it unfolds gradually across social strata. This pattern reminds policymakers that equitable reform must include strategies for both early and late adopters, ensuring that no community is left behind in the digital transition. Systems Theory reframes India's health governance as a living, adaptive network that depends on feedback loops and interdependence among multiple stakeholders. Finally, Transformational Leadership Theory positions human agency, empathy, and vision as the driving forces that align technological innovation with ethical and inclusive outcomes. Collectively, these frameworks reveal that technology by itself cannot deliver transformation; sustainable progress arises from continuous learning, feedback integration, and leadership that bridges innovation with compassion.

While digital technologies have revolutionized India's public health communication and accessibility, they have also introduced new psychological and behavioral vulnerabilities. The rapid integration of mobile devices, social media, and online health platforms has reshaped patterns of interaction, often blurring the boundary between connection and dependency. Excessive screen exposure, smartphone overuse, and digital fatigue are increasingly influencing health behaviors and social relationships.

To ensure that the phygital transformation remains both humane and inclusive, India's health governance must evolve toward a "compassionate digital paradigm." This approach emphasizes empathy, accessibility, and psychological safety alongside technological innovation. It requires policies that integrate behavioral science, mental health literacy, and participatory feedback mechanisms into digital health programs. Digital transformation should aim not only to connect devices and databases but also to connect people—bridging emotional gaps and restoring a sense of community within the technological landscape. In essence, India's phygital health reform will achieve its fullest potential only when it harmonizes innovation with empathy, ensuring that the digital revolution enhances human connection rather than diminishes it.

In synthesizing these perspectives, the discussion concludes that India's phygital health reform embodies both a technological revolution and a moral experiment. Its success depends not only on how effectively digital tools are deployed but on how meaningfully they transform citizens' relationships with health knowledge and public institutions. The reform's long-term viability lies in fostering an environment where economic efficiency coexists with ethical governance, marketing creativity aligns with cultural authenticity, and leadership inspires both participation and accountability. Ultimately, the discussion affirms that the true measure of progress in national health reform is not in digital reach or fiscal prudence alone, but in the creation of a *conscious, connected, and compassionate citizenry*—capable of navigating the phygital world with both wisdom and dignity.

RECOMMENDATIONS AND SOLUTIONS

The analysis and discussion have identified several interrelated bottlenecks in India's health reform, including fragmented health literacy governance, inequitable digital access, limited behavioral integration, and variable leadership capacity across institutional levels. Based on these identified challenges—and informed by the theoretical and conceptual frameworks developed earlier—the following recommendations respond directly to these systemic constraints by proposing integrated, scalable, and equity-oriented strategies for strengthening India's phygital health ecosystem.

Building on the insights derived from the analysis and discussion, this section presents a set of comprehensive recommendations and practical solutions for strengthening India's phygital national health reform by integrating economic rationality, marketing innovation, and transformational leadership into a coherent, inclusive, and sustainable model. The central premise is that India's public health system must evolve from fragmented, program-specific interventions to an ecosystem-based framework that fosters continuous learning, digital inclusion, and behavioral transformation. First and foremost, it is recommended that health literacy be institutionalized as a core component of national policy, enshrined in measurable indicators across states and districts. Establishing a National Health Literacy Mission (NHLM) under NITI Aayog could ensure strategic coordination, data integration, and inter-ministerial collaboration, aligning health education with the objectives of digital governance and social equity. This mission should create a unified Health Literacy Index (HLI) to measure progress in awareness, accessibility, and behavioral adoption, enabling data-driven policy design and performance benchmarking. Such institutionalization would transform health literacy from a rhetorical ideal into an operational reality within India's developmental agenda.

Economically, health reform must be guided by the principle of equitable efficiency, balancing fiscal responsibility with universal accessibility. To achieve this, the government should adopt participatory budgeting models that allocate resources based on local needs, leveraging community health audits and citizen feedback loops. Investment in digital infrastructure, such as telemedicine hubs, regional data servers, and multilingual health portals, should be prioritized not as a luxury but as a public good. Moreover, tax incentives and CSR frameworks can encourage private-sector participation in health literacy campaigns, digital health startups, and innovation accelerators focused on low-cost health technologies. The use of public–private–people partnerships (PPPP)—expanding the traditional PPP model—can institutionalize community ownership, ensuring that the economic returns of digital health innovation are distributed equitably across regions. These economic strategies would strengthen both the resilience and inclusivity of India's phygital health system, creating a virtuous cycle of investment, trust, and citizen empowerment.

From a communication and marketing perspective, it is imperative to reimagine health communication as a dialogic, data-informed, and culturally contextual process rather than a top-down dissemination exercise. Public health campaigns must integrate *social marketing* principles that appeal to emotion, identity, and belonging while maintaining factual accuracy and ethical integrity. Multi-lingual, multimedia content—ranging from short-form videos and podcasts to vernacular mobile apps—should be tailored to specific demographic groups, particularly women, adolescents, and rural populations. Additionally, digital influencers, community leaders, and faith-based organizations can act as mediators between national policies and local realities, fostering trust in digital platforms. Establishing regional health communication labs under public universities could facilitate research on message framing, digital engagement, and misinformation management. Furthermore, health gamification models, where citizens earn digital rewards for maintaining wellness behaviors (such as vaccination or fitness tracking), can merge behavioral economics with motivational psychology, reinforcing health-positive habits. These marketing innovations would ensure that health literacy is not perceived as an imposed message but as a participatory and aspirational movement.

In terms of leadership, India's health reform requires a new generation of phygital leaders who blend emotional intelligence with technological fluency. Leadership development programs for district health officers, ASHA supervisors, and policy planners should include training in *digital ethics, data analytics, and participatory governance*. Transformational leadership practices—rooted in empathy, shared vision, and inclusivity—should be embedded in the culture of public administration, enabling leaders to respond adaptively to feedback and change. Leadership networks can also promote intersectoral collaboration, connecting ministries of health, education, technology, and rural development in a unified policy matrix. To institutionalize such collaboration, Health Leadership Forums (HLFs) could be established at state and district levels, tasked with coordinating digital health initiatives, monitoring impact metrics, and ensuring alignment with sustainable development goals (SDGs). In addition, fostering women's leadership in digital health governance is essential for achieving gender equity, as women often serve as primary health communicators within families and communities.

To ensure sustainability, the phygital transformation must be underpinned by robust monitoring and evaluation (M&E) *systems* that integrate qualitative and quantitative indicators. These systems should track not only digital reach and program efficiency but also psychological metrics such as trust, satisfaction, and empowerment. Adopting *real-time data dashboards* and AI-based analytics could provide continuous policy feedback and resource optimization. Simultaneously, data privacy and ethical governance frameworks must be strengthened to protect citizens from digital exploitation and surveillance. The government, in collaboration with civil society, should develop a Digital Health Ethics Charter that outlines clear standards for consent, transparency, and data stewardship. Integrating these safeguards will build the moral foundation of India's digital health ecosystem.

Finally, long-term sustainability requires embedding health literacy and digital competence within the education system. Introducing age-appropriate curricula on nutrition, hygiene, mental health, and digital wellness from the school level can cultivate an informed and responsible citizenry. Collaborations between educational institutions, public broadcasters, and technology firms can expand digital health outreach through interactive e-learning modules, particularly in regional languages. Encouraging universities to integrate phygital health research incubators and cross-disciplinary labs can further stimulate innovation in behavioral health, community medicine, and AI-enabled public health analytics. By aligning education, economy, and ethics under a single vision, India can transform its health reform into a model of inclusive modernization.

In sum, these recommendations converge on one guiding principle: the success of India's national health reform depends on synergizing technological progress with human-centered governance. Economic investment without communication fails to inspire; communication without leadership fails to endure; leadership without ethics fails to transform. The path forward lies in constructing a *phygital ecosystem* that is efficient yet empathetic, innovative yet inclusive—where every citizen, regardless of geography or income, participates not as a passive recipient but as an active co-creator of the nation's health destiny.

FUTURE RESEARCH DIRECTIONS

Future research on India's phygital national health reform must extend beyond descriptive policy analysis to develop empirically grounded, interdisciplinary models that assess how digital transformation interacts with human behavior, institutional capacity, and social equity. The complexity of the phygital ecosystem—where economics, marketing, and leadership intersect—requires methodological pluralism that combines quantitative data analytics, qualitative ethnography, and systems modeling.

One promising direction lies in developing empirical indicators to measure phygital health literacy (PHL), capturing not only access and awareness but also comprehension, trust, and behavioral application of health information. Researchers could design large-scale national surveys using psychometric instruments to quantify the digital health competence of different socio-economic groups, enabling comparisons across gender, region, and educational strata. This would establish the empirical foundation for a *National Health Literacy Index (NHLI)* capable of guiding targeted interventions and evaluating longitudinal progress. Parallel to this, micro-level case studies in rural and semi-urban India could explore how community health workers, telemedicine practitioners, and citizens negotiate technological and cultural barriers in everyday contexts. Such ethnographic insights would enrich the understanding of how health messages travel through hybrid communication networks that combine oral traditions, social media, and institutional channels.

Another crucial research avenue concerns the economics of phygital health governance. Scholars should examine cost–benefit ratios, sustainability models, and public–private–people partnership (PPPP) mechanisms to determine how digital innovations can enhance efficiency without exacerbating inequality. Comparative studies between states or countries could illuminate how fiscal strategies influence digital health adoption, highlighting the economic implications of infrastructural investment, human resource training, and data-driven governance. In parallel, researchers in public policy and behavioral economics can analyze the return on investment (ROI) of digital health campaigns—measuring their effectiveness in improving compliance, reducing disease burden, and promoting preventive behavior. These analyses would allow policymakers to link fiscal prudence with social outcomes, thereby transforming health communication from a cost center into a strategic driver of national productivity.

The marketing and communication dimension offers another rich field for inquiry. Future studies should explore how digital storytelling, gamification, and influencer-based campaigns shape public perception and behavioral intent across demographic cohorts. Mixed-method approaches combining sentiment analysis, social media analytics, and focus group studies could help uncover the emotional and cognitive mechanisms underlying message reception and misinformation resistance. Given the surge of artificial intelligence and machine learning in health communication, future research could also evaluate the ethical and psychological impact of algorithmic personalization—how AI-curated health advice affects autonomy, consent, and trust. Similarly, comparative experiments could test the relative efficacy of human-led versus AI-assisted communication in promoting adherence to health interventions. These lines of inquiry would deepen our understanding of how digital marketing principles can be ethically integrated into public health communication to maximize engagement while safeguarding individual dignity and data sovereignty.

In the realm of leadership and governance, future research should focus on developing a Phygital Leadership Competency Framework (PLCF) for the public health sector. This framework could define the digital, emotional, and ethical competencies required for effective health governance in a technology-mediated environment. Longitudinal studies on leadership development among district health officials, ASHA coordinators, and policy administrators can shed light on how training, mentoring, and institutional culture shape adaptive leadership capacity. Additionally, organizational psychology research could investigate how transformational and servant leadership models translate into digital contexts, where authority is diffused and communication is instantaneous. These insights could inform leadership training modules, ensuring that the human element remains at the center of India's rapidly digitizing health system.

Given India's linguistic and cultural diversity, cross-cultural and multilingual research is also essential. Future studies can explore how regional language interfaces, traditional healing practices, and community-based knowledge systems can be integrated into digital health content to enhance cultural resonance and local ownership. Researchers might also investigate the sociolinguistic barriers that limit comprehension of digital health information, particularly among marginalized groups. Integrating principles of *cultural epidemiology* and *anthropology of technology* would allow for a more inclusive understanding of how health meanings are negotiated in a multicultural society.

Furthermore, as artificial intelligence, wearable technology, and the Internet of Things (IoT) increasingly redefine the boundaries of healthcare, ethical, legal, and policy research must anticipate emerging challenges. Scholars should examine the implications of biometric surveillance, data commodification, and AI-driven diagnostics for privacy, consent, and governance. Future work should aim to design AI ethics frameworks specifically tailored to the Indian context—balancing innovation with human rights protection. Comparative legal research across countries could inform India's policy architecture on digital health regulation, providing evidence for robust data protection laws and public oversight mechanisms.

Finally, future research should adopt a futures and foresight perspective, using scenario planning and systems dynamics modeling to anticipate how global trends—such as pandemics, climate change, or geopolitical shifts—might influence India's phygital health landscape over the next two decades. Interdisciplinary research collaborations between technologists, economists, sociologists, and behavioral scientists could simulate different policy trajectories to identify resilient pathways toward *Health Literacy 5.0*—a future model integrating artificial intelligence, personalized health ecosystems, and participatory governance. The establishment of Phygital Health Research Hubs in universities and policy think tanks could facilitate these long-term studies, enabling continuous innovation and evidence-based policymaking.

In essence, future research must evolve from documenting India's health reform to co-creating *it*, positioning scholars not as external observers but as active contributors to the nation's health transformation. The integration of behavioral science, digital technology, and leadership theory offers a fertile ground for developing new paradigms of public health governance—ones that are data-informed yet deeply human, technologically advanced yet ethically grounded. The ultimate aim of future inquiry should be to ensure that India's journey toward phygital health reform is not only efficient and innovative but also equitable, reflective, and compassionate—anchored in the principle that the future of healthcare lies in the seamless union of *human wisdom and digital intelligence*.

CONCLUSION

India's journey in healthcare reform illustrates a powerful evolution—from the early decades of public awareness and civic hygiene campaigns to the emergence of participatory, technology-driven "phygital" models that unite physical outreach with digital engagement. Over seventy years, health literacy has transformed from a mode of instruction to a mechanism of empowerment, enabling citizens to navigate health systems, exercise informed choices, and co-create public health outcomes. Economic priorities shaped through successive Five-Year Plans have guided this evolution, aligning welfare, efficiency, and innovation with national development goals.

The transition from the Planning Commission to NITI Aayog marks a shift from centralized planning to adaptive, data-driven, and collaborative leadership. Yet, the challenge remains to ensure that economic growth and technological advancement are matched by ethical leadership, inclusivity, and equitable access. Phygital action must move beyond awareness campaigns to real-time community engagement, transparent governance, and digitally supported behavioral change.

Ultimately, India's healthcare reform represents both progress and paradox—a nation advancing in communication and innovation while still confronting disparities in access and understanding. True reform demands human-centered governance where economic insight, digital inclusion, and moral leadership converge to transform awareness into action and information into dignity. As India steps deeper into the phygital era, its capacity to sustain health literacy and leadership across sectors will determine the enduring success and ethical legacy of its national health vision.

REFERENCES

Djakeli, K. (2024). Healthcare marketing: Meaning, historical development, applications, and current status. In Djakeli, K. (Ed.), *Modern Healthcare Marketing in the Digital Era* (pp. 1–25). IGI Global Scientific Publishing., DOI: 10.4018/979-8-3693-0679-6.ch001

Gigauri, I., & Djakeli, K. (2021). National health reforms in Georgia during 1994–2021 and their success. HOLISTICA – Journal of Business and Public Administration, 12(2), 102–108. https://reference-global.com/download/article/10.2478/hjbpa-2021-0017.pdf

Ministry of Health and Family Welfare. (Various years). *Annual reports*. Government of India. https://www.mohfw.gov.in/?q=en/documents/publication

Planning Commission, Government of India. (1951–1956). *First Five-Year Plan*. Government of India. https://archive.org/download/dli.ernet.449278/449278-The%20First%20Five%20Year%20Plan_text.pdf

Planning Commission, Government of India. (1974–1979). *Fifth Five-Year Plan*. Government of India. https://niti.gov.in/planning-commission-archive

Planning Commission, Government of India. (1985–1990). *Seventh Five-Year Plan* (Vols. 1–2). Government of India. https://niti.gov.in/planning-commission-archive

Planning Commission, Government of India. (1992–1997). *Eighth Five-Year Plan* (Vols. 1–2). Government of India. https://niti.gov.in/planning-commission-archive

Planning Commission, Government of India. (2002–2007). *Tenth Five-Year Plan* (Vols. 1–3). Government of India. https://niti.gov.in/planning-commission-archive

Planning Commission, Government of India. (2007–2012). *Eleventh Five-Year Plan* (Vols. 1–3). Government of India. https://niti.gov.in/planning-commission-archive

Planning Commission, Government of India. (2012–2017). *Twelfth Five-Year Plan* (Vols. 1–3). Government of India. https://niti.gov.in/planning-commission-archive

KEY TERMS AND DEFINITIONS

Digital Health Reform: Digital Health Reform refers to the transformation of healthcare systems through digital technologies such as telemedicine, electronic health records, mobile health (mHealth) apps, and AI-based platforms. It aims to improve accessibility, efficiency, and equity in healthcare delivery by integrating technology into traditional health governance and service frameworks.

Health Literacy: Health Literacy is the ability of individuals to access, comprehend, evaluate, and apply health information to make informed decisions about their well-being. It encompasses cognitive, social, and digital skills that empower people to navigate healthcare systems effectively, adopt preventive behaviors, and contribute to community health improvement.

Phygital Health Governance: Phygital Health Governance combines physical and digital elements in healthcare systems to create a seamless, participatory model of health service delivery. It integrates human interaction with digital tools like AI, mobile applications, and data analytics to enhance communication, monitoring, and decision-making across institutional and community levels.

Public Health Communication: Public Health Communication involves the strategic use of communication techniques to inform, influence, and motivate individuals and communities toward healthier behaviors. It includes campaigns, social marketing, and health education programs designed to disseminate accurate, culturally sensitive, and accessible information to diverse audiences.

Socio-Economic Policy: Socio-Economic Policy refers to governmental strategies that link economic planning with social welfare objectives. In healthcare, it ensures equitable distribution of resources, addresses social determinants of health such as income and education, and aligns economic efficiency with inclusive health development and national growth.

Social Marketing: Social Marketing applies principles of commercial marketing to promote behaviors that benefit individuals and society. In health reform, it uses audience segmentation, emotional appeal, and persuasive messaging to encourage preventive care, healthy lifestyles, and active participation in public health programs.

Sustainable Health Development: Sustainable Health Development focuses on creating long-term, resilient healthcare systems that balance economic growth, environmental stewardship, and social equity. It aims to ensure continuous access to quality healthcare, reduce inequalities, and integrate health goals with broader sustainable development objectives.

Transformational Leadership: Transformational Leadership in health reform refers to visionary, empathetic leadership that inspires collective commitment and innovation. Such leaders motivate stakeholders to embrace change, foster collaboration across sectors, and uphold ethical governance while driving digital transformation and inclusive health policy implementation.

Chapter 12
Phygital Transformation in Healthcare:
Bridging Technology, Trust, and Accessibility in the Modern Health Economy

Ryan Stephen
http://orcid.org/0009-0008-9975-2857
Christ University, Bengaluru, India

ABSTRACT

The healthcare industry is at a critical juncture as it grapples with the rapid adoption of new technology while trying to integrate these advancements into traditional care models in order to respond to the increasing demands of society and economy. This chapter discusses how phygital healthcare can help improve the efficiency, access, and engagement of patients when using digital technology by addressing issues that have historically plagued the industry such as trust and access to affordable options. An analysis of how these technologies will change the way we deliver healthcare and how we will manage it financially is presented along with an exploration of the economic and marketing implications of digital health in relation to building patient-centered systems and sustainable health markets. Through case studies and literature reviews, this chapter lays out a model for integrating digital innovation into ethical leadership to ensure that health care reform occurs in a socially inclusive and technologically progressive manner.

DOI: 10.4018/979-8-3373-7173-3.ch012

1. INTRODUCTION

The fast, radical shift of the Health care in terms of accessing and delivering care is mirrored in the increasing use of digital means in our daily lives where conventional visits were a part of the medical care. The digital care alternatives are steadily finding their way into the everyday experiences of patients and represent a more convenient, faster and efficient way of delivery and they address the needs of patients. The convergence of physical care and digital care is called phygital health care that transforms how care is accessed, how patients experience their healthcare provider and how care is given to the people with access, phygital health care. The emergence of Digital Health through Teleconsults, AI based diagnostics, Remote Monitoring System, Electronic Health Records and Digital Public Health Initiatives are just but a few examples of how this industry will continue to change structurally. The potential efficiencies in health economics that can be created by the use of digital health tools will decrease the overall cost of long-term health through the potential to eliminate transaction costs, manage resources in a more efficient way, and create more access points to preventative care pathways. Better communication and personalized care with the help of DHTs will lead to better marketing and engagement of patients in the domain of their health as they will develop more active interest in their health due to the creation of a more profound understanding of their needs and confidence in their provider. Other topics that will involve more work on the part of DHTs include paying more attention to the spheres of leadership and ethical concerns in digital health. The issues of reasonable use of patient data, adherence to the requirements of the regulatory bodies, and equitable access to both DHT and innovative medical technologies are the issues that will demand further attention and care. Digital applications could become useful in Health Economics in the form of the decrease in the transaction costs; the increased possibility of optimisation of resource allocation; and the added preventive care models which will lead to the decreased total expenditures, through the long-term expenditure cuts. Moreover, digital platforms are a value addition in a Marketing and Patient Engagement perspective since they enhance the quality of communication and give patients a higher degree of personalisation and trust, thereby allowing patients to be much more proactive in their health care process. Besides this advantage in the patients, the Leadership and Ethics in Digital Health issue is also gaining relevance regarding ensuring the adequate use of data, the adherence to the regulations regarding the usage of the digital health tools, and the equal opportunities of all people to enjoy the advantages of the Digital Age innovations. The chapter offers a complete insight into how Phygital Healthcare Ecosystems will be established, develop and will be sustainable in a dynamic Global Economy of Health. This chapter aims at giving valuable information that can be applied by Policymakers, Healthcare Administrators, Digital Health Startups, and Researchers who wish to transform the National Health Policy.

2. LITERATURE REVIEW

The phygital healthcare concept is a product of a number of related research fields such as digital health, telemedicine, healthcare innovation, patient engagement, and health economics. The growing use of digital technologies in the healthcare delivery process has created a great academic concern in the knowledge about how hybrid models could enhance healthcare accessibility, efficiency, and patient outcomes. Digital Health and Telemedicine 2.1. Digital health Digital health is the use of information and communication technologies (ICT) to provide healthcare services, health information systems, and health management of the population. As discussed by the World Health Organization (2021), digital health is vital in enhancing health care systems as it has the ability to enhance the accessibility of data and clinical decision-making and efficiency of service delivery. The most notable use of digital health technologies has become telemedicine. Teleconsultation services increased exponentially in healthcare systems all over the world during the COVID-19 pandemic. Research has demonstrated that telemedicine can greatly enhance the access to healthcare, especially among the rural and underserved groups, because it decreases geographical barriers and travel expenses (Thomas et al., 2021). Companies like Practo and Apollo 24/7 in India have shown that it is possible to scale up the provision of healthcare by using virtual appointments, online prescriptions, and diagnostic tools.

According to research conducted by Menachemi and Collum (2011), the EHR systems enhance clinical records, sharing of information among healthcare providers and decrease the occurrence of multiple medical tests. Nonetheless, the problems associated with interoperability, data security, and integration with the current clinical processes are some of the key challenges.

2.1 Wearable and Predictive Analytics Technology

Remote patient monitoring systems and wearable health technologies have become very significant in the management of chronic diseases. The technologies enable continuous measurement of such vital health indicators as blood levels, glucose, blood pressure, and physical activity. Steinhubl et al. (2015) underline that wearable devices make it possible to pursue active healthcare because it is possible to detect the possible dangers to health before they occur. On this note, artificial intelligence and machine learning-based predictive analytics can enable healthcare providers to conduct a large-scale analysis to discover patterns and predict deterioration of patients, as well as aid clinical decision-making (Rajkomar et al., 2019). Such technologies bring into place the more personalized and preventive healthcare models.

2.2 Phygital Healthcare as a Hybrid Healthcare Model

Philosophy The term phygital was first coined in the marketing literature to refer to a combination of physical and digital customer experience. According to Pantano and Gandini (2017), phygital environments provide a smooth flow between digital and physical points of interaction to increase customer engagement and satisfaction.

Phygital models in the field of healthcare entail integrating digital healthcare technologies with conventional healthcare services to develop a continuous care ecosystem. The patients can enter their healthcare journey over online platforms including teleconsultation applications or symptom checkers and subsequently obtain the clinical services in person when it is necessary. According to Sharma et al. (2022), phygital healthcare implementation requires trust, usability, and continuity of care as the key elements to success.

2.3 Economic Digital Healthcare Implications

The transformation of digital healthcare is currently analyzed more economically. The global healthcare is under increasing financial strain as a result of the aging population, increasing incidences of chronic diseases, and high costs of healthcare.

Digital monitoring technologies and telemedicine have been demonstrated to cut on the cost of healthcare by limiting hospital readmissions and decreasing administrative costs and enhancing the management of preventive care (Kruse et al., 2017). The OECD (2020) states that digital health technologies have the potential to improve the efficiency of healthcare by improving timely diagnosis and the management of the disease, which will lead to the decrease in long-term healthcare spending.

2.4 Patient Engagement, Healthcare Marketing

The delivery of healthcare is moving more towards patient-centred methods of care where patient experience, engagement, and trust are focused upon. The digital platform (patient portal, mobile health apps, and online communication tool) allows healthcare professionals to keep in touch with patients at all times.

It is proposed in the research that digital engagement tools enhance treatment adherence, patient satisfaction, and healthcare outcomes (Yeow et al., 2018). Digital marketing is another approach through which healthcare institutions are educating patients about preventive care and utilizing it to promote the introduction of digital healthcare services.

The paper addresses two topics: leadership and ethical governance in digital health.

Healthcare Digital transformation needs a robust leadership and governance framework. West et al. (2020) emphasize the role of transformational leadership in leading healthcare organizations through the technological change and restructuring of the organization.

Digital healthcare adoption is also centered on ethical considerations. Patient data privacy and informed consent issues, cybersecurity risks, and the possibility of algorithmic bias are some of the issues that should be taken into consideration to use the digital technologies responsibly (Vayena et al., 2018). These issues are all the more crucial in phygital systems of healthcare where small amounts of sensitive patient information are being transferred back and forth on a constant stream across various digital platforms.

3. THE PHYGITAL HEALTHCARE MODEL

The redesign of healthcare systems using digital technologies has also resulted in the formation of the phygital healthcare model combining physical healthcare services with digital health technologies. The phygital approach also integrates digital and physical healthcare to form a continuous and uninterrupted healthcare experience in patients instead of viewing them as two distinct systems. This integrated model can help healthcare systems to provide care more effectively and enhance access, coordination and patient participation.

Practically, the phygital healthcare model enables patients to start their healthcare experience on the digital platform in the form of mobile applications, chatbots, teleconsultation portals, and remote monitoring devices. As soon as it is required, patients will be able to move to face-to-face treatment using a hospital, clinic, diagnostic center, or a specialty facility. Phygital healthcare correlates with improved patient satisfaction, care continuity, and resource use in healthcare organizations through the integration of digital and physical healthcare delivery systems, which results in an increased adoption of the benefits of each approach.

3.1 Phygital Healthcare Defined

Phygital healthcare is a combination of physical and digital healthcare that enables the development of a unified and patient-centered care system. Physical healthcare services encompass the physical medical consultations, in-hospital diagnostics, surgery and emergency medical services. Digital health services, in turn, are telemedicine websites, diagnostic applications based on artificial intelligence, mobile health applications, distant visits, wearable health monitors, and electronic health records.

The main aim of the phygital healthcare is to build a daily and linked healthcare experience to allow patients to seamlessly transition between digital and physical healthcare spaces. The model seeks to establish a healthcare ecosystem that is data-linked, and that patient information can be safely distributed among healthcare providers to enhance clinical decision-making and care coordination. Secondly, phygital healthcare fosters patient-centered experiences through providing more convenient healthcare services, accelerated access to healthcare services, and more individually targeted treatment routes.

Notably, there is no intention to substitute physical healthcare services with the phygital model. Rather, digital technologies are employed to supplement and optimize the traditional way of healthcare delivery and improve the interaction with patients, track their well-being, and diagnose and intervene at the earliest.

3.2 Phygital Healthcare Ecosystems Core Components

An effective phygital healthcare ecosystem consists of a number of interrelated elements that together facilitate the process of integrating digital and physical healthcare services.

Digital Access Layer

The digital access layer is the beginning of the healthcare experience of numerous patients. This layer comprises of digital tools and platforms that allows the patients to communicate with the healthcare providers and receive medical services remotely. The most frequent aspects of this layer are teleconsultation systems, online appointment systems, symptom checkers, medical triage chatbots, and mobile health apps. Such technologies help to decrease the waiting periods, geographical boundaries, and allow the patients to consult medical guidance at earlier stages of a disease.

Diagnostic and Monitoring Layer

The diagnostic and monitoring layer combines the digital diagnostic tools with the conventional medical testing method. The systems that enable healthcare providers to monitor patient health indicators constantly include remote patient monitoring systems, wearable health devices, artificial intelligence-assisted imaging systems, and smart diagnostic devices. These technologies enhance the early detection of the diseases, assist in the planning of the personalized treatment, as well as allow the healthcare professionals to track the patients in the environments other than the traditional hospitals.

Computerized Information and Electronic Health Records

The presence of electronic health record (EHR) systems is at the core of the data integration of phygital healthcare ecosystem. EHR systems can facilitate efficient sharing of patient data among healthcare professionals when implemented appropriately, therefore, lessening the repetition of medical tests and enhancing the communication among hospitals, clinics, laboratories, and pharmacies. The interoperability of healthcare information systems is a critical success factor in the implementation of phygital healthcare since it enables medical data to be transferred across various healthcare organizations with ease.

Physical Infrastructure of Healthcare

Although the role of the digital technologies is getting bigger, the physical healthcare infrastructure will also be a part of the phygital model. Surgeries, emergency medical care, and complicated diagnostic processes are some of the key services that can not be entirely substituted by digital platforms. Hospitals, clinics, laboratories, and pharmacies offer such services. The physical infrastructure hence supplements the digital healthcare systems by providing face-to-face medical services where necessary.

Healthcare Marketing Layer and Patient Engagement

Sustaining continuity of care and enhancing patient-healthcare provider relationships are some of the roles of patient engagement tools. Online interaction tools encompass medication reminder services, online prescriptions, customized patient portals, preventive health systems and online patient communities. Digital marketing strategies are also used by healthcare organizations to inform patients, promote preventive healthcare practices, as well as encourage the use of digital healthcare services.

4. FINANCIAL ASPECTS OF PHYGITAL HEALTHCARE

Digital transformation of healthcare systems is not merely a technological change but also an economic policy that aims at enhancing sustainability of healthcare. The rising costs of healthcare provision are coupled with the world experiencing greater financial pressure in the form of aging and the increasing number of chronic illnesses, which is coupled with the growing prevalence of chronic illnesses. Phygital healthcare provides the chance to enhance the cost-effectiveness through minimizing the medical spending on unnecessary and non-essential medical expenses and maximizing the utilization of healthcare resources.

4.1 Resource Optimization and Cost Efficiency

Digital healthcare technologies have a role to play in cost efficiency in a number of ways. Teleconsultation services help decrease the operational costs of having physical healthcare facilities as well as lowering the administrative costs. Telemedicine lowers the number of expenses spent on traveling by patients to healthcare facilities and enhances the streamlining process of healthcare delivery overall, as healthcare providers can remotely organize consultations.

Remote patient monitoring system has also proved to be capable of decreasing hospital rehospitalization of chronic illnesses like heart failure, diabetes, hypertension, and chronic obstructive pulmonary disease. Studies have shown that one of the potential ways to lower the readmission rates in hospitals is remote monitoring, which can decrease it by as much as 25-30 percent (Dinh-Le et al., 2019). Moreover, predictive analytics tools enable healthcare providers to detect possible health risks in advance and work on them before they get serious, which contributes to the decrease of costly emergency treatment.

Healthcare supply chain management can also be enhanced with the help of digital technologies. With e-procurement systems, the levels of transparency have been improved, inventory shortages are reduced, and waste is minimized through the improvements in the coordinating of the healthcare providers with the medical suppliers.

4.2 Macroeconomic Effect on the National Healthcare Systems

Digital healthcare transformation has economic value not just to individual healthcare organizations but also to the healthcare systems of a country. Digital health infrastructure can help governments to enhance access to healthcare, and manage long-term healthcare spending.

As an illustration, telemedicine services save time and time wastage through patient travel and preventeeism respectively. Moreover, online health platforms generate the emergence of new healthcare markets, such as online pharmacies, digital diagnostics, preventive healthcare subscription business models, and medical startups based on artificial intelligence.

According to industry estimates, the Indian health technology market may grow to about 50 billion dollars by 2030, and phygital innovation may be an important part of this market expansion.

4.3 Healthcare Affordability/Equity

Affordability in healthcare is a significant issue with most of the developing economies. Phygital healthcare solutions can contribute to this issue by making rural patients travel cheaper, allowing low-priced online consultancy, and offering remote follow-ups. The solutions enhance access to healthcare and reduce the cost burden by patients.

The Ayushman Bharat Digital Mission (ABDM) of India shows that the government is dedicated to the growth of affordable digital healthcare. ABBM will enhance the accessibility of healthcare and efficient patient data management within the healthcare ecosystem by developing digital health identities and interoperable health records.

4.4 Economic Disincentives to Adoption

Although it has the potential benefits, phygital healthcare systems are facing a number of economic challenges in their implementation. Costs to establish digital healthcare infrastructure may be high, and especially when a public healthcare institution is involved, especially if it does not have adequate funds. Medical professionals should also be trained and digitally literate through workforce training to help the providers to use digital health technologies properly.

Moreover, the fear of not getting a payback on a particular digital healthcare technology can put healthcare organizations off the use of the system. The policymakers should thus come up with long-term planning measures that can contribute to the evolution of sustainable infrastructural development of digital healthcare.

5. ENGAGEMENT AND DIGITAL TRUST WITH PATIENTS

The transformation of phygital healthcare is not merely a technological change but also a patient behavioral change as well as a change in communication strategies. Before the benefits of phygital healthcare systems are realized to the full extent, patients need to comprehend, have faith, and embrace digital healthcare services.

Modern patients are much more demanding in the form of convenient, transparent, personalized, and conveniently accessible healthcare services. Digital platforms fulfill these requirements as they provide patients with access to healthcare data and information, help to make appointments, get medical consultations, and control their health status using online platforms.

5.1 Building Digital Trust

In the adoption of digital healthcare services, trust is of great importance as the information in the healthcare is very sensitive. Digital healthcare tools have higher chances of being adopted by patients in case the healthcare providers explain to the patient how patient data is collected, stored, and used. Making sure that the cybersecurity protection measures are adequate, privacy policy is clear, and digital user experiences are trustworthy assist in enhancing patient trust.

Weak user interface design, a high number of technical problems, or ambiguous data privacy policies can have a great impact on decreasing patient trust in the digital healthcare systems.

5.2 Digital Healthcare Marketing Strategies

Digital marketing is a growing trend in healthcare organizations as the strategy is used to market healthcare services to customers and inform patients about preventative healthcare practices. These plans involve search engine optimization, education social media campaigns, partnership with medical influencers, patient testimonials and customized health education material.

Such big healthcare organizations like the Mayo Clinic and Apollo Hospitals have shown how digital communication plans can reinforce patient involvement and enhance awareness in healthcare.

5.3 Patient Experience and Personalization

Involved patients tend to comply with treatment regimens and make routine follow-up visits and engage in preventive health interventions. The use of digital tools like patient portals, mobile health apps, and real-time communication platforms can help healthcare providers to ensure that there is constant interaction between themselves and patients.

Technologies in artificial intelligence are also useful in facilitating customized healthcare experiences through offering individualized treatment plans, behavioral health alerts and personalized wellness insights.

6. ONE OF THE MAIN CONCERNS ABOUT THE PHYGITAL HEALTHCARE IS LEADERSHIP AND ETHICAL GOVERNANCE

Phygital healthcare systems should rely not just on technological innovation in order to be successfully implemented but also on proper leadership and ethical governance systems. The healthcare leaders should make sure that the digital transformation initiatives should meet the needs of patients, healthcare professionals and national healthcare priorities.

Transformational leadership is especially significant in the process of leading healthcare organizations towards digital transformation. By means of transformational leaders, innovation is stimulated, disciplinary cooperation is encouraged, and an attitude of constant learning in the healthcare organization is encouraged (Bass and Riggio, 2006).

Clearly, healthcare institutions like the Cleveland Clinic have shown the value of leadership in digital transformation by investing in digital infrastructure long before the COVID-19 pandemic increased the rate of telemedicine use. Likewise, the Indian healthcare providers, including Apollo Hospitals and Fortis Healthcare, have adopted digital-first healthcare models that unify teleconsultation service with online pharmacy and remote diagnostics and conventional hospital services.

6.1 Digital Healthcare Ethical Concerns

The implementation of digital medical technologies also comes with a number of ethical issues that go beyond the scope of conventional medical ethics. The privacy of patient data is among the most critical issues, where health systems contain high amounts of sensitive health information about patients. Healthcare data breaches or unauthorized access to healthcare data could be a serious deterrent to the general public.

Another ethical concern that is relevant in digital healthcare systems is informed consent. It is necessary to show patients how their medical information is being used and how AI systems can be used to assist in clinical decision-making. But the digital consent forms may be complicated and hard to comprehend by the patients.

Another emerging issue within the healthcare systems based on artificial intelligence is algorithmic bias. The use of AI models, which have been trained on a small or biased dataset, can result in faulty forecasting of specific populations, which could result in unequal healthcare results.

It is also necessary to assure digital equity. Lack of access to internet, smartphones and low digital literacy may limit the ability of some populations accessing digital healthcare services.

7. CASE STUDIES

Case studies are used to demonstrate the way of how phygital healthcare models are implemented in the real-life healthcare system.

India Case Studies

Apollo 24/7 is a complex phygital healthcare ecosystem, comprising of teleconsultations, AI-driven symptom checkers, digital pharmacies, home diagnostics services, and physical hospital networks. The platform has millions of users and shows how digital and physical healthcare services are possible to be combined into one healthcare system.

It has transformed Practo into a massive online healthcare network comprising of teleconsultations, online pharmacy delivery, laboratory testing services and digital health records, since it is now more than a typical doctor-booking platform.

The eSanjeevani telemedicine portal headed by the government has been able to carry out more than 150 million consultations and offer telemedicine services to underserved communities and rural areas.

Global Case Studies

The Mayo Clinic in America has adopted artificial intelligence, remote monitoring, and tele-intensive care systems in its network of healthcare facilities. These are the technologies that help healthcare professionals to check the cardiac irregularities with the assistance of smartphone-based ECG monitors, which illustrates how specialized healthcare services can be enhanced with the aid of digital innovation.

8. THE OBSTACLES TO PHYGITAL HEALTHCARE

Although it has its advantages, phygital healthcare implementation has technological, economic, and behavioral as well as regulatory obstacles.

Some of the technological barriers are the lack of interoperability in electronic health record systems, lack of digital infrastructure in the rural regions, and lack of cybersecurity measures. There are economic issues such as high start up costs and lack of assurance on financial pay off of digital healthcare technologies.

Behavioral barriers are also very important. Patients might be reluctant to use telemedicine services because some of them like to attend the real-life consultation. On the same note, medical practitioners might oppose the reforms to the traditional clinical practices.

The regulatory issues comprise the absence of international uniform digital health policies and legal ambiguities regarding telemedicine malpractice and artificial intelligence-based clinical decision-making.

9. PHYGITAL HEALTHCARE ADOPTION STRATEGIES

Policymakers and healthcare institutions need to undertake various strategic initiatives in order to facilitate the uptake of the phygital healthcare systems.

Investment in digital infrastructure including broadband internet access, low-cost smartphones, and 5G networks enabling remote diagnostics should be one of the priorities of governments. The digital literacy programs also play a crucial role in ensuring that healthcare providers as well as patients are able to use digital healthcare technologies effectively.

Healthcare systems should also enhance interoperability through setting the national health data standards, promoting the open application programming interface, and implementing international data exchange frameworks like the HL7 FHIR.

Another strategy would be training healthcare professionals in digital competencies in health. These are telemedicine practices, digital diagnostic tools, artificial intelligence decision support systems, cybersecurity awareness, and electronic health record management, which should be part of medical education programs.

Hybrid Chronic Disease Management

One of the major contributors to the healthcare spending in the world is the chronic diseases. Phygital healthcare models promise a lot in enhancing the management of chronic diseases by constantly monitoring and intervening.

Remote patient monitoring, virtual follow-ups, artificial intelligence-driven health alerts, and programs where the nurse is in charge of telemanagement, enable medical practitioners to follow-up with patients more efficiently outside of the traditional hospital environment. These hybrid care models will allow an early intervention and increase the long-term health outcomes and decrease the hospital readmissions.

10. CONCLUSION

Phygital healthcare can be seen as a paradigm shift in the contemporary healthcare systems as it combines digital technologies with conventional medical services. The hybrid model empowers the healthcare providers to provide more affordable, effective, and patient-focused care and helps to overcome most of the structural problems of global health systems.

Telemedicine, artificial intelligence, remote patient monitoring, and electronic health record have integrated to increase healthcare accessibility and enhance clinical efficiency to a great degree. Simultaneously, the digital medium can enable healthcare organizations to enhance patient interaction and create individual care journeys.

Nevertheless, technological adoption is not the only factor that can lead to the successful implementation of phygital healthcare systems. The problems of data privacy, ethical governance, digital infrastructure, and healthcare staff training should be taken into consideration. The reduction of the digital divide is another issue of concern to policymakers and leaders in the healthcare sector to ensure equal access to digital health services.

In the case of emerging economies like India, phygital healthcare will offer a chance to develop its healthcare delivery systems and enhance the accessibility of healthcare to vast populations. Digital infrastructures like the Ayushman Bharat Digital Mission, which are national programs, indicate the possibility of utilizing large-scale healthcare innovation using digital infrastructures.

On the whole, the future of healthcare is more and more hybrid in character. Digital and physical healthcare services integration can help to increase the efficiency of healthcare, improve patient experiences, and support more sustainable healthcare systems in the world.

REFERENCES

Bass, B. M., & Riggio, R. E. (2006). *Transformational leadership*. Psychology Press. DOI: 10.4324/9781410617095

Dinh-Le, C., Chuang, R., Chokshi, S. K., & Mann, D. (2019). An electronic health record and wearable health technology integration: Scoping review. *JMIR mHealth and uHealth*, *7*(9). Advance online publication. DOI: 10.2196/12861 PMID: 31512582

Kruse, C. S., Krowski, N., & Rodriguez, B. (2017). Patient satisfaction and telehealth: A systematic review. *BMJ Open*, *7*(8). Advance online publication. DOI: 10.1136/bmjopen-2017-016242 PMID: 28775188

Menachemi, N., & Collum, T. H. (2011). Suits and limitations of electronic health record systems. Healthcare Policy and Risk Management, 4.

Pantano, E., & Gandini, A. (2017). The connection between the types of sociality mediated by new technologies in retail environments. *Computers in Human Behavior*, •••, 77.

Rajkomar, A., Dean, J., & Kohane, I. (2019). Artificial intelligence in healthcare. *The New England Journal of Medicine*, •••, 380.

Steinhubl, S. R., Muse, E. D., & Topol, E. J. (2015). The new sphere of mobile health. *Science Translational Medicine*, *7*(283). PMID: 25877894

Thomas, E. E., Haydon, H. M., & Mehrotra, A. (2021). It is based on the fast adoption of telehealth in COVID-19. *Journal of Medical Internet Research*, *23*(10).

Vayena, E., Haeusermann, T., Adjekum, A., and Blasimme, A. (2018). The case of why we require ethics in digital health. Nature Digital Medicine, 1(1).

WHO (2023). Digital Health Global Strategy Update. The Lancet Digital Health (2022). Healthcare system digital health transformation. Health Affairs (2021). Adoption of telemedicine and delivery of health care. OECD (2022). Health IT and Economic Value.

World Health Organization. (2021). Online health global strategy 20202025. Topol, E. (2019). Deep Medicine: Artificial Intelligence Can Save Healthcare by Moving It Back to Humans.

Chapter 13
Refugee Health Reform in the Phygital Era:
Economic, Legal, and Leadership Perspectives From India and Germany

Abhinash Mohanta
http://orcid.org/0000-0002-8732-3202
KIIT University, India

Anuj Kumar Sinha
http://orcid.org/0009-0003-5953-8454
Amity University, Ranchi, India

Shaikh Sahanwaz Islam
http://orcid.org/0009-0006-2068-8959
Madhusudan Law University, India

ABSTRACT

Refugee health is a key indicator of how inclusive and resilient national health reforms are in the digital age. This chapter offers a comparative doctrinal analysis of refugee health governance in India and Germany, asking how economic capacity, legal design, and leadership shape access to care in phygital systems. Germany follows a structured asylum and insurance model that limits entitlements during the initial asylum period, while India relies on constitutional guarantees, executive discretion, and fragmented welfare measures in the absence of a refugee law. The analysis links health financing with digital tools such as telemedicine, electronic records, and data protection rules to assess effects on inclusion and accountability. Drawing on doctrinal analysis and expert opinion, the chapter treats refugee health

DOI: 10.4018/979-8-3373-7173-3.ch013

as both a moral benchmark and a diagnostic lens. It concludes that durable phygital inclusion requires legal entitlements, viable risk pooling, privacy-conscious governance, and adaptive leadership that builds public trust.

INTRODUCTION

Refugee health is one of the indicators of a nation's commitment to inclusive health reforms. Providing fair care for refugees who are among the most vulnerable and demonstrates progress toward universal health coverage and social solidarity. How a country addresses the health needs of refugees is a telling indicator of how well the health system is functioning and how broad the social policies are. In the past few years, several governments have begun to add refugees to national health strategies. As of 2021, 76 per cent of states surveyed had introduced refugees to health plans, up from 62 per cent in 2019 (Refugee and Migrant Health at the Centre of Discussions during the 77th UN General Assembly, 2022). This change indicates that governments are approaching refugee health within the framework of national public health and development. But policy inclusion is no guarantee of actual access. Studies suggest persistently problematic access, coverage gaps, access barriers, and unmet chronic and psychosocial needs (Olabi et al., 2025). Sustainable integration models are poorly researched. Therefore, how refugees are treated is a moral test as well as a diagnostic tool. It reflects the depth of national reform, the inclusiveness of institutions and the political will for health equity. Examining the health issues faced by refugees in various countries can illuminate broader reform paths.

Healthcare receives a big dose of digital transformation too. The emerging phygital ecosystem integrates physical and digital health services and is transforming the care of patients. In this model, in-person visits work in conjunction with digital tools to create a seamless experience. The arrival of telemedicine in the mainstream is due to the impact of the Covid-19 pandemic. Meanwhile, consumer technology has heightened expectations for seamless and user-centred care (Coulter, 2024). Today's ecosystem includes teleconsultations, mobile health apps, electronic health records, and AI- assisted decision tools. These digital components are complementary to traditional care and offer new opportunities to reach underserved groups. Digital solutions have the potential to reduce structural barriers, which has benefits for refugees in remote settlements or urban fringes. Mobile units, telehealth platforms, digital information systems and information enhance access where providers are scarce. Early evidence indicates that such innovations are cost-effective and flexible and offer practical ways to reach hard-to-reach populations (Hou et al., 2024). Grasping this evolving phygital landscape is important to assessing how inclusive the future of health reforms will be, particularly for refugees who often slip through the cracks of service delivery.

India and Germany offer a useful juxtaposition in studying refugee health in a phygital setting. They vary in economic size, health system structure, and legal rules for refugees, yet both are faced with similar pressures at the intersection of migration and health. A lower-middle-income country home to 1.4 billion people, India continues to increase accessibility to health services through reform and innovation. It is home to over 250,000 refugees but not a signatory of the 1951 Refugee Convention and has no national refugee legislation (Shanker & Raghavan, 2020). As a result, refugees are living in a patchwork of administrative arrangements, often with unclear legal status and inconsistent access to services. This situation makes the question of refugee health a revealing test of India's reforms. Access is subject to discretionary policies and aid agencies and a strained public health system. At the same time, India is a world leader in experimentation in digital health. Telemedicine pilots, rural digital platforms and a national digital health ID system provide an opportunity for researchers to observe whether tools such as phygital can fill gaps in infrastructure and legal protection.

Germany provides a contrast. It is a nation of high incomes and universal health coverage with strong insurance structures, but they faced an abrupt onrush of refugees that strained their resources. From 2015 to 2016, Germany received more than one million asylum applications, becoming Europe's refugee crisis (Stafford, 2016). The increase served to challenge its legal and health frameworks. Under the Asylum Seekers' Benefits Act, asylum seekers are only given emergency and essential care for the first 18 months. Full coverage comes after that period or once their status is recognised (Ziegler & Bozorgmehr, 2024). Although the purpose of this policy was to let the little government limit costs and baseless claims, it created regional differences and administrative delays. Germany's experience shows that even well-funded systems have trouble when legal rules limit access. Comparing India and Germany can provide a rich picture: India uses voluntary, innovative approaches within limits, and Germany is a wealthy country, using structured legal entitlements in a tech-savvy system. The contrast speaks to the impact of economic strength, legal rules and governance priorities on the use of phygital tools and the inclusiveness of health reforms.

The study is based on three disciplinary lenses i.e. economics, law, and leadership. The economic lens examines the role of resources, incentives and costs in determining the outcomes of refugees. It also takes into account the fiscal implications of integrating refugees into local systems in the country and the cost-effectiveness of digital interventions. Earlier studies have indicated that investing in the health of the refugees yields long-term benefits, such as improved public health and productivity. The legal lens is important because refugee access to care is dependent on international conventions, regional directives, and either the presence or absence of domestic statutes. Germany's limited benefits established structural obstacles that later spawned reforms, such as the electronic health cards to make access easier. India's absence of legislation on refugees leaves refugees in a legal limbo, and they are dependent on constitutional rights or temporary orders to be cared for. Law also influences the digital space, including data protection and telemedicine regulations. The leadership lens emphasises the fact that reforms are often contingent upon political will, institutional vision, and cross-sector coordination. Leadership drove Germany's reforms in the 2015 influx and India's efforts to propagate the Ayushman Bharat Digital Mission. Local leaders also led efforts to implement digital tools, such as electronic cards for asylum seekers, and telemedicine projects in marginalised communities.

Based on this framework, the study raises three research questions. First, how is the state of refugee health a barometer of health reforms in India and Germany? Second, how does the emergence of a phygital ecosystem impact the provision of refugee healthcare? Third, how do economic, legal, and leadership factors interact to influence the health outcomes of refugees and the adoption of innovation?

LITERATURE REVIEW

The intersection of refugee health, digital transformation, and comparative health governance forms a multidisciplinary research field that has gained increased academic attention, especially in the wake of the global migration crisis and the COVID-19 pandemic. Despite the existence of well-developed individual strands in this literature, they typically remain isolated within disciplinary boundaries. No prior study has systematically examined refugee health governance through a simultaneous economic, legal, and leadership lens within a phygital framework, nor has any comparative analysis been conducted across a non-Convention low-middle-income country and a high-income European Union member state. The following survey maps out five thematic domains that provide context to the current analysis and highlight the specific gaps that are addressed in the study.

Refugee Health & Universal Health Coverage & Barriers to Access

Refugees represent one of the most medically underserved populations in the world, and research shows this in a significant body of work that spans cross-national research. Olabi et al. (2025) synthesised findings from low- and middle-income countries and identified enduring structural gaps in refugees' integration into national health systems, including fragmented service provision, barriers to documentation, and poor mental health provision. The World Health Organization (2022) reported that although 76 per cent of surveyed states have formally included refugees in national health plans by 2021, policy inclusion does not necessarily equate to actual access, since gaps in coverage, financial barriers and exclusions on the basis of location and/or national belonging continue to lead to adverse health outcomes, even where systems are formally inclusive.

Refugee health has been framed increasingly in the scholarly literature as a barometer of systemic health equity. Hou et al. (2024) suggested that digital health platforms, if carefully designed, could potentially lessen structural barriers to access for migrants and refugees, especially in geographically underserved areas, although they also warned that digital solutions that are not coupled with legal recognition reproduce rather than resolve structural exclusion. Faroqi and Sundaram (2022) described the specific vulnerability of refugees in India, where a lack of formal legal status leaves them with near-total reliance on non-governmental organisations for primary care. Shanker and Raghavan (2020) further established that India's undocumented refugee populations were disproportionately marginalised during the COVID-19 pandemic due to their exclusion from the welfare database and public health infrastructure. These studies together suggest that access to refugee healthcare services is mediated not simply by health system capacity, but by the legal and administrative architecture within which health systems exist. A comparative analysis putting this problem in the context of two different legal and economic regimes, however, is still missing from the existing literature.

Comparative Health Law: Legal Contexts for Entitlements of Refugees

The issue of legal regulation of refugee health entitlements has been studied in depth within European contexts. Ziegler and Bozorgmehr (2024) performed an ethnographic study of the meaning of Germany's Asylum Seekers' Benefits Act in clinical practice and found that there is considerable discretionary variation in how healthcare staff interpret the necessary treatment provisions under Section 4, leading to inconsistencies in the healthcare access and quality that refugees receive across different regions. Riemer et al. (2025) documented how the 2023 change of the restricted benefit period from 15 to 36 months led to constitutional, above-board concerns due to its compatibility with the ruling of the Federal Constitutional Court in 2012, which declared that minimum benefits may not violate human dignity. Wenner et al. (2022) provided population-based evidence that there are measurable inequalities in access to healthcare at the level of states within Germany which create what the authors call a postcode lottery of refugee health entitlements.

Scholarship on India's legal framework exposes a structurally different and no less significant set of problems. Birla (2023) analysed India's refugee law regime and found that judicial responses to refugee claims, while often protective, are reactive rather than systemic. The lack of domestic refugee legislation has left refugees vulnerable to the construction of Article 21 and the administrative will of the executive. Vijayaraghavan (2020) recorded the way this gap was made particularly harmful at the time of the pandemic, as the indeterminate legal status of refugees meant they were excluded from relief programmes. Tiwari (2024) analysed the Foreigners' Act of 1946 as a poor and outdated legal basis for the governance of refugees and argued for codified statutory reform. Debbarma (2024) explored community-level effects of the lack of a refugee law in India, linking the legal gap with material health and welfare deficits. Despite these rich individual country analyses, no prior scholarly work has conducted a doctrinal comparative analysis of India and Germany as a pairing, focusing on the interaction between the existence or non-existence of codified refugee health entitlements, the constitutional structure, international obligations, and digital health governance.

Digital Health Transformation & Phygital Healthcare Models

The idea of phygital healthcare, characterised by the convergence of physical clinical infrastructure and digital means of teleconsultation, electronic health records, and diagnostics assisted by AI, has emerged as the defining paradigm for health systems after the pandemic. Coulter (2024) characterised this hybrid model as opening new possibilities for extending care to populations who were previously excluded from the physical infrastructure for health. Sood et al. (2025) conducted a detailed evaluation of India's eSanjeevani national telemedicine platform, which has used a federated architecture, connecting 1.3 lakh spoke facilities to specialist hubs and delivering over 36 crore consultations to patients as of April 2025; the approach shows significant uptake by women and rural populations. This makes eSanjeevani a globally significant case study of government-operated phygital healthcare.

Germany's digital health transformation has mainly been examined with respect to institutional design and adoption issues. McKinsey (2022) reported near-universal integration of outpatient physicians and pharmacies into the national telematics network but continued disintegration between hospital and ambulatory systems. Compu Group Medical (2024) stated that the nationwide implementation of electronic prescriptions in 2024 resulted in 51 million prescriptions in the first few months of operation, made possible by the scale of Germany's telematics infrastructure. Mishra and Anand (2025) analysed India's Ayushman Bharat Digital Mission as a federated digital health ecosystem, which states that the generation of more than 760 crore Ayushman Bharat Health Account identifiers is unprecedented in terms of scale of digital health onboarding. The application of phygital frameworks to the specific population of refugees and migrants, however, has received little attention from scholarly literature. Steinbrink et al. (2021) is a key study that provides real data on how asylum seekers in Germany feel about their digital privacy and shows that their fear of being watched significantly made them less likely to use digital health and welfare services. Berg (2025) built on this analysis by linking digital exclusion to broader processes of social othering amongst refugee communities. These studies suggest a critical lacuna: very little attention has been paid to the equity implications of the design principles of phygital health systems for legally marginalised populations.

Health Financing, Risk Pooling and Economic Efficiency

The health economics literature on the inclusion of refugees has developed evidence to directly challenge the fiscal justification for limited access policies. Bozorgmehr and Razum (2015) used a quasi-experimental approach with 20 years of German data and found that treating asylum seekers with only emergency healthcare led to higher per capita costs than if access to full healthcare were provided, because of the escalation of untreated conditions to costly acute episodes. Niedermaier et al. (2020) supported this in data from the claims of Halle (Saale) by showing that asylum seeker medical care could be better managed with integration into statutory insurance, instead of the fragmented welfare model. Spiegel et al. (2018) provided a global review of innovative health financing mechanisms for refugees and argued that blended models of combinations of national insurance inclusion, international co-financing from UNHCR and multilateral development banks and community risk pooling represent the most sustainable pathways. They found that parallel systems that are run by humanitarian organisations alone are more costly and less clinically effective than integrated national systems.

Health financing scholarship in India has been led more by the Ayushman Bharat programme. Angell et al. (2019) critically analysed the governance and stewardship issues in AB-PMJAY, such as low reimbursement rates and public-private tensions that limit its effectiveness. Garg et al. (2024) evaluated the four-year impact of the programme and found significant benefits in terms of financial protection with more than 1.25 lakh crore in out-of-pocket savings; however, the benefits were disproportionate as geographic disparities remained. Bukhari (2025) reported on the 2023 crisis of the withdrawal of private hospitals from the scheme, highlighting structural weaknesses of the public-private partnership model. A gap that persists without getting addressed throughout this body of work is an analysis of how refugees could be financially integrated into the AB-PMJAY risk pool or how international co-financing could supplement national schemes to cover non-citizen populations, which are considered in this study.

Leadership, Governance & Health Reform Communication

Leadership scholarship in the health reform literature has recognised, at increasing rates, the centrality of political will, institutional vision, and communication strategy to the success of major health initiatives. Kneuer and Wallaschek (2022) analysed the crisis communication of Chancellor Angela Merkel during the Covid-19 pandemic and found that her style of crisis communication (fact-based, transparent) added considerably to the courageous public compliance with health measures and the comparatively effective early pandemic management in Germany. Susanto (2020) has analysed the governance structures of the pandemic in Germany as the ideal case of a superior coordination of welfare states modelling and explains its success by both leadership style and the institutional framework of cooperative federalism. Gottlieb et al. (2024) contributed a narrative analysis of the legitimisation or delegitimization of inclusionary migration and health policies through public discourse, ensuring that framing refugee health as a public investment instead of a burden significantly enhances the durability of such policies. These studies shed light on how communicative choices among political leaders affect public legitimacy of health policies that impact vulnerable populations.

In the Indian context, Kamath and Brand (2023) examined the political framing of Ayushman Bharat as a mission-mode scheme implementation by top-level political advocacy, which had to be present for the fast implementation of the scheme at scale. Agrawal et al. (2024) examined five years of the National Health Policy 2017 and revealed ongoing interministerial coordination breakdown as the key governance challenge of health reform efforts in India, which has hindered effective implementation and responsiveness to the needs of vulnerable populations. The literature on leadership has not taken a systematic approach to understanding the interactions between governance structures and political communication strategies and digital health deployment among refugee populations. The accountability mechanisms, cross-sectoral coherence requirements, and ethical dimensions of phygital refugee health governance are still underdeveloped, however, in current scholarship.

Synthesis and Research Gap

As in, the existing literature offers rich individual analyses of refugee access to health, comparative health law, digital health transformation, health financing, and governance leadership. Three big gaps persist in these bodies of work. First, there has never been a comparative study of India and Germany as a couple, although there is an analytical value in comparing a non-Convention developing country with a high-income EU member state. Second, the use of the phygital framework for a particular group of people in the context of refugee populations in a way that intersects digital and physical dimensions of care in rights-based analysis is not theorised or empirically investigated. Third, the combined use of economic, legal, and leadership lenses for the governance of refugee health as a single interdisciplinary categorisation has not yet been introduced into the literature. The present study resolves all three gaps, making a novel contribution, both in its comparative design and in its interdisciplinary methodology.

METHODOLOGY

The research methodology employed a legal research method known as the doctrinal approach, which is the traditional black-letter research method that focuses on law as it is written. It comprises the detailed investigation of authoritative sources of law by means of logical analysis. In practice, the doctrinal method interprets statutes, codes, and judicial decisions to ascertain the law (Choudhary, 2024). The researcher is a critical analysis of legal rules that existed and their interrelationship, organising and systematising propositions and reasoning and deduction. By combining legislation and case precedents, this approach clarifies the current state of the law regarding specific issues. Rooted in the tradition of common law scholarship, this methodology is still essential to questions of legal interpretation. In this research, doctrinal analysis provides a structure for addressing issues in artificial intelligence and digital rights through known legal texts and principles.

Along with the doctrinal analysis, the study included expert opinion for enrichment and validation of the findings. Interviews in the purely legal sense are rare in pure legal research, unless there is a socio-legal or empirical perspective, but experts can be used to fill the gaps left by solely textual sources . A semi-structured interview with Prof. Sneha, Assistant Professor at XIM University, and an AI and digital rights expert brought in specialised knowledge and practical context. Her understandings contributed to the research going beyond abstract rules and addressing more subtle issues and current developments that may not have been already reflected in literature or case law. Using the input of experts ensured that the analysis was grounded and relevant, that readings of the law were checked, and that emerging issues were foreseen, complementing the doctrinal qualities of the finding with a contemporary understanding.

The crux of the research was based on primary legal materials. Statutes and legislation were the starting point because this is where the formal rules on technology and digital rights exist. The study exhaustively reviewed key legislative frameworks, including data-protection laws, cyber laws, etc., to extract provisions that are relevant to AI and personal rights. Judicial case law was also examined to understand the court's interpretation and application of those statutes. By analysing leading cases in digital privacy and technology, the researchers identified how principles are implemented or tested. Following the doctrinal method, the analysis immediately referred to primary legal sources that provided the most authoritative evidence. International conventions and treaties were taken into further consideration to integrate global norms. Instruments such as human rights treaties or international guidelines on artificial intelligence governance have been scrutinised in view of their harmonisation with more general standards that may exist in domestic law. For example, a similar doctrinal study of national laws read in comparison with treaties such as the Berne Convention or TRIPS Agreement methodically interpreted national laws to assess the adequacy of the laws (Albnian et al., 2025). Similarly, this research analysed domestic laws in the context of international principles on digital rights. Important court decisions, domestic and international, were surveyed to illustrate enforcement of these principles. Through this extensive review of statutes, cases and conventions, the research ensured that its analysis was based on the most direct sources, which control AI and digital rights.

Finally, a series of secondary materials complemented and contextualised the primary research. Scholarly works, including journal articles, legal commentaries, and academic books, were engaged to take advantage of existing analysis and debates. These sources provide critical commentary and interpretations of complex issues, often emphasising the background and real-life consequences of the law. Drawing upon academic literature ensured that the research was reflective of contemporary academic conversations and of the differing perspectives of experts. Further, relevant reports and policy documents, such as committee reports on AI policy or NGO reports on digital rights, have been considered to include factual data and current developments. Such reports provided real-world context, such as statistics or case studies that might not be found in pure doctrinal sources. The interview with the expert Prof. Sneha was also a great secondary source and supported the written information as well as providing new perspectives where they were lacking in the literature. By blending these secondary materials, authoritative analyses and practical reports, the methodology was kept well-rounded and informed. This combination served to strengthen research, as the secondary sources were helpful to interpret primary law and identify areas of consensus or controversy, thus enriching the overall research.

COMPARATIVE LEGAL FRAMEWORKS

In Germany, entitlement to healthcare for asylum seekers is mainly regulated by the benefits used of the Asylum Seekers' Act. During the first phase of residence, recently extended to thirty-six months with a 2023 amendment, healthcare coverage is limited. It is limited to the treatment of acute illnesses and pain and important preventive services. Section 4 guarantees the necessary medical and dental treatment, medication and basic therapeutic measures. It also has certain protections for pregnant women and recent mothers. Section 6 provides for additional health benefits where the treatment is required in individual circumstances in order to protect a person's health. After the expiry of this restrictive phase, asylum seekers are entitled to regular social welfare benefits under the Social Code and to healthcare at a comparable level to the benefits available to citizens receiving social assistance. The extension of the restrictive period from fifteen to thirty-six months has been criticised for its possible negative effect on refugee health and for raising constitutional concerns. German jurisprudence has made it clear that “necessary treatment” doesn't only refer to emergency treatment but also to treatment of chronic conditions that cause significant pain or deterioration and protects the right to health (Riemer et al., 2025).

Germany's overall healthcare system is laid out under Social Code Book V (SGB V), which is the legislation governing the operation of the statutory health insurance system. Health insurance is obligatory for residents, and recognised refugees or persons who have been given protection status are normally insured under the same conditions as citizens. Once a resort of lawful status is achieved or the limitation period has passed, resettlement of asylum seekers is typically provided with the issuance of an electronic health insurance card with a connection to a statutory insurance provider, allowing them full access to medical services. Section 264 of SGB V provides for the administration of healthcare for persons not insured so far by statutory health insurance funds on behalf of local authorities, e.g., asylum seekers receiving welfare benefits (Refugees and Asylum, 2024). The costs are reimbursed by the social welfare offices. This mechanism allows integrating eligible refugees into the framework of the regular insurances, instead of having fragmented systems based on emergency needs. Several different federal states in Germany have already introduced ordinary health insurance cards for asylum seekers even in earlier stages, which allow for direct access to the physicians without excessive administrative barriers. Through this structure, refugees with established legal status are entitled to healthcare under the same statutory conditions as other insured residents (Riemer et al., 2025).

As a member state of the European Union, the refugee health policy in Germany is also determined by European law. The EU Reception Conditions Directive (2013/33/EU) requires Member States to guarantee decent living conditions for asylum applicants (including access to necessary healthcare). Article 19 prescribes emergency treatment and necessary care for diseases and severe mental illness. The corresponding needs are reflected in German legislation, which provides for acute medical treatment during the asylum process. The Qualification Directive (2011/95/EU) further establishes that Persons who are granted refugee status or subsidiary protection are entitled to equal access to employment, social welfare and healthcare as nationals of the host country under Articles 26 and 29 to 30 (Refugees and Asylum, 2024). This European framework is the basis for Germany's legal obligations. Recognised refugees obtain full access to the statutory health insurance system, and those who are in the process of having their status determined obtain basic medical services in accordance with EU standards.

In processing information for the purpose of registration in the case of refugees, German authorities must adhere to strict data protection rules. The General Data Protection Regulation treats health data as a special category of data requiring extra protection. Processing such data, including medical histories or sharing patient data, is prohibited unless a lawful basis is present for processing, including explicit consent or statutory processing in healthcare or vital public interests. Germany's Federal Data Protection Act (Bundesdatenschutzgesetz, BDSG) supplements the GDPR by outlining how public authorities have to process sensitive personal data in accordance with principles of necessity, proportionality and confidentiality (Jahn et al., 2021). Refugee health records should be securely held and used for legitimate purposes such as medical treatment or for epidemiological monitoring. Unauthorised disclosure or misuse would be against EU and country law, thus showing the importance of privacy within refugee health governance.

In contrast, in India there is no specific statute dealing with refugees. The legal framework is mainly of constitutional origin and administrative law. Article 21 of the Constitution ensures the right to life and personal liberty, according to Art. 21 of the Constitution. The Supreme Court has construed this provision very broadly to encompass the right to live with dignity, which includes the right to health. Healthcare has therefore been perceived as an integral part of Article 21 and hence imposes a duty on the state to provide medical facilities (Mathiharan, 2006). In *State of Punjab v. Mohinder Singh Chawla (1997)*, the Supreme Court held that the right to health is an integral part of the right to life and laid stress on the duty of the government to provide adequate healthcare services. In *Paschim Banga Khet Mazdoor Samity Vs. State of West Bengal*, the court held that if emergency treatment was not given in a timely manner, it constituted a violation of Article 21. Importantly, Article 21 is applicable to all persons and not limited to the citizens. Refugees and asylum seekers present in India are therefore entitled to minimum life and health protections under this fundamental right. In *Ktaer Abbas Habib Al Qutaifi & Anr. V. Union Of*

India & Ors., Court have used this principle to order authorities to cover medical care and humane treatment regardless of nationality.

In the absence of special laws dealing with refugees, the Indian asylum seekers are mainly governed by the Foreigners Act, 1946. This statute provides wide executive powers to control the entry, stay and expulsion of foreigners without distinguishing between refugees and other migrants (Vijayaraghavan, 2020). Those who are fleeing persecution could potentially be treated as illegal migrants if they have no authorised entry because no formal statutory asylum procedure exists. Decisions relating to stay and welfare are usually made by executive discretion rather than through codified law. The United Nations High Commissioner for Refugees can grant refugee certificates to some people, but such certificates do not automatically confer legal status under Indian law unless the government recognises them. Consequently, refugees often spend considerable time in a legal grey area, relying on administrative decision-making and judicial intervention to access services and protection against deportation.

Although India is not a party to the 1951 Refugee Convention, international principles have shaped the judicial approach in India. The Supreme Court acknowledged that customary international law may inform domestic rights in the absence of conflicting legislation. In National Human Rights Commission vs. State of Arunachal Pradesh (1996), the Court restrained expulsion of Chakma refugees on the basis of Article 21 and the doctrine of non-refoulement. Similarly, in the case of *Ktaer Abbas Habib Al Qutaifi (1998)*, the Gujarat High Court believed that non-refoulement is part of Article 21, so there is no difference between the reading of the constitution and international norms (Katrak, 2021). Indian courts have often relied upon international human rights instruments to advance refugee-protective interpretations of constitutional guarantees even though there is no explicit statute granting asylum (Kumar, 2024).

Prof. Sneha emphasises that comparative refugee health entitlements must be read not merely as statutory design but as operational justice. She observes that Germany's tiered benefits regime under the Asylum Seekers' Benefits Act reflects a structured legal hierarchy of access, whereas India's reliance on constitutional jurisprudence produces a rights discourse without uniform administrative clarity. According to her, "legal architecture determines predictability." In Germany, codified entitlements despite limitations generate administrative consistency. In India, however, the absence of refugee-specific legislation produces variability, where implementation depends heavily on executive discretion and judicial intervention. She further argues that constitutional guarantees like Article 21 remain powerful normative tools, but without statutory embodiment and procedural rules, they risk remaining aspirational rather than systemic

ECONOMIC AND MANAGERIAL ARCHITECTURE

Germany's health system exemplifies a highly organised system of financing with wide pooling of risk and selective protection for vulnerable groups. Refugee health care is funded mainly from public funds under the Asylum Seekers' Benefits Act, which isolates the welfare of asylum seekers from the general social insurance package. During their first 15 months in Germany, or until their status is resolved, asylum seekers receive a limited benefits package funded out of local social welfare offices. Municipalities therefore have the immediate financial responsibility towards the healthcare of refugees. For example, the city of Halle (Saale) spent about EUR 2.825 million on the medical care of asylum seekers in 2015, which corresponded to roughly EUR 1,584 per person per year. While this decentralised model offers minimum coverage, it has been criticised for causing administrative complexity and barriers to getting timely care (Niedermaier et al., 2020).

There is evidence that restricting refugees to emergency-only services is not necessarily cost-effective (Fehr, 2018)Studies found that the restricted-access asylum seekers had had higher annual per capita costs incurred compared with those who gained full access to healthcare, with an estimated excess cost of about EUR 376 per person (Bozorgmehr & Razum, 2015) These additional expenses are incurred as a result of untreated conditions that become more severe, and they eventually require emergency treatment. Recognising this inefficiency, many German states started to issue electronic health insurance cards to asylum seekers earlier in the process and integrate asylum seekers into the statutory insurance mechanisms in an effort to reduce bureaucracy without increasing treatment costs.

Once refugees have been granted legal status or once they have completed the waiting period, they then pass into the statutory health insurance (SHI) system in Germany. Recognised refugees are subject to mandatory SHI coverage as well as enjoying the same entitlements as the citizens. Financing is by income-based insurance contributions with general tax revenues (State of Health in the EU, Germany - Country Health Profile 2023, 2023). Germany's overall expenditure on health care is among the highest in the world, amounting to roughly EUR 5,159 per capita in 2021, more than 85% of which is publicly funded. Out-of-pocket payments represent a small portion of the overall health expenditure, only around 12%, indicating robust risk pooling and financial protection. In contrast, India spends slightly over 1% of the GDP on public health in India (Angell et al., 2019), and out-of-pocket payments are more than 50 percent of the total health expenditure, indicating a much higher financial burden on individuals (Bukhari, 2025).

One root of Germany's model is its risk equalisation and insurance pooling system. Approximately 88-90% of the population participates in SHI, which contributes income-based premiums to a central health fund (Gesundheitsfonds). These pooled contributions are then redistributed as on a risk-adjusted per capita basis to 96 competing sickness funds (Germany - Health Systems in Transition, 2023). The morbidity-based risk adjustment formula (morbi-RSA), introduced in the 1990s and updated since 2009, takes into account demographic factors (such as age and sex) and diagnosed medical conditions (Blümel & Busse, 2020). This mechanism neutralises incentives for insurance companies for selecting only the healthy ones.

By replacing older or sicker populations with younger and healthier ones, Germany distributes predictable risk among the entire pool of insured. The result is a level playing field where funds are competing on the basis of efficiency and quality of service, instead of on the basis of risk selection. Government subsidies also add to solidarity; children's coverage is supported by federal grants, and the contributions of pensioners are partially supported by pension funds. Since 2021, Germany has also introduced the use of a high-cost risk pool for reimbursing about 80% of the annual expenditure over a certain threshold (McGuire et al., 2020). This ensures that extreme cases in costs do not destabilise individual insurers.

Through these mechanisms, Germany supports community-rated premiums and comprehensive benefits and remains financially viable. Catastrophic health expenditures are relatively exceptional and coverage is nearly universal. However, this system needs huge costs in terms of capital, with health spending reaching approx. 12-13% of GDP in the past years (State of Health in the EU, Germany - Country Health Profile 2023, 2023). The high degree of pooled funding dramatically lowers individual financial risk and is an example of the power of solidarity-based insurance.

Prof. Sneha underscores that digital health expansion must be accompanied by enforceable consent frameworks and grievance safeguards (Sneha et al., 2024). She explains that Germany's eGK and telematics infrastructure illustrate how privacy-by-design strengthens legitimacy, while India's ABDM reflects scale-driven innovation that must now prioritise digital literacy and awareness. In her view, phygital governance succeeds only when refugees trust that their data will not be used for immigration surveillance or discrimination. She stresses that audit trails, multilingual consent interfaces, and clear separation between welfare and enforcement databases are essential to prevent deterrence from healthcare access. "Digital inclusion without digital protection," she argues, "can unintentionally reproduce vulnerability." Therefore, technological efficiency must remain subordinate to human dignity and informed autonomy.

Germany's provider payment system enshrines accountability with regulation of fees and prospective payment models. Ambulatory physicians are self-employed professionals who are paid on a self-serving fee-for-service basis based on a standardized fee schedule (EBM). However, regional budgets put caps on reimbursable service volumes per physician per quarter (Blümel & Busse, 2020). Once a physician moves past the quarterly case threshold, marginal reimbursement decreases, making it a soft cap on service expansion. Although gatekeeping is not strict in Germany, sickness funds encourage voluntary gatekeeping models for chronic care management.

Hospital financing is based on Diagnosis-Related Groups (DRGs), for which hospitals are paid on fixed basis of the cases based on DRG weight and Regional Base Rates (Blümel & Busse, 2020). These payments are used for running expenses, with capital investments to be separately raised by the states. Introduced in the 2000s, the DRG system motivates efficiency by penalising hospitals that try to stay unnecessarily long or intervene when unnecessary by requiring them to manage with essentially fixed payments.

Quality safeguards are part of payment reforms. The Federal Joint Committee (G-BA) defines binding guidelines for treatment and quality indicators (Blümel & Busse, 2020). Providers must report performance data such as surgical outcomes and the rate of infection to outside quality assurance bodies. Persistent under performance may lead to financial penalties or exclusion from SHI contracts. The corporatist model of governance, where physician associations and sickness fund associations negotiate tariffs and enforce standards together, allows for accountability by regulation and peer control instead of competition in the market alone.

In contrast, India launched Ayushman Bharat–Pradhan Mantri Jan Arogya Yojana (AB-PMJAY) in 2018 as a large-scale reform to expand financial protection. The scheme provides coverage of 5 lakh per family annually for secondary and tertiary hospitalization, targeting the poorest 40% of the population, approximately 500 million individuals (Angell et al., 2019). Financing is shared between central and state governments, typically at a 60:40 ratio, with poorer states receiving 90:10 or full central funding.

Despite its scale, per capita expenditure under AB-PMJAY has been low due to India's huge eligible population. The scheme regulates costs with standardised package rates for over 1,600 procedures (Bukhari, 2025). Hospitals are reimbursed at fixed tariffs covering all the associated costs. While these ceilings are the source of affordability and predictability, providers frequently complain that rates are not high enough to pay for complex cases and rising input costs. Analysis show that tertiary care procedures are often priced below reimbursement levels and the loss must be absorbed by the hospitals.

Nonetheless, AB-PMJAY has reduced the financial burdens significantly (Garg et al., 2024)Till 2025, it saved families more than 1.25 lakh crores in out-of-pocket expenditure, it reportedly said. The scheme covered more than 42 crore people and empanelled more than 33,000 hospitals. Strategic purchasing mechanisms such as periodic revision of rates and treatment guidelines are intended to balance cost containment with service delivery . However, the central allocation is only a small share of total health spending so that per beneficiary there is a limitation (Towards Universal Healthcare: Ayushman Bharat Pradhan Mantri-Jan Arogya Yojana, 2025)

Public-private partnership is one of the cornerstones of AB-PMJAY. Approximately half of empanelled hospitals are private institutions, which includes tertiary care centres. While the expansion of private participation opened the door to more people, tensions arose as a result of low reimbursement rates and delayed settlements of claims. In a number of states, hospitals reported waiting six to nine months to get paid, undercutting financial sustainability.

In 2023 hundreds of private hospitals suspended the services of AB-PMJAY beneficiaries because of unpaid dues (Bukhari, 2025)The government is also blamed for the politics in Haryana, where about 650 private hospitals refused collectively to admit new patients until the power arrears were cleared. Similar jolts were felt in Gujarat and Jammu & Kashmir. Reduced private participation has led to patients being confined to overburdened public hospitals or compelled to travel considerable distances for care (Sarthe, 2025)Fraud control and audit measures made matters even more difficult. Government lookout for exaggerated claims and unnecessary procedures associated with it resulted in a tougher verification system involving electronic claims and pre-authorisation procedure. While necessary for accountability, these measures provided a slowdown in reimbursements and a deficit of trust. Efforts to revise package rates and streamline claims processing continue, but incentive alignment is still tenuous.

India also has constraints in terms of efficiency that are based on the low levels of infrastructure and workforce capacity. Public health expenditure is currently slightly above 1% of GDP and therefore chronically under-invested. Although India has thousands of primary health centres and district hospitals, many were already stressed before the increased demand by AB-PMJAY. In the rural areas, there are supply-side bottlenecks from the shortage of doctors, nurses, and equipment.

Administrative capacity varies from state to state, resulting in uneven implementation. States with more digitised systems and governance have higher utilisation rates compared to poor states which have low utilisation despite high need. Persistent out-of-pocket expenditure among those who have insurance reflects geographic gaps and shortages of services (Angell et al., 2019).

Recognising such constraints, complementary schemes such as the National Health Mission and the PM Ayushman Bharat Health Infrastructure Mission (PM-ABHIM) were launched by the government to build up the facilities and work force capacity. However, until the infrastructure, human resources and governance systems are improved uniformly, the efficiency and equity of AB-PMJAY will be limited by structural limitations of low-resource settings.

DIGITAL TRANSFORMATION & PHYGITAL HEALTH GOVERNANCE

Germany has established an organized digital health strategy with its national electronic health insurance card system at its heart. Every statutorily insured person is issued an electronic health card (eGK) incorporating a chip which acts as proof of insurance and as a digital entry for healthcare services (Adam, 2025). The eGK includes administrative information (name, date of birth and insurance information, etc.) and allows safe access to digital applications such as electronic prescriptions and electronic patient records (ePA), with patient consent ("The Electronic Medical Data Card (eGK)," 2025). Governance of this infrastructure is coordinated with gematik, the federal agency which operates the nationwide telematics infrastructure which securely connects clinics, medical practices, pharmacies, and insurers together. The system has strict data protection standards. Access to medical information requires two-level authentication via professional smartcards used in combination with a patient PIN. All data transmission is encrypted. Although the eGK is mandatory and universally used, patients have control over what health information is shared and may limit what can be shared with others within a patient's records.

Prof. Sneha underscores that digital health expansion must be accompanied by enforceable consent frameworks and grievance safeguards. She explains that Germany's eGK and telematics infrastructure illustrate how privacy-by-design strengthens legitimacy, while India's ABDM reflects scale-driven innovation that must now prioritise digital literacy and awareness. In her view, phygital governance succeeds only when refugees trust that their data will not be used for immigration surveillance or discrimination. She stresses that audit trails, multilingual consent interfaces, and clear separation between welfare and enforcement databases are essential to prevent deterrence from healthcare access. "Digital inclusion without digital protection," she argues, "can unintentionally reproduce vulnerability." Therefore, technological efficiency must remain subordinate to human dignity and informed autonomy.

Recent reforms involve extending digital records usage. From late 2025, healthcare providers will have to actively use ePA by uploading key medical documents such as diagnoses, discharge summaries, lab findings and medication plans into each patient's record ("German E-Health Offerings Expand, but Adoption Remains Uneven," 2022). This movement away from a system of opt-in has been aimed at overcoming historically low uptake under the previous voluntary system. In the first year of voluntary ePA implementation, the number of people activating electronic records was scarce, only about 500,000 people, or 0.7 per cent of the total number of insured, and very few clinical documents were uploaded. The low participation reflected both hesitation by the patient and uncertainty by providers about workflow integration. By making electronic records the norm and incorporating electronic records into the eGK infrastructure, Germany hopes to improve continuity of care, avoid the duplication of tests and provide better coexistence between sectors while maintaining high standards of data security and individual autonomy ("German E-Health Offerings Expand, but Adoption Remains Uneven," 2022).

Interoperability and continuity of care are key elements of the digital transformation in Germany. As of 2022, around 96 per cent of outpatient physicians and 99 per cent of pharmacies were linked to the national telematics network close to universal integration of infrastructure ("German E-Health Offerings Expand, but Adoption Remains Uneven," 2022). This connectivity allowed nationwide electronic prescriptions (e-Rezept). Although the first test phases in 2022 met with resistance because of privacy issues and technical errors, by 2024, e-prescriptions were standard in ambulatory treatment. In the first month of the nationwide rollout, approximately 12 million electronic prescriptions were issued, as opposed to in earlier pilot stages ("E-Prescriptions New Standard in Germany: CGM with Positive Interim Assessment," 2024). By the beginning of 2024, more than 51 million e-prescriptions had been dispensed, and almost all of Germany's 17,500 pharmacies were set up to process them. Each prescription is also stored securely within the telematics infrastructure and accessed through the scanning of the eGK or a secure mobile application, ensuring that the coordination between doctors and pharmacies is seamless and that paper-based errors are reduced ("The Electronic Medical Data Card (eGK)," 2025).

Digital tools like secure messaging systems (KIM and TIM) enable providers and insurers to exchange clinical documents electronically, and patients can give physicians access to emergency summary data as needed. Despite such progress, there is still not full cross-sector interoperability. In 2021, only around 12 per cent of German hospitals exchanged electronic data with outside physicians on a regular basis although this was an improvement, considering that in 2020, it was 4 per cent ("E-Prescriptions New Standard in Germany: CGM with Positive Interim Assessment," 2024). Persistent fragmentation between hospital and outpatient systems still limits continuity of care. In response, the government implemented mandatory shared standards and offers of financial incentives to encourage digital adoption and system compatibility. Integration of electronic medication plans into ePA is expected to help overcome issues of data continuity across care settings to move comprehensive patient histories across multiple providers and mitigate inefficiencies created by siloed information systems.

Germany's approach to refugee health data highlights the importance of governance, oversight, and transparency in digital health administration. During the influx of refugees in 2015 and 2016, a Refugee Digitisation System was developed in Germany to make the registration process more efficient and to maintain consistency of personal information among agencies ("German Refugee Digitisation

System," 2019). Under the Data Sharing Improvement Law, relevant authorities, such as immigration offices, social services, and health, had access to a shared common core data platform, which is administered by the Federal Office for Migration. A refugee's information at first contact is thus fed into one database and used by different competent agencies, reducing duplication, avoiding confusion about who is who, and speeding up service provision. Biometric identification, such as fingerprinting, improves accuracy and helps avoid misidentification or nosing around the benefit of an individual.

This centralised system requires people to register in a digital system more easily to access housing, welfare and healthcare services, as registration in the digital system is a prerequisite to receive services. However, the concentration of sensitive personal data raises privacy concerns. Although by law Germany limits use of data and puts strict access controls in place, trust problems still exist among vulnerable groups. Undocumented migrants do not seek healthcare due to fear that personal information will be shared with immigration authorities. Social welfare offices are mandated by law to report undocumented patients to immigration enforcement, which has been criticised because it has a deterrent effect on medical care and may violate the right to health. Advocacy groups have contested this obligation in constitutional debates, holding that it violates equitable access. These tensions indicate the need for regular audits, judicial oversight and transparency mechanisms. Germany's experience shows that digital efficiency must be complemented by strong legal protections and structures of accountability to ensure that administrative integration does not involve the compromising of privacy or discourage people from obtaining necessary health services (Steinbrink et al., 2021).

India's digital health transformation is altogether very different in scale, speed, and architecture. The Ayushman Bharat Digital Mission (ABDM) launched in 2021 aims at building a federated national information ecosystem of health rather than a centralised database. At the heart of it all is the Ayushman Bharat Health Account (ABHA), a unique health ID that would allow the people to connect medical records across facilities and providers. As the system of issuing ABHA IDs in India has been rapidly implemented in diverse regions and socioeconomic groups, more than 76 crore (760 crore) ABHA IDs had been generated by 2025 (Mishra & Anand, 2025). Unlike with centralised storage, ABDM is based on a federated architecture: health records are stored by respective hospitals, clinics or laboratories but are shared securely when needed, with the consent of patients themselves.

To make this system operational, ABDM developed foundational digital registries. The Health Professional Registry lists close to six lakh verified healthcare providers, and the Health Facility Registry has more than three lakh healthcare institutions with a unique digital identifier. These registries provide reliability and authentication in digital transactions such as referrals or prescription sharing or laboratory reporting. Additional building blocks include its Health Information Exchange and Consent Manager, or HIE-CM, Unified Health Interface, or UHI, and upcoming drug and claims registries. UHI offers a standardised protocol for service discovery and digital interoperability as a financial sector counterpart to India's Unified Payments Interface. Through HIE-CM, individuals can provide granular and time-bound consent for access to their records, enhancing patient autonomy in the data-sharing construct.

Security and consent are the backbone of ABDM's architecture, and it is consistent with the evolving data protection standards in India. By the end of 2024, over 42 crore digital health records linked with their ABHA IDs included prescriptions, diagnostic reports, and discharge summaries. The speed and scope of onboarding is in stark contrast to Germany's incremental model of adoption. However, rapid infrastructures are a challenge in terms of ensuring consistency of use, provider training, and integration across the various healthcare settings.

Telemedicine has become a backbone of digital strategy for India through the initiation of the eSanjeevani platform, which was launched in 2020. Operating both in doctor-to-doctor and direct-to-consumer mode, the platform links primary health centres to specialist hubs as well as facilitating public online outpatient consultations. By April 2025, eSanjeevani had facilitated more than 36 crore consultations and is the largest government-operated telemedicine initiative for primary care in the world. The network is comprised of over 17,000 hub centres and 1.3 lakh spoke facilities integrated with health and wellness centres across the country (Sood et al., 2025).

Patients are able to access health professionals through smartphones or community kiosks and receive electronic prescriptions and referrals for face-to-face treatments. Usage has been particularly high among women as well as rural populations, suggesting that digital platforms are helping to address sections of society that had previously been left out of access. Consultation records can be attached to ABHA IDs, allowing continuity of care within the federated ecosystem. By comparison, Germany had about 3.5 million tele-consultations in 2021, reflecting the more gradual integration which depends on institutional structure and differences in scale of the population ("German E-Health Offerings Expand, but Adoption Remains Uneven," 2022).

India's Digital Personal Data Protection Act (DPDP) of 2023 institutes a complete legal framework over digital health data (Naithani, 2024). The Act brings in the concept of a data fiduciary, which includes any entity deciding the purpose and means for processing personal data. Hospitals, clinics, telemedicine platforms, and health technology companies are fiduciaries and mandated to act in best interest of the individuals. Informed consent is required unless there are certain legal exceptions, such as in cases of a medical emergency or public health requirements.

Consent is to be free, particular, informed and unambiguous, and people have the right to withdraw consent at any time.

Data fiduciaries must implement strong security measures such as encryption, access controls, and breach notification mechanisms. Serious penalties (up to a penalty of Rs 250 per sq km) apply in case of serious violations. Entities playing the role of Significant Data Fiduciaries have additional compliance requirements, such as independent auditing and appointing Data Protection Officers. The DPDP Act helps strengthen ABDM's consent-based architecture by codifying fiduciary duties and accountability standards into India's developing digital health ecosystem, which are enforceable by law (Naithani, 2025).

LEADERSHIP, GOVERNANCE ETHICS & PUBLIC COMMUNICATION

In Germany, effective leadership in health is based on institutionalised multi-level coordination at the federal, state, and local levels. The federal structure allows for a high level of autonomy for the Länder (states), and health initiatives from the federal level and those aimed at the nation as a whole require consensus and cooperation, not top-down mandates. Formal mechanisms and regular meetings contribute to ensuring an integration of policies: state governments are represented at the federal level (e.g., in the Bundesrat and in regular conferences of ministers and heads of government), while their participation leads to regional voices as part of the health decisions. For example, the National Conference of Health Ministers (Gesundheitsministerkonferenz) provides a forum for all the state and federal health authorities to establish a consensus for health legislation (Geffert et al., 2024). This highly structured coordination has been part of the governance of Germany. It allows for the central government to set direction but lets the subnational authorities supplement the guidance with implementation geared to local realities. During the Covid-19 crisis, for example, Chancellor Angela Merkel held regular videoconferences with the heads of the 16 states to agree on common measures against the pandemic (Kneuer & Wallaschek, 2022). Her government even created special people's intergovernmental task forces to coordinate lockdown rules among jurisdictions. Such collaborative leadership helped Germany mount a united response to its decentralised system. By combining this type of federal guidance with decentralised execution, German leaders kept policies coherent and took advantage of administrative strengths at the local level.

German health governance also stresses the importance of clear communication approaches to maintain public trust. Leaders have learned that communication transparency and empathy in messaging are as important as good policy. Angela Merkel, with her habit of calm and fact-based communication, demonstrated this form of communication during the pandemic. In a rare televised address, she insisted open democracy requires "political decisions to be made transparent and explained" to the public. By honestly explaining the scientific reasoning behind restrictions and accepting hardships, she tried to take citizens with her instead of just imposing rules. This honesty played its role in strengthening credibility; observers attributed this candour to shoring up public confidence. Merkel herself emphasised that public trust and transparent communication, coupled with social togetherness, were important for overcoming the crisis. Consistent and clear messaging from regular press conferences to public health campaigns has thus been an integral part of the leadership approach taken by Germany in relation to health reform to ensure understanding and acceptance of necessary measures.

In India, health leadership is frequently programmatic in the form of ambitious flagship schemes. Ayushman Bharat, launched in 2018 as a national scheme for universal healthcare coverage and popularly called "Modicare" by some, is an excellent example of a mission-driven endeavour (Kamath & Brand, 2023). Prime Minister Narendra Modi himself was a major proponent of the scheme as a historic leap in the social welfare movement. He cast it as a moral imperative, "a great opportunity to serve the poor" even calling it the greatest campaign ever for the underprivileged. The scale of the scheme is unprecedented; it is billed as the "world's largest" government-funded health assurance initiative, providing coverage of up to 5 lakh per family for over 500 million individuals (D. Sharma, 2018). Its rapid implementation has been lauded as a demonstration of effective leadership. Within months of birth, authorities empanelled over 13,000 hospitals. This was a "Herculean task" to accomplish in just 6 months. Ayushman Bharat's success story highlighted the importance of top-level initiative and political will in the successful implementation of major health reforms in India. He later praised the outcome of the scheme, describing it as a "revolution in public healthcare" that showed how "scale, compassion, and technology" can contribute to improving human welfare.

In India, hierarchical and siloed organization in the public sector has frequently impeded inter-ministerial coordination in health. Recognising this, recent policies promote more collaborative governance. The National Health Policy 2017, for instance, demands institutionalising inter-sectoral coordination through bodies with non-health ministries as a result of recognising that many determinants of health are external to the health department (Agrawal et al., 2024). Joint initiatives have been promoted; for example, the Swachh Bharat (Clean India) mission to improve the sanitation situation had to involve health authorities in devising joint initiatives with other departments. In practice, it is often the strong impetus of the Prime Minister's Office that is required to bring disparate agencies to the same table. High-level committees and "mission mode" task forces to bring several ministries and states under the same tie-up. Through such efforts and an emphasis on "cooperative federalism" (close centre-state partnership), India's leadership is slowly breaking bureaucratic barriers so that health programmes can be implemented in a more holistic, cross-sectoral manner.

In Germany, the story around the inclusion of refugees in health services is the embodiment of ethical leadership in action. Leaders have argued for refugee access to care as both a humanitarian imperative and a measured policy. Studies found that attempts to limit the access of asylum seekers to healthcare undermined equity and even the efficiency of the system, reinforcing the case for an inclusive healthcare system (Gottlieb et al., 2024). Merkel set the tone with sympathetic rhetoric. In a speech in 2015, amidst a massive influx of refugees, she urged Germans not to adopt a "cynical" attitude, arguing that such perspectives render all our ideas "inhuman". Instead, she urged Germans to view the new arrivals as a "opportunity for tomorrow" and emphasised that Germany would undoubtedly fulfil its obligation to aid those seeking refuge (Müller, 2021). By framing inclusion of refugees in positive moral terms and drawing on national values of solidarity, the leadership in Germany built support, as public sentiment favoured incorporating newcomers into social services. This framing of the narrative was an effective way of 'marketing' health reforms by appealing to ethics and shared identity to help make potentially controversial policies more palatable and legitimate (Susanto, 2020).

Finally, transparency in decision-making is crucial to building legitimacy in Germany's and India's health reforms. By openly explaining policies and sharing data, leaders build public trust. Merkel provided a good example of such transparency with his ability to clearly explain what the government was doing to the citizens. Such honesty engenders buy-in and makes health policies more credible.

Prof. Sneha highlights that refugee health reform ultimately reflects ethical leadership choices. She notes that Germany's communicative transparency during crises particularly under Merkel's leadership illustrates how moral framing can legitimise inclusive policy. In India, mission-mode programmes such as Ayushman Bharat demonstrate how political will accelerates reform, but sustained coordination across ministries remains critical. She argues that leadership must not only initiate reform but also institutionalise accountability and cross-sectoral coherence. According to her, refugee inclusion becomes politically sustainable when framed not as burden-sharing but as public health investment. Ethical governance therefore requires transparent communication, evidence-based justification, and a consistent reaffirmation of constitutional values.

DOCTRINAL CHALLENGES AND STRUCTURAL GAPS

India's refugee health governance is marked by the lack of any formal legal guarantees and by improvised policy measures. India is not a signatory to the 1951 Refugee Convention and does not have any specific domestic law on refugees. As a result, there is no codified entitlement to healthcare/welfare for those fleeing persecution in Indian territory. Refugees are covered by general immigration laws and do not enjoy specific statutory protections. This gap in the law means that refugees and asylum seekers are unable to claim health services on the basis of an entitlement enforceable by law. Although the courts in India have at times construed the constitutional "right to life" under Article 21 to comprehend dimensions of healthcare, such interventions by judicial bodies are haphazard in nature and cannot replace comprehensive legislation (Birla, 2023). Consequently, refugees still find themselves effectively cut off from public healthcare schemes and welfare infrastructure. Unlike citizens, who can legally demand government support, refugees are often left outside state medical programmes (Faroqi & Sundaram, 2022).

The absence of legal status and documentation adds to the exclusion. Many refugees lack Aadhaar identification, and any other recognised identity document is often required to enter a public hospital or clinic. In reality, this barrier to documentation means that consistent access to subsidised medical services is unachievable. As a result, refugees often rely on UNHCR and non-governmental organisations' ad hoc assistance for basic support with healthcare. Their access to care remains predicated on the administrative discretion of court administrators and not guaranteed entitlement, so without statutory recognition, they have been "stuck" in a lengthy legal grey area.

Prof. Sneha observes that doctrinal fragmentation creates structural insecurity for refugees in India. While courts have advanced non-refoulement principles and health protections through constitutional interpretation, she argues that litigation-driven protection is reactive rather than preventive. Without statutory clarity, administrative discretion fills the vacuum, resulting in uneven access and accountability deficits. In Germany, she notes, doctrinal clarity exists but fiscal and political contestation complicate uniform implementation across federal states. She emphasises that legal certainty and administrative coherence must function together. "Rights must be codified, operationalised, and monitored," she asserts, otherwise protection remains contingent. She further stresses that grievance redress systems must be accessible, language-sensitive, and independent to ensure that digital and welfare reforms do not marginalise vulnerable populations.

This governance gap is reinforced by India's refugee management system, which is fragmented and executive-driven. In lieu of a homogeneous law, refugee policy is based on colonial-era legislation such as the Foreigners Act of 1946 and the Registration of Foreigners Act of 1939 (Tiwari, 2024). These statutes give the authorities wide discretionary powers to regulate, detain or deport non-citizens, making no distinction between refugees and other migrants. Successive governments have defined this basic framework with ad hoc administrative orders geared towards individual refugee communities. Policy decisions are often informed by geopolitics, however, rather than uniform humanitarian principles.

India has informally recognised and supported certain groups, notably the Tibetan refugees and Sri Lankan Tamils, providing them with land and access to education and healthcare facilities. In contrast, other communities like the Rohingya from Myanmar (Mitra, 2024) or ethnic Chakma refugees have not had similar recognition (Saha, 1999). Official classifications usually only recognise Tibetans (Bloch, 2023) and Sri Lankan Tamils as "refugees", with everyone else being considered as illegal immigrants (Goreau-Ponceaud, 2024). This unequal recognition has resulted in a hierarchy of protection on the basis of nationality and political expediency. Critical health and welfare matters are dealt with, if at all, by executive discretion, judicial orders or state-level practices. Without a unified statutory framework, there is inconsistency in entitlements. A refugee's access to healthcare may be dependent upon the state of residence or the interpretation of local officials and not based on any standard national guarantee. This delegated and fragmenting system undercuts accountability and maintains uncertainty.

India's desires to bring digital tools into the governance of healthcare also have to reckon with established inequalities in the digital and infrastructural realms. The vision of "phygital" health integration, coupling digital platforms with physical healthcare services, is limited by socio-economic disparities. Internet connectivity is still patchy where only around a quarter of rural households have internet access compared with around two-thirds in urban areas. Limited connectivity and poor digital literacy limit access to telemedicine platforms, online health portals, and electronic medical records. Many rural clinics do not have reliable electricity, broadband or computing infrastructure, limiting the reach of digital health initiatives.

Healthcare infrastructure itself is unevenly distributed. Rural areas still suffer from a lack of doctors, diagnostic laboratories, and hospital facilities, and urban centres are relatively better equipped. Refugees and other vulnerable groups often live in impoverished urban settings or in rural areas where infrastructure gaps are pronounced. Placing digital health applications in the hands of people who lack smartphones, stable connectivity, or digital literacy is of little practical use. Over-reliance on digital platforms runs the risk of exacerbating existing inequities. While efforts are being made by government programmes to increase coverage of broadband and digital literacy, progress is slow. Until connectivity, infrastructure and user capacity are strengthened, digital health integration may inadvertently deepen disparities in access and outcomes.

Germany operates within a comprehensive system of asylum but is facing different kinds of fiscal and political pressures. The refugee flood in 2015-2016, with more than one million asylum seekers held, put the German humanitarian commitment to the test. Much public expenditure was orientated toward programmes of emergency housing, healthcare and integration. Later arrivals, such as more than one million Ukrainian refugees in 2022, caused further fiscal pressures. By late 2023, in the face of economic slowdown and rising budgetary pressures, the federal government announced its intention to slash financial transfers to states for refugee support from EUR 3.75 billion in 2023 down to around EUR 1.25 billion per year thereafter (Robelski et al., 2020).

State governments warned that housing, education and healthcare services were already strained and that lowered federal contributions could doom refugee programmes. The protests indicated fiscal fatigue among layers of the public and increasing political polarisation around refugee policy. The initial *Willkommenskultur* gave way to more scepticism in regard to integration and security (Windel et al., 2020). The Alternative für Deutschland (AfD) was able to feed on these fears, joining the Bundestag in 2017 as the third-largest party on an anti-immigration platform. Political debates became so polarised that asylum regulations were tightened, for example, by temporarily suspending family reunion for some refugees and expanding the list of designated "safe" countries to speed up deportations (Mast & Šuber, 2024).

The Asylum Seekers' Benefits Act also became a politically contested issue. In 2012, Germany's Federal Constitutional Court held that minimal asylum benefits violated the principle of human dignity, confirming that dignity cannot be subordinated to migration policy considerations. The judgement ordered a rise in the level of support for asylum seekers. Nevertheless, political pressures for cost containment persist and represent a tension between constitutional commitments and fiscal constraint ("Judgment of the Federal Constitutional Court in the Proceeding 1 BvL 10/10," 2012).

Germany's federal structure compounds refugee health governance. While the federal government is responsible for legislation on asylum and immigration policy, the implementation of housing, welfare, and medical services falls to the Landers and municipalities. This division causes periodic friction, especially in times of surges in arrivals (Berg, 2025). States complain the federal transfers are not sufficient to cover local costs. Differences in political leadership from state to state lead to differences in administration.

Access to healthcare services varies from state to state for asylum seekers. As a result of a reform in 2014, electronic health insurance cards for asylum candidates, for example, have been introduced in the states of Berlin and Bremen to make direct access to physicians easier (Wenner et al., 2022). Other states kept the voucher system with pre-approval from welfare offices for medical consultations. The voucher mechanism can cause delays in care and place administrative burdens. As a result, access conditions differ by location, leaving invisible inequalities similar to a postcode lottery. Efforts to harmonise practices have been resisted because of state autonomy in administrative matters. Major policy adjustments demand negotiations between the federal government and sixteen Lander, which slows nationwide implementation of reforms.

Despite the different contexts, issues of privacy literacy and grievance redress are the common thread for India and Germany in their digital health governance systems. Both countries are rapidly depending on digitised health records and data-sharing systems. In India, there is not much awareness about data privacy, despite the recognition of it as a fundamental right by the judiciary. The waves of data protection legislation have not converted into a mass understanding of digital rights. Many patients are unaware of the potential uses of their health data, and they lack trust in digital platforms.

In Germany, while generally refugees have more access to digital devices, many have fears of surveillance and misuse of personal information. Studies have shown that asylum seekers tend to avoid using some digital tools for fear of being monitored by the state or non-state actors. Such distrust can constrain engagement with beneficial digital health services from mental health applications or pandemic tracing contacts. Strengthening digital and privacy literacy through multilingual outreach and concrete safeguards is therefore needed in both countries.

Grievance redress mechanisms for refugees are still limited. While citizens may approach consumer forums, ombuds institutions, or courts, refugees are often unaware, lack legal status, or have inadequate knowledge of the language necessary to seek remedies. In India, refugees who have been denied treatment or charged excessive fees have no committed authority to handle complaints. In Germany, refugees are required to go through general administrative or judicial systems to challenge unwarranted denial of benefits or misuse of data (Palmiotto, 2023). Civil society litigation against unlawful mass extraction of the mobile phone data of asylum seekers is indicative of reliance on lengthy legal procedures. The lack of available refugee-specific grievance channels leaves many reliant on official discretion and protracted court proceedings, exposing structural gaps in accountability in both systems.

POLICY & LEGAL RECOMMENDATIONS

India does not have a specific law dealing with refugees and has, therefore, a need for the development of a Refugee Health Protection Framework (Debbarma, 2024). As India does not sign the 1951 Refugee Convention, protection for refugees developed on an ad hoc basis under general laws, such as the Foreigners Act. There is no codified statutory guarantee of healthcare or other related rights for refugees. Establishing a formal framework would make it clear that refugees, as non-citizens, have the right to preventive and curative healthcare without discrimination. Such legislation would make constitutional principles work. Article 21 of the Indian Constitution provides for the right to life and personal liberty, and Article 14 provides for equality before the law of all persons, including foreigners. Codifying refugee health rights through legislation would offer consistency and transparency. Whether the Afghan in Delhi or the Rohingya in Jammu, every refugee would be familiar with the extent of his/her entitlements and services available.

The framework could counterfeit to international standards for example the WHO Global Action Plan on Refugee and Migrant Health. The experience of Germany provides a practical illustration. Section 4 of the Asylum Seekers' Benefits Act of Germany explicitly ensures basic medical treatment and additional support for vulnerable individuals (Annual Policy Report by the German National Contact Point for the European Migration Network (EMN), 2016). An Indian framework would be able to similarly list services like emergency, immunisation, maternal and mental health, as well as chronic diseases. Legal clarity would give healthcare institutions the power to treat refugees consistently, thus eliminating the current uncertainty that is leading to uneven access. In the long term, integration of refugees in the public health schemes would reinforce the targets of universal health coverage and the inclusive agenda of development in India. A well-defined statutory policy would also improve international cooperation because global partners are more willing to support countries with transparent national frameworks. Codification would make reliance less on sporadic intervention by the judiciary. The Supreme Court has already held that foreigners have the right of protection as per Article 21. A legislative act would embody in structured policy the principles established by the courts instead of allowing executive discretion.

Prof. Sneha supports the proposal for a Refugee Health Protection Framework in India, arguing that codification would transform judicial principles into enforceable entitlements. She recommends a tiered legislative approach: primary legislation defining rights and non-discrimination guarantees, supplemented by delegated rules specifying enrolment procedures, benefit packages, and oversight mechanisms. She also advocates integration of refugees into national insurance pools with international co-financing models to ensure fiscal sustainability. From a digital governance perspective, she emphasises embedding privacy-by-design standards, audit mechanisms, and explicit consent architecture within refugee health programmes. She concludes that inclusive reform must align law, financing, and technology under a rights-based framework. Without such integration, policy innovation risks remaining fragmented and uneven in impact.

However, even an effective primary law requires detailed delegated legislation to ensure its effective implementation. Secondary rules and regulations should explicitly prescribe procedures, record-keeping requirements and standards for service delivery. In the Indian federal structure, clear central guidelines are necessary to avoid inconsistent application across states. Without the rules being set out in detail, implementation could be very different across different areas, creating a "postcode lottery" of entitlements. For instance, when the government makes refugees eligible for any government insurance schemes, then rules have to define the enrolment procedures, acceptable documentation, benefit packages, and grievance procedures. Ambiguity in these matters is attractive to a bureaucratic arbitrariness.

The experience of Germany shows this is a difficult challenge. Despite a national regulation, differences emerged between the German states in terms of accessing healthcare for asylum seekers. Some introduced electronic health insurance cards, and others retained voucher systems with prior approval required (Gottlieb et al., 2019). This divergence made it important for the presence of clear administrative directives. India could empower a nodal agency like the Ministry of Health or NITI Aayog to issue uniform guidelines, monitor its compliance and periodically revise the rules of implementation. Strong delegated legislation lessens court burdens by resolving what disputes one can foresee at the regulatory level. It gives frontline administrators a clear working framework, taking the legislative intent and turning it into consistent practice, and ensuring refugees get timely care without procedural wrangling.

Financing refugee healthcare requires economic sustainability. Establishing refugee risk pools can spread costs in an efficient manner and avoid undue pressure on host systems. Risk pooling involves spreading healthcare costs across a group of people, rather than having them pay for coverage. The integration of refugees into existing national insurance schemes is a practical approach. For example, Azerbaijan amended its laws to bring refugees under mandatory health insurance systems free of charge (Bakunina et al., 2020). India could extend schemes such as Ayushman Bharat or Employees' State Insurance to recognised refugees with premiums subsidised through government and international contributions (Spiegel et al., 2018).

Inclusion in the national risk pools promotes solidarity and efficiency. Many refugees are young and economically active, which means that their participation can help shore up the insurance base. A blended financing model might involve low contributions from the employed refugees and full subsidies for the most vulnerable. Studies show that the larger the participation, the more resilient the risk pools become and can sustain targeted subsidies. International burden-sharing mechanisms further enhance sustainability. Funds presently spent by UNHCR and donor agencies on parallel healthcare programmes could be incorporated into the national systems, reducing duplication and administrative fragmentation.

Regional sharing of risk provides other options. A South Asian refugee health fund, modelled on disaster insurance pools, could distribute resources when there are major influxes. Germany's enrolment of asylum seekers into the country's statutory health insurance after a waiting period proves the efficiency of the long-term implementation of this model. Evidence indicates that early access to primary care reduces the cost of expensive complications and does not dramatically raise overall costs (Gottlieb et al., 2019). For India, actuarial analysis and pilot projects in association with insurers and international experts would be imperative. A well-designed risk pool shifts refugee health from the sphere of emergency expenditure to that of structured national financing underpinned by domestic resources and international solidarity.

International co-financing partnerships are also strengthening this approach and capturing the spirit of Sustainable Development Goal 17. Refugee health cannot be carried by the host countries alone; there is a need for collective responsibility. The Global Compact on Refugees explicitly promotes burden-sharing and resource mobilisation. Partnerships could include grants, concessional loans, technical support, or private sector contributions. Germany's international contributions to health demonstrate this principle. In 2023, Germany contributed more than EUR 50 million to the humanitarian health programmes of WHO to support vulnerable people worldwide (Germany: Partner in Global Health, 2025).

India could similarly work with institutions like the World Bank and UNHCR for co-financing of refugee health. International support may be directed at funding vaccination campaigns, tuberculosis and HIV programmes, and infrastructure expansion of refugee hosting areas. Joint initiatives could involve training healthcare workers in trauma-informed care and multilingual communication. Private-sector participation via corporate social responsibility or impact investment could be used to supplement the public funds. Pharmaceutical companies can donate medicines or equipment in the framework of structured partnerships. Transparent coordination frameworks would ensure accountability and avoid duplication. Regular reporting on refugee health outcomes would boost donor confidence and measure impact. Co-financing partnerships not only take off fiscal burdens, but they also build institutional capacity and innovation.

Digital solutions offer extra possibilities for enhancing refugee health governance. Interoperability guarantees that health information systems can communicate between or across institutions and borders (Cascini, 2025). Refugees tend to travel between locations, and portable health records are essential. India's National Digital Health Mission has the potential to integrate refugees into digital health identification systems with the secure storage and sharing of medical histories with consent. European implementation, like the European Health Data Space, focuses on cross-border compatibility, which offers important lessons for international cooperation.

Alongside interoperability, audit trails are critical to trust and accountability. Audit trails keep track of who accessed whom, when and why they accessed health data. This transparency is of enormous importance to vulnerable groups who are worried about data misuse. Under NDH, the recommendations are to provide individuals with access to logs of data (RESPONSE TO THE INVITATION FOR PUBLIC COMMENT NATIONAL DIGITAL HEALTH BLUEPRINT, 2019). Implementing such mechanisms would give refugees a better means to track how their information is being used. Audit systems also discourage abuse by providing accountability among officials and healthcare providers.

Germany's electronic health insurance card for asylum seekers serves as a prime example of the advantages of digital systems. Replacing paper vouchers increased transparency in billing and tracking services while reducing fraud. Interoperability with auditing could one day facilitate safe transfer of refugee health records between countries at the time of resettlement or return. Achieving this objective requires global standards like Fast Healthcare Interoperability Resources (FHIR), as well as formal agreements between nations. Investment in connectivity and staff training in refugee settlements is also critical. These measures encourage continuity of care, especially for long-term monitoring of chronic conditions.

Privacy protections remain a key part of any digital or policy intervention. Refugees often come from environments where they were persecuted, and if their data are not handled sensitively, they or their family could be exposed to harm. Data minimisation principles dictate that only information needed for delivery of healthcare is collected. Health data must be subject to strict legal control. The European Union's General Data Protection Regulation sets a standard, with explicit consent and data rights for individuals. India's Digital Personal Data Protection Act provides a new and potential framework for extending protection to refugees irrespective of their citizenship status.

A secure storage, encryption, and access controls must be put into place with digital integration. Data-sharing agreements between NGOs and government hospitals should prohibit non-health uses of information on refugees. Safeguards that prevent disclosure of personal details to the authorities in the countries of origin of refugees. Privacy-by-design techniques like anonymous reporting for disease surveillance enable public health monitoring without infringing on individual privacy. Strong legal penalties for a breach reinforce compliance.

Embedding privacy in refugee health policy helps build trust and support service use. Refugees are more likely to access treatment and communicate accurate medical information when they know they will not be discriminated against or threatened with reprisal. Legal and technological safeguards combined to ensure that humanitarian assistance does not compromise dignity or safety.

CONCLUSION

The manner in which such a society handles the health of the refugees is a telling measurement of the society's leadership in health reform and equity. Fulfilling the pledge of the Sustainable Development Goals to "leave no one behind" means no one is left, including refugees and migrants, to have their health needs met. Refugee health challenges stimulate governments to integrate humanitarian commitments into policy and action. In India, the absence of a formal asylum law has meant that some 250,000 refugees are managed under ad hoc measures, and many are left in poverty with limited access to quality health. This policy gap became highly apparent during times of crises such as the pandemic of Covid-19, where the ambiguous legal status of refugees meant that they struggled to receive the most basic of medical care and relief. In contrast, Germany's health system operates within a clearly defined legal framework for asylum seekers, yet it also puts leadership to the test. The Asylum Seekers' Benefits Act only provides limited care (for acute illness, pregnancy, etc.) to asylum seekers during the first 18 months in the country. Faced with a huge influx of refugees, German authorities had to find innovative ways to work within this system: some areas offered electronic health insurance cards to asylum seekers to facilitate access to services, while others continued with burdensome voucher systems. These choices created a kerfuffle over equity or cost. This case study illustrates the extent of refugee health policy as a litmus test of a country's commitment to inclusive health reform. Bold leadership is needed so refugees are not left at the margins but are integrated into health systems as a matter of human rights and social responsibility. Successful reform leadership is characterised by a willingness to extend health protection to those with the least voice. Refugee health is therefore a testing ground for health system inclusiveness more generally.

A comparison of the approaches in India and Germany yields important insights on health reform dynamics and how these have wider implications. Despite profound differences in the health system capacity and economic resources, both countries face the same challenge of ensuring vulnerable populations are not left out. The well-funded system in Germany ensures near-universal coverage. Yet the exclusion of asylum seekers from full benefits initially points to a struggle between resource constraints and the principle of equity. India, on the other hand, has engaged in ambitious reforms to increase coverage for its citizens, like the Ayushman Bharat scheme and a National Digital Health Mission envisaged in its 2017 National Health Policy, but is still grappling with infrastructural gaps and low public health spending. Notably, in India there is no refugee policy, and therefore refugee healthcare relies on ad hoc arrangements, rather than guaranteed rights. The implication is that policy frameworks have an impactful effect on health outcomes. Inclusive legislation and sufficient investment can provide protection for marginalised groups, whereas policy vacuums or piecemeal approaches leave them vulnerable. At the same time, both countries are turning to digital innovation to close care gaps. Germany's Digital Healthcare Act, for instance, has enabled the prescription of health apps, whereas India's digital health mission aims to modernise healthcare delivery at scale. The comparative lesson is that leadership in health reform must be coupled with innovation and inclusion. In practice, this involves a combination of new technologies and policies with an unwavering commitment to equity so that improvements benefit all segments of society. Countries can also learn from each other's experiences. Germany may be able to learn from the population-based digital initiatives in India, as India can learn from the formal health protections for refugees and other patients in Germany. Such exchange aids in balancing trade-offs through efficiency, cost, and social justice in health policy.

Looking ahead, health reforms need to become more consistent with the ideals of the SDGs and achieve universal health coverage. In practice, this involves the use of both physical and digital strategies, which is basically a "phygital" approach to better healthcare delivery. The concept of phygital health involves integrating on-the-ground services with digital technologies to improve access and quality. For example, phygital models, which combine physical care with telehealth and digital applications, are championed by experts in India to address the urban-rural healthcare divide. Realising this vision by 2030 will require transformational leadership as well as supportive policy in both countries. India has put out a blueprint with initiatives such as the Ayushman Bharat Digital Mission with the aim of developing a national digital health ecosystem. However, technology alone will not be enough. It needs to be coupled with investments in health infrastructure and workforce capacity, particularly in underserved areas. Germany, with its strong institutions, is able to pilot models of integrated care to better serve ageing populations and migrant communities using digital innovations. Both countries must ensure that their digital health reform processes explicitly prioritise inclusivity, building the principle of "leave no one behind" into their design and implementation. These initiatives could involve efforts to tailor digital services to non-citizens and hard-to-reach groups, enhance multilingual platforms, and ensure data privacy and ethics. International frameworks like the WHO's Global Strategy on Digital Health outline guidance on scaling such innovations according to the global standard. Successful SDG-aligned health reforms in the coming years will most likely be characterised by an agile combination of e-health and traditional care, ensuring maximum reach. This will also require them to be guided by evidence-based policy and cross-sector collaboration. Medical professionals, technologists and policymakers need to collaborate in order to adapt to emerging challenges. By pledging to this phygital and inclusive way forward, countries such as India and Germany can show genuine reformist leadership. Such leadership would fortify their own health systems and, at the same time, be part of the global search for health equity and sustainable development.

REFERENCES

Adam, R. (2025). *Electronic Health Card (eGK): Information & frequently asked questions*. https://www.getnelly.de/en/blog/elektronische-gesundheitskarte-egk

Agrawal, S., Chauhan, G., Galhotra, A., & Goel, S. (2024). Five Years of National Health Policy in India: Critical Analysis of the Public Health Expenditure from 2017 to 2022 and Way Forward. *Indian Journal of Community Medicine : Official Publication of Indian Association of Preventive & Social Medicine*, *49*(6), 883–885. DOI: 10.4103/ijcm.ijcm_823_22 PMID: 39668924

Albnian, A., Alghathian, G. A., & Allouzi, A. (2025). Challenges of protecting electronic works in the era of artificial intelligence: A legal and doctrinal perspective. *Frontiers in Human Dynamics*, *7*, 1701267. Advance online publication. DOI: 10.3389/fhumd.2025.1701267

Angell, B., Prinja, S., Gupt, A., Jha, V., & Jan, S. (2019). The Ayushman Bharat Pradhan Mantri Jan Arogya Yojana and the path to universal health coverage in India: Overcoming the challenges of stewardship and governance. *PLoS Medicine*, *16*(3), e1002759. Advance online publication. DOI: 10.1371/journal.pmed.1002759 PMID: 30845199

Bakunina, N., Gil, A., Polushkin, V., Sergeev, B., Flores, M., Toskin, I., Madyanova, V., & Khalfin, R. (2020). Health of refugees and migrants from former Soviet Union countries in the Russian Federation: A narrative review. *International Journal for Equity in Health*, *19*(1), 180. Advance online publication. DOI: 10.1186/s12939-020-01279-0 PMID: 33050933

Berg, M. (2025). Refugee Integration in Germany: The Interplay of Othering, Digital Exclusion, and Identity Negotiation. *Journal of International Migration and Integration*, *26*(1), 235–254. DOI: 10.1007/s12134-025-01238-0

Birla, A. (2023). Evaluating the Indian Refugee Law Regime: How Has the Judiciary Responded to Refugee Claims in Light of International Law Obligations, and How Can It Do Better? *International Journal of Refugee Law*, *35*(1), 81–100. DOI: 10.1093/ijrl/eead013

Bloch, N. (2023). Boundary-Making and Political Activism in Protracted Exile: Second-Generation Tibetan Refugees in India. *Journal of Refugee Studies*, *38*(2), 340–356. DOI: 10.1093/jrs/fead013

Blümel, M., & Busse, R. (2020). International Health Care System Profiles - Germany. *The Commonwealth Fund*. https://www.commonwealthfund.org/international-health-policy-center/countries/germany

Bozorgmehr, K., & Razum, O. (2015). Effect of Restricting Access to Health Care on Health Expenditures among Asylum-Seekers and Refugees: A Quasi-Experimental Study in Germany, 1994–2013. *PLoS One, 10*(7), e0131483. Advance online publication. DOI: 10.1371/journal.pone.0131483 PMID: 26201017

Bukhari, A. (2025). Private Hospitals Suspend Services for India's Health Insurance Members, Leaving Millions Without Care. *Health Policy Watch*. https://healthpolicy-watch.news/private-hospitals-suspend-services-for-indias-health-insurance-members-leaving-millions-without-care

Cascini, F. (2025). Enabling Factors and Opportunities to Maximize Health Data Reuse. *SpringerBriefs in Public Health, 101*, 101–119. Advance online publication. DOI: 10.1007/978-3-031-88497-9_3

Choudhary, K. (2024). Which Method Should I Select for My Legal Research – Doctrinal, Empirical, Multi-Method or Something Else? *Teisė*, *132*, 135–144. DOI: 10.15388/Teise.2024.132.10

Coulter, L. (2024). Exploring the "Phygital" Future of Healthcare. *HCO News*. https://hconews.com/2024/11/29/exploring-the-phygital-future-of-healthcare/

Debbarma, M. (2024). Refugees Experience and the Host Communities: Critical Analyses on Absence of Refugee Law in India. *Journal of Asian and African Studies*, *60*(5), 3204–3218. DOI: 10.1177/00219096241228804

E-prescriptions new standard in Germany: CGM with positive interim assessment. (2024). *CompuGroup Medical*. https://www.cgm.com/corp_en/magazine/articles/press-releases/2024/e-rezept-neuer-standard-cgm-zieht-positive-zwischenbilanz.html

Faroqi, T., & Sundaram, J. R. (2022). Healthcare for refugees in India. *The Routledge Handbook of Refugees in India*, 842. DOI: 10.4324/9781003246800-77

Fehr, A. (2018). Health monitoring and health indicators in Europe. *PubMed, 2*(1), 3. DOI: 10.17886/rki-gbe-2017-020.2

Garg, S., Bebarta, K. K., & Tripathi, N. (2024). The Ayushman Bharat Pradhan Mantri Jan Arogya Yojana (AB-PMJAY) after four years of implementation – is it making an impact on quality of inpatient care and financial protection in India? *BMC Health Services Research*, *24*(1), 919. Advance online publication. DOI: 10.1186/s12913-024-11393-2 PMID: 39135015

Geffert, K., Voss, S., Rehfuess, E., & Rechel, B. (2024). The role of the public health service in the implementation of heat health action plans for climate change adaptation in Germany: A qualitative study. *Health Research Policy and Systems, 22*(1), 161. Advance online publication. DOI: 10.1186/s12961-024-01231-6 PMID: 39639289

German e-health offerings expand, but adoption remains uneven. (2022). *McKinsey & Company*. https://www.mckinsey.com/industries/life-sciences/our-insights/german-e-health-offerings-expand-but-adoption-remains-uneven#/

German Refugee Digitisation System. (2019). *European Commission*. https://ec.europa.eu/digital-building-blocks/sites/spaces/DIGITAL/blog/2019/07/31/533366012/German+Refugee+Digitisation+System

Germany - Health systems in transition. (2023). World Health Organization. https://eurohealthobservatory.who.int/countries/germany

Germany: Partner in global health. (2025). World Health Organization. https://www.who.int/about/funding/contributors/deu

Goreau-Ponceaud, A. (2024). Lives in exile? Perspectives on the resettlements of Sri Lankan refugees in Tamil Nadu, India. *World Development, 180*, 106629. DOI: 10.1016/j.worlddev.2024.106629

Gottlieb, N., Gold, A. W., Palla, I., Dimaku, I. C., Güell, B., Legarda Díaz-Aguado, I., & Bozorgmehr, K. (2024). Narrative change for inclusionary health and migration policies. *The Lancet Regional Health. Europe, 41*, 100835. DOI: 10.1016/j.lanepe.2024.100835 PMID: 39119100

Gottlieb, N., Ohm, V., & Knörnschild, M. (2019). A first assessment of the electronic health insurance card for asylum seekers in Berlin. *European Journal of Public Health, 29*(Supplement_4), ckz187.015. Advance online publication. DOI: 10.1093/eurpub/ckz187.015

Hou, L., An, N., Lin, V., & Lin, V. K. (2024). Can Digital Health Improve Healthcare Access for Migrants. *NAM Perspectives, 2024*. Advance online publication. DOI: 10.31478/202408b PMID: 39830819

Jahn, R., Rohleder, S., Qreini, M., Erdmann, S., Kaur, S., Aluttis, F., & Bozorgmehr, K. (2021). Health monitoring of refugees in reception centres for asylum seekers: Decentralized surveillance network for the analysis of routine medical data. *PubMed, 6*(1), 30. Judgment of the Federal Constitutional Court in the proceeding 1 BvL 10/10. (2012). *ESCR-Net – International Network for Economic, Social & Cultural Rights*. https://www.escr-net.org/caselaw/2012/judgment-federal-constitutional-court-proceeding-1-bvl-1010/DOI: 10.25646/7865

Kamath, R., & Brand, H. (2023). A Critical Analysis of the World'S Largest Publicly Funded Health Insurance Program: India's Ayushman Bharat. *International Journal of Preventive Medicine, 14*(1). Advance online publication. DOI: 10.4103/ijpvm.ijpvm_39_22 PMID: 37033284

Katrak, M. (2021). REFOULING ROHINGYAS: THE SUPREME COURT OF INDIA'S UNEASY ENGAGEMENT WITH INTERNATIONAL LAW. *Journal of Liberty and International Affairs Institute for Research and European Studies - Bitola, 7*(2), 116. DOI: 10.47305/JLIA2172011 6k

Kneuer, M., & Wallaschek, S. (2022). Framing COVID-19: Public Leadership and Crisis Communication By Chancellor Angela Merkel During the Pandemic in 2020. *German Politics, 32*(4), 686–709. DOI: 10.1080/09644008.2022.2028140

Kumar, R. S. K. (2024). Strict implementation of the right to health as a fundamental right: Ensuring universal access and equity in India. *Law and Safety, 93*(2), 151–162. DOI: 10.32631/pb.2024.2.14

Mast, J. L., & Šuber, D. (2024). Societalized Politics in the German Civil Sphere: The 2015 "Refugee Crisis" and Post-Potsdam Civil Backlash. *International Journal of Politics Culture and Society, 38*(2), 157–186. DOI: 10.1007/s10767-024-09490-5

Mathiharan, K. (2006). The fundamental right to health care. *PubMed, 11*(4), 123. https://pubmed.ncbi.nlm.nih.gov/16335519

McGuire, T. G., Schillo, S., & van Kleef, R. C. (2020). Very high and low residual spenders in private health insurance markets: Germany, The Netherlands and the U.S. Marketplaces. *The European Journal of Health Economics, 22*(1), 35–50. DOI: 10.1007/s10198-020-01227-3 PMID: 32862358

Migration, Integration, Asylum: Political Developments in Germany 2016. (2016). Federal Office for Migration and Refugees, Germany. https://www.bamf.de/SharedDocs/Anlagen/EN/EMN/Politikberichte/emn-politikbericht-2016-germany.pdf?__blob=publicationFile&v=7

Mishra, N., & Anand, R. (2025). *A Milestone in the Modernization of Indian Healthcare: How Digital Integration is Transforming the Country's Health System*. https://nextbillion.net/milestone-modernization-indian-healthcare-digital-integration-transforming-health-system/

Mitra, R. (2024). From the Translocal to the Multi-Sited Transnational: Tracing Rohingya Refugee Networks in India. *Global Networks, 25*(1), e12494. Advance online publication. DOI: 10.1111/glob.12494

Müller, T. R. (2021). Reshaping conceptions of citizenship? German Business sector engagement and refugee integration. *Citizenship Studies*, *25*(3), 409–425. DOI: 10.1080/13621025.2021.1873916

Naithani, P. (2024). Analysis of India's Digital Personal Data Protection Act, 2023. *International Journal of Law and Management*, *67*(5), 543–553. DOI: 10.1108/IJLMA-05-2024-0174

Naithani, P. (2025). Article: Strengthening Legitimate Use in India's Digital Personal Data Protection Act, 2023. *Global Privacy Law Review*, *6*(2), 61–65. DOI: 10.54648/GPLR2025011

Niedermaier, A., Freiberg, A., Tiller, D., Wienke, A., & Führer, A. (2020). Outpatient health care utilization and health expenditures of asylum seekers in Halle (Saale), Germany - an analysis of claims data. *BMC Health Services Research*, *20*(1), 961. DOI: 10.1186/s12913-020-05811-4 PMID: 33081775

Olabi, A., Palmer, N., Bertone, M. P., Loffreda, G., Bou-Orm, I. R., Sempé, L., Espinoza, M. V., Dakessian, A., Kadetz, P., Ager, A., & Witter, S. (2025). Refugee integration in national health systems of low- and middle-income countries (LMICs): Evidence synthesis and future research agenda. *Social Science & Medicine*, *385*, 118546. DOI: 10.1016/j.socscimed.2025.118546 PMID: 41061533

Palmiotto, F. (2023). „Like Handing My Whole Life Over". *Verfassungsblog: On Matters Constitutional*. DOI: 10.17176/20230228-185227-0

Refugee and migrant health at the centre of discussions during the 77th UN General Assembly. (2022). WHO. https://www.who.int/news/item/21-09-2022-refugee-and-migrant-health-at-the-centre-of-discussions-during-the-77th-un-general-assembly

Refugees and asylum. (2024). Federal Ministry of Labour and Social Affairs, Germany. https://www.bmas.de/EN/Europe-and-the-World/Europe/Migration-from-third-countries/refugees-and-asylum.html

RESPONSE TO THE INVITATION FOR PUBLIC COMMENT NATIONAL DIGITAL HEALTH BLUEPRINT. (2019). https://mittalsouthasiainstitute.harvard.edu/wp-content/uploads/2019/08/Response-to-the-Invitation-for-Public-Comment-National-Digital-Health-Blueprint.pdf

Riemer, L., Rau, L., & Schalast, R. (2025). *Asylum Database Information, Germany*. AIDA. https://asylumineurope.org/reports/country/germany/reception-conditions/health-care/

Robelski, S., Mette, J., Wirth, T., Kiepe, N., Nienhaus, A., Harth, V., & Mache, S. (2020). (Un)bounded Social Work?—Analysis of Working Conditions in Refugee and Homeless Aid in Relation to Perceived Job Stress and Job Satisfaction. *International Journal of Environmental Research and Public Health, 17*(2), 601. DOI: 10.3390/ijerph17020601 PMID: 31963446

Saha, K. C. (1999). The Chittagong Hill Tracts Peace Accord: A Landmark Model for a Viable Solution to the Refugee Problem. *Refuge: Canada's Journal on Refugees, 10*, 10–15. Advance online publication. DOI: 10.25071/1920-7336.22008

Sarthe, A. (2025). Over 600 Private Hospitals Exit AB-PMJAY; Gujarat Leads Opt-Outs. *DNA*. https://www.digitalhealthnews.com/over-600-private-hospitals-exit-ab-pmjay-gujarat-leads-opt-outs

Shanker, R., & Raghavan, P. (2020). The Invisible Crisis: Refugees and COVID-19 in India. *International Journal of Refugee Law, 32*(4), 680–684. DOI: 10.1093/ijrl/eeab011

D. Sharma, S. (2018). Health Care for India's 500 Million: The Promise of the National Health Protection Scheme. *HPHR Journal, 18*. DOI: 10.54111/0001/R1

Sneha, M. (2024). Advances in Finance, Accounting, and Economics: Vol. 399. *A., Chatterjee, S., & Rout, P. C.* Can Medical AI Bridge the Gender Gap for Sustainable Healthcare., DOI: 10.4018/979-8-3693-7580-8.ch017

Sood, S., Lal, K., Bhatia, M., Kapoor, G., Singh, S., Kaushish, R. K., Bisht, D., Sharma, V. K., Chakraborty, S., Shete, M., Solanki, N. K., Naskar, A., Sharma, M., Subramaniyan, E. U., Waikar, S., & Verma, N. (2025). Adoption and utilization of India's eSanjeevani national telemedicine service. *Oxford Open Digital Health, 3*, oqaf025. Advance online publication. DOI: 10.1093/oodh/oqaf025 PMID: 41158553

Spiegel, P., Chanis, R., & Trujillo, A. (2018). Innovative health financing for refugees. *BMC Medicine, 16*(1), 90. Advance online publication. DOI: 10.1186/s12916-018-1068-9 PMID: 29903046

Stafford, N. (2016). Voices unite to demand free healthcare for refugees in Germany. *BMJ (Clinical Research Ed.), 352*, i884. Advance online publication. DOI: 10.1136/bmj.i884 PMID: 26867757

State of Health in the EU, Germany - Country Health Profile 2023. (2023). European Union. https://health.ec.europa.eu/system/files/2023-12/2023_chp_de_english.pdf

Steinbrink, E., Reichert, L., Mende, M., & Reuter, C. (2021). Digital Privacy Perceptions of Asylum Seekers in Germany: An Empirical Study about Smartphone Usage during the Flight. *Proceedings of the ACM on Human-Computer Interaction*, *5*(CSCW2), 1–24. DOI: 10.1145/3479526

Susanto, S. R. (2020). Germany's Strategy in Handling COVID-19: The Role of National Leadership Strength and The Maximization of Welfare State Continental System Support. *Jurnal Global &amp. Strategis*, *14*(2), 403. DOI: 10.20473/jgs.14.2.2020.403-420

The electronic medical data card (eGK). (2025). *Bundesministerium Für Gesundheit*. https://gesund.bund.de/en/the-electronic-medical-data-card

Tiwari, G. (2024). Promoting Effective Refugee Protection in India: Balancing National Interests and International Obligations. *Athens Journal of Law*, *10*(2), 221–232. DOI: 10.30958/ajl.10-2-3

Towards Universal Healthcare: Ayushman Bharat Pradhan Mantri-Jan Arogya Yojana. (2025). Govt. of India. https://www.pib.gov.in/PressNoteDetails.aspx?NoteId=155855&ModuleId=3&reg=3&lang=2

Vijayaraghavan, H. (2020). Gaps in India's Treatment of Refugees and Vulnerable Internal Migrants Are Exposed by the Pandemic. *Migration Policy Institute*. https://www.migrationpolicy.org/article/gaps-india-refugees-vulnerable-internal-migrants-pandemic

Wenner, J., Biddle, L., Gottlieb, N., & Bozorgmehr, K. (2022). Inequalities in access to healthcare by local policy model among newly arrived refugees: Evidence from population-based studies in two German states. *International Journal for Equity in Health*, *21*(1), 11. Advance online publication. DOI: 10.1186/s12939-021-01607-y PMID: 35073919

Windel, F., Balaram, A., & Perkins, K. M. (2020). Discourses of the Willkommenskultur (Welcoming culture) in Germany. *Critical Discourse Studies*, *19*(1), 93–116. DOI: 10.1080/17405904.2020.1839921

Ziegler, S., & Bozorgmehr, K. (2024). Translating restrictive law into practice: An ethnographic exploration of the systemic processing of legally restricted health care access for asylum seekers in Germany. *International Journal for Equity in Health*, *23*(1), 208. DOI: 10.1186/s12939-024-02251-y PMID: 39390515

ADDITIONAL READINGS

Bjerneld, M., Ismail, N., & Puthoopparambil, S. J. (2018). Experiences and reflections of Somali unaccompanied girls on their first years in Sweden: A follow-up study after two decades. *International Journal of Migration, Health and Social Care*, *14*(3), 305–317. DOI: 10.1108/IJMHSC-03-2018-0018 PMID: 30333858

Corona Maioli, S., & Burgess, R. A. (2025). Protecting unaccompanied migrant youth in transit through Mexico: Frontline perspectives on appropriate policy implementation. *Health Policy and Planning*, *40*(7), 719–726. DOI: 10.1093/heapol/czaf037 PMID: 40468994

Davitian, K., Noack, P., Eckstein, K., Hübner, J., & Ahmadi, E. (2024). Barriers of Ukrainian refugees and migrants in accessing German healthcare. *BMC Health Services Research*, *24*(1), 1112. Advance online publication. DOI: 10.1186/s12913-024-11592-x PMID: 39317924

Forcier, M. B., Gallois, H., Mullan, S., & Joly, Y. (2019). Integrating artificial intelligence into health care through data access: Can the GDPR act as a beacon for policymakers? *Journal of Law and the Biosciences*, *6*(1), 317–335. DOI: 10.1093/jlb/lsz013 PMID: 31666972

Müllerschön, J., Koschollek, C., Santos-Hövener, C., Kuehne, A., Müller-Nordhorn, J., & Bremer, V. (2019). Impact of health insurance status among migrants from sub-Saharan Africa on access to health care and HIV testing in Germany: A participatory cross-sectional survey. *BMC International Health and Human Rights*, *19*(1), 10. Advance online publication. DOI: 10.1186/s12914-019-0189-3 PMID: 30832665

Pelters, P., Lindgren, E.-C., Kostenius, C., Lydell, M., & Hertting, K. (2021). Health-related integration interventions for migrants by civil society organizations: An integrative review. *International Journal of Qualitative Studies on Health and Well-being*, *16*(1), 1927488. Advance online publication. DOI: 10.1080/17482631.2021.1927488 PMID: 34053417

Peprah, P., Lloyd, J., & Harris, M. (2024). Responding to health literacy of refugees in Australian primary health care settings: A qualitative study of barriers and potential solutions. *BMC Health Services Research*, *24*(1), 757. Advance online publication. DOI: 10.1186/s12913-024-11192-9 PMID: 38907354

KEY TERMS AND DEFINITIONS

Comparative Health Law: Comparative health law is the analytical study of how different legal systems regulate healthcare access, financing, and rights, with the aim of identifying similarities, divergences, and reform lessons across jurisdictions.

Data Protection: Data protection involves the legal and technical safeguards designed to ensure the privacy, security, and lawful processing of personal and sensitive health information.

Digital Health Governance: Digital health governance encompasses the legal, regulatory, ethical, and institutional frameworks that oversee the use, management, and protection of digital health technologies and data within healthcare systems.

Health Financing: Health financing refers to the mechanisms through which funds are raised, pooled, and allocated to ensure equitable access to healthcare services while protecting individuals from catastrophic expenditure.

India–Germany Comparison: India–Germany comparison refers to the structured analytical contrast between two distinct health systems to evaluate how economic capacity, legal frameworks, and governance approaches influence refugee health integration.

Leadership in Health Reform: Leadership in health reform signifies the strategic direction, political will, and institutional coordination exercised by decision-makers to design, implement, and sustain equitable healthcare policies.

Phygital Healthcare: Phygital healthcare denotes the integrated delivery of health services through a hybrid model that combines physical clinical care with digital technologies such as telemedicine, electronic health records, and mobile health platforms.

Refugee Health: Refugee health refers to the physical, mental, and social well-being of displaced persons, shaped by legal status, access to healthcare systems, and the socio-economic conditions of host countries.

Compilation of References

Abbasi, N., & Smith, D. A. (2024). Cybersecurity in Healthcare: Securing Patient Health Information (PHI), HIPPA compliance framework and the responsibilities of healthcare providers. *Journal of Knowledge Learning and Science Technology ISSN: 2959-6386 (Online), 3*(3), 278–287.

Abdulwahab, L. O., Daniel, O., Gul, A., & Bubari, H. U. (2026). The Economic Impact of Digital Health Innovations on Disease Prevention: Cost-Effectiveness, ROI, and Policy Implications. In *Reshaping Health Promotion and Disease Prevention Through Digital Innovation* (pp. 29–56). IGI Global Scientific Publishing. DOI: 10.4018/979-8-3373-3531-5.ch002

Abdulwahab, L. O., Daniel, O., Halabi, K. A., & Umar, H. B. (2026). Healthcare Entrepreneurship and Global Talent: Navigating Visa Barriers, Health Innovation, and Startup Survival as an International Graduate. In *International Student Narratives in Globalized Higher Education* (pp. 401–434). IGI Global Scientific Publishing. https://www.igi-global.com/chapter/healthcare-entrepreneurship-and-global-talent/400509

Abubakari, M. S., & Olamilekan, L. A. (2026). Digital Competency's Role in Promoting Equity in the Digital Healthcare Ecosystem: An Overview. *Reshaping Health Promotion and Disease Prevention Through Digital Innovation*, 129–152.

Ackerknecht, E. H. (1957). Medical education in 19th century France. *Academic Medicine, 32*(2), 148–153. PMID: 13398763

Acts of the Ministry of Labor, Health and Social Protection of Georgia. (2014). Matsne Press. Source: https://matsne.gov.ge

Adam, R. (2025). *Electronic Health Card (eGK): Information & frequently asked questions*. https://www.getnelly.de/en/blog/elektronische-gesundheitskarte-egk

Adegoke, K., Adegoke, A., Dawodu, D., Bayowa, A., & Adekoya, A. (2025). Interoperability in digital healthcare: Enhancing consumer health and transforming care systems.

Adusumalli, S., Aragam, G. G., & Patel, M. S. (2020). A Nudge Towards Cardiovascular Health: Applications of Behavioral Economics for Primary and Secondary Cardiovascular Prevention. *Current Treatment Options in Cardiovascular Medicine*, *22*(9), 1–17. DOI: 10.1007/s11936-020-00824-y

Agarwal, R., Bjarnadottir, M., Rhue, L., Dugas, M., Crowley, K., Clark, J., & Gao, G. (2023). Addressing algorithmic bias and the perpetuation of health inequities: An AI bias aware framework. *Health Policy and Technology*, *12*(1), 100702. DOI: 10.1016/j.hlpt.2022.100702

Agarwal, R., Gupta, A., & Fendrick, A. M. (2018). Value-Based Insurance Design Improves Medication Adherence Without An Increase In Total Health Care Spending. *Health Affairs*, *37*(7), 1057–1064. DOI: 10.1377/hlthaff.2017.1633 PMID: 29985690

Agrawal, S., Chauhan, G., Galhotra, A., & Goel, S. (2024). Five Years of National Health Policy in India: Critical Analysis of the Public Health Expenditure from 2017 to 2022 and Way Forward. *Indian Journal of Community Medicine : Official Publication of Indian Association of Preventive & Social Medicine*, *49*(6), 883–885. DOI: 10.4103/ijcm.ijcm_823_22 PMID: 39668924

Aguilar-Gaxiola, S., Loera, G., Méndez, L., Sala, M., & Kopelowicz, A. (2011). Community-defined solutions for Latino mental-health care disparities: A community-based participatory-research project. *American Journal of Public Health*, *101*(12), 2255–2263. DOI: 10.2105/AJPH.2010.192021

Ahn, H., & Park, E. (2022). Determinants of consumer acceptance of mobile healthcare devices: An application of the concepts of technology acceptance and coolness. *Telematics and Informatics*, *70*, 101810. DOI: 10.1016/j.tele.2022.101810

Ajzen, I. (2015). *Belief, Attitude, Intention and Behaviour: An Introduction to Theory and Research*. Addison-Wesley.

Ajzen, I., & Fishbein, M. (1977). Attitude-Behavior Relations: A Theoretical Analysis and Review of Empirical Research. *Psychological Bulletin*, *84*(5), 888–918. DOI: 10.1037/0033-2909.84.5.888

Al Dahdah, M., & Mishra, R. K. (2023). Digital health for all: The turn to digitized Healthcare in India. *Social Science & Medicine*, *319*, 114968. DOI: 10.1016/j.socscimed.2022.114968 PMID: 35459554

Albalawi, A. F., Yassen, M. H., Almuraydhi, K. M., Althobaiti, A. D., Alzahrani, H., & Alqahtani, K. M. (2024). *Ethical Obligations and Patient Consent in the Integration of Artificial Intelligence in Clinical Decision-Making*. JOURNAL OF HEALTHCARE SCIENCES., DOI: 10.52533/JOHS.2024.41241

Albarari, S. S. A., & Phagava, H. (2025). Georgia's healthcare system: A journey of reform, investment and progress. *International Journal of Health Governance*, •••, 1–13.

Albnian, A., Alghathian, G. A., & Allouzi, A. (2025). Challenges of protecting electronic works in the era of artificial intelligence: A legal and doctrinal perspective. *Frontiers in Human Dynamics*, *7*, 1701267. Advance online publication. DOI: 10.3389/fhumd.2025.1701267

Alford-Teaster, J. A., Wang, F., Moen, E. L., Cowan, L., Smith, R. E., Tosteson, A., & Onega, T. (2023). *Broadband Data Forensics: Spatiotemporal Variations of the Download/Upload Speed Metric Commonly Used to Evaluate Potential Telehealth Accessibility. Telemedicine Journal and E-Health*. The Official Journal of the American Telemedicine Association., DOI: 10.1089/tmj.2023.0320

Alrebh, A. H., Aljadher, A. M., Alghaith, B., Baothman, M. S., Al-Shaban, W. R., & Tufaif, T. A. A. (2024). *Ethical Considerations in Telemedicine and Remote Patient Care*. JOURNAL OF HEALTHCARE SCIENCES., DOI: 10.52533/JOHS.2024.41233

Amin, K. (2019). Impact of Out-of-Network Service Utilization and State Policy Changes on Payments and Follow-Up Visits.

Anastasiadou, O., Tsipouras, M., Mpogiatzidis, P., & Angelidis, P. (2025, April). Digital Healthcare Innovative Services in Times of Crisis: A Literature Review. []. MDPI.]. *Health Care*, *13*(8), 889. PMID: 40281838

Anderson, M., Pitchforth, E., Edwards, N., Alderwick, H., McGuire, A., & Mossialos, E. (2022). United Kingdom: Health System Review. *Health Systems in Transition*, *24*(1), 1–194. PMID: 35579557

Angell, B., Prinja, S., Gupt, A., Jha, V., & Jan, S. (2019). The Ayushman Bharat Pradhan Mantri Jan Arogya Yojana and the path to universal health coverage in India: Overcoming the challenges of stewardship and governance. *PLoS Medicine*, *16*(3), e1002759. Advance online publication. DOI: 10.1371/journal.pmed.1002759 PMID: 30845199

Armstrong, S. M., & Lamm, S. L. (2024). The Changing Healthcare Environment. Clinical Laboratory Management, 67–91.

Arrow, K. J. (1963). Uncertainty and the welfare economics of medical care. *The American Economic Review, 53*(5), 941–973. https://www.jstor.org/stable/1812044

Arrow, K., Auerbach, A., Bertko, J., Brownlee, S., Casalino, L. P., Cooper, J., Crosson, F. J., Enthoven, A., Falcone, E., Feldman, R. C., Fuchs, V. R., Garber, A. M., Gold, M. R., Goldman, D., Hadfield, G. K., Hall, M. A., Horwitz, R. I., Hooven, M., Jacobson, P. D., & Van De Ven, W. P. (2009). Toward a 21st-century health care system: Recommendations for health care reform. *Annals of Internal Medicine, 150*(7), 493–495. DOI: 10.7326/0003-4819-150-7-200904070-00115 PMID: 19258550

Arts, J. W., Frambach, R. T., & Bijmolt, T. H. (2011). Generalizations on consumer innovation adoption: A meta-analysis on drivers of intention and behavior. *International Journal of Research in Marketing, 28*(2), 134–144. DOI: 10.1016/j.ijresmar.2010.11.002

Ashimi, T. A. (2018). The contribution of Muslim scholars to the field of medicine (with particular reference to Ibn Sina and Al-Razi during the Islamic Golden Age). *Journal of Education and Social Sciences, 9*(3), 73–77.

Asthana, S., & Prime, S. (2023). The role of digital transformation in addressing health inequalities in coastal communities: Barriers and enablers. *Frontiers in Health Services, 3*, 1225757. Advance online publication. DOI: 10.3389/frhs.2023.1225757 PMID: 37711604

Aytekin, A., Alan, H., Demirel, H., Onur, N., Yalman, A., Livberber, T., & Yiğit-Açıkgöz, F. (2025). Digital health technologies in patient experience literature: A scoping review and future outlook for sustainable digital health interventions. *Sustainability (Basel), 17*(2), 456. DOI: 10.3390/su17020456

Bachuk, O. (2024). *DIGITAL TRANSFORMATION IN THE HEALTH CARE SYSTEM. Odesa National University Herald*. Economy., DOI: 10.32782/2304-0920/3-101-6

Bajunaied, K., Hussin, N., & Kamarudin, S. (2023). Behavioral intention to adopt FinTech services: An extension of unified theory of acceptance and use of technology. *Journal of Open Innovation, 9*(1), 100010. DOI: 10.1016/j.joitmc.2023.100010

Bakunina, N., Gil, A., Polushkin, V., Sergeev, B., Flores, M., Toskin, I., Madyanova, V., & Khalfin, R. (2020). Health of refugees and migrants from former Soviet Union countries in the Russian Federation: A narrative review. *International Journal for Equity in Health, 19*(1), 180. Advance online publication. DOI: 10.1186/s12939-020-01279-0 PMID: 33050933

Balabanova, D., Roberts, B., Richardson, E., Haerpfer, C., & McKee, M. (2012). Health Care Reform in the former Soviet Union: Beyond the transition. *Health Services Research*, *47*(2), 840–864. DOI: 10.1111/j.1475-6773.2011.01323.x PMID: 22092004

Balak, D. M. W., Deprez, E., Hilhorst, N., Hoorens, I., Gutermuth, J., Bos, W. J. W., & Lambert, J. (2024). Value-Based Healthcare: A Primer for the Dermatologist. *Dermatology (Basel, Switzerland)*, *240*, 814–822. DOI: 10.1159/000539372 PMID: 38934138

Bandura, A. (1986). *Social foundations of thought and action: A social cognitive theory*. Prentice Hall. https://psycnet.apa.org/record/1985-98423-000

Barello, S., Graffigna, G., & Vegni, E. (2012). Patient engagement as an emerging challenge for healthcare services: Mapping the literature. *Nursing Research and Practice*, *2012*(1), 905934. DOI: 10.1155/2012/905934 PMID: 23213497

Barisevičius, G., Coste, M., Geleta, D., Juric, D., Khodadadi, M., Stoilos, G., & Zaihrayeu, I. (2018, September). Supporting digital healthcare services using semantic web technologies. In *International Semantic Web Conference* (pp. 291-306). Cham: Springer International Publishing. DOI: 10.1007/978-3-030-00668-6_18

Bass, B. M., & Riggio, R. E. (2006). *Transformational leadership* (2nd ed.). Lawrence Erlbaum Associates., https://www.taylorfrancis.com/books/mono/10.4324/9781410617095/transformational-leadership-bernard-bass-bruce-riggio DOI: 10.4324/9781410617095

Berardi, C., Antonini, M., Jordan, Z., Wechtler, H., Paolucci, F., & Hinwood, M. (2024). Barriers and facilitators to the implementation of digital technologies in mental health systems: A qualitative systematic review to inform a policy framework. *BMC Health Services Research*, *24*(1), 243. DOI: 10.1186/s12913-023-10536-1 PMID: 38408938

Berg, M. (2025). Refugee Integration in Germany: The Interplay of Othering, Digital Exclusion, and Identity Negotiation. *Journal of International Migration and Integration*, *26*(1), 235–254. DOI: 10.1007/s12134-025-01238-0

Beveridge, W. (2000). Social insurance and allied services. 1942. *Bulletin of the World Health Organization*, *78*(6), 847. PMID: 10916922

Beverid, W. (2000). Social insurance and allied services. *Bulletin of the World Health Organization*, *78*(6), 847–855. PMID: 10916922

Bhattacherjee, A. (2001). Understanding information systems continuance: An expectation-confirmation model. *Management Information Systems Quarterly*, *25*(3), 351–370. DOI: 10.2307/3250921

Bhugra, D. (2004). Migration and mental health. *Acta Psychiatrica Scandinavica*, *109*(4), 243–258. DOI: 10.1046/j.0001-690X.2003.00246.x PMID: 15008797

Birla, A. (2023). Evaluating the Indian Refugee Law Regime: How Has the Judiciary Responded to Refugee Claims in Light of International Law Obligations, and How Can It Do Better? *International Journal of Refugee Law*, *35*(1), 81–100. DOI: 10.1093/ijrl/eead013

Blake, H. A., Sharples, L. D., Harron, K., van der Meulen, J. H., & Walker, K. (2023). Linkage of multiple electronic health record datasets using a 'spine linkage ' approach compared with all 'pairwise linkages'. *International Journal of Epidemiology*, *52*(1), 214–226. DOI: 10.1093/ije/dyac130 PMID: 35748342

Blanke, B., & Perschke-Hartmann, C. (1994). The 1992 health reform victory over pressure group politics. *German Politics*, *3*(2), 233–248. DOI: 10.1080/09644009408404363

Bloch, N. (2023). Boundary-Making and Political Activism in Protracted Exile: Second-Generation Tibetan Refugees in India. *Journal of Refugee Studies*, *38*(2), 340–356. DOI: 10.1093/jrs/fead013

Blümel, M., & Busse, R. (2020). International Health Care System Profiles - Germany. *The Commonwealth Fund*. https://www.commonwealthfund.org/international-health-policy-center/countries/germany

Bocean, C., & Vărzaru, A. (2025). Health status in the era of digital transformation and sustainable economic development. *BMC Health Services Research*, *25*(1), 343. Advance online publication. DOI: 10.1186/s12913-025-12498-y PMID: 40045359

Bonati, I. (2019). The (un) healthy poor: Wealth, poverty, medicine and Health care in the Greco-Roman world. *Akroterion*, *2019*(64), 15–43.

Bozorgmehr, K., & Razum, O. (2015). Effect of Restricting Access to Health Care on Health Expenditures among Asylum-Seekers and Refugees: A Quasi-Experimental Study in Germany, 1994–2013. *PLoS One*, *10*(7), e0131483. Advance online publication. DOI: 10.1371/journal.pone.0131483 PMID: 26201017

Brandt-Rauf, P. W., & Brandt-Rauf, S. I. (1987). History of occupational medicine: Relevance of Imhotep and the Edwin Smith papyrus. *British Journal of Industrial Medicine*, *44*(1), 68–70. DOI: 10.1136/oem.44.1.68 PMID: 3545281

Braun, V., & Clarke, V. (2006). Using thematic analysis in psychology. *Qualitative Research in Psychology*, *3*(2), 77–101. DOI: 10.1191/1478088706qp063oa

Braveman, P., & Gruskin, S. (2003). Defining equity in health. *Journal of Epidemiology and Community Health*, *57*(4), 254–258. DOI: 10.1136/jech.57.4.254 PMID: 12646539

Bukhari, A. (2025). Private Hospitals Suspend Services for India's Health Insurance Members, Leaving Millions Without Care. *Health Policy Watch*. https://healthpolicy-watch.news/private-hospitals-suspend-services-for-indias-health-insurance-members-leaving-millions-without-care

Burke, S., Parker, S., Fleming, P., Barry, S., & Thomas, S. (2021). Building health system resilience through policy development in response to COVID-19 in Ireland: From shock to reform. *The Lancet Regional Health. Europe*, *9*, 9. DOI: 10.1016/j.lanepe.2021.100223 PMID: 34642676

Burton-Jones, A., & Straub, D. W.Jr. (2006). Reconceptualizing system usage: An approach and empirical test. *Information Systems Research*, *17*(3), 228–246. DOI: 10.1287/isre.1060.0096

Buse, K., Hein, W., & Drager, N. (2009). *Making sense of global health governance*. Palgrave Macmillan.https://link.springer.com/book/9780230209923

Carpenter, S., Rigaud, M., Barile, M., Priest, T. J., Perez, L., & Ferguson, J. B. (2006). The Ebers Papyrus. *Bard College, 3*.

Cascini, F. (2025). Enabling Factors and Opportunities to Maximize Health Data Reuse. *SpringerBriefs in Public Health*, *101*, 101–119. Advance online publication. DOI: 10.1007/978-3-031-88497-9_3

Cassidy, R. (2021). Attitudes towards digital health technology: introducing the digital health scale. medRxiv, 2021-09. DOI: 10.1101/2021.09.03.21262482

Champion, V. L., & Skinner, C. S. (2008). The Health Belief Model. In Glanz, K., Rimer, B. K., & Viswanath, K. (Eds.), *Health behavior and health education: Theory, research, and practice* (4th ed., pp. 189–193). Jossey-Bass.

Chandak, P. (2024). *Advancing Telemedicine Through Adaptive UX: A Systematic Review of Interface Design for Equity and Accessibility in Diverse Healthcare Settings*. Progress in Medical Sciences., DOI: 10.47363/PMS/2024(8)E178

Chatterjee, S., & Kulkarni, P. (2021). Healthcare consumer behaviour: The impact of digital transformation of healthcare on consumer. *Cardiometry*, (20), 134–143. DOI: 10.18137/cardiometry.2021.20.134143

Chen, J., Lin, Z., Li, L. A., Li, J., Wang, Y., Pan, Y., Yang, J., Xu, C., Zeng, X., Xie, X., & Xiao, L. (2021). Ten years of China's new healthcare reform: A longitudinal study on changes in health resources. *BMC Public Health*, *21*(1), 2272. DOI: 10.1186/s12889-021-12248-9 PMID: 34903184

Chen, K., & Chan, A. H. (2014). Predictors of gerontechnology acceptance by older Hong Kong Chinese. *Technovation*, *34*(2), 126–135. DOI: 10.1016/j.technovation.2013.09.010

Chin, M. H., Afsar-Manesh, N., Bierman, A. S., Chang, C., Colón-Rodríguez, C. J., Dullabh, P., Duran, D. G., Fair, M., Hernandez-Boussard, T., Hightower, M., Jain, A., Jordan, W. B., Konya, S., Moore, R. H., Moore, T. T., Rodriguez, R., Shaheen, G., Snyder, L. P., Srinivasan, M., & Ohno-Machado, L. (2023). Guiding principles to address the impact of algorithm bias on racial and ethnic disparities in health and health care. *JAMA Network Open*, *6*(12), e2345050–e2345050. DOI: 10.1001/jamanetworkopen.2023.45050 PMID: 38100101

Chinn, D. (2011). Critical health literacy: A review and critical analysis. *Social Science & Medicine*, *73*(1), 60–67. DOI: 10.1016/j.socscimed.2011.04.004

Chiruvella, V., & Guddati, A. K. (2021). Ethical issues in patient data ownership. *Interactive Journal of Medical Research*, *10*(2), e22269. DOI: 10.2196/22269 PMID: 34018968

Chong, A. Y. L., Blut, M., & Zheng, S. (2022). Factors influencing the acceptance of healthcare information technologies: A meta-analysis. *Information & Management*, *59*(3), 103604. DOI: 10.1016/j.im.2022.103604

Choudhary, K. (2024). Which Method Should I Select for My Legal Research – Doctrinal, Empirical, Multi-Method or Something Else? *Teisė*, *132*, 135–144. DOI: 10.15388/Teise.2024.132.10

Chumachenko, D., & Yakovlev, S. (2024). Artificial intelligence algorithms for healthcare. *Algorithms*, *17*(3), 105. DOI: 10.3390/a17030105

Coetzer, J. A., Goedhart, N. S., Schuitmaker-Warnaar, T. J., Dedding, C., & Zuiderent-Jerak, T. (2025). Health Equity in the Digital Age: Exploring health policy and inclusive digital care. *Health Policy and Technology*, *14*(5), 101039. DOI: 10.1016/j.hlpt.2025.101039

Cole, A. A., Breakwell, L. M., & Hutton, M. J. (2018). The National Health Service (NHS) in England: Trying to Achieve Value-Based Healthcare. Quality Spine Care: Healthcare Systems, Quality Reporting, and Risk Adjustment, 171–198.

Cornejo, J. A., Cruz-Ausejo, L., Alejandro, J. C., Burgos-Flores, M., Ambrosio-Melgarejo, J., Rimache, J. R., & Cruz, S. G. (2025). Barriers and limitations to the development of a telemental health service for workers in Peru- A user-centered approach. *PLoS One*, *20*(4), e0321401. Advance online publication. DOI: 10.1371/journal.pone.0321401 PMID: 40202969

Coulter, L. (2024). Exploring the "Phygital" Future of Healthcare. *HCO News*. https://hconews.com/2024/11/29/exploring-the-phygital-future-of-healthcare/

Creswell, J. W., & Plano Clark, V. L. (2018). *Designing and Conducting Mixed Methods Research* (3rd ed.). SAGE.

Croke, K., & Ogbuoji, O. (2023). Health reform in Nigeria: The politics of primary health care and universal health coverage. *Health Policy and Planning*, *39*(1), 22–31. DOI: 10.1093/heapol/czad107 PMID: 37978878

Cruz, K. D., Hermosura, J. C., Vigonte, F. G., & Abante, M. V. (2023). Analyzing the Real-World Application of the Elasticity Theory of Demand and Supply and its Impact on Pricing Strategies, Consumer Behavior, and Policy Decisions. SSRN *Electronic Journal*. DOI: 10.2139/ssrn.4447159

Cunningham, C., Hutchings, T., Henderson, J. L., Rimas, H. M., & Chen, Y. (2016). Modeling the hospital safety partnership preferences of patients and their families: A discrete choice conjoint experiment. *Patient Preference and Adherence*, *10*, 1359–1372. DOI: 10.2147/PPA.S105605 PMID: 27555752

Curatsio International Foundation. (2025). Healthcare Barometer, February. DOI: DOI: 10.13140/RG.2.2.24611

Curioso, W. H., Coronel-Chucos, L. G., & Oscuvilca-Tapia, E. (2024). Empowering the digital health workforce in Latin America in the context of the COVID-19 pandemic: The Peruvian case. *Informatics for Health & Social Care*, *49*(1), 73–82. DOI: 10.1080/17538157.2024.2315266 PMID: 38349775

Czech, H., Hildebrandt, S., Reis, S. P., Chelouche, T., Fox, M., González-López, E., Lepicard, E., Ley, A., Offer, M., Rotzoll, A. M., Sachse, C., Siegel, S., Šimůnek, M., Teicher, A., Uzarczyk, K., von Villiez, A., Wald, H., Wynia, M., & Roelcke, V. (2023). The Lancet Commission on medicine, Nazism, and the Holocaust: Historical evidence, implications for today, teaching for tomorrow. *Lancet*, *402*(10415), 1867–1940. DOI: 10.1016/S0140-6736(23)01845-7 PMID: 37951225

D. Sharma, S. (2018). Health Care for India's 500 Million: The Promise of the National Health Protection Scheme. *HPHR Journal, 18*. DOI: 10.54111/0001/R1

Dada, S. A., & Adekola, A. D. (2024). Leveraging digital marketing for health behavior change: A model for engaging patients through pharmacies. *International Journal of Science and Technology Research Archive*. DOI: 10.53771/ijstra.2024.7.2.0063

Dailah, H. (2021). Understanding the determinants of digital health marketing strategies: A comparison of private and public sector hospitals *(Preprint)*. DOI: 10.2196/preprints.27844

Dal Mas, F., Massaro, M., Rippa, P., & Secundo, G. (2023). The challenges of digital transformation in healthcare: An interdisciplinary literature review, framework, and future research agenda. *Technovation, 123*, 102716. DOI: 10.1016/j.technovation.2023.102716

Datareportal. (2024). Digital 2024: Georgia. Retrieved from: https://datareportal.com/reports/digital-2024-georgia#:~:text=The%20state%20of%20digital%20in%20Georgia%20in%202024&text=Georgia%20was%20home%20to%202.85,percent%20of%20the%20total%20population

David, A. R. (2008). The ancient Egyptian medical system. Egyptian mummies and modern science, 181–194.

Davis, F. D. (1989). Perceived usefulness, perceived ease of use, and user acceptance of information technology. *Management Information Systems Quarterly, 13*(3), 319–340. DOI: 10.2307/249008

Deal, K. (2013). Segmenting Patients and Physicians Using Preferences from Discrete Choice Experiments. *The Patient - Patient-Centered Outcomes Research, 7*, 5–21. DOI: 10.1007/s40271-013-0037-9

Debbarma, M. (2024). Refugees Experience and the Host Communities: Critical Analyses on Absence of Refugee Law in India. *Journal of Asian and African Studies, 60*(5), 3204–3218. DOI: 10.1177/00219096241228804

Del Vecchio, P., Secundo, G., & Garzoni, A. (2023). Phygital technologies and environments for breakthrough innovation in customers' and citizens' journey. A critical literature review and future agenda. *Technological Forecasting and Social Change, 189*, 122342. DOI: 10.1016/j.techfore.2023.122342

Deng, Z., Mo, X., & Liu, S. (2014). Comparison of the middle-aged and older users' adoption of mobile health services in China. *International Journal of Medical Informatics, 83*(3), 210–224. DOI: 10.1016/j.ijmedinf.2013.12.002 PMID: 24388129

Deshingkar, P., & Akter, S. (2009). *Migration and human development in India* (UNDP Human Development Report No. 13). United Nations Development Programme.

Devassy, B., & George, A. (2021). The social integration and health of migrant labourers in Kerala. *Indian Journal of Public Health Research & Development, 12*(3), 184–191.

Di Bernardo, I., Marzullo, M., Mele, C., & Spena, T. R. (2023). AI-Based Technologies in the Phygital Care Journey. In *Impact of Artificial Intelligence in Business and Society* (pp. 212–230). Routledge. DOI: 10.4324/9781003304616-14

Dillon, M., & McCaskey, P. H. (2018). *Quality Elasticity of Demand in Healthcare: Unraveling the Puzzle*. https://consensus.app/papers/quality-elasticity-of-demand-in-healthcare-unraveling-the-mccaskey-dillon/5d310935a4a05224a945a56aa71fb588/

Dinh-Le, C., Chuang, R., Chokshi, S. K., & Mann, D. (2019). An electronic health record and wearable health technology integration: Scoping review. *JMIR mHealth and uHealth, 7*(9). Advance online publication. DOI: 10.2196/12861 PMID: 31512582

Djakeli, K. (2011, April). Milton Friedman's ideas influenced the Health Care Reform of Georgia. In the 6th Silk Road International Conference" Globalization and Security in Black and Caspian Seas Region".

Djakeli, K. (2023). Sustainable Healthcare Reforming Model Based on Marketing: Case of Georgia. In Handbook of Research on Achieving Sustainable Development Goals With Sustainable Marketing (pp. 271-287). IGI Global.

Djakeli, K. (2024 A). Social Marketing: Past, Current Period. Phygital Approaches to Social Marketing, IGI Global.

Djakeli, K. (2025 A). Social Marketing: Past, Current Period, and the Future. In Phygital Approaches to Social Marketing (pp. 1-20). IGI Global Scientific Publishing.

Djakeli, K. (2025 B). Social Marketing and Public Health in the Phygital Era. In Phygital Approaches to Social Marketing (pp. 43-66). IGI Global Scientific Publishing.

Djakeli, K. (2025 C). History of Branding, Its Current Status, and the Future of Phygitalization. In Brand Creation and Management in the Phygital Era (pp. 1-30). IGI Global Scientific Publishing.

Djakeli, K. (2025B). Social Marketing and Public Health in the Phygital Era. In Phygital Approaches to Social Marketing (pp. 43-66). IGI Global Scientific Publishing.

Djakeli, K. (2025C). Strategic Management for Digital Platform Brands in the Phygital Era. In Brand Creation and Management in the Phygital Era (pp. 499-520). IGI Global Scientific Publishing.

Djakeli, K., & McElroy[1], J. W. (2025, March). The Power of Customer Journey Mapping with Artificial Intelligence: A Case Study. In Reliability and Statistics in Transportation and Communication: Human Sustainability and Resilience in the Digital Age: Selected Papers from the 24th International Multidisciplinary Conference on Reliability and Statistics in Transportation and Communication, RelStat-2024, Riga, Latvia, September 25-28, 2024 (Vol. 1337, p. 244). Springer Nature.

Djakeli, K. (2013). Analyzing success and failure of two health reforms in independent Georgia. *The Journal of Business*, *2*(2), 5–14.

Djakeli, K. (2024). B). Healthcare marketing: meaning, historical development, applications, and current status. In *Modern Healthcare Marketing in the Digital Era* (pp. 1–25). IGI Global Scientific Publishing.

Djakeli, K. (2025A). Phygitalization of Palliative Care and Its Social Marketing. In *Phygital Approaches to Social Marketing* (pp. 267–288). IGI Global Scientific Publishing.

Djakeli, K., & Jakeli, T. (2016). Health Reforms Need Marketing-Analyzing Current Georgian Healthcare Model through Reform Marketing Matrix (RMM). *The Journal of Business*, *5*(2), 7–15. DOI: 10.31578/.v5i2.106

Domecq, J. P., Prutsky, G., Elraiyah, T., Wang, Z., Nabhan, M., Shippee, N., Brito, J. P., Boehmer, K., Hasan, R., Firwana, B., Erwin, P., Eton, D., Sloan, J., Montori, V., Asi, N., Abu Dabrh, A. M., & Murad, M. H. (2014). Patient engagement in research: A systematic review. *BMC Health Services Research*, *14*(1), 89. DOI: 10.1186/1472-6963-14-89 PMID: 24568690

Donohue, J. M., Cole, E. S., James, C. V., Jarlenski, M., Michener, J. D., & Roberts, E. T. (2022). The US Medicaid program: Coverage, financing, reforms, and implications for health equity. *Journal of the American Medical Association*, *328*(11), 1085–1099. DOI: 10.1001/jama.2022.14791 PMID: 36125468

Dunleavy, P., Margetts, H., Bastow, S., & Tinkler, J. (2006). *Digital era governance: IT corporations, the state, and e-government*. Oxford University Press., DOI: 10.1093/acprof:oso/9780199296194.001.0001

Eagly, A. H., & Chaiken, S. (1993). *The psychology of attitudes*. Harcourt, Brace, & Janovich.

Ebert, R. H., & Ginzberg, E. (1988). The reform of medical education. *Health Affairs*, *7*(suppl 2), 5–38. DOI: 10.1377/hlthaff.7.2.5 PMID: 3378732

Elliott, D., Robinson, E. J., Anthony, K., & Stillman, P. (2013). Patient-centered outcomes of a value-based insurance design program for patients with diabetes. *Population Health Management, 16*(2), 99–106. DOI: 10.1089/pop.2012.0031 PMID: 23405873

Emswiler, T., & Nichols, L. M. (2009). *Baylor Health Care System: High-Performance Integrated Health Care*. Commonwealth Fund.

Engström, J., Norin, O., & Varennes, S. (2022, December 19). de G. de, & Valtakoski, A. (2022). Service design in healthcare: A segmentation-based approach. *Journal of Service Management, 33*(6), 50–78. Advance online publication. DOI: 10.1108/JOSM-06-2021-0239

E-prescriptions new standard in Germany: CGM with positive interim assessment. (2024). *CompuGroup Medical.* https://www.cgm.com/corp_en/magazine/articles/press-releases/2024/e-rezept-neuer-standard-cgm-zieht-positive-zwischenbilanz.html

Eriksen, J., Ebbesen, M., Eriksen, K. T., Hjermitslev, C., Knudsen, C., Bertelsen, P., Nøhr, C., & Weber, D. (2023). Equity in digital healthcare – the case of Denmark. *Frontiers in Public Health, 11*, 1225222. Advance online publication. DOI: 10.3389/fpubh.2023.1225222 PMID: 37744503

Fabra, M. E., Jung, J., & Katz, R. (2025). The contribution of ICTs and Telemedicine to COVID-19 vaccination: Evidence from the United States. *Health Policy and Technology, 14*(2), 100980. Advance online publication. DOI: 10.1016/j.hlpt.2025.100980

Fahad, M. (2024). *Technological Transformation in Healthcare: A Global Perspective. Journal of Digitainability, Realism & Mastery*. DREAM., DOI: 10.56982/dream.v3i12.294

Fan, C., Zou, G., Yang, C., & Zhao, Z. (2024). Can the digital transformation of pharmaceutical enterprises' finance improve healthcare equity? *Finance Research Letters, 67*, 105911. Advance online publication. DOI: 10.1016/j.frl.2024.105911

Faroqi, T., & Sundaram, J. R. (2022). Healthcare for refugees in India. *The Routledge Handbook of Refugees in India*, 842. DOI: 10.4324/9781003246800-77

Fehr, A. (2018). Health monitoring and health indicators in Europe. *PubMed, 2*(1), 3. DOI: 10.17886/rki-gbe-2017-020.2

Ferrara, L., & Tozzi, V. (2018). Bundled payment for mental health care: A realist review. *International Journal of Integrated Care, 18*(s2), 155. Advance online publication. DOI: 10.5334/ijic.s2155

Ferrigno, G., Del Sarto, N., Piccaluga, A., & Baroncelli, A. (2023). Industry 4.0 base technologies and business models: A bibliometric analysis. *European Journal of Innovation Management*, *26*(7), 502–526. DOI: 10.1108/EJIM-02-2023-0107

Fidler, D. P. (2010). *The challenges of global health governance* (Working paper). Council on Foreign Relations. https://www.cfr.org/report/challenges-global-health-governance

Finnegan, H., & Mountford, N. (2025). 25 years of electronic health record implementation processes: Scoping review. *Journal of Medical Internet Research*, *27*, e60077. DOI: 10.2196/60077 PMID: 40053758

Fitzpatrick, R. (2022). Satisfaction with health care. In *The experience of illness* (pp. 154–176). Routledge. DOI: 10.4324/9781003283966-8

Flexner, A. (1910). Medical education in the United States and Canada. *Science*, *32*(810), 41–50. DOI: 10.1126/science.32.810.41 PMID: 17745880

Floridi, L., Cowls, J., Beltrametti, M., Chatila, R., Chazerand, P., Dignum, V., & Vayena, E. (2018). AI4People: An ethical framework for a good AI society. *Minds and Machines*, *28*(4), 689–707. DOI: 10.1007/s11023-018-9482-5 PMID: 30930541

Folkman, S., & Moskowitz, J. T. (2004). Coping: Pitfalls and promise. *Annual Review of Psychology*, *55*(1), 745–774. DOI: 10.1146/annurev.psych.55.090902.141456 PMID: 14744233

Ford, C., & Ashkenazy, Q. (2025). The Legal Innovation Sandbox. *The American Journal of Comparative Law*. Advance online publication. DOI: 10.1093/ajcl/avae029

Fotopoulou, A., Barratt, H., & Marandet, E. (2021). A data-based participatory approach for health equity and digital inclusion: Prioritizing stakeholders. *Health Promotion International*. Advance online publication. DOI: 10.1093/heapro/daab166 PMID: 34967901

Friedman, M. (1962). *Capitalism and freedom*. University of Chicago Press. https://press.uchicago.edu/ucp/books/book/chicago/C/bo68666099.html

Friedman, M., & Friedman, R. (1980). *Free to choose: A personal statement*. Harcourt Brace Jovanovich. https://archive.org/details/freetochoosepers0000frie

Friedman, E. (1998). What Price Survival?: The Future of Blue Cross and Blue Shield. *Journal of the American Medical Association*, *279*(23), 1863–1869. DOI: 10.1001/jama.279.23.1863 PMID: 9634248

Friedman, M. (2016). Capitalism and freedom. In *Democracy: a reader* (pp. 344–349). Columbia University Press. DOI: 10.7312/blau17412-074

Fulton, J. F. (1953). History of medical education. *British Medical Journal*, *2*(4834), 457–461. DOI: 10.1136/bmj.2.4834.457 PMID: 13066760

Gabelaia, I. (2025). Brand Resonance in the Phygital Era: Fostering Loyalty Through Hybrid Engagement. In *Brand Creation and Management in the Phygital Era* (pp. 31-46). IGI Global Scientific Publishing. DOI: DOI: 10.4018/979-8-3373-0948-4.ch002

Gabelaia, I., Djakeli, K., & McElroy, J. W. (2024, September). The Power of Customer Journey Mapping with Artificial Intelligence: A Case Study Method. In *International Conference on Reliability and Statistics in Transportation and Communication* (pp. 244–257). Cham: Springer Nature Switzerland.

Gabelaia, I. (2025). The Relevance of AI-Driven Marketing Through Design Thinking for a Strategic Approach to Resilient Problem-Solving and Communication for SMEs. *Sustainability (Basel)*, *17*(20), 8994. DOI: 10.3390/su17208994

Gagnon, M. P., Desmartis, M., Labrecque, M., Car, J., Pagliari, C., Pluye, P., Frémont, P., Gagnon, J., Tremblay, N., & Légaré, F. (2012). Systematic review of factors influencing the adoption of information and communication technologies by healthcare professionals. *Journal of Medical Systems*, *36*(1), 241–277. DOI: 10.1007/s10916-010-9473-4 PMID: 20703721

Gallegos-Rejas, V. M., Thomas, E., Kelly, J. T., & Smith, A. C. (2022). A multi-stakeholder approach is needed to reduce the digital divide and encourage equitable access to telehealth. *Journal of Telemedicine and Telecare*, *29*(1), 73–78. DOI: 10.1177/1357633X221107995 PMID: 35733379

Ganesh, N. B., Siddineni, D., Reddy, V. V., Lateef, K., & Sharma, R.N Balaji Ganesh. (2025). Corporate Governance in the Age of AI: Ethical Oversight and Accountability Frameworks. *Journal of Information Systems Engineering & Management*, *10*(35s), 1141–1148. Advance online publication. DOI: 10.52783/jisem.v10i35s.6285

Ganji, K., &Afshan, N. (2024). Elevating Patient Loyalty in Modern Healthcare through Phygital Frontier.

Garg, S., Bebarta, K. K., & Tripathi, N. (2024). The Ayushman Bharat Pradhan Mantri Jan Arogya Yojana (AB-PMJAY) after four years of implementation – is it making an impact on quality of inpatient care and financial protection in India? *BMC Health Services Research*, *24*(1), 919. Advance online publication. DOI: 10.1186/s12913-024-11393-2 PMID: 39135015

Geffert, K., Voss, S., Rehfuess, E., & Rechel, B. (2024). The role of the public health service in the implementation of heat health action plans for climate change adaptation in Germany: A qualitative study. *Health Research Policy and Systems*, *22*(1), 161. Advance online publication. DOI: 10.1186/s12961-024-01231-6 PMID: 39639289

George, J., & Karalam, S. B. R. (in progress). Research work related to migrant workers in Kerala [Unpublished working thesis]. Department of social work, Christ University, Bengaluru.

German e-health offerings expand, but adoption remains uneven. (2022). *McKinsey & Company*. https://www.mckinsey.com/industries/life-sciences/our-insights/german-e-health-offerings-expand-but-adoption-remains-uneven#/

German Refugee Digitisation System. (2019). *European Commission*. https://ec.europa.eu/digital-building-blocks/sites/spaces/DIGITAL/blog/2019/07/31/533366012/German+Refugee+Digitisation+System

Germany - Health systems in transition. (2023). World Health Organization. https://eurohealthobservatory.who.int/countries/germany

Germany: Partner in global health. (2025). World Health Organization. https://www.who.int/about/funding/contributors/deu

Gigauri, I., & Djakeli, K. (2021). National health reforms in Georgia during 1994–2021 and their success. HOLISTICA – Journal of Business and Public Administration, 12(2), 102–108. https://reference-global.com/download/article/10.2478/hjbpa-2021-0017.pdf

Gigauri, I., & Djakeli, K. (2021). *National Health Reforms in Georgia during 1994–2021 and their Success*. HOLISTICA Journal of Business and Public Administration, 12(2), 102–108. https://reference-global.com/download/article/10.2478/hjbpa-2021-0017.pdf

Gigauri, I., & Djakeli, K. (2021). A). Expecting Transformation of Marketing During the Post-Pandemic New Normal: Qualitative Research of Marketing Managers in Georgia. [IJSEM]. *International Journal of Sustainable Economies Management*, *10*(2), 1–18. DOI: 10.4018/IJSEM.2021040101

Gigauri, I., & Djakeli, K. (2021). B). Remote working challenges for Georgian social enterprises amid the current pandemic. *HOLISTICA–Journal of Business and Public Administration*, *12*(3), 39–53. DOI: 10.2478/hjbpa-2021-0021

Gigauri, I., & Djakeli, K. (2021). National Health Reforms in Georgia during 1994-2021 and their Success. *HOLISTICA Journal of Business and Public Administration*, *12*(2), 102–108. DOI: 10.2478/hjbpa-2021-0017

Giulio de Belvis, A., Meregaglia, M., Morsella, A., Adduci, A., Perilli, A., Cascini, F., & Scarpetti, G. (2022). Italy: Health System Review. *Health Systems in Transition, 24*(4), 1–236. PMID: 36951263

Global strategy on digital health 2020-2025 ISBN 978-92-4-002092-4, World Health Organization (WHO) — Global Strategy on Digital Health 2020–2025 (2021)

Godiyal, M., & Mishra, A. (2025). *Impact of Digital Marketing in Consumer Purchasing Behaviour.* International Journal For Multidisciplinary Research., DOI: 10.36948/ijfmr.2025.v07i02.40554

Golinelli, D., Boetto, E., Carullo, G., Nuzzolese, A. G., Landini, M. P., & Fantini, M. P. (2020). Adoption of digital technologies in health care during the COVID-19 pandemic: Systematic review of early scientific literature. *Journal of Medical Internet Research, 22*(11), e22280. DOI: 10.2196/22280 PMID: 33079693

Goodwin, I. (2022). Programmatic alcohol advertising, social media and public health: Algorithms, automated challenges to regulation, and the failure of public oversight. *The International Journal on Drug Policy, 109*, 103826. DOI: 10.1016/j.drugpo.2022.103826 PMID: 35994939

Goreau-Ponceaud, A. (2024). Lives in exile? Perspectives on the resettlements of Sri Lankan refugees in Tamil Nadu, India. *World Development, 180*, 106629. DOI: 10.1016/j.worlddev.2024.106629

Gostin, L. O., Moon, S., & Meier, B. M. (2021). Reimagining Global Health Governance in the Age of COVID-19. *American Journal of Public Health, 110*(11), 1615–1619. DOI: 10.2105/AJPH.2020.305933 PMID: 33026872

Gotsadze, G., Zoidze, A., & Vasadze, O. (2005). Reform strategies in Georgia and their impact on health care provision in rural areas: Evidence from a household survey. *Social Science & Medicine, 60*(4), 809–821. DOI: 10.1016/j.socscimed.2004.06.017 PMID: 15571898

Gottlieb, N., Gold, A. W., Palla, I., Dimaku, I. C., Güell, B., Legarda Díaz-Aguado, I., & Bozorgmehr, K. (2024). Narrative change for inclusionary health and migration policies. *The Lancet Regional Health. Europe, 41*, 100835. DOI: 10.1016/j.lanepe.2024.100835 PMID: 39119100

Gottlieb, N., Ohm, V., & Knörnschild, M. (2019). A first assessment of the electronic health insurance card for asylum seekers in Berlin. *European Journal of Public Health, 29*(Supplement_4), ckz187.015. Advance online publication. DOI: 10.1093/eurpub/ckz187.015

Government of India. (2020). *Economic survey 2019–2020.* Ministry of Finance International Labour Organization. (2018). *Women and men in the informal economy: A statistical picture* (3rd ed.). ILO.

Grbic, M., Grbić, D. S., Štimac, L., & Šostar, Z. (2019). Digital marketing in healthcare. *European Journal of Public Health, 29*(Supplement_4), ckz186.077. Advance online publication. DOI: 10.1093/eurpub/ckz186.077

Greenleaf, R. K. (1977). *Servant leadership: A journey into the nature of legitimate power and greatness*. Paulist Press.

Grudtsyn, N. A. (2024). Transformative impact of the COVID-19 pandemic on medical tourism. *ВестникСанкт-Петербургскогоуниверситета. Науки о Земле, 69*(4), 646–666.

Hair, J. F., Hult, G. T. M., Ringle, C. M., & Sarstedt, M. (2022). *A Primer on Partial Least Squares Structural Equation Modeling (PLS-SEM)* (3rd ed.). Sage., DOI: 10.1007/978-3-030-80519-7

Hair, J.Jr, Sarstedt, M., Hopkins, L., & Kuppelwieser, G., V. (. (2014). Partial least squares structural equation modeling (PLS-SEM) An emerging tool in business research. *European Business Review, 26*(2), 106–121. DOI: 10.1108/EBR-10-2013-0128

Hajdini, J., Za, S., & Iaia, L. (2025). State of art and future research directions for marketing technologies in healthcare: A bibliometric analysis. [REMOVED HYPERLINK FIELD]. *Technological Forecasting and Social Change, 218*, 124226. Advance online publication. DOI: 10.1016/j.techfore.2025.124226

Halwani, T., & Takrouri, M. (2006). Medical laws and ethics of Babylon, as read in Hammurabi's code (History). The Internet Journal of Law. *Healthcare and Ethics, 4*(2), 1–8.

Hamzah, N. H., Radzi, N. M., & Omar, I. M. (2025). DIGITAL LEADERSHIP COMPETENCIES THROUGH A SYSTEMATIC LITERATURE REVIEW: BRIDGING EDUCATIONAL DEVELOPMENT AND ORGANIZATIONAL SUCCESS. *International Journal of Modern Education.* DOI: 10.35631/IJMOE.724003

Hansen, A., Herrmann, M., Ehlers, J. P., Mondritzki, T., Hensel, K. O., Truebel, H., & Boehme, P. (2019). Perception of the progressing digitization and transformation of the German health care system among experts and the public: Mixed methods study. *JMIR Public Health and Surveillance, 5*(4), e14689. DOI: 10.2196/14689 PMID: 31661082

Haris, A. (2023). Digital Marketing and Consumer Engagement: A Systematic Review. *Amkop Management Accounting Review (AMAR)*. DOI: 10.37531/amar.v3i2.1442

He, A. J., & Ma, L. (2021). Citizen participation perceived public service performance, and trust in government: Evidence from health policy reforms in Hong Kong. *Public Performance & Management Review*, *44*(3), 471–493. DOI: 10.1080/15309576.2020.1780138

Heinrich, A. (2022). The emergence of the socialist healthcare model after the First World War. In *International Impacts on Social Policy: Short Histories in Global Perspective* (pp. 35–46). Springer International Publishing. DOI: 10.1007/978-3-030-86645-7_4

Hellinger, F. J. (1995). Selection bias in HMOs and PPOs: A review of the evidence. *Inquiry : a Journal of Medical Care Organization, Provision and Financing*, •••, 135–142. PMID: 7601511

Hermes, S., Riasanow, T., Clemons, E., Böhm, M., & Krcmar, H. (2020). The digital transformation of the healthcare industry: Exploring the rise of emerging platform ecosystems and their influence on the role of patients. *Business Research*, *13*(3), 1033–1069. Advance online publication. DOI: 10.1007/s40685-020-00125-x

Hollimon, L. A., Taylor, K. V., Fiegenbaum, R., & Seixas, A. A. (2025). Redefining and solving the digital divide and exclusion to improve healthcare: Going beyond access to include availability, adequacy, acceptability, and affordability. *Frontiers in Digital Health*, *7*, 1508686. Advance online publication. DOI: 10.3389/fdgth.2025.1508686 PMID: 40330871

Holum, M. (2023). Citizen participation: Linking government efforts, actual participation, and trust in local politicians. *International Journal of Public Administration*, *46*(13), 915–925. DOI: 10.1080/01900692.2022.2048667

Hone, T., Macinko, J., & Millett, C. (2018). Revisiting Alma-Ata: What is the role of primary health care in achieving the Sustainable Development Goals? *Lancet*, *392*(10156), 1461–1472. DOI: 10.1016/S0140-6736(18)31829-4 PMID: 30343860

Hoque, R., & Sorwar, G. (2017). Understanding factors influencing the adoption of mHealth by the elderly: An extension of the UTAUT model. *International Journal of Medical Informatics*, *101*, 75–84. DOI: 10.1016/j.ijmedinf.2017.02.002 PMID: 28347450

Hou, L., An, N., Lin, V., & Lin, V. K. (2024). Can Digital Health Improve Healthcare Access for Migrants. *NAM Perspectives*, *2024*. Advance online publication. DOI: 10.31478/202408b PMID: 39830819

Hsiao, C. H., & Tang, K. Y. (2015). Examining a model of mobile healthcare technology acceptance by the elderly in Taiwan. *Journal of Global Information Technology Management, 18*(4), 292–311. DOI: 10.1080/1097198X.2015.1108099

Huang, C. Y., Yang, M. C., & Huang, C. Y. (2021). An empirical study on factors influencing consumer adoption intention of an AI-powered chatbot for health and weight management. *International Journal of Performability Engineering, 17*(5), 422. DOI: 10.23940/ijpe.21.05.p2.422432

Hu, P. J. H., Chau, P. Y., & Sheng, O. R. L. (2002). Adoption of telemedicine technology by health care organizations: An exploratory study. *Journal of Organizational Computing and Electronic Commerce, 12*(3), 197–221. DOI: 10.1207/S15327744JOCE1203_01

Hurley, R. E., Strunk, B. C., & White, J. S. (2004). The puzzling popularity of the PPO. *Health Affairs, 23*(2), 56–68. DOI: 10.1377/hlthaff.23.2.56 PMID: 15046131

Ibrahim, H., Mahmood, H. S., & Ali, R. (2020). The significant healthcare merits of insurance models: A review study. *Karbala J Pharm Sci, 18*, 12–19.

Ii, R. R., van Mierlo, T., & Fournier, R. (2022). Testing Behavioral Nudges and Prompts in Digital Courses for the Treatment of Depression and Anxiety: Protocol for 3-Arm Randomized Controlled Trial *(Preprint)*. DOI: 10.2196/preprints.37231

Ikhalea, N., Chianumba, E. C., Mustapha, A. Y., Forkuo, A. Y., & Osamika, D. (2024). A Model for Strengthening Health Systems in Low-Resource Settings Using AI and Telemedicine. *International Journal of Future Engineering Innovations*. DOI: 10.54660/IJFEI.2024.1.1.86-92

Israelowich, I. (2015). *Patients and healers in the High Roman Empire*. JHU Press. DOI: 10.1353/book.39295

Ivers, N., Brown, A. D., & Detsky, A. S. (2018). Lessons from the Canadian experience with single-payer health insurance: Just comfortable enough with the status quo. *JAMA Internal Medicine, 178*(9), 1250–1255. DOI: 10.1001/jamainternmed.2018.3568 PMID: 30083756

Jackson, C. M., Chow, S., & Leitch, R. A. (1997). Toward an understanding of the behavioral intention to use an information system. *Decision Sciences, 28*(2), 357–389. DOI: 10.1111/j.1540-5915.1997.tb01315.x

Jahn, R., Rohleder, S., Qreini, M., Erdmann, S., Kaur, S., Aluttis, F., & Bozorgmehr, K. (2021). Health monitoring of refugees in reception centres for asylum seekers: Decentralized surveillance network for the analysis of routine medical data. *PubMed, 6*(1), 30. Judgment of the Federal Constitutional Court in the proceeding 1 BvL 10/10. (2012). *ESCR-Net – International Network for Economic, Social & Cultural Rights*. https://www.escr-net.org/caselaw/2012/judgment-federal-constitutional-court-proceeding-1-bvl-1010/DOI: 10.25646/7865

Jakeli, K., Lobjanidze, T., & Lobjanidze, M. (2025). Healthcare Digitalization Reforms around the World and Georgia's Path. *International Journal Chemistry and Human Health*, (2), 85–91. DOI: 10.52340/ijch.2025.02.06

Jan Dijk, J. (2020). *The digital divide*. Polity Press., DOI: 10.1002/asi.24355

Janlöv, N., Blume, S., Glenngård, A. H., Hanspers, K., Anell, A., & Merkur, S. (2023). *Sweden: health system review* (Vol. 25, No. 4). World Health Organization. Regional Office for Europe.

Jayanagara, O. (2024). APPLICATION OF LEADERSHIP STYLES IN DIGITAL HEALTHCARE SYSTEMS. *Milestone: Journal of Strategic Management*. DOI: 10.19166/ms.v4i1.8304

Jedličková, A. (2024). Ethical dimensions in telemedicine—Balancing technology, responsible care, and patient protection. *Casopis Lekaru Ceskych, 163*(3), 106–114. PMID: 38981731

Jeon, S., & Tuuminen, R. (2024). Healthcare quality indicators for value-based reimbursement in ophthalmology. *Acta Ophthalmologica, 102*(6), 625–626. Advance online publication. DOI: 10.1111/aos.16698 PMID: 38656704

Jiangliu, Y., Kim, H. T., Lazar, M., Liu, E., Mantri, S., Qiu, E., Berube, M., Sood, H., Walia, A. S., Biondi, B. E., Mesias, A. M., Mishuris, R., & de la Vega, P. B. (2024). A Medical Student-Led Multipronged Initiative to Close the Digital Divide in Outpatient Primary Care. *Applied Clinical Informatics, 15*(4), 808–816. DOI: 10.1055/a-2370-2298 PMID: 39038793

Jiang, X., Ming, W., & You, J. (2019). The Cost-Effectiveness of Digital Health Interventions on the Management of Cardiovascular Diseases: Systematic Review. *Journal of Medical Internet Research, 21*(6), e13166. Advance online publication. DOI: 10.2196/13166 PMID: 31210136

Jones, C. H., & Dolsten, M. (2024). Healthcare on the brink: Navigating the challenges of an aging society in the United States. *npj. Aging (Albany NY), 10*(1), 22. DOI: 10.1038/s41514-024-00148-2 PMID: 38582901

Jorbenadze, A., Zoidze, A., Gzirirshvili, D., & Gotsadze, G. (1999). Health reform and hospital financing in Georgia. CMJ Online, 40(2).

Joseph, T., & Nair, K. S. (2020). Informal sector and mental health: A comparative study of natives and migrants in Tamil Nadu. *Labor Studies Journal, 45*(4), 293–310. DOI: 10.1177/0160449X20941023

Joshi, K. J., Vala, J., & Katoch, C. (2023). *Revolutionising Healthcare: The Pinnacle Role of Artificial Intelligence in Medical Institutes of National Importance*. NMO Journal., DOI: 10.4103/JNMO.JNMO_10_23

Joy, Z. H., Rahman, M. M., Uzzaman, A., & Maraj, M. A. A. (2024). INTEGRATING MACHINE LEARNING AND BIG DATA ANALYTICS FOR REAL-TIME DISEASE DETECTION IN SMART HEALTHCARE SYSTEMS. *Global Mainstream Journal*. DOI: 10.62304/ijhm.v1i3.162

Joynt, K. E., Figueroa, J., Beaulieu, N., Wild, R. C., Orav, E., & Jha, A. (2017). Segmenting high-cost Medicare patients into potentially actionable cohorts. *Health Care, 5*(1-2), 1–2, 62–67. DOI: 10.1016/j.hjdsi.2016.11.002 PMID: 27914968

Kamath, R., & Brand, H. (2023). A Critical Analysis of the World'S Largest Publicly Funded Health Insurance Program: India's Ayushman Bharat. *International Journal of Preventive Medicine, 14*(1). Advance online publication. DOI: 10.4103/ijpvm.ijpvm_39_22 PMID: 37033284

Kaplan, B. (2020). REVISITING HEALTH INFORMATION TECHNOLOGY ETHICAL, LEGAL, and SOCIAL ISSUES and EVALUATION: TELEHEALTH/TELEMEDICINE and COVID-19. *International Journal of Medical Informatics, 143*, 104239–104239. DOI: 10.1016/j.ijmedinf.2020.104239 PMID: 33152653

Karamanou, M., Tsoucalas, G., Papaioannou, T. G., & Sfikakis, P. (2019). Healthcare policy in Ancient Greece: Insights from the Golden Age of Athens (5th century BC) may be helpful in medical Care in the 21st century.

Karnik, H., Barbiero, J., Zemmel, D. J., Weiss, N. M., Kulik, P. K. G., Power, L. E., & Leider, J. P. (2025). Building Adaptive Leaders: A Formative Evaluation of the Region V Public Health Leadership Institute Using Ripple Effect Mapping and Focus Groups. *Journal of Public Health Management and Practice, 31*(4), 591–599. DOI: 10.1097/PHH.0000000000002150 PMID: 40172981

Katoue, M. G., Cerda, A. A., García, L. Y., & Jakovljevic, M. (2022). Healthcare system development in the Middle East and North Africa region: Challenges, endeavors and prospective opportunities. *Frontiers in Public Health, 10*, 1045739. DOI: 10.3389/fpubh.2022.1045739 PMID: 36620278

Katrak, M. (2021). REFOULING ROHINGYAS: THE SUPREME COURT OF INDIA'S UNEASY ENGAGEMENT WITH INTERNATIONAL LAW. *Journal of Liberty and International Affairs Institute for Research and European Studies - Bitola, 7*(2), 116. DOI: 10.47305/JLIA21720116k

Keesara, S., Jonas, A., & Schulman, K. (2020). COVID-19 and healthcare's digital revolution. *The New England Journal of Medicine, 382*(23), e82. DOI: 10.1056/NEJMp2005835 PMID: 32240581

Khan, I., Saleh, M. A., Quazi, A., & Johns, R. (2021). Health consumers' social media adoption behaviours in Australia. *Health Informatics Journal, 27*(2), 14604582211009917. DOI: 10.1177/14604582211009917 PMID: 33887968

Khan, M., Abimbola, S., Aloudat, T., Capobianco, E., Hawkes, S., & Rahman-Shepherd, A. (2021). Decolonising global health in 2021: A roadmap to move from rhetoric to reform. *BMJ Global Health, 6*(3), e005604. DOI: 10.1136/bmjgh-2021-005604 PMID: 33758016

Khan, W. U., Shachak, A., & Seto, E. (2021). Understanding Decision-Making in the Adoption of Digital Health Technology: The Role of Behavioral Economics' Prospect Theory. *Journal of Medical Internet Research, 24*(2), e32714. Advance online publication. DOI: 10.2196/32714 PMID: 35129459

Khodayari-zarnaq, R., Mobasseri, K., Ghasemyani, S., Sadeghi-Ghyassi, F., Naghshi, M., & Kabiri, N. (2024). Challenges and Weaknesses of Leadership and Governance-related Health Policies in Iran: A Systematic Review. *Archives of Iranian Medicine, 27*(9), 508–521. DOI: 10.34172/aim.28907 PMID: 39465526

Kickbusch, I., Pelikan, J. M., Apfel, F., & Tsouros, A. D. (2013). *Health literacy: The solid facts.* World Health Organization, Regional Office for Europe. https://apps.who.int/iris/bitstream/handle/10665/128703/e96854.pdf

Kickbusch, I., Leung, G. M., Bhutta, Z. A., Matsoso, M. P., Ihekweazu, C., & Abbasi, K. (2020). COVID-19: How a virus is turning the world upside down. *BMJ (Clinical Research Ed.), 369*, m1336. DOI: 10.1136/bmj.m1336 PMID: 32245802

Kickbusch, I., Silberschmidt, G., & Buss, P. (2017). Global health diplomacy: The need for new perspectives, strategic approaches and skills in global health. *Bulletin of the World Health Organization, 95*(3), 159–159A. DOI: 10.2471/BLT.13.118596 PMID: 17486216

Kim, E., & Han, S. (2023). Investigating the digital health acceptance of Korean baby boomers: Comparative study of telemedicine and wearable healthcare devices. *Health Policy and Technology, 12*(1), 100727. DOI: 10.1016/j.hlpt.2023.100727

Kim, T. H., & Kim, H. S. (2016). Delivery app understanding and acceptance among food tech customers using the modified technology acceptance model. *Journal of Tourism Science, 40*(5), 127–144.

Kleisiaris, C. F., Sfakianakis, C., & Papathanasiou, I. V. (2014). Health care practices in ancient Greece: The Hippocratic ideal. *Journal of Medical Ethics and History of Medicine, 7*, 6. PMID: 25512827

Kneuer, M., & Wallaschek, S. (2022). Framing COVID-19: Public Leadership and Crisis Communication By Chancellor Angela Merkel During the Pandemic in 2020. *German Politics, 32*(4), 686–709. DOI: 10.1080/09644008.2022.2028140

Kodali, R. K., Swamy, G., & Lakshmi, B. (2015, December). An implementation of IoT for healthcare. In *2015 IEEE Recent Advances in Intelligent Computational Systems (RAICS)* (pp. 411-416). IEEE. DOI: 10.1109/RAICS.2015.7488451

Kotler, P., Shalowitz, J., & Stevens, R. J. (2021). *Strategic marketing for health care organizations: Building a customer-driven health system* (2nd ed.). Jossey-Bass., https://www.wiley.com/en-us/Strategic+Marketing+For+Health+Care+Organizations%3A+Building+A+Customer-Driven+Health+System%2C+2nd+Edition-p-9781118355831

Krack, G. (2019). How to make value-based health insurance designs more effective? A systematic review and meta-analysis. *The European Journal of Health Economics, 20*(6), 841–856. DOI: 10.1007/s10198-019-01046-1 PMID: 30923986

Kraus, S., Schiavone, F., Pluzhnikova, A., & Invernizzi, A. C. (2021). Digital transformation in healthcare: Analyzing the current state-of-research. *Journal of Business Research, 123*, 557–567. DOI: 10.1016/j.jbusres.2020.10.030

Krejcie, R. V., & Morgan, D. W. (1970). Determining sample size for research activities. *Educational and Psychological Measurement, 30*(3), 607–610. DOI: 10.1177/001316447003000308

Kruse, C. S., Krowski, N., & Rodriguez, B. (2017). Patient satisfaction and telehealth: A systematic review. *BMJ Open, 7*(8). Advance online publication. DOI: 10.1136/bmjopen-2017-016242 PMID: 28775188

Kumar, R. S. K. (2024). Strict implementation of the right to health as a fundamental right: Ensuring universal access and equity in India. *Law and Safety, 93*(2), 151–162. DOI: 10.32631/pb.2024.2.14

Kumar, R., & Singh, A. (2022). Digital divide and health governance in India: Challenges of inclusion in the phygital era. *The Indian Journal of Public Administration, 68*(2), 175–192. DOI: 10.1177/00195561221091332

Kurek, A. A., Shah, R., Inman, E., & Quiroga, A. (2023). Primary Care Redesign for Value-Based Care. *NEJM Catalyst Innovations in Care Delivery*, *4*(12). Advance online publication. DOI: 10.1056/CAT.22.0285

Kuzmanović, M., & Savić, G. (2020). Avoiding the Privacy Paradox Using Preference-Based Segmentation: A Conjoint Analysis Approach. *Electronics (Basel)*, *9*(9), 1382. Advance online publication. DOI: 10.3390/electronics9091382

Lang, C., Meier zu Biesen, C., & Burchardt, M. (2024). Digital technologies and the future of health: Aspirations, design, use and resistance. [REMOVED HYPERLINK FIELD]. *Health Risk & Society*, *31*(3), 201–214. Advance online publication. DOI: 10.1080/13648470.2024.2397921 PMID: 39508152

Lazarus, R. S., & Folkman, S. (1984). *Stress, appraisal, and coping*. Springer.

Leake, C. D. (1952). The old Egyptian medical papyri.

Leckenby, E., Dawoud, D., Bouvy, J., & Jónsson, P. (2021). The Sandbox Approach and its Potential for Use in Health Technology Assessment: A Literature Review. *Applied Health Economics and Health Policy*, *19*(6), 857–869. DOI: 10.1007/s40258-021-00665-1 PMID: 34254275

Lemak, C., Pena, D., Jones, D. A., Kim, D. H., & Guptill, J. (2024). Leadership to Accelerate Healthcare's Digital Transformation: Evidence From 33 Health Systems. *Journal of Healthcare Management*, *69*(4), 267–279. DOI: 10.1097/JHM-D-23-00210 PMID: 38976787

Leung, L. B., Rose, D., Stockdale, S. E., McGowan, M., Yano, E., Graaff, A. L., Dresselhaus, T., & Rubenstein, L. (2019). Regional Adoption of Primary Care-Mental Health Integration in Veterans Health Administration Patient-Centered Medical Homes. *Journal for Healthcare Quality*, *41*(5), 297–305. Advance online publication. DOI: 10.1097/JHQ.0000000000000206 PMID: 31135605

Leyland, M., Archer, N., Deal, K., & Hassanein, K. (2011). PDB76 DESIGNING A SERVICE FRAMEWORK FOR ELECTRONIC PERSONAL HEALTH RECORDS: A PATIENT-CENTRED APPROACH. *Value in Health*, *14*(3), A105. Advance online publication. DOI: 10.1016/j.jval.2011.02.584

Liang, S., Stults, C., Jones, V. G., Huang, Q., Sutton, J., Tennyson, G., & Chan, A. S. (2021). Effects of Behavioral Economics–Based Messaging on Appointment Scheduling Through Patient Portals and Appointment Completion: Observational Study. *JMIR Human Factors*, *9*(1), e34090. Advance online publication. DOI: 10.2196/34090 PMID: 35353051

Li, J., Ma, Q., Chan, A. H., & Man, S. (2019). Health monitoring through wearable technologies for older adults: Smart wearables acceptance model. *Applied Ergonomics, 75*, 162–169. DOI: 10.1016/j.apergo.2018.10.006 PMID: 30509522

Lim, W. M., & Weissmann, M. A. (2023). Toward a Theory of Behavioral Control. *Journal of Strategic Marketing, 31*(1), 185–211. DOI: 10.1080/0965254X.2021.1890190

Lindsay, S., Smith, S., Bellaby, P., & Baker, R. (2009). The health impact of an online heart disease support group: A comparison of moderated versus unmoderated support. *Health Education Research, 24*(4), 646–654. DOI: 10.1093/her/cyp001 PMID: 19251770

Liu, J. X., Vallin, J., Chiu, C., Cabrera, F. A., Hunter, L., Rao, A., Njau, P., & McCoy, S. (2023). Designing for two: How enhancing human-centered design with behavioral nudges unlocked breakthroughs to promote young women's psychological safety and access to reproductive care in Tanzania. *Social Science & Medicine, 320*, 115683. Advance online publication. DOI: 10.1016/j.socscimed.2023.115683 PMID: 36709692

Liu, X., Sun, M., & Li, J. (2018). Research on gender differences in online health communities. *International Journal of Medical Informatics, 111*, 172–181. DOI: 10.1016/j.ijmedinf.2017.12.019 PMID: 29425630

Li, Y.-H., Li, Y., Wei, M.-Y., & Li, G. (2024). Innovation and challenges of artificial intelligence technology in personalized healthcare. *Scientific Reports, 14*(1), 18994. Advance online publication. DOI: 10.1038/s41598-024-70073-7 PMID: 39152194

Li, Z., Li, X., & Guo, S. (2020). Mental-health status of Chinese rural-urban migrant workers and influencing factors: A meta-analysis. *Journal of Affective Disorders, 276*, 1102–1110. DOI: 10.1016/j.jad.2020.05.076 PMID: 32663938

Lopes, H. T., & Pereira, R. G. G. (2021). *The Gynecological Papyrus Kahun*. BoD–Books on Demand. DOI: 10.5772/intechopen.95311

Love-Koh, J., Griffin, S., Kataika, E., Revill, P., Sibandze, S., & Walker, S. (2020). Methods to promote equity in health resource allocation in low- and middle-income countries: An overview. *Globalization and Health, 16*(1), 6. Advance online publication. DOI: 10.1186/s12992-019-0537-z PMID: 31931823

Lu, J., Lu, C., Yu, C. S., & Yao, J. E. (2003). Exploring factors associated with wireless internet via mobile technology acceptance in Mainland China. *Communications of the IIMA, 3*(1), 101–120.

MacMillan, A., & Thomas, P. (2024). Hybrid healthcare models: The rise of phygital medicine. *Journal of Telemedicine Practices, 18*(1), 22–33.

Macrae, C., & Ansell, C. K. (2024). Generative Spaces: Collaboration, Learning and Innovation in a Regulatory Sandbox. SSRN *Electronic Journal*. DOI: 10.2139/ssrn.4825907

Mair, J., Hashim, J., Thai, L., Tai, E. S., Ryan, J. C., Kowatsch, T., Müller-Riemenschneider, F., & Edney, S. (2025). Understanding and overcoming barriers to digital health adoption: A patient and public involvement study. *Translational Behavioral Medicine*, *15*(1), ibaf010. Advance online publication. DOI: 10.1093/tbm/ibaf010 PMID: 40167046

Maita, K. C., et al. (2024). *The impact of digital health solutions on bridging the health-care access gap in rural areas: A scoping review.* BMC Health Services Research. [REMOVED HYPERLINK FIELD]PMC.DOI: 10.1186/s12913-024-11402-4

Major, R. H. (1930). The Papyrus Ebers. *Annals of Medical History*, *2*(5), 547. PMID: 33944361

Malhotra, N. (2020). *Marketing research: An applied orientation* (7th ed.). Pearson Education Limited.

Mallidi, R. K., Sharma, M., & Singh, J. (2021). Legacy Digital Transformation: TCO and ROI Analysis. *International Journal of Electrical and Computer Engineering Systems*. DOI: 10.32985/ijeces.12.3.5

Margetts, H., & Dunleavy, P. (2013). The second wave of digital-era governance: A quasi-paradigm for government on the web. *Philosophical Transactions of the Royal Society A, 371*(1987), 20120382. DOI: 10.1098/rsta.2012.0382

Marjoua, Y., & Bozic, K. J. (2012). Brief history of quality movement in US healthcare. *Current Reviews in Musculoskeletal Medicine*, *5*(4), 265–273. DOI: 10.1007/s12178-012-9137-8 PMID: 22961204

Marmot, M., Allen, J., Goldblatt, P., Herd, E., & Morrison, J. (2020). *Build back fairer: The COVID-19 Marmot review*. Institute of Health Equity. https://www.instituteofhealthequity.org/resources-reports/build-back-fairer-the-covid-19-marmot-review

Marmot, M. (2017). The Health Gap: The Challenge of an Unequal World: the argument. *International Journal of Epidemiology*, *46*(4), 1312–1318. DOI: 10.1093/ije/dyx163 PMID: 28938756

Mashar, M., Chawla, S., Chen, F., Lubwama, B., Patel, K., Kelshiker, M. A., Bachtiger, P., & Peters, N. S. (2023). Artificial intelligence algorithms in health care: Is the current food and drug administration regulation sufficient? *JMIR AI*, *2*(1), e42940. DOI: 10.2196/42940 PMID: 38875544

Massaro, M. (2023). Digital transformation in the healthcare sector through blockchain technology. Insights from academic research and business developments. *Technovation*, *120*, 102386. DOI: 10.1016/j.technovation.2021.102386

Mast, J. L., & Šuber, D. (2024). Societalized Politics in the German Civil Sphere: The 2015 "Refugee Crisis" and Post-Potsdam Civil Backlash. *International Journal of Politics Culture and Society*, *38*(2), 157–186. DOI: 10.1007/s10767-024-09490-5

Masyuri, R. I. (2024). Towards Equitable Healthcare: Redesigning Informed Consent Regulations. *Journal of Ecohumanism*. DOI: 10.62754/joe.v3i8.5447

Mathiharan, K. (2006). The fundamental right to health care. *PubMed, 11*(4), 123. https://pubmed.ncbi.nlm.nih.gov/16335519

Mattei, P. (2020). Digital governance in tax-funded European healthcare systems: From the Back office to patient empowerment. *Israel Journal of Health Policy Research*, *9*(1), 3. Advance online publication. DOI: 10.1186/s13584-020-0361-1 PMID: 31952548

Mauro, M., Noto, G., Prenestini, A., & Sarto, F. (2024). Digital transformation in healthcare: Assessing the role of digital technologies for managerial support processes. *Technological Forecasting and Social Change*, *209*, 123781. DOI: 10.1016/j.techfore.2024.123781

Mbunge, E., Muchemwa, B., Jiyane, S. E., & Batani, J. (2021). Sensors and healthcare 5.0: Transformative shift in virtual care through emerging digital health technologies. *Global Health Journal (Amsterdam, Netherlands)*, *5*(4), 169–177. DOI: 10.1016/j.glohj.2021.11.008

McGuire, E., Al-Zu'bi, M., Boa-Alvarado, M., Luu, T. T. G., Sylvester, J. M., & Leñero, E. M.-V. (2024). Equity principles: Using social theory for more effective social transformation in agricultural research for development. *Agricultural Systems*, *218*, 103999. Advance online publication. DOI: 10.1016/j.agsy.2024.103999

McGuire, T. G., Schillo, S., & van Kleef, R. C. (2020). Very high and low residual spenders in private health insurance markets: Germany, The Netherlands and the U.S. Marketplaces. *The European Journal of Health Economics*, *22*(1), 35–50. DOI: 10.1007/s10198-020-01227-3 PMID: 32862358

McNeil, C. D. W., Professor, P. E. M. E., Pereira, D. B., Ensz, O. S., Lukose, K., Harrell, G., & Feller, D. B. (2024). Toward a Comprehensive Model of Medical-Dental-Behavioral Integration. *JDR Clinical and Translational Research*, *9*(1_suppl), 23–31. DOI: 10.1177/23800844241273836 PMID: 39558739

Menachemi, N., & Collum, T. H. (2011). Suits and limitations of electronic health record systems. Healthcare Policy and Risk Management, 4.

Merchán-Cruz, E. A., Gabelaia, I., Savrasovs, M., Hansen, M. F., Soe, S., Rodriguez-Cañizo, R. G., & Aragón-Camarasa, G. (2025). Trust by Design: An Ethical Framework for Collaborative Intelligence Systems in Industry 5.0. *Electronics (Basel)*, *14*(10), 1952. DOI: 10.3390/electronics14101952

Merino, M., del Barrio, J., Nuño, R., & Errea, M. (2024). Value-based digital health: A systematic literature review of the value elements of digital health care. *Digital Health*, *10*, 20552076241277438. Advance online publication. DOI: 10.1177/20552076241277438 PMID: 39403712

Meskó, B., & Spiegel, B. (2022). A revised Hippocratic oath for the era of digital health. *Journal of Medical Internet Research*, *24*(9), e39177. DOI: 10.2196/39177 PMID: 36069845

Metwaly, A. M., Ghoneim, M. M., Eissa, I. H., Elsehemy, I. A., Mostafa, A. E., Hegazy, M. M., Afifi, W. M., & Dou, D. (2021). Traditional ancient Egyptian medicine: A review. *Saudi Journal of Biological Sciences*, *28*(10), 5823–5832. DOI: 10.1016/j.sjbs.2021.06.044 PMID: 34588897

Migration, Integration, Asylum: Political Developments in Germany 2016. (2016). Federal Office for Migration and Refugees, Germany. https://www.bamf.de/SharedDocs/Anlagen/EN/EMN/Politikberichte/emn-politikbericht-2016-germany.pdf?__blob=publicationFile&v=7

Ministry of Health and Family Welfare (MoHFW). (Various years). *Annual reports*. Government of India. https://www.mohfw.gov.in/?q=en/documents/publication

Ministry of Health and Family Welfare. (Various years). *Annual reports*. Government of India. https://www.mohfw.gov.in/?q=en/documents/publication

Mishra, A. (2025, August 25). *Strategy and examples for phygital marketing in healthcare*. Valuebound Blog.[REMOVED HYPERLINK FIELD]https://www.valuebound.com/resources/blog/Phygital-Marketing-in-Healthcare

Mishra, N., & Anand, R. (2025). *A Milestone in the Modernization of Indian Healthcare: How Digital Integration is Transforming the Country's Health System*. https://nextbillion.net/milestone-modernization-indian-healthcare-digital-integration-transforming-health-system/

Mitra, R. (2024). From the Translocal to the Multi-Sited Transnational: Tracing Rohingya Refugee Networks in India. *Global Networks*, *25*(1), e12494. Advance online publication. DOI: 10.1111/glob.12494

Mohammad, A. A. S., Alzyoud, M., Samara, E. I. M., Al-shanableh, N., Salameh, W. E. M. K. B., Alshurideh, M. T., Al-Ayed, S., Alqahtani, M., Al-Momani, A., & Al-Hawary, S. I. S. (2025). Electronic health records adoption: a bibliometric analysis. In *Intelligence-Driven Circular Economy: Regeneration Towards Sustainability and Social Responsibility–Volume 1* (pp. 301–314). Springer Nature Switzerland. DOI: 10.1007/978-3-031-73899-9_24

Montagu, I., & Maplethorpe, N. (2024). British Social Attitudes 41| Five years of unprecedented challenges.

Moore, C. M. (2022). The challenges of health inequities and AI. *Intelligence-Based Medicine*, *6*, 100067. DOI: 10.1016/j.ibmed.2022.100067

Moores, T. T. (2012). Towards an integrated model of IT acceptance in healthcare. *Decision Support Systems*, *53*(3), 507–516. DOI: 10.1016/j.dss.2012.04.014

Morley, I. (2007). City chaos, contagion, Chadwick, and social justice. *The Yale Journal of Biology and Medicine*, *80*(2), 61. PMID: 18160991

Müller, T. R. (2021). Reshaping conceptions of citizenship? German Business sector engagement and refugee integration. *Citizenship Studies*, *25*(3), 409–425. DOI: 10.1080/13621025.2021.1873916

Musa, S., Abdulwahab, L. O., & Beri, M. H. (2026). The Impact of AI Technologies in Transforming Financial Systems and Driving Innovation. In *Promoting Inclusivity and Accessibility With FinTech* (pp. 153–182). IGI Global Scientific Publishing., https://www.igi-global.com/chapter/the-impact-of-ai-technologies-in-transforming-financial-systems-and-driving-innovation/387218

Nadhamuni, S., John, O., Kulkarni, M., Nanda, E., Venkatraman, S., Varma, D., Balsari, S., Gudi, N., Samantaray, S., Reddy, H., & Sheel, V. (2021). Driving digital transformation of comprehensive primary health services at scale in India: An enterprise architecture framework. *BMJ Global Health*, *6*(Suppl 5), e005242. Advance online publication. DOI: 10.1136/bmjgh-2021-005242 PMID: 34312149

Naithani, P. (2024). Analysis of India's Digital Personal Data Protection Act, 2023. *International Journal of Law and Management*, *67*(5), 543–553. DOI: 10.1108/IJLMA-05-2024-0174

Naithani, P. (2025). Article: Strengthening Legitimate Use in India's Digital Personal Data Protection Act, 2023. *Global Privacy Law Review*, *6*(2), 61–65. DOI: 10.54648/GPLR2025011

Narayana, D., & Venkiteswaran, C. S. (2021). Migration and exclusion in Kerala's informal sector. *Kerala Development Report*, *3*(1), 22–35.

Nazari-Shirkouhi, S., Badizadeh, A., Dashtpeyma, M., & Ghodsi, R. (2023). A model to improve user acceptance of e-services in healthcare systems based on technology acceptance model: An empirical study. *Journal of Ambient Intelligence and Humanized Computing*, *14*(6), 7919–7935. DOI: 10.1007/s12652-023-04601-0 PMID: 37228695

Niedermaier, A., Freiberg, A., Tiller, D., Wienke, A., & Führer, A. (2020). Outpatient health care utilization and health expenditures of asylum seekers in Halle (Saale), Germany - an analysis of claims data. *BMC Health Services Research*, *20*(1), 961. DOI: 10.1186/s12913-020-05811-4 PMID: 33081775

Nordal, K. C. (2012). Healthcare reform: Implications for independent practice. *Professional Psychology, Research and Practice*, *43*(6), 535–544. DOI: 10.1037/a0029603

Nordberg, S. S., Jaso-Yim, B., Sah, P., Schuler, K., Eyllon, M., Pennine, M., Hoyler, G. H., Barnes, J. B., Murillo, L., O'Dea, H., Orth, L., Rogers, E., Welch, G., Peloquin, G. D., & Youn, S. J. (2024). Evaluating the Implementation and Clinical Effectiveness of an Innovative Digital First Care Model for Behavioral Health Using the RE-AIM Framework: Quantitative Evaluation. *Journal of Medical Internet Research*, *26*, e54528. Advance online publication. DOI: 10.2196/54528 PMID: 39476366

North, D. C. (1990). *Institutions, institutional change and economic performance*. Cambridge University Press., DOI: 10.1017/CBO9780511808678

Northouse, P. G. (2021). *Leadership: Theory and practice* (9th ed.). SAGE Publications., https://www.scirp.org/reference/referencespapers?referenceid=3786973

Nunnally, J. C. (1967). *Psychometric Theory*. McGraw-Hill Book Company.

Nutbeam, D. (2000). Health literacy as a public health goal. *Health Promotion International*, *15*(3), 259–267. DOI: 10.1093/heapro/15.3.259

Nutbeam, D. (2008). The evolving concept of health literacy. *Social Science & Medicine*, *67*(12), 2072–2078. DOI: 10.1016/j.socscimed.2008.09.050

Nwadiokwu, O. T. (2025). *Ethical AI and machine learning integration in health innovation information systems for clinical excellence. Computer Science &amp.* IT Research Journal., DOI: 10.51594/csitrj.v6i3.1872

O'Laughlin, B. (2016). Pragmatism, Structural Reform and the Politics of Inequality in Global Public Health. *Development and Change*, *47*(4), 686–711. DOI: 10.1111/dech.12251

Oberlander, J. (2010). Long time coming: Why health reform finally passed. *Health Affairs*, *29*(6), 1112–1116. DOI: 10.1377/hlthaff.2010.0447 PMID: 20530339

Ochinanwata, N., Ezepue, P., Nwankwo, T., Ochinanwata, C., & Igwe, P. (2021). Public–private entrepreneurial financing partnership model in Nigeria. *Thunderbird International Business Review*, *63*(3), 369–379. Advance online publication. DOI: 10.1002/tie.22194

Olabi, A., Palmer, N., Bertone, M. P., Loffreda, G., Bou-Orm, I. R., Sempé, L., Espinoza, M. V., Dakessian, A., Kadetz, P., Ager, A., & Witter, S. (2025). Refugee integration in national health systems of low- and middle-income countries (LMICs): Evidence synthesis and future research agenda. *Social Science & Medicine*, *385*, 118546. DOI: 10.1016/j.socscimed.2025.118546 PMID: 41061533

Oluwagbade, E. (2025). Bridging the healthcare Gap: The role of AI-Driven Telemedicine in Emerging Economies. *International Journal of Research Publication and Reviews*. DOI: 10.55248/gengpi.6.0125.0531

Organisation for Economic Co-operation and Development (OECD). (2021). *Centre stage: Driving inclusive growth through inclusive policy making*. OECD Publishing.

Organisation for Economic Co-operation and Development. (2020). *Health in the 21st century: Putting data to work for stronger health systems*. OECD Publishing. DOI: 10.1787/e3b23f8e-en

Orosz, E., Ellena, G., & Jakab, M. (1998). Reforming the Healthcare System. The Unfinished Agenda. Public Finance Reform during the Transition: The Experience of Hungary.

Osborne, R. H., Batterham, R. W., Elsworth, G. R., Hawkins, M., & Buchbinder, R. (2013). The grounded psychometric development and initial validation of the Health Literacy Questionnaire (HLQ). *BMC Public Health*, *13*(1), 658. DOI: 10.1186/1471-2458-13-658

Osipov, V. S., & Skryl, T. V. (2021). Impact of digital technologies on the efficiency of healthcare delivery. In *IoT in healthcare and ambient assisted living* (pp. 243–261). Springer Singapore. DOI: 10.1007/978-981-15-9897-5_12

Oso, O. B., Alli, O. I., Babarinde, A., & Ibeh, A. I. (2025). Impact-Driven Healthcare Investments: A Conceptual Framework for Deploying Capital and Technology in Frontier Market. *International Journal of Multidisciplinary Research and Growth Evaluation*. DOI: 10.54660/.IJMRGE.2025.6.1.1702-1720

Palmiotto, F. (2023). „Like Handing My Whole Life Over". *Verfassungsblog: On Matters Constitutional*. DOI: 10.17176/20230228-185227-0

Palombini, M., Vereen, T., Taghiani, J., & Chitre, T. (2023). Building a Framework for a More Inclusive Healthcare System. *Telehealth and Medicine Today*, *8*(3). Advance online publication. DOI: 10.30953/thmt.v8.414

Panch, T., Mattie, H., & Atun, R. (2019). Artificial intelligence and algorithmic bias: Implications for health systems. *Journal of Global Health*, *9*(2), 020318. DOI: 10.7189/jogh.09.020318 PMID: 31788229

Pantano, E., & Gandini, A. (2017). The connection between the types of sociality mediated by new technologies in retail environments. *Computers in Human Behavior*, •••, 77.

Papa, A., Mital, M., Pisano, P., & Del Giudice, M. (2020). E-health and wellbeing monitoring using smart healthcare devices: An empirical investigation. *Technological Forecasting and Social Change*, *153*, 119226. DOI: 10.1016/j.techfore.2018.02.018

Parikh, R. B., Basen-Enquist, K. M., Bradley, C., Estrin, D., Levy, M., Lichtenfeld, J. L., Malin, B., McGraw, D., Meropol, N. J., Oyer, R. A., Sheldon, L. K., & Shulman, L. N. (2022). Digital health applications in oncology: An opportunity to seize. *Journal of the National Cancer Institute*, *114*(10), 1338–1339. DOI: 10.1093/jnci/djac108 PMID: 35640986

Park, J. H., Lee, C. W., & Do, C. (2025). Examining Users' Acceptance Intention of Health Applications Based on the Technology Acceptance Model. *Health Care*, *13*(6), 596. PMID: 40150446

Pascoe, E. A., & Richman, L. S. (2009). Perceived discrimination and health: A meta-analytic review. *Psychological Bulletin*, *135*(4), 531–554. DOI: 10.1037/a0016059 PMID: 19586161

Philip, J., Gilli, K., & Knappstein, M. (2023). Identifying key leadership competencies for digital transformation: Evidence from a cross-sectoral Delphi study of global managers. *Leadership &amp. Leadership and Organization Development Journal*, *44*(3), 392–406. Advance online publication. DOI: 10.1108/LODJ-02-2022-0063

Planning Commission, Government of India. (1951). *First Five-Year Plan (1951–1956)*. Government of India. https://archive.org/details/dli.ernet.449278

Planning Commission, Government of India. (1951–1956). *First Five-Year Plan*. Government of India. https://archive.org/download/dli.ernet.449278/449278-The%20First%20Five%20Year%20Plan_text.pdf

Planning Commission, Government of India. (1974). *Fifth Five-Year Plan (1974–1979)*. Government of India. https://niti.gov.in/planning-commission-archive

Planning Commission, Government of India. (1974–1979). *Fifth Five-Year Plan.* Government of India. https://niti.gov.in/planning-commission-archive

Planning Commission, Government of India. (1985–1990). *Seventh Five-Year Plan* (Vols. 1–2). Government of India. https://niti.gov.in/planning-commission-archive

Planning Commission, Government of India. (1985–1990). *Seventh Five-Year Plan* (Vols. I & II). Government of India. https://niti.gov.in/planning-commission-archive

Planning Commission, Government of India. (1992–1997). *Eighth Five-Year Plan* (Vols. 1–2). Government of India. https://niti.gov.in/planning-commission-archive

Planning Commission, Government of India. (1992–1997). *Eighth Five-Year Plan* (Vols. I & II). Government of India. https://niti.gov.in/planning-commission-archive

Planning Commission, Government of India. (2002–2007). *Tenth Five-Year Plan* (Vols. 1–3). Government of India. https://niti.gov.in/planning-commission-archive

Planning Commission, Government of India. (2002–2007). *Tenth Five-Year Plan* (Vols. I–III). Government of India. https://niti.gov.in/planning-commission-archive

Planning Commission, Government of India. (2007–2012). *Eleventh Five-Year Plan* (Vols. 1–3). Government of India. https://niti.gov.in/planning-commission-archive

Planning Commission, Government of India. (2007–2012). *Eleventh Five-Year Plan* (Vols. I–III). Government of India. https://niti.gov.in/planning-commission-archive

Planning Commission, Government of India. (2012). *Twelfth Five-Year Plan (2012–2017): Faster, more inclusive, and sustainable growth* (Vols. 1–3). SAGE Publications India. https://niti.gov.in/planning-commission-archive

Planning Commission, Government of India. (2012–2017). *Twelfth Five-Year Plan* (Vols. 1–3). Government of India. https://niti.gov.in/planning-commission-archive

Planning Commission, Government of India. (2012–2017). *Twelfth Five-Year Plan* (Vols. I–III). Government of India. https://niti.gov.in/planning-commission-archive

Pooyan, E. J., Sakha, M. A., Mohtasham, F., & Mostafavi, H. (2018). The Effect of Resource Allocation Decisions on Efficiency and Equity in the Health Sector: A Systematic Review. *Journal of Health Research*, *3*(1), 28–34. DOI: 10.29252/cjhr.3.1.28

Poveda, J., Bretón-Romero, R., del Rio-Bermudez, C., Taberna, M., & Medrano, I. H. (2022). How can artificial intelligence optimize value-based contracting? *Journal of Pharmaceutical Policy and Practice*, *15*(1), 85. Advance online publication. DOI: 10.1186/s40545-022-00475-3 PMID: 36401303

Puri, A. (2024). Legal Challenges and Considerations in Implementing Telemedicine Services. *International Journal of Social Science and Economic Research.* DOI: 10.46609/IJSSER.2024.v09i09.017

Putera, I. (2017). Redefining health: Implication for value-based healthcare reform. *Cureus, 9*(3). PMID: 28409068

Rahimi, K. (2019). Digital health and the elusive quest for cost savings. *The Lancet. Digital Health, 1*(3), 108–109. DOI: 10.1016/S2589-7500(19)30056-1 PMID: 33323258

Raimo, N., De Turi, I., Albergo, F., & Vitolla, F. (2023). The drivers of the digital transformation in the healthcare industry: An empirical analysis in Italian hospitals. *Technovation, 121*, 102558. DOI: 10.1016/j.technovation.2022.102558

Rajan, S. I., & Zachariah, K. C. (2019). *Emigration and remittances: New evidence from the Kerala migration survey 2018.* Centre for Development Studies.

Rajkomar, A., Dean, J., & Kohane, I. (2019). Artificial intelligence in healthcare. *The New England Journal of Medicine*, •••, 380.

Ramachander, A., & Gowri, D. P. (2025). The future of digital health in transforming healthcare. In *Digital Technology in Public Health and Rehabilitation Care* (pp. 363–385). Academic Press. DOI: 10.1016/B978-0-443-22270-2.00021-6

Ratwani, R. M., Sutton, K., & Galarraga, J. E. (2024). Addressing AI algorithmic bias in health care. *Journal of the American Medical Association, 332*(13), 1051–1052. DOI: 10.1001/jama.2024.13486 PMID: 39230911

Raven, J., Mansour, W., Aikins, M., Bulthuis, S., Chikaphupha, K., Dieleman, M., Kok, M., Martineau, T., Ssengooba, F., Wyss, K., & Vallières, F. (2024). From PERFORM to PERFORM2Scale: Lessons from scaling-up a health management strengthening intervention to support Universal Health Coverage in three African countries. *Health Policy and Planning, 39*(8), 841–853. DOI: 10.1093/heapol/czae063 PMID: 38978193

Rawls, J. (1971). *A theory of justice.* Harvard University Press. DOI: 10.4159/9780674042605

Reddy, K. S., Sharma, A., Kumar, P., Gupta, V., & Singh, A. (2018). Towards achieving global health equity: Opportunities and challenges of health promotion. *Lancet, 392*(10165), 1225–1237. DOI: 10.1016/S0140-6736(18)32380-6

Reddy, P., & Sharma, B. (2016). DIGITALISATION: THE FUTURE OF HEALTH CARE. *Journal of Business and Management*, •••, 11.

Reed, M. E., Warton, E. M., Kim, E., Solomon, M. D., & Karter, A. (2017). Value-Based Insurance Design Benefit Offsets Reductions In Medication Adherence Associated With Switch To Deductible Plan. *Health Affairs*, *36*(3), 516–523. DOI: 10.1377/hlthaff.2016.1316 PMID: 28264954

Refugee and migrant health at the centre of discussions during the 77th UN General Assembly. (2022). WHO. https://www.who.int/news/item/21-09-2022-refugee-and-migrant-health-at-the-centre-of-discussions-during-the-77th-un-general-assembly

Refugees and asylum. (2024). Federal Ministry of Labour and Social Affairs, Germany. https://www.bmas.de/EN/Europe-and-the-World/Europe/Migration-from-third-countries/refugees-and-asylum.html

Relman, A. S., Todd, J. S., Schramm, C. J., & Seidman, B., BROMBERG, M. D., ROSENBERG, N., & BRUNTON, R. S. (1990). Reforming the health care system. *Issues in Science and Technology*, *7*(1), 6–11. PMID: 2402264

RESPONSE TO THE INVITATION FOR PUBLIC COMMENT NATIONAL DIGITAL HEALTH BLUEPRINT. (2019). https://mittalsouthasiainstitute.harvard.edu/wp-content/uploads/2019/08/Response-to-the-Invitation-for-Public-Comment-National-Digital-Health-Blueprint.pdf

Richard, L., Furler, J., Densley, K., Haggerty, J., Russell, G., Levesque, J., & Gunn, J. (2016). Equity of access to primary healthcare for vulnerable populations: The IMPACT international online survey of innovations. *International Journal for Equity in Health*, *15*(1), 64. Advance online publication. DOI: 10.1186/s12939-016-0351-7 PMID: 27068028

Richardson, S., Lawrence, K., Schoenthaler, A. M., & Mann, D. M. (2022). A framework for digital health equity. *NPJ Digital Medicine*, *5*(1), 119. Advance online publication. DOI: 10.1038/s41746-022-00663-0 PMID: 35982146

Riegler, J. (2023). *Comparative Ethics of Modern Payment Models*. Voices in Bioethics., DOI: 10.52214/vib.v9i.10310

Riemer, L., Rau, L., & Schalast, R. (2025). *Asylum Database Information, Germany*. AIDA. https://asylumineurope.org/reports/country/germany/reception-conditions/health-care/

Ringen, K. (1979). Edwin Chadwick, the market ideology, and sanitary reform: On the nature of the 19th-century public health movement. *International Journal of Health Services*, *9*(1), 107–120. DOI: 10.2190/LR4G-X2NK-9363-F1EC PMID: 370032

Rivera, M., Gregory, A., & Cobos, L. (2015). Mobile application for the timeshare industry: The influence of technology experience, usefulness, and attitude on behavioral intentions. *Journal of Hospitality and Tourism Technology*, *6*(3), 242–257. DOI: 10.1108/JHTT-01-2015-0002

Robelski, S., Mette, J., Wirth, T., Kiepe, N., Nienhaus, A., Harth, V., & Mache, S. (2020). (Un)bounded Social Work?—Analysis of Working Conditions in Refugee and Homeless Aid in Relation to Perceived Job Stress and Job Satisfaction. *International Journal of Environmental Research and Public Health*, *17*(2), 601. DOI: 10.3390/ijerph17020601 PMID: 31963446

Rogers, E. M. (2003). *Diffusion of innovations* (5th ed.). Free Press., https://books.google.com/books?id=9U1K5LjUOwEC

Romanovskaya, O. V., & Romanovskiy, G. B. (2024). Law and digitalization of modern healthcare. *RUDN Journal of Law*, *28*(3), 565–583. DOI: 10.22363/2313-2337-2024-28-3-565-583

Rosenberg, M. (1965). *Society and the adolescent self-image*. Princeton University Press. DOI: 10.1515/9781400876136

Rosenstock, I. M. (1974). Historical origins of the health belief model. *Health Education Monographs*, *2*(4), 328–335. DOI: 10.1177/109019817400200403

Rothstein, W. G. (1987). *American medical schools and the practice of medicine: A history*. Oxford University Press. DOI: 10.1093/oso/9780195041866.001.0001

Rouidi, M., Hamdoune, A., Choujtani, K., & Chati, A. (2022). TAM-UTAUT and the acceptance of remote healthcare technologies by healthcare professionals: A systematic review. *Informatics in Medicine Unlocked*, *32*, 101008. DOI: 10.1016/j.imu.2022.101008

Ryff, C. D., & Keyes, C. L. M. (1995). The structure of psychological well-being revisited. *Journal of Personality and Social Psychology*, *69*(4), 719–727. DOI: 10.1037/0022-3514.69.4.719 PMID: 7473027

Saha, K. C. (1999). The Chittagong Hill Tracts Peace Accord: A Landmark Model for a Viable Solution to the Refugee Problem. *Refuge: Canada's Journal on Refugees*, *10*, 10–15. Advance online publication. DOI: 10.25071/1920-7336.22008

Saifudin, A., Aima, M., Sutawidjaya, A., & Sugiyono, S. (2021). Hospital digitalization in the era of industry 4.0 based on GHRM and service quality. *International Journal of Data and Network Science*, *5*(2), 107–114. DOI: 10.5267/j.ijdns.2021.2.004

Salvi, A., Vitolla, F., Rubino, M., Giakoumelou, A., & Raimo, N. (2021). Online information on digitalisation processes and its impact on firm value. *Journal of Business Research, 124*, 437–444. DOI: 10.1016/j.jbusres.2020.10.025

Santos, P., & Nazaré, I. (2025). The doctor and patient of tomorrow: Exploring the intersection of artificial intelligence, preventive medicine, and ethical challenges in future healthcare. *Frontiers in Digital Health, 7*, 1588479. Advance online publication. DOI: 10.3389/fdgth.2025.1588479 PMID: 40248038

Sarthe, A. (2025). Over 600 Private Hospitals Exit AB-PMJAY; Gujarat Leads Opt-Outs. *DNA*. https://www.digitalhealthnews.com/over-600-private-hospitals-exit-ab-pmjay-gujarat-leads-opt-outs

Saxena, N., & Pillai, P. (2021). Trust and technology adoption in India's e-governance ecosystem. *Information Polity, 26*(4), 465–480. DOI: 10.3233/IP-210289

Schiavone, F., & Ferretti, M. (2021). The FutureS of healthcare. *Futures, 134*, 102849. DOI: 10.1016/j.futures.2021.102849 PMID: 34584276

Schmitt, M. T., Branscombe, N. R., Postmes, T., & Garcia, A. (2014). The consequences of perceived discrimination for psychological well-being: A meta-analytic review. *Psychological Bulletin, 140*(4), 921–948. DOI: 10.1037/a0035754 PMID: 24547896

Schulenburg, J. M. G. (1983). Report from Germany: Current conditions and controversies in the health care system. *Journal of Health Politics, Policy and Law, 8*(2), 320–351. DOI: 10.1215/03616878-8-2-320 PMID: 6413572

Schutte, L. (2024). Advancing Digital Health Equity: An Interdisciplinary Educational Approach to Digital Health Access and Inclusivity. *Studies in Health Technology and Informatics, 315*, 511–514. DOI: 10.3233/SHTI240201 PMID: 39049311

Schwenk, U., Gesundheit, D. P., Stiftung, B., Strotbek, J., Wehling, H., & Meier, F. (2023). Entwicklung und Anwendung eines Composite Measures für die Qualitätsdarstellung von Krankenhäusern.

Scuffham, P. (2002). Systematic review of cost effectiveness in telemedicine. *BMJ (Clinical Research Ed.), 325*(7364), 598.1. Advance online publication. DOI: 10.1136/bmj.325.7364.598 PMID: 12228145

Sebastian, R. (2024). The Role of Artificial Intelligence in Telemedicine: Legal Considerations under Indonesian Health Laws. *Devotion : Journal of Research and Community Service*. DOI: 10.59188/devotion.v5i12.20694

Semenova, Y., Lim, L., Salpynov, Z., Gaipov, A., & Jakovljevic, M. (2024). Historical evolution of healthcare systems of post-soviet Russia, Belarus, Kazakhstan, Kyrgyzstan, Tajikistan, Turkmenistan, Uzbekistan, Armenia, and Azerbaijan: A scoping review. Heliyon, 10(8). vd Schulenburg, J. M. G. (2019). The German health care system: concurrent solidarity, freedom of choice, and cost control. In Health Care Systems and Their Patients (pp. 83-104). Routledge.

Sen, A. (1999). *Development as freedom*. Oxford University Press., https://global.oup.com/academic/product/development-as-freedom-9780198297581

Senbekov, M., Saliev, T., Bukeyeva, Z., Almabayeva, A., Zhanaliyeva, M., Aitenova, N., Toishibekov, Y., & Fakhradiyev, I. (2020). The recent progress and applications of digital technologies in healthcare: A review. *International Journal of Telemedicine and Applications*, *2020*(1), 8830200. DOI: 10.1155/2020/8830200 PMID: 33343657

Senge, P. M. (2006). *The fifth discipline: The art and practice of the learning organization* (Rev. ed.). Doubleday.

Settou, H., & Aomari, A. (2024). *The impact of the social digital influencer on the attitudinal change of his virtual community*. South Florida Journal of Development., DOI: 10.46932/sfjdv5n11-028

Shanker, R., & Raghavan, P. (2020). The Invisible Crisis: Refugees and COVID-19 in India. *International Journal of Refugee Law*, *32*(4), 680–684. DOI: 10.1093/ijrl/eeab011

Sheiman, I., & Fleck, F. (2013). Rocky road from the Semashko to a new health model. *Bulletin of the World Health Organization*, *91*(5), 320–321. DOI: 10.2471/BLT.13.030513 PMID: 23678194

Sheiman, I., Shishkin, S., & Shevsky, V. (2018). The evolving Semashko model of primary health care: The case of the Russian Federation. *Risk Management and Healthcare Policy*, *11*, 209–220. DOI: 10.2147/RMHP.S168399 PMID: 30464661

Shen, Y., Yu, J., Zhou, J., & Hu, G. (2025). Twenty-five years of evolution and hurdles in electronic health records and interoperability in medical research: A comprehensive review. *Journal of Medical Internet Research*, *27*, e59024. DOI: 10.2196/59024 PMID: 39787599

Shkeer, A. S., Sharabati, A., Samarah, T., Alqurneh, M. I. M., & Ali, A. (2024). The influence of social media content marketing on consumer engagement: A mediating of the role of consumer cognition. *International Journal of Data and Network Science*. DOI: 10.5267/j.ijdns.2024.5.015

Shuliuk, B. (2021). CORPORATE FINANCING OF PUBLIC-PRIVATE PARTNERSHIP PROJECTS: ASSESSMENT OF FINANCIAL OPPORTUNITIES AND RISKS. *Financial and Credit Activity: Problems of Theory and Practice*. DOI: 10.18371/fcaptp.v3i38.237422

Shyshka, I., Mashchenko, O., & Tomareva, V. (2023). Theoretical And Methodological Foundations Of The Healthcare System Of Ukraine. *Baltic Journal of Economic Studies*, *9*(4), 253–261. DOI: 10.30525/2256-0742/2023-9-4-253-261

Siddiqi, S., Masud, T. I., Nishtar, S., Peters, D. H., Sabri, B., Bile, K. M., & Jama, M. A. (2009). Framework for assessing governance of the health system in developing countries: Gateway to good governance. *Health Policy (Amsterdam)*, *90*(1), 13–25. DOI: 10.1016/j.healthpol.2008.08.005 PMID: 18838188

Siddique, S. M., Tipton, K., Leas, B., Jepson, C., Aysola, J., Cohen, J. B., Flores, E., Harhay, M. O., Schmidt, H., Weissman, G. E., Fricke, J., Treadwell, J. R., & Mull, N. K. (2024). The impact of health care algorithms on racial and ethnic disparities: A systematic review. *Annals of Internal Medicine*, *177*(4), 484–496. DOI: 10.7326/M23-2960 PMID: 38467001

Simons, M., Golas, S., Agboola, S., & Buijs, J. op den, Felsted, J., Fischer, N., & Orenstein, A. (2018). *Maximizing Potentially Avoidable Hospitalizations and Cost Savings Beyond Targeting the Most Costly Patients (Preprint)*. DOI: 10.2196/preprints.11731

Simpson, J., Albani, V., Bell, Z., Bambra, C., & Brown, H. (2021). Effects of social security policy reforms on mental health and inequalities: A systematic review of observational studies in high-income countries. *Social Science & Medicine*, *272*, 113717. DOI: 10.1016/j.socscimed.2021.113717 PMID: 33545493

Smith, H. (2000). A Quaker Inheritance: An Analysis of Family Values, Religion and the Childhood and Youth of George Newman (1870-1948). *Quaker Studies*, *5*(1), 4.

Smyshlyaev, A. (2022). Public-private partnership in the system of compulsory health insurance: Features and trends. *Spravočnik Vrača Obŝej Praktiki (Journal of Family Medicine)*. DOI: 10.33920/med-10-2206-02

Sneha, M. (2024). Advances in Finance, Accounting, and Economics: Vol. 399. *A., Chatterjee, S., & Rout, P. C.* Can Medical AI Bridge the Gender Gap for Sustainable Healthcare., DOI: 10.4018/979-8-3693-7580-8.ch017

Snigdha, E. Z., Jalil, M. S., Dahwal, F. M., Saeed, M., Mehedy, M. T. J., & Hasan, S. K. (2025). Cybersecurity in Healthcare IT Systems: Business Risk Management and Data Privacy Strategies. *The American Journal of Engineering and Technology*, *7*(03), 163–184. DOI: 10.37547/tajet/Volume07Issue03-15

Socha-Dietrich, K. (2021). Empowering the health workforce to make the most of the digital revolution. *OECD Health Working Papers*, (129), 0_1-67. DOI:DOI: 10.1787/18152015

Solar, O., & Irwin, A. (2010). *A conceptual framework for action on the social determinants of health.* World Health Organization. https://apps.who.int/iris/handle/10665/44489

Sood, S., Lal, K., Bhatia, M., Kapoor, G., Singh, S., Kaushish, R. K., Bisht, D., Sharma, V. K., Chakraborty, S., Shete, M., Solanki, N. K., Naskar, A., Sharma, M., Subramaniyan, E. U., Waikar, S., & Verma, N. (2025). Adoption and utilization of India's eSanjeevani national telemedicine service. *Oxford Open Digital Health*, *3*, oqaf025. Advance online publication. DOI: 10.1093/oodh/oqaf025 PMID: 41158553

Spiegel, P., Chanis, R., & Trujillo, A. (2018). Innovative health financing for refugees. *BMC Medicine*, *16*(1), 90. Advance online publication. DOI: 10.1186/s12916-018-1068-9 PMID: 29903046

Stafford, N. (2016). Voices unite to demand free healthcare for refugees in Germany. *BMJ (Clinical Research Ed.)*, *352*, i884. Advance online publication. DOI: 10.1136/bmj.i884 PMID: 26867757

Stanić, T., Avşar, T. S., & Gomes, M. (2023). Economic Evaluations of Digital Health Interventions for Children and Adolescents: Systematic Review. *Journal of Medical Internet Research*, *25*, e45958. Advance online publication. DOI: 10.2196/45958 PMID: 37921844

State of Health in the EU, Germany - Country Health Profile 2023. (2023). European Union. https://health.ec.europa.eu/system/files/2023-12/2023_chp_de_english.pdf

Stecker, E., Ayanian, J., & Fendrick, A. M. (2015). Value-Based Insurance Design: Aligning Incentives to Improve Cardiovascular Care. *Circulation*, *132*(16), 1580–1585. Advance online publication. DOI: 10.1161/CIRCULATIONAHA.114.012584 PMID: 26481563

Steinbrink, E., Reichert, L., Mende, M., & Reuter, C. (2021). Digital Privacy Perceptions of Asylum Seekers in Germany: An Empirical Study about Smartphone Usage during the Flight. *Proceedings of the ACM on Human-Computer Interaction*, *5*(CSCW2), 1–24. DOI: 10.1145/3479526

Steinhubl, S. R., Muse, E. D., & Topol, E. J. (2015). The new sphere of mobile health. *Science Translational Medicine*, *7*(283). PMID: 25877894

Stewart, M. (2023). The public health crisis created by UK social policy reforms. *Justice. Power and Resistance*, *6*(2), 217–228. DOI: 10.1332/GQDH4178

Stiefel, M., Shaner, A., & Schaefer, S. D. (2006). The Edwin Smith Papyrus: The birth of analytical thinking in medicine and otolaryngology. *The Laryngoscope*, *116*(2), 182–188. DOI: 10.1097/01.mlg.0000191461.08542.a3 PMID: 16467701

Stiglitz, J. E. (2000). *Economics of the public sector* (3rd ed.). W. W. Norton & Company., https://www.academia.edu/37552359/Economics_of_the_Public_Sector_Joseph_E_Stiglitz

Stoumpos, A. I., Kitsios, F., & Talias, M. A. (2023). Digital transformation in healthcare: Technology acceptance and its applications. *International Journal of Environmental Research and Public Health*, *20*(4), 3407. DOI: 10.3390/ijerph20043407 PMID: 36834105

Stratton, E., Jones, N., Peters, S. E., Torous, J., & Glozier, N. (2021). Digital mHealth Interventions for Employees. *Journal of Occupational and Environmental Medicine*, *63*(8), 512–525. DOI: 10.1097/JOM.0000000000002267 PMID: 34050095

Straub, D., Limayem, M., & Karahanna-Evaristo, E. (1995). Measuring system usage: Implications for IS theory testing. *Management Science*, *41*(8), 1328–1342. DOI: 10.1287/mnsc.41.8.1328

Strull, W. M., Lo, B., & Charles, G. (1984). Do patients want to participate in medical decision making? *Journal of the American Medical Association*, *252*(21), 2990–2994. DOI: 10.1001/jama.1984.03350210038026 PMID: 6502860

Sukriti, K. C., Tewolde, S., Laverty, A. A., Costelloe, C., Papoutsi, C., Reidy, C., Gudgin, B., Shenton, C., Majeed, A., Powell, J., & Greaves, F. (2023). Uptake and adoption of the NHS App in England: An observational study. *The British Journal of General Practice*. PMID: 37783512

Summers, C., & Curtis, K. (2020). Novel Digital Architecture of a "Low Carb Program" for Initiating and Maintaining Long-Term Sustainable Health-Promoting Behavior Change in Patients with Type 2 Diabetes. *JMIR Diabetes*, *5*(1), e15030. Advance online publication. DOI: 10.2196/15030 PMID: 32130113

Sun, T. Q. (2021). Adopting artificial intelligence in public healthcare: The effect of social power and learning algorithms. *International Journal of Environmental Research and Public Health*, *18*(23), 12682. DOI: 10.3390/ijerph182312682 PMID: 34886404

Surabhi, P. K. (2025). Digital transformation in healthcare technology: A technical perspective. *European Journal of Computer Science and Information Technology, 13*(30), 50–66. DOI: 10.37745/ejcsit.2013/vol13n305066

Susanti, D. (2021). DIGITAL MARKETING TO CUSTOMER VALUE AND CUSTOMER ENGAGEMENT IN REPEAT PURCHASE ON THE MARKETPLACE. *SULTANIST: Jurnal Manajemen Dan Keuangan*. DOI: 10.37403/sultanist.v9i2.339

Susanto, S. R. (2020). Germany's Strategy in Handling COVID-19: The Role of National Leadership Strength and The Maximization of Welfare State Continental System Support. *Jurnal Global &amp. Strategis, 14*(2), 403. DOI: 10.20473/jgs.14.2.2020.403-420

Swan, E. L., Peltier, J. W., & Dahl, A. J. (2023). Artificial intelligence in healthcare: The value co-creation process and influence of other digital health transformations. *Journal of Research in Interactive Marketing*. Advance online publication. DOI: 10.1108/JRIM-09-2022-0293

Swartz, A., Lefevre, A., Perera, S., Kinney, M., & George, A. (2020). Multiple pathways to scaling up and sustainability: An exploration of digital health solutions in South Africa. *Globalization and Health, 17*(1), 77. Advance online publication. DOI: 10.1186/s12992-021-00716-1 PMID: 34229699

Swenson, E. R., Bastian, N. D., & Nembhard, H. (2016). Data analytics in health promotion: Health market segmentation and classification of total joint replacement surgery patients. *Expert Systems with Applications, 60*, 118–129. DOI: 10.1016/j.eswa.2016.05.006

Sytnyk, Y., & Tarkanii, M. (2024). Trends in development of digital literacy of the staff of medical institutions. *Management and Entrepreneurship in Ukraine: The Stages of Formation and Problems of Development*. DOI: 10.23939/smeu2024.02.138

Thaler, R. H., & Sunstein, C. R. (2008). *Nudge: Improving decisions about health, wealth, and happiness.* Yale University Press. https://yalebooks.yale.edu/book/9780300122237/nudge

The electronic medical data card (eGK). (2025). *Bundesministerium Für Gesundheit.* https://gesund.bund.de/en/the-electronic-medical-data-card

Thomas, E. E., Haydon, H. M., & Mehrotra, A. (2021). It is based on the fast adoption of telehealth in COVID-19. *Journal of Medical Internet Research, 23*(10).

Thomas, J., Rajeev, P. V., & Philip, S. (2020). The plight of interstate migrant workers in Kerala: A policy analysis. *Economic and Political Weekly, 55*(7), 15–20.

Tikhomirov, A. (2024). Semashko Model: Critical Overview. Available at *SSRN* 4906897.

Tiwari, G. (2024). Promoting Effective Refugee Protection in India: Balancing National Interests and International Obligations. *Athens Journal of Law*, *10*(2), 221–232. DOI: 10.30958/ajl.10-2-3

Todua, N., & Todua, N. (2025). The Influence of Digital Media Marketing Activities on Healthcare Consumer Behavior. In *International Scientific-Practical Conference* (pp. 208-221). Cham: Springer Nature Switzerland. DOI: 10.1007/978-3-031-88052-0_16

Todua, N., Babilua, P., & Dochviri, T. (2013). On the multiple linear regression in marketing research. *Bull. Georg. Natl. Acad. Sci*, *7*(3), 135–139.

Todua, N., & Jashi, C. (2018). Influence of social marketing on the behavior of Georgian consumers regarding healthy nutrition. *Bull. Georg. Natl. Acad. Sci*, *12*(2), 183–190.

Todua, N., Jashi, C., & Todua, N. (2024). The role of social media in healthcare marketing. In *Modern healthcare marketing in the digital era* (pp. 26–41). IGI Global Scientific Publishing.

Todua, N., & Urotadze, E. (2025). Effect of Social Media Influencers on Consumer Brand Engagement and Its Implications on Purchase Intention. In *Brand Creation and Management in the Phygital Era* (pp. 541–562). IGI Global Scientific Publishing. DOI: 10.4018/979-8-3373-0948-4.ch021

Topol, E. (2019). *Deep medicine: How artificial intelligence can make healthcare human again*—basic Books. https://www.basicbooks.com/titles/eric-topol/deep-medicine/9781541644632/

Tortorella, G. L., Fogliatto, F. S., Kurnia, S., Thürer, M., & Capurro, D. (2022). Healthcare 4.0 digital applications: An empirical study on measures, bundles and patient-centered performance. *Technological Forecasting and Social Change*, *181*, 121780. DOI: 10.1016/j.techfore.2022.121780

Tortorella, G. L., Fogliatto, F. S., Tlapa Mendoza, D., Pepper, M., & Capurro, D. (2023). Digital transformation of health services: A value stream-oriented approach. *International Journal of Production Research*, *61*(6), 1814–1828. DOI: 10.1080/00207543.2022.2048115

Tountas, Y. (2009). The historical origins of the basic concepts of health promotion and education: The role of ancient Greek philosophy and medicine. *Health Promotion International*, *24*(2), 185–192. DOI: 10.1093/heapro/dap006 PMID: 19304737

Towards Universal Healthcare: Ayushman Bharat Pradhan Mantri-Jan Arogya Yojana. (2025). Govt. of India. https://www.pib.gov.in/PressNoteDetails.aspx?NoteId=155855&ModuleId=3&reg=3&lang=2

Trevisanato, S. I. (2006). Six medical papyri describe the effects of Santorini's volcanic ash, and provide Egyptian parallels to the so-called biblical plagues. *Medical Hypotheses*, *67*(1), 187–190. DOI: 10.1016/j.mehy.2006.01.008 PMID: 16513290

Tulchinsky, T. H. (2018). Bismarck and the long road to universal health coverage. *Case studies in public health, 131*. vd Schulenburg, J. M. G. (2019). The German health care system: concurrent solidarity, freedom of choice, and cost control. In Health Care Systems and Their Patients (pp. 83-104). Routledge.

Turner, M., Kitchenham, B., Brereton, P., Charters, S., & Budgen, D. (2010). Does the technology acceptance model predict actual use? A systematic literature review. *Information and Software Technology*, *52*(5), 463–479. DOI: 10.1016/j.infsof.2009.11.005

Tynkkynen, L. K., Pulkki, J., Tervonen-Goncalves, L., Schön, P., Burström, B., & Keskimäki, I. (2022). Health system reforms and the needs of the ageing population—An analysis of recent policy paths and reform trends in Finland and Sweden. *European Journal of Ageing*, *19*(2), 221–232. DOI: 10.1007/s10433-022-00699-x PMID: 35465210

Usuemerai, P. A., Ibikunle, O. E., Abass, L. A., Alemede, V., Nwankwo, E. I., & Mbata, A. O. (2024). *A conceptual framework for digital health marketing strategies to enhance public health outcomes in underserved communities*. World Journal of Advanced Pharmaceutical and Medical Research., DOI: 10.53346/wjapmr.2024.7.2.0044

Vahedi, S., Yazdi-Feyzabadi, V., Amini-Rarani, M., Mohammadbeigi, A., Khosravi, A., & Rezapour, A. (2020). Tracking socio-economic inequalities in healthcare utilization in Iran: A repeated cross-sectional analysis. *BMC Public Health*, *20*(1), 929. Advance online publication. DOI: 10.1186/s12889-020-09001-z PMID: 32539734

Vaishali, P. M., Boopathy, N., & Boobalan, N. (2024). Edwin Chadwick: A Pioneer of Public Health Reform and His Role in Sanitary Awakening. *Cureus*, *16*(9). Advance online publication. DOI: 10.7759/cureus.68858 PMID: 39376875

Van Middendorp, J. J., Sanchez, G. M., & Burridge, A. L. (2010). The Edwin Smith papyrus: A clinical reappraisal of the oldest known document on spinal injuries. *European Spine Journal : Official Publication of the European Spine Society, the European Spinal Deformity Society, and the European Section of the Cervical Spine Research Society*, *19*(11), 1815–1823. DOI: 10.1007/s00586-010-1523-6 PMID: 20697750

Vayena, E., Haeusermann, T., Adjekum, A., and Blasimme, A. (2018). The case of why we require ethics in digital health. Nature Digital Medicine, 1(1).

Venkatesh, V., & Davis, F. D. (2000). A theoretical extension of the technology acceptance model: Four longitudinal field studies. *Management Science*, *46*(2), 186–204. DOI: 10.1287/mnsc.46.2.186.11926

Venkatesh, V., Morris, M. G., Davis, G. B., & Davis, F. D. (2003). User acceptance of information technology: Toward a unified view. *Management Information Systems Quarterly*, *27*(3), 425–478. DOI: 10.2307/30036540

Venkatesh, V., Thong, J. Y., & Xu, X. (2012). Consumer acceptance and use of information technology: Extending the unified theory of acceptance and use of technology. *Management Information Systems Quarterly*, *36*(1), 157–178. DOI: 10.2307/41410412

Venkateswaran, S., Slaria, S., & Mukherjee, S. (2022). Political motivation as a key driver for universal health coverage. *Frontiers in Public Health*, *10*, 922578. Advance online publication. DOI: 10.3389/fpubh.2022.922578 PMID: 36457324

Verhoef, P. C., Broekhuizen, T., Bart, Y., Bhattacharya, A., Dong, J. Q., Fabian, N., & Haenlein, M. (2021). Digital transformation: A multidisciplinary reflection and research agenda. *Journal of Business Research*, *122*, 889–901. DOI: 10.1016/j.jbusres.2019.09.022

Verulava, T. (2023). Managed competition and health insurance reforms in Georgia. Bull. Georg. Natl. Acad. Sci, 17(1).

Vijayaraghavan, H. (2020). Gaps in India's Treatment of Refugees and Vulnerable Internal Migrants Are Exposed by the Pandemic. *Migration Policy Institute*. https://www.migrationpolicy.org/article/gaps-india-refugees-vulnerable-internal-migrants-pandemic

Vlădescu, C., Rădulescu, S., & Cace, S. (2005). The Romanian healthcare system: between Bismarck and Semashko. Decentralization in Healthcare: Analyses and Experiences in Central and Eastern Europe in the 1990s, 435-485.

von der Schulenburg J-Matthias, G. (2018). Pricing and reimbursement policies in Germany: current and future trends. European Medicines Pricing and Reimbursement, 19-38.

Von Klein, C. H. (1905). The Medical Features of the Papyrus Ebers. *Journal of the American Medical Association*, *45*(26), 1928–1935. DOI: 10.1001/jama.1905.52510260014001e

Waddell, K. J., Shah, P., Adusumalli, S., & Patel, M. S. (2020). Using Behavioral Economics and Technology to Improve Outcomes in Cardio-Oncology. *JACC. CardioOncology*, *2*(1), 84–96. DOI: 10.1016/j.jaccao.2020.02.006 PMID: 34396212

Wang, C.-J., Liu, S., Yang, H., Guo, J., Wu, Y., & Liu, J. (2023). Ethical Considerations of Using ChatGPT in Health Care. *Journal of Medical Internet Research*, *25*, e48009. Advance online publication. DOI: 10.2196/48009 PMID: 37566454

Wang, Q., Su, M., Zhang, M., & Li, R. (2021). Integrating digital technologies and public health to fight Covid-19 pandemic: Key technologies, applications, challenges and outlook of digital healthcare. *International Journal of Environmental Research and Public Health*, *18*(11), 6053. DOI: 10.3390/ijerph18116053 PMID: 34199831

Wang, X., & Luan, W. (2022). Research progress on digital health literacy of older adults: A scoping review. *Frontiers in Public Health*, *10*, 906089. DOI: 10.3389/fpubh.2022.906089 PMID: 35991040

Weinberger, N., Hery, D., Mahr, D., Adler, S. O., Stadlbauer, J., & Ahrens, T. D. (2025). Beyond the gender data gap: Co-creating equitable digital patient twins. *Frontiers in Digital Health*, *7*, 1584415. Advance online publication. DOI: 10.3389/fdgth.2025.1584415 PMID: 40370708

Weissert, W. G., & Weissert, C. S. (2019). *Governing health: The politics of health policy*. Johns Hopkins University Press. DOI: 10.56021/9781421428932

Wenner, J., Biddle, L., Gottlieb, N., & Bozorgmehr, K. (2022). Inequalities in access to healthcare by local policy model among newly arrived refugees: Evidence from population-based studies in two German states. *International Journal for Equity in Health*, *21*(1), 11. Advance online publication. DOI: 10.1186/s12939-021-01607-y PMID: 35073919

WHO (2023). Digital Health Global Strategy Update. The Lancet Digital Health (2022). Healthcare system digital health transformation. Health Affairs (2021). Adoption of telemedicine and delivery of health care. OECD (2022). Health IT and Economic Value.

Williams, K., & Williams, J. (2021). Social Insurance and the Allied Services: the Political Utopia of 1942. In *The Works of William H. Beveridge* (pp. Vol7-43). Routledge.

Williams, D. R., & Mohammed, S. A. (2009). Discrimination and mental health: A review. *Annual Review of Clinical Psychology*, *5*, 335–361. DOI: 10.1146/annurev.clinpsy.032408.153610

Wilson, E. V., & Lankton, N. K. (2004). Modeling patients' acceptance of provider-delivered e-health. *Journal of the American Medical Informatics Association : JAMIA, 11*(4), 241–248. DOI: 10.1197/jamia.M1475 PMID: 15064290

Wimalasena, L. M. D. O., & Jayasinghe, C. (2025). Digital Marketing and Brand Engagement Behavior: A Conceptual Review. *Sri Lanka Journal of Marketing*. DOI: 10.4038/sljmuok.v10i2.197

Windel, F., Balaram, A., & Perkins, K. M. (2020). Discourses of the Willkommenskultur (Welcoming culture) in Germany. *Critical Discourse Studies, 19*(1), 93–116. DOI: 10.1080/17405904.2020.1839921

Wolff, B., Nielsen, S., & Kiwanuka, A. (2024). Practical guidelines for developing digital health solutions to increase equity in dementia care in the UK. *Frontiers in Digital Health, 6*, 1490156. Advance online publication. DOI: 10.3389/fdgth.2024.1490156 PMID: 39749098

Wong, C. B., Huang, H., Ning, Y., & Xiao, J. (2024). Probiotics in the new era of Human Milk Oligosaccharides (HMOs): HMO utilization and beneficial effects of Bifidobacterium longum subsp. Infantis M-63 on infant health. *Microorganisms, 12*(5), 1014. DOI: 10.3390/microorganisms12051014 PMID: 38792843

World Health Organization (WHO). (2010). *Monitoring the building blocks of health systems: A handbook of indicators and their measurement strategies*. WHO Press.

World Health Organization. (1986). *Ottawa charter for health promotion.* World Health Organization. https://www.who.int/publications/i/item/ottawa-charter-for-health-promotion

World Health Organization. (2010). *Health systems financing: The path to universal coverage*. WHO Press. https://www.who.int/publications/i/item/9789241564021

World Health Organization. (2018). *Digital technologies: Shaping the future of primary health care*.https://www.who.int/docs/default-source/primary-health-care-conference/digital-technologies.pdf

World Health Organization. (2021). *Global strategy on digital health 2020–2025.* WHO Press.

World Health Organization. (2021). *Global strategy on digital health 2020–2025.* World Health Organization. https://www.who.int/publications/i/item/9789240020924

World Health Organization. (2021). Online health global strategy 20202025. Topol, E. (2019). Deep Medicine: Artificial Intelligence Can Save Healthcare by Moving It Back to Humans.

World Health Organization. (2022). *Global oral health status report: towards universal health coverage for oral health by 2030*. World Health Organization.

World Health Organization. (2023). *Global report on digital health 2023*. World Health Organization. https://www.who.int/publications/i/item/9789240071303

Xu, K., Soucat, A., Kutzin, J., Brindley, C., Maele, N. V., Touré, H., Garcia, M. A., Li, D., Barroy, H., Flores, G., & Wang, H. (2018). *Public spending on health: A closer look at global trends*. World Health Organization & World Bank Group. https://www.hst.org.za/publications/NonHST%20Publications/WHO-HIS-HGF-HF-WorkingPaper-18.3-eng.pdf.

Yap, Y. Y., Tan, S. H., & Choon, S. W. (2022). Elderly's intention to use technologies: A systematic literature review. *Heliyon*, *8*(1), e08765. DOI: 10.1016/j.heliyon.2022.e08765 PMID: 35128090

Yarmohammadi, H., Mojahedian, M. M., & Zargaran, A. (2012). Medicine and economy in Ancient Persia. *The Journal of Research on History of Medicine*, *1*(3).

Yoo, B.-K., Kim, M., Sasaki, T., Hoch, J., & Marcin, J. (2017). Selected Use of Telemedicine in Intensive Care Units Based on Severity of Illness Improves Cost-Effectiveness. *Telemedicine Journal and e-Health*, *24*(1), 21–36. DOI: 10.1089/tmj.2017.0069 PMID: 28661790

Yu, P., & Qian, S. (2018). Developing a theoretical model and questionnaire survey instrument to measure the success of electronic health records in residential aged care. *PLoS One*, *13*(1), e0190749. DOI: 10.1371/journal.pone.0190749 PMID: 29315323

Żak, A., Djakeli, K., & Bielińska-Dusza, E. (2024). Cross-Sector Partnerships and Relationship Marketing in Healthcare: The Example of Fairy Tale Therapy in Children's Hospitals in Poland. In Modern Healthcare Marketing in the Digital Era (pp. 164-192). IGI Global Scientific Publishing.

ZDROWIA, T. C. W. O., & MARKETINGOWY, I. J. W. (2023). Digital transformation in health care and its marketing dimension. MARKETING, 49(3), 27-46

Zhang, C., & Wang, Y. (2024). Is enterprise digital transformation beneficial to shareholders? Insights from the cost of equity capital. *International Review of Financial Analysis*, *92*, 103104. Advance online publication. DOI: 10.1016/j.irfa.2024.103104

Zhang, S., & Song, J. (2024). An empirical investigation into the preferences of the elderly for user interface design in personal electronic health record systems. *Frontiers in Digital Health*, *5*, 1289904. Advance online publication. DOI: 10.3389/fdgth.2023.1289904 PMID: 38348367

Zhong, M., Qiang, D., Wang, J., & Sun, W. (2024). Improving health and reducing health inequality: An innovation of digitalization? *Social Science & Medicine*, *348*, 116847. DOI: 10.1016/j.socscimed.2024.116847 PMID: 38569285

Ziegler, S., & Bozorgmehr, K. (2024). Translating restrictive law into practice: An ethnographic exploration of the systemic processing of legally restricted health care access for asylum seekers in Germany. *International Journal for Equity in Health*, *23*(1), 208. DOI: 10.1186/s12939-024-02251-y PMID: 39390515

Zin, K. S. L. T., Kim, S., Kim, H. S., & Feyissa, I. F. (2023). A study on technology acceptance of digital healthcare among older Korean adults using extended tam (extended technology acceptance model). *Administrative Sciences*, *13*(2), 42. DOI: 10.3390/admsci13020042

About the Contributors

Kakhaber Djakeli is a Health Economist and Health Marketer. He wrote his PhD Thesis in Germany, being a Doctoral Student at Leibniz University Hannover (LUH) under the mentorship of the renowned German health Economist, Prof. Dr. Mathias Graf von der Schulenburg at IVBL. During 2006-2007, Kakhaber Djakeli was invited to Yale University's School of Public Health by Professor Hong Wang, where he worked on health reform concepts in the Soviet countries, particularly in Georgia. During 2007-2008, Kakhaber Djakeli was hired by the World Bank to assist the government of Georgia in developing the Health Reform Concept. With a team of Health Reformers, Kakhaber Djakeli elaborated the Concept of Georgian Healthcare Reform, which the government implemented. During 2008-2013, Georgia improved its Healthcare Potential, which was the result of reforms in the National Health System. Between 1998 and 2017, Kakhaber Djakeli was invited by DAAD to German universities for research on healthcare concept development. In 2017, Kakhaber Djakeli was a Visiting Professor at Kennesaw State University (USA). He currently works at the University of Georgia's School of Health Sciences, where he continues to study Healthcare Markets and Healthcare Reform opportunities in response to Global and Local Challenges. The digitalization and innovative information technologies implemented in the Healthcare Market and industry enable Professor Djakeli to study global and local challenges in national and international markets, promoting new concepts and ideas for better patient satisfaction. Kakhaber Djakeli has published numerous scientific articles and books on digitalization in the healthcare market. He continues to consult with Healthcare Companies, Hospitals, Healthcare Managers, and Marketers.

***

Jince George is a Ph.D. Scholar in the Department of Social Work at Christ (Deemed to be University), Bengaluru. His research focuses on contemporary social issues and community development, with a particular interest in evidence-based social interventions and inclusive policy practices.

Shaikh Sahanwaz Islam is an accomplished legal academic and administrator, presently serving as Associate Professor of Law and Head of the P.G. Department of Law at Capital Law College, Bhubaneswar under Madhusudan Law University. With a distinguished teaching career of 25 years, he has contributed extensively to legal education through classroom teaching, academic leadership, research, and public engagement in Odisha and beyond. His career includes five years as Associate Professor at Uttaranchal University, Dehradun, and eighteen years as Assistant Professor at Capital Law College under Utkal University, reflecting a sustained commitment to mentoring generations of law students and strengthening institutional academic standards. Dr. Islam holds a Ph.D. in Law from Utkal University on the theme "Right to Information as a Tool of Good Governance," a subject that places him at the intersection of transparency, accountability, and democratic governance in India. His diverse academic background includes an LL.M. in Commercial Law from Utkal University and a second LL.M. with specializations in Cyber Law, Competition Law, and Intellectual Property Law from Karnataka University, equipping him with strong expertise across contemporary and technology- driven legal domains. Complementing his legal qualifications, he has obtained an MBA in Human Resource Management from Pondicherry University, a Post- Graduate Degree in Human Rights and Duties Education from Utkal University, and a Post-Graduate Degree in Sociology from Utkal University, Bhubaneswar, which together enrich his interdisciplinary perspective on law, policy, and society. An active author and researcher, Dr. Islam has written four books: "Consumer Protection Act, 1986 with Orissa Rules" (2016), "Orissa Public Works Department Code" (2016), "Odisha Pension Rules" (2017), and "Scheduled Caste and Scheduled Tribe (Prevention of Atrocities) Act, 1989" (2017), all published by OJR Publishing Company, Cuttack. These works demonstrate his engagement with statutory interpretation, social justice, public administration, and welfare legislation, and serve as practical resources for students, practitioners, and administrators. In addition to his authored books, he has edited nine books and published 14 national and 15 international research articles, contributing to scholarly discourse on constitutional law, human rights, governance, and emerging areas of legal regulation. Dr. Islam has actively participated in academic and professional forums, having attended 64 seminars, conferences, and workshops at national and international levels. His academic visibility further extends through visiting lectures at key institutions, including delivering lectures on the Indian Penal Code at the Mahatma Gandhi Institute of Prison Administration and Correctional Homes, Bhubaneswar, and on the National Commission for Protection of Child Rights at the Navodaya Leadership Institute, Konark, under the

Navodaya Vidyalaya Samiti, Ministry of Education, Government of India. He has also spoken on the Right to Information at the Judicial Academy, Cuttack, and on the new criminal law and its implementation at the Biju Patnaik Police Academy, Bhubaneswar, thereby engaging directly with judges, police officers, and public officials on critical legal reforms. Beyond law faculties, Dr. Islam has served as visiting faculty in Labour Law at both the Department of Botany and the Department of PMIR at Utkal University, underlining his interdisciplinary teaching profile and his ability to connect labour and employment law with diverse academic fields. His broad qualifications and long experience as a teacher, researcher, author, and trainer make him a respected figure in legal academia and a resource person for institutions seeking to strengthen legal awareness and governance- related capacities. Through his work in classrooms, research publications, books, and training programmes, Dr. Shaikh Sahanwaz Islam continues to contribute meaningfully to the advancement of legal education and the promotion of rights- based governance in India.

Sunitha Abhay Jain is a Professor at the School of Law, CHRIST (Deemed to be University), Bengaluru. She holds a Doctoral Degree in Law from NLSIU, Bengaluru, and has over two decades of teaching experience. She has served as the Coordinator for the LLM and MPhil programs at CHRIST for more than ten years. Dr. Jain holds LL.B. and LL.M. degrees from Bangalore University, where she secured Second Rank in her BA LLB (Hons.) program. She also earned a Master of Human Rights from Pondicherry University and a Postgraduate Diploma in Cyber Laws from NALSAR, Hyderabad. Currently pursuing her Post-Doctoral Research at SUSU, Russia, she has also cleared the UGC NET examination. Her areas of expertise include Corporate and Commercial Laws, International Trade Law, Constitutional Governance, and Human Rights. A prolific researcher, she has published extensively and contributed to national policy discussions, including the Expert Consultation Workshop on the Karnataka Municipalities Bill, 2019.

Shruti Jose is a Research Enthusiast and an Assistant Professor in the Department of Professional Studies under the School of Commerce, Finance and Accountancy at CHRIST (Deemed to be) University, Bangalore (India). Her research interests lie in banking, finance, technology adoption, consumer behaviour, payments, eCommerce, artificial intelligence, and innovation research.

Sheeja Karalam is a dedicated faculty member in the Department of Social Work at Christ (Deemed to be University), Bengaluru. She brings extensive experience in social work education, research, and community engagement, with a strong commitment to promoting social justice, empowerment, and sustainable development through her academic and field initiatives.

Abhinash Mohanta pursued a three-year LLB program at Ganjam Law College, Berhampur, under Berhampur University. He further advanced his academic journey by enrolling in the Master of Laws (LLM) program in Business Law at the P.G. Department of Law, Berhampur University, graduating in 2017. Currently, he is pursuing a Ph.D. in Law at KIIT Deemed to be University, with a research focus on critical areas such as refugee and human rights. In addition to his academic endeavors, Abhinash has authored several Scopus-indexed papers covering diverse topics, including AI, environment, migration, crime, intellectual property, and refugee studies.

Babitha Nadampalli is a dedicated law academician and researcher specializing in Constitutional and Administrative Law. She holds an LL.M. and is currently pursuing her Ph.D. in Law at Christ University, Bengaluru. With teaching experience at esteemed institutions such as University Law College, Bangalore University, and School of Law, Christ University, she has played a vital role in nurturing future legal professionals. Her doctoral research focuses on the intersection of Public Health Education and the Right to Health, exploring how constitutional principles can enhance healthcare access and human rights. Her scholarship bridges legal theory and social relevance, contributing to both academic discourse and policy development. ORCID: 0000-0003-2955-6531

Farjana Farvin Sahapudeen is an accomplished academician and researcher in Computer Science and Engineering with over 15 years of teaching experience. She holds a Ph.D. in Information and Communication Engineering from Anna University, specializing in deep neural network optimization for lung cancer segmentation. Her expertise spans artificial intelligence, machine learning, deep learning, computer vision, and natural language processing. She has authored several high-impact journal publications, IEEE conference papers, and book chapters in the domains of medical imaging and IoT. Dr. Farvin has contributed to NPTEL as a certified translator and earned multiple elite certifications and top performer recognitions. She is a patent holder with innovative projects in AI-driven healthcare, cybersecurity, and cloud-based diagnostics. She actively serves as a reviewer for reputed journals and engages in knowledge dissemination through invited talks, workshops, and FDPs. Her technical skills include proficiency in Python, Java, TensorFlow, PyTorch, and modern analytics frameworks. She is passionate about leveraging AI to address real-world challenges in healthcare and society. Currently, she continues to contribute to research, teaching, and innovation as an Assistant Professor at SASTRA Deemed University, Kumbakonam.

Ranjit Singha is a Doctorate Research Fellow at Christ (Deemed to be University) and holds a prestigious membership in the American Psychological Association (APA). With a strong background in Research and Development, he has significantly contributed to various fields such as Mindfulness, Addiction Psychology, Women Empowerment, UN Sustainable Development Goals, and Data Science. With over 15 years of experience in Administration, Teaching, and Research, both in Industry and Higher Education Institutions (HEI), Mr Ranjit has established himself as a seasoned professional. Mr Ranjit is dedicated to research and teaching endeavours, primarily focusing on mindfulness and compassion-based interventions. His work in these areas aims to promote well-being and foster positive change in individuals and communities.

Surjit Singha is an academician with a broad spectrum of interests, including UN Sustainable Development Goals, Organizational Climate, Workforce Diversity, Organizational Culture, HRM, Marketing, Finance, IB, Global Business, Business, AI, K12 & Higher Education, Gender and Cultural Studies. Currently a faculty member at Kristu Jayanti (Deemed to be University), He serves as an Editor, reviewer, and author for prominent global publications and journals, including being on the Editorial review board of Information Resources Management Journal and contributor to various publications. With over 16 years of experience in Administration, Teaching, and Research, Dr. Surjit is dedicated to imparting knowledge and guiding students in their research pursuits. As a research mentor, Dr. Surjit has nurtured young minds & fostered academic growth. Dr. Surjit has an impressive track record of over 150+ publications (SCOPUS Indexed 100+), including articles, book chapters, and textbooks, holds 2 US Copyrights, 1 patent granted, and has successfully completed and published 2 fully funded minor research projects from Kristu Jayanti (Deemed to be University).

Anuj Sinha is a legal academic and researcher specializing in Competition Law, Constitutional Law, and Jurisprudence. He was awarded the Doctor of Philosophy (Ph.D.) in Law by Hemwati Nandan Bahuguna Garhwal (A Central) University, Uttarakhand, in December 2024. His doctoral thesis, Combating Cartelization and Bid-Rigging: A Critical Study with Reference to The Competition Act, 200z, offers a doctrinal and policy-oriented analysis of anti-competitive agreements with emphasis on collusive bidding and cartel conduct. The work critically evaluates the implementation of the Competition Act, 2002, the role of the Competition Commission of India (CCI), and judicial interpretations in promoting market fairness, regulatory effectiveness, and consumer welfare. Before pursuing his doctorate, Dr. Sinha completed his LL.M. at HNB Garhwal University, where his dissertation, Euthanasia and Right to Die under Article 21 of the Indian Constitution:

An Analysis, explored the constitutional dimensions of personal liberty and the emerging discourse on end-of-life rights in India. He holds a B.A. LL.B. (Hons.) from IMS, Dehradun, where he excelled academically and participated in moot courts, debates, and legal awareness programmes. A UGC-NET qualified scholar in Law (2019, 2021, 2022), he was awarded the Junior Research Fellowship (JRF), later upgraded to Senior Research Fellowship (SRF) in 2024. His academic journey is further distinguished by teaching experience, postgraduate supervision, and active contributions to institutional innovation and outreach. Dr. Sinha has published more than ten research papers in peer-reviewed and indexed journals, including European Economic Letters (ABDC) and the Journal of Social Research & Marketing (ABDC), alongside Indian journals such as Shodh Sarita, Sanshodhak, and Inclusive. His research spans a wide spectrum of contemporary issues: ESG compliance, diaital economv reaulation. privacv and data protection. consumer riahts. and iudicial decision-makina. He has contributed book chapters to edited volumes from leading publishers such as Thomson Reuters, Taxmann, and Satyam Law Publishers. He has presented more than 25 papers at national and international conterences hosted by institutions including ISIL, HNLU Kaipur, Jamia Millia Islamia, Panjab University, and Amity University. His paper, Competition Law during the COVID-19 Pandemic: An Analysis of the Approach Adopted by the Regulatory Authorities, won Best Paper Presentation at a national e-conference organized by Symbiosis Law School, Hyderabad. At present, Dr. Sinha serves as Programme Leader for the LL.M. programme and Member Secretary of the Board of Studies at Amity Law School, Amity University Jharkhand. He is also actively engaged in intellectual property awareness and institutional innovation, having convened multiple seminars and workshops under the Institution's Innovation Council. He has successfully supervised postgraduate dissertations on contemporary themes, including digital privacy under the Data Protection Act, 2023, and online crimes against women. His teaching and research interests cover competition Law. Constitutional Law, Research Methodology, Media Law, and Legal Theory. Committed to interdisciplinary learning and evidence-based policy analysis, Dr. Sinha continues to guide the next generation of legal professionals and researchers, combining rigorous scholarship with practical engagement in pressing issues of law and governance.

Ryan Stephen is a BBA Data Analytics student with a strong interest in digital health, patient experience, and technology-driven healthcare transformation.

A. Sumathi is working as an Assistant Professor in the Department of Computer Science and Engineering, SRC, SASTRA Deemed to be University, Kumbakonam, TN, India. Research areas include Data Mining, Machine Learning, Data Science, and Healthcare applications.

Index

A

B

C

D

E

G

H

I

L

M

N

P

R

www.ingramcontent.com/pod-product-compliance
Lightning Source LLC
LaVergne TN
LVHW062334300926
849161LV00007B/1687